Educational Software Directory

Educational Software Directory
A Subject Guide to
Microcomputer Software

Compiled by
Marilyn J. Chartrand and Constance D. Williams
for Corporate Monitor, Inc.

Libraries Unlimited, Inc.   Littleton, Colorado
1982

LIBRARIES UNLIMITED, INC.
P.O. Box 263
Littleton, Colorado 80160

Library of Congress Cataloging in Publication Data

Main entry under title:

Educational software directory.

    Bibliography: p. 261.
    Includes indexes.
    1. Computer-assisted instruction--Equipment and supplies--Catalogs. 2. Microcomputers--Equipment and supplies--Catalogs. I. Corporate Monitor, Inc.
LB1028.7.E38   1982   016.3713'9445   82-20400
ISBN 0-87287-352-8 (pbk.)

Libraries Unlimited books are bound with Type II nonwoven material that meets and exceeds National Association of State Textbook Administrators' Type II nonwoven material specifications Class A through E.

ACKNOWLEDGMENTS

The information in this Directory was collected and compiled by Connie Williams. Marilyn Chartrand directed the data base efforts. Editorial assistance was provided by Douglas Tanner and Beth Warner. Gary Cook coordinated the publication efforts, including layout, graphic design, and photocomposition.

CONTENTS

INTRODUCTION

SCOPE

The *Educational Software Directory: A Subject Guide to Microcomputer Software* (ESD)contains listings of software packages (more than one program sold as a set) and programs for use in the classroom. All items are for use in kindergarten through grade 12. Materials chosen may overlap into other grades also, such as programs which can be used in high school through college.

Software included falls into three types: 1.) programs used by students; 2.) software used to create programs for students; and 3.) programs used by the teacher for demonstration purposes. Administrative programs such as grade books are not included. Many programs listed do have selective administrative functions, but not as the primary function of the program.

All information in this directory has been obtained from publisher and distributor literature, published reviews, hardware manufacturers, and telephone interviews with vendors. No software has been examined by the compilers.

Material has been chosen on the basis of its educational value. While educational content cannot be completely apparent without examination of the software itself, several indicators have been taken into account. First, the subject matter must be appropriate to the learning environment and to the computer medium itself. Adventure games, while exciting, are not usually of much value in the classroom; nor is a program that simply reproduces a book, such as an atlas, of much value as a computer program. Second, the program must be usable for the grade level for which it is intended. For example, kindergarten and first grade students cannot be expected to type lengthy responses. The third criteria used pertains to the producer of the software. If the catalog has cursory or unclear descriptions, and the company has not provided better information, or preview or purchase policies, or has not replied to our questions at all, their software has not been included. The exception to this rule is software that has been favorably reviewed in the journal literature.

Over 300 organizations were contacted for information and catalogs. About 100 did not respond at all; and an additional 100 were rejected as unsuitable because their software did not fall within the scope of the ESD.

HOW TO USE THIS PUBLICATION

The ESD contains five sections—Software, Publishers and Distributors, Bibliography, Subject Index, and Title Index—described below.

Software

Subject Categories—The software listings are arranged by 12 broad subject categories. Entries appear within the sections in alphabetical order by title. Because many packages contain programs on several subjects, the subject index should be used to supplement the categories. For example, a vocabulary package in section H (LANGUAGE ARTS) contains three foreign language programs. These programs can be identified through the use of the Subject Index.

Software is listed once, with all known distribution sources included. During the compilation of the ESD it may not have been evident that two pieces of software are the same, since the name or description may have been changed by the supply house. Therefore, the editors cannot absolutely claim to have eliminated all duplicates.

A. General—This section includes software that encompasses more than one subject, as well as those items which do not fit into any subject category, such as programs that teach test-taking skills.

B. Basic Living Skills—Programs on skills that a learner needs to function independently, such as driver education, consumer skills, and job finding skills, are in section B. Also found here is software on telling time, money, safety, and reading signs and labels. Many programs in this section are useful for the special education curriculum.

C. Business Education—Business Education includes traditional topics, such as bookkeeping and clerical skills (filing, typing, etc.), as well as nontraditional topics, like the use of a microcomputer for small business accounting.

D. Computer Literacy—This section covers all aspects of using a microcomputer, especially in the classroom. The majority of software in this section teaches programming on the student's level.

E. Courseware Development—The section on Courseware Development includes software that enables the teacher to create Computer-Aided Instruction drills, lessons and tests. There are many programs in the remainder of the directory which may have this feature, but the items in this section have no subject content associated with them. The Subject Index should be consulted to find more programs which will perform this function. Specific terms for this topic are ''Lesson development,'' ''Test development,'' and ''Puzzle building.'' These listings from the other sections include packages that have a program which will enhance or add to existing software.

F. Fine Arts—This section includes music, drawing, and art education programs. The music programs make especially imaginative use of the computer for learning purposes.

G. Foreign Languages—Many programs that drill in vocabulary and grammar are found in this section. Languages covered are French, German, Italian, Japanese, Latin, Russian and Spanish.

H. Language Arts—Language Arts is a large category, covering grammar skills, reading, vocabulary, spelling, and literature. Many of the packages in this section are extensive series of lessons and are intended to be used as a complete language arts curriculum.

I. Library Skills—The programs in the Library Skills section cover all aspects of using the library and books. Skills covered include using the card catalog, reference books, indexes and finding books on the shelf. Programs concerned with books cover such topics as book indexes, title pages, and copyright.

J. Mathematics—This section covers a wide range of skills from basic programs on counting and numeral recognition, through drills in arithmetic skills, to specialized programs on trigonometry and calculus.

K. Science—Science programs also cover a wide range of topics, from body organs and sex education to ecology simulations and physics labs. Other topics include astronomy, geology, and genetics. Many programs make use of the computer to simulate tedious and time-consuming lab conditions.

L. Social Sciences—The section on social sciences includes history, geography, economics, and civics. There are many simulations in this section.

Entry Format—The Software entries contain product information needed by purchasers to identify software that will fulfill their needs. Information on each entry is arranged in the format described below. For material not printed in catalogs, every attempt has been made to contact the publisher. For any information not provided, contact the vendor directly.

The Software entries may be for software programs or packages. Software listed in the publisher's catalog as a package is listed in the ESD under the package name.

(A package is a series of programs that can be purchased together from the vendor.) If the entry is for a package, the individual program names and descriptions are also included. Programs not included in packages are separate entries in the Software section.

ID—The first item in an entry is the ID number, which begins with a letter indicating the subject section (A1, A2, etc.). These numbers arrange the software titles alphabetically.

Package (or Program) Name—The package (or program name if not a package) appears next in capital letters.

Publisher's Name—The publisher's name is the next item given. Address, phone numbers, and other information can be found in the Publishers and Distributors section.

Availability—The names of the distributors and supply houses that also carry the software appear after ''Also available from:''. They are arranged in alphabetical order and separated by a bullet (•). If an individual program (and not the package) is available from a distributor, it will be noted in that program's description. Information on these companies will also be found in the Publishers and Distributors section.

Date—The next item in the entry is the original release date, which may be quite useful in selection for purchase. For example, programs that have been available for some time will probably have all the bugs corrected; however, the content of some programs may be outdated (such as scientific programs).

Grade—Grade level has been expressed, in most cases, in the language of the producer. Occasionally, reading levels have been given in place of, or in addition to, the grade. No attempt has been made to grade programs which have not been graded by the producer.

Format—Format refers to the media in which the package is available. If the publisher has provided information on the number of cassettes or diskettes, then the number is included. When an entry reads ''cassette'' or ''diskette'' without a specific number, it means that the number of cassettes or diskettes was unavailable. In most cases, the format is cassette or diskette (5 1/4-inch floppy disk). In the case of Texas Instrument machines, however, some software is available in Solid State Software™ Command Modules. TSC® is available only in a sealed hard disk.

Hardware—The next entry item is the hardware requirement. Since many programs are available for more than one microcomputer model, the separate machine requirements are listed here, separated by a bullet (•). The first part of each hardware entry is the model name and number; the second is the minimum Random Access Memory (RAM) required, followed by other requirements for ROM and DOS. Peripherals are listed last (printers, game paddles, light pens, etc.). There are several listings for computers other than micros. Minicomputer models are included in cases where microcomputer software is listed by the publisher as being available for both.

Language—The language in which the software has been written is listed next. The majority of the programs in the ESD have been written in BASIC.

Price—All prices are as listed by the manufacturer and are subject to change. Often there are discounts available for schools or volume purchasers. Check the Publishers and Distributors section for that information.

Source Code—Source code availability refers to the availability of the original program code or statements which enable the user to make modifications to the software.

Description—A description of the package or program is the next part of the entry. This includes informative material taken from catalogs, or published reviews in some cases, on intent, type of feedback, method of presentation, sequencing, reports to the instructor, and documentation.

Program Names; Program Descriptions—If the listing is a package, this part of the entry includes the names and descriptions of the programs that are part of the package.

Publishers and Distributors

The Publishers and Distributors section includes publishers, software houses, distributors, and consortia that provide the software found in the Software section.

Organizations are arranged in alphabetical order. Each entry includes name, address and telephone number, if available. The annotations include preview and purchase policies, warranty and copyright information, statement of shipping and handling charges, and discounts. Each company has been asked to provide a copy of its preview policy. Contact the organizations directly for any information not included.

Bibliography

A three-part annotated bibliography is included to assist educators in using microcomputers. The first section, "Getting Started," contains references that present the considerations to be made before purchasing a computer. The following topics are encompassed by this section: hardware components and their selection; determination of user needs; current developments in hardware and software; definition of computer terminology; costs; maintenance; and computer languages.

The second section, "Selecting and Designing Software," provides references on how to evaluate and design software. The last section, "Case Studies," provides reports on the use of microcomputers by specific schools both in the U.S. and abroad.

Copies of journal articles should be obtained from a local library system. References to documents listed as

"ERIC Document Reproduction Service No...." are available for purchase from:

ERIC Clearinghouse/IR
School of Education
Syracuse University
Syracuse, N.Y. 13210

$1.00 handling should be added to the microfiche (MF) or paper copy (PC) price listed. ERIC prices are subject to change without notice.

Subject Index

The Subject Index lists each item separately with its title and ID number. The letter in this identifier indicates the major subject category in the Software section. Each program or package is listed only once; duplicate titles indicate that several programs have the same name. (e.g., CAPITALIZATION is listed several times, indicating several different programs with that title.)

"See" references refer to the term used for that topic. For example, "Mortgages *see* Loans," indicates that "Loans" is the index term used. "*See also*" refers to related or more specific terms in the index, e.g., "Biology *see also* Botany, Zoology, etc." Broad terms have been chosen in the case of subjects for which all narrower subjects are included in the one package. For example, if the software covers addition, subtraction, multiplication, and division, the term "Arithmetic" is used. If several parts of speech are covered, such as "Nouns," "Adverbs," "Verbs," etc., "Parts of speech" has been chosen. For programs on very specific mathematical or scientific concepts, subject terms reflect that specificity. (For example, GAS LAWS AND KINETIC MOLECULAR THEORY has been indexed under "Gases," "Chemistry," and "Kinetic Theory."

Most of the subject terms have been chosen from the following sources:

National Information Center for Education Media. *NICSEM Special Education Thesaurus.* Los Angeles, CA: University of Southern California, c1978, 79.

U.S. Dept. of Health, Education, and Welfare. National Center for Educational Statistics. *Combined Glossary: Terms and Definitions from the Handbook of the State Education Records and Reports Series.* U.S. Government Printing Office, 1974.

Engineers Joint Council. *Thesaurus of Engineering and Scientific Terms.* New York: EJC, 1967.

International Dictionary of Applied Mathematics. Princeton, NJ: Van Nostrand Company, 1960.

Title Index

The Title Index provides access to program or package names. Programs that are part of a package are not included in the Title Index, as these titles are usually not descriptive. In this index also, all packages with the same name will be listed, along with their respective ID number.

NOTES

The use of microcomputers for educational purposes is a relatively recent innovation. In the past two years the number of schools acquiring microcomputers has been growing, as has the number of home computers available for this purpose. The amount of software available for education is increasing every day, and more and more publishers are adapting their software for all of the popular microcomputer models. This is a trend that will provide more software options for current microcomputer owners. The problem now for teachers and parents is not finding software to purchase, but selecting quality programs that will actually aid the student in the learning process. There are many computer and software salesmen available to assist in selection, but unfortunately, too few understand the educational process. Software users must think about their needs and make them known to producers.

Many of the programs in the ESD are excellent; however, there are likely to be some that are marginal. Prospective purchasers should take the time to become familiar with software by reading reviews, discussing results with current users, and carefully evaluating the options before purchase. Publishers will continue to produce good software if they are supported by purchasers. Users must also be fair to producers and respect their investment by not violating the copyright laws.

Many organizations with software listed in the ESD have been producing educational software for a very short time. For the most part, these companies have no formulated preview policy. Hopefully, as educators make their needs known, these companies will become aware of the need for stated policies.

During the data collection effort, the editors were in some cases unable to get full software descriptions from publishers and distributors, making it difficult to provide complete entries in the ESD. As the educational software market develops, it is hoped that better and more complete information will become available.

The editors welcome comments and suggestions for improvement of future editions of this directory. Communications should be sent to:

Corporate Monitor, Inc.
14618 West 6th Avenue,
Suite 201
Golden, CO 80401
(303) 278-4890
Attn: Connie Williams

The following models, operating systems, and languages are registered trademarks and/or trading names of the companies indicated. Registered trademarks of individual programs are noted in the text.

3-G Company, Inc.: 3G Light Pen

Apple Computer, Inc.: Apple, Apple II, Apple II Plus, Applesoft, Muffin

Atari,Inc.: Atari, Atari 400, Atari 800, Atari 810 disk drive, Atari BASIC

Bell & Howell Microcomputer Systems: Bell & Howell

Chatsworth Data Corp.: Mark Sense Card Reader

Commodore Business Machines, Inc.: Commodore, Commodore 64, 2001, 4000, 4016, 8000, 8032, PET 2000, 4000 series, VIC 20, 2031, 2040, 4040, 8050 disk drives, C2N recorder

Digital Equipment Corp.: PDP-8, PDP-11

Digital Research, Inc.: CP/M

Exidy Systems, Inc.: Sorcerer

Hewlett-Packard Co.: HP-3000

International Business Machines: IBM

North Star Computers, Inc.: North Star

Prime Computer, Inc.: Prime

Regents of the University of California: U.C.S.D. Pascal

TSC[T.M.] A Houghton Mifflin Company: Dolphin

Tandy Corp.: TRS-80 Color Computer, TRS-80 Model I, TRS-80 Model II, TRS-80 Model III, TRSDOS 1.3, Disk BASIC, Extended BASIC, Level II BASIC, Model III BASIC, CTR-80A cassette recorder

Texas Instruments: TI, TI 99/4, TI 99/4A

Wang Laboratories: Wang

Software

A

ID: A1

ALPHABET/ GUESS THE NUMBER/ REVERSE

Publisher: Edu-Soft[T.M.]

Also available from: Academic Software • Scholastic Software

Format: 3 programs on cassette or diskette

Hardware: Apple II; 16K (cassette) or 32K (diskette) with Applesoft in ROM (DOS 3.2 or 3.3)

Price: $14.95/cassette; $19.95/diskette

Three programs are designed to help users learn the alphabet or typing, learn relative sizes of numbers and play an educational strategy game.

ALPHABET - The user presses the keys and the letters of the alphabet appear in color or black-and-white while the alphabet song is played. Different colors are used each time. A repeat feature is provided to help users when they get stuck.

GUESS THE NUMBER - Program aids users in recognizing relative size of different numbers. Computer asks user to guess a number between 1 and 500. The guess will "sink" or "float" on the screen depending on whether it is too large or too small. The speed of the sinking or floating varies according to how close the guess is to the computer's secret number.

REVERSE - This is an educational strategy game using a list of digits. The digits are scrambled and the object is to get them in the correct order through a series of moves called "reverses".

ID: A2

APPLE DISSEMINATION DISK #1

Publisher: San Mateo County Office of Education and Computer-Using Educators

Format: 1 diskette

Hardware: Apple; 8 to 32K (DOS 3.2 or 3.3)

Language: BASIC

Source Code: yes

Price: $10.00

This disk contains 16 programs in the public domain. Topics range from fractions to French hangman to an Oregon Trail simulation.

ARTILLERY - Student selects trajectory to hit a target. (S 8K)FP

CHRISTMAS TREE SONG/DECK THE HALLS - Plays "We Wish You a Merry Christmas" and "Deck the Halls" as words appear on screen. (E/S 16K)INT

OREGON TRAIL - Simulates a pioneer wagon train trip from Independence, MO to Oregon City, OR. (E/S 32K)FP

STATES & CAPITALS - Fill-in-blanks to identify states and their capitals. (E/S 8K)FP

NATIONS & CAPITALS - Matching and fill-in-blanks to identify nations and their capitals. (E/S 8K)FP

GUESS MY FRACTION - Practice converting fractions to decimals. (E/S 8K)FP

CONNECTION - Logic game for 2 players based on the commercial board game "Connect 4". (E/S 8K)INT

MULTIPLICATION - Player chooses to practice a specific multiplication table or practices mixed tables. (E/S 16K)FP

MICROSCOPE - Drill program on parts of the microscope, using a high-resolution microscope loaded from within the program. (S 48K)FP

APPLE ROSE/FANCY ROSE - Plotting routine utilizing independent variables for the function R = SIN (N*THETA) (E/S 8K)FP

CHEMIST - Practice in ratio and proportion using chemistry as a gimmick. (S 16K)INT

REVERSE - Arrange digits 1-9 in correct sequence by reversing a selected number of digits. (E/S 8K)INT

HANGMAN (FRENCH) - Traditional HANGMAN with instructions and words in French. (E/S 8K)INT

HANGMAN FOR ONE - Word guessing game. (E/S 8K)INT

TITRATION - Student neutralizes an unknown acid with a base of known concentration. (S 8K)FP

MEET THE ROMANS - Practice converting Roman numerals to Arabic and reverse. (E/S 8K)FP

ID: A3

APPLE DISSEMINATION DISK #2

Publisher: San Mateo County Office of Education and Computer-Using Educators

Hardware: Apple; 8 to 32K (DOS 3.2 or 3.3)

Language: BASIC

Source Code: yes

Price: $10.00

This disk contains 16 programs in the public domain. Topics covered include mortgages, interest, quadrant plotting and a California driving test.

PET PIT PAT POT - Guess the word from definition for a word starting with Pet, Pit, Pat, or Pot. (E 8K)FP

A & AN - Practice in using "a" or "an". (E 8K)FP

SCRAMBLED WORD - Unscramble letters to spell the word. (E/S 8K)FP

CINQUAIN - Demonstrates what a cinquain is and gives student an opportunity to create a poem. (E/S 32K)FP

HOME MORTGAGES - Practice in computing mortgage data. (S 8K)FP

SAVINGS AND LOANS - Computes interest values at varying interest rates. (S 8K)FP

FUNCTION GAME - Program presents a function and a target number; user must identify two numbers which will yield target number when put into the function. (S 16K)FP

MATH QUIZ - Random math problems in levels of difficulty. (E/S 8K)FP

ADDITION RACE - Two students race on individual sets of addition problems. (ES/ 16K)FP

IMPOSSIBLE FIGURE - Draws figure in high-resolution graphics which defies laws of perspective. (ES/8K)FP

TRAP - Number guessing game requires the development of strategy to guess a number in the least possible tries. (E/S 16K)FP

CALIFORNIA DRIVING TEST - Multiple-choice questions on California traffic laws. (S 32K)INT

ADVANCED GUESS MY FRACTION - Practice converting fractions to decimals by guessing a fraction selected by the computer. (E/S 8K)FP

CRYPTOGRAM - Practice in solving puzzles. (E/S 8K)INT

PLOTTING POINTS - Demonstrates first quadrant plotting. (S 32K)INT

BAGELS - Classic number guessing game. (E/S 8K)FP

ID: A4

APPLE DISSEMINATION DISK #3

Publisher: San Mateo County Office of Education and Computer-Using Educators

Format: 1 diskette

Hardware: Apple; 8 to 48K (DOS 3.2 or 3.3)

Language: BASIC

Source Code: yes

Price: $10.00

This disk includes 13 programs in the public domain. The majority cover math topics.

FORECAST - Gives forecast for data entered, and converts to metric if necessary. (S 48K)FP

SINE WAVES - Graphs curve for values input by user. (S 32K)FP

GRAPHICS GAME - Two players compete in plotting lines using BASIC commands to make a rectangle. (E/S 8K)INT

SEQUENCES - Computer presents a sequence of 5 numbers; user predicts next number. (E/S 16K)FP

MUSIC GENERATOR - Composes music from information input by user. (S 16K)INT

NAME THE STATES - Student types names of states from memory. (E/S 8K)FP

MULTIPLICATION BINGO - Multiplication tables drill (1-9) with correct answers filling in a BINGO card. (E/S 16K)FP

FLASHCARD - Student selects operation to practice math facts within time limits. (E 16K)INT

DYNOMATH - Math facts practice in addition & subtraction. (E/S 16K)INT

EQUATIONS - Demonstrates the graph of a quadratic equation. (S 8K)INT

GEOGRAPHY - Word game using geographic names of nations, states, world cities, oceans and rivers. (E/S 8K)FP

SURVIVAL - Multiple-choice quiz on survival tactics. (E/S 16K)FP

LAF ISLAND - Survival simulation game based on cooperative action. (E/S 16K)FP

ID: A5

APPLE DISSEMINATION DISK #4

Publisher: San Mateo County Office of Education and Computer-Using Educators

Format: 1 diskette

Hardware: Apple; 8 to 48K (DOS 3.2 or 3.3)

Language: BASIC

Source Code: yes

Price: $10.00

This disk includes 14 programs in the public domain.

DISTANCE - Program teaches how to calculate the distance between points on a straight line graph. Uses high-resolution graphics. (S 32K)FP

CHARGE - This is the Millikan Oil Drop Experiment. User enters voltage and must determine charge on stopped drop. (S 8K)FP

PLANK - Given the frequency of X-rays being used, user determines voltage necessary to decrease collector current to zero. (S 8K)FP

MIDPOINT - Teaches how to find midpoint of a line segment. Uses high-resolution graphics. (S 48K)FP

GUESSING GAME - The computer will guess your number of letter. (E/S 8K)INT

MAD CHEMIST - Uses ratio and proportion to mix chemicals. Low-resolution graphics. (E/S 8K)FP

X-Y GRAPHER - Graphs equations of the form Y = (function of X). High- resolution graphics. (S 48K)FP

STAR LANES - Simulates business world, buying and selling interstellar trading lanes. (E/S 16K)FP

ADD-LIBS - Like "Mad Libs", with user entering parts of speech to create humorous stories. (E/S 32K)INT

MATH SPELL - Spelling of math-related words. (E/S 8K)FP

SLOPES - Teaches how to calculate slope of a line segment. High- resolution graphics. (S 48K)FP

ECO-SIMULATION - The classic "Graze-Huntington simulation" of the interaction among cattle, birds, and grassland. (E/S 8K)FP

CRAYFISH - Test on crayfish external anatomy. High-resolution graphics. (S 48K)FP

MATH DICE - User adds, subtracts, multiplies and divides the numbers on 5 dice to get the highest score. Simulated graphics. (E/S 8K)FP

ID: A6

APPLE DISSEMINATION DISK #5

Publisher: San Mateo County Office of Education and Computer-Using Educators

Format: 1 diskette

Hardware: Apple; 48K (DOS 3.3). Will not run until HIGHER TEXT (Synergistic Software) has been added.

Language: Applesoft BASIC

Source Code: yes

Price: $10.00; $32.50/HIGHER TEXT (Synergistic Software)

This disk includes 3 simulation programs.

ROAD TRIP - High-resolution graphics simulation of a trip from from Dullsville to Greenstone Park. One has a car, $200 and a map. One's goal is to complete the 900-mile trip in two days. As one drives, one sees the scenery and the road ahead, the road behind (in the rearview mirror), and the dashboard of the car. One must make decision about which routes to take and the amount of money to spend for gas, food and lodging. One must also be able to handle unexpected events. (E/S 48K)FP

POWERSAT - High-resolution graphics energy resources simulation. One is in charge of supplying the materials for the solar panel assembly phase of a power satellite. One must decide how to provision space shuttle for each flight, what fuel to use (nuclear, coal, natural gas, oil), and what cargo to carry. One will be required to dock shuttle on the space platform, using keyboard commands (it's not easy...). (E/S 48K)FP

MOONWALK - High-resolution graphics simulation. One's mission is to rendezvous with the mother ship in the Mare "Nectaris" on the moon. Uses keboard commands to move about the moon. (E/S 48K)FP

ID: A7
APPLE DISSEMINATION DISK #6

Publisher: San Mateo County Office of Education and Computer-Using Educators

Format: 1 diskette

Hardware: Apple; 16 to 32K (DOS 3.2 or 3.3)

Language: Applesoft BASIC

Source Code: yes

Price: $10.00

This disk includes 9 programs in the public domain.

ASSERTIVENESS TRAINING - As one goes through a school day one responds to various situations. Responses determine assertiveness rating. (S 32K)FP

TIC TAC ADD - Tic-Tac-Toe-like game where user picks a box and solves the problem displayed. Low-resolution graphics gameboard. (E 16K)FP

PERIMETER & AREA DRILL - Student finds perimeter or area on either a square, rectangle or triangle. Figures are shown in low-resolution graphics and length of sides is randomly generated. (E/S 16K)FP

FOOTBALL - Two teams choose offensive and defensive plays to simulate a game. Ball moves on field and scoreboard shows results. (E/S 16K)FP

LINEAR EQUATIONS - Computer graphs an equation (e.g., $4X + 2Y = 8$), then helps student to solve the equation for Y and to develop a table of X and Y values. Students can then enter other equations and graph them. (S 16K)FP

LOGIC PRACTICE - Logic quiz asks students to choose "either/or," "if/then," or "subgrouping." Pre- and post-test included. (S 16K)FP

VOWEL SEARCH - Practice in: identifying vowels; short vowel in one- syllable words: long vowel with silent E in one-syllable words. (E 16K)FP

ALPHABET ANTICS - Student types the letter to: match the letter shown; follow the letter shown; find previous letter in alphabetical order; fill in middle letter in a three-letter alphabetical sequence. (E 16K)FP

COLT RACE - Two students solve decimal division problems to win a race. (E/S 16K)FP

ID: A8
APPLE II TAPE

Publisher: University Software

Date: 1981

Format: cassette

Hardware: Apple II; 24K

Language: BASIC

Source Code: no

Price: $29.95

Sampling of six ready-to-run programs from vendor's library of more than 100 printed programs in areas of small business,

education and science, fun and games, and home economics.

PRESIDENTS QUIZ - Identifies presidents and teaches American history.

REVERSI - Challenging board game offering various skill levels.

SAVINGS & LOAN - Handles all standard S & L computations.

BUDGET - Provides interactive home budget analysis.

CROSS

SPELL - Offers computer-aided instruction for beginning reader.

ID: A9
ATARI DISSEMINATION DISK #1

Publisher: San Mateo County Office of Education and Computer-Using Educators

Format: 1 diskette

Hardware: Atari; 8 to 16K

Source Code: yes

Price: $10.00

This disk includes 13 programs in the public domain.

MEET THE ROMANS - Practice converting Roman numerals to Arabic and reverse. (E/S 8K)

BAGELS - Classic number guessing game. (E/S 8K)

TRAP - Number guessing game requires the development of strategy to guess a number in the least possible tries. (E/S 16K)

GEOGRAPHY - Word game using geographic names of nations, states, world cities, oceans and rivers. (E/S 8K)

MULTIPLICATION BINGO - Multiplication tables drill (1-9) with correct answers filling in a BINGO card. (E/S 16K)

SCRAMBLED WORD - Unscramble letters to spell the word. (E/S 8K)

SINE WAVES - Graphs curve for values input by user. (S 32K)

HANGMAN FOR ONE - Word guessing game. (E/S 8K)

BOURREAU - Traditional HANGMAN with instructions and words in French. (E/S 8K)

FANCY ROSE - Plotting routine utilizing independent variables for the function $R = SIN (N*THETA)$. (E/S 8K)

NAME THE STATES - Student types names of states from memory. (E/S 8K)

MATH QUIZ - Random math problems in levels of difficulty. (E/S 8K)

STATES & CAPITALS - Fill-in-blanks to identify states and their capitals. (E/S 8K)

ID: A10
ATARI VOL. II - EDUCATION & SCIENTIFIC

Publisher: University Software

Date: 1981

Format: cassette

Hardware: Atari 400/800; 24K

Language: BASIC

Source Code: no

Price: $29.95

Sampling of seven ready-to-run programs from vendor's library of more than 100 printed programs in areas of small business, education and science, fun and games, and home and economics.

PRESIDENTS QUIZ - Identifies presidents and teaches American history.

SIMULTANEOUS EQUATIONS - Enables user to solve simultaneous equations.

SPEED READER - Offers computer-aided instruction in speed reading.

QUANTUM CHEMISTRY - Computes quantum numbers of atoms.

PYTHAGOREAN THEOREM - Reviews geometric theorems.

OCTA-DEC - Computes octal to decimal conversions and vice-versa.

KINEMATICS - Provides computer-aided instruction in study of motion.

ID: A11
COLLEGE BOARD SAT PREP SERIES/EDUCATOR EDITION

Publisher: Krell Software Corporation

Also available from: Academic Software • MARCK • McKilligan Supply Corp. • Opportunities For Learning, Inc. • Queue, Inc.

Hardware: TRS-80; 16K • PDP-11 • PET; 16K • Atari; 16K • Apple; 16K • CP/M

Price: $229.95/educator ed.

The 25 programs in this series confront the user with a virtually limitless series of questions and answers. Each is based on past exams and presents material in the same level of difficulty and in the same form used in the S.A.T. Covers vocabulary, word relationships, reading comprehension, sentence completion, and mathematics. Independent lists of S.A.T. series performance show a mean total increase of 70 points in students' scores.

ID: A12
COMPETENCY/PROFICIENCY TEST PREPARATION SERIES

Publisher: Krell Software Corporation

Also available from: Academic Software • MARCK • McKilligan Supply Corp. • Queue, Inc.

Grade: 4-6

Hardware: Apple II; 48K with Applesoft in ROM • TI99/4A; 48K (available 1983) • PET; 32K • TRS-80 MOD I or III; 48K (available 1983) • Atari 800; 48K (available 1983) • IBM (available 1983) • CP/M (available 1983)

Price: $2,499.00

There are 3 editions of this software - national, New York, and California. All provide structured, sequential curricula in reading, writing and math. The programs consist of simulated examination modules, a thorough diagnostic package, and a complete set of instructional programs. Topical areas covered are: reading - phonetic analysis, structural analysis, vocabulary, and comprehension; writing - sentence recognition and manipulation, punctuation, capitalization, paragraph format, word forms, usage, spelling, business letter, report based on

data, and persuasive composition; mathematics - arithmetic facts, computation, comprehension, applications, expressions, equations, formulas, geometry, measurement, charts and tables; functional transfer - filling blank forms, charts, maps, matrices and graphs, and measurement - scales and diagrams. The instruction modules are designed for independent use by students, containing self-testing features to ensure that the rate of progress within each module is controlled by the student's progress in understanding and mastering the concepts presented.

ID: A13
EARLY ELEMENTARY I

Publisher: COMPU-TATIONS, Inc.

Also available from: Academic Software • Opportunities For Learning, Inc.

Grade: Preschool-2

Format: 4 programs on diskette

Hardware: Apple II; (DOS 3.2 or 3.3)

Price: $29.95; $34.95 for disk compatible with the VOTRAX speech synthesizer

This is a series of four programs requiring little keyboard skill. Each program provides a positive comment, graphics and optional music reinforcement when the student answers a problem correctly. A comprehensive teacher management file is included and the documentation includes ten behavioral objectives. All of the programs include personalized congratulatory messages, music and happy or sad faces in response to each answer. The TEACHER MANAGEMENT FILE offers the following options: adjust the number of problems; turn the music on or off; turn the recordkeeping on or off; view the class file; delete a name from the file; erase the entire class file; print a copy of the file; and vary the speed of the presentation.

COUNT THE SHAPES - This program places one of 12 objects at the top of the screen. When the number shown at the bottom of the screen matches the number counted at the top, the student is asked to press any key.

COLOR MATCH - This program requires the student to identify and match the color of a block at the top of the screen with one of several randomly generated colored blocks displayed at the bottom of the screen.

NUMBER DRILL - This program displays a numeral at top of screen and asks the student to match it with randomly spelled numbers at the bottom. The highest number to be worked on can be selected prior to running the program.

SHAPE MATCH - This program produces seven different shapes and asks the student to press any key when two of the same shapes are displayed on the screen.

ID: A14
EARLY ELEMENTARY II

Publisher: COMPU-TATIONS, Inc.

Also available from: Academic Software • Opportunities For Learning, Inc.

Grade: Preschool-2

Format: 4 programs on diskette

Hardware: Apple II; (DOS 3.2 or 3.3)

Price: $29.95; $34.95 for disk compatible with the VOTRAX speech synthesizer

This disk is a continuation of a series of programs designed for the preschool through second grade levels. It also includes four classroom-tested programs, a password- protected teacher management file and documentation of behavioral objectives. These programs also include personalized congratulatory messages, music and happy or sad faces in response to each answer. The TEACHER MANAGEMENT FILE offers the following options: adjust the number of problems; turn the music on or off; turn record-keeping on or off; view the class file; delete a name from the file; erase the entire class file; vary the speed of presentation; and select upper or lower case.

ALPHA DRILL - This program requires that the student press any key when the randomly displayed lower case alpha character matches the upper case one displayed at the top of the screen.

ALPHABET LINE - This program asks the student to fill in the missing letter in a section of the alphabet. An incorrect answer results in a listing of the alphabet to assist the student.

INSIDE OUT - Teaches the concepts of ''inside'' and ''outside'' by having the student press any key when various shapes which move about the screen appear inside a rectangle.

NUMBER LINE - Similar to ALPHABET LINE in that it asks the student to fill in the missing number of a sequential listing of numbers.

ID: A15
EDUCATIONAL PACKAGE II

Publisher: Micro Learningware

Also available from: Academic Software • MARCK • Queue, Inc.

Format: cassette or diskette

Hardware: TRS-80 MOD I or III; 16K cassette or 32K diskette • PET cassette

Language: BASIC

Source Code: yes

Price: $24.95

Package contains miscellaneous game and drill and practice programs. For all computers listed unless otherwise noted in descriptions. Written instructions provided.

CHANGE MAKER - Provides drill and practice on making change, based on randomly selected purchase and payment amounts. Individual program available from K-12 Micro Media.

HANGMAN - Word guessing game in which user attempts to guess spelling of word before computer draws scaffold and hangs him. Program is written in such a way that it is very easy to substitute any set of words. Individual program available from K-12 Micro Media.

NAME THAT LETTER - Two-player game in which players bid against each other on number of turns required to guess the letter the computer is thinking of. Computer gives clues after each guess as to whether correct letter is lower or higher in alphabet.

ANIMALS - Program tries to guess the animal the user has in mind. As program asks questions about animals, it learns more and more about animals as it continues, demonstrating computer's ability to ask questions and learn.

KINGDOM - Simulation of ancient kingdom where user plays role of ruler of kingdom, and makes decisions in an attempt to manage people and resources. For Commodore computer only.

ID: A16
ELEMENTARY - VOLUME 4

Publisher: Minnesota Educational Computing Consortium

Also available from: Academic Software • Creative Computing • K-12 Micromedia • Scholastic Software • Sunburst Communications

Date: June 82

Grade: 3-6

Format: diskette

Hardware: Apple II; 32K with Applesoft in ROM (DOS 3.3)

Language: Applesoft BASIC

Source Code: no

Price: $39.70

Package consists of mathematics, ecology, and astronomy programs for elementary classroom. Support booklet included.

ESTIMATE, MATHGAME - Two math programs provide reinforcement on estimating skills and basic facts.

ODELL LAKE - Deals with food chains in fish.

ODELL WOODS - Deals with food chains in animals.

SOLAR DISTANCE - Teaches concepts of distances in space.

URSA - Provides tutorial on constellations.

ID: A17
ELEMENTARY - VOLUME 7

Publisher: Minnesota Educational Computing Consortium

Also available from: Sunburst Communications

Date: June 82

Grade: K-2

Format: diskette

Hardware: Apple II; 32K with Applesoft in ROM (DOS 3.3)

Language: Applesoft BASIC

Source Code: no

Price: $38.50

Package is comprised of language arts, cognitive skills, and mathematics programs for the classroom. Support booklet includes information on teacher options to change words used in programs. Support booklet included.

CATERPILLAR, TRAIN - Drills student on sequence of alphabet.

SOUNDS - Drills student on initial sound of a word.

PICTURES, WORDS, SHAPES - Uses concentration game format to reinforce skills.

SMILE, WUZZLE, SPACESHIPS - Develop mathematics concepts such as counting, order of numerals, and simple addition.

ID: A18
ELEMENTARY PACKAGE V

Publisher: Micro Learningware

Also available from: Academic Software

Grade: Elementary

Format: diskette

Hardware: Apple II; 32K or 48K with Applesoft in ROM (DOS 3.2 or 3.3)

Language: Applesoft BASIC

Source Code: yes

Price: $24.95

Package consists of variety of programs designed to appeal to elementary students.

SPELLING TUTOR - Program tutors students on instructor's word lists, using definition to identify each word, thereby encouraging long- term retention. Unique and highly effective presentation goes beyond drill and practice. Requires 32K.

MATHFILES - While drilling class on any of four basic math operations, program keeps detailed records on every student. Easy-to- read display tells instructor who is having trouble and in exactly what area. All information is stored on disk for easy access at any time. Teacher sets specific limits on range of problems tested. 48K.

STOCK MARKET - Game for elementary students teaches basics of stock market operation in highly entertaining format, while promoting understanding of basic record-keeping and, if instructor chooses, encouraging practice in arithmetic. 48K.

HUMAN CALCULATOR - Helps instructor or students check calculations by requiring that calculations be done by same method. Makes it easy to locate errors in complicated problems. 32K.

ID: A19

FACTS AND FORMULAS

Publisher: Aquarius Publishers Inc.

Date: Aug. 82

Format: cassette or diskette

Hardware: TRS-80 MOD I or III

Language: BASIC

Source Code: no

Price: $14.95

Completely menu-driven program introduces many facts and formulas used in everyday life. Input from keyboard allows student to apply knowledge acquired. One in series of programs authored by The Programming Force and distributed exclusively by vendor.

ID: A20

IQ BUILDER SERIES

Publisher: Program Design, Inc.

Also available from: Academic Software • Queue, Inc.

Date: Apr. 81

Grade: 7 and up

Format: cassette or diskette

Hardware: PET; cassette • TRS-80 MOD I; with Level II BASIC; cassette • Atari; 8K cassette; 16K diskette • Apple II Plus; 32K • Apple II; 32K with Applesoft in ROM

Price: $16.95/PET and TRS-80; $16.95/Atari cassette; $23.95/diskette; $23.95/Apple

Group of 4 courses prepares high school student for college board examinations or adult for aptitude tests.

VOCABULARY BUILDER 1: BEGINNING - Eleven programs include set of graded vocabulary questions on synonyms and antonyms, which are the most common type of vocabulary question on an IQ test. Last lesson is vocabulary test. Total of 400 questions, 2000 words in course.

VOCABULARY BUILDER 2: ADVANCED - Eleven programs are like those in VOCABULARY 1, but use a more advanced word list.

NUMBER SERIES - Series contains 8 programs that provide practice in a common math problem type. First lesson teaches how to approach number series and how to analyze their patterns. Later lessons provide practice with increasingly difficult problems, giving clues to problems with which student has greatest difficulty. Final lesson is test of abilities.

ANALOGIES - Program contains six lessons that teach what an analogy is and what the common types are. Program provides method for analyzing analogies and practice in handling all types. Final lesson is analogies test. This individual program is also available from Texas Instruments and K-12 Micromedia.

ID: A21

KID'S PROGRAMS #1

Publisher: Santa Cruz Educational Software

Also available from: GRAFex Company

Grade: 1-7

Format: cassette or diskette

Hardware: Atari 400; 14K; cassette • Atari 400: 24K; diskette • Atari 800; 14K; cassette • Atari 800; 24K; diskette

Source Code: yes

Price: $14.95

Package includes 3 programs on one tape or disk. User modifiable.

MATH QUIZ - Unlike many of the math quizzes, this allows one to input the highest numbers students can handle in their math drills. This means that combined with the nice little musical pieces and a few graphic rewards, they won't get bored as easily.

DIALOGUE - Talk to the computer! It may answer like a wise guy, but it can always be turned off. This is a computer classic translated for the Atari. (Minor adult language).

LOST TREASURE - See what fun kids can have trying to search over a small island looking for a treasure when they have to figure out the clues as to where they are. A good lesson in learning North & South directions. Also, a few graphics are included.

ID: A22

KID'S PROGRAMS #2

Publisher: Santa Cruz Educational Software

Also available from: GRAFex Company

Grade: 1-10

Format: cassette or diskette

Hardware: Atari 400; 16K; cassette • Atari 400; 24K; diskette •
Atari 800; 16K; cassette • Atari 800; 24K; diskette

Source Code: yes

Price: $14.95

Package includes 2 spelling games and a third game called TOUCH. User modifiable.

SPELLING BEE - Allows input of spelling list and then it flashes the words and checks student's spelling. The flashes get longer as they misspell the words so that eventually they will get them right.

SCRAMBLE - This learning game gives a bunch of letters to make words out of. Two players then try to outscore each other, requesting more letters when needed. It has some nice touches that make it fun for all ages.

TOUCH - Follow the computer's instructions to touch knees, elbows, etc. to those of other players.

ID: A23

LEARNING CAN BE FUN #5

Publisher: Jensen Software

Grade: 4 and up

Format: cassette or diskette

Hardware: TRS-80 MOD I or III; with Level I or III BASIC

Price: $19.95/cassette; $24.95/diskette

This series includes five programs that teach state and foreign capitals, reading comprehension and memory, spelling, and synonyms.

STATE CAPITALS - Lists the states, then gives capitals one at a time for identification.

FOREIGN CAPITALS - Covers the major countries of the world. Tests how many capital cities child can identify.

CUB REPORTER - Tests reading comprehension and memory.

TEST YOUR SPELLING - Many commonly misspelled words are used. One of the words given is spelled correctly.

TEST YOUR VOCABULARY - Student is given a word and must choose the correct synonym from the given list.

ID: A24

LEARNING CAN BE FUN #6

Publisher: Jensen Software

Grade: 4 and up

Format: cassette or diskette

Hardware: TRS-80 MOD I or III; with Level I or II BASIC

Price: $19.95/cassette; $24.95/diskette

This package contains five programs that teach spelling, test knowledge of state entry into the Union, and test the order of the presidents in office.

SPELLING - GRADE 4 - Program uses some of the most commonly misspelled words at this level.

SPELLING - GRADE 5 - Program uses some of the most commonly misspelled words at this level. More difficult than SPELLING - GRADE 4.

HANGMAN - A spelling game for all age levels. Difficulty can be changed by changing data lines in the program.

STATES - ORDER OF ENTRY - Object is to list the states in order of their entry into the Union.

PRESIDENTS - ORDER OF OFFICE - Object is to list U.S. presidents in order of their terms of office.

ID: A25

LOGIC AND DEDUCTION

Publisher: Educational Micro Systems Inc.

Also available from: MARCK

Grade: 4-9

Format: cassette or diskette

Hardware: TRS-80 MOD I; 32K (DOS 2.3) or 16K cassette
TRS-80 MOD III; 32K (DOS 1.2) or 16K cassette

Price: $23.95/diskette; $18.95/cassette

This program is a modified version of Mastermind, which may be played as a game or effectively incorporated in lesson plans by introducing deductive reasoning concepts. Exposure to this program should help the player appreciate the importance of: 1. thoroughly understanding the problem; 2. carefully identifying what is known and what is unknown; 3. establishing and limiting the universe of the unknown; 4. determining the relationships that exist between the known and the unknown; 5. making well thought out guesses (trial and error); 6. continually re-evaluating the known and the unknown; their relationships, and developing new relationships based on information learned from each trial; 7. using the "new" information to shrink the unknown universe to provide insight for the next trial. The object of the game is for the codebreaker (who may be one or more students) to break a numerical code "hidden" by a codemaker (who may be teacher, student, or computer). Three game options determine the difficulty of breaking the code: (1) the number of columns (and therefore the number of numbers in the code); (2) the number of possibilities per column (the size of the range of numbers from which the codemaker selects the code for each column); and (3) whether "direct" or "indirect" hints are supplied by the computer after each turn.

ID: A26

MEDALIST SERIES

Publisher: Hartley Courseware, Inc.

Date: Sept. 82

Grade: 3-10

Format: 4 diskettes

Hardware: Apple II; 48K with Applesoft in ROM (DOS 3.2 or 3.3)

Language: Applesoft BASIC

Price: $39.95/diskette

Series of social studies programs enable students to study ever-changing facts about states, presidents, continents, or major historical events.

MEDALIST - STATES - Helps students learn about states through provision of clues to a state's identity. Student tries to guess name of state by "buying" clues. Easier clues are more expensive than harder ones. Teacher may change clues. Student may compete with his/her own score or challenge three students with highest scores, who are known as Medalists.

MEDALIST - CONTINENTS - Operates in same manner as STATES program. Student must buy clues to guess identity of continent.

MEDALIST - PRESIDENTS - Similar in structure to STATES/CONTINENTS programs. Provides hundreds of facts about U.S. presidents.

MEDALIST - CREATE - Enables instructor to define topics and enter clues in any subject area.

ID: A27
MEMORY BUILDER: CONCENTRATION

Publisher: Program Design, Inc.

Also available from: Academic Software • GRAFex Company • MARCK • Queue, Inc.

Date: Apr. 81

Grade: 1 and up

Format: cassette or diskette

Hardware: PET; cassette • TRS-80 MOD I; with Level II BASIC; cassette • Atari; 16K cassette; 24K diskette • Apple II Plus; 32K • Apple II; 32K with Applesoft in ROM

Price: $16.95/PET and TRS-80; $16.95/Atari cassette, $23.95/diskette; $23.95/Apple

Series of educational games improves memory, attention span, and concentration. Letters and 3-letter words are used. Player has 3 options: play against computer, play against him or herself, and play against another player. Game is especially good for parent and child to play together.

ID: A28
MICROCOSM I

Publisher: Basics and Beyond, Inc.

Also available from: MARCK • Queue, Inc.

Grade: 3 and up

Format: cassette or diskette

Hardware: TRS-80 MOD I or III; 16K (cassette) or 48K (diskette)

Language: BASIC

Source Code: yes

Price: $24.95

Package contains 30 programs of varied educational, recreational, and practical content intended to promote computer literacy. A sampling of the more educationally oriented of these programs follows. A user handbook is included.

SOUTH POLE - Program simulates exploration of earth's most mysterious region, requiring user to rely on instincts and make sound decisions.

METRIC CONVERSION - Program helps user solve many conversion problems.

MUSIC TRANSPOSITION - User selects two keys and program transposes entire piece. Program is intended for practical and reviewing use.

MATH TABLES DRILL - Practice program helps students learning arithmetic. Twenty problems per "game" test skills in addition, subtraction, multiplication, and division.

COUNTRY-GUESS - User selects any country in world, and computer guesses country after asking only a few questions.

SPELLING DRILL - User enters words once, and computer drills user in spelling those words correctly.

ID: A29
MICROCOSM II

Publisher: Basics and Beyond, Inc.

Also available from: MARCK • Queue, Inc.

Grade: 3 and up

Format: cassette or diskette

Hardware: TRS-80 MOD I or III; 16K (cassette) or 48K (diskette)

Language: BASIC

Source Code: yes

Price: $24.95

Package contains 20 programs of varied educational, recreational, and practical content intended to promote computer literacy. A sampling of the more educationally oriented of these programs follows.

BLANK SLATE - Allows user to "paint" pictures on TRS-80 screen, then preserve these pictures on tape.

STATE GUESS - Reviews geographic facts about states of U.S. User selects any state in Union, and computer is able to guess state after asking only a few yes/no questions.

PLANET FINDER - Computer will calculate positions of all planets on any date after 1 January 1900.

ALGEBRAIC FACTORING - Program assists first-year algebra students in learning six different methods for factoring polynomials.

SPELLING BEE - Two-person competition features phonetic spelling of high- school level word list. Words must then be spelled correctly.

PREFIX STUDY AND QUIZ - Program intended for high school and college students helps increase vocabulary by introducing/reviewing most commonly used prefixes and their definitions.

ID: A30
MIND-MEMORY IMPROVEMENT AND STUDY SKILLS COURSE

Publisher: TYC Software (Teach Yourself by Computer)

Also available from: MARCK • Queue, Inc.

Grade: 7 and up

Format: cassette or diskette

Hardware: TRS-80 MOD I or III; 16K, with Level II BASIC; cassette • Apple II; 16K (cassette) or 48K (diskette) (DOS 3.3)

Language: BASIC

Price: Step 1 $26.50/cassette; $31.50/diskette Step 2 $31.50/cassette; $36.50/diskette

Course consists of introductory and advanced programs in memorization techniques. Tutorial and exercise programs utilize proven psychological techniques to improve study and memorization skills. Accompanying manuals include explanations, readings, and suggested additional activities.

MIND - STEP 1 - Ten lessons provide introductory course in memory techniques. Paced tutorial and exercise lessons introduce and reinforce copyrighted mnemonic system which has been used with both students and business executives.

MIND - STEP 2 - Broadens focus of techniques taught in MIND - STEP 1 to other areas. Includes analysis and memorization of poetry, textual material, development of good listening habits, and remembering visual information such as names and faces. Includes audio cassette for listening skill practice.

ID: A31

PET DISSEMINATION DISK #3

Publisher: San Mateo County Office of Education and Computer-Using Educators

Format: 1 diskette

Hardware: PET; 8K; disk drive 2031, 2040, 4040, 8050

Source Code: yes

Price: $10.00

This disk includes 18 programs in the public domain.

AFRICA & ASIA - Drill on capitals of African and Asian nations. (E/S 8K)

ANDROID NIM - Compete against computer in removing game figures -- practice in number manipulation and logical thinking. (E/S 8K)

BAGELS - Student logically guesses a 3-digit number using word clues. (E/S 8K)

CHEMIST - Ratio problems for adding proper quantity of water to acid. (S 8K)

DENSITY - Computes density upon input of volume and mass. (S 8K)

GEOGRAPHY - Word game using geographic names of nations, states, world cities, oceans and rivers. (E/S 8K)

HAMMURABI - Try to maintain a stable population, controlling the ancient kingdom of Babylon. (E/S 8K)

LIFE EXPECTANCY - Computes life expectancy based on response to questions about life style and medical history. (S 8K)

MORSE CODE - Presents code and asks for letter. (E/S 8K)

OTHELLO - Board game in which players alternately try to outflank and capture opponent's pieces on an 8 X 8 board. (E/S 8K)

PICTURE KINGDOM - Kingdom game with objective of achieving and maintaining a stable population. (E/S 8K)

PIZZA - Logic game to teach coordinates and position. (E 8K)

PRESIDENT'S QUIZ - Gives data of President's term and asks for name of President. (E/S 8K)

RADIOACTIVE DECAY - Calculates radioactive decay or population growth using the formula: $X = AE^{KT}$. (S 8K)

STATES & CAPITALS - Identify state when capital is given or capital when state is given. (E/S 8K)

WEATHERMAN - Program finds humidity index, wind chill factor, relative humidity, and/or temperature conversion. (S 8K)

WORLD CAPITALS - Identify capital cities of world nations. (E/S 8K)

YAHTZEE - Computerized version of board game, using dice rolls to develop logical thinking skills. (E/S 8K)

ID: A32

PET DISSEMINATION DISK #5

Publisher: San Mateo County Office of Education and Computer-Using Educators

Format: 1 diskette

Hardware: PET; 8K; disk drive 2031, 2040, 4040, 8050

Source Code: yes

Price: $10.00

The disk includes 18 math programs in the public domain.

HEART'S DESIRE - Chase and target game.

GRIBBET - Search and strategy game.

RACETRACK - User controls acceleration of car around track.

METEOR - Reaction time test.

KALAH - Computer version of ancient board game.

ZONE X - Strategic guessing game using advanced graphics.

NUMBER-TOE - Mathematical tic-tac-toe game (two players).

NIM - Computer version of a classic strategy game.

MATCHES - User and computer take turns removing matches from a row of 11 matches; player taking the last match loses.

MUGWUMP - User must locate all 4 mugwumps hiding on a two-dimensional grid.

SNARK - User must locate snark on a 10x10 grid.

BAGELS - Strategy number guessing game.

ACEY DEUCY - Traditional betting game; excellent graphics.

PAK JANA - User controls movements of a dancing figure with a simple animation programming language. [Requires 16K]

BART - Simulation tests whether user should drive to a given destination or take public transportation (BART = Bay Area Rapid Transit).

JARGON - User asks questions which the computer answers with sentences that are mostly nonsense and filled with jargon.

COMPUTER POETRY - Computer invites user to write simple poems.

WORD LADDER - User changes one letter at a time to move from original given word to the target word assigned by the computer.

ID: A33

PET DISSEMINATION DISK #6

Publisher: San Mateo County Office of Education and Computer-Using Educators

Format: 1 diskette

Hardware: PET; 8 to 32K; disk drive 2031, 2040, 4040, 8050

Source Code: yes

Price: $10.00

This disk includes 19 programs in the public domain.

BIG LETTER - Prints large alphabet letters and numerals on the screen. (E 8K)

CLEF DRILL - Identifying notes on bass, alto, tenor and treble clefs. (E/S 8K)

COMPUTER HAIKU - Generates random haiku using computer-related words. (E/S 8

ELEMENT HANGMAN - Traditional hangman game using element names. (S 16K)

GAS LAW SOLVER - Solve for an unknown using combined gas law equation. (S 8K

GIFT WRAP PART A - Generates random patterns. (E/S 8K)

GIFT WRAP PART B - Prints out worksheet for logic exercises based on GIFT WRAP PART A (E/S 8K). (requires printer)

HANG MATH2 - Challenges user to replace letters in a multiplication problem with correct numerals in a limited number of tries. (E/S 8K)

LONG DIVISION - Tutorial illustration of long division process. (E 16K)

MATH PLUS - Instructional drill on addition and subtraction. (E 16K)

MILLION PL VALUE - Place values using numbers from 3 to 7 digits. (E 8K)

NAMING COMPOUNDS - Write name or formula for randomly presented compounds. (S 16K)

OREGON TRAIL 32K - Simulates a pioneer wagon train trip from Independence MO to Oregon City, OR. (E/S 32K)

PETALS - Object of the program is to figure out the object of the program. (E/S 8K)

REFERENCE BALLOON - Identifying the appropriate reference book to use for various types of questions. (E/S 16K)

REG'D POWER SUP - Provides design specifications for a regulated power supply. (S 16K)

SPELL ENDINGS - Drill on ed, ing and plural endings. (E 8K)

STORY - Randomly generated math story problems with data statements that can be changed to use the names and hobbies of students in the class. (E 8K)

SUBJECTS - Identify subjects of the sentences. (E/S 8K)

ID: A34
PET TAPE

Publisher: University Software

Date: 1981

Format: cassette

Hardware: PET; 24K

Language: BASIC

Source Code: no

Price: $29.95

Sampling of six ready-to-run programs from vendor's library of printed programs in areas of small business, education & science, fun & games, and home & economics.

PRESIDENTS QUIZ - Identifies presidents and teaches American history.

CONVERT

SAVINGS & LOAN - Handles all standard S&L computations.

SPELL - Game program that offers computer-aided instruction for beginning reader.

INVESTMENT MANAGEMENT - Provides analysis of stocks, funds, debentures, and real estate.

SCRAMBLE - Computer scrambles words entered by players.

ID: A35
POT POURRI

Publisher: Educational Courseware

Also available from: Academic Software • MARCK

Format: diskette

Hardware: Apple; 48K (DOS 3.3 or 3.2)

Price: $24.00

This disk, containing programs created by students, illustrates how algorithms are developed, solving some problems with the aid of computers. Includes NUMBER RACE, a game in logic; PIPELINE, a minimum path and cost logic; CONVERSIONS, which converts any English unit to metric or metric to English; and CALCULATOR, which converts Apple into a powerful calculator for science, math, astronomy, and physics.

ID: A36
PREPARING FOR THE S.A.T.

Publisher: Program Design, Inc.

Date: June 82

Grade: High School-College Prep

Format: 6 cassettes

Hardware: Atari 400/800; 16K

Language: BASIC

Source Code: no

Price: $125.00

Package teaches students how to take Scholastic Aptitude Test (SAT) and other intelligence and aptitude tests, develops problem-solving skills, and provides practice in answering questions typically found on such tests. Except for NUMBER SERIES, which is self-testing, there is a test at the end of each course. All programs except TAKING APTITUDE TESTS are also available individually. Package includes user's manual and copy of booklet, ''Making the Grade.''

TAKING APTITUDE TESTS - Cassette explains purpose of standardized IQ and aptitude tests; discusses some false beliefs surrounding such tests; describes ways to improve test-taking skills; and presents strategy for answering questions that are most likely to pay off with correct answers.

VOCABULARY BUILDERS I AND II - Two cassettes are designed to help develop student's vocabulary, and build skills needed to answer synonym and antonym questions. This individual program is available from Queue, Inc.

ANALOGIES - Course describes common types of analogies and provides practice in analyzing and solving analogy problems. This individual program is also available from Texas Instruments and K-12 Micromedia.

NUMBER SERIES - Course teaches students how to analyze number series patterns and provides practice in number series problems.

QUANTITATIVE COMPARISONS - Course reviews mathematics, from elementary arithmetic through algebra and plane geometry, and provides practice in solving types of math problems found on standardized tests.

ID: A37
PRESCHOOL IQ BUILDER

Publisher: Program Design, Inc.

Also available from: Academic Software • GRAFex Company •
MARCK • Queue, Inc. • Texas Instruments

Date: Apr. 81

Grade: Preschool-1

Format: cassette or diskette

Hardware: PET; cassette • TRS-80 MOD I; with Level II BASIC;
cassette • Atari; 8K cassette; 16K diskette • Apple II Plus;
32K • Apple II; 32K with Applesoft in ROM

Price: $16.95/PET and TRS-80; $16.95/Atari cassette, $23.95/
diskette; $23.95/Apple

Program teaches vital cognitive skills that children must learn
in order to do well in school. In Part 1, SAME AND DIF-
FERENT, child discriminates between two forms. In Part 2, LET-
TER BUILDER, child matches letter on TV monitor to one on
keyboard. Accompanying parent's guide gives instructions.

ID: A38

PROBLEM-SOLVING STRATEGIES; A UNIQUE AP-
PROACH TO THINKING THROUGH PROBLEMS IN
MATH, SCIENCE AND READING

Publisher: Readers Digest

Date: Oct. 82

Grade: 5-7, 7-9

Format: 2 series of 4 diskettes

Hardware: Apple II • Apple II Plus • TRS-80 MOD I or III

Source Code: no

Price: $174.00/series set; $29.70/30 extra workbooks

These programs teaching logical thinking and decision making can be used to enhance any mathematics, science, or
reading program. Two different levels permit extensive flexibility in grade use, with arithmetic skills in the Green series at
levels 5.0-7.0, and at 7.0-9.0 in the Blue Series. A teacher's
guide and 32 workbooks are included with each series.

ID: A39

S.A.T. TUTOR

Publisher: Aquarius Publishers Inc.

Date: Aug. 82

Grade: High School-College Prep

Format: diskette

Hardware: TRS-80 MOD III

Source Code: no

Price: $55.00

Program prepares students for SAT test through computer
tutorial that makes effective use of advanced graphics and
sound. Student is given instruction in strategies and approaches
to the various question types. After this preparation, student
may elect to review background information in different
primary subject areas, or go directly to series of practice testing
drills.

ID: A40

SCHOOLHOUSE I

Publisher: COMPU-TATIONS, Inc.

Also available from: Academic Software • Opportunities For
Learning, Inc.

Grade: Elementary

Format: diskette

Hardware: Apple II; (DOS 3.2 or 3.3)

Price: $24.95

This is a collection of ten educational programs on one disk.

SPELLING WORDS - Words are shown briefly on the screen
for recognition. The user is then asked to type in the word.
Score is summarized and reruns are available.

HANGMAN - A secret word is entered by one player, and
the others try to guess it by choosing letters. Wrong guesses
add features to hangman display.

WORD FUN - A form of ad-lib stories. The program explains,
gives examples of and requests 5 nouns, adjectives, adverbs
and verbs along with some information about the user. The
computer creates a story from the information submitted.

ROMAN NUMERALS - Roman numerals are displayed and
the user is taught and quizzed on principles of Roman
numerals and can view facts or return to quiz.

GUESS MY NUMBER - This program teaches bracketing
techniques to find an unknown number.

ADDING COLUMNS - The user enters figures for addition or
subtraction and this program displays a tape of the item
number, entry and cumulative total rounded to two decimal
places. It also scrolls to show the last 18 entries.

DIVISION WITH R - This program involves division problems with remainders instead of decimals. The user enters the
dividend and divisor. The program displays the problem and
quotient with remainder.

LEARN A POEM - This program helps in the programmed
learning of poems, theatrical lines, etc. through the use of data
statements and display.

UNKNOWN VARIABLES - This program presents simple
equation problems and asks for the values of the unknown
variable "n". It teaches the algebra concept and keeps score.

FRACTION PROBLEMS - The user enters any two fractions
and the computer screen gives the compound fraction, simple
fraction equivalents, the fractions in lowest common
denominator, and the final compound fraction solution in
lowest terms for the four basic operations: a + b, a-b, axb, a/b.

ID: A41

SCRAMBLED/DECIMAL

Publisher: Cow Bay Computing

Format: 1 cassette

Hardware: PET; any model except VIC 20 or 8032

Price: $15.00

SCRAMBLED includes 150 words to choose from, or teachers
can do their own list. Students score points for spelling jumbled
words correctly. DECIMAL calculates the decimal after the user
enters the numerator, denominator, and the number of
decimal places to be calculated.

ID: A42

SOFTWARE LIBRARY

Publisher: Dr. Daley's Software

Grade: K-12

Format: 6 cassettes or 2 diskettes

Hardware: PET; 8K; 40 column • Apple II; 24K with Applesoft in ROM (DOS 3.2 or 3.3)

Language: BASIC

Source Code: no

Price: $69.95/cassette set; $79.95/diskette set

Package contains fifty game and tutorial programs grouped into eight categories. Package as whole is menu-driven, with programs in package being called and loaded automatically from central menu. Written documentation is included.

SOCIAL SCIENCE AND SPORTS - Includes following programs: Hamurabi, Dictator, Market, Football, Football for 2, and Baseball.

PRESCHOOL CHILDREN'S PROGRAMS - Includes following programs: Letter, Big Letter, Math Test, Faces, and Hurkle.

ELEMENTARY SCHOOL CHILDREN'S PROGRAMS - Includes following programs: Math, Divide, Spell, Synonym, and Hangman.

ARCADE-TYPE GAMES - Includes following programs: Tag, Deflection, Horse Race (Snake in Apple version), Breakout, ZZZAPPP!, Racetrack, Chase, and Mad Bomber.

SCIENCE FICTION GAMES - Includes following programs: Capture, TREK3, Swarms, and Starbattle (Popshot in Apple version).

BOARD GAMES - Includes following programs: Qubic, Checkers, Othello, Othello for 2, Fox, Black Box, Backgammon, Conundrum, and Obsession.

MORE SERIOUS PROGRAMS - Includes following programs: Checkbook, Calendar, Mail List, Dual Density Plot (HIRES Plotting in Apple version), Histogram Plot, and Bar Plot.

THE REST - Includes following programs: Bible Book, Bible Quiz, Maze, Wumpus, Biorhythm, Eliza, and Morse Code.

ID: A43

SORCERER TAPE

Publisher: University Software

Date: 1981

Format: cassette

Hardware: Sorcerer; 24K

Language: BASIC

Source Code: no

Price: $29.95

Sampling of eight ready-to-run programs from vendor's library of more than 100 printed programs in areas of small business, education and science, fun and games, and home and economics.

SAVINGS & LOAN - Handles all standard S & L computations.

BUDGET - Provides interactive home budget analysis.

TEDIT - Text editor for composing and correcting notes, letters, and invoices.

SPELL - Offers computer-aided instruction for beginning reader.

CROSS

REVERSI - Challenging board game offering various skill levels.

PRESIDENTS QUIZ - Identifies presidents and teaches American history.

MATH

ID: A44

TRAIL WEST

Publisher: Micro-Ed, Inc.

Also available from: K-12 Micromedia • Opportunities For Learning, Inc. • Queue, Inc.

Grade: Elementary-Adult

Format: cassette or diskette

Hardware: Commodore 64 • PET • TI 99/4

Language: BASIC

Source Code: no

Price: $7.95; $9.95/TI ed.

This is a game of options and events. The player is trying to get to the gold fields of California two thousand miles away. At the outset, some units of food, ammunition, clothes and supplies are available. Reserve units are also on hand. Reserve units can be transferred to the other categories as needed. Units of food can be created by hunting. The hunting sequence works as follows: A target animal appears on the right side of the screen. The player uses the numbers 1 to 20 to shoot at the target. The farther down on the screen the target is, the larger will be the number needed to hit the target. Each time the player enters a number and presses the return key, a bullet shoots across the screen. The hunting sequence continues until it is successful. Then it is time to travel. Each leg of the journey has a destination shown on the screen. Miles are traveled according to how far west the player (also shown on the screen) goes to reach that destination. After this, random events occur. A big storm might hit, a wagon may overturn in a river, and so forth. Sometimes, good things happen as well. In order to win the game, the player must reach the gold fields before running out of units in any category.

ID: A45

TRS-80 DISSEMINATION DISK #2

Publisher: San Mateo County Office of Education and Computer-Using Educators

Format: 1 diskette

Hardware: TRS-80 MOD I or III; 8 to 16K

Source Code: yes

Price: $10.00

This disk contains 14 programs in the public domain.

EYE - Graphic quiz on parts of the human eye. (E/S 16K)

HEART - Graphic quiz on parts of the human heart. (E/S 16K)

NEPHRON - Graphic quiz on parts of the kidney unit, nephron. (S 16K)

COCHLEA - Graphic quiz on parts of the cochlea of the inner ear. (E/S 16K)

MIRRDEMO - Demonstration of ray diagrams on a concave mirror. (S 16K)

REFFRDMO - Demonstration of reflecting light on a lens. (S 8K)

LENSDEMO - Demonstration of light passing through a lens. (S 8K)

POOL - Uses pool table graphic to demonstrate geometric angles. (S 16K)

DECFRAC - Practice problems converting decimals to fractions. (E/S 8K

CONFRAC - Drill converting fractions. (E/S 8K)

LOWEST - Drill in finding lowest common denominator. (E/S 16K)

MULTTEST - Very flexible teacher assistance program that administers a multiple-choice test prepared by a teacher in DATA statements. (Professional 16K)

STATES - Graphic quiz for identifying U.S. states, capital cities and state abbreviations. (E/S 8K)

SPLBOUND - Versatile language arts activity involving words, spelling and memory exercises. (E/S 16K)

ID: A46
TRS-80 DISSEMINATION DISK #3

Publisher: San Mateo County Office of Education and Computer-Using Educators

Format: 1 diskette

Hardware: TRS-80 MOD I or III; 4 to 16K

Source Code: yes

Price: $10.00

This disk contains 5 programs in the public domain.

SERVICE AND FILOAD - A business accounting application that generates a Trial Balance, Income Statement, and Balance Sheet for a service- oriented business. Teacher uses FILOAD to enter the correct account numbers, names and balances. Students use SERVICE program to enter their trial balance amounts from which are generated the financial statements. (S 16K)

WORMPLUS - A CLOAD program (April 1978) for practice of coordination and spatial skills. (E/S 4K)

UTILITY - A menu program of instructions to aid in the use of Apparat's NEWDOS80. (Professional 16K)

MCHMAKER (MATH AND MATCHMAKER) - A Concentration-like game using phrases and with a matchmaking program which allows the user to create new versions which can be saved on the disk. (E/S 16K)

MATCHD - The same game as above, but using data statements rather than data files. (E/S 16K)

BASIC LIVING SKILLS

ID: B1

ADVERTISING TECHNIQUES; PERSUASION...WITH WORDS

Publisher: Micro Power & Light Company

Also available from: Academic Software • K-12 Micromedia • Queue, Inc.

Format: diskette

Hardware: Apple II; 32K with Applesoft in ROM

Price: $24.95

The program describes four techniques: join the crowd, decide for yourself, remember me?, and act now! Each of the four techniques consists of: instruction with illustrative examples, exercises affording practice opportunities, mastery quiz and a concluding mastery exercise, to determine consumer intelligence level! Each technique requires about 10-15 minutes.

ID: B2

CALENDAR SKILLS

Publisher: Hartley Courseware, Inc.

Also available from: Academic Software • Opportunities For Learning, Inc. • Queue, Inc.

Grade: 2-5

Format: 1 diskette

Hardware: Apple II; 48K with Applesoft in ROM (DOS 3.2 or 3.3)

Language: Applesoft BASIC

Price: $29.95

Lessons drill student on days of week and months of year, as well as on seasons and holidays. Student must type correct answer. Both questions and answers may be changed by teacher. Includes total of 10 lessons with 20 presentations each.

ID: B3

CHANGE MAKING

Publisher: Robert R. Baker, Jr.

Date: June 82

Format: cassette or diskette

Hardware: TRS-80 MOD I or III; 16K

Language: BASIC

Source Code: yes

Price: $29.85

Program gives students practice in making correct change. Students are checked and timed by computer. Different levels of difficulty make program interesting to all students. Average program running time is 2-3 minutes at each level of difficulty. Written documentation is provided, and program is self-documented as well.

ID: B4

CLOCK

Publisher: Hartley Courseware, Inc.

Also available from: Academic Software • Scholastic Software

Grade: 1-5

Format: 1 diskette

Hardware: Apple II; 48K with Applesoft in ROM (DOS 3.2 or 3.3)

Language: Applesoft BASIC

Price: $39.95

Helps student learn to tell time by representing clock graphically on screen and enabling student to set hands of clock or type in digital time corresponding to setting of clock hands. Five levels of difficulty ranging from 1 hour to 1 minute. Graphic reinforcement is provided when 5 correct responses are made.

ID: B5

CLOCK

Publisher: Micro-Ed, Inc.

Also available from: Texas Instruments

Grade: Primary

Format: cassette or diskette

Hardware: Commodore 64 • PET • TI 99/4

Language: BASIC

Source Code: no

Price: $7.95; $9.95/TI ed.

This program presents problems in telling time by the hour or half-hour. Each lesson consists of twelve randomly selected clock faces showing various times, such as 9:00, 10:30, etc. The learner answers by first typing the number of the hour, then a colon, then the minutes. If the learner does not know the answer, pressing the question mark key will cause the right answer to be revealed. A unique feature of this program is that the computer will not print any incorrect key if pressed. Thus, the learner is guided, stroke by stroke, to the correct answer. At the end of each lesson, the learner's performance is summarized, including a listing of the specific times that gave trouble. If the same time trouble is listed twice in the summary, this means that the learner first made an incorrect response, then asked for the answer.

ID: B6

COLOR GUESS

Publisher: Ideatech Company

Also available from: MARCK

Grade: Preschool-2

Format: diskette

Hardware: Apple II; 16K with ROM Integer • Apple II PLUS; 16K with ROM Integer

Language: BASIC

Price: $12.95

COLOR GUESS teaches the reading and spelling of color words by associating the color with the correct color word as displayed on the screen. COLOR GUESS gives the student an opportunity to learn to read and to spell ten color words. During the introduction, a smiling face and the matching color word are shown. The student may choose to watch as each of the ten faces and color words are shown or may choose to proceed to the reading or spelling portion of the program.

ID: B7
COMPARATIVE BUYING

Publisher: Interpretive Education, Inc.

Also available from: Queue, Inc.

Grade: Junior-Senior High

Format: 4 diskettes

Hardware: Apple II Plus; 48K Apple II; 48K with Applesoft in ROM

Language: Applesoft BASIC

Source Code: no

Price: $225.00 with backup; $165.00 without

This program explains the concepts of comparative buying. It provides the learner with interactive experiences in determining items to purchase based on a number of variables. Subjects covered are: concepts of comparative buying; decisions before buying; effective sales buying; and cash buying versus credit buying. The teacher may control entry reading level (2nd, 3rd, 5th, or 7th), speed of program, reentry points at concept intervals, and optional music or sound. Software also has an enrichment level with simulation and problem solving. Content makes program useful with special education students.

ID: B8
CONTEMPORARY LIVING

Publisher: Aquarius Publishers Inc.

Also available from: Academic Software

Date: 1982

Grade: 3-5

Format: cassette or diskette

Hardware: Apple II; 48K with Applesoft in ROM (DOS 3.2 or 3.3) • TRS-80 MOD I or III; 16K

Source Code: no

Price: $24.95/cassette; $145.00/6 in package $29.95/diskette; $175.00/6 in package

Written on theme of how to make it in the real world, these programs use branching techniques to present material either at fifth or third grade reading level, depending on student's comprehension. Part of 27-program Survival Skills series ($775.00 diskettes or $640.00 cassettes). Teacher's guide is included. Average running time is 20 minutes.

FRIENDS AND YOU

AGE OF RESPONSIBILITY

MAP READING

SUCCEEDING

DECISION MAKING

LAW

ID: B9
DIRECTION AND DISTANCE

Publisher: Micro-Ed, Inc.

Also available from: Opportunities For Learning, Inc. • Queue, Inc. • Texas Instruments

Grade: Primary

Format: cassette or diskette

Hardware: Commodore 64 • PET • TI 99/4

Language: BASIC

Source Code: no

Price: $7.95; $9.95/TI ed.

This program uses a game format to teach primary grade children the eight directions of north, south, east, west, northeast, southeast, southwest, and northwest. Students must also estimate the distance between two objects on the screen.

ID: B10
DOLLAR AND CHANGE

Publisher: Micro-Ed, Inc.

Grade: Elementary

Format: cassette or diskette

Hardware: Commodore 64 • PET • VIC; 3K memory enhancement

Language: BASIC

Source Code: no

Price: $14.95

How fast can the student make change from a dollar bill? The player is given $5.00 in nickels, dimes and half- dollars that are to be returned as change to customers for certain purchases. A clock on the screen records the speed of the transactions.

ID: B11
DRESSING

Publisher: Aquarius Publishers Inc.

Date: Aug. 82

Grade: Special ed., Preschool

Format: 2 diskettes

Hardware: Apple II; 48K with Applesoft in ROM (DOS 3.2 or 3.3)

Language: Applesoft BASIC

Source Code: no

Price: $65.00; $34.95/diskette

Clothes and dressing are subjects of these Basic Education Programs. Each program includes multi-use disk lesson, controlled vocabulary books (single copy of each title), and cut-out dolls and doll clothing. Programs feature large print on screen display; sound; multicolor rewards; simple "space bar only" operation; automatic advancement after three tries; random word selection from pool of 31 words; full-color, controlled vocabulary books; and colorful reinforcement games.

DRESSING I - Getting dressed, getting undressed

DRESSING II - What will they wear? Special clothes

ID: B12
DRIVER EDUCATION SET

Publisher: Micro-Ed, Inc.

Grade: Junior High and up

Format: 4 programs on cassette or diskette

Hardware: VIC; 3K memory enhancement

Language: BASIC

Source Code: no

Price: $39.95

This four-program set presents the core of a course in driver's education that prepares the student for the written test. Topics include lane identification, signs, and signals, as well as a review test.

LANE IDENTIFICATION - The student is tested on the laws and rules for proper turns and passing maneuvers. One-way and two-way roads, along with their intersections, are graphically illustrated in traffic situations with which the learner must cope.

SIGNS - Proper interpretation of traffic signs, their shapes and colors, leads to safe and effective driving skills. These signs - regulatory, informational, and warning - are clearly displayed on the screen. The student is then tested on their identification and purpose.

SIGNALS - Stop, go, turn, lane control - these red, yellow, and green traffic signals are colorfully shown on the screen. The student must demonstrate knowledge of these signals by reacting properly in various situations.

DRIVER'S TEST - This wrap-up quiz covers the basic rules a driver must know before getting behind the wheel. Key elements include lane identification, the shapes and colors of traffic signs, and the interpretation of signal lights.

ID: B13
DRIVER'S AID
Publisher: Aquarius Publishers Inc.

Date: Aug. 82

Grade: High School

Format: diskette

Hardware: TRS-80 MOD III; 48K

Language: BASIC

Source Code: no

Price: $55.00

Comprehensive driver's education program combines text and graphics to serve as accompaniment to drivers education course. Completely menu-driven program allows student to directly access materials needed and to break material down into manageable study units. Simulated driving lesson creates student interest as it provides review of concepts introduced in lesson. Program is ideal for use before first driving test or just to keep in practice. Written documentation provided.

RULES OF THE ROAD
SIGNS AND SIGN SHAPES
DRIVING LAWS
SAFETY TIPS
SAMPLE TEST QUESTIONS
PEDESTRIAN RULES

ID: B14
DRIVER'S EDUCATION/INDUSTRIAL ARTS - VOLUME 1
Publisher: Minnesota Educational Computing Consortium

Date: June 82

Grade: Junior High-High School

Format: diskette

Hardware: Apple II; 32K with Applesoft in ROM (DOS 3.3)

Language: Applesoft BASIC

Source Code: no

Price: $32.90

Programs include support manual.

DRIVER EDUCATION - Two programs prepare students to take Minnesota driver permit test.

MICROMETER - Drills student graphically on use of micrometer.

RAFTER, STAIRS - Programs do calculations needed to build rafter in building and stairs in home.

ID: B15
ELEMENTARY - VOLUME 13
Publisher: Minnesota Educational Computing Consortium

Date: June 82

Grade: 5-8

Format: diskette

Hardware: Apple II; 32K with Applesoft in ROM (DOS 3.3)

Language: Applesoft BASIC

Source Code: no

Price: $38.70

Nutrition package designed by Rochester, Minnesota Public Schools contains programs which analyze student's diet and correlate exercise with diet. Support booklet (included) contains listings of foods and exercises used with programs.

ID: B16
GERTRUDE'S PUZZLES
Publisher: Learning Company

Date: 1982

Grade: 1 and up

Format: diskette

Hardware: Apple II; 48K with Applesoft in ROM (DOS 3.3); color monitor recommended • Apple II Plus; color monitor recommended

Language: Applesoft BASIC

Source Code: no

Price: $75.00

Games help child develop reasoning skills by moving puzzle pieces of different shapes and colors provided by Gertrude the Goose to form color and shape patterns. Players move to six different puzzle rooms, each with a new challenge. Sometimes they arrange game pieces according to given rules, and sometimes they must guess rule. Children then learn how to analyze what they *see* and how to solve problems with incomplete information. Gertrude the Goose delivers sets of puzzle pieces and prizes. Children can design their own sets of pieces using this powerful new Discovery Tool game.

ID: B17
GERTRUDE'S SECRETS
Publisher: Learning Company

Date: 1982

Grade: K-4

Format: diskette

Hardware: Apple II; 48K with Applesoft in ROM (DOS 3.3); color monitor recommended • Apple II Plus; color monitor recommended

Language: Applesoft BASIC

Source Code: no

Price: $75.00

Series of games helps child learn logical thinking while playing with colors and shapes. Players solve puzzles by arranging game pieces provided by Gertrude the Goose according to given rules or by guessing secret rule. They can play with sets of shapes that come with each game or create special shapes of their own. All puzzles involve thinking about colors and shapes of pieces in each game set. With this gentle tool, child learns to create order and to plan ahead.

ID: B18

GOOD HEALTH HABITS

Publisher: RIGHT ON PROGRAMS

Date: July 82

Grade: 1

Format: cassette or diskette

Hardware: Apple II; 48K with Applesoft in ROM (DOS 3.2 or 3.3) • PET; 16K

Language: BASIC

Source Code: yes

Price: $13.00/cassette; $15.00/diskette

Humorous program for young children covers weight and height, care of teeth and visits to dentist, nutrition, good sleep habits, and care of mind. Game follows.

ID: B19

GRADUATED CYLINDER

Publisher: Cow Bay Computing

Format: cassette

Hardware: PET; any model except VIC 20 or 8032

Price: $15.00

The student using this program will learn to read a scale using graphic representation.

ID: B20

HICKORY DICKORY

Publisher: APX (Atari Program Exchange)

Also available from: Academic Software

Date: June 82

Grade: K-6

Format: cassette or diskette

Hardware: Atari 400 or 800; 16K (cassette) or 24K (diskette); joystick controller optional

Language: BASIC

Source Code: no

Price: $15.95

Program uses high-resolution graphics to help student learn to tell time on traditional clockface and translate time into

digital terms using either keyboard or joystick for input. Six skill levels are offered, with time intervals from hours to minutes. Student selects number of examples to try; running score displays after each example, and total score displays at end of session. User manual is included.

ID: B21

HOME SAFE HOME

Publisher: Interpretive Education, Inc.

Also available from: MARCK • Queue, Inc.

Grade: Elementary-Junior High

Format: 4 diskettes

Hardware: Apple II Plus; 48K • Apple II; 48K with Applesoft in ROM

Language: Applesoft BASIC

Source Code: no

Price: $225.00 with backup; $165.00 without

This informative safety program highlights the major household hazards of fire, electrical shocks, falls and poisoning. Preventative suggestions are emphasized. The program uses color graphics extensively and links sound and music to the concepts presented. Branching provides options of 3 reading levels - 2nd, 3rd, and 5th. Content makes this program appropriate for special education students.

ID: B22

INCOME MEETS EXPENSES

Publisher: Interpretive Education, Inc.

Also available from: MARCK • Queue, Inc.

Grade: Elementary-Junior High

Format: 8 diskettes

Hardware: Apple II Plus; 48K • Apple II; 48K with Applesoft in ROM

Language: Applesoft BASIC

Source Code: no

Price: $460.00 with backup; $340.00 without

This program introduces students to the concept of budgeting by learning about income and its relationship to fixed and variable expenses based on needs and wants. Disk subjects are: introduction and definition of budget; income and expenses; definition of needs and wants and their relationship to expenses; categorization of fixed and variable expenses in relationship to needs and wants; and practice in using concepts taught using worksheets. The program combines instruction with practice exercises and practical experience in basic budgeting concepts. Branching will place student in one of three reading levels - 2nd, 3rd, or 5th. Includes worksheets. Content makes this program useful with special education students.

ID: B23

JOB READINESS - ASSESSMENT AND DEVELOPMENT

Publisher: Interpretive Education, Inc.

Also available from: MARCK • Queue, Inc.

Grade: Junior High

Hardware: Apple II Plus; 48K • Apple II; 48K with Applesoft in ROM

Language: Applesoft BASIC

Source Code: no

Price: $225.00 with backup; $165.00 without

This innovative program combines the techniques of assessment and instruction in supplying the student with the information to develop job readiness attitudes. It also provides the practical knowledge necessary for filling out applications, interviews, and locating job placement agencies. Subjects covered are assessment of learner attitudes about work (pretesting, tutorial, post-testing), filling out job applications, job interviews, and job placement resources. Branching provides testing at two reading levels - 6th or 3rd; and a tutorial on 3 levels - 6th, 4th, or 3rd. The software also includes pre- and post- test. Includes worksheets.

ID: B24
JUGGLES' RAINBOW

Publisher: Learning Company

Date: 1982

Grade: Preschool-K

Format: diskette

Hardware: Apple II Plus • Apple II; 48K with Applesoft in ROM (DOS 3.3); color monitor recommended

Language: Applesoft BASIC

Source Code: no

Price: $45.00

Program is designed to enable children aged three to six to play spatial games on computer using keyboard even before they can read, after only a few adult-supervised sessions. Keyboard is divided into sections with blue strips, and child presses any key in given sector to make games appear. Picture clues let child work alone or with friends while melodies play and patterns appear. Colors and patterns are used to help child learn such concepts as above and below, left and right. Child also works with lines and circles that help teach letters p, d, b, and q, considered the most difficult in the alphabet. (Apple Educational Foundation awarded JUGGLES' RAINBOW a prize for program and design excellence.)

ID: B25
LIFE CHALLENGES

Publisher: Aquarius Publishers Inc.

Date: Aug. 82

Grade: High School

Format: 5 diskettes

Hardware: Apple II; 48K with Applesoft in ROM (DOS 3.2 or 3.3)

Language: Applesoft BASIC

Source Code: no

Price: $34.95/diskette; $169.00/set

Series is designed to simulate variety of real life situations, then enable student to explore various options and methods of coping, and finally *see* potential effects. Programs enhance student's judgment and critical thinking regarding cause-and-effect relationships, encourage student reaction and interpreta-

tion, foster solutions to problem situations, and provide an opportunity for sharing these solutions. Documentation is provided.

ARREST - Unique simulation of arrest of an adolescent suspected of committing a crime contains detailed evidence followed by options. Each option includes cause-and-effect relationships.

DEATH - Stages of death and dying are presented as they affect a high school student. Program emphasizes identification through a gaming situation.

INVOLVED IN AN ACCIDENT - Object in simulation is to deal with having been involved in a traffic accident, identifying what must be done, and by whom.

BEING FIRED - Simulation involving employee-employer relationships teaches student how to try to avoid being fired, or to handle the situation if fired.

VIOLATED CONSUMER RIGHTS - Object of simulation is to identify how and why consumer rights have been violated. Once learned, student challenges computer to restore his or her rights.

ID: B26
MAP READING

Publisher: Micro Power & Light Company

Also available from: Academic Software • K-12 Micromedia • Queue, Inc.

Grade: 4 and up

Format: diskette

Hardware: Apple II; 32K with Applesoft in ROM

Price: $19.95

This program is an introduction to direction and distance. It can be used for anyone who has at least 4th grade reading skills and can multiply single-digit whole numbers. Topics covered include the compass, the concept of scale, and notation. Each topic includes instruction, examples, practice exercises and review.

ID: B27
MARKET SURVEY

Publisher: Comaldor

Format: cassette or diskette

Hardware: PET

Price: $20.00

A good program for family studies, consumer education and mathematics. By keeping track of different stores and various items as chosen by the class, the program performs cost analysis by store, by item, and by selective shopping. It calculates savings in dollars and cents as well as percentage, and tallies the number of bargains at each store. Results may appear on screen or via printer.

ID: B28
MATH - MONEY

Publisher: RIGHT ON PROGRAMS

Also available from: Academic Software • Queue, Inc.

Grade: 4

Format: cassette or diskette

Hardware: Apple II; 48K with Applesoft in ROM (DOS 3.2 or 3.3) • PET; 16K

Language: BASIC

Source Code: yes

Price: $13.00/cassette; $15.00/diskette

The student is given several reasons why understanding of money and the ability to add, subtract, multiply and divide money are so important. Examples are given and incorrect answers are corrected.

ID: B29
MATH - TELLING TIME
Publisher: RIGHT ON PROGRAMS

Also available from: Academic Software • Queue, Inc.

Grade: 2

Format: cassette or diskette

Hardware: Apple II; 48K with Applesoft in ROM (DOS 3.2 or 3.3) • PET; 16K

Language: BASIC

Source Code: yes

Price: $13.00/cassette; $15.00/diskette

Basic concepts of the clock and telling time are introduced. Not only is the traditional clock faced used, but digital clocks and watches are also included.

ID: B30
MEMORY MYTH
Publisher: Micro Power & Light Company

Also available from: Academic Software • Queue, Inc.

Format: diskette

Hardware: Apple II; 32K with Applesoft in ROM

Price: $19.95

This program is for anyone who wants to challenge and develop their memory skills and have a good time doing it. Each program consists of 12 levels of exercises. Each successive level is still more challenging. Challenge #1 is to be able to do all 12 levels - how quickly can an image be placed in the user's memory. Challenge #2 is to do so as quickly as possible. The user can start at any level.

ID: B31
MONEY MANAGEMENT ASSESSMENT
Publisher: Interpretive Education, Inc.

Also available from: MARCK • Queue, Inc.

Grade: Junior-Senior High

Format: 4 diskettes

Hardware: Apple II Plus; 48K Apple II; 48K with Applesoft in ROM

Language: Applesoft BASIC

Source Code: no

Price: $225.00 with backup; $165.00 without

This is a prescriptive, diagnostic program with error analysis. A unique program which assesses basic mathematical skills, vocabulary and money management concepts. The results, when used for pre- and post-testing, will assist the teacher in the implementation and evaluation of money management programs. The program assesses vocabulary of money management, concepts of money management, calendar concepts and money symbols, and skills needed to manage money. MONEY MANAGEMENT ASSESSMENT provides automatic placement of student on one of two reading levels - 2nd or 5th. It also includes concept and math skill testing and a tutorial review. Content makes this software useful in special education programs. Includes worksheets.

ID: B32
MONEY! MONEY!
Publisher: Hartley Courseware, Inc.

Date: Sept. 82

Grade: 2-5

Format: 1 diskette

Hardware: Apple II; 48K with Applesoft in ROM (DOS 3.2 or 3.3)

Language: Applesoft BASIC

Price: $39.95

Provides practice in working with concepts involving money, using high-resolution graphics to develop pictures of bills and coins. Student is required to determine amounts shown, work with concept of more and less, determine correct amount to give for specific item, and be able to count correct change. Reinforcers are presented after five correct responses.

ID: B33
PERSONAL CONSUMERISM
Publisher: Aquarius Publishers Inc.

Also available from: Academic Software • Opportunities For Learning, Inc.

Date: 1982

Grade: 3-5

Format: cassette or diskette

Hardware: Apple II; 48K with Applesoft in ROM (DOS 3.2 or 3.3) • TRS-80 MOD I or III; 16K

Source Code: no

Price: $24.95/cassette; $195.00/8 in package $29.95/diskette; $235.00/8 in package

Written on theme of how to make it in the real world, these programs use branching techniques to present material either at fifth or third grade reading level, depending on student's responses. This is part of a 27-program Survival Skills Series ($775.00/diskettes or $640.00/cassettes). A teacher's guide is included. Average running time is 20 minutes.

TIPS ON BUYING A USED CAR

READING AN ADVERTISEMENT

CONSUMERISM AND YOU

SHOPPING IN A COMPARATIVE WAY

LAWS FOR CONSUMERS

CONSUMER FRAUD

CONSUMER HELP

UNDERSTANDING PACKAGING

ID: B34

PERSONAL FINANCE

Publisher: Aquarius Publishers Inc.

Also available from: Academic Software • Opportunities For Learning, Inc.

Date: 1982

Grade: 3-5

Format: cassette or diskette

Hardware: Apple II; 48K with Applesoft in ROM (DOS 3.2 or 3.3) • TRS-80 MOD I or III; 16K

Source Code: no

Price: $24.95/cassette; $165.00/7 in package $29.95/diskette; $199.00/7 in package

Written on theme of how to make it in the real world, these programs use branching techniques to present material, either at fifth or third grade reading level, depending on student's comprehension. Part of 27-program Survival Skills series ($775.00 diskettes or $640.00 cassettes). Teacher's guide is included. Average running time is 20 minutes.

> HOW TO FINANCE A CAR
>
> MONEY
>
> ALL ABOUT INTEREST
>
> METRICS AND YOU
>
> EATING FOR GOOD HEALTH
>
> YOU AND INSURANCE
>
> CREDIT

ID: B35

POISON PROOF YOUR HOME

Publisher: Interpretive Education, Inc.

Also available from: MARCK • Queue, Inc.

Grade: Elementary-Junior High

Format: 4 diskettes

Hardware: Apple II Plus; 48K • Apple II; 48K with Applesoft in ROM

Language: Applesoft BASIC

Source Code: no

Price: $285.00 with backup: $210.00 without

This is a concept-oriented, interest program describing ways in which one may be poisoned, types of poisons, preventative techniques and what to do if a poisoning occurs. Subjects covered are categories of poisons, poison prevention concepts, places poisons are found in the home, suggestions for poison prevention, and what to do if a poisoning occurs. Branching allows student to learn at 2nd, 3rd, or 5th reading levels.

ID: B36

ROCKY'S BOOTS

Publisher: Learning Company

Date: 1982

Grade: 2 and up

Format: diskette

Hardware: Apple II; 48K with Applesoft in ROM (DOS 3.3); color monitor recommended • Apple II Plus; color monitor recommended

Language: Applesoft BASIC

Source Code: no

Price: $75.00

Games help child develop logic skills that will be of use throughout life. Players build animated logic machines in order to score points in game. While building machines, children learn basics of computer circuits. Machines operate kicking boot, and players score or lose points for "booting" particular objects. Game features color graphics that support learning, as well as music and sound effects that can be turned on and off. ROCKY'S BOOTS has appeal of arcade game with content of logic course.

ID: B37

SURVIVAL MATH

Publisher: Sunburst Communications

Grade: 4 and up

Format: diskette

Hardware: Apple II; 32K

Price: $50.00

This package includes 4 simulations that apply math skills to everyday life. Each puts the student in a situation that requires the use of math as a basis for making sound judgments.

SMART SHOPPER MARATHON - This program takes the student on a shopping trip. As a consumer, the student tries to decide on the best buys, using unit prices and percent discounts.

HOT DOG STAND - In this program students run a hot dog stand at football games to raise money.

TRAVEL AGENT CONTEST - The student becomes a contestant in a trip-planning contest. The aim is to plan a 7-day, 6-night trip without exceeding a prescribed spending limit. Money must be allocated for transportation, meals, lodging and special events.

FOREMAN'S ASSISTANT - The student helps plan a playroom and buys materials for building it, keeping in a budget and time-frame. Covers area, perimeter, and units of measure.

ID: B38

TELLING TIME COMPUTER SET

Publisher: Orange Cherry Media

Also available from: Academic Software • K-12 Micromedia • Queue, Inc.

Grade: K-3

Format: cassette or diskette

Hardware: PET 2000 or 4000; 16K • TRS-80 MOD I or III; 16K • Apple; 16K • Apple II; 16K

Price: $15.00/cassette; $28.00/cassette set of 2; $34.00/diskette

Explaining how to tell time is not a simple task. But this clear microcomputer program simplifies the task for youngsters learning about clocks and time.

> HOURS OF THE DAY
>
> MINUTES IN AN HOUR

ID: B39
TIME MASTER

Publisher: Micro Power & Light Company

Format: diskette

Hardware: Apple II; 48K with Applesoft in ROM

Price: $29.95

The program offers three types of instruction. One type asks the student to enter the time, first hours then minutes. The program then positions the hands on the clock face accordingly. The second type of instruction reverses these roles. The program asks the student to position the hands to show a specified time. The hands can be moved either clockwise or counterclockwise by repetitive pressing of either the Forward or Back Arrow keys. When the hour and minute hands are set in the desired position, the student so informs the program by pressing the Return key. Students have two chances to set the hands correctly. After each successful attempt a happy face is displayed on the monitor. After a second unsuccessful attempt to set the hands, TIME MASTER positions the hands correctly for the student to see! With this type of instruction the student first learns hours, then half hours, quarter hours and finally minutes. The third type of instruction enables the student to actually start the clock at a time of his or her choice. After entering the starting hour and minutes, the clock face is displayed with the hands set to the specified time. The clock begins to tick! A minute later the hands move to their new position, and the clock ticks on. With but little initial support from teacher (or parent), TIME MASTER can be used by kindergarten age children, discovering that telling time is lots of fun! And early elementary students frequently operate the program quite on their own, without the teacher's help!

ID: B40
U.S. TIME ZONES

Publisher: Micro-Ed, Inc.

Also available from: Queue, Inc.

Grade: Elementary and up

Format: cassette or diskette

Hardware: Commodore 64 • PET

Language: BASIC

Source Code: no

Price: $7.95

The focus in this program is on telling time from one zone to another. The structure is the same as for the Micro-Ed program CLOCK.

ID: B41
USING A CALENDAR

Publisher: Hartley Courseware, Inc.

Date: Sept. 82

Grade: 2-4

Format: 1 diskette

Hardware: Apple II; 48K with Applesoft in ROM (DOS 3.2 or 3.3)

Language: Applesoft BASIC

Price: $39.95

Presents calendar concepts, including simple date/day relationships, as well as more general interpretations, using picture of calendar with information and questions scrolled below. Teacher can create calendar lesson by specifying month and first day, then entering appropriate questions.

ID: B42
USING MONEY AND MAKING CHANGE

Publisher: Orange Cherry Media

Also available from: Academic Software • K-12 Micromedia

Grade: 2-4

Format: cassette or diskette

Hardware: PET 2000 or 4000; 16K • TRS-80 MOD I or III; 16K • Apple; 16K • Apple II; 16K

Price: $15.00/cassette; $42.00/cassette set of 3; $50.00/diskette

An effective and practical use of the computer's capabilities to teach the value of coins and currency for younger students. Pupils also learn how money is used to pay for things and how to calculate the correct change in purchases.

LET'S LOOK AT MONEY

EVERYDAY USE OF MONEY

IF YOU RAN A COOKIESHOP

ID: B43
WORK SERIES

Publisher: Aquarius Publishers Inc.

Also available from: Academic Software • Opportunities For Learning, Inc.

Date: 1982

Grade: 3-5

Format: cassette or diskette

Hardware: Apple II; 48K with Applesoft in ROM (DOS 3.2 or 3.3) • TRS-80 MOD I or III; 16K

Source Code: no

Price: $24.95/cassette; $145.00/6 in package $29.95/diskette; $175.00/6 in package

Written on theme of how to make it in the real world, these programs use branching techniques to present material either at fifth or third grade reading level, depending on student's comprehension. Part of 27-program Survival Skills series ($775.00 diskettes or $640.00 cassettes). Teacher's guide is included. Average running time is 20 minutes.

HOW TO GET AND HOLD A JOB

JOB AND YOU

SELF-CONCEPT AND YOUR WORK

PART-TIME JOBS

NEW ON THE JOB

INTERVIEWING

ID: B44
YOU CAN BANK ON IT

Publisher: Interpretive Education, Inc.

Also available from: MARCK • Queue, Inc.

Grade: Junior-Senior High

Format: 6 diskettes

Hardware: Apple II Plus; 48K • Apple II; 48K with Applesoft in ROM

Language: Applesoft BASIC

Source Code: no

Price: $375.00/with backup; $285.00 without

This program introduces the concept of a bank. Through interaction with presentations on the banking services of checking and savings, the learner is provided opportunities to apply the newly acquired knowledge. Subjects covered are concepts and rationale of a bank, beginning a savings account, depositing money into a savings account, withdrawing money from a savings account, beginning a checking account, writing checks and keeping records. The program combines instruction with practice exercises on three reading levels - 2nd, 3rd, and 5th. Includes worksheets.

BUSINESS EDUCATION

C

ID: C1
10-KEY DRILL
Publisher: Robert R. Baker, Jr.
Also available from: Queue, Inc.
Date: June 82
Grade: 5-12
Format: cassette or diskette
Hardware: TRS-80 MOD I or III; 16K
Language: BASIC
Source Code: yes
Price: $19.85

Computer displays up to 30 numbers to key. Student keys numbers as rapidly and accurately as possible, using 10-key pad on computer. After all numbers are keyed, computer checks for errors and calculates keying speed in strokes per minute. Immediate feedback makes program interesting and challenging. Average program running time is 2-3 minutes at each level of difficulty. Written documentation is provided, and program is self-documented as well.

ID: C2
ACCOUNTING EXAM
Publisher: Robert R. Baker, Jr.
Date: June 82
Grade: 9-12
Format: cassette or diskette
Hardware: TRS-80 MOD I or III; 16K
Language: BASIC
Source Code: yes
Price: $23.85

Program gives student an accounting test on computer. Questions appear in different order each time program runs. Test is scored and timed, and missed questions are reviewed. New questions may be added through DATA statement in BASIC. Average program running time is 2-3 minutes at each level of difficulty. Written documentation is provided, and program is self-documented as well.

ID: C3
ACCOUNTS PAYABLE POSTING DRILL
Publisher: Robert R. Baker, Jr.
Date: June 82
Grade: 9-12
Format: cassette or diskette
Hardware: TRS-80 MOD I or III; 16K
Language: BASIC
Source Code: yes
Price: $23.85

Drill gives students practice in posting accounts payable into computer. Transactions and appropriate posting format are self-contained within program. Each program is timed, and time and error scores are displayed. Average program running time is 2-3 minutes at each level of difficulty. Written documentation is provided, and program is self- documented as well.

ID: C4
ACCOUNTS RECEIVABLE POSTING DRILL
Publisher: Robert R. Baker, Jr.
Date: June 82
Grade: 9-12
Format: cassette or diskette
Hardware: TRS-80 MOD I or III; 16K
Language: BASIC
Source Code: yes
Price: $23.85

Drill gives students practice in posting accounts receivable into computer. Transactions and appropriate posting format are self-contained within program. Each problem is timed, and time and error scores are displayed. Average program running time is 2-3 minutes at each level of difficulty. Written documentation is provided, and program is self- documented as well.

ID: C5
BUSINESS - VOLUME 1
Publisher: Minnesota Educational Computing Consortium
Date: June 82
Grade: High School and up
Format: diskette
Hardware: Apple II; 32K with Applesoft in ROM (DOS 3.3)
Language: Applesoft BASIC
Source Code: no
Price: $34.80

Package contains basic business programs to calculate interest and loans. Includes support booklet.

BANK - Solves three types of bank problems.

INTEREST - Compares simple and compound interest.

LOANAM - Prints loan amortization tables.

MANAGE - Simulation program in which teams of students compete against each other to run a business.

MONEY - Tests user on monetary principles.

PAYROLL - Simulates payroll program.

TYPING - Gives users practice in improving typing speed.

ID: C6
BUSINESS - VOLUME 2
Publisher: Minnesota Educational Computing Consortium
Date: June 82
Grade: Junior High and up
Format: diskette
Hardware: Apple II; 32K with Applesoft in ROM (DOS 3.3); dual disk drives; 132-column printer
Language: Applesoft BASIC
Source Code: no
Price: $38.80

Program simulates payroll system, including company files, employee files, and tax files. Program prints checks, quarterly reports, and yearly reports. Support booklet included.

ID: C7

BUSINESS - VOLUME 3

Publisher: Minnesota Educational Computing Consortium

Also available from: Sunburst Communications

Date: June 82

Grade: High School and up

Format: diskette

Hardware: Apple II; 32K with Applesoft in ROM (DOS 3.3); dual disk drives; 132-column printer

Language: Applesoft BASIC

Source Code: no

Price: $63.10

Microcomputer Integrated Computerized Accounting System (MICAS) provides a realistic experience with automated accounting systems. Package consists of four integrated systems: (1) general ledger; (2) accounts payable; (3) accounts receivable; and (4) inventory control. Support booklet is necessary to use programs. Answer key provides solution to student exercises in support booklet.

ID: C8

BUSINESS PACKAGE I

Publisher: Micro Learningware

Also available from: MARCK

Format: cassette or diskette

Hardware: TRS-80 MOD I or III; 16K cassette or 32K diskette

Language: BASIC

Source Code: yes

Price: $24.95

Package consists of four programs dealing with basic accounting concepts. Written instructions provided.

ACCOUNTING I - Presents basic accounting concepts, including double entry concepts with many graphic illustrations.

ACCOUNTING II - Introduces journals, ledgers, and financial statements, with many graphic illustrations.

GENERAL LEDGER - Provides simulated computerized system that allows user to enter transactions, print trial balance of general ledger balances and financial statements. General ledger provides means of gaining practice without drudgery of handwritten journal and ledger entries.

DEPRECIATION - Calculates depreciation according to straight line, double declining balance, or sum-of-years digit methods. Methods of computation accord with IRS guidelines. Program will also display depreciation schedule.

ID: C9

BUSINESS PACKAGE II

Publisher: Micro Learningware

Also available from: Academic Software • MARCK

Format: cassette or diskette

Hardware: TRS-80 MOD I or III; 16K cassette or 32K diskette • PET; 8K cassette • Apple II; 32K with Applesoft in ROM (DOS 3.2 or 3.3);

Language: BASIC

Source Code: yes

Price: $24.95

Package presents advanced business concepts and guides student in use. Individual programs are for all computers listed unless otherwise noted in descriptions. For Apple II, this package is known as BUSINESS PACKAGE I. Written instructions provided.

ANNUITIES - Calculates amount that can be accumulated with initial investment for specified number of periods at specified interest rate. For all computers except Apple II.

LOAN AMORTIZATION - Complete loan analysis program calculates either payment amounts, number of periods, rate of interest, length of loan, or total interest, and prints amortization schedule if desired.

BANK RECONCILIATION - Accepts bank balance, checkbook balance, checks written, outstanding checks, charges, and reconciles bank statement.

STOCK MARKET SIMULATION - Players buy and sell stocks, with object of game being to increase their net worth. Simulation allows selection from 26 stocks that fluctuate in price based on market indicators such as prime interest rate and inflation rate.

DEPRECIATION - Calculates depreciation according to straight line, double declining balance, or sum-of-years digit methods. Methods of computation accord with IRS guidelines. Program will also display depreciation schedule. For Commodore and Apple II only.

ID: C10

BUSINESS PACKAGE III

Publisher: Micro Learningware

Also available from: Academic Software • MARCK

Format: diskette

Hardware: TRS-80 MOD I or III; 32K • Apple II; 32K with Applesoft in ROM (DOS 3.2 or 3.3); printer

Language: BASIC

Source Code: yes

Price: $24.00

Series of programs including two accounting projects with solutions. Written instructions provided.

CHART OF ACCOUNTS ENTRY - Program maintains chart of accounts disk file, allowing student to add new accounts, change or delete accounts, and print new chart of accounts.

JOURNAL ENTRY - Program accepts journal entries, prints proof of journal entries, allows corrections, and posts entries to ledger.

REPORT PRINT - Prints trial balance of general ledger, profit and loss statement, and balance sheet.

ID: C11

DECISION-MAKING SIMULATIONS IN ACCOUNTING FOR THE MICROCOMPUTER

Publisher: Gregg/ McGraw-Hill

Date: Feb. 82

Grade: Secondary

Format: 3 diskettes

Hardware: TRS-80 MOD III; 32K (TRSDOS 1.3); • Apple II Plus; 32K (DOS 3.3);

Language: BASIC

Price: $350.00

Designed as supplement to *Accounting: Systems and Procedures*, 4th edition, by Weaver, Brower, Smiley, and Porreca, programs enable students to apply content of each chapter in text to making realistic business decisions. Each simulation requires student to interact with computer for approximately 15 minutes. Management component provides teachers with complete control over use of simulations, and serves as means of tracking and diagnosing problems. Teacher's manual contains background material and sample solutions to simulations. Teacher's manual is included.

ID: C12
FILING TEST

Publisher: Robert R. Baker, Jr.

Date: June 82

Grade: 9-12

Format: cassette or diskette

Hardware: TRS-80 MOD I or III; 16K

Language: BASIC

Source Code: yes

Price: $23.85

Test increases student knowledge of correct filing practices. Missed questions are corrected by student as soon as they are missed. Total score and time are displayed at end of exercise. Average program running time is 2-3 minutes at each level of difficulty. Written documentation is provided, and program is self-documented as well.

ID: C13
GENERAL LEDGER POSTING DRILL

Publisher: Robert R. Baker, Jr.

Date: June 82

Grade: 9-12

Format: cassette or diskette

Hardware: TRS-80 MOD I or III; 16K

Language: BASIC

Source Code: yes

Price: $23.85

Program gives students practice in posting general ledger into computer. Transactions and appropriate posting format are self-contained within program. Each problem is timed, and time and error scores are displayed. Average program running time is 2-3 minutes at each level of difficulty. Written documentation is provided, and program is self- documented as well.

ID: C14
HIRE-SAFE COMPUTER OPERATOR TEST

Publisher: Robert R. Baker, Jr.

Date: June 82

Grade: 9-12

Format: cassette or diskette

Hardware: TRS-80 MOD I or III; 16K

Language: BASIC

Source Code: yes

Price: $59.85

Program time-tests prospective employees in computer operation, including typing, ten-key, and computer knowledge. Individual skill scores and overall scores are displayed so that job applicants may be compared. Average program running time is 2-3 minutes at each level of difficulty. Written documentation is provided, and program is self-documented as well.

ID: C15
INVENTORY POSTING DRILL

Publisher: Robert R. Baker, Jr.

Date: June 82

Grade: 9-12

Format: cassette or diskette

Hardware: TRS-80 MOD I or III; 16K

Language: BASIC

Source Code: yes

Price: $23.85

Drill gives students practice in posting inventory into computer. Transactions and appropriate posting format are self-contained within program. Each problem is timed, and time and error scores are displayed. Average program running time is 2-3 minutes at each level of difficulty. Written documentation is provided, and program is self- documented as well.

ID: C16
KEYPUNCH DRILL

Publisher: Robert R. Baker, Jr.

Date: June 82

Grade: 9-12

Format: cassette or diskette

Hardware: TRS-80 MOD I or III; 16K

Language: BASIC

Source Code: yes

Price: $29.00

Provides practice in keypad data entry. Drills appear on computer screen to be keyed by student. Correct keys for keypunch numeric data must be used. Keying rate and number of errors are displayed at end of exercise. Average program running time is 2-3 minutes at each level of difficulty. Written documentation is provided, and program is self-documented as well.

ID: C17
MARKET PLACE

Publisher: Minnesota Educational Computing Consortium

Date: June 82

Grade: 3-8

Format: diskette

Hardware: Atari 400/800; 16K with Atari BASIC in cartridge

Language: BASIC

Source Code: no

Price: $37.90

Series of four business simulations casts elementary students in role of decision-makers. Graphics help stimulate high interest in programs, each of which teaches different aspect of business marketing. Support booklet included.

SELL APPLES

SELL PLANTS

SELL LEMONADE

SELL BICYCLES

ID: C18

MASTER TYPE

Publisher: Aquarius Publishers Inc.

Date: 1982

Format: cassette or diskette

Hardware: Apple II; (DOS 3.2 or 3.3) • TRS-80 MOD I or III

Source Code: no

Price: $34.95/diskette; $24.95/cassette

Action-packed space game uses arcade-like color graphics to teach touch typing. Enemy words appear on screen and launch missiles toward student's star base. Student must type attacking words accurately and rapidly to prevent missiles from reaching star base and blowing it up. Average running time is 20 minutes; documentation is provided.

ID: C19

MICRO TYPING

Publisher: Sheridan College

Grade: Junior High-College

Format: 1 diskette

Hardware: PET 4016 or 8032; 8K (DOS 1.0 or 2.0) • Apple II Plus; 8K (DOS 3.1)

Price: $100.00

A basic typing program, designed to teach the keyboard and improve speed and accuracy, including testing and marking for both. The lessons and drills include: Starting on the Keyboard; The Index Fingers; The Alphabet; The Shift Keys; The Number Keys; Sentences for Speed and Accuracy.

ID: C20

MICROCOMPUTER ACCOUNTING APPLICATIONS

Publisher: Gregg/ McGraw-Hill

Date: Feb. 82

Grade: Secondary

Format: 4 diskettes

Hardware: PET; 32K; printer • TRS-80 MOD III; 32K (TRSDOS 1.3); printer • Apple II Plus; 32K (DOS 3.3); printer

Language: BASIC

Source Code: no

Price: $125.00

Applications require student to maintain complete set of financial records for service and merchandising business. They include general ledger, accounts payable, accounts receivable,

and payroll systems. All programs needed to complete problem materials are contained on disks. Students work partly at computer and partly at desks. Teacher's manual and key contains suggestions for setting up and managing microcomputer instruction in accounting as well as keys for all problems found in student workbook. Programs are designed as complement to *Accounting: Systems and Procedures*, 4th edition, by Weaver, Brower, Smiley, and Porreca. Text workbook and teacher's manual and key are included.

ID: C21

MICROCOMPUTER TESTING PROGRAM FOR ACCOUNTING: SYSTEMS AND PROCEDURES, FOURTH EDITION

Publisher: Gregg/ McGraw-Hill

Date: Feb. 82

Grade: Secondary

Format: 4 diskettes (3 for TRS-80)

Hardware: PET; 32K; printer • TRS-80 MOD III; 32K; (TRSDOS 1.3); printer • Apple II Plus; 32K (DOS 3.3); printer

Language: BASIC

Source Code: no

Price: $100.00

Program provides objective test for every chapter of Accounting: Systems and Procedures, 4th edition, by Weaver, Brower, Smiley, and Porreca. Randomly generated, multiple-choice vocabulary and concept questions provide reinforcement for correct answers and immediate feedback to student and teacher in the form of computer-generated session reports. There are 25-30 questions per chapter; each test should take about 15 minutes. Teacher's manual is included.

ID: C22

PAYROLL POSTING DRILL

Publisher: Robert R. Baker, Jr.

Date: June 82

Grade: 9-12

Format: cassette or diskette

Hardware: TRS-80 MOD I or III; 16K

Language: BASIC

Source Code: yes

Price: $23.85

Drill gives students practice in posting payroll into computer. Transactions and appropriate posting format are self-contained within program. Each problem is timed, and time and error scores are displayed. Average program running time is 2-3 minutes at each level of difficulty. Written documentation is provided, and program is self- documented as well.

ID: C23

PROFIT AND LOSS: A MICROCOMPUTER SIMULATION

Publisher: Gregg/ McGraw-Hill

Date: Jan. 82

Grade: Secondary

Format: diskette

Hardware: TRS-80 MOD III; (TRSDOS 1.3) • Apple II Plus; (DOS 3.3)

Language: BASIC

Source Code: no

Price: $50.00

This 5-class teacher-administered simulation provides an introduction to economic concepts. Course uses fictional company to stimulate student interest in pricing and demand, supply and demand, and advertising and demand. Student teams try to come up with winning combination for company after studying concepts. Printouts show company's resulting profit or loss. Simulation is designed as short unit in courses in free enterprise, economics, general business, and retailing. Teacher's manual includes reproducible handouts.

ID: C24

SHORTHAND TAKE

Publisher: Robert R. Baker, Jr.

Date: June 82

Grade: 9-12

Format: cassette or diskette

Hardware: TRS-80 MOD I or III; 16K

Language: BASIC

Source Code: yes

Price: $39.85

Three-minute shorthand dictation is given on cassette and transcribed into computer by student. Computer tests spelling and accuracy by checking key words. Instructions for creating new takes are included. Average program running time is 2-3 minutes at each level of difficulty. Written documentation is provided, and program is self- documented as well.

ID: C25

STENO

Publisher: Robert R. Baker, Jr.

Also available from: Queue, Inc.

Date: June 82

Grade: 9-12

Format: cassette or diskette

Hardware: TRS-80 MOD I or III; 16K

Language: BASIC

Source Code: yes

Price: $19.85

STENO teaches brief forms the easy way. Computer dictates brief forms which student then transcribes by typing words back into computer. Computer then scores dictation, showing errors and correct word. Average program running time is 2-3 minutes at each level of difficulty. Written documentation is provided, and program is self-documented as well.

ID: C26

T-ACCOUNTS

Publisher: Robert R. Baker, Jr.

Also available from: Queue, Inc.

Date: June 82

Grade: 6-12

Format: cassette or diskette

Hardware: TRS-80 MOD I or III; 16K

Language: BASIC

Source Code: yes

Price: $19.85

Provides practice in posting ten transactions to T-Accounts. Computer displays T's, and as transactions are posted account information appears in correct locations on T's. Average program running time is 2-3 minutes at each level of difficulty. Written documentation is provided, and program is self-documented as well.

ID: C27

TYPING

Publisher: Robert R. Baker, Jr.

Date: June 82

Format: cassette or diskette

Hardware: TRS-80 MOD I or III; 16K

Language: BASIC

Source Code: yes

Price: $19.85

Provides timed typing drill as supplement to normal typing class. As student types, words per minute are displayed on screen. Average program running time is 2-3 minutes at each level of difficulty. Written documentation is provided, and program is self-documented as well.

ID: C28

TYPING TEACHER

Publisher: COMPU-TATIONS, Inc.

Also available from: Academic Software

Format: 1 program on diskette

Hardware: Apple II; (DOS 3.2 or 3.3)

Price: $14.95

This is a hands-on educational program which utilizes behavioral learning principles to teach anyone to master the typewriter or keyboard. Written by a behavioral psychologist, the program concentrates on drill, practice and reinforced learning through eight phases of instruction. In each of the eight practice levels, there are ten exercises to be completed at the student's own pace. The screen displays the relevant keyboard positions and identifies where to place fingers. The student is asked to successfully type four repetitions of each of ten exercises.

ID: C29

TYPING TEACHER

Publisher: Instant Software[T.M.]

Also available from: MARCK

Grade: 3 and up

Format: cassette

Hardware: TRS-80 MOD I or III; 16K with Level II BASIC

Language: BASIC

Source Code: no

Price: $12.95

Complete seven-part package guides user from familiarization with keyboard through typing of words and phrases to mastery of touch-typing. Video monitor becomes bottomless page for typing practice. Written documentation is provided.

ID: C30

TYPING TUTOR

Publisher: Aquarius Publishers Inc.

Date: 1982

Format: cassette or diskette

Hardware: TRS-80 MOD I or III

Source Code: no

Price: $34.95/diskette; $24.95/cassette

Typing tutorial program is designed for beginning student, who progresses from keyboard appearing in graphics on screen, (letters must be pressed on computer keyboard to advance score) to typing tests given a line at a time on screen. Student must type line given before next one appears. Number right and wrong are displayed throughout testing. Average running time is 20 minutes; documentation is provided.

COMPUTER LITERACY

D

ID: D1
ALICE IN LOGOLAND

Publisher: Krell Software Corporation

Format: 4 diskettes

Hardware: Apple II

Language: LOGO

This is a 20-program tutorial series for intermediate and experienced programmers new to the LOGO language. It is a clever series of adventures in which Alice and her friends introduce the user to LOGO.

ID: D2
BASIC TUTOR

Publisher: Aquarius Publishers Inc.

Date: Aug. 82

Format: diskette

Hardware: TRS-80 MOD III; 48K

Source Code: no

Price: $59.50

Package teaches skills necessary for BASIC programmer. Written by a professional programmer, program progresses from learning commands to actually writing programs. All instructions are given on-line; there are no manuals to fill out or coding forms to use. Trade secrets are offered about the language used for a more efficient use of available memory.

ID: D3
BASIC TUTOR SERIES

Publisher: Educational Courseware

Also available from: Academic Software • MARCK • Queue, Inc.

Format: 9 diskettes

Hardware: Apple; 48K (DOS 3.3 or 3.2)

Language: Applesoft BASIC

Price: $32.00/diskette; $250.00/series

This series of disks is designed for the persons wishing to learn how to write programs on a computer. There are more than 100 programs written in Applesoft BASIC in the series. The BASIC TUTOR SERIES is organized to provide a sequential study and practice of programming skills and techniques. With periodic self-paced practice, user can learn how to create original programs. All of these disks are menu- driven and are user-friendly.

SYSTEMS COMMANDS - BASIC TUTOR 1 will introduce the novice to how the keys on the Apple's keyboard can be used to command the computer. The most often used systems commands are introduced and are illustrated in animation. Programs include: GETTING STARTED; KEYBOARD COMMANDS; SYSTEM COMMANDS - LOAD, LIST, RUN, SAVE, NEW, CATALOG, DELETE, LOCK & UNLOCK, RENAME, NEW, and others; PRINT, STRINGS AND NUMERIC VARIABLES; STUDY FUNCTIONS; INVERSE & NORMAL; STUDY HELP; TEXT GRAPHICS; and ANIMATION OF COMMANDS. Once this first TUTOR disk is mastered, the user is ready to learn how to write his first program with BASIC TUTOR 2.

PROGRAMMING COMMANDS - This second disk in the TUTOR SERIES presents the most often used programming commands. Sample listings and examples are provided for study. With some experimentation and practice, the user should be writing his first brief programs after working with these tutorial programs. PROGRAMMING COMMANDS covers: LET, PRINT, GOTO, IF-THEN, VTAB & HTAB, REM, GOSUB-RETURN, READ-DATA, SPEED, END, INPUT & GET, FOR-NEXT, and others; STUDY MID & RIGHT & LEFT & CHR$; STUDY LOOPS; STUDY INPUT; STUDY ASCII; and STUDY LEN & VAL.

GRAPHIC COMMANDS - Designed to help the user learn how to create programs in high- and low-resolution graphics. The graphics features of the Apple are superior to most computers. Programs on this disk include: TUTOR GRAPHICS PLUS GR, COLOR, FLIN and HLIN, PLOT, HGR, HCOLOR, HPLOT, and others; PLOTS OF ORBITING PLANETS; GRAPHICS OF A BOUNCING BALL; GRAPHS OF SOME EQUATIONS; STARS IN A CONSTELLATION; BAR CHARTS; and other graphic demonstrations.

CREATING MUSIC & SOUNDS - The programs on this disk help the user learn to: create music on the Apple; play back compositions; save compositions on the disk; transfer songs to another program; create various other sounds; and show students how to compose music. There are examples of the use of the poke command and the use of text-files within this disk. The notes have been calibrated to be in tune with the piano's notes so music plays on pitch.

TEXT-FILE COMMANDS - The use of text-files is the basis of most data processing, business, and educational programming. This powerful feature is very useful in many programming creations. Bank accounts, inventories, address and phone lists, word processing, keeping records, and many other applications use text-file procedures. Covers: sequential vs. random access text-files; writing text-files; reading files; altering text-files; searching for records; appending records to text-files; file structures; and examples of inventory and addresses. From this point on the user will be able to process data and information that he has written into his text files. Searching, sorting, evaluating, and updating information are possible once these techniques are mastered.

SHAPES & PICTURES - SHAPES & PICTURES provides some techniques and routines that teach how to create pictures and draw shapes with the Apple. Some of the features help to: draw shapes; change their size and rotate the shapes; put text in the graphic page; move shapes across the screen; present pictures that have been saved; produce animations; and flip graphic pages for smooth display.

PROGRAM SAMPLE STUDIES - Disk #7 in this series includes many brief program samples for study and use. Some techniques and routines that will help polish skills are: sorting; gas economy; primes; text- in-graphics; simulations; presidents; animals; day of dates; number race; multiple-choice test; spelling word drill; and six more programs.

ADVANCED TOPICS - By the time one reaches this disk of the BASIC Tutor Series, one will be ready to learn about these advanced topics: poking information into memory; peeking at information in memory; calling ROM and other routines; changing pointers and addresses; organizing and memory mapping; altering the screen color background; and setting Lomem and Himem.

PROGRAMMING AIDS - This last disk in the Tutor Series includes many useful routines and programs that will speed up programming creations and make work more efficient. Includes: BONES - start any program with this set of subroutines; ERROR TRAPPING; HOUSE CLEANING; FIND CONTROLS - to find hidden controls; BINARY ADDRESS - to find B-file addresses; LENGTH - to find program length; sources of other utilities available; and quiz on programming (review).

ID: D4
COMPUTER IS: TERMS, DEVICES, SHAPES AND SIZES

Publisher: Micro Power & Light Company

Grade: Junior High and up

Format: diskette

Hardware: Apple II; 32K with Applesoft in ROM

Price: $34.95

The first time through the material the student is led by the program, thereby ensuring readiness for each new idea presented. Whenever the user stops, the program assigns a Progress ID Number. Later the program will resume in the same place when this same number is entered. If after a second chance the assigned number is not entered the program acts as if all sections have been completed, allowing the user to start at any point identified on the Main Menu screen: 1 Basic Definitions, 2 Computer Architecture, 3 Peripheral Devices, 4 Useful Configurations, H Help, and Q Quit. The HELP and QUIT options are available each time the user returns to the Main Menu, or to any of the four lesson sections. By choosing Help the user is able to turn (most of) the program's sound effects On or Off, adjust the presentation speed, display a report of progress, or use the Glossary. The four lesson sections include: BASIC DEFINITIONS: This section introduces basic concepts and terminology common to the world of computers. It does so through a number of clever graphics and tutorial; COMPUTER ARCHITECTURE: With the user's help the program actually builds a computer step-by-step, to solve a specific problem. Then the user can *see* it work! PERIPHERAL DEVICES: The most common microcomputer input and output devices are described. The user sees what's under the floppy disk jacket; hears data being written to cassette tape!; USEFUL CONFIGURATIONS: The user now gets a chance to select the type and size of computer to run a business, play games, do word processing, simulate experiments, etc.

ID: D5
COMPUTER POWER: A FIRST COURSE IN USING THE COMPUTER

Publisher: Gregg/ McGraw-Hill

Grade: Secondary

Format: 7 diskettes

Hardware: Apple II; 48K (DOS 3.3); Pascal language system; color monitor

Language: PASCAL

Source Code: no

Price: $385.00; $10.00 hardbound or $7.50 softbound/ student textbook

This 18-week computer literacy course guides average students to become beginning programmers. Discovery exercises guide students through command structures. Make- it-yourself projects require creation of actual programs. Programs

provide immediate execution of commands in a variety of musical, still, and moving picture graphics modes. Course is designed to be used by 15 students per microcomputer system. Teacher's manual is included.

ID: D6
ELECTRONIC TOOL

Publisher: Micro Power & Light Company

Also available from: Academic Software • Queue, Inc.

Grade: 7 and up

Format: diskette

Hardware: Apple II; 32K with Applesoft in ROM

Price: $34.95

Using this program, the student will learn how computers store data, select and retrieve records, reorganize records in files, perform calculations, and how they can be used. The student is taught what a computer record is, and is then given a chance to build a few, thereby constructing a computer file. The program then uses this file to demonstrate how the computer can retrieve specific records, and reorganize them. A variety of calculation possibilities are demonstrated. The program also demonstrates one way computers are used as a teaching tool - presenting the student with a number of drill and practice exercises, in language arts as well as mathematics. The student can choose to *see* either of two simulations. One is an ecology study involving the interaction of two animal populations. The other involves predicting job success from personality traits. In both, the student is invited to enter the critical variables - and to observe "what if...''!

ID: D7
INTRODUCTION TO USING THE COMPUTER

Publisher: Academic Computing Association

Date: Sept. 81

Grade: 5-Adult

Format: cassette or diskette

Hardware: Apple • TRS-80 • PET

Source Code: no

Price: $6.95

This program is part of ACA's CODES software. This lesson gives instruction on the following four skills relating to the operation of a computer terminal: (1) Indicating the end of one's response; (2) Correcting typing errors; (3) Spacing between words; and (4) Typing numbers (the number 1 versus the letter I, etc.). The lesson is intended for use by students who will use the computer for drill and instruction. In addition, the lesson is an excellent example for instructors who write CODES lessons.

ID: D8
MIT-LOGO FOR APPLE

Publisher: Krell Software Corporation

Also available from: Academic Software • MARCK

Hardware: Apple II; 64K

Language: LOGO

Price: $179.95

LOGO is a unique computer programming language. Developed at M.I.T., under the sponsorship of the National Science Foundation, LOGO was created primarily to foster education. It is a complete and powerful programming language. Its exceptionally rich graphic power and its simple command structure make LOGO ideal for introducing children and, indeed, all new programmers, to the world of computers. M.I.T.'s LOGO for Apple II can be quickly learned by even the youngest and most inexperienced user. Because new users can rapidly master LOGO's color, sound, and graphic capabilities, LOGO is able to convey the crucial sense of mastery to the learner. It is this mastery that fundamentally changes the way in which the user perceives his relationship to the computer. The student is now the creator. As he interacts with the microcomputer the student is transformed from mere passive recipient of information to the motive force commanding, directing, and animating the reality he produces. In this way, the user establishes an intimate relationship with the process of knowledge information. He begins to view himself as personally responsible for creating that knowledge. LOGO is designed to enhance that dialogical process by which the learner and his computer interact. As the student acquires skill with LOGO, he uses the language to draw, to animate his fantasies, and to simulate the behavior of objects in the real world. Thus, for whatever purpose he employs LOGO, the user is placed in the most active role. He must continually reexamine the state of his own understanding and must reformulate the procedures by which he instructs the computer. Gaps, deficiencies, contradictions, ambiguities are all revealed as he builds a LOGO program. Package includes 2 copies of LOGO, a utility disk, ALICE IN LOGOLAND - a 20-program tutorial series, a technical manual, Logo for the Apple by Harold Abelson, the *Alice in Logoland Primer*, a wall chart and a year's subscription to the *Logo and Educational Computing Newsletter*.

ID: D9
PART 1: INTRODUCTION TO BASIC

Publisher: Radio Shack®

Also available from: McKilligan Supply Corp.

Date: 1982

Grade: Secondary-College

Hardware: TRS-80 MOD I; 4K with Level II BASIC • TRS-80 MOD III; 16K with Model III BASIC

Language: BASIC

Price: $159.00

Instructional materials are designed to serve as introduction to computer programming, using TRS-80 computer and BASIC language as vehicles. Each lesson consists of overview, statement of objectives, guided note-taking, quick quiz, and "hands-on" activity experience. Objectives of instructional package are to assist beginners in identifying programming concepts, principles, and techniques; to provide means of checking knowledge gained; and to give practice in applying programming skills learned. Complete classroom package includes teacher's manual, 143 transparencies for overhead projector, and 25 student workbooks.

ID: D10
PART 2: BASIC PROGRAMMING

Publisher: Radio Shack®

Also available from: McKilligan Supply Corp.

Date: 1982

Grade: Secondary-College

Hardware: TRS-80 MOD I; 4K with Level II BASIC • TRS-80 MOD III; 16K with Model III BASIC

Language: BASIC

Price: $199.00

Instructional materials are designed to continue and extend programming concepts introduced in PART 1: INTRODUCTION TO BASIC. Using same format, course covers such topics as editing program lines, arrays, error messages, memory management, and string manipulation. Complete classroom package includes teacher's manual, 164 transparencies for overhead projector, and 25 student workbooks.

ID: D11
PROGRAM: THE ART OF TALKING TO COMPUTERS

Publisher: Micro Power & Light Company

Grade: Junior High and up

Format: diskette

Hardware: Apple II; 32K with Applesoft in ROM

Price: $34.95

This computer literacy program is intended for use at junior high level and beyond, by teachers and parents as well as students! This program can be used alone or with two other computer literacy programs available from Micro Power & Light Co. This program, THE PROGRAM, addresses software and programming; A COMPUTER IS covers hardware and configurations; THE ELECTRONIC TOOL illustrates common uses of computers. Through entertaining graphics and tutorials THE PROGRAM provides understandable answers to such frequently-asked questions as: (1) Just what is a program?, (2) How is a program used by the computer?, (3) What's this about decimal, binary, and "hex"?, (4) Why the different types of programs?, (5) What is a program language?, (6) Why are there different languages?, (7) How do languages compare?, (8) How easy is it to program?, (9) What characterizes a "good" program?, and (10) Is there more to it than programming? The PROGRAM does not teach a programming language, but rather illustrates the principal features and characteristics common to most program languages. It takes the user step by step through a simple program at work. It shows how a specific problem is solved using first one program language, then a second, and then a third. The user gets a good feel and appreciation for what programming is all about and how it works.

ID: D12
PROGRAMMING IN APPLE INTEGER BASIC: SELF-TEACHING SOFTWARE

Publisher: Hayden Book Company, Inc.

Format: cassette or diskette

Hardware: Apple II

Language: BASIC

Price: $29.95/cassette; $39.95/diskette

Interactive programmed instruction format to teach yourself Apple Integer BASIC. Twelve lessons cover BASIC 2 programming concepts, emphasizing the writing of simple programs.

ID: D13
PROGRAMS FOR BEGINNERS ON THE TRS-80

Publisher: Hayden Book Company, Inc.

Hardware: TRS-80 MOD I or III

Price: $10.95; $8.95 /book.

Series of interesting programs for home use that can be understood and used immediately by the beginner in personal computer programming. Teaches step by step how 21 sample TRS-80 programs work. Blechman explains the same 21 programs in his book, *Programs for Beginners on the TRS-80*.

ID: D14
SIMULATED COMPUTER

Publisher: Edu-Soft[T.M.]

Also available from: Academic Software • Opportunities For Learning, Inc. • Queue, Inc.

Format: cassette or diskette

Hardware: Apple II; 16K (cassette) or 32K (diskette) with Applesoft in ROM (DOS 3.2 or 3.3) • Atari 400 or 800; 16K (cassette) or 24K (diskette)

Price: $14.95/cassette; $19.95/diskette

Program is designed to acquaint user with Z-80 or 6502 microprocessor. Program simulates operation of small machine-language computer. Player can input programs, run them, single step them and watch every machine cycle on the screen. Ten different instructions enable viewer to write a variety of programs. A "display" option causes the computer to display a message describing each operation as performed. Eight different error messages help user debug programs. Program comes with a 5-lesson tutorial and complete manual. Documentation can be reviewed by typing "HELP".

ID: D15
SPELL WRITER

Publisher: Texas Instruments

Also available from: Scott, Foresman and Co.

Format: cassette or diskette

Hardware: TI

Source Code: no

Price: $24.95/cassette; $29.95/diskette

Three Speak & Spell[T.M.] packages using Text-to-Speech technology. Consists of a program enabling the design of customized spelling lessons, a program in word games and a file transfer program to make additional copies of word lists. Virtually unlimited vocabulary is attainable using required Terminal Emulator II package and Speech Synthesizer.

ID: D16
STEP BY STEP

Publisher: Program Design, Inc.

Also available from: Academic Software • Aquarius Publishers Inc. • K-12 Micromedia • MARCK • Queue, Inc.

Date: Apr. 81

Grade: 7-Adult

Format: cassette or diskette

Hardware: PET; cassette • TRS-80 MOD I; with Level II BASIC; cassette • Apple II Plus; 32K • Apple II; 32K with Applesoft in ROM

Price: $49.95/PET and TRS-80; $79.95/Apple

Thirty-two programs teach programming in BASIC for beginner. Course introduces all important BASIC commands and programming logic, including simple string logic and one-dimensional arrays. Lessons are interactive, presented in question-and-answer format on the screen. NEW STEP BY STEP Apple version teaches Applesoft BASIC through 20 hours of instruction that includes computer graphics, animation, sound effects, and an audio cassette voice track. Programs use combination of instruction, structured practice, and frequent skills testing. Workbook included.

ID: D17
TERRAPIN LOGO LANGUAGE

Publisher: Terrapin, Inc.

Format: diskette

Hardware: Apple II; 48K with 16K RAM card or language card

Language: LOGO

Price: $149.95; $5.00/backup diskette

LOGO is a powerful, easy-to-use computer language designed to be as friendly as possible to the user. It is an ideal first language. Though easy to understand and simple to work with, it places enough power in the hands of its user so that he or she can begin to use the computer right away. First-grade students using the LOGO language have learned to program so quickly they were teaching their teachers. LOGO was the first language ever to use turtle graphics -- an intuitive way of doing computer graphics. Turtle graphics uses the idea of a turtle -- a cybernetic animal that lives on a computer screen and responds to the user's commands to move forward or backward, to turn left or right. The turtle leaves a trail behind it as it moves. Terrapin LOGO language users can easily write programs to draw complex figures on the screen in high-resolution color graphics. Although the traditional coordinate graphics is also available, most people prefer turtle graphics. LOGO was developed at MIT.

ID: D18
TI LOGO

Publisher: Texas Instruments

Also available from: Scott, Foresman and Co.

Format: module

Hardware: TI; memory expansion unit

Source Code: no

Price: $129.95

Computer language represents innovative approach to developing computer awareness, plus children's math, logic, and communications skills.

ID: D19
TURTLE
Publisher: Edu-Soft[T.M.]

Also available from: Academic Software

Format: diskette

Hardware: Apple II; 64K with U.C.S.D. Pascal in ROM (D0S
3.2 or 3.3)

Language: PASCAL

Price: $29.95/diskette

Program enables user to learn commands of Apple Pascal,
which are identical to Turtle commands. The Turtle commands
enable the user to learn the Apple Pascal commands. Both the
"turtle" and the command typed remain visible on the screen
as the Turtle obeys the command. The package includes
worksheets and fully documented source code.

COURSEWARE DEVELOPMENT

E

ID: E1
ADAPTABLE SKELETON

Publisher: Micro Power & Light Company

Also available from: Academic Software • Queue, Inc.

Format: diskette

Hardware: Apple II; 32K with Applesoft in ROM

Price: $34.95

Using this program, the teacher creates exercises for student use. At the teacher's choice material can be presented to each student either as drill and practice or as a quiz. In the quiz mode the teacher tells the program the type of material and number of exercises each student is to be given. As individual students sign on the computer the program presents each with the specified number of exercises, one at a time, selected randomly from the list of all possible exercises. Student scores are recorded by the program on disk, for subsequent review by the teacher. The drill and practice mode works similarly except each student (rather than the teacher) tells the computer how many exercises he or she is to work, and the program does not record any scores. Exercises are entered by the teacher in the multiple-choice format. The statement of each question is followed by up to four answer choices. The teacher can associate a brief feedback message with each answer choice, and can also arrange for a review screen to be shown the student each time a particular answer choice is selected. Wording of the questions, answer choices, feedback messages and review screens - all at the teacher's choice. As many as 15 exercises can be used any way the teacher finds useful. Common uses include grouping exercises according to levels of difficulty, grade level or subject matter. The program has a "Teacher Section" accessible only after the teacher-defined password has been entered. Here the teacher can add, change, or delete exercises, as well as review and delete student records. THE ADAPTABLE SKELETON can be used in most any subject area, at any grade level beyond fourth. In addition to being a valuable tool in the classroom it is well adapted for use at home and in tutoring situations.

ID: E2
APPLE PILOT

Publisher: Apple Computer, Inc.

Date: 1982

Format: 2 diskettes

Hardware: Apple II; 48K (DOS 3.3); 2 disk drives

Language: PILOT

Price: $100.00

Apple PILOT is a specialized programming language developed to utilize capabilities of Apple computer for interactive teaching and learning. An extension of PILOT (which is itself a subset of Pascal), Apple PILOT enables user to create graphics, sound, and special characters without any particular programming expertise. System consists of PILOT author diskette, which enables user to create, print, or edit lessons; and a lesson diskette designed to record lessons created. Only one disk drive is required to run lessons once they have been created and saved. Two user manuals included.

ID: E3
BLOCKS AUTHOR LANGUAGE SYSTEM AND GRAPHICS LIBRARY

Publisher: San Mateo County Office of Education and Computer-Using Educators

Format: 7 diskettes

Language: INTEGER

Source Code: yes

Price: $70.00

The BLOCKS AUTHOR SYSTEM is a series of programs designed to enable teachers without any programming knowledge to create and illustrate computerized lesson material for any subject, at any grade level. All materials in this system were developed with funds from a California Title IV-C project and are in the public domain. The version listed here was contributed to the SOFTSWAP by the California School for the Deaf. Extensive documentation is included with each packet. Questions, comments, or requests for workshops should be directed to Margaret Irwin, California School for the Deaf, 39350 Gallauden Drive, Fremont, CA 94538. Companion packages are GRAPHICS CREATION and GRAPHICS LIBRARY.

BLOCKS AUTHOR DISK - Used to create lessons.

BLOCKS LESSON DISK - The storage disk on which lessons are saved.

BLOCKS CLASS DISK - Runs the lesson for the student, manages teacher prepared lesson plans for individual pupils, records grades and reports them via screen or printer.

BLOCKS LESSON SAMPLER DISK - A group of 20 lessons illustrates applications of the system.

BLOCKS UTILITIES DISK - Facilitates use of the system.

BLOCKS COPYCAT - A graphics utility disk for use with the GRAPHICS LIBRARY.

BLOCKS GRAPHICS LIBRARY DEMO DISK - Contains two images from each of the GRAPHICS LIBRARY disks.

ID: E4
CAI - MANAGER

Publisher: Mathware/Math City

Format: 10 diskettes and 1 VHS videotape (for use as a backup)

Hardware: Apple II; 48K; 5M, 10M, 20M, or multiple Corvus hard disk; printer optional

Price: $1500.00

This system may be used for two purposes - management of a multiple software curriculum, with its complex record-keeping, and a lesson authoring program, with which any teacher can write lessons and tests in a variety of formats and have them assigned to students. Record-keeping capabilities include: 1) 50 students per class / 40 classes per subject / 9 subjects; 2) current-month student and class detail reports; 3) current-month class summary reports; 4) year-to-date summary reports; 5) year-to-date class summary reports; 6) student test result reports; 7) class test result reports; 8) printouts of all report displays.

ID: E5
CAIWARE

Publisher: MicroGnome

Also available from: MARCK • Queue, Inc.

Format: 2 cassettes

Hardware: TRS-80 MOD I & III

Price: $44.95

CAIWARE is a three program course-authoring system, featuring text and multiple-choice or fill-in question formats; forward branching; and key-word or alternate answer recognition. The performance levels may be set by author.

ID: E6
CAIWARE-3D

Publisher: MicroGnome

Format: diskette

Hardware: TRS-80; 32K

Language: BASIC

Price: $219.00

This is a menu-driven system of 9 programs. It allows the instructor to create courseware for any subject. Text screens provide built-in word processing and graphics art. Question screens allow multiple-choice, true/false, fill-ins (alternate answer and keyword recognition). Lessons can be updated and saved on a diskette or may be copied from diskette to tape for use on 16K tape systems. The second part of this software provides for Computer-Managed Instruction, which schedules, tracks progress, records statistics and reports to the instructor.

ID: E7
CO-PILOT

Publisher: Apple Computer, Inc.

Date: June 82

Format: 2 diskettes

Hardware: Apple II; 48K (DOS 3.3)

Language: PILOT

Source Code: no

Price: $35.00

Self-contained, self-paced, interactive tutorial teaches how to program in Apple PILOT.

ID: E8
COMPUTER MATH GAMES - VOLUME 7

Publisher: Addison-Wesley Publishing Company

Grade: 1-9

Format: 2 programs on diskette, with backup

Hardware: Apple II; 32K (DOS 3.3) • Apple II Plus

Price: $36.00

This package provides a method for the teacher to write and administer quizzes on math problems.

QUIZ - This program provides a unique way to administer quizzes or tests that are entered into the computer by the instructor.

HANGMAN - This program provides vocabulary and spelling practice.

ID: E9
CREATE - ELEMENTARY

Publisher: Hartley Courseware, Inc.

Grade: 1-6

Format: 1 diskette

Hardware: Apple II; 48K with Applesoft in ROM (DOS 3.2 or 3.3)

Language: Applesoft BASIC

Price: $26.95

Allows teachers to create tutorial lessons, tests, or drills in their own content areas, using format that allows for four lines of stimulus input and for more than one acceptable response. Large letters and numerals limit line length to around fifteen spaces. Holds 50 different files of up to 20 presentations per file; 30 to 100 students' records can be saved.

ID: E10
CREATE - FILL IN THE BLANK

Publisher: Hartley Courseware, Inc.

Grade: K-6

Format: 1 diskette

Hardware: Apple II; 48K with Applesoft in ROM (DOS 3.2 or 3.3); CCD required

Language: Applesoft BASIC

Price: $26.95

Allows teacher to create series of elementary lessons with visual and aural components, with at least one blank and one correct response. Only one line of 15 characters is presented at a time. Holds 50 different files of up to 20 presentations per file. Can save 30 to 100 students' records.

ID: E11
CREATE - INTERMEDIATE

Publisher: Hartley Courseware, Inc.

Grade: 4-10

Format: 1 diskette

Hardware: Apple II; 48K with Applesoft in ROM (DOS 3.2 or 3.3)

Language: Applesoft BASIC

Price: $26.95

Allows teacher to create tutorial lessons, tests, or drills in their own content areas, in format which allows room for 9 lines of instruction or text material at beginning of each lesson, and six lines for questions or additional information. Line length is limited to 25 spaces. Program is similar to CREATE - ELEMENTARY except that it allows for longer sentences. Holds 50 different files of up to 20 presentations per file; 30 to 100 students' records can be saved.

ID: E12
CREATE - SPELL IT

Publisher: Hartley Courseware, Inc.

Also available from: Academic Software

Grade: 1-10

Format: 1 diskette

Hardware: Apple II; 48K with Applesoft in ROM (DOS 3.2 or 3.3); CCD required

Language: Applesoft BASIC

Price: $26.95

Enables teacher to record and present spelling or other oral tests to student, using computer to control tape recorder and keep track of student responses. Provides printout or screen listing for easy grading. Each disk holds fifty different files of up to 20 presentations per file; 100 students' records can be saved.

ID: E13

CREATE VOCABULARY

Publisher: Hartley Courseware, Inc.

Grade: 1-10

Format: 1 diskette

Hardware: Apple II; 48K with Applesoft in ROM (DOS 3.2 or 3.3); CCD required

Price: $26.95

Program enables teachers to build own word lists for vocabulary drill and individualized testing. Student sees and says word, then hears word recorded by teacher, using cassette control device (CCD). Student indicates on computer if he or she knows word. Computer stores any errors for future review and teacher planning.

ID: E14

CROSSWORD MAGIC

Publisher: L & S Computerware

Also available from: McKilligan Supply Corp.

Grade: Adjustable

Format: 2 diskettes

Hardware: Apple II; 48K (DOS 3.3); printer • Atari 800; printer • Apple II Plus; 48K (DOS 3.3); printer

Price: $49.95

This program creates puzzles by automatically interconnecting words. If the desired words do not immediately fit, the program will store it for future use.

ID: E15

DISK SPELL-BOUND

Publisher: Robert R. Baker, Jr.

Date: June 82

Grade: 7-12

Format: diskette

Hardware: TRS-80 MOD I or III; 16K

Language: BASIC

Source Code: yes

Price: $24.85

Program runs like SPELL-BOUND and includes simple editor for easily creating new spelling list. Editor allows user to title

word groups and correct any errors made while creating spelling lists. Average program running time is 2-3 minutes at each level of difficulty. Written documentation is provided, and program is self-documented as well.

ID: E16

DISK STENO

Publisher: Robert R. Baker, Jr.

Also available from: Queue, Inc.

Date: June 82

Grade: 9-12

Format: diskette

Hardware: TRS-80 MOD I or III; 16K

Language: BASIC

Source Code: yes

Price: $24.85

Program runs like STENO and includes simple editor program for easily creating new dictation lists. Instructor simply titles each list and types in words for computer to dictate to student. Excellent program for those unfamiliar with DATA statement in BASIC programming language. Average program running time is 2-3 minutes at each level of difficulty. Written documentation is provided, and program is self-documented as well.

ID: E17

EDUCATORS' LESSON MASTER

Publisher: Aquarius Publishers Inc.

Date: Aug. 82

Format: 6 diskettes

Hardware: Apple II; 48K with Applesoft in ROM (DOS 3.3)

Language: Applesoft BASIC

Source Code: no

Price: $150.00

Teacher-friendly authoring system enables educator to design virtually any type of lesson without prior programming knowledge. Menu-driven system places no limit on type of lessons that can be created, making it adaptable for use in any area of curriculum. Lessons created can be saved onto storage disks for later use, and program design allows for continuous lesson editing and update. System features selectable graphic rewards and student management system preprogrammed to operate with whatever lesson is developed and to identify specific items missed. Package consists of authoring disk, master lesson disk, four blank lesson storage disks, easy-to-understand documentation, and directions for program use.

ID: E18

EUREKA[T.M.] LEARNING SYSTEM

Publisher: Eiconics, Inc.

Format: cassette or diskette

Hardware: Apple II; 32K with Applesoft in ROM • Apple II Plus; 32K • TRS-80 MOD I; 32K with Level II BASIC • TRS-80 MOD III; 32K with BASIC

Language: BASIC

Price: $495.00/license; $49.50/each additional computer used; $25.00/Demo package; $10.00/Addl. Teacher Guide; $100.00/Yr. software maint. after 1st yr.; $1.00/copy of lesson distributed, royalty fee

This program allows design of educational courses without having any programming experience.

TEXT WRITER - Menu-driven program takes information divided by "Subjects", "Attributes" and "Entities" and puts it into language the computer understands. Presentation formats include several kinds of declarative and interrogative sentence structures, graphics capabilities and information modifiers. Information is stored in the Text Volume and Illustrator Volume.

EDUCATOR - Program presents lesson to the student. Copy of the "Educator" program together with the "Text Volume" and "Illustrator Volume" for a lesson make up a lesson tape for student use. Practice Mode allows student to practice answering questions. Evaluator Mode scores answers.

ID: E19
EXAM

Publisher: Robert R. Baker, Jr.

Also available from: Queue, Inc.

Date: June 82

Format: cassette or diskette; printer version requires diskette

Hardware: TRS-80 MOD I or III; 16K

Language: BASIC

Source Code: yes

Price: $19.85; $24.85/printer version

EXAM allows instructor to create multiple-choice examinations, using DATA statement in BASIC to enter questions, answers, and number of correct answers. Each time program is run, questions are placed in random order so that student cannot memorize answer sequence. After student completes exam, all questions and correct answers are displayed for review. Separate printer version prints out all student names and scores at end of exam. Average program running time is 2-3 minutes at each level of difficulty. Written documentation is provided, and program is self-documented as well.

ID: E20
EXAM-ANALYSIS SYSTEM

Publisher: Microphys Programs

Format: 2 diskettes

Hardware: PET 4032 or 8032; 32K; 4040 or 8050 disk drive; 4022 or 8022 printer; and Chatsworth Data Mark Sense Card Reader

Language: BASIC

Source Code: yes

Price: $200.00

System is designed to enable instructors and administrators to analyze objective exams which have been given to the entire student body or to a particular class or group. Software is ideal for use with various standardized tests, such as achievement, IQ, statewide competency, or regents exams. Answers to exam are recorded on mark-sense cards and fed into a reader. Computer then scores exam and generates detailed analysis of individual and group scores.

ID: E21
EXAM-GENERATING SYSTEM

Publisher: Microphys Programs

Format: 2 diskettes

Hardware: PET 4032 or 8032; 32K; 4040 or 8050 disk drive; 4022 or 8022 printer

Language: BASIC

Source Code: yes

Price: $200.00/system; $100.00/question files

Menu-driven and fully annotated system permits instructor to create unlimited number of question files which may be accessed in either an exam-generating mode or a student-interactive mode, depending on whether an exam or lesson session is preferred. Question files for use with system contain approximately 300 questions each, and are available in the six subject areas given below. Complete documentation is provided on the use of programs.

SENIOR HIGH VOCABULARY
JUNIOR HIGH VOCABULARY
SENIOR HIGH MATHEMATICS
JUNIOR HIGH MATHEMATICS
INTRODUCTORY PHYSICS
INTRODUCTORY CHEMISTRY

ID: E22
GENIS (GENERALIZED INSTRUCTIONAL SYSTEMS)

Publisher: Bell & Howell Microcomputer Systems

Format: 3 programs on diskette

Hardware: Bell & Howell • Apple II Plus

Language: PILOT

Price: $300.00

GENIS is a series of three programs for creating Computer-Assisted-Instruction. It is composed of two interrelated software systems, which can be used independently or in conjunction with one another.

CDSI - The Courseware Development System enables educators and trainers to develop interactive instructional materials on any subject matter. CDSI is actually comprised of two parts: An authoring system which allows a teacher or trainer to create curriculum materials; and a presentation system which provides a means for presenting these materials to the student. During the authoring session, the microcomputer "asks" the instructor for the information that it needs to create and present the student's lesson. The instructor provides the microcomputer with the information he or she wants presented to the student: questions to ask, hints to be given, correct answers and responses, incorrect answers and responses, and other presentation parameters. Each authoring session may continue for as long as the instructor desires and go into as much detail as he or she wishes. The lesson can be constructed to be sensitive to each student's individuality, responding to particular needs and speed of learning. During the student's instructional session, CDSI keeps detailed records of the student's progress. These records are available to the instructor in the form of reports which can be used to diagnose areas of student progress or to develop future curriculum.

MARK-PILOT - MARK-PILOT is an enhanced Computer-Assisted Instruction language. It functions as a type of computer shorthand allowing educators to develop Computer Assisted Instruction materials quickly and efficiently. MARK-PILOT is Bell & Howell's own version of the computer language Pilot with special routines that provide automatic record-keeping and assist in student performance management. MARK-PILOT consists of two sections: an authoring system which enables educators and trainers to create instructional materials, and a presentation system which facilitates the presentation of these materials to the student. When utilizing the authoring system the instructor may use up to 22 simple commands which direct the microcomputer to execute specific instructional tasks. From the instructor's perspective, these commands are quite simple to use. For example, the instructor is able to develop complex curriculum material without acquiring microcomputer programming skills. The instructor may interrupt the development of a lesson, edit it or change it. After the MARK-PILOT curriculum has been created, the instructor may compile a student class list, and instruct the computer to maintain student records and evaluate student performance. During the student's instructional session, the lesson is presented to the student in the form specified by the instructor during the authoring session. The instructional sequence may be composed of drill and practice, question and answer dialog, new knowledge or a computer simulation of real-world phenomena. The instructor may use animation, graphics, and color to make the lesson more descriptive and attractive, and the instructor may make available to the student MARK-PILOT's built-in calculating ability to help with numerical problems. The instructor has complete control over the speed of lesson presentation and the format of the presentation.

SYNER-GENIS - SYNER-GENIS is a means of combining the power of CDSI with the flexibility of Bell & Howell's MARK-PILOT to design microcomputer-assisted instruction. Using the SYNER-GENIS capability, users may assess MARK-PILOT programs at any time through CDSI and return to CDSI without affecting student records. With SYNER-GENIS, a person using the CDSI authoring system may utilize the capability of MARK-PILOT to enhance lesson presentation.

ID: E23
GRAPHICS CREATION

Publisher: San Mateo County Office of Education and Computer-Using Educators

Format: 3 diskettes

Hardware: Apple; 48K (DOS 3.2); 2 disk drives

Language: Applesoft BASIC

Source Code: yes

Price: $30.00

These 3 programs enable the teacher to create graphics compatible with the BLOCKS AUTHOR SYSTEM.

EDU-PAINT - Allows easy drawing of illustrations utilizing straight or free lines, frames, boxes, open circles or solid disks, color fill, and saving of full screen pictures or images compatible with the BLOCKS System, all while using a menu or more than four billion colors and patterns. Use game paddles, or joystick; program works with or without an Apple Graphics Tablet.

SHAPER - Allows user to create sophisticated line drawings using the computer keyboard only. Shapes may be in color, in any scale from 1 to 255, rotated, viewed in two scales simultaneously.

PAINT CHIP - Converts shapes or pictures created on an Apple Graphics Tablet into images which can be utilized by the BLOCKS Author System. It also creates rubber-band lines, does point plotting for fine enhancement of graphics, and initialized Graphics Library Disks.

ID: E24
GRAPHICS LIBRARY

Publisher: San Mateo County Office of Education and Computer-Using Educators

Format: 24 diskettes

Hardware: Apple; 48K (DOS 3.2); 2 disk drives

Language: INTEGER

Source Code: yes

Price: $180.00; $10.00/disk

The GRAPHICS LIBRARY is a group of 699 images designed for use in teacher-written BLOCKS lessons. The images are stored in 20 classifications according to the Dewey Decimal System. The BLOCKS copycat program is used to view and to transfer the images onto lesson disks. New images can be drawn using the GRAPHICS CREATION package or the Apple Graphics Tablet.

SYMBOLS
FOOD
CARTOONS
DECORATIVE ARTS
MANUAL COMMUNICATION
HOLIDAYS
EARTH SCIENCES
ASTRONOMY
ANIMALS
MATH
TIME
PLANTS
PEOPLE I
PEOPLE II
APPLIED SCIENCE
TRANSPORTATION
TOOLS I
TOOLS II
RECREATION
BUILDINGS
MAPS I
MAPS II
MAPS III
SCENERY

ID: E25
INDIVIDUAL STUDY CENTER

Publisher: TYC Software (Teach Yourself by Computer)

Also available from: K-12 Micromedia • MARCK

Grade: 1-12

Format: 4 cassettes or 1 diskette; more than 50 subject tapes available

Hardware: TRS-80 MOD I or III; 16K, with Level II BASIC • Apple II Plus • Apple II; 16K (cassette) or 48K (diskette) with Applesoft in ROM (DOS 3.3)

Language: BASIC

Price: $49.95/cassette; $54.95/diskette; $5.95/subject data tape or diskette

Flexible drill and test package gives teacher ability to make up questions and answers or to use prepared questions and answers on over 50 different topics. Package comes with six activity programs listed below, each having a different educational objective. Any of six may be used with any of more than 50 subject tapes or with questions provided by teacher on blank tape supplied with system. Demonstration tape/disk file and teaching/instruction manual included.

HOUSE ON FIRE - Suspense-filled game format especially designed for elementary student, in which student is rewarded for right answers, and appropriately corrected for wrong answers.

AROUND THE BALL PARK - Baseball game presentation provides interesting and enjoyable way to encourage students to learn difficult material.

BEAT THE CLOCK - Object is to increase speed of student's answers by setting time limit in seconds or minutes, either on question-by-question basis or as overall limit for set of questions.

PUZZLER - Crossword-type game which allows student to fill in puzzle while answering questions.

MATCHING - Program enables student to drill on material or take test in matching format.

COMPLETION - Requires student to fill in correct answer. Program allows student to review, do drills on material, or take test.

SUBJECT DATA TAPES/FILES - Library includes more than 50 graded lessons, each with at least 80 questions and answers, in following subject areas: French, Spanish, and German languages; English vocabulary, parts of speech, grammar and spelling; mathematics; American and world history; geography; and biology.

ID: E26
K-8 MATH WORKSHEET GENERATOR

Publisher: Radio Shack®

Date: 1982

Grade: K-8

Format: 1 diskette

Hardware: TRS-80 MOD I; 32K with Level II BASIC; printer • TRS-80 MOD III; 32K with Model III BASIC; printer

Language: BASIC

Source Code: yes

Price: $89.95

Program enables teacher to print worksheets and answer sheets for exercises in addition, subtraction, multiplication, and division, using selected problem sequences from K-8 MATH PROGRAM. Using program, teacher can use pre-designed worksheet headings, or create new ones; choose subject, lesson number, and number of problems from each lesson; specify number of worksheets to be printed at particular levels of difficulty; save worksheet designs on disk; and protect saved worksheets with password. Teacher's manual included.

ID: E27
MICRO BRAILLE TRANSLATOR

Publisher: Duxbury Systems, Inc.

Grade: Handicapped

Format: diskette

Hardware: North Star; 64K; 2 disk drives; Triformation LED-120 braille embosser (120 char/sec); letter-quality printer terminal optional

Price: $9850.00/software, terminal, and computer; $7400-$14500/embosser; $2900/printer

This system provides for both automatic translation of text to braille and conventional word processing. A person with no knowledge of braille may enter and edit material. The micro is capable of Grade I and II braille in American, British and Spanish, as well as Grade I in four other languages.

ID: E28
MICROTEACH

Publisher: Compumax, Inc.

Also available from: Academic Software

Date: 1981

Format: diskette

Hardware: Atari 800; 48K; 2 Atari 810 disk drives; monitor (preferably color); printer optional • Apple II; 48K; 2 disk drives; monitor (preferably color); printer optional

Language: BASIC

Source Code: yes

Price: $150.00/OS/A+ and BASIC A+; $195.00/TEACHERS AIDE; $80.00/ STUDENT PAK; $39.95/ACCOUNTING PRIMER; $39.95/SALES PRIMER

MICROTEACH system consists of three integrated packages designed to facilitate courseware development without programming, using Apple and Atari color graphics capabilities to advantage. Menu-driven system leads novice users through available options, prompting them through design and use of courseware developed with system. English and Spanish language versions of TEACHERS AIDE and STUDENT PAK modules are available. OS/A+ is an operating system that is compatible with both Atari and Apple, and BASIC A+ is a dialect of BASIC in which the program was written; both are necessary to modify the system. Written documentation is included.

TEACHER'S AIDE - Program transforms computer into automatic courseware generator, allowing user to create course materials for any subject or level. Text can be written either in single "page" mode or in multipage "scroll" mode, and instructor can choose among wide range of color options. Many different test formats can be written, including multiple choice, true/false, matching, yes/no, and fill-in. Author can determine how long page will remain on screen, making it possible to integrate audo aids with course. Twenty-six user-assignable reporting categories help user track student responses in the next program in a wide variety of ways. Versatile text editing mode makes writing and changing of text, questions, and illustrations easy to accomplish.

STUDENT PAK - Program performs essential record-keeping functions, enabling students to take courses generated by TEACHER'S AIDE and enabling teacher to channel, guide, and monitor student progress. Instructor can assign any portion of courseware to one or more students through ID and password system. Students can enter answers to test questions, and tests are then automatically graded and results tabulated and analyzed through student report/review section.

COURSEWARE - Courseware written using TEACHER'S AIDE may be adopted for distribution by vendor. Currently, two programs are available in this series: ACCOUNTING PRIMER and SALES PRIMER. Courses can cover any subject at any level, from spelling to physics, from elementary to post-graduate. Each diskette or "volume" may contain up to around 2200 lines of text, illustrations, or pages (roughly 120 "pages"). Length of chapters and sections is left entirely to author's discretion. Royalty arrangements will vary depending on amount of program support author is willing to provide.

ID: E29
MULTIPLE CHOICE FILES
Publisher: COMPU-TATIONS, Inc.

Also available from: Academic Software • Queue, Inc.

Grade: Elementary-College

Format: diskette

Hardware: Apple II; (DOS 3.2 or 3.3)

Price: $24.95

This program allows the creation of multiple choice tests. It contains randomized questioning and immediate feedback learning techniques. Five choices are provided for each question. Complex questions and longer answer choices are possible. The user selects the letter identifying his answer.

ID: E30
PILOT ANIMATION TOOLS
Publisher: Apple Computer, Inc.

Date: Feb. 82

Format: diskette

Hardware: Apple II; 48K

Language: PILOT

Price: $75.00

Package brings Computer-Assisted-Instruction (CAI) programs to life by enabling instructor to take graphic images created with PILOT Author System (available separately) and build, edit, and call these images in animated sequences. Package also includes Maxwell demonstration program; Hormuz and Dr. Memory, two sample PILOT lessons; and Immediate, a program for on-the-spot review of animation sequences created. Instructions included.

ID: E31
PROCTOR
Publisher: Comaldor

Format: cassette or diskette

Hardware: PET; 32K; 4040 disk drive

Price: $150.00/set; $110.00/PROCTOR; $20.00/program for remaining 3 programs

This program can be used by classroom teachers to create drills, tests, and exams in their own subject areas using questions and answers they supply. The PROCTOR will present these questions on the computer and evaluate the responses typed in by the students. The teacher can specify partial marks for misspelled answers, which are added into a cumulative score as the student progresses through the test. A test of teacher-specified length is randomly selected from the question bank, which may contain up to 300 questions per subject or unit within a subject. No question is given twice during the same sequence. The student may or may not be given a running account of his progress. The teacher may specify the following details of answer processing for each separate question: alternate answers; mark weighting; spelling variation with part marks; ignore capitalization; ignore blanks and/or punctuation; look for only numeric portions of response; scan response for a correct keyword. Requires the teacher's KEY which plugs on cassette port in order to work, thereby ensuring security of files.

PROCTOR-PRINT - Works in conjunction with PROCTOR. Produces hard copy tests for class presentations. Choice of listing mark values of question. Also produces answer sheet if requested. These may then be duplicated in class sets. One may call for 3 or 4 tests in a row; each will contain randomly selected questions from the bank, eliminating the problem of giving same test to absent student later.

PROCTOR-STATS - This program displays data regarding the success of students' attempts to answer PROCTOR questions. During teacher review of a student's use of the PROCTOR main program, an option is offered to update the STATS file with the results of current usage. If the option is accepted, PROCTOR records, into running totals for each question given during the session on the computer, the results of the student's answers - whether the question was correct, misspelled, or incorrect for each question tried. These totals are now accessible with STATS, which will retrieve them from the STATS file on the disk and display the results in both literal and graphic representations. It is thus a simple matter for the teacher to find out whether the questions contained are serving their intended purpose.

PROCTOR-MERGE - This program will combine several existing PROCTOR question banks into one large bank.

ID: E32
QUESTION & ANSWER GROUP
Publisher: Educational Courseware

Also available from: Academic Software • Queue, Inc.

Format: diskette

Hardware: Apple; 48K (DOS 3.3 or 3.2)

Price: $32.00/diskette

Lessons can be created using this series. Three subjects are currently available. Each disk allows the instructor to combine unique classroom work with prewritten material.

AMERICAN HISTORY - Covers Colonial period, presidents, wars, national expansion, and court decisions.

GENERAL CHEMISTRY - Topics covered include atoms, ions, elements, compounds, and crude oils.

GENERAL BIOLOGY - This disk covers plant and animal classification, digestion, endocrine glands, enzymes, hormones, and circulation.

ID: E33

QUESTION, ANSWER & VOCABULARY FACILITIES

Publisher: TIES, Minnesota School Districts Data Processing Joint Board

Date: Dec. 81

Format: 3 diskettes with backup

Hardware: Apple II; 32K with Applesoft in ROM (DOS 3.3) • Apple II Plus

Price: $99.95; $10.00/documentation

Using this software, the teacher can create, edit and display question and answer lessons in any subject area. The two student diskettes focus on increasing word facility.

TEACHER UTILITIES - The teacher can create and edit lessons or word lists which are saved on the Student Presentation diskettes.

MICRO QUEST STUDENT PRESENTATION - The lessons stored on the MICRO QUEST STUDENT PRESENTATION diskette are multiple-choice lessons and may be used in any subject area. The teacher may create a maximum of 99 questions per lesson in two possible formats.

VOCAB STUDENT PRESENTATIONS - The word lists stored on this diskette may be used by the student with 5 programs - HANGMAN, SCRAMBLE, SPELL1, SPELL2, and WORDER.

ID: E34

QUIZ MASTER

Publisher: APX (Atari Program Exchange)

Also available from: Academic Software

Date: June 82

Grade: 3 and up

Format: diskette

Hardware: Atari 400 or 800; 32K; joystick controller optional

Language: BASIC

Source Code: no

Price: $22.95

Teachers and parents can use program to create five kinds of computer-assisted instruction (CAI) quizzes, and students can use it to take resulting quizzes. Types of quizzes include vocabulary or spelling; true/false; and multiple choice with three, four, or five choices. Quiz questions can be revised as needed. Menu-driven quiz is stored on cassette or disk, and is then available as needed. Program provides encouraging responses to both correct and incorrect answers; final score displays at end of quiz. User manual is included.

ID: E35

READABILITY; FORMULA RESULTS, GRAPHS AND STATISTICS

Publisher: Micro Power & Light Company

Format: diskette

Hardware: Apple II; 48K with Applesoft in ROM

Price: $44.95

The READABILITY Program measures the difficulty level of text material according to nine different formulas. Results are displayed in both text and graphic formats. One graph shows Fry formula scores. The other is a composite graph showing all scores! The formulas applied include: Dale- Chall, Fry, Flesch, Flesch-Kincaid, Fog, ARI, Coleman, Powers, and Holmquist. This program package is very comprehensive. It includes all of the following "user- friendly" features. It: (1) Produces reading grade levels according to nine different formulas, (2) Shows the results graphically as well as numerically, (3) Accepts normal text entry, with but a few helpful guidelines to be followed, (4) Supports entry of lengthy text passages in piecemeal manner, and (5) Comes with an easy-to-follow User Manual, including tutorial sample run. This program is easy to use! It can be of real value to teachers, curriculum specialists, authors and librarians.

ID: E36

SIMULATED COMPUTER/COMPUTA-DOODLE

Publisher: Edu-Soft[T.M.]

Format: 2 programs on cassette or diskette

Hardware: TRS-80 MOD I or III; 16K (cassette) or 32K (diskette) with with Level II BASIC

Price: $14.95/cassette; $19.95/diskette

One program enables player to be a computer artist; the other simulates the operation of a small machine-language computer.

COMPUTA-DOODLE - Program allows player to draw pictures or graphs on screen and to save them on tape. Pictures can be incorporated into player's own programs. Fine-tuning control allows drawing of smooth curves.

SIMULATED COMPUTER - Program simulates operation of small machine-language computer. Player can input programs, run them, single-step them and watch every machine cycle on the screen. Ten different instructions enable viewer to write a variety of programs. A "display" option causes the computer to display a message describing each operation as performed. Eight different error messages help user debug programs. Program comes with a 5-lesson tutorial and complete manual. Documentation can be reviewed by typing "HELP". This program is available individually from Queue, Inc., and Academic Software.

ID: E37

STUDY QUIZ FILES

Publisher: COMPU-TATIONS, Inc.

Also available from: Academic Software • Queue, Inc.

Grade: Elementary-College

Format: diskette

Hardware: Apple II; (DOS 3.2 or 3.3) • Atari

Price: $24.95

This is a user-oriented host program that allows the user to create lessons in quiz form on any subject without programming knowledge. An entire course can be placed on the disk with modular lessons which can be retrieved, run or revised at will. Items are scrambled and represented until the material is mastered. A word-match format is used.

STUDY QUIZ FILES - There are 2 versions available. One version requires the user to type in the number of his answer choice. The FULL-ANSWER version requires the user to type in the full response, thereby reinforcing spelling skills.

ID: E38
SUPER-CAI
Publisher: MicroGnome

Also available from: MARCK • Queue, Inc.

Format: 2 cassettes

Hardware: TRS-80; 16K

Price: $66.95

This is an enhanced version of CAIWARE. Added features include updating, copying and compressing of existing lessons on tape. Text screens provide three levels of remedial material. Length of a lesson is not limited by memory size because the lesson is saved as a data file on tape. A second part of this program is Computer-Managed Instruction, with which students get immediate feedback on performance and recaps at the end of the topic and lesson.

ID: E39
SUPERPILOT
Publisher: Apple Computer, Inc.

Date: June 82

Format: diskette

Hardware: Apple II Plus; 64K (DOS 3.3) • Apple II; 64K (DOS 3.3)

Language: PILOT

Source Code: no

Price: $200.00

SuperPILOT is versatile extension of Apple PILOT programming language designed to help educators and industrial trainers create lessons and illustrations for Computer-Aided-Instruction. Designed for interactive video and graphics applications, SuperPILOT offers all capabilities of Apple PILOT plus added features for graphic enhancement, easy debugging, and external video control. Capabilities include control of external videodisc and videotape through user and computer command and response; "turtle" learning; display of color text on color background; and display of double-sized characters for emphasis. Included in SuperPILOT package is a diskette tutorial program, Co-SuperPILOT.

ID: E40
T.E.S.T.
Publisher: TYC Software (Teach Yourself by Computer)

Also available from: MARCK • Queue, Inc.

Format: cassette

Hardware: TRS-80 MOD I or III; 16K; printer optional

Language: BASIC

Price: $13.95

Package enables teacher or student to build library of test and drill programs on any subject simply and cheaply for classroom, resource room, or home. Includes complete instruction manual.

MAINTENANCE PROGRAM - Allows user to create test of up to 35 questions and save it on cassette for use immediately or whenever it is needed. In order to produce test, question of up to 240 characters is typed. Type of question (true-false, multiple choice, or completion) is then entered, along with correct answer. Test may then be saved onto blank tape for future use.

TEST AND DRILL - Utility program is designed to accept test prepared by maintenance program. Using program, students can either use questions as review or take scored test, or teacher can have computer prepare printed test or worksheet with answer key.

ID: E41
TEACHER'S AIDE
Publisher: Instant Software[T.M.]

Also available from: MARCK • Queue, Inc.

Format: diskette

Hardware: TRS-80 MOD I; 16K, espansion interface

Language: BASIC

Source Code: no

Price: $39.95

This program allows the user to create a teaching system for any conceivable subject, creating a question-and-answer lesson of up to 8000 characters, saving lesson on disk, and creating entire sequences of lessons. The program also permits optional review of material prior to taking lesson, provision of hints to help answer questions, and graphics display as reward for answering questions correctly. Program even allows for spelling errors. Written documentation is provided.

ID: E42
TESTING SERIES
Publisher: Educational Courseware

Format: 5 diskettes

Hardware: Apple; 48K (DOS 3.3 or 3.2)

Price: $32.00/diskette; $140.00/series

This series provides a method for the teacher to create tests. The five disks cover multiple choice, matching, true or false, completion, and spelling and parts of speech. Each one allows for saving the test, altering it at any time, printing out a copy, erasing any test, and scoring as they are used by students. Each time a test is used the answers are shuffled to give a variety of forms.

ID: E43
TRS-80 PILOT PLUS
Publisher: Radio Shack®

Date: 1982

Format: 1 diskette

Hardware: TRS-80 MOD I; 32K with Level II BASIC

Language: BASIC

Source Code: yes

Price: $49.95

Based on PILOT computer language, TRS-80 PILOT Plus is command-oriented author language that allows teacher to create Computer-Assisted Instruction courseware, or to adapt such courseware from pre-existing curriculum. Language has extended capabilities for graphics generation and student file handling. While not required, a basic knowledge of computer programming would be helpful. Teacher's manual includes full reference aids, as well as sample lesson program.

ID: E44
VOCABULARY - ELEMENTARY

Publisher: Hartley Courseware, Inc.

Also available from: Academic Software • Queue, Inc.

Grade: 1-4

Format: 1 diskette with backup

Hardware: Apple II; 48K with Applesoft in ROM (DOS 3.2 or 3.3); CCD required

Language: Applesoft BASIC

Price: $64.95

Sixty-three lesson lists of up to 30 words each, already programmed into computer or added by teacher. Words are presented orally by use of cassette control device (CCD). Student sees and says word, then hears word and indicates on computer if he or she knows word. Computer stores errors for future review by teacher. Lessons closely follow Harcourt-Brace ''Bookmark'' reading series.

ID: E45
WORD PREP (ADVANCED); VOCABULARY DRILL...MAKE YOUR OWN

Publisher: Micro Power & Light Company

Format: diskette

Hardware: Apple II; 32K with Applesoft in ROM

Price: $29.95

The program includes: (1) 1000 vocabulary-expanding words and associated definitions, appropriate for use by senior high students and those preparing for college; (2) randomization routines which ensure a novel selection of words and purported definitions, each time the program is used; (3) facilities enabling modification of the word list to better fit a set of preferred words or definitions; and (4) instructions and facilities enabling creation of sets of word lists.

ID: E46
WORD WISE AUTHORING

Publisher: TIES, Minnesota School Districts Data Processing Joint Board

Date: Sept. 81

Grade: 1-3

Format: 2 diskettes with backup

Hardware: Apple II; 48K with Applesoft in ROM (DOS 3.3) • Apple II Plus

Price: $74.95; $9.50/documentation

WORD WISE is designed as an authoring system used to create sight vocabulary exercises for primary-level students. The students either fill in a blank in a sentence with a word (or phrase), or match a word (or phrase) with a picture. After the student completes a lesson, a bar graph is displayed which illustrates the number of questions the student answered right and wrong. Teachers who wish to develop picture lessons should also obtain the PICTURE LIBRARY program (available for $324.95).

TEACHER UTILITIES - Teachers may use the WORD WISE TEACHER UTILITIES diskette to create and edit sentence lessons, picture lessons, and menus. These lessons are stored on the STUDENT PRESENTATION diskette for use by students.

STUDENT PRESENTATION - The student will complete a sentence with a word or phrase choice. The sentence and picture choices are those created by the teacher. Picture lessons include an image which would match a word or phrase.

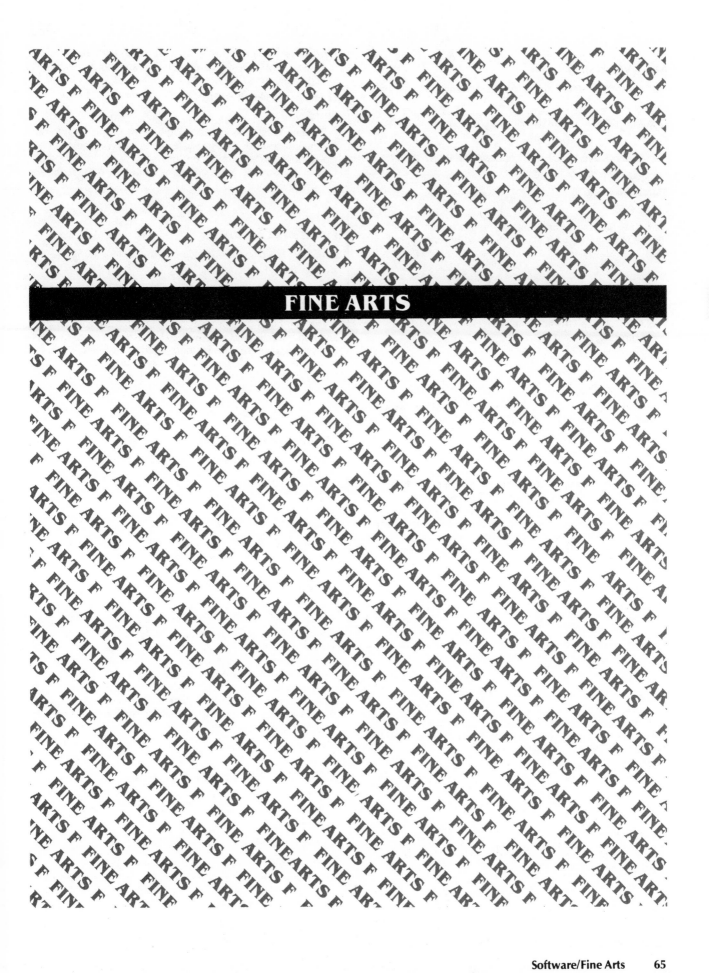

FINE ARTS

ID: F1

ART - VOLUME 1

Publisher: Minnesota Educational Computing Consortium

Date: June 82

Grade: 6-12, Vocational

Format: diskette

Hardware: Apple II; 32K with Applesoft in ROM

Language: Applesoft BASIC

Source Code: no

Price: $35.50

Module presents tutorials on one- and two-point perspective for use in junior high art classes. Support booklet included.

ID: F2

CHORD MANIA

Publisher: Micro Music Software Library (distributed by Musitronic)

Date: Nov. 81

Grade: Junior High-Adult

Format: diskette

Hardware: Apple II Plus • Apple II; 48K with Applesoft in ROM; MMI DAC sound production board (available separately for $175.00)

Language: Applesoft BASIC

Price: $190.00

Basic drill program is designed for practice of chords, including recognition of four-voice chords in any combination of chord qualities (all triads and five different seventh chords) and inversions. Presented in game context where one or two players try to "beat the clock", program allows either teacher or student to tailor sessions to unique set of drill patterns.

ID: F3

COMPOSE

Publisher: Comaldor

Format: cassette or diskette

Hardware: PET

Price: $20.00

Program enables user to convert PET into a sound organ, on which to compose songs and play them back with varying tempos and tone qualities. Program will save compositions on cassette to be played later or revised. The newest PETS have built-in sound but on models before the "Fat 40" the user will need a PETSOUND or a Radio Shack mini-amp (available from publisher for $25).

ID: F4

DOREMI

Publisher: Micro Music Software Library (distributed by Musitronic)

Date: Nov. 81

Format: diskette

Hardware: Apple II Plus • Apple II; 48K with Applesoft in ROM; MMI DAC sound production board (available separately for $175.00)

Language: Applesoft BASIC

Price: $100.00

Program teaches students to identify (by sound only) the individual degrees of a major scale using scale degree or solfeggio responses. Recommended for beginner ear training skills. One in Benward Series of programs written by music educator Dr. Bruce Benward.

ID: F5

ELEMENTS OF MUSIC

Publisher: Electronic Courseware Systems, Inc. (ECS)

Format: diskette

Hardware: Apple II; (DOS 3.2 or 3.3)

Price: $175.00

This computer program was developed for use with children and non-music majors who wish to learn the elements in music at an entry level. Lessons include: pitch names, pitches on the keyboard and key signatures. All lessons have been developed with a student router and data- keeping options for collecting student progress.

ID: F6

HARMONIOUS DICTATOR

Publisher: Micro Music Software Library (distributed by Musitronic)

Date: Nov. 81

Grade: Junior High-Adult

Format: diskette

Hardware: Apple II Plus • Apple II; 48K with Applesoft in ROM and MMI DAC sound production board (available separately for $175.00)

Language: Applesoft BASIC

Price: $190.00

Program in game format teaches students to hear chord progressions. Each progression heard is notated using traditional Roman numerals for chord functions and numerical symbols for chord inversions. Program covers material beginning with simple tonic-dominant patterns and advances to all diatonic chords, selected seventh chords, and secondary dominants with inversions. All musical patterns are uniquely "dictated" by computer, in infinite variety. Summary of student's progress is provided at end of session.

ID: F7

HARMONY DRILLS: SET 1

Publisher: Micro Music Software Library (distributed by Musitronic)

Date: Nov. 81

Grade: Junior High-College

Format: diskette

Hardware: Apple II Plus • Apple II; 48K with Applesoft in ROM; MMI DAC sound production board (available separately for $175.00)

Language: Applesoft BASIC

Price: $110.00

Package includes comprehensive supplement written by Dr. Bruce Benward and J. Timothy Kolosick to accompany a selection of harmony drills in Benward's textbook *Ear Training, A Technique for Listening*, published by Wm. C. Brown Co. Drills promote aural recognition of diatonic chord progression, at five levels of difficulty beginning with simple tonic/dominant root position chords.

ID: F8
HIGHER, SAME, LOWER

Publisher: Micro-Ed, Inc.

Also available from: Academic Software • MARCK • Queue, Inc. • Texas Instruments

Grade: Elementary

Format: cassette

Hardware: PET

Language: BASIC

Source Code: no

Price: $7.95; $9.95 TI ed.

Each lesson consists of ten problems in which two notes are played. Is the second note higher than, lower than, or the same as the first note? Each pair of notes is randomly selected from a bank of sixty-seven pairs. Each problem is repeated until the learner responds correctly. At the end of the lesson, the learner's performance is summarized.

ID: F9
INSTRUMENT DRILL

Publisher: Comaldor

Format: cassette or diskette

Hardware: PET

Price: $20.00 each; $200.00/14 programs

This series allows the student to practice his fingering on the instrument he plays while reviewing names of notes on the staff - all on the PET! The valves and keys move, and strings are highlighted, as he indicates how to produce the given notes. Student is given a number of tries before the correct answer is provided. The computer simulates a trumpet, trombone, French horn, tuba, baritone, flute, oboe, English horn, clarinet, saxophone, violin, viola, cello, or bass guitar.

ID: F10
INTERVAL DRILLMASTER

Publisher: CONDUIT

Date: 1982

Grade: 9-College

Format: diskette

Hardware: Apple II; 48K with Applesoft in ROM (DOS 3.2.1)

Language: BASIC

Source Code: no

Price: $75.00; $10.00/add'l software copy; $3.00/add'l student manual; add'l teacher manual - free

Provides students with practice in identifying and notating simple melodic intervals. The software includes 22 levels of interval training and gives students the option of taking each level either as an assisted drill or timed test. Students using the programs without officially "enrolling" may enter INTERVAL DRILLMASTER at any level, an option particularly valuable as review in advanced ear training. Students who actually enroll in the DRILLMASTER course, however, must satisfactorily pass each level before moving on to the next. A record-keeping facility of the package allows the instructor to follow each student's progress. The package also includes a number of diagnostic and self-evaluation facilities, so that each student can track his own progress, analyze his weaknesses, and find valuable help in correcting them.

ID: F11
INTERVAL MANIA

Publisher: Micro Music Software Library (distributed by Musitronic)

Date: Nov. 81

Format: diskette

Hardware: Apple II Plus • Apple II; 48K with Applesoft in ROM; MMI DAC sound production board (available separately for $175.00)

Language: Applesoft BASIC

Price: $190.00

Basic drill program is designed for practice of melodic and harmonic intervals with any combination of interval sizes and qualities (major, minor, diminished, augmented, and perfect), and practice in bass or treble clefs or the full great staff. Presented in game context where one or two players try to "beat the clock". Allows either teacher or student to tailor drill session to unique set of drill patterns.

ID: F12
KEY SIGNATURE DRILLS

Publisher: Micro Music Software Library (distributed by Musitronic)

Date: Nov. 81

Hardware: Apple II Plus • Apple II; 48K with Applesoft in ROM; MMI DAC sound production board (available separately for $175.00)

Language: Applesoft BASIC

Price: $110.00

Package includes series of programs for drill in recognition and identification of major and minor key signatures. Key signature game is included. One in Makas Series of basic musicianship programs written by Dr. George Makas, author of "Hello, I'm Music".

ID: F13
KOLOSICK SERIES

Publisher: Micro Music Software Library (distributed by Musitronic)

Date: Nov. 81

Format: diskette

Hardware: Apple II Plus • Apple II; 48K with Applesoft in ROM; MMI DAC sound production board (available separately for $175.00)

Language: Applesoft BASIC

Price: $190.00/program

Series includes two programs written by Dr. J. Timothy Kolosick, with field testing at the University of Wisconsin. Both programs keep track of student progress on disk for review purposes.

SIR WILLIAM WRONG NOTE - Comprehensive program written for junior high and above allows student to practice pitch-error detection within any combination of four-voiced chord types. Once chord type is selected, program presents visual notation of chord, then sounds chord with one note sounded incorrectly. Student must identify incorrectly sounded voice as well as actual pitch sounded by note.

ARNOLD - Written for all grades in five skill levels, ARNOLD is program of patterns taken from 95 graded melodies that is designed to teach tone recognition and melodic memory skills. Program asks student to recall and enter tones of ever-increasing melody by using solfeggio syllables or scale degree numbers.

ID: F14
LINES AND SPACES OF THE TREBLE CLEF

Publisher: Micro-Ed, Inc.

Also available from: Academic Software • MARCK • Queue, Inc.

Grade: Elementary

Format: cassette

Hardware: PET

Language: BASIC

Source Code: no

Price: $7.95

Using whole notes, the computer teaches the student the names of the lines and spaces that make up the treble clef. As each note is displayed, it is sounded. When the instructional phase of the program is finished, a test is given in which notes are randomly displayed and sounded. If the student makes a mistake during the test, the test starts over. This continues until the student achieves complete mastery of the material. (If the student does not know the answer and types the question mark, the computer will give the answer).

ID: F15
MATCHING EQUIVALENT NOTES

Publisher: Micro-Ed, Inc.

Also available from: Academic Software • MARCK • Queue, Inc.

Grade: Elementary

Format: cassette

Hardware: PET

Language: BASIC

Source Code: no

Price: $7.95

This program gives the student practice in matching equivalent notes on the treble clef. For example, G-flat and F-sharp have the same pitch. They are equivalent notes. Each problem consists of the computer sounding and displaying a note selected at random. The student must type the name of the equivalent note. Each lesson consists of ten problems. The computer summarizes the results of the lesson, including the names of the specific notes that gave trouble during the lesson.

ID: F16
MATCHING RHYTHMS

Publisher: Micro-Ed, Inc.

Also available from: Academic Software • MARCK • Queue, Inc.

Grade: Elementary

Format: cassette

Hardware: PET

Language: BASIC

Source Code: no

Price: $7.95

The computer selects one of ten rhythmic patterns and plays this as it displays matching quarter notes and eighth notes on the screen. The learner attempts to match the rhythm by pressing the space bar. If the learner can do this successfully, the computer selects and plays another rhythm. Otherwise, the same rhythm is repeated. Ten rhythms in all are presented. The computer is a fairly strict drill-master, so the learner must match a given rhythm quite well before proceeding to the next pattern.

ID: F17
MELODIOUS DICTATOR

Publisher: Micro Music Software Library (distributed by Musitronic)

Date: Nov. 81

Format: diskette

Hardware: Apple II Plus • Apple II; 48K with Applesoft in ROM; MMI DAC sound production board (available separately for $175.00)

Language: Applesoft BASIC

Price: $190.00

Program in game format teaches students to hear single line melodies and to notate these melodies on a traditional treble clef staff. Student interacts with computer, first listening to a melody, then notating pitches on a staff using graphic representation of keyboard. Program begins with two-note pattern based upon major and minor seconds, and increases in difficulty to seven-note patterns utilizing all harmonic intervals within octave. Summary of student's progress is provided at end of session.

ID: F18
MODE DRILLS

Publisher: Micro Music Software Library (distributed by Musitronic)

Date: Nov. 81

Format: diskette

Hardware: Apple II Plus • Apple II; 48K with Applesoft in ROM; MMI DAC sound production board (available separately for $175.00)

Language: Applesoft BASIC

Price: $110.00

Package presents series of programs for visual and aural drill in recognition and identification of major, minor and church modes. One in Makas Series of basic musicianship programs written by Dr. George Makas, author of ''Hello, I'm Music''.

ID: F19
MUSIC I: TERMS AND NOTATIONS

Publisher: Minnesota Educational Computing Consortium

Also available from: APX (Atari Program Exchange)

Date: June 82

Format: diskette

Hardware: Atari 400/800; 16K with Atari BASIC in cartridge

Language: BASIC

Source Code: no

Price: $37.90

Five programs drill on note and rest types, treble and bass clefs, key signatures, fifty-seven music terms, and enharmonics, using Atari computer's tone generation and high-resolution graphics capabilities. First of three music theory disks; used together with other two, programs provide sequential learning for beginning to advanced music theory students. Students can choose level of difficulty of problems presented and can select exercises of increasing difficulty as they improve. Support booklet included.

INTRODUCTION - Demonstration program helps acquaint students with Atari computer and features used in some of the other programs.

NOTE TYPES - Drill for recognizing different types of notes and rests.

NAME THE NOTE - Drill for identifying notes on both bass and treble clefs.

KEY SIGNATURES - Drill for recognizing major and minor key signatures.

TERMS - Drill for identifying 57 musical terms. Program has three levels of difficulty.

ENHARMONICS - Drill for identifying notes that are equivalent in pitch but can be written differently. Students decide whether exercises include double sharps and double flats.

ID: F20
MUSIC III: SCALES AND CHORDS

Publisher: Minnesota Educational Computing Consortium

Date: June 82

Format: diskette

Hardware: Atari 400/800; 16K with Atari BASIC in cartridge

Language: BASIC

Source Code: no

Price: $36.80

Drills provide aural discrimination of whole and half steps, triads, major and minor scales, and seventh chords. Third in

series of music theory diskettes; used together with other two, programs provide sequential learning for beginning to advanced music theory students. Support booklet included.

ID: F21
MUSIC IN THEORY AND PRACTICE TUTOR (VOLUME 1: 2ND EDITION): A COMPUTER-ASSISTED SUPPLEMENT

Publisher: Micro Music Software Library (distributed by Musitronic)

Date: Nov. 81

Grade: Junior High-College

Format: 13 diskettes

Hardware: Apple II Plus • Apple II; 48K with Applesoft and Integer BASIC in ROM; MMI DAC sound production board (available separately for $175.00)

Language: INTEGER

Price: $500.00

Package includes comprehensive supplement of some 70 assignments written by Dr. Bruce Benward to accompany his nationally recognized text, *Music in Theory and Practice*, 2nd edition, published by Wm. C. Brown Co. Programs are offered as supplements to existing text by arrangement with publisher.

ID: F22
MUSIC LOVER'S GUIDES TO LEARNING SERIES

Publisher: Micro Music Software Library (distributed by Musitronic)

Date: Nov. 81

Format: diskette

Hardware: Apple II Plus • Apple II; 48K with Applesoft in ROM; MMI DAC sound production board (available separately for $175.00)

Language: Applesoft BASIC

Price: $90.00/program

Challenging, interactive format presents spelling, recognition and recall of basic music information. Difficulty level may be controlled by student, and self- adjusts to student performance. Special sound effects and graphics make learning fun as well as rewarding. Programs in series include guides to composers, music symbols, general music terms, Italian music terms, standard instrument names, general music terms, and foreign instrument names (latter for junior high to adult).

ID: F23
MUSIC MAKER

Publisher: Texas Instruments

Also available from: Scholastic Software • Scott, Foresman and Co.

Format: module

Hardware: TI; data storage system recommended

Source Code: no

Price: $39.95

A music introduction tool which allows a novice composer to create computer music by arranging notes on an electronic musical staff.

ID: F24

MUSIC SKILLS TRAINER

Publisher: Texas Instruments

Also available from: McKilligan Supply Corp. • Scholastic Software • Scott, Foresman and Co.

Format: diskette or cassette

Hardware: TI; disk drive or cassette recorder

Source Code: no

Price: $29.95/diskette; $24.95/cassette

A package of four music drills that test musical ability and improve skills. Drills cover pitch guess, interval recognition, chord recognition and phrase recall.

ID: F25

MUSIC THEORY SERIES

Publisher: Comaldor

Format: cassette or diskette

Hardware: PET

Price: $20.00/program

A new series especially useful to the teacher who wishes to introduce students to music theory. The lessons require student-computer interaction in order to master each concept. Frequent review helps consolidate gains.

NOTES AND STAVES - An introduction to letter names of notes, grand staff, treble staff, bass staff, ledger lines, bass and treble clef, and names of lines and spaces, with helpful hints to remember them.

NOTES AND PITCH - Contains a quick review of notes and staves with a *sight and sound* introduction to pitch, treble and bass notes, and octave. Uses notes and pitch to play a tune.

ID: F26

NAME THAT TUNE

Publisher: Micro Music Software Library (distributed by Musitronic)

Date: Nov. 81

Hardware: Apple II Plus • Apple II; 48K with Applesoft in ROM; MMI DAC sound production board (available separately for $175.00)

Language: Applesoft BASIC

Price: $100.00

Familiar tunes are utilized in game context to teach identification (by sound) of the degrees of the scale, using solfeggio syllables or scale degree numbers. One in Benward series of programs written by music educator Dr. Bruce Benward.

ID: F27

NAME THAT TUNE

Publisher: Comaldor

Format: cassette or diskette

Hardware: PET

Price: $20.00

Volume 1 contains 20 songs selected at random to stump the player. Notes appear on the staff as they are presented one by one for the player to hear. Starting with $25, the player wagers an amount of his or her choice that he or she can name the song. With each successive note required, possible winnings are diminished. After four notes, the player loses and hears the entire song. Then it's on to the next song. Other volumes are under development.

ID: F28

PITCH DRILLS WITH ACCIDENTALS

Publisher: Micro Music Software Library (distributed by Musitronic)

Date: Nov. 81

Hardware: Apple II Plus • Apple II; 48K with Applesoft in ROM; MMI DAC sound production board (available separately for $175.00)

Language: Applesoft BASIC

Price: $110.00

Package includes series of programs for drill on names of lines and spaces for treble and bass clefs with accidentals added. Pitch game is also included as well as pitch transposition exercises. One in Makas Series of basic musicianship programs written by Dr. George Makas, author of "Hello, I'm Music".

ID: F29

PITCH DRILLS WITHOUT ACCIDENTALS

Publisher: Micro Music Software Library (distributed by Musitronic)

Date: Nov. 81

Format: diskette

Hardware: Apple II Plus • Apple II; 48K with Applesoft in ROM; MMI DAC sound production board (available separately for $175.00)

Language: Applesoft BASIC

Price: $110.00

Package presents series of programs for visual drill of names of lines and spaces in treble and bass clefs. Program also includes pitch game and exercises in pitch transposition. One in Makas Series of basic musicianship programs written by Dr. George Makas, author of "Hello, I'm Music".

ID: F30

RHYTHM DRILLS

Publisher: Micro Music Software Library (distributed by Musitronic)

Date: Nov. 81

Format: diskette

Hardware: Apple II Plus • Apple II; 48K with Applesoft in ROM; MMI DAC sound production board (available separately for $175.00)

Language: Applesoft BASIC

Price: $110.00

Package includes series of graded programs for rhythmic dictation in melodic context. One in Makas Series of basic musicianship programs written by Dr. George Makas, author of "Hello, I'm Music".

ID: F31

RHYTHMIC DICTATOR

Publisher: Micro Music Software Library (distributed by Musitronic)

Date: Nov. 81

Grade: Junior High-Adult

Format: diskette

Hardware: Apple II Plus • Apple II; 48K with Applesoft in ROM; MMI DAC sound production board (available separately for $175.00)

Language: Applesoft BASIC

Price: $190.00

Program in game format teaches students to hear basic rhythmic patterns and to notate these patterns on a one- line rhythmic staff. Program systematically sequences through rhythmic phrases which increasingly stress syncopation and rest values. All musical patterns are uniquely "dictated" by computer, and program provides infinite library of patterns for dictation practice. Summary of student's progress is provided at end of session.

ID: F32

SEBASTIAN

Publisher: Micro Music Software Library (distributed by Musitronic)

Date: July 82

Format: diskette

Hardware: Apple II Plus • Apple II; 48K with Applesoft in ROM; MMI DAC sound production board (available separately for $175.00)

Language: Applesoft BASIC

Price: $145.00

Melodic dictation program teaches melodic, rhythmic, and tempo identification through detection of musical airs within melodic structure. Unlimited variety of melodies may be added to program by user.

ID: F33

SKETCH-A-DRAWING

Publisher: Aquarius Publishers Inc.

Date: Aug. 82

Format: cassette or diskette

Hardware: TRS-80 MOD I or III

Language: BASIC

Source Code: no

Price: $14.95

Program allows user to design any picture, graph, or text on full screen, and will create BASIC program to reproduce drawing just made. Second part allows recall and modification of any drawing. One in series of programs authored by The Programming Force and distributed exclusively by vendor.

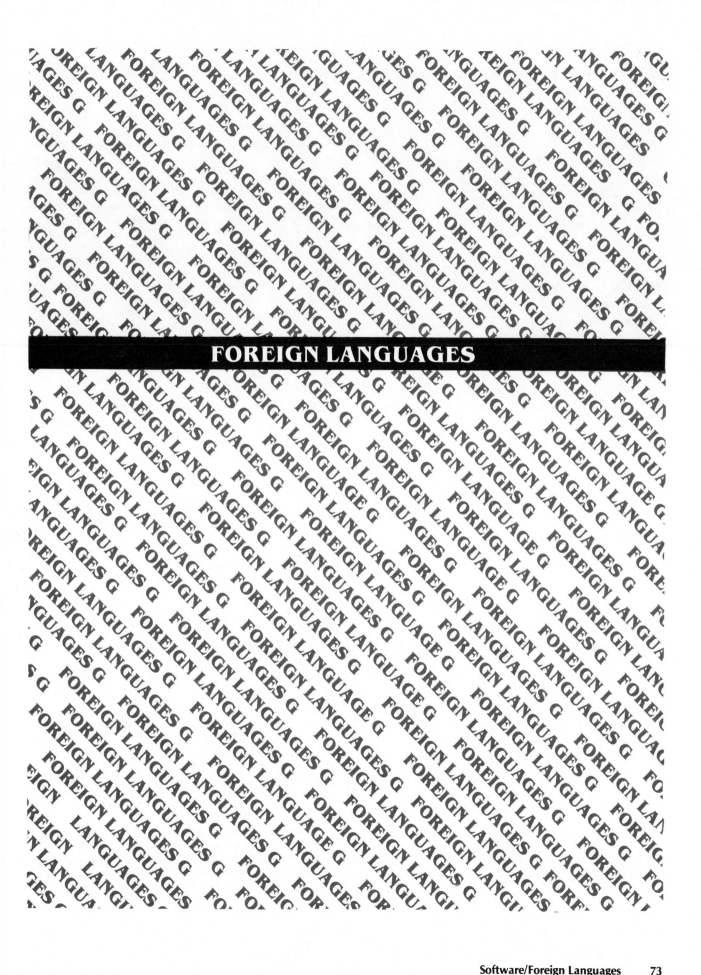

FOREIGN LANGUAGES

ID: G1
DEFINITIVE ARTICLE, GERMAN LANGUAGE
Publisher: Avant-Garde Creations
Also available from: Academic Software • Queue, Inc.
Grade: Up to 10
Format: diskette
Hardware: Apple; 48K with Applesoft in ROM
Price: $29.95

This lesson in German covers classification, analysis and grammar.

ID: G2
FOREIGN LANGUAGE VOCABULARY DRILL
Publisher: COMPU-TATIONS, Inc.
Grade: Elementary-College
Format: 1 program on diskette
Hardware: Apple II
Price: $24.95

This is a drill and practice program for German, French, or Spanish to English translation and vice versa. The program includes several practice files and allows the teacher, parent or student to develop additional specific files. A score summary is presented at the end of this program. The program is available in German, French or Spanish.

ID: G3
FOREIGN LANGUAGES
Publisher: SEI (Sliwa Enterprises Inc.)
Also available from: Queue, Inc.
Date: May 82
Grade: 9-12 and up
Format: 3 diskettes
Hardware: Apple II; 32K with Applesoft in ROM (DOS 3.2 or 3.3)
Language: Applesoft BASIC
Source Code: yes
Price: $30.00/diskette

Programs present enjoyable ways of learning vocabulary of foreign languages. Each diskette has over 800 entries, in following formats: foreign to English, English to foreign, foreign to foreign (synonyms), and foreign phrases to English. Each data base is divided into files such as Easy Nouns 2 or Hard Verbs 1. Programs are generally at beginning and intermediate levels. Each program has all of special characters required for implementing that particular language. Menu-driven programs require no documentation. Each program comes with resident editor for easy modification, updating, or expansion of data base by teacher or student.

SPANISH
GERMAN
FRENCH

ID: G4
FRENCH
Publisher: TYCOM Associates
Also available from: Queue, Inc.
Format: 2 programs on cassette
Hardware: PET; 8K; 40 column screen; C2N cassette recorder
Price: $15.95

This set of programs is intended as a vocabulary builder for the French student. Several modes of operation exist for both noun and verb practice. The user may choose to be passively drilled with the computer supplying English words followed by the French equivalent at regular time intervals, or may choose to be a participant. As a participant, the user may opt for multiple-choice answers, or may type in an answer. In both modes, the computer tallies right answers and gives a final score. For each question incorrectly answered, the computer will immediately give the correct answer.

ID: G5
FRENCH DELICACY
Publisher: Curriculum Applications
Grade: 7-8
Format: cassette
Hardware: TRS-80 MOD I or III; 16K with Level II BASIC
Language: BASIC
Price: $19.95

This program is a French version of DIETING DINOSAUR. It is designed to fit into a first-year French curriculum.

ID: G6
FRENCH VERB CONJUGATIONS
Publisher: TYCOM Associates
Format: cassette
Hardware: PET; 16K; 40 column screen; C2N cassette recorder
Price: $15.95

This program drills and tests the intermediate French student's mastery of verb conjugations. Following instructions, in French or English, the student is given one of several common and representative verbs in the infinitive, a subject pronoun and one of eight tenses. The student must provide the appropriate conjugated verb. For instance, the student is given "ELLES-VENIR-PASSE DU CONDITIONNEL," and he or she must type "SERAIENT VENUES" for a correct answer. Included are regular verbs of the three conjugations, irregular verbs (among them "avoir", "etre", and "aller"), a reflexive verb and verbs conjugated with both "avoir" and "etre" in compound tenses. Tenses included are the present, imparfait, futur, conditionnel, passe simple, passe compose, plus-que-parfait and passe du conditionnel. The program gives the student an extra chance in case of error, will provide correct answers, and gives a grade at the end of the drill.

ID: G7
GERMAN

Publisher: TYCOM Associates

Format: 2 programs on cassette

Hardware: PET; 8K; 40 column screen; C2N cassette recorder

Price: $19.95

This set of programs provides vocabulary practice for the German student. Both noun and verb vocabulary builders operate in either a passive or active mode. In the active mode, the student may choose to enter synonyms to given words, or may opt for a multiple choice question format. The German nouns include gender and plural formation. In all active modes, the computer instantly provides the correct answer to any missed question, and upon exiting, gives a final score.

ID: G8
GERMAN PACKAGE I

Publisher: Micro Learningware

Also available from: MARCK

Format: cassette or diskette

Hardware: TRS-80 MOD I or III; 16K cassette or 32K diskette

Language: BASIC

Source Code: yes

Price: $24.95

Package of programs presents exercises in mastering fundamentals of German language. Written instructions are provided.

SEIN AND HABEN - Provides exercise in mastering the two fundamental strong verbs. Presents first-, second-, and third-person conjugated forms, both singular and plural.

NOUNS - Presents nouns and their articles for exercises in vocabulary building. Any of these or user's input nouns may be declined in all four cases, singular or plural.

ADJECTIVES - Presents adjectives and menu of options with which to practice them. User may exchange language formats while program is running.

BASIC VERBS - Helps build useful vocabulary of action words. Options allow flexibility within programs.

COMPARATIVE AND SUPERLATIVE OF ADJECTIVES - Presents exercises in comparative and superlative forms of some common adjectives.

STRONG AND IRREGULAR VERBS - User has choice of exercises in strong and irregular verbs for translation or for principal parts.

ID: G9
GERMAN PACKAGE II

Publisher: Micro Learningware

Also available from: MARCK • Opportunities For Learning, Inc.

Format: cassette or diskette

Hardware: TRS-80 MOD I or III; 16K cassette or 32K diskette

Language: BASIC

Source Code: yes

Price: $24.95

Package continues presentation of fundamental grammatical aspects of German language. Written instructions provided.

ADVERBS AND CONJUNCTIONS - Provides practice with useful set of adverbs and conjunctions. Includes menu of options.

PERSONAL PRONOUNS - Deals with case forms of personal pronouns. User is prompted for response in accusative, dative, or genitive.

POSSESSIVE PRONOUNS - User supplies inflectional endings to possessive pronouns. Whole sentences are given as prompts.

REFLEXIVE PRONOUNS - Provides exercise in using reflexive pronouns with accusative and dative cases. When personal pronoun and case are given, user responds with reflexive form.

RELATIVE PRONOUNS - User fills in blank with relative pronoun. Whole sentences are provided as prompts.

SEPARABLE PREFIX WITH STRONG VERB PARTS - When prompted with German infinitive, user responds with third-person singular of separable prefix verb.

ID: G10
GERMAN PACKAGE III

Publisher: Micro Learningware

Also available from: MARCK • Opportunities For Learning, Inc.

Format: cassette or diskette

Hardware: TRS-80 MOD I or III; 16K cassette or 32K diskette

Language: BASIC

Source Code: yes

Price: $24.95

Package continues presentation of fundamental grammatical aspects of German language. Written instructions provided.

MODAL (AUXILIARY) VERBS - When prompted with English sentence, user responds with German translation, including article and noun, modal verb, and non-modal infinitive.

SEPARABLE PREFIX/DATIVE OBJECT/AND REFLEXIVE VERBS - When prompted with English verb, user responds with German infinitive. Hint is given for each verb, telling what type of verb it is.

PREPOSITIONS - User responds to German sentence with correct case form. If it is two-way preposition, user decides whether it answers question "Wo?" or "Wohin?".

SUBORDINATING AND COORDINATING CONJUNCTIONS - User responds to conjunctions prompt with correct type. Two separate sentences are given, then combined using conjunction.

STRONG AND WEAK ADJECTIVE ENDINGS - User is prompted with sentence description for correct adjective ending. Successful use requires familiarity with preceding subjects in series.

ID: G11
LANGUAGE TEACHER SERIES

Publisher: Acorn Software Products, Inc.

Date: Sept. 81

Grade: High School and up

Format: diskette

Hardware: TRS-80 MOD I or III; 32K

Language: BASIC

Source Code: no

Price: $29.95/language

Series includes French, Italian, German I and II, and Spanish I and II. Each program offers hundreds of word combinations, verb conjugations, and phrases. Student does essential vocabulary study by choosing topic of drill and whether it is foreign-language-to-English format or vice versa. Options permit multiple-choice answers and retesting on missed items. Program provides running percentage of correct answers, ample documentation, and printout capability for quizzes.

ID: G12

PRACTICANDO ESPANOL CON LA MANZANA II (COMPUTER-ASSISTED INSTRUCTION IN SPANISH)

Publisher: CONDUIT

Also available from: MARCK • Queue, Inc.

Date: 1980

Grade: 7-College

Format: 2 diskettes

Hardware: Apple II; 48K with Applesoft in ROM

Language: BASIC

Source Code: yes

Price: $100.00; $3.00/add'l copy of instructor's guide $20.00/add'l copy of software

These computer-assisted instruction materials in Spanish provide (1) verb drills covering virtually all tenses of Spanish verbs (excluding the perfect subjunctive and the future and conditional perfects), and (2) vocabulary drills which can be keyed to any textbook of the instructor's choice. The drills are appropriate at all levels of Spanish language courses from the seventh grade through second-year college, whenever students need drill in vocabulary (English to Spanish) or in verb forms. Students can use the drills as soon as they learn to read and write vocabulary items and verb tenses. Includes Instructor's Guide (30 pages).

ID: G13

ROMAN BANQUET

Publisher: Curriculum Applications

Grade: 7-8

Format: cassette

Hardware: TRS-80 MOD I or III; 16K with Level II BASIC

Language: BASIC

Price: $19.95

This is a Latin version of DIETING DINOSAUR. Designed with English hints, it will fit into the first-year Latin curriculum.

ID: G14

RUSSIAN LANGUAGE SERIES

Publisher: Instant Software[T.M.]

Also available from: MARCK • Queue, Inc.

Grade: 4-Adult

Format: cassette or diskette

Hardware: TRS-80 MOD I; 16K with Level II BASIC, expansion interface • Apple II; 32K

Language: BASIC

Source Code: no

Price: $9.95/program, cassette; $24.95/both, diskette

Basic instruction and quizzes in Russian language, designed to enable student to master language that is vital to today's international politics and commerce. Written documentation is provided.

BEGINNER'S RUSSIAN - Three programs give on-screen displays of Cyrillic letters, detailed instruction in their proper pronunciation, and exercises designed to enable students to recognize and speak simple Russian words.

EVERYDAY RUSSIAN - Programs acquaint student with words for various foods, places to eat, signs, and names of stores, as well as the order of the Cyrillic alphabet. Each of three parts in package will not only teach these words but will also present student with quiz as well, using words student wishes to work on. Computer will score results of lesson. Programs also allow user to type in letters or words using complete Cyrillic alphabet.

RUSSIAN DISK - BEGINNER'S RUSSIAN and EVERYDAY RUSSIAN are available together on a single disk.

ID: G15

SPANISH

Publisher: TYCOM Associates

Format: 3 programs on cassette

Hardware: PET; 8K; 40 column screen; C2N recorder

Price: $19.95

This set of programs provides vocabulary and verb conjugation practice for the Spanish student. Both noun and verb vocabulary builders operate in either a passive mode, with the computer displaying either an English or Spanish word, followed after a brief pause with the synonym from the other language, or an active mode, in which an English or Spanish word is given and the student must type in the corresponding word from the other language. In addition, passive review and active practice of the endings in the three regular Spanish conjugations are provided. In all active modes, the computer instantly provides the correct answer to any missed question.

ID: G16

SPANISH SIRLOIN

Publisher: Curriculum Applications

Grade: 7-8

Format: cassette

Hardware: TRS-80 MOD I or III; 16K with Level II BASIC

Language: BASIC

Price: $19.95

This program is a Spanish version of DIETING DINOSAUR. It will cover a first-year Spanish curriculum and includes English hints.

ID: G17

SUPER PROMPTER (JAPANESE KATAKANA)

Publisher: Jagdstaffel Software

Date: 1981

Format: diskette

Hardware: Apple II Plus • Apple II; 32K with Applesoft in ROM (DOS 3.3)

Language: Applesoft BASIC

Source Code: no

Price: $39.95

Programmed learning utility package enables use of Japanese Katakana character set by language arts student and/or instructor in study of Japanese language. Program enables student or instructor to create data lists and files, then use them for study and/or testing purposes. Under study and test options, program presents prompt and response in random sequences. Given data files can handle from one to fifty pairs of prompts and responses at one time. All study and test options are scored with percentage of correct to incorrect responses. Written documentation is provided.

ID: G18

SUPER PROMPTER (RUSSIAN CYRILLIC)

Publisher: Jagdstaffel Software

Date: 1981

Format: diskette

Hardware: Apple II Plus • Apple II; 32K with Applesoft in ROM (DOS 3.3)

Language: Applesoft BASIC

Source Code: no

Price: $39.95

Programmed learning utility package enables use of Russian Cyrillic character set by language arts student and/or instructor in study of Russian language. Program enables student or instructor to create data files and lists, then use them for study and/or testing purposes. Under study and test options, program presents prompt and response in random sequences. Given data files can have from one to fifty pairs of prompts and responses at one time. All study and test options are scored with percentage of correct to incorrect responses. Written documentation provided.

LANGUAGE ARTS

ID: H1
20,000 LEAGUES UNDER THE SEA
Publisher: Radio Shack®

Date: 1982

Grade: 4-6

Format: cassette

Hardware: TRS-80 Color Computer; 4K; CTR-80A cassette recorder

Source Code: yes

Price: $14.95

Package includes illustrated reader, read-along audio cassette, and computer tape with vocabulary and spelling exercises. Designed for home use, package is part of Reading Is Fun series.

ID: H2
ABC
Publisher: Comaldor

Grade: K-3

Format: cassette or diskette

Hardware: PET

Price: $20.00

This program helps teach the letters of the alphabet. The teacher may specify large case or mixed large and small cases. In this entertaining game the child is presented with a letter on the screen and thinks of the next letter in the alphabet. S/he then touches that letter on the keyboard. If correct, one of a number of entertaining graphics with sound "does its thing" on the screen. If incorrect, s/he is led through the "alphabet song" up to the letter which was the correct answer, thereby consolidating the order of the letters. The only computer knowledge required is being able to recognize the letters on the keyboard, and pressing the correct key.

ID: H3
ACRONYMS
Publisher: SEI (Sliwa Enterprises Inc.)

Date: May 82

Grade: 9-12 and up

Format: 1 diskette

Hardware: Apple II; 32K with Applesoft in ROM (DOS 3.2 or 3.3)

Language: Applesoft BASIC

Source Code: yes

Price: $25.00

Program contains over 1000 acronyms and abbreviations ranging from governmental to technical, athletics to computers, and popular to military. Spelling counts, but hints are given after each try. Menu-driven program requires no documentation. Program comes with resident editor for easy modification, updating, or expansion of data base by teacher or student.

ID: H4
ACTIVE READER - WORLD OF NATURE SERIES
Publisher: Orange Cherry Media

Also available from: Academic Software • Queue, Inc.

Grade: 2-5

Format: cassette or diskette

Hardware: PET 2000 or 4000; 16K • TRS-80 MOD I or III; 16K • Apple; 16K • Apple II; 16K

Price: $56.00/4 cassettes; $15.00/cassette; $67.00/2 diskettes

Using the computer, students take an active role in reading about these high-interest topics. Reading becomes fun and easy with the help of the friendly computer who motivates, establishes a personal relationship with students, and monitors progress. A happy face and wild computer graphics reward all correct answers to questions.

READING ABOUT UNUSUAL ANIMALS

READING ABOUT SHARKS - ANIMALS OF THE SEA

READING ABOUT EARTHQUAKES AND VOLCANOES

READING ABOUT THE PLANETS

ID: H5
ADJECTIVE
Publisher: Micro-Ed, Inc.

Also available from: Academic Software • EISI (Educational Instructional Systems, Inc.) • K-12 Micromedia • MARCK • Queue, Inc.

Grade: Elementary and up

Format: cassette or diskette

Hardware: Commodore 64 • PET

Language: BASIC

Source Code: no

Price: $7.95

This program uses a game-playing format to teach its subject matter. The student plays against the computer to see which one can score the most points. Each time the student answers a problem, the upper left-hand corner of the screen reveals whether the answer is right or wrong, and some numbers begin to whiz by in a little box. Hitting the RETURN key will then get the student one of these numbers. If the answer was right, this number will be added to the student's game score. If the answer was wrong, this number will be subtracted from the student's game score. The computer always adds 3 to its own game score. If the student does not know the answer to a problem, typing the question mark will cause the answer to be revealed. At the end of the lesson, the student's performance is summarized.

ID: H6
ADJECTIVES
Publisher: Convergent Systems Inc.

Grade: Upper Elementary and up

Format: diskette

Hardware: Apple II; 48K with Applesoft in ROM; shift key adapter • Apple II Plus; shift key adapter

Source Code: no

Price: $75.00

The 4 lessons in this program will take 60 minutes to complete. ADJECTIVES is part of the Basic English Skills Lesson Series. Its 4 lessons are: What is an Adjective; Adjective Degree Forms; Let's Classify Adjectives!; and A or An? A specific learning objective is selected for each lesson. To accomplish the objective the lessons are programmed in several stages: the first is the tutorial section, which provides the learner with definitions, examples and clues for use and identification of parts of speech. Student performance is evaluated through a practice session during which review options are available if the learner has difficulty with a particular area. To proceed, the student must respond correctly. After 3 or 4 attempts, the student is given the correct answer. Upon completion of the basic skills lesson, scores are given and problem areas are identified with recommendations for review. To enhance learning reinforcement, feedback is given for both correct and incorrect responses.

ID: H7

ADVENTURES AROUND THE WORLD

Publisher: Orange Cherry Media

Also available from: Academic Software • K-12 Micromedia • Queue, Inc.

Grade: 3-6

Format: cassette or diskette

Hardware: PET 2000 or 4000; 16K • TRS-80 MOD I or III; 16K • Apple; 16K • Apple II; 16K

Price: $56.00/cassette set of 4; $15.00/cassette; $67.00/diskette set of 2

This high-interest reading series helps students to develop their reading skills in an enjoyable manner. The student actively participates in the adventures with the computer acting as a friendly guide. Questions to monitor comprehension are placed throughout the programs.

LET'S TAKE AN AFRICAN SAFARI

CLIMBING MOUNT EVEREST

JOURNEY UNDER THE SEA

FROZEN TRIP TO ANTARCTICA

ID: H8

ADVERB

Publisher: Micro-Ed, Inc.

Also available from: Academic Software • EISI (Educational Instructional Systems, Inc.) • K-12 Micromedia • Queue, Inc.

Grade: Elementary and up

Format: cassette or diskette

Hardware: Commodore 64 • PET

Language: BASIC

Source Code: no

Price: $7.95

This program deals with the adverb, a word that modifies a verb, an adjective, or another adverb. First, the subject matter is defined and taught. Then the student is tested on what has been presented. If the student does not know the answer to a problem, the question mark can be typed and the computer will give the answer. At the end of the lesson, the student's performance is summarized.

ID: H9

ADVERBS

Publisher: Convergent Systems Inc.

Grade: Upper Elementary and up

Format: diskette

Hardware: Apple II; 48K with Applesoft in ROM; shift key adapter • Apple II Plus; shift key adapter

Source Code: no

Price: $30.00

ADVERBS, part of the Basic Engligh Skills Lesson Series, includes 2 lessons. Topics covered are distinguishing between adjectives and adverbs in statements and questions, and the use of adjectives and adverbs according to the type of verb used in the sentence. This software will take 60 minutes to run. A specific learning objective is selected for each lesson. To accomplish the objective the lessons are programmed in several stages: the first is the tutorial section, which provides the learner with definitions, examples and clues for use and identification of parts of speech. Student performance is evaluated through a practice session during which review options are available if the learner has difficulty with a particular area. To proceed, the student must respond correctly. After 3 or 4 attempts, the student is given the correct answer. Upon completion of the basic skills lesson, scores are given and problem areas are identified with recommendations for review. To enhance learning reinforcement, feedback is given for both correct and incorrect responses.

ID: H10

AGREEMENT OF SUBJECT AND VERB

Publisher: Micro-Ed, Inc.

Also available from: Academic Software • EISI (Educational Instructional Systems, Inc.) • K-12 Micromedia • MARCK • Queue, Inc.

Grade: Elementary and up

Format: cassette or diskette

Hardware: Commodore 64 • PET

Language: BASIC

Source Code: no

Price: $7.95

Problems consist of sentences with missing words. Word choices (singular and plural) are provided for each problem. The learner types the answer. At the bottom of the problem screen, the learner and the computer have a steam engine race. Getting the answers right will help the learner win. Each lesson consists of from nine to thirteen problems, depending on the progress of the race. Because the problems are selected randomly from a bank of thirty-two problems, it is unlikely that any two lessons will present exactly the same sets of problems. At the conclusion of each lesson, the learner's performance is summarized.

ID: H11

ALPHABETIZE

Publisher: Robert R. Baker, Jr.

Date: June 82

Grade: 9-12

Format: cassette or diskette

Hardware: TRS-80 MOD I or III; 16K

Language: BASIC

Source Code: yes

Price: $23.85

Program drills students in alphabetizing. Word lists that appear on computer are typed by student in alphabetical order. Each answer is timed and checked. Total score and time are displayed at end of exercise. Average program running time is 2-3 minutes at each level of difficulty. Written documentation is provided, and program is self- documented as well.

ID: H12

ALPHABETIZING

Publisher: Little Bee Educational Programs

Grade: 2-4

Format: cassette

Hardware: TRS-80 MOD I or III; 16K with Level II BASIC

Price: $10.95

On the left side of the screen, the student is presented with a list of words. These are to be placed in alphabetical order by zipping them to the right side of the screen. The words are selected from a list of 125 words. The program can be made to increase in difficulty as the program progresses. The words in any sequence are selected randomly. Scoring is given at the end of the session.

ID: H13

ALPHAKEY

Publisher: Radio Shack®

Also available from: McKilligan Supply Corp.

Date: 1982

Grade: K-1

Format: cassette or diskette

Hardware: TRS-80 MOD I; 16K with Level II BASIC • TRS-80 MOD III; 16K with Model III BASIC

Language: BASIC

Source Code: yes

Price: $29.95

AlphaKey is alphabet and keyboard familiarization program for children four to six years old. Parts 1 and 2 teach children to discriminate capital letters and to associate capital and lowercase letters. Part 3 gives practice typing letters of alphabet in order. ''Happy face'' appears on screen to reinforce correct answers. Comprehensive reporting function gives teachers report on each student after session is over. Teacher's manual included.

ID: H14

ALPINE SKIER

Publisher: Data Command

Also available from: EISI (Educational Instructional Systems, Inc.) • K-12 Micromedia

Grade: 5-6; Junior High remedial

Format: 4 diskettes

Hardware: Apple II; 48K with Applesoft in ROM • Apple II Plus; 48K • TRS-80 MOD I; 16K (cassette) or 32K (diskette) with Level II BASIC • TRS-80 MOD III; 32K with MOD III BASIC

Language: BASIC

Price: $113.75/set; $29.95/program (1 diskette/program)

Entertaining programs let student become Olympic class skier on way to improving important reading comprehension skills. Lesson is presented as downhill slalom course which student must negotiate by giving correct answers. Programs use animated graphics and self-paced, menu-driven, interactive learning techniques. Each program is available individually and consists of 3 rounds of 12 races each. Student may select which round he or she wishes to run. Summary of student's progress is retained for use by teacher. Average running time is 15-20 minutes.

DETERMINING FACT AND OPINION - Program is designed to improve student's comprehension skills by helping him or her tell difference between fact and opinion. Student is given pairs of sentences and must identify which sentence in each pair represents fact or opinion.

SEEING CAUSE AND EFFECT - Student is challenged to think critically about cause and effect. He or she reads phrases which are carefully written to contain both cause and effect, and must identify first part of each phrase as cause or effect.

CATEGORIZING WORDS AND PHRASES - Program guides student in thinking critically about meanings of words and phrases and in organizing thoughts. Computer gives sets of four or five words or phrases, and student must determine which word or phrase does not belong in each set. Difficulty level increases through three rounds of program.

GETTING SENTENCE MEANINGS - Program will aid student in getting greater meaning from what he or she reads. Computer gives two carefully worded sentences; student must determine whether they mean the same thing, or have different meanings. Difficulty level increases through 3 rounds of program.

ID: H15

ANAGRAMS

Publisher: Microphys Programs

Also available from: EISI (Educational Instructional Systems, Inc.) • MARCK

Format: 10 cassettes or 1 diskette

Hardware: VIC-20; 3K expansion cartridge • PET; 8K • Commodore 64; 8K • Apple II; 24K • TRS-80 MOD I or III; 16K • Bell & Howell

Language: BASIC

Source Code: yes

Price: $15.00/cassette; $180.00/diskette

Series of ten programs randomly generates scrambled words which are to be identified by means of clues provided. Many of words used are those selected for vendor's spelling and vocabulary series. Programs thus reinforce reading, vocabulary, and spelling skills. Same sequence of words generated may be requested, thus making match play possible. Five level-of-difficulty categories each consist of two programs. Complete instructions are included. Also available on diskette for price noted above, along with six WHEEL-OF-FORTUNE WORD GAME programs. User must specify machine for which diskette is intended.

RECREATIONAL (PV340-341)

COLLEGE (PV342-343)

HIGH SCHOOL (PV344-345)

JUNIOR HIGH (PV346-347)

ELEMENTARY (PV348-349)

ID: H16

ANALOGIES; CHALLENGES IN MEANING AND ORDER

Publisher: Micro Power & Light Company

Grade: High School, Adjustable

Format: diskette

Hardware: Apple II; 32K with Applesoft in ROM

Price: $34.95

The ANALOGIES program contains 100 analogy exercises. Some are quite apparent, others equally devious! Work as many exercises as one likes, choosing any of the following types: Synonyms and antonyms, Geometry, Cause and effect, Comparison and degrees, and Is a part of. The material is grouped into 5 sets of 20 exercises each. Each exercise consists of the following entries: The first pair of terms in the analogy; Four answer choices of the best pair of terms to complete the analogy; and Four feedback responses, one associated with each of the answer choices. A review screen can be associated with any answer choice. The program supports up to 10 such review screens in total. As supplied, ANALOGIES is ready for use by high school students and older. But with the facilities described above, it can easily be adapted to any level! At the teacher's choice the ANALOGIES program saves student scores on disk. As many as 200 student records can be saved before it is necessary to delete them from disk, making room for the next 200. These student records can be reviewed by the teacher according to any of the several selection criteria - by student name, period, date or type of analogy. The ANALOGIES program actually runs in either of two modes or "sections". In the Teacher Section exercises can be reviewed, changed, deleted and added, and student records can be reviewed and deleted. In the Student Section exercises are presented and student scores written to disk.

ID: H17

ANTONYM MACHINE

Publisher: Micro-Ed, Inc.

Also available from: EISI (Educational Instructional Systems, Inc.) • MARCK • Texas Instruments

Grade: Elementary

Format: cassette or diskette

Hardware: TI 99/4 • Commodore 64 • PET

Language: BASIC

Source Code: no

Price: $7.95; $9.95/TI ed.

The computer randomly selects a pair of words with opposite meanings. One of the two words is displayed flashing on and off in the upper left corner of the screen. What is the other word, the one that is its antonym? After the learner responds, an antonym machine processes the first word so that it becomes its antonym. Each lesson is designed to work with twenty pairs of words chosen randomly from a bank of fifty pairs. However, the lesson may be terminated at any point, at which time the learner's performance will be summarized according to the following categories: number of problems, number of errors, number of times computer gave answer, time used on the lesson, and specific antonyms that gave trouble.

ID: H18

ANTONYM/SYNONYM TIC-TAC-TOE

Publisher: Little Bee Educational Programs

Grade: 2-4

Format: cassette

Hardware: TRS-80 MOD I or III; 16K with Level II BASIC

Price: $10.95

This program presents students with an interesting drill as they become familiar with common antonyms and synonyms by means of a Tic-Tac-Toe game. The student selects a block and if he correctly responds, that block becomes his. Two students can compete against each other or a single student can match wits with the computer. The instructor can select either antonyms or synonyms or both. There are over 50 common antonyms and synonyms included in the program. Scoring is obtained at the end of the session.

ID: H19

ANTONYMS

Publisher: RIGHT ON PROGRAMS

Also available from: Queue, Inc.

Grade: 11

Format: 5 programs on 5 cassettes or diskette

Hardware: Apple II; 48K with Applesoft in ROM (DOS 3.2 or 3.3) • PET; 16K

Language: BASIC

Source Code: yes

Price: $13.00/cassette; $15.00/diskette; $70.00/5 programs on 1 diskette

This program is part of a series designed to help students improve their performance on standardized tests. This program emphasizes the correct selection of a word opposite in meaning to the given word. Different words appear in each program and answers are explained.

ID: H20

ANTONYMS/SYNONYMS

Publisher: Hartley Courseware, Inc.

Also available from: Academic Software

Grade: 3-8

Format: 1 diskette

Hardware: Apple II; 48K with Applesoft in ROM (DOS 3.2 or 3.3)

Language: Applesoft BASIC

Price: $39.95

Twenty-one lessons providing reinforced drill on recognition and use of synonyms and antonyms, in gradually increasing levels of difficulty.

ID: H21

APOSTROPHE

Publisher: Micro-Ed, Inc.

Also available from: Academic Software • EISI (Educational Instructional Systems, Inc.) • K-12 Micromedia • MARCK • Queue, Inc.

Grade: Elementary and up

Format: cassette or diskette

Hardware: Commodore 64 • PET

Language: BASIC

Source Code: no

Price: $7.95

This program teaches the use of the apostrophe. First, the subject matter is presented in an instructional format. Then the learner is tested on his understanding of this material. At the end of the lesson, the learner's performance is summarized.

ID: H22

ARC SEQUENCE

Publisher: Little Bee Educational Programs

Grade: K-1

Format: cassette

Hardware: TRS-80 MOD I or III; 16K with Level II BASIC

Price: $10.95

Marching letters motivate children to learn the sequence of the letters of the alphabet. A staircase is formed upon which the letters of the alphabet march. A face at the center of the screen smiles with a correct entry and frowns with an incorrect entry. After all 26 letters have been entered, the letters fly to the top of the screen. Scoring is obtained at the end of the session.

ID: H23

BASIC LANGUAGE SKILLS

Publisher: Orange Cherry Media

Also available from: Academic Software • K-12 Micromedia • Queue, Inc.

Grade: 3-6

Format: cassette or diskette

Hardware: PET 2000 or 4000; 16K • TRS-80 MOD I or III; 16K • Apple; 16K • Apple II; 16K

Price: $15.00/cassette; $70.00/cassette set of 5; $84.00/diskette set of 2

Students learn the parts of speech through definition and examples. They are then eligible to play games which create funny stories and poetry. From a list of words supplied by the student, the computer makes up an amusing story. Programs also include other exercises and review questions as students learn the function of words in creative expression.

USING NOUNS

USING VERBS
USING ADJECTIVES
USING ADVERBS
CREATING SENTENCES

ID: H24

BEGINNING GRAMMAR

Publisher: Texas Instruments

Also available from: McKilligan Supply Corp. • Scholastic Software • Scott, Foresman and Co.

Grade: 2-5

Format: module

Hardware: TI

Source Code: no

Price: $29.95

Introduces the basic parts of speech and how they are used to build sentences.

ID: H25

BEGINNING/ENDING SOUNDS

Publisher: Little Bee Educational Programs

Grade: 1-2

Format: cassette

Hardware: TRS-80 MOD I or III; 16K with Level II BASIC

Price: $10.95

This program provides practice in making new words by changing either the beginning or ending sound. The student is shown a word and below it the same word with either the first or last letter missing. Three choices are given from which a new word is to be formed. A correct answer scores a bulls-eye; an incorrect answer misses the bulls-eye. Scoring is given at the end of the session.

ID: H26

BIG DOOR DEAL

Publisher: Data Command

Also available from: EISI (Educational Instructional Systems, Inc.) • K-12 Micromedia

Grade: 5-6; Junior High remedial

Format: 12 cassettes or 4 diskettes

Hardware: Apple II; 48K with Applesoft in ROM • Apple II Plus; 48K • TRS-80 MOD I; 16K (cassette) or 32K (diskette) with Level II BASIC • TRS-80 MOD III; 32K with MOD III BASIC

Language: BASIC

Source Code: no

Price: $113.75/set; $29.95/program (1 diskette or 3 cassettes/program)

Programs are takeoffs on popular big-money TV game shows, in which student earns points toward grand prizes by using reading skills to open correct doors. Programs use animated graphics and self-paced, menu-driven interactive learning techniques. Each program is available individually, and consists of three complete games or rounds of 15 exercises each. Student may select which round he or she wishes to play. Summary of student's progress is retained for review by teacher.

USING CONTEXT CLUES - Program aids student in using context to determine word meanings. Computer provides sentence containing unfamiliar word, and student uses context of sentence to determine which of three meanings is correct. Difficulty of exercises increases throughout three rounds of program.

RECOGNIZING FIGURATIVE LANGUAGE - Program builds student's comprehension skill by creating familiarity with colorful language. Student is given incomplete sentence and must determine which of three endings for sentence uses figurative language.

MAKING ANALOGIES - Program enhances student's ability to think critically as he or she reads. Computer provides one part of analogy, and student must select which of three words correctly completes analogy. Difficulty of exercises increases through three rounds of programs.

SEQUENCING EVENTS - Program helps student organize information logically as he or she reads. Computer provides group of four or five words or phrases, then shows them arranged in three different ways. Student must decide which arrangement is correct.

ID: H27

C-V-C (CONSONANT-VOWEL-CONSONANT)

Publisher: Microcomputer Workshops

Also available from: Academic Software • K-12 Micromedia • MARCK

Date: July 82

Grade: Elementary

Format: cassette

Hardware: PET; 16K

Language: BASIC

Source Code: no

Price: $20.00

Program for elementary reading classes makes excellent use of graphics to guide student up set of steps as reward for making simple three-letter words of consonant-vowel-consonant form. Feedback for correct and incorrect answers is given by happy and unhappy faces on SCREEN. When learner reaches top step, huge happy face fills screen and learner may then continue with new set of steps. Written documentation is provided.

ID: H28

CALENDAR TIC-TAC-TOE

Publisher: Little Bee Educational Programs

Grade: 2-4

Format: cassette

Hardware: TRS-80 MOD I or III; 16K with Level II BASIC

Price: $14.95

Three in a row wins! This challenging Tic-Tac-Toe game provides a means of drill on the order of the days of the week and months of the year. Each block contains a question about a day of the week or month of the year. To put an ''X'' in the block

the question must be answered correctly. This program can be used by a single student against the computer or with two students competing against each other. A session consists of 5 Tic-Tac-Toe games with different questions each time. Scoring for each student is given at the end of the program.

ID: H29

CAPITALIZATION

Publisher: Educational Activities, Inc.

Also available from: Queue, Inc.

Grade: Upper Elementary

Format: diskette

Hardware: Apple II Plus; (DOS 3.2.1 or 3.3) • TRS-80 MOD I or III; with Level II BASIC • PET • Commodore 2001 • Commodore 4000; 40 or 80 column • Commodore 8000; 80 column

Source Code: no

Price: $49.00

This program covers the various uses of capital letters. It includes capitalization in letter headings, addresses, quotations, and names. It also illustrates the use of capital letters with the end punctuation marks covered in PUNCTUATION I. Drill is used throughout the lesson to allow a continuously interactive format throughout both tutorial and drill sections. Several different drill formats are used to maintain student interest.

ID: H30

CAPITALIZATION

Publisher: Instant Software[T.M.]

Also available from: Queue, Inc.

Grade: 7 and up

Format: diskette

Hardware: Apple II; 32K with Applesoft in ROM

Language: Applesoft BASIC

Source Code: no

Price: $24.95

This program teaches and reviews rules governing capital letters. Written documentation is provided.

ID: H31

CAPITALIZATION

Publisher: Hartley Courseware, Inc.

Also available from: Academic Software • Queue, Inc.

Grade: 3-7

Format: 2 diskettes

Hardware: Apple II; 48K with Applesoft in ROM (DOS 3.2 or 3.3)

Language: Applesoft BASIC

Price: $49.95

Presents basic rules of capitalization, followed by examples and 25 practice sentences. Students work from menu to modify each sentence until they believe it is correct. In case of error, corrected sentence appears directly below student's work. Series includes both practice disk and test disk. Latter contains complete student management files which keep record on student responses.

ID: H32

CAPITALIZATION AND PUNCTUATION

Publisher: RIGHT ON PROGRAMS

Date: July 82

Grade: 2

Format: cassette or diskette

Hardware: Apple II; 48K with Applesoft in ROM (DOS 3.2 or 3.3) • PET; 16K

Language: BASIC

Source Code: yes

Price: $13.00/cassette; $15.00/diskette

Principles of beginning a sentence with capital letter and ending it with a period or question mark are taught. There are many examples given so child can be sure he or she understands idea. In second part of program, game is used to reinforce skills taught. If an incorrect answer is given, it is corrected with no rewards or penalties given.

ID: H33

CAPITALIZATION SERIES

Publisher: Micro-Ed, Inc.

Also available from: EISI (Educational Instructional Systems, Inc.) • Opportunities For Learning, Inc.

Grade: Elementary and up

Format: 20 programs on cassette or diskette

Hardware: Commodore 64 • PET

Language: BASIC

Source Code: no

Price: $140.00

Each lesson in this series has two parts. The first one (Part A) is tutorial. The second (Part B) features drill and practice on the material covered in Part A. Part B uses a standardized achievement test format in order to help students become familiar with this sort of testing. The series also includes a 50-item pre-test which concludes with a recommendation concerning student placement within the series, and a 50-item post-test that suggests which lessons ought to be reviewed.

ID: H34

CATCH THE RHYMING FISH

Publisher: Micro-Ed, Inc.

Also available from: Academic Software • MARCK

Grade: Elementary

Format: cassette or diskette

Hardware: Commodore 64 • PET • VIC; 3K memory enhancement

Language: BASIC

Source Code: no

Price: $7.95

A word flashes on and off at the top of the screen. Then three fish begin pulling other words across the screen. One of these words rhymes with the word at the top of the screen. Which

one? The student uses a fishing pole to catch the right answer fish. At the end of the lesson, the learner's performance is summarized.

ID: H35

CLOZE TECHNIQUE FOR DEVELOPING COMPREHENSION

Publisher: Orange Cherry Media

Also available from: Academic Software • K-12 Micromedia • Queue, Inc.

Grade: 3-6

Format: cassette or diskette

Hardware: PET 2000 or 4000; 16K • TRS-80 MOD I or III; 16K • Apple; 16K • Apple II; 16K

Price: $15.00/cassette; $28.00/cassette set of 2; $34.00/diskette

In these programs, certain words are deleted from the reading passages. The deletions are then supplied by the pupils, who select from the alternatives provided them. Only one answer is correct when judged within the context of the entire reading selection.

CLOZE: BUILDING UNDERSTANDING (I)

CLOZE: BUILDING UNDERSTANDING (II)

ID: H36

COLLEGE ENTRANCE EXAMINATION PREPARATION

Publisher: Borg-Warner Educational Systems

Grade: Senior High

Format: part 1 - 5 diskettes; part 2- 7 diskettes

Hardware: Apple II Plus; 48K

Language: Applesoft BASIC

Source Code: no

Price: $575.00/Part 1, $75.00/subscription; $875.00/Part 2, $105.00/subscription

The College Entrance Examination Preparation series (CEEP) provides students with individualized instruction and practice to help them prepare for the Scholastic Aptitude Test (SAT) and other standardized achievement and aptitude tests. CEEP contains a total of 56 instructional modules on 12 disks, organized according to the SAT's major test categories. The test questions in these modules are presented in a sequence of instruction that includes the use of two and sometimes all three of the following modes: 1) the test mode - simulates test conditions and provides an overall evaluation of student performance; scoring includes speed of response as well as correctness; this mode also itemizes questions requiring additional study; 2) the lesson mode - includes helpful hints and explanations of questions as well as simple "right" and "wrong" reinforcement of student response; and 3) the information mode - provides the student with exhaustive background information on correct responses as well as information about the distractors used in the questions presented. The CEEP management system will provide an instant, detailed analysis of student performance in all categories; recommend items needing further study; display student performance on the SAT scale; determine if altering the amount of time spent on each item could improve the student's score; and offers several other features to help the student in overall learning and in practicing test-taking strategies.

PART 1 - VERBAL SERIES - Disk A - Synonyms; Disk B - Synonyms; Disk C - Synonyms/ Antonyms; Disk D - Synonyms/Antonyms; Disk E - Synonyms/ Antonyms

PART 2 - VERBAL STRATEGIES/MATHEMATICS SERIES - Disk V - Representative Verbal Items; Disk Q - Analogies; Disk R - Reading Comprehension; Disk S - Sentence Completion; Disk P - Prerequisite and Representative Math Items; Disk M - Math: Quantitative Comparisons; Disk N - Math; Logic; Geometry; Algebra.

ID: H37

COMMAS; TWELVE COMMON USES

Publisher: Micro Power & Light Company

Also available from: Academic Software • Queue, Inc.

Format: diskette

Hardware: Apple II; 32K with Applesoft in ROM

Price: $29.95

The COMMAS program states the rule related to each of twelve common uses of the comma. Each use is in turn illustrated, and then an opportunity is afforded the student to apply the rule to a number of exercises. The rules covered deal with: (1) Items in a series, (2) More than one adjective, (3) Nouns in a direct address, (4) Titles and degrees, (5) The adverb "too", (6) Interrupting elements, (7) Successive independent clauses, (8) Introductory clauses and phrases, (9) Nonessential modifiers, (10) Explanatory words and phrases, (11) Contrasts and alternatives, and (12) Long phrases of identification. The program alerts the student to the fact that the implementation of certain rules may vary from one text or teacher to the next - and may even change merely with the passage of time! The rules are presented more as "guidelines", to help make meaning clear, and not to unnecessarily restrict the writer. The rules are presented in the form of a menu, making it easy to start today's review where appropriate. The student can cause the program to present as many (or as few) drill and practice exercises as desired - being able to stop or to return to the menu after working each exercise. In addition, while working the exercises, the student can ask to *see* the rule stated again - to reinforce his or her understanding on the spot.

ID: H38

COMPOUND WORD MATCHUP

Publisher: Little Bee Educational Programs

Grade: 2-4

Format: cassette

Hardware: TRS-80 MOD I or III; 16K with Level II BASIC

Price: $10.95

The student is presented with two lists of words from which he/she must form compound words. The compound words are formed by pointing an arrow at the selected pair of words. If a proper compound word is formed, the two words will come from opposite sides of the screen and crash together, forming the compound word. Scoring is obtained at the end of the session.

ID: H39

COMPOUND WORDS

Publisher: Micro-Ed, Inc.

Also available from: EISI (Educational Instructional Systems, Inc.) • MARCK • Queue, Inc.

Grade: Elementary

Format: cassette or diskette

Hardware: Commodore 64 • PET • TI 99/4; extended BASIC module

Language: BASIC

Source Code: no

Price: $7.95; $9.95/TI ed.

A compound word is made up of two smaller words. Each problem in this program consists of a compound word drawn at random from a bank of twenty-five words. The job of the student is to type the two smaller words that make up the compound word being presented. At the end of ten problems, the student's performance is summarized.

ID: H40

COMPU-READ[T.M.] 3.0

Publisher: Edu-Ware Services

Also available from: Academic Software • EISI (Educational Instructional Systems, Inc.) • K-12 Micromedia • MARCK • McKilligan Supply Corp. • Opportunities For Learning, Inc. • Queue, Inc.

Format: diskette

Hardware: Apple; 48K (DOS 3.2 or 3.3) • Atari; 48K with BASIC

Language: Applesoft BASIC

Price: $29.95

This program , designed to improve reading speed and recall, covers letters, words, synonyms and antonyms, and sentences. The Learning Manager provides capability for building and editing word files and adjusting difficulty. A graphic/ numeric reporting system will display complete data on a learner's progress and reading rate.

ID: H41

COMPU-SPELL[T.M.]

Publisher: Edu-Ware Services

Also available from: Academic Software • EISI (Educational Instructional Systems, Inc.) • K-12 Micromedia • MARCK • McKilligan Supply Corp. • Opportunities For Learning, Inc. • Queue, Inc.

Grade: 4-Adult

Format: diskette

Hardware: Apple; 48K (DOS 3.2 or 3.3)

Language: Applesoft BASIC

Price: $29.95/system disk; $19.95/data disk

This program is an instructional system which teaches spelling through positive reinforcement. Its operating system accommodates 1 to 60 learners. The system consists of a system diskette and data diskette for grades 4, 5, 6, 7, 8 and Adult-Secretarial. Each individual's progress is monitored and continuously updated. All spelling words are displayed in sentence context. A list of review words missed by each learner is retained. Each data diskette contains 800 to 1200 spelling words.

ID: H42
CONJUNCTIONS

Publisher: Convergent Systems Inc.

Grade: Upper Elementary and up

Format: diskette

Hardware: Apple II; 48K with Applesoft in ROM; shift key adapter • Apple II Plus; shift key adapter

Source Code: no

Price: $30.00

CONJUNCTIONS is part of the Basic English Skills Lesson Series. Taking approximately 60 minutes to run, this software consists of two lessons. The first covers the identification of coordinating, subordinating and correlative conjunctions in questions and statements. The second teaches the student to determine the correct conjunction to use according to the meaning of the sentence. A specific learning objective is selected for each lesson. To accomplish the objective the lessons are programmed in several stages: the first is the tutorial section, which provides the learner with definitions, examples and clues for use and identification of parts of speech. Student performance is evaluated through a practice session during which review options are available if the learner has difficulty with a particular area. To proceed, the student must respond correctly. After 3 or 4 attempts, the student is given the correct answer. Upon completion of the basic skills lesson, scores are given and problem areas are identified with recommendations for review. To enhance learning reinforcement, feedback is given for both correct and incorrect responses.

ID: H43
CONSONANTS

Publisher: Hartley Courseware, Inc.

Also available from: Academic Software • Queue, Inc.

Grade: 1-4

Format: 1 diskette with backup

Hardware: Apple II; 48K with Applesoft in ROM (DOS 3.2 or 3.3); CCD required

Language: Applesoft BASIC

Price: $79.95

Complete series of phonics lessons on consonant sounds and blends, including initial and final consonants along with initial, final, and medial blends. Teacher presents instructions to student on tape, using cassette control device (CCD). Develops listening skills and helps student discriminate among consonant sounds.

ID: H44
CONTRACTIONS

Publisher: Micro-Ed, Inc.

Also available from: EISI (Educational Instructional Systems, Inc.)

Grade: Elementary

Format: cassette or diskette

Hardware: Commodore 64 • PET • TI 99/4; extended BASIC module

Language: BASIC

Source Code: no

Price: $7.95; $9.95/TI ed.

For each problem, the computer will randomly display either a contraction or an uncontracted expression. If what is presented is a contraction, the student should type the uncontracted expression. If an uncontracted expression is presented, then the student should type the contraction. There are ten problems to a lesson. If the student makes no mistakes, two space warriors will honor the student.

ID: H45
CONTRACTIONS

Publisher: Little Bee Educational Programs

Also available from: K-12 Micromedia • Queue, Inc.

Grade: 2-4

Format: cassette

Hardware: TRS-80 MOD I or III; 16K with Level II BASIC

Price: $10.95

Causing the two words to "crash" together to form the contraction offers fun and drill for recognizing and spelling contractions. The student has 2 chances to identify the contraction for the two given words and produce the "crash." Scoring is given at the end of the session.

ID: H46
CRITICAL READING

Publisher: Borg-Warner Educational Systems

Grade: Adjustable; 4-Adult

Format: up to 8 diskettes

Hardware: Apple II Plus; 48K

Language: Applesoft BASIC

Source Code: no

Price: $750.00/series A-H, $120.00/subscription; $350.00/series A-D; $400.00/series E-H

The Critical Reading series is an individual supplemental program designed to introduce students to the fundamental skill of critical thinking. The purpose is to help students master rules of inference that will help them to a better understanding of written material. Each level of the program begins with a pretest to determine where a student should begin working and concludes with a post-test to assess mastery. The reading settings in which each rule of inference is used progress from simple, two-sentence presentations to longer, more complex paragraphs. Each rule is taught by example; first in the simplest setting, and then in contexts which grow increasingly more demanding. Student records are maintained in the management system and may be permanently recorded with the use of an optional printer. The Teacher's Guide allows the instructor or student to begin the program immediately, even if a novice with microcomputers.

DISK A - USE OF THE LOGICAL "OR"

DISK B - USE OF THE LOGICAL "OR"

DISK C - USE OF THE LOGICAL "ALL"

DISK D - USE OF THE LOGICAL "ALL"

DISK E - CONDITIONAL STATEMENT: "IF"

DISK F - CONDITIONAL STATEMENT: "IF"

DISK G - INDUCTIVE REASONING

DISK H - INDUCTIVE REASONING

ID: H47

DEFINITIONS

Publisher: RIGHT ON PROGRAMS

Also available from: Queue, Inc.

Grade: 11

Format: 3 programs on 3 cassettes or diskette

Hardware: Apple II; 48K with Applesoft in ROM (DOS 3.2 or 3.3) • PET; 16K

Language: BASIC

Source Code: yes

Price: $13.00/cassette; $15.00/diskette

This program is part of a series designed to help students improve their performance on standardized exams. This series emphasizes the correct selection of words by definition.

ID: H48

DIASCRIPTIVE READING

Publisher: Educational Activities, Inc.

Also available from: K-12 Micromedia • Queue, Inc.

Grade: 3-8

Format: cassette or diskette

Hardware: Apple II Plus; (DOS 3.3 or 3.2.1) • PET • Commodore 2001 • TRS-80 MOD I or III; with Level II BASIC • Commodore 4000; 40 or 80 column • Commodore 8000; 80 column

Source Code: no

Price: $245.00/15 cassettes; $245.00/7 diskettes

Contains 6 diagnostic tests and 36 developmental reading programs which diagnose student reading skills, prescribe what is needed for improvement and evaluate performance at each level. Student is either advanced to next level or directed to lower level for remediation. Student reads selections and responds to questions. Each lesson is self- directing and self-correcting. A management system (diskette version) records student's progress and remediates or advances student automatically. Teacher can obtain scores from the diskette.

DIAGNOSTIC TEST FOR ALL SKILL AREAS

VOCABULARY

SEQUENCE

MAIN IDEA

FACT/OPINION

DETAILS

INFERENCE

ID: H49

DICTIONARY GUIDE WORDS

Publisher: Micro-Ed, Inc.

Also available from: Academic Software

Grade: Elementary

Format: cassette or diskette

Hardware: Commodore 64 • PET • TI 99/4; extended BASIC module

Language: BASIC

Source Code: no

Price: $7.95; $9.95/TI ed.

At the top of each page in a dictionary are two words called guide words. The first guide word is the same as the first entry word on that page. The second guide word is the same as the last entry word on that page. There are four lessons in this program. Each lesson consists of two columns of words. The student's job is to match each word in Column A with the pair of guide words in Column B that represent the dictionary page on which the Column A word would be found. At the end of each lesson, the computer lists the words from Column A that were not matched correctly with the guide words from Column B.

ID: H50

DIETING DINOSAUR

Publisher: Curriculum Applications

Also available from: K-12 Micromedia

Grade: 3-5, 7-8

Format: 2 programs on cassette

Hardware: TRS-80 MOD I or III; 16K with Level II BASIC

Language: BASIC

Price: $29.95

These programs use the Hangman format to promote vocabulary, spelling and writing skills. To play the game, the class is divided into teams to compete for total points. (It is intended for use with entire class, but utilizes only one computer.) The class "goes to dinner" with Ludwig Van Dinosaur. Most elements of the game correspond to the meal. The lower case drives must be loaded or the program will not run. Game is hosted by the resident dinosaur who is on a strict diet and can only eat letters which fit into the word to be guessed. Students have the opportunity to feed the creature while expanding their vocabulary. Major features include extensive error-checking capabilities which do not allow bad keyboard entry, large printing throughout for easy visual comprehension, teacher adjustments for upper/lower case option, hints allowed, random or sequential word selection and size of word bank to be used. Games feature sound and extensive documentation for teachers with complete details and recommendations for tailoring to specific student needs, as well as the ability for teachers to replace the word bank with their own chosen words and hints.

ID: H51

DRACULA

Publisher: Radio Shack®

Date: 1982

Grade: 4-6

Format: cassette

Hardware: TRS-80 Color Computer; 4K; CTR-80A cassette recorder

Source Code: yes

Price: $14.95

Package includes illustrated reader, read-along audio cassette, and computer tape with spelling and vocabulary exercises. Designed for home use, package is part of Reading Is Fun series.

ID: H52
DRAGON GAME SERIES FOR LANGUAGE ARTS
Publisher: Educational Activities, Inc.

Grade: 3-6

Format: cassette or diskette

Hardware: Apple II Plus; (DOS 3.2.1 or 3.3) • TRS-80 MOD I or III; with Level II BASIC • PET • Commodore 2001 • Commodore 4000; 40 or 80 column • Commodore 8000; 80 column

Source Code: no

Price: $49.00

This series of programs uses a game format that allows the student to review and practice parts of speech. Each game in the series focuses on a different part of speech. The student must move along a game board displayed on the computer monitor by correctly answering questions or end up in the fiery dragon's den. Animated graphics make the game motivational and exciting! The student must reach the end of the game board in order to receive the reward. Incorrect answers are explained by branching. A brief review of each part of speech precedes each game. It's a sound way to give students the drill work they need in a way they will enjoy.

THE DRAGON OF NOUNS

THE DRAGON OF VERBS

THE DRAGON OF ADJECTIVES

THE DRAGON OF SYNONYMS

THE DRAGON OF ANTONYMS

THE DRAGON OF CONTRACTIONS

ID: H53
DROPPING THE FINAL E
Publisher: Micro-Ed, Inc.

Also available from: EISI (Educational Instructional Systems, Inc.) • MARCK • Queue, Inc.

Grade: Elementary

Format: cassette or diskette

Hardware: Commodore 64 • PET • TI 99/4; extended BASIC module

Language: BASIC

Source Code: no

Price: $7.95; $9.95/TI ed.

Each problem begins with a base word. The first job of the student is to type the base word plus an ED or ING ending. Finally, working from an ED or ING ending, the student must type the base word. Each problem word has been randomly drawn from a bank of fifty words. Each lesson consists of ten problems. At the end of the lesson, the student's performance is summarized.

ID: H54
ELEMENTARY - VOLUME 2
Publisher: Minnesota Educational Computing Consortium

Also available from: Academic Software • Creative Computing • K-12 Micromedia • Opportunities For Learning, Inc. • Scholastic Software • Sunburst Communications

Date: June 82

Grade: 1-6

Format: diskette

Hardware: Apple II; 32K with Applesoft in ROM (DOS 3.3); printer for some programs

Language: Applesoft BASIC

Source Code: no

Price: $40.40

Package consists of spelling, vocabulary, and computer education programs for elementary classroom. Teacher can enter lists of words and have them used by computer. Support booklet included.

SPELL - Drills students on spelling.

MIXUP - Presents spelling words in mixed-up order.

WORD FIND - Creates word-find puzzle for teacher to duplicate.

CROSS WORD - Creates crossword puzzle from words and definitions entered by teacher.

WORD GAME - Creates word game to be played using words and definitions entered by teacher.

TALK - Designed to introduce students to computer.

AMAZING - Prints out worksheet mazes.

ID: H55
ELEMENTARY - VOLUME 5
Publisher: Minnesota Educational Computing Consortium

Also available from: Academic Software • CONDUIT • K-12 Micromedia • Scholastic Software

Date: June 82

Grade: 1-4

Format: diskette

Hardware: Apple II; 32K with Applesoft in ROM (DOS 3.3)

Language: Applesoft BASIC

Source Code: no

Price: $37.80

Package contains five lessons which both teach and allow practice on prefixes of UN, RE, DIS, PRE, and IN. Also includes two review drills, DRAGON FIRE and PRE-APPII. Support booklet included.

ID: H56
ELEMENTARY - VOLUMES 11 & 12
Publisher: Minnesota Educational Computing Consortium

Date: June 82

Grade: 1-4

Format: 2 diskettes

Hardware: Apple II; 32K with Applesoft in ROM (DOS 3.3)

Language: Applesoft BASIC

Source Code: no

Price: $65.40

Module consists of two diskettes produced by TIES (Total Information Educational Systems). First provides drills on elements of phonetics, such as suffixes, sound association, syllable contraction, and homonyms. Second contains language arts games, which use words based on SIMS word list. Support booklet (included) is necessary to describe drill numbers.

ID: H57

ELEMENTARY PACKAGE III

Publisher: Micro Learningware

Also available from: Academic Software • MARCK • Opportunities For Learning, Inc. • Queue, Inc.

Grade: Elementary

Format: cassette or diskette

Hardware: TRS-80 MOD I or III; 16K (cassette) or 32K (diskette) • TRS-80 Color Computer; 16K; cassette

Language: BASIC

Source Code: yes

Price: $24.95

Package consists of word exercises and games. Disk versions are more flexible than cassette versions. Certain programs are for certain models of computers only, as noted in descriptions. Written instructions provided.

SPELLING - Maintains disk or tape file(s) of word lists. Words can be added, changed, or deleted from files. Words are selected randomly and flashed on screen. Student is then asked to spell word.

WORD SCRAMBLE - Words selected randomly by computer from word files are scrambled and displayed on screen. Student is asked to "unscramble" word.

RAT MAZE - Student specifies dimension of maze. Computer displays maze graphically on screen. Student is timed as he or she directs rat through maze.

WORD PUZZLE - Makes word puzzles from list of words provided by teacher. Words can be displayed either on screen or on printer. Available for TRS-80 MOD I or III only.

RHYMING - Words are randomly selected and displayed on screen along with short list of words from which to choose rhyming word. Available for TRS-80 Color Computer only.

ID: H58

END PUNCTUATION

Publisher: Micro-Ed, Inc.

Also available from: Academic Software • EISI (Educational In-

structional Systems, Inc.) • K-12 Micromedia • MARCK • Queue, Inc.

Grade: Elementary

Format: cassette or diskette

Hardware: Commodore 64 • PET

Language: BASIC

Source Code: no

Price: $7.95

This program teaches the use of the three different kinds of punctuation marks that end sentences. These are the period, the question mark and the exclamation point. At the end of the lesson, the learner's performance is summarized.

ID: H59

ENGLISH - VOLUME 1

Publisher: Minnesota Educational Computing Consortium

Also available from: Sunburst Communications

Date: June 82

Grade: High School, General Education

Format: diskette

Hardware: Apple II; 32K with Applesoft in ROM

Language: Applesoft BASIC

Source Code: no

Price: $41.70

Module provides diagnostic drills and tutorials on parts of speech, including nouns, pronouns, adjectives, adverbs, verbs, conjunctions, and interjections. Teacher option to create tests is also available. Support booklet (included) describes classroom use of module and lists sentences used in drills.

ID: H60

ENGLISH ACHIEVEMENT I-V

Publisher: Microcomputer Workshops

Also available from: Academic Software • K-12 Micromedia

Date: July 82

Grade: 9-12

Format: 5 cassettes or diskettes

Hardware: PET; 16K • Apple II; 48K

Language: BASIC

Source Code: no

Price: $100.00/set of 5 cassettes; $175.00/set of 5 diskettes; $20.00/cassette; $39.95/diskette

Programs cover five formats appearing on CEEB's English achievement examination. Sentences containing errors are presented at random in batches of 16 to student, who indicates part of sentence containing error. Program then supplies corrected rewrite. Analysis is made of types of errors student is prone to make, and approximate SAT score is given. Analysis is updated as program is continued. Written documentation is provided.

ID: H61

ENGLISH BASICS

Publisher: Educational Activities, Inc.

Also available from: K-12 Micromedia • MARCK • Opportunities For Learning, Inc. • Queue, Inc.

Grade: Upper Elementary

Format: cassette or diskette

Hardware: Apple II Plus; (DOS 3.2.1 or 3.3) • TRS-80 MOD I or III; with Level II BASIC • PET • Commodore 2001 • Commodore 4000; 40 or 80 column • Commodore 8000; 80 column

Source Code: no

Price: $145.00/set (cassette), $170.00/set (diskette), PROGRAM I; $85.00/set (cassette), $99.95/set (diskette), PROGRAM II; $34.95/cassette, $39.95/diskette, PROGRAM I & II

The following English skills are reviewed and reinforced with student interaction: nouns, pronouns, verbs, adjectives, adverbs, homonyms, synonyms, and antonyms, contractions. Each program focuses on a single problem experienced by students. The programs first display text material and highlight it in examples. The student is then quizzed on the skill presented and "reward" messages are displayed for correct answers. If the student gives an incorrect answer, s/he is encouraged to try again. Finally, if the student keeps giving incorrect responses, the answer is displayed.

PROGRAM I - PARTS OF SPEECH - Includes NOUNS I and II; PRONOUNS I and II; VERBS I and II; ADJECTIVES I and II; and ADVERBS I and II.

PROGRAM II - CONCEPTS IN LANGUAGE ARTS - Includes HOMONYMS I and II; SYNONYMS I and II; and CONTRACTIONS I and II.

ID: H62

ENGLISH COMPUTORIALS I-V

Publisher: Educulture

Date: 1982

Grade: High School and up

Format: 27 diskettes; 10 audio cassettes

Hardware: Apple II Plus; 48K (DOS 3.2 or 3.3); disk drive; audio cassette player; printer optional

Language: Applesoft BASIC

Source Code: no

Price: $625.00 including audio cassette player; $125.00/ Computorial; $125.00/audio cassette player separately

Package includes sequence of basic English mechanics tutorials with accompanying audio narrative covering topics from sentence patterns through clauses, phrases, and subordination. Self-paced, interactive instruction features automatic branching based on student answers. Answer judging and immediate corrective feedback are accompanied by a management system which provides thorough analysis of pre- and post-test lesson material, including summary reports on student performance. Each "computorial" package consists of 18-22 lessons and provides a minimum of 2 hours of student exposure

time. Typical lesson is given in two parts: tutoring in audio with supporting displays on screen, followed by intensive drill exercises on lesson topic. Each computorial contains two data diskettes, two coded backup diskettes, one proctor's diskette and coded backup, two audio cassettes, and user's guide. Package as whole adds five student diskettes and audio cassette player.

COMPUTORIAL I - BASIC SENTENCE PATTERNS - Student will identify words and sentences according to their parts of speech; identify and supply words according to their functions in given sentences; and identify and write sentences that conform to the four basic sentence patterns.

COMPUTORIAL II - SENTENCE PATTERNS WITH MODIFIERS - Student will distinguish among four basic sentence patterns; identify and use adjectives and adverbs in sentences conforming to those patterns; identify and use prepositional phrases in sentences distinguishing between preposition and object; and distinguish between prepositional phrases used as adjectives and those used as adverbs.

COMPUTORIAL III - USING INDEPENDENT CLAUSES - Student will identify compound elements in sentences; distinguish between simple and compound sentences; punctuate compound sentences correctly; and identify and correctly use coordinating conjunction transition words.

COMPUTORIAL IV - USING SUBORDINATE CLAUSES - Student will identify and analyze functions of adjective, adverb, and noun clauses in given sentences; identify and correctly use relative pronouns, subordinating conjunctions and other "signal" words; correctly punctuate sentences containing subordinate clauses; and write sentences using subordinate clauses.

COMPUTORIAL V - USING SUBORDINATE PHRASES - Student will distinguish between phrases and clauses; analyze sentences containing appositive, participial, gerund and infinitive phrases; distinguish between essential and nonessential subordinate phrases; identify and supply correct punctuation for subordinate phrases in sentences; and write sentences containing appositive, participial, gerund, and infinitive phrases.

ID: H63

ENGLISH LESSONS - SET ONE

Publisher: Academic Computing Association

Date: Nov. 80

Grade: 7-12

Format: cassette or diskette

Hardware: Apple • TRS-80 • PET

Source Code: no

Price: $13.95/diskette; $45.00/set of cassettes; $6.95/lesson on cassette

This set is part of the ACA's CODES software. This package teaches and provides drill on ten rules of capitalization.

RULE 1 - 101 - This lesson covers titles people may hold.

RULE 2 - 102 - Covers words that show family relationships.

RULE 3 - 103 - Covers the names of places.

RULE 4 - 104 - This program is a review of rules 1 through 3.

RULES 5, 6 and 7 - 105 - The names of businesses, organizations, institutions, and brand names are included in this lesson.

RULES 8, 9, and 10 - 106 - Capitalization of nationalities, languages, races and religious groups are covered in Rule 8. Rule 9 includes words in titles; Rule 10 covers compass points.

REVIEW OF RULES 1-10 - 107

TEST ON RULES 1-10 - 108

ID: H64

ENGLISH LESSONS - SET TWO

Publisher: Academic Computing Association

Grade: 7-12

Format: cassette or diskette

Hardware: Apple • TRS-80 • PET

Source Code: no

Price: $13.95/diskette; $45.00/set of cassettes; $6.95/cassette

This set is part of the ACA's CODES software. It teaches and gives drill on sentence fragments and run-on sentences.

SENTENCE FRAGMENTS - 201 - This program covers the subject and verb of a sentence.

SENTENCE FRAGMENTS - 202 - After completing this lesson, the student should be able to tell a complete sentence from a fragment.

SENTENCE FRAGMENTS - 203 - This program is a final test on fragments.

RUN-ON SENTENCES - 204 - This lesson covers comma splice.

RUN-ON SENTENCES - 205 - Covers the key words it, she/he, then, and therefore.

RUN-ON SENTENCES - 206 - Covers the key words it, then, and therefore.

RUN-ON SENTENCES - 207 - More practice.

RUN-ON SENTENCES - 208 - This lesson is review on run-on sentences.

RUN-ON SENTENCES - 209 - A test on run-on sentences.

ID: H65

ETYMOLOGY

Publisher: RIGHT ON PROGRAMS

Also available from: Queue, Inc.

Grade: 11

Format: 5 programs on 5 cassettes or diskette

Hardware: Apple II; 48K with Applesoft in ROM (DOS 3.2 or 3.3) • PET; 16K

Language: BASIC

Source Code: yes

Price: $13.00/cassette; $15.00/diskette; $70.00/5 programs on 1 diskette

This program recognizes the importance of Greek and Latin prefixes and roots. Many roots and prefixes are explained and

defined. This is part of a larger series of programs designed to help students improve their performance on standardized examinations.

GREEK ROOTS AND PREFIXES - Review is given of Greek roots and prefixes.

LATIN ROOTS AND PREFIXES - Review is given of Latin roots and prefixes.

GROUP B

GROUP C

FOREIGN WORDS AND PHRASES - Common foreign words and phrases are introduced and reviewed through exercises.

ID: H66

EXACTOSPELL

Publisher: Comaldor

Format: cassette or diskette

Hardware: PET

Price: $20.00

With this individualized spelling program, each student has his own data tape to which words that give him difficulty are added. The words are mastered through various drills and study routines over a number of successive sessions, at which time the option is given of removing the word from the list. It will generate progress charts on the screen or printer for each student's words giving the success rate for each, and allowing teachers to "zero in" on weak skill areas.

ID: H67

EXTRA PRACTICE SPELLING SERIES

Publisher: Micro-Ed, Inc.

Also available from: EISI (Educational Instructional Systems, Inc.) • K-12 Micromedia • MARCK • Queue, Inc.

Grade: 2-6

Format: 7 programs per level on cassette or diskette; 5 levels

Hardware: Commodore 64 • PET • VIC

Language: BASIC

Source Code: no

Price: $249.75/set; $49.95/level

This series is designed for students who need extra practice, and lots of it, in order to develop their spelling skills. The patterns into which the words are grouped for practice are the same as the patterns listed for the regular drill and practice series. However, the instructional format is different. Each lesson works as follows. A word appears on the screen and remains visible while the student tries to type it at the computer keyboard. The student makes as many attempts as may be necessary in order to accomplish this. When the word has been typed correctly, the screen is cleared and the student is asked to type the word from memory. If this is not done successfully, the word reappears and the procedure begins anew. When the student types the word correctly from memory, a new word is presented and the cycle starts over. Words are selected at random from a bank usually containing between 30 and 50 words per lesson. The lesson may be terminated at any time, after which the student's performance is summarized, including a listing of the specific words that gave trouble. If the student works with at least 10 words during the lesson, and does so without making any mistakes, the computer displays two space warriors who honor the student's achievement. The total program includes grades 2 through 6 with word banks containing more than 7,000 spelling words. There are 36 lessons per grade level for a total of 180 lessons in all. Each grade level may be purchased separately.

EXTRA PRACTICE GRADE 2

EXTRA PRACTICE GRADE 3

EXTRA PRACTICE GRADE 4

EXTRA PRACTICE GRADE 5

EXTRA PRACTICE GRADE 6

ID: H68

FLASH SPELL HELICOPTER

Publisher: Microcomputer Workshops

Also available from: Academic Software • K-12 Micromedia • MARCK

Date: July 82

Grade: K-12

Format: cassette

Hardware: PET; 16K

Language: BASIC

Source Code: no

Price: $20.00

Program designed for any grade level combines spelling practice with graphics in which helicopter game provides incentive to student to spell words correctly. For each word spelled correctly, student earns ten seconds of helicopter time. At the end of the session, student plays helicopter game for total number of seconds earned. Teacher may enter any number of spelling words by entering or replacing data lines. Words are then presented to student at random from data list. Written documentation is included.

ID: H69

FLASH SPELLING

Publisher: Educational Activities, Inc.

Also available from: Academic Software • Opportunities For Learning, Inc. • Queue, Inc.

Grade: Adjustable

Format: cassette or diskette

Hardware: Apple II Plus; (DOS 3.2.1 or 3.3) • TRS-80 MOD I or III; with Level II BASIC • PET • Commodore 2001 • Commodore 4000; 40 or 80 column • Commodore 8000; 80 column

Source Code: no

Price: $14.95/cassette; $28.50/cassette set (Scrambled Letters and Flash Spelling); $33.50/diskette (Scrambled Letters)

The new spelling words are flashed one by one on the screen. The student can attempt typing in the correctly spelled word. A correct response receives a "reward." If the student gives an incorrect response, the same word is flashed again for a longer period of time. Instructions which describe how teachers may add their own words to the program are included.

ID: H70

FOREIGN/ENGLISH

Publisher: SEI (Sliwa Enterprises Inc.)

Date: May 82

Grade: 9-12 and up

Format: 1 diskette

Hardware: Apple II; 32K with Applesoft in ROM (DOS 3.2 or 3.3)

Language: Applesoft BASIC

Source Code: yes

Price: $30.00

Program contains over 900 American vocabulary words that come directly? from foreign languages. Each multiple-choice question is accompanied by correct definition, pronunciation, originating language, and literal translation if applicable. Special characters are used in generating foreign words and pronunciations. Menu-driven program requires no documentation. Program comes with resident editor for easy modification, updating, or expansion of data base by teacher or student.

ID: H71

FOUR BASIC READING SKILLS/BASIC SKILLS PRACTICE

Publisher: BrainBank, Inc.

Also available from: Academic Software • K-12 Micromedia • Queue, Inc.

Grade: 5 and up

Format: 5 units of 5 programs each on cassette or diskette

Hardware: Apple; 16K • PET; 16K • TRS-80; 16K

Price: $50.00/unit

The first unit, Four Basic Reading Skills, is an introduction and must be used before any of the others. Includes Courseware Kit with Teacher's Guide.

FOUR BASIC READING SKILLS - Topics include how to recall details, identifying the main idea, how to draw conclusions, how to put things in order, and a review.

BASIC SKILLS PRACTICE A - Stories are: A Bicycle Trip; Fish for the Queen; Rent-A-Cow; Asparagus; and People Bites.

BASIC SKILLS PRACTICE B - Stories are: A Fisherman's Catch; Dieting; Toadstools; Prehistoric Life; The Face of the Moon.

BASIC SKILLS PRACTICE C - Stories are: Tiny Nibbling Rabbits; Sleep Without Snoring; A Pretty Fancy Fur; An Insect Sense; A Lost Ocean Liner.

BASIC SKILLS PRACTICE D - Stories are: A Most Popular Pet; A Little Glitter; The Old Globe; The Longest Day; Right Things.

ID: H72

GLOSSARY OF USAGE

Publisher: RIGHT ON PROGRAMS

Also available from: Queue, Inc.

Grade: High School

Format: 5 programs on 5 cassettes or diskette

Hardware: Apple II; 48K with Applesoft in ROM (DOS 3.2 or 3.3) • PET; 16K

Language: BASIC

Source Code: yes

The program includes a series of constructions accepted as standard English with particular emphasis on words frequently confused. Each program provides a review of different words or phrases and has many exercises to reinforce the user's ability to recognize and correct these errors.

ID: H73
GRAMMAR PACKAGE I

Publisher: Micro Learningware

Also available from: Academic Software • K-12 Micromedia • MARCK • Opportunities For Learning, Inc. • Queue, Inc.

Format: cassette or diskette

Hardware: TRS-80 MOD I or III; 16K cassette or 32K diskette • TRS-80 Color Computer; 16K with extended BASIC; cassette • Apple II; 32K with Applesoft in ROM (DOS 3.2 or 3.3)

Language: BASIC

Source Code: yes

Price: $24.95

Drill and practice programs instruct students in recognition of various parts of speech and types of noun constructs. Written instructions provided.

ADJECTIVE RECOGNITION - Student tries to identify adjectives from words in sentences selected and displayed at random by computer. Little robot on screen nods or shakes head at correct and incorrect answers, and gives student another chance if answer is incorrect.

NOUN RECOGNITION - Student attempts to identify nouns among words presented from sentences chosen at random by computer.

ADVERB RECOGNITION - Student attempts to identify adverbs, using above methodology.

VERB RECOGNITION - Student attempts to identify verbs, using above methodology.

PRONOUN RECOGNITION - Student attempts to identify pronouns, using above methodology.

PERSON, PLACE, THING - Student attempts to identify as person, place, or thing, a noun selected at random by computer and placed in one of three boxes, then moved to another until student feels it is in properly labeled box.

ID: H74
GRAMMAR PACKAGE II

Publisher: Micro Learningware

Also available from: Academic Software • MARCK

Format: cassette or diskette

Hardware: TRS-80 MOD I or II; 16K cassette or 32K diskette • Apple II; 32K with Applesoft in ROM (DOS 3.2 or 3.3)

Language: BASIC

Source Code: yes

Price: $24.95

Tutorial programs offer instruction in various types of grammatical constructs. For all computers listed unless otherwise noted in descriptions. Written instructions provided.

CONTRACTIONS - Tutorial on contractions includes detailed explanations with examples and drills.

POSSESSIVE CASE - Tutorial program on possessive case of pronouns and nouns. Includes explanations with numerous examples and drills.

PREFIX/SUFFIX - Tutorial includes prefixes, suffixes and their meanings. Includes explanations with numerous examples and drills.

SPELLING RULES - Tutorial on most of spelling rules includes many examples and user-selected drills.

SUBJECT-VERB AGREEMENT - Tutorial with definitions, examples, and drills. When incorrect answer is given, explanation follows. For Apple II only.

ID: H75
GRAMMAR PROBLEMS FOR PRACTICE

Publisher: Milliken Publishing Company

Also available from: EISI (Educational Instructional Systems, Inc.) • McKilligan Supply Corp.

Grade: 3-9

Format: 5 programs on 10 diskettes

Hardware: Apple II Plus; 48K

Price: $375.00/set of 10; $565.00/set of 10 with backup; $80.00/each for HOMONYMS, VERBS or PRONOUNS; $40.00/ MODIFIER; $120.00/SPELLING

The five modules cover skills that are generally introduced in the 3rd through 6th grades, but the programs are also suited to remediation in the 7th through 9th grades. These modules provide interesting and extensive practice in troublesome grammar and usage aras. Generally, each module consists of practice exercises followed by a post-test; however, the types of exercises and flow of work will vary due to the nature of the curriculum in each module. The HOMONYMS module, for example, begins with a pre-test of the words covered in the assigned lesson. If mastery is demonstrated, the student proceeds to the next lesson. If he can either review definitions of the homonyms that were missed or work practice exercises. These exercises provide immediate feedback and reinforcement. The student also has access to a "help" option whenever an incorrect response is entered. Once the practice exercises are completed, the student must demonstrate mastery on a post-test before advancing to the next lesson. The VERBS module, on the other hand, does not have a pre-test and the activities are completely different, but the movement from practice exercises to a post-test is the same. Each diskette in the GRAMMAR PROBLEMS FOR PRACTICE package contains a Manager Program which allows teachers to maintain records for up to 100 students. The teacher can make individual assignments, review student performance, identify student problem areas. Hard-copy printouts may be generated. The Manager Program keeps all data confidential.

HOMONYMS - This module covers contraction homonyms, triple homonyms, and confusing pairs.

VERBS - Module covers verbs, irregular verb pairs, and subject-verb agreement. All lessons suitable for grades 3-9.

PRONOUNS - Using correct cases and antecedent agreement are covered in this module.

MODIFIERS - Topics covered are modifiers and making comparisons.

SPELLING - Module covers making plurals, adding endings, special variations, and a lesson for teacher-entered words.

ID: H76

GUESS THAT WORD

Publisher: Micro-Ed, Inc.

Also available from: K-12 Micromedia • MARCK

Grade: Elementary and up

Format: cassette or diskette

Hardware: Commodore 64 • PET • TI 99/4; extended BASIC module

Language: BASIC

Source Code: no

Price: $7.95; $9.95/TI ed.

This instructional program makes it easy for the user (or his students) to create spelling lessons using words of his choice. Simply type in the words on the appropriate data lines. The needed data lines are so easy to create that even elementary school students (grades four and up) should be able to do the job. Lines 7000-7999 should be used for entering spelling words as data. Multiple spelling lists can be entered. Each list should be preceded by a number identifying the list. An arrow pointing up concludes each list. All data entries should be separated by commas. The program as it comes when purchased already has five lists of words sometimes identified as spelling demons. These lists can be changed simply by changing the data line entries. Here is how GUESS THAT WORD works when the program is run. As requested by the computer, the student types in the number of the desired word list. Then the computer randomly selects a word from the list and, near the top of the screen, prints a row of gray boxes equivalent in length to the length of the chosen word. The student now has three choices. He/she can try to guess the entire word, guess a single letter, or ask the computer to reveal a letter of the word. If the student tries to guess the word, 100 points are won if the guess is right, and 5 points are lost if the guess is wrong. If the student tries to guess a letter, the cost of the guess (regardless of its accuracy) is 1 point. If the student guesses correctly, all such letters in the word are revealed. If the student's guess is wrong, no letters are revealed. If the student asks the computer to show a letter, only one letter is revealed even though more than one such letter may be in the word. The cost of this option is always 2 points. When the student finally guesses the word, the computer summarizes the results on an ongoing basis. This includes the average score per word, plus a list of the specific words presented by the computer.

ID: H77

HAIKU

Publisher: Micro-Ed, Inc.

Also available from: EISI (Educational Instructional Systems, Inc.) • K-12 Micromedia

Grade: Elementary and up

Format: cassette or diskette

Hardware: Commodore 64 • PET

Language: BASIC

Source Code: no

Price: $7.95

Haiku is a Japanese form of poetry. It calls for seventeen syllables in three lines. These lines have syllable counts of five, seven, and five. Three other general rules must also be followed if the end result deserves to be called haiku. First, a haiku must refer in some way to nature. The poem doesn't have to be "about" nature, but there must be a nature clue or reference included in it. The second requirement of haiku is that the poem refer to a particular event as it is presently taking place. Generalizations do not belong in haiku. Rule three requires that the haiku suggest to the reader the emotions the poet feels while describing the particular event. A bank of words appropriate to the writing of haiku has been written into this program and, choosing them, the computer writes poetry in seventeen syllables - three lines of five, seven, five syllables each. An exciting thing about this program is the ability of the computer to revise its poem, line by line, at the request of the student. In practice then, this unusual program can be used to encourage students to write creatively. Individual lines can be copied down on paper by the student for use in other poetry. Interesting images can be used as a jumping-off place for a single student, or a whole class, to create further images and further poetry - whether haiku is the ultimate result or not. The ability of the computer to revise its own poem, line by line, gives the student a chance to become a critical recognizer of good haiku. In a classroom setting, students can be encouraged to explain why one group of 17 syllables is acceptable as haiku, while another misses the mark.

ID: H78

HALLOWEEN JUMBLE/THANKSGIVING CROSSWORD/CHRISTMAS WORD SEARCH

Publisher: Little Bee Educational Programs

Also available from: Queue, Inc.

Grade: 2-4

Format: cassette

Hardware: TRS-80 MOD I or III; 16K with Level II BASIC

Price: $8.00/each

These programs offer a fun way to learn the common words associated with the listed holidays. These programs can be used with first-grade students if a word list is displayed. Scoring is given at the end of each of these programs.

ID: H79

HANGMAN

Publisher: Comaldor

Format: cassette or diskette

Hardware: PET

Price: $20.00

This spelling program includes built—in words, but allows the instructor to enter his own list.

ID: H80

HANGMAN

Publisher: Aquarius Publishers Inc.

Date: Aug. 82

Format: cassette or diskette

Hardware: TRS-80 MOD I or III

Language: BASIC

Source Code: no

Price: $14.95

User has up to seven misses to guess hidden word before being shot by arrow. Words included range from easy to very hard. One in series of programs authored by The Programming Force and distributed exclusively by vendor.

ID: H81

HARD AND SOFT C

Publisher: Micro-Ed, Inc.

Also available from: EISI (Educational Instructional Systems, Inc.) • Queue, Inc.

Grade: Elementary

Format: cassette or diskette

Hardware: Commodore 64 • PET • TI 99/4; extended BASIC module

Language: BASIC

Source Code: no

Price: $7.95; $9.95/TI ed.

Each problem in this program consists of a word containing either a SOFT C or a HARD C. The student is to identify the C in the problem word by pressing S for SOFT C or by pressing K for HARD C. Each problem word is randomly selected from a bank of fifty words. Each lesson consists of ten problems. At the end of each lesson, the student's performance is summarized.

ID: H82

HARD AND SOFT G

Publisher: Micro-Ed, Inc.

Also available from: EISI (Educational Instructional Systems, Inc.) • MARCK

Grade: Elementary

Format: cassette or diskette

Hardware: Commodore 64 • PET • TI 99/4; extended BASIC module

Language: BASIC

Source Code: no

Price: $7.95; $9.95/TI ed.

Each problem in the program consists of a word containing either a SOFT G or a HARD G. The student is to identify the G in the problem word by pressing J for SOFT G or by pressing G for HARD G. Each problem word is randomly selected from a bank of fifty words. Each lesson consists of ten problems. At the end of each lesson, the student's performance is summarized.

ID: H83

HOMONYM JUGGLER

Publisher: Little Bee Educational Programs

Also available from: Queue, Inc.

Grade: 2-4

Format: cassette

Hardware: TRS-80 MOD I or III; 16K with Level II BASIC

Price: $10.95

The student strikes the juggler's arm containing the word that the student believes to fit the blank in the sentence. If the student is correct, the word will move into the blank space and flash on and off. Scoring is obtained at the end of the session.

ID: H84

HOMONYM MACHINE

Publisher: Micro-Ed, Inc.

Also available from: EISI (Educational Instructional Systems, Inc.) • MARCK • Queue, Inc. • Texas Instruments

Grade: Elementary

Format: cassette or diskette

Hardware: Commodore 64 • PET • TI 99/4

Language: BASIC

Source Code: no

Price: $7.95; $9.95/TI ed.

The computer randomly selects a pair of words with the same sound but different meanings (examples: meat, meet). In all other respects, this homonym program works in exactly the same way as the ANTONYM MACHINE. The difference is that the desired word in each case is a homonym rather than an antonym.

ID: H85

HOMONYMS

Publisher: Hartley Courseware, Inc.

Also available from: Academic Software

Grade: 3-8

Format: 1 diskette

Hardware: Apple II; 48K with Applesoft in ROM (DOS 3.2 or 3.3)

Language: Applesoft BASIC

Price: $39.95

Includes 17 tutorial/drill lessons introducing homonyms in an increasing order of difficulty; and 3 review lessons requiring students to write correct homonym in context of sentence. Lessons are at five different graded reading levels.

ID: H86

HOMONYMS

Publisher: RIGHT ON PROGRAMS

Date: July 82

Grade: 2

Format: cassette or diskette

Hardware: Apple II; 48K with Applesoft in ROM (DOS 3.2 or 3.3) • PET; 16K

Language: BASIC

Source Code: yes

Price: $13.00/cassette; $15.00/diskette

First part of program explains what homonym is and gives examples in sentences. Children have many opportunities to show they understand the material. Second part of program consists of game which rewards child for right answer. There is no penalty for an incorrect answer.

ID: H87
HOMONYMS II
Publisher: RIGHT ON PROGRAMS

Date: July 82

Grade: 2

Format: cassette or diskette

Hardware: Apple II; 48K with Applesoft in ROM (DOS 3.2 or 3.3) • PET; 16K

Language: BASIC

Source Code: yes

Price: $13.00/cassette; $15.00/diskette

Same principle as HOMONYMS using slightly more sophisticated homonyms. Second part of program consists of game which rewards child for right answer. There is no penalty for an incorrect answer.

ID: H88
HOUND OF THE BASKERVILLES
Publisher: Radio Shack®

Date: 1982

Grade: 4-6

Format: cassette

Hardware: TRS-80 Color Computer; 4K; CTR-80A cassette recorder

Source Code: yes

Price: $14.95

Package includes illustrated reader, read-along audio cassette, and computer tape with spelling and vocabulary exercises. Designed for home use, package is part of Reading Is Fun series.

ID: H89
HOW TO READ IN THE CONTENT AREAS
Publisher: Educational Activities, Inc.

Also available from: Academic Software • Activity Resources Company, Inc. • K-12 Micromedia • Opportunities For Learning, Inc. • Queue, Inc.

Grade: 5-6; Remedial 7-8

Format: cassette or diskette

Hardware: Apple II Plus; (DOS 3.3 or 3.2.1) • TRS-80 MOD I or III; with Level II BASIC • PET • Commodore 2001 • Commodore 4000; 40 or 80 column • Commodore 8000; 80 column

Source Code: no

Price: $49.00/content area; $189.00/complete package

A skills development program that utilizes the unique capabilities of the computer to personalize, individualize, and interact with the student to help him/her learn content area reading. Concepts taught include: spotlighting, surveying, detecting, recalling, and utilizing. The program is easy to use and follow. The self-correcting features let the learner know immediately whether or not each response is correct. If incorrect, the program provides for immediate reteaching and reinforcement of the particular skill before the student tries again. Through the clever use of graphics, the microcomputer rewards successful student performance with visual prizes. At the end of each lesson, the learner sees a summary of his/her performance.

SCIENCE
SOCIAL STUDIES
LITERATURE
MATHEMATICS

ID: H90
IDENTIFYING COMPLETE SENTENCES
Publisher: Micro-Ed, Inc.

Also available from: Academic Software • MARCK • Queue, Inc.

Grade: Elementary

Format: cassette or diskette

Hardware: Commodore 64 • PET • VIC • TI 99/4

Language: BASIC

Source Code: no

Price: $7.95; $9.95/TI ed.

Groups of words are presented on the screen. For each group, the student must identify whether or not it is a complete sentence. The groups are presented in random sequence, and it is unlikely that any given lesson will have exactly the same groups of words as the lesson preceding it or the lesson following it. At the end of each lesson, the student's performance is summarized.

ID: H91
IMPROVING WRITING STYLE (ADVANCED)
Publisher: RIGHT ON PROGRAMS

Also available from: Academic Software • Queue, Inc.

Grade: High School

Format: 5 programs on 5 cassettes or diskette

Hardware: Apple II; 48K with Applesoft in ROM (DOS 3.2 or 3.3) • PET; 16K

Language: BASIC

Source Code: yes

Price: $13.00/cassette; $15.00/diskette; $70.00/5 programs on 1 diskette

These programs will enable the writer to become a more mature and sophisticated writer.

PARALLEL STRUCTURE (A&B) - The programs illustrate errors in parallel structure in words, phrases and clauses. Recognition and correction of errors is stressed.

SENTENCE BEGINNINGS (A&B) - The user is encouraged to improve style through varying sentence beginnings. The use of adverbs, phrases, and subordinate clauses is explained and illustrated. The recognition of technique is stressed.

EXCESS WORDS - This program emphasizes a writing style that avoids wordiness and encourages "blue penciling" the user's writing.

ID: H92

IMPROVING WRITING STYLE (BASIC)

Publisher: RIGHT ON PROGRAMS

Also available from: Academic Software • Queue, Inc.

Grade: High School

Format: 5 programs on 5 cassettes or diskette

Hardware: Apple II; 48K with Applesoft in ROM (DOS 3.2 or 3.3) • PET; 16K

Language: BASIC

Source Code: yes

Price: $13.00/cassette; $15.00/diskette; $70.00/5 programs on 1 diskette

These 5 programs are designed to help the user become a more effective writer.

COORDINATION (A&B) - The user is given practice in combining short, choppy sentences. The use of appropriate coordinating conjunctions is shown.

FAULTY COORDINATION - Exercises are provided to give the user practice in recognizing and correcting faulty sentence coordination. Explanations are provided for errors given.

SUBORDINATION (A&B) - The user learns to combine sentences through use of subordination. Subordinating conjunctions are shown and explained. Exercises provide opportunity to use the most appropriate conjunction for sentence clarity.

ID: H93

INTERMEDIATE READING SKILLS

Publisher: BLS Inc.

Date: Apr. 82

Grade: 4 and up (reading level 5-6)

Format: 13 diskettes

Hardware: Apple II; 48K with Applesoft in ROM (DOS 3.2 or 3.3); color monitor optional

Language: Applesoft BASIC

Source Code: no

Price: $663.00/series; $60.00/diskette; $162.00/COMPOUND WORDS; $324.00/PREFIXES AND SUFFIXES; $216.00/INFERENCES.

TUTORCOURSE BLS85 series provides practice and instruction in compound words, prefixes and suffixes, and use of inference. Color graphics reinforce instruction and review throughout, helping student focus on key concepts as well as measuring progress. Three programs contain total of nine lessons, each ending with a summary and test. Programs utilize self-paced, branch-programmed instruction methods. Comprehensive user documentation is provided. Series study time: 6-9 hours.

COMPOUND WORDS - TUTORPROGRAM BLS85A includes two lessons, covering following topics: making compound words (parts 1 and 2); and meanings of compound words.

PREFIXES AND SUFFIXES - TUTORPROGRAM BLS85B includes three lessons, covering following topics: prefixes parts 1-3; suffixes parts 1 and 2; and final test.

INFERENCES - TUTORPROGRAM BLS85C includes four

lessons, covering following topics: using "what" and "where"; using "when" and "how"; using "why"; and final test.

ID: H94

ITS/IT'S - YOUR/YOU'RE

Publisher: Micro-Ed, Inc.

Also available from: EISI (Educational Instructional Systems, Inc.) • MARCK • Queue, Inc.

Grade: Elementary

Format: cassette or diskette

Hardware: Commodore 64 • PET

Language: BASIC

Source Code: no

Price: $7.95

Each lesson consists of twenty problems. There are sentences with blanks to be filled by the appropriate homonyms. At the end of the lesson, the learner's performance is summarized. Among other things, this summary lists the specific homonyms that may have given the learner trouble during the lesson.

ID: H95

JUNIOR HIGH VOCABULARY

Publisher: Microphys Programs

Also available from: Academic Software • EISI (Educational Instructional Systems, Inc.) • K-12 Micromedia • MARCK

Grade: 7-9

Format: 15 cassettes or 1 diskette

Hardware: PET; 8K; cassette or 4040 dual disk drive • Apple II; 24K (DOS 3.2 or 3.3) • TRS-80 MOD I or III; 16K • Bell & Howell

Language: BASIC

Source Code: yes

Price: $180.00/diskette; $20.00/cassette

Package consists of 15 interactive vocabulary programs which present approximately 30 words each in contextual usage. Individualized-instruction versions generate a unique set of problems for each student, including exams and homework assignments. Grades and overall evaluation are compiled by programs for each student. Complete instructions are included.

VOCABULARY I-V: 9TH GRADE (PC416-420)

VOCABULARY I-V: 8TH GRADE (PC421-425)

VOCABULARY I-V: 7TH GRADE (PC426-430)

ID: H96

JUNIOR/SENIOR HIGH SPELLING

Publisher: Microphys Programs

Also available from: Academic Software • EISI (Educational Instructional Systems, Inc.) • MARCK • Queue, Inc.

Grade: 7-12

Format: 12 cassettes or 1 diskette

Hardware: PET; 8K; cassette or 4040 dual disk drive • Apple II; 24K (DOS 3.2 or 3.3) • TRS-80 MOD I or III; 16K • Bell & Howell

Language: BASIC

Source Code: yes

Price: $180.00/diskette; $20.00/cassette

Package consists of 12 interactive spelling programs for different grade levels. Each program contains 60 words, presented in randomly selected groups of five words, any one of which may be spelled incorrectly. Individualized-instruction versions generate a unique set of problems for each student, including exams and homework assignments. Grades and overall evaluation are compiled by programs for each student. Complete instructions are included. Also available through Queue, Inc. in diskette format only.

SPELLING I & II: GRADE 12 (PC601-602)

SPELLING I & II: GRADE 11 (PC606-607)

SPELLING I & II: GRADE 10 (PC611-612)

SPELLING I & II: GRADE 9 (PC616-617)

SPELLING I & II: GRADE 8 (PC621-622)

SPELLING I & II: GRADE 7 (PC626-627)

ID: H97

LANGUAGE ARTS

Publisher: TSC® , A Houghton Mifflin Company

Grade: 3-8

Format: sealed disk

Hardware: Dolphin

Language: PASCAL

Source Code: no

Price: $1500.00/year license

Based on the Houghton Mifflin Language for Meaning Series, this program covers skills in grammar, usage, and mechanics usually taught in grades 3-8. It can be used to remediate reinforce, or enrich skills in conjunction with a student's regular daily assignments. Topics are concentrated in three areas: grammar - sentence characteristics, types, parts and patterns, and parts of speech; usage - verb, pronoun, adjective, adverb, preposition and conjunction usage; and mechanics - capitalization and punctuation. Documentation includes a "drill booklet" detailing each skill exactly.

ID: H98

LANGUAGE ARTS: STUDY SKILLS

Publisher: Milliken Publishing Company

Also available from: EISI (Educational Instructional Systems, Inc.) • McKilligan Supply Corp.

Grade: 1-8

Format: 2 diskettes

Hardware: Apple II Plus; 48K

Price: $75.00

The LANGUAGE ARTS package provides a variety of exercises covering Letter Recognition and Alphabetization skills. Students move through sequence levels by achieving individualized mastery criteria. Both skill and performance objectives may be individualized by the teacher. Student interaction requires a minimum of direct supervision, so the sequences may be implemented in various learning environments. A teacher

management program and comprehensive documentation are included with the package. The scope of the Language Arts Curriculum is substantial, with sequence levels appropriate for use in grades one through eight. The skills covered at the primary level include recognizing lower case forms of letters, recalling alphabetical sequences of letters, and alphabetizing by the first letter. The balance of the curriculum is directed toward alphabetization skills through the fifth letter and beyond. This is accomplished through a variety of exercises which include listing words and names, creating sentences, recognizing interruptions in order, and determining word placement in a list. The package contains a Manager Program which enables teachers to maintain individualized records for up to 100 students on each diskette. The teacher can make personalized assignments for an entire class. Student performance records are automatically updated and hard-copy printouts may be generated. Progress graphs make it very easy to identify student problem areas.

ID: H99

LANGUAGE PACK I

Publisher: Ideatech Company

Format: 3 programs on diskette

Hardware: Apple II Plus; 16K • Apple II; 16K with Applesoft in ROM

Price: $24.95

This package contains three programs also available seperately. See individual program entries for descriptions.

COLOR GUESS

WORD FLASH

QUESTIONS & STORY

ID: H100

LANGUAGE SKILLS

Publisher: Aquarius Publishers Inc.

Date: Aug. 82

Format: cassette or diskette

Hardware: Apple II; 48K with Applesoft in ROM (DOS 3.2 or 3.3) • TRS-80 MOD I or III; 16K

Language: BASIC

Source Code: no

Price: $24.95/cassette; $225.00/10 in package. $29.95/diskette; $275.00/10 in package

Series of lessons introduces and teaches parts of speech through narrative conversation with computer. Personal relationship is established between student and computer as computer first explains and then provides practice with each of the parts of speech. Design of series makes it useful for individual students, small groups, or classroom. It is most useful in team-like instructional setting. Programs include detailed Teacher's Guide and management system. When entire series is purchased, diagnostic program is included at no charge.

NOUNS

PRONOUNS

ADJECTIVES

VERBS AND ADVERBS

VERB TENSES (PAST, PRESENT, FUTURE)

PREPOSITIONS AND CONJUNCTIONS
PHRASES AND CLAUSES
WORD CHOICE
PUNCTUATION AND CAPITALIZATION
POSSESSIVE CASE (ADJECTIVES, NOUNS, PRONOUNS)

ID: H101
LAY/LIE

Publisher: Micro-Ed, Inc.

Also available from: EISI (Educational Instructional Systems, Inc.) • MARCK • Queue, Inc.

Grade: Elementary and up

Format: cassette or diskette

Hardware: Commodore 64 • PET

Language: BASIC

Source Code: no

Price: $7.95

This program instructs the student in the proper use of the verbs lay and lie. Twenty problems are given requiring the student to select the appropriate verb to use.

ID: H102
LEARNING CAN BE FUN #3

Publisher: Jensen Software

Grade: K-5

Format: cassette or diskette

Hardware: TRS-80 MOD I or III; with Level I or II BASIC

Price: $19.95/cassette; $24.95/diskette

This package includes five programs teaching word-to-picture matching, spelling, homonyms, and story fact retention.

LEARN TO READ - Child must match word to corresponding picture from an accompanying page.

LEARN TO SPELL - Partial words are displayed and child is to add a letter to form a complete word.

SOUNDS LIKE - Assists in understanding words which sound alike but are spelled differently and have different meanings.

LEARN MORE WORDS - Similar to LEARN TO READ but words are longer and more difficult.

STORY TELLING - Child reads a short story and is tested on ability to remember facts from the story. Each time the program is run, certain key words are changed.

ID: H103
LETTER RECOGNITION

Publisher: Hartley Courseware, Inc.

Also available from: Academic Software • Opportunities For Learning, Inc. • Queue, Inc.

Grade: K-1

Format: 1 diskette

Hardware: Apple II; 48K with Applesoft in ROM (DOS 3.2 or 3.3)

Language: Applesoft BASIC

Price: $26.95

Presents easy-to-read letters and numerals, with choice of uppercase letters only, lowercase letters only, numerals or mixed characters. Student must find corresponding letter or numeral on keyboard.

ID: H104
LISTEN AND SPELL

Publisher: Little Bee Educational Programs

Grade: 2-4

Format: cassette

Hardware: TRS-80 MOD I or III; 16K with Level II BASIC

Price: $10.95

Scoring a "bulls-eye" provides an interesting drill on troublesome wh and th words. The words are given orally from the cassette. The screen has a sentence with blanks for the missing word. The student types in the word; a correct response results in a "bulls-eye." With an incorrect response, the student is given a second opportunity before the correct spelling is shown. Scoring is given at the end of the session.

ID: H105
LONG/SHORT VOWEL SPACE SHIPS

Publisher: Little Bee Educational Programs

Also available from: K-12 Micromedia

Grade: 1-2

Format: cassette

Hardware: TRS-80 MOD I or III; 16K with Level II BASIC

Price: $10.95

The student is "Commander" of the space station and must clear the skies of the alien "vowel sound" spaceships by "zapping" them. The computer assigns the student to either "zap" the long vowel or short vowel spaceships. The "Commander" must be a good "zapper" because there are only 20 rockets to clear the sky. Two word lists with different degrees of difficulty are provided. Scoring is obtained at the end of the session.

ID: H106
MAKE A SENTENCE

Publisher: Micro-Ed, Inc.

Also available from: Academic Software • MARCK • Queue, Inc.

Grade: 1

Format: cassette

Hardware: PET

Language: BASIC

Source Code: no

Price: $7.95

Some scrambled words appear on the screen. The learner must use some of these words (but only these words) to type a complete sentence. Each sentence must end with a period. At the end of each sentence, the learner should press the return key. The computer will then perform according to what sentence was typed. Six different sentences are possible.

ID: H107
MAKING AN OUTLINE
Publisher: Micro-Ed, Inc.

Also available from: Academic Software • MARCK • Texas Instruments

Grade: Elementary

Format: cassette or diskette

Hardware: Commodore 64 • PET • TI 99/4

Language: BASIC

Source Code: no

Price: $7.95; $9.95/TI ed.

The computer presents an article for the student to read. The student must then finish a partly completed outline by selecting subtopics in the order in which they appear in the article. The student may review the article as often as necessary in order to complete the work. At the end of the lesson, the student's performance is summarized.

ID: H108
MATCHING CAPITAL LETTERS
Publisher: Micro-Ed, Inc.

Also available from: Academic Software

Grade: K

Format: cassette or diskette

Hardware: Commodore 64 • PET; light pen optional (specify program RE-4) • VIC

Language: BASIC

Source Code: no

Price: $7.95

A large capital letter appears on the screen. What letter on the computer keyboard matches it? The student tries to find and press the key with the matching letter. At the bottom of the screen, two little rectangles of light have a race. One belongs to the computer. The other belongs to the student. Which one will win? It all depends on how well the student matches the capital letter displayed by the computer. (If the student does not know the answer, and types the question mark, the computer will give the answer.)

ID: H109
MATCHING SMALL WITH CAPITAL LETTERS
Publisher: Micro-Ed, Inc.

Grade: K-1

Format: cassette or diskette

Hardware: Commodore 64 • PET • VIC

Language: BASIC

Source Code: no

Price: $7.95

The computer selects one of several lower case letters that appear on the screen. Which capital letter on the computer keyboard matches it? The learner tries to find and press the key with the matching letter. If the learner does not know the answer, and presses the question mark, the computer will give the answer.

ID: H110
MATCHING WORDS
Publisher: Micro-Ed, Inc.

Also available from: Academic Software

Grade: K-1

Format: cassette or diskette

Hardware: Commodore 64 • PET; light pen optional (specify program RE-8)

Language: BASIC

Source Code: no

Price: $7.95

Each problem consists of a moving word and two possible matching words randomly selected from a bank of 40 pairs of words. The student must choose the matching word. The two words in each pair are similar in appearance so as to require relatively fine visual discrimination by the student. Examples of these word pairs include the following: SOAP, SOUP; LAND, LEND; SWEAT, SWEET. At the end of each lesson, the student's performance is summarized.

ID: H111
MECHANICS
Publisher: RIGHT ON PROGRAMS

Also available from: Academic Software • Queue, Inc.

Grade: High School

Format: 6 programs on cassettes or diskette

Hardware: Apple II; 48K with Applesoft in ROM (DOS 3.2 or 3.3) • PET; 16K

Language: BASIC

Source Code: yes

Price: $13.00/cassette; $15.00/diskette; $70.00/6 programs on 1 diskette

This series reviews the rules of the mechanics of correct writing.

END MARKS - This program focuses on the correct use of the period, question mark, and exclamation mark. The user is given practice making corrections in sentences and paragraphs.

COMMAS - The user receives practice in inserting commas in word series, introductory phrases, nonrestrictive clauses, parenthetical expressions and appositives.

QUOTATIONS - Illustrations are provided for punctuation of direct quotes, as well as rules for capitalization and end punctuation, with quotes. The user is requested to correct errors.

CAPITALIZATION (A) - The program covers capitalization of proper nouns and adjectives, personal titles and geographical names. The user receives practice in correcting errors.

CAPITALIZATION (B) - Review is provided for capitalization of day, month, holidays, historical data, names of organizations, nationalities, etc.

CAPITALIZATION (C) - Review is provided for capitalization of a deity, direct quotes, poetry, and titles.

ID: H112
MECHANICS OF ENGLISH
Publisher: BLS Inc.

Date: Apr. 82

Grade: 6-9 (reading level 7-8)

Format: 23 diskettes

Hardware: Apple II; 48K with Applesoft in ROM (DOS 3.2 or 3.3)

Language: Applesoft BASIC

Source Code: no

Price: $1173.00/series; $60.00/diskette; $270.00/SENTENCE PATTERNS; $378.00/VERBS, NUMBER...; $324.00/ CAPITALIZATION; $270.00/ PUNCTUATION

TUTORCOURSE BLS93 series has been designed by California Test Bureau for students who require assistance to understand and apply basic skills needed for correct sentence construction, capitalization, and punctuation. Four programs contain total of 23 lessons, each ending with summary and test. Programs utilize self-paced, branch-programmed instruction method. Comprehensive user documentation is provided. Series study time: 8-16 hours.

SENTENCE PATTERNS - TUTORPROGRAM BLS93A includes five lessons, covering the following topics: proper sentence construction, subjects, verbs, and modifiers; dummy-verb-subject pattern, prepositions, direct objects, and objects of a preposition; forms of ''be'', and subject-linking verb complement patterns; adjectives and adverbs, and adjectival and adverbial phrases; and active and passive verbs, along with noun and adjective complements.

VERBS, NUMBER, AND CASE - TUTORPROGRAM BLS93B includes seven lessons, covering the following topics: forming tenses of regular verbs; irregular verbs; passive and progressive verb construction, and participles and gerunds; helper verbs, and third principle part of some irregular verbs; verb number, including subject-verb agreement; and pronouns and case.

CAPITALIZATION - TUTORPROGRAM BLS93C includes six lessons, covering the following topics: rules of capitalization; capitalization of places and things; capitalization of schools and times; and capitalization of historical documents and written works.

PUNCTUATION - TUTORPROGRAM BLS93D includes five lessons, covering the following topics: end punctuation and punctuating quotations; title punctuation and special quotation rules; appositives and parenthetical expressions; other uses of commas; and uses of the apostrophe.

ID: H113

MECHANICS OF ENGLISH

Publisher: BLS Inc.

Date: Apr. 82

Grade: 4-9 (reading level 5-6)

Format: 18 diskettes

Hardware: Apple II; 48K with Applesoft in ROM (DOS 3.2 or 3.3)

Language: Applesoft BASIC

Source Code: no

Price: $918.00/series; $60.00/diskette; $216.00/SENTENCE PATTERNS and CAPITALIZATION; $270.00/VERBS... and PUNCTUATION

TUTORCOURSE BLS92 series has been designed by California Test Bureau for students who require assistance to understand and apply basic skills needed for correct sentence construction, capitalization, and punctuation. Four programs contain total of 18 lessons, each ending with summary and test. Programs utilize self-paced, branch-programmed instruction method. Comprehensive user documentation is provided. Series study time: 8-16 hours.

SENTENCE PATTERNS - TUTORPROGRAM BLS92A includes four lessons, covering following topics: subject-predicate construction, and complete subjects; simple and compound subjects, noun and pronoun subjects, and you-understood subjects; verbs, predicates, and helping verbs; and declarative, interrogative, exclamatory, and imperative sentences.

VERBS, MODIFIERS, AND PRONOUNS - TUTORPROGRAM BLS92B includes five lessons, covering following topics: subject-verb agreement; regular and irregular verbs; adjectives, articles, and comparison; adverbs and prepositions; and pronouns, and nominative, objective, and possessive cases.

CAPITALIZATION - TUTORPROGRAM BLS92C includes four lessons, covering following topics: rules of capitalization (parts 1 and 2); capitalization of places and languages; and capitalization of names and times.

PUNCTUATION - TUTORPROGRAM BLS92D includes five lessons, covering following topics: end punctuation; punctuation of abbreviations, quotations, and titles; use of commas; other uses of commas; and use of apostrophe.

ID: H114

MISPLACED OR DANGLING MODIFIERS

Publisher: Micro-Ed, Inc.

Also available from: EISI (Educational Instructional Systems, Inc.) • MARCK

Grade: Elementary and up

Format: cassette or diskette

Hardware: Commodore 64 • PET • TI 99/4; extended BASIC module

Language: BASIC

Source Code: no

Price: $7.95; $9.95/TI ed.

A phrase or clause modifying a word that it should not modify is a misplaced or dangling modifier. In this program, twenty sentences are presented in random sequence. Some of these sentences are worded correctly. Others need to be changed. The student must indicate for each sentence whether or not it needs to be rewritten. At the end of the lesson, the student's performance is summarized, and the sentences that gave trouble during the lesson are listed.

ID: H115

MISSILE SPELLING

Publisher: Microphys Programs

Grade: 4-12

Format: 36 cassettes

Hardware: VIC-20; 3K expansion cartridge

Language: BASIC

Source Code: yes

Price: $15.00/cassette

Series of 36 programs consists of four programs in each of nine grade levels. Programs enable students to develop and practice basic spelling skills by identifying missiles launched for that purpose. Each program contains 60 graded words from which five at a time are chosen randomly for display. Words chosen for grades 7-12 correspond to vendor's vocabulary series. Complete instructions are included.

GRADE 12 (PV601-604)

GRADE 11 (PV606-609)

GRADE 10 (PV611-614)

GRADE 9 (PV616-619)

GRADE 8 (PV621-624)

GRADE 7 (PV626-629)

GRADE 6 (PV631-634)

GRADE 5 (PV636-639)

GRADE 4 (PV641-644)

ID: H116

MISSING LETTER

Publisher: Little Bee Educational Programs

Grade: K-1

Format: cassette

Hardware: TRS-80 MOD I or III; 16K with Level II BASIC

Price: $10.95

A challenging program to provide drill in the sequence of the letters of the alphabet. The student is presented with a sequence of letters and must respond with the missing letter in the sequence. The student has 2 opportunities to correctly identify the missing letter, then the letter is identified for the student. Scoring is given at the end of the session.

ID: H117

MOBY DICK

Publisher: Radio Shack®

Date: 1982

Grade: 4-6

Format: cassette

Hardware: TRS-80 Color Computer; 4K; CTR-80A cassette recorder

Source Code: yes

Price: $14.95

Package includes illustrated reader, read-along audio cassette, and computer tape with spelling and vocabulary exercises. Designed for home use, package is part of Reading Is Fun series.

ID: H118

MORE PREFIXES

Publisher: Micro-Ed, Inc.

Also available from: EISI (Educational Instructional Systems, Inc.) • K-12 Micromedia

Grade: Elementary

Format: cassette or diskette

Hardware: Commodore 64 • PET • TI 99/4; extended BASIC module

Language: BASIC

Source Code: no

Price: $7.95; $9.95/TI ed.

The problems in this program consist of incomplete words and suggested prefixes. The student must choose the right prefix. The prefixes covered are PRE, PRO, DE, DIS, and UN.

ID: H119

MORE SUFFIXES

Publisher: Micro-Ed, Inc.

Also available from: EISI (Educational Instructional Systems, Inc.) • K-12 Micromedia

Grade: Elementary

Format: cassette or diskette

Hardware: Commodore 64 • PET • TI 99/4; extended BASIC module

Language: BASIC

Source Code: no

Price: $7.95; $9.95/TI ed.

The problems in this program consist of incomplete words and suggested suffixes. The student must choose the right suffix. The problems are randomly selected by the computer, and there are ten problems in a lesson. The suffixes are FUL, LESS, ANT, ENT, ABLE, IBLE, and OUS.

ID: H120

MR LONG/MR SHORT

Publisher: Little Bee Educational Programs

Grade: K-1

Format: cassette

Hardware: TRS-80 MOD I or III; 16K with Level II BASIC

Price: $10.95

The student is presented with a word and she/he must decide whether it is a long vowel word or a short vowel word. With a correct long vowel response, a stick figure of a man grows longer. If the word is a short vowel word, the stick figure will shrink right before one's eyes. Scoring is given at the end of the session.

ID: H121

MULTIPLE SKILLS

Publisher: Hartley Courseware, Inc.

Also available from: Academic Software

Grade: 1-3

Format: 1 diskette with backup

Hardware: Apple II; 48K with Applesoft in ROM (DOS 3.2 or 3.3); CCD required

Language: Applesoft BASIC

Price: $92.95

Variety of lessons with over 800 presentations covering root words, affixes, homonyms, compound words, plurals, and contractions. Lessons include 1-3 level vocabulary; each lesson indicates appropriate reading level. Instructions are presented to student on tape with use of cassette control device (CCD); student responds on computer.

ID: H122

NEWBERY WINNERS

Publisher: Sunburst Communications

Grade: 3-6

Format: 5 diskettes

Hardware: Apple II; 32K

Price: $79.00

Five Newbery winners-*The Cricket in Times Square, The Great Gilly Hopkins, The Island of the Blue Dolphins, My Side of the Mountain,* and *Sounder*-are accompanied by one diskette containing four programs of vocabulary and comprehension drills and games. A story guide for each book provides story synopses, reading levels and printouts of each program's contents.

ID: H123

NOUN

Publisher: Micro-Ed, Inc.

Also available from: Academic Software • EISI (Educational Instructional Systems, Inc.) • K-12 Micromedia • MARCK

Grade: Elementary and up

Format: cassette or diskette

Hardware: Commodore 64 • PET

Language: BASIC

Source Code: no

Price: $7.95

This program deals with common and proper nouns. The subject matter is first defined and taught through examples. Then the learner is tested on what has been presented. At the end of the lesson, the learner's performance is summarized.

ID: H124

NOUNS

Publisher: Convergent Systems Inc.

Grade: Upper Elementary and up

Format: diskette

Hardware: Apple II; 48K with Applesoft in ROM; shift key adapter • Apple II Plus; shift key adapter

Source Code: no

Price: $49.00

NOUNS, part of the Basic English Skills Lesson Series, includes 6 lessons. They are: What's a Noun, which identifies nouns; Proper and Common Nouns, teaching the difference between proper and common nouns in statements and questions; 3 lessons on Noun Plurals, including -s, -es and nouns that end in o, f and y; and Collective Nouns. These lessons are instructor-independent and flexible. The entire 6 lessons will take approximately 100 minutes. A specific learning objective is selected for each lesson. To accomplish the objective the

lessons are programmed in several stages: the first is the tutorial section, which provides the learner with definitions, examples and clues for use and identification of parts of speech. Student performance is evaluated through a practice session during which review options are available if the learner has difficulty with a particular area. To proceed, the student must respond correctly. After 3 or 4 attempts, the student is given the correct answer. Upon completion of the basic skills lesson, scores are given and problem areas are identified with recommendations for review. To enhance learning reinforcement, feedback is given for both correct and incorrect responses.

ID: H125

NOUNS/PRONOUNS

Publisher: Hartley Courseware, Inc.

Also available from: Academic Software • Queue, Inc.

Grade: 3-8

Format: 1 diskette

Hardware: Apple II; 48K with Applesoft in ROM (DOS 3.2 or 3.3)

Language: Applesoft BASIC

Price: $32.95

Comprehensive, multilevel program of vocabulary lessons on nouns and pronouns. Each lesson includes introductory frame and simple examples, with difficult words and concepts presented at least twice in different formats. Includes recognition of common and proper nouns; possessives; noun plurals, both regular and irregular; and identification of pronouns and pronoun antecedents. Vocabulary in lessons is controlled to allow for each skill to be presented at different reading levels.

ID: H126

O'BRIEN VOCABULARY PLACEMENT TEST

Publisher: Educational Activities, Inc.

Also available from: Academic Software • K-12 Micromedia • Opportunities For Learning, Inc. • Queue, Inc.

Grade: 1-7

Format: cassette or diskette

Hardware: Apple II Plus; (DOS 3.3 or 3.2.1) • PET • Commodore 2001 • Commodore 4000; 40 or 80 column • Commodore 8000; 80 column • TRS-80 MOD I or III; with Level II BASIC

Source Code: no

Price: $14.95/cassette; $19.95/diskette

A graduated vocabulary test that will find a student's independent reading level quickly. Validated on over 7000 students, it is culturally unbiased, discounts guessing, and has a placement range of readiness through a seventh-grade reading level. Scores are stored for display to teacher only.

ID: H127

OPPOSITES

Publisher: Hartley Courseware, Inc.

Grade: 1-10

Format: 1 diskette

Hardware: Apple II; 48K with Applesoft in ROM (DOS 3.2 or 3.3);

Language: Applesoft BASIC

Price: $29.95

Vocabulary building program, with lessons beginning at third-grade level and building to tenth. Presents words and choices of opposites. Instructor can use words provided or add words. Correct words are indicated by arrow if student's answer is incorrect. In each lesson, missed words are repeated at end of lesson. Student planning feature saves errors for review by teacher.

ID: H128

P/SAT PREPARATORY

Publisher: Aquarius Publishers Inc.

Date: Aug. 82

Grade: High School-College Prep

Format: 2 sets of 2 diskettes each

Hardware: Apple II; 48K with Applesoft in ROM (DOS 3.2 or 3.3)

Language: Applesoft BASIC

Source Code: no

Price: $49.00/set

Package consists of two programs that prepare college-bound students specifically for ''antonyms'' portion of Scholastic Aptitude Test, giving them the edge on mastering vocabulary and deciphering new words. Each program contains two diskettes: Prefixes, and Roots. Vocabulary words, carefully selected for frequent appearance on PSAT/SAT, are grouped into six lessons. In each lesson, student first pinpoints word's meaning by selecting its synonym, then reviews word through definition, sample sentences, analysis of its components (roots or prefixes), and a test question. Timed test then prepares student to function under pressure.

    PSAT WORD ATTACK SKILLS

    SAT WORD ATTACK SKILLS

ID: H129

PAL READING PROGRAM

Publisher: Universal Systems for Education, Inc. (USE)

Also available from: Avant-Garde Creations

Grade: 2-6

Format: diskette

Hardware: Apple; 48K with Applesoft in ROM

Price: $99.95/master diskette; $99.95/grade level; $10.00/demo diskette

The PAL rading program teaches reading by evaluation, diagnosis, prescription, and remediation directly targeted at each reading program. Up to 40 major skills and 160 subskills are covered on each level.

ID: H130

PET DISSEMINATION DISK #1

Publisher: San Mateo County Office of Education and Computer-Using Educators

Format: 1 diskette

Hardware: PET; 8 to 16K; disk drive 2031, 2040, 4040, 8050

Source Code: yes

Price: $10.00

This disk includes 21 language arts programs in the public domain.

A OR AN - Completing sentences for practice in using a or an. (E 8K)

ASK - Practice and drill in using nouns and verbs. (E 8K)

BILINGUAL SPELL - Student chooses English or Spanish, then spells correctly the word that flashes on the screen (10 words in data lines can be changed). (E/S 8K)

CINQUAIN - Helps student write a short poem. (E/S 8K)

COMPUTER POETRY - Three short poetry samples. (E/S 8K)

FRENCH SENTENCES - Fill in blanks in sentences with correct form of three verbs - etre, aller, avoir. (E/S 8K)

FRENCH VERBS - Student is asked to conjugate choice of 16 verbs and/or tenses in French (regular and irregular verbs). (E/S 8K)

HANGMAN 1 - Word guessing game. (E/S 16K)

HANGMAN 2 - Word guessing game, can be adapted for grade level. (E/S 8K)

HANGMAN 3 - Word guessing game with five levels of difficulty. (E/S 8K)

HANGMAN 4 - Word guessing game. (E/S 16K)

PET PIT PAT POT - Given the definition of a word beginning with Pet, Pit, Pat, or Pot, user guesses the word. (E 8K)

Q'S & Z'S - Identifying words beginning with Q or Z from given definitions. (E 8K)

SCRAMBLED WORD - Unscramble the letters to spell the word. (E/S 8K)

SPEED READ - Helps students to improve ability to recognize printed phrases quickly (Vocabulary for grades 3 to 10). (E/S 8K)

SPEED READ 2 - Program flashes words/phrases on screen and student types words (Vocabulary and speed can be varied). (E/S 16K)

SWAP NEW ROM - Exchange words on a list until they are arranged alphabetically. (E/S 8K)

SWAP OLD ROM - This program is the same as SWAP NEW ROM.

TACHISTOSCOPE - Increase reading speed and concentration by recognizing word or phrase flashed on screen. (List can be changed) .(E/S 8K)

WORD MARKET - Spelling a word correctly will give a reward. (E 8K)

WORD HUNT - Given clues, student identifies the fugitive word. (E/S 8K)

ID: H131

PHONET

Publisher: TIES, Minnesota School Districts Data Processing Joint Board

Date: Sept. 80

Grade: 1-6

Format: 1 program on diskette with backup

Hardware: Apple II; 32K with Applesoft in ROM (DOS 3.3) •
Apple II Plus

Price: $49.95; $5.00/documentation

PHONET allows a student to work through a set of prepared phonetic exercises in sound associations, affixes, syllables, contractions and homonyms. After each lesson, a summary is displayed which includes the total questions asked, the number correct on the first try, the number correct on the second try, and the number of incorrect answers. PHONET exercises include sound associations, affixes, syllables, and contractions.

ID: H132
PHRASES AND CLAUSES

Publisher: Avant-Garde Creations

Also available from: Academic Software • Opportunities For
Learning, Inc. • Queue, Inc.

Grade: Up to 10

Format: diskette

Hardware: Apple; 48K with Applesoft in ROM

Price: $29.95

This program covering classification of phrases and clauses is comprised of a series of graded questions with revision questions to reinforce principles in the event of incorrect answers.

ID: H133
PIK-PEK-PUT

Publisher: Data Command

Also available from: EISI (Educational Instructional Systems,
Inc.) • Opportunities For Learning, Inc.

Grade: 5-6; Junior High remedial

Format: 24 cassettes or 8 diskettes

Hardware: Apple II; 48K with Applesoft in ROM • Apple II
Plus; 48K • TRS-80 MOD I; 16K (cassette) or 32K (diskette)
with Level II BASIC • TRS-80 MOD III; 32K with MOD III
BASIC

Language: BASIC

Price: $227.50/set; $29.95/program (1 diskette or 3 cassettes/
program)

Programs challenge student to put word skills to work to beat computer in game of strategy much like Tic-Tac-Toe, only with a word or words in each square. Programs use animated graphics and self-paced, interactive, menu-driven learning techniques. Each program is available individually and consists of 3 rounds of 6 games each. In disk format, student may select round he or she wishes to play. Summary of student's progress is retained for review by teacher. Average running time is 15-20 minutes.

SUFFIXES, PART I - Program gives student valuable experience affixing six common suffixes to as many as 152 base words. Difficulty of words increases as rounds progress.

SUFFIXES, PART II - Instructional methods are same as those in PART I; however, the six suffixes and 160 base words are entirely different.

PREFIXES, PART I - Students build word recognition skills by affixing six common prefixes to as many as 166 base words.

PREFIXES, PART II - Instructional methods and number of words are same as in PART I, but prefixes and base words used are completely different.

CONTRACTIONS - Program builds ability to identify and correctly use 50 different contractions. Each round is a bit more difficult than the one before it.

BASE WORDS - Program helps student gain proficiency in recognizing bases of up to 185 affixed words. Each round is a little more difficult than the one before it.

PLURALS - Provides meaningful experiences with correct spelling of plural endings of 164 different singular words supplied by computer.

POSSESSIVES - Game requires correct spellings of singular or plural possessive forms of up to 189 singular words. Difficulty of word choices increases throughout the three rounds.

ID: H134
PLURAL NOUNS

Publisher: Micro-Ed, Inc.

Grade: Elementary

Format: cassette or diskette

Hardware: VIC; 3K memory enhancement

Language: BASIC

Source Code: no

Price: $7.95

The computer randomly selects ten problems from a bank of forty. For each problem, the student must type the plural form of a given noun. The rules for forming plurals are presented within the program and may be reviewed by the student at any time during the lesson. Student performance is summarized.

ID: H135
PLURALS

Publisher: Comaldor

Format: cassette or diskette

Hardware: PET

Price: $20.00

Drill and review in game form provide choice of Canadian or American spelling at beginning of game. One, two, or three players may participate. Program gives correct answer if needed, and keeps running score. Marquee messages keep students informed as to results. 12" PETs feature optional built-in sound.

ID: H136
POETRY

Publisher: Avant-Garde Creations

Also available from: Academic Software • Queue, Inc.

Grade: Up to 10

Format: diskette

Hardware: Apple; 48K with Applesoft in ROM

Price: $29.95

Questions and comparisons of simple poetic forms are covered in this lesson. Revision questions reinforce concepts.

ID: H137

PREFIXES

Publisher: Micro-Ed, Inc.

Also available from: EISI (Educational Instructional Systems, Inc.) • K-12 Micromedia

Grade: Elementary

Format: cassette or diskette

Hardware: Commodore 64 • PET • TI 99/4; extended BASIC module

Language: BASIC

Source Code: no

Price: $7.95; $9.95/TI ed.

The problems in this program consist of incomplete words and suggested prefixes. The student must choose the right prefix. The problems are randomly selected by the computer, and there are ten problems in a lesson. At the end of the lesson, the student's performance is summarized. The prefixes treated in this program are RE, CON, COM, EX, EN, IM, and IN.

ID: H138

PREPOSITIONS

Publisher: Convergent Systems Inc.

Grade: Upper Elementary and up

Format: diskette

Hardware: Apple II; 48K with Applesoft in ROM; shift key adapter • Apple II Plus; shift key adapter

Source Code: no

Price: $15.00

This software, part of the Basic English Skills Series, teaches the student to use prepositions correctly in statements. It takes 30 minutes to run. A specific learning objective is selected for each lesson. To accomplish the objective the lessons are programmed in several stages. The first is the tutorial section, which provides the learner with definitions, examples and clues for use and identification of parts of speech. Student performance is then evaluated through a practice session during which review options are available if the learner has difficulty with a particular area. To proceed, the student must respond correctly. After 3 or 4 attempts, the student is given the correct answer. Upon completion of the basic skills lesson, scores are given and problem areas are identified with recommendations for review. To enhance learning reinforcement, feedback is given for both correct and incorrect responses.

ID: H139

PRONOUNS

Publisher: Convergent Systems Inc.

Grade: Upper Elementary and up

Format: diskette

Hardware: Apple II; 48K with Applesoft in ROM; shift key adapter • Apple II Plus; shift key adapter

Source Code: no

Price: $49.00

PRONOUNS, part of the Basic English Skills Lesson Series, takes about 100 minutes to complete 4 lessons. Topics covered are identification and use of pronouns in the nominative and objective case and the use of who and whom. A specific learning objective is selected for each lesson. To accomplish the objective the lessons are programmed in several stages: the first is the tutorial section, which provides the learner with definitions, examples and clues for use and identification of parts of speech. Student performance is evaluated through a practice session during which review options are available if the learner has difficulty with a particular area. To proceed, the student must respond correctly. After 3 or 4 attempts, the student is given the correct answer. Upon completion of the basic skills lesson, scores are given and problem areas are identified with recommendations for review. To enhance learning reinforcement, feedback is given for both correct and incorrect responses.

ID: H140

PUNCTUATION

Publisher: Educational Activities, Inc.

Also available from: K-12 Micromedia • Opportunities For Learning, Inc. • Queue, Inc.

Grade: Upper Elementary

Format: diskette

Hardware: Apple II Plus; (DOS 3.3 or 3.2.1) • TRS-80 MOD I or III; with Level II BASIC • PET • Commodore 2001 • Commodore 4000; 40 or 80 column • Commodore 8000; 80 column

Source Code: no

Price: $49.00/diskette; $93.00/set

These delightful programs take full advantage of the computer's color, graphics, animation, and sound producing qualities, using the vehicle of a written letter to the student, to teach and reinforce basic punctuation. An interactive tutorial method is used to immediately involve the student with the lesson. As the punctuation is introduced, the student is also given drill work consisting of inserting the correct punctuation where needed. Each mark is given an identifying sound which is heard only when the mark is correctly used by the student and provides an instant reward for work done correctly. The program branches back to instruction when the student makes an error. Additional drill material is provided for students who make more than four errors in the first twenty sentences to be punctuated. Reproducible Activity Masters are included to complement the microcomputer programs.

PUNCTUATION I - Teaches the period, question mark, and exclamation point.

PUNCTUATION II - Teaches use of the comma.

ID: H141

PUNCTUATION CIRCUS

Publisher: Micro Power & Light Company

Grade: 3-6

Format: diskette

Hardware: Apple II; 32K with Applesoft in ROM

Price: $34.95

It's a real three-ring circus! In the first ring are periods, the center ring presents question marks, and the third ring features exclamation points! Children in grades 3-6 will find the brief tutorial informative and the practice opportunities unlimited. And on occasion a clown winks and a lion yawns! The program disk comes with 15 exercises involving final periods, 15 more on question marks and 15 on exclamation marks. The student can work exercises selected from any one set, or can choose to work five from each set consecutively, finishing with a colorful quiz containing all three types of exercises. Not only do the exercises include declarative, interrogative and exclamatory sentences, but incomplete sentences as well. This provides additional practice in not only choosing correct end punctuation, but in deciding whether any punctuation is appropriate at all. The disk includes programs enabling the user (teacher or parent) to include his own sets of exercises. The user can either replace those that come furnished on the disk, or they can be stored on the disk as additional exercises.

ID: H142

PUNCTUATION SERIES

Publisher: Micro-Ed, Inc.

Also available from: Academic Software • EISI (Educational Instructional Systems, Inc.) • K-12 Micromedia • MARCK

Grade: Elementary and up

Format: cassette or diskette

Hardware: Apple II Plus; 48K (DOS 3.3) • PET • TRS-80 Color Computer; 32K • TI 99/4 • VIC; 3K memory enhancement

Language: BASIC

Source Code: no

Price: $56.00

These lessons provide drill and practice using a standardized test format. The computer randomly selects and presents a problem sentence. The student must identify where (if at all) a mistake in punctuation occurs. As the learner responds, the computer not only says whether the answer was right or wrong, but sets forth the applicable rule for the correction (if any). Each lesson covers from two to seven rules of punctuation. In order to prevent the student from identifying a mistake because of the content of a given problem sentence, many of the problem sentences are identical in content except for a specific mistake in punctuation. At the end of each lesson, the learner's performance is summarized.

PROGRAM 1 - This program covers using an apostrophe in contractions and with the possessive; and using a comma in written conversation and after the greeting of a letter.

PROGRAM 2 - Covers commas between city and state, month and day, after a mild interjection, between words in a series, to set off a name in direct address, and between a last name and first name.

PROGRAM 3 - Covers using a comma to set off a word group, after Yes or No at the beginning of a sentence, to set off a transitional word or phrase, or the explanatory words in conversation.

PROGRAM 4 - Covers using a comma before the connective in a compound sentence, between a name and title, using a period after an abbreviation, after an initial, after a statement, after a command or request, and using a comma to indicate a pause between adjectives.

PROGRAM 5 - Covers using a colon after the name of a speaker in a play, in writing time, to introduce a list, after the greeting in a business letter, and using an exclamation point.

PROGRAM 6 - Covers using question marks and quotation marks in written conversation.

PROGRAM 7 - Covers using quotation marks with the titles of songs, stories, poems, chapters and articles.

PROGRAM 8 - Covers quotation marks with more than one sentence and with commas and periods, semicolons, and hyphens.

ID: H143

PUNCTUATION SKILLS: COMMAS

Publisher: Milton Bradley

Also available from: McKilligan Supply Corp. • Opportunities For Learning, Inc.

Grade: 6-8

Format: 1 diskette

Hardware: Apple II; 48K with Applesoft in ROM (DOS 3.3)

Language: Applesoft BASIC

Price: $44.95

This program includes introductory elements, items in a series, interrupting elements, independent clauses, dates, addresses, letters, and titles. It has three instructional modes: statement of rule, in which rules are broken down into more specific subrules; practice mode, in which students practice with examples; and review game mode, which reviews and then rewards the student with Alien Raiders game. Includes a Teacher's Guide and reproducible activity sheets.

ID: H144

PUNCTUATION SKILLS: END MARKS, SEMICOLON, COLON

Publisher: Milton Bradley

Also available from: McKilligan Supply Corp. • Opportunities For Learning, Inc.

Grade: 6-8

Format: 1 diskette

Hardware: Apple II; 48K with Applesoft in ROM (DOS 3.3)

Language: Applesoft BASIC

Price: $44.95

Allowing student to move at his own speed, this program includes three instructional modes. The first explains the marks; the second provides practice; the third gives review and a reward in the form of a game. Covers period, question mark, exclamation point, semicolon and colon. Includes Teacher's Guide and reproducible activity sheets.

ID: H145

QUESTIONS AND STORY

Publisher: Ideatech Company

Also available from: K-12 Micromedia • MARCK

Grade: 2-6, Remedial

Format: diskette

Hardware: Apple II Plus; 16K • Apple II; 16 K with Applesoft in ROM

Language: BASIC

Price: $9.95

This program promotes reading as a fun activity, encourages creativity and provides practice in categorization. QUESTIONS AND STORY provides reading practice for all students and motivates the most reluctant readers to participate. Seven questions are presented to the student. The answers are incorporated into one of three randomly chosen stories and presented to the student at one of three reading speeds.

ID: H146
QUOTATION MARKS
Publisher: Educational Activities, Inc.

Grade: Upper Elementary

Format: cassette or diskette

Hardware: Apple II Plus; (DOS 3.2.1 or 3.3) • TRS-80 MOD I or III; with Level II BASIC • PET • Commodore 2001 • Commodore 4000; 40 or 80 column • Commodore 8000; 80 column

Source Code: no

Price: $49.00

This is a series of six programs which illustrates and reviews the many uses of quotation marks and the proper punctuation of quotations. The programs provide an interactive-tutorial presentation. Each lesson begins with a review of a particular usage followed by a drill exercise. Concepts taught include: the direct quotation; the indirect quotation; capital letters in direct quotations; interrupting expressions in the quoted sentence; the direct quotation and commas; and closing punctuation in direct quotations. Correct responses in the drill exercises are reinforced with animated, graphic rewards. After an incorrect response the computer branches to an appropriate tutorial section to review the concept. Reproducible Activity Masters are included with the series. They may be used to further reinforce and review the material covered by the computer lesson.

ID: H147
READABILITY ANALYSIS
Publisher: TIES, Minnesota School Districts Data Processing Joint Board

Date: Feb. 81

Format: 1 program on diskette with backup

Hardware: Apple II; 48K with Applesoft in ROM (DOS 3.3) • Apple II Plus

Price: $49.95

READABILITY ANALYSIS calculates the reading level of written materials, using the following formulas: Spache, Dale-Chall, Raygor, Fry, Flesch, Gunning Fog, and SMOG. It also displays a helpful graphic comparison of the various tests at the end of the program. READABILITY ANALYSIS is designed as a tool to aid in the selection of textbooks and outside readings. READABILITY ANALYSIS does the complicated and time-consuming work to free the user to make informed selections.

ID: H148
READING
Publisher: TSC®, A Houghton Mifflin Company

Grade: 3-8

Format: sealed disk

Hardware: Dolphin

Language: PASCAL

Source Code: no

Price: $1500.00/year license

This program is based on the reading skills list for the Individual Pupil Monitoring System of the Houghton Mifflin reading materials; it can, however, be used with any reading program for remediation. Divided into three sections, READING covers: word attack - phonics, structure, and context; vocabulary/comprehension - literal, interpretive and evaluative comprehension; and study skills - reference material, pictorial and graphic skills, organizing information, and following directions. The software is available in two parts, grades 3-5 and 6-8. Documentation includes a "skill booklet" which details each skill covered in the program.

ID: H149
READING COMPREHENSION
Publisher: Milliken Publishing Company

Also available from: EISI (Educational Instructional Systems, Inc.) • McKilligan Supply Corp.

Format: 48 diskettes (12 levels of 4 each)

Hardware: Apple II Plus; 48K

Price: $150.00/each level; $425.00/3 levels; $635.00/3 levels with backup

The READING COMPREHENSION package is an inductive skill-building program for students at reading levels one through twelve. Developed in conjunction with Instructional/Communications Technology, the program contains a wide range of informative, interesting reading selections and helps to improve twenty-five major comprehension skills through extensive and varied reading experiences. Each lesson consists of three parts: preparation, preview, and comprehensive reading. During the preparation segment, the student reviews new vocabulary words presented in context sentences. The preview segment, which is optional, provides the student with key sentences from the reading selection for a general understanding of the selection. The comprehensive reading segment may be used in either of two formats. In the "timed" format, the reading rate is set by the teacher or, if desired, by the student and the story is presented line by line at the designated rate. Students may periodically adjust their reading rate. When using the "manual" format, which is not timed, several lines are displayed at a time and the student advances these pages as desired. Both formats present the story in segments with comprehension questions at the end of each segment. Students have the option to reread segments before answering the comprehension questions. There are four diskettes with a total of twelve reading selections at each of 12 levels. Selection topics include adventure, contemporary issues, sports, career awareness, life adjustments, etc. The following comprehension skills are treated in the questions which accompany each reading selection - literal understanding, interpretation, analysis, evaluation, and appreciation.

ID: H150
READING COMPREHENSION (BLS79)
Publisher: BLS Inc.

Date: Apr. 82

Grade: 3-6 (reading level 3-4)

Format: 15 diskettes

Hardware: Apple II; 48K with Applesoft in ROM (DOS 3.2 or 3.3)

Language: Applesoft BASIC

Source Code: no

Price: $714.00/series; $60.00/diskette; $162.00/REFERENCE SKILLS and FOLLOWING DIRECTIONS; $216.00/READING INTERPRETATIONS I and II

TUTORCOURSE BLS79 series has been designed by California Test Bureau for help in mastering basic reading skills. Programs offer remedial instruction in reading comprehension, following directions, and using reference sources. Four programs contain total of 15 lessons, each ending with summary and test. Programs utilize self-paced, branch-programmed instruction methods. Comprehensive user documentation is provided. Series study time: 8-16 hours.

REFERENCE SKILLS - TUTORPROGRAM BLS79A includes three lessons, covering following topics: parts of books, and information available in books; book classes, using book titles, and library book numbers; and using calendar, alphabet, and graphs.

FOLLOWING DIRECTIONS - TUTORPROGRAM BLS79B includes three lessons, covering following topics: reading words and letters; using directions to go places; and doing things in order.

READING INTERPRETATIONS I - TUTORPROGRAM BLS79C includes five lessons, covering following topics: reading carefully and completely; understanding what one reads; order of events; interpreting what one reads; and remembering what one reads.

READING INTERPRETATIONS II - TUTORPROGRAM BLS79D includes four lessons, covering following topics: facts, sentence meaning, inference, and motivation; main idea, inference, and reality; actions and feelings of characters and order of action; and conversation, relationship of characters, and motivation.

ID: H151

READING COMPREHENSION (BLS80)

Publisher: BLS Inc.

Date: Apr. 82

Grade: 4-7 (reading level 5-6)

Format: 16 diskettes

Hardware: Apple II; 48K with Applesoft in ROM (DOS 3.2 or 3.3)

Language: Applesoft BASIC

Source Code: no

Price: $612.00/series; $60.00/diskette; $162.00/program

TUTORCOURSE BLS80 series has been designed by California Test Bureau for help in mastering basic reading skills. Programs offer remedial instruction in reading comprehension skills, following directions, and using reference sources. Four programs contain total of 12 lessons, each ending with a test. Programs utilize self-paced, branch-programmed instruction methods. Comprehensive user documentation is provided. Series study time: 12-20 hours.

REFERENCE SKILLS - LIBRARY - TUTORPROGRAM BLS80A includes three lessons, covering following topics: dictionaries, indexes, and table of contents; using the Dewey Decimal System and card catalog; and graph and map reading. Test diskette is supplied at no additional cost.

FOLLOWING DIRECTIONS - TUTORPROGRAM BLS80B includes three lessons, covering following topics: counting; Roman numerals; exercises in following directions; prefixes; compound words; and homonyms. Test diskette is supplied at no additional cost.

READING INTERPRETATIONS I - TUTORPROGRAM BLS80C includes three lessons, covering following topics: related words and phrases, and identification of paragraphs; figures of speech, and inferences; and main idea, point of view, and turning point. Test diskette is supplied at no additional cost.

READING INTERPRETATIONS II - TUTORPROGRAM BLS80D includes three lessons, covering following topics: related sentences, paragraphs, and titles; facts in different words, and indirect knowledge; and fact and fantasy, and imagination exercise. Test diskette is supplied at no additional cost.

ID: H152

READING COMPREHENSION SERIES

Publisher: Micro-Ed, Inc.

Also available from: EISI (Educational Instructional Systems, Inc.)

Grade: 1-3

Format: 4 sets of programs on cassette (34 programs)

Hardware: VIC

Language: BASIC

Source Code: no

Price: $35.00/Set A; $42.00/Set B; $77.00/Set C; $84.00/Set D

This READING COMPREHENSION series is designed to be used in connection with the TYPE TO READ series. Whereas TYPE TO READ is intended to help students upgrade their beginning word attack skills, READING COMPREHENSION programs are meant to give students practice in understanding what they read. To serve this purpose, the Comprehension series uses a variation of the popular Cloze method - an approach which uses words in context as a means of assessing understanding. Each lesson begins with four lines of text printed on the screen. Each line has a missing word. Near the bottom of the screen are five numbered words. Four of these words belong in the four "blanks" or "holes" in the text. The fifth does not belong anywhere. The problem for the student is to identify which words belong where. It is strongly recommended that the various Comprehension exercises be used only after certain exercises have been successfully completed for the TYPE TO READ series. The reason for this is that the words used in the Comprehension series are the words used in the TYPE TO READ series. Both series are based on a step-by-step progression that has been carefully worked out to cover a substantial sequence of lessons.

ID: H153

READING COMPREHENSION: WHAT'S DIFFERENT?

Publisher: Program Design, Inc.

Also available from: Academic Software • GRAFex Company • K-12 Micromedia • MARCK • Queue, Inc.

Date: Apr. 81

Grade: 3 and up

Format: cassette or diskette

Hardware: PET; cassette • TRS-80 MOD I; with Level II BASIC; cassette • Atari; 8K cassette, 16K diskette • Apple II Plus; 32K • Apple II; 32K with Applesoft in ROM

Price: $16.95/PET and TRS-80; $16.95/Atari cassette, $23.95/diskette; $23.95/Apple

Package includes five reading comprehension programs which present logical problems where student picks one word in four which does not belong with rest. Programs build analytical skills essential for understanding what student reads.

ID: H154

READING LESSONS - SET ONE

Publisher: Academic Computing Association

Date: Sept. 81

Grade: 7-12

Format: cassette or diskette

Hardware: Apple • TRS-80 • PET

Source Code: no

Price: $45.00/set of cassettes; $6.95/cassette; $13.95/diskette

This package is a part of ACA's CODES software. This set of lessons gives the student drill and instruction on nine specific reading skills.

AFFIXES - This lesson gives instruction in defining and recognizing prefixes, suffixes and roots.

PREFIXES - An instructional lesson in six common prefixes.

ALPHABETIZING - This program asks students to choose which of three words comes first in alphabetical order.

AU AND AW - These irregular vowel digraphs are covered in instruction and drill.

CLASSIFICATION - This program asks the student to recognize the word in a short list that does not belong in the same category as the other words.

CONTEXT CLUES - The student is asked to choose the word or words which best define the indicated word in each sentence.

IRREGULAR CONSONANT DIGRAPHS - In this lesson, the student is asked to pick the correct consonant digraphs for a particular word in each sentence.

TWO SOUNDS OF EA - Instruction and drill are given in the long and short sounds of this irregular vowel digraph.

ENDS OF WORDS - This program is intended for the student who is not attentive to the ends of words.

ID: H155

READING LESSONS - SET TWO

Publisher: Academic Computing Association

Date: Nov. 81

Grade: 7-12

Format: cassette or diskette

Hardware: Apple • TRS-80 • PET

Source Code: no

Price: $45.00/set of cassettes; $6.95/lesson on cassette; $13.95/diskette

This package is part of the ACA's CODES software. This set gives the student drill and instruction on nine specific reading skills.

OI AND OY - This lesson gives instruction and drill in these irregular vowel digraphs.

TWO SOUNDS OF OO - Gives instruction and drill.

SOUNDING OU AND OW - This lesson covers some of the sounds of these very irregular vowel digraphs.

SOUNDS VOWEL PAIRS - Students are given practice in sounding words and identifying which one of four words is a nonsense word.

PREFIXES - This lesson introduces mis-, out-, under-, in-, and over-.

RECOGNIZING PREFIXES - The student is asked to identify the word not containing a prefix.

VOWELS WITH "R" - A review of R- vowel sounds is presented. Then the student is asked to sound or recognize the word with an R- vowel that goes in the blank of each sentence.

BLENDS WITH "S" - The drill in this lesson asks the student to pick the correct blend of the letter "s" to complete the partially spelled word in each sentence.

MAKING ADJECTIVES WITH SUFFIXES - After a brief explanation, the student is asked to choose the correct suffix.

ID: H156

READING MACHINE

Publisher: SouthWest EdPsych Services

Date: 1982

Grade: K-3

Format: 1 diskette with backup

Hardware: Apple II; 48K with Applesoft in ROM (DOS 3.3); color monitor; printer and cassette recorder optional

Language: Applesoft BASIC

Source Code: no

Price: $59.95; $9.95/ manual. $49.95/cassette interface; $12.95/ pre-recorded audio tape

Program supplements classroom instruction to improve basic reading skills by offering step-by-step individualized lessons at over 28 skill levels on the range of grammatical elements in the basic reading domain. A phonetic approach corresponds to elementary reading series throughout the country. High-resolution graphic pictures match each word presented with a corresponding visual image; large size upper and lower case letters are used throughout to improve readability. Immediate feedback and an innovative reinforcement system help motivate child to succeed. Comprehensive management and record-keeping systems help control and monitor student's progress. Separately available cassette interface and pre-recorded audio tape match picture and word with spoken voice. Manual and student record forms included.

ID: H157

READING RACER ONE

Publisher: Micro-Ed, Inc.

Also available from: Academic Software • EISI (Educational Instructional Systems, Inc.) • K-12 Micromedia • MARCK

Grade: Elementary

Format: cassette

Hardware: PET

Language: BASIC

Source Code: no

Price: $7.95

This program is designed to give a student practice in reading six short passages at a speed chosen by the student. After each passage, a comprehension question is asked. At the end of the exercise, the student's performance is summarized. If the student goes through the exercise a second time, new questions are asked.

ID: H158
READING SKILLS GRADE 1

Publisher: Scott, Foresman and Co.

Also available from: McKilligan Supply Corp. • Scholastic Software • Texas Instruments

Date: Jan. 82

Grade: 1

Format: 2 modules

Hardware: TI 99/4A

Source Code: no

Price: $58.95/module

Two separately packaged modules in reading courseware series for grades 1-6 supplement basal reading programs in skill areas of word identification, comprehension, study and research, and literary appreciation. Developed in cooperation with Texas Instruments, modules follow publisher's reading instruction pattern of teach/practice/ apply/assess. Teacher's guide and pupil reader are included with each module.

EARLY READING (PACKAGE 1A)

READING RAINBOWS (PACKAGE 1B)

ID: H159
READING SKILLS GRADE 2

Publisher: Scott, Foresman and Co.

Date: Jan. 82

Grade: 2

Format: 2 modules

Hardware: TI 99/4A

Source Code: no

Price: $58.95/module

Two separately packaged modules in reading courseware series for grades 1-6 supplement basal reading programs in skill areas of word identification, comprehension, study and research, and literary appreciation. Developed in cooperation with Texas Instruments, modules follow publisher's reading instruction pattern of teach/practice/ apply/assess. Teacher's guide and pupil reader are included with each module.

READING FUN (PACKAGE 2A)

READING CHEERS (PACKAGE 2B)

ID: H160
READING SKILLS GRADE 3

Publisher: Scott, Foresman and Co.

Date: Jan. 82

Grade: 3

Format: 2 modules

Hardware: TI 99/4A

Source Code: no

Price: $58.95/module

Two separately packaged modules in reading courseware series for grades 1-6 supplement basal reading programs in skill areas of word identification, comprehension, study and research, and literary appreciation. Developed in cooperation with Texas Instruments, modules follow publisher's reading instruction pattern of teach/practice/ apply/assess. Teacher's guide and pupil reader are included with each module.

READING ON (PACKAGE 3A)

READING ADVENTURES (PACKAGE 3B)

ID: H161
READING SKILLS GRADE 4

Publisher: Scott, Foresman and Co.

Date: Jan. 82

Grade: 4

Format: 2 modules

Hardware: TI 99/4A

Source Code: no

Price: $58.95/module

Two separately packaged modules in reading courseware series for grades 1-6 supplement basal reading programs in skill areas of word identification, comprehension, study and research, and literary appreciation. Developed in cooperation with Texas Instruments, modules follow publisher's reading instruction pattern of teach/practice/ apply/assess. Teacher's guide and pupil reader are included with each module.

READING ROUNDUP (PACKAGE 4A)

READING TRAIL (PACKAGE 4B)

ID: H162
READING SKILLS GRADE 5

Publisher: Scott, Foresman and Co.

Date: Jan. 82

Grade: 5

Format: 2 modules

Hardware: TI 99/4A

Source Code: no

Price: $58.95/module

Two separately packaged modules in reading courseware series for grades 1-6 supplement basal reading programs in skill areas of word identification, comprehension, study and research, and literary appreciation. Developed in cooperation with Texas Instruments, modules follow publisher's reading instruction pattern of teach/practice/ apply/assess. Teacher's guide and pupil reader are included with each module.

READING RALLY (PACKAGE 5A)

READING POWER (PACKAGE 5B)

ID: H163

READING SKILLS GRADE 6

Publisher: Scott, Foresman and Co.

Date: Jan. 82

Grade: 6

Format: 2 modules

Hardware: TI 99/4A

Source Code: no

Price: $58.95/module

Two separately packaged modules in reading courseware series for grades 1-6 supplement basal reading programs in skill areas of word identification, comprehension, study and research, and literary appreciation. Developed in cooperation with Texas Instruments, modules follow publisher's reading instruction pattern of teach/practice/ apply/assess. Teacher's guide and pupil reader are included with each module.

READING FLIGHT (PACKAGE 6A)

READING WONDERS (PACKAGE 6B)

ID: H164

RECOGNIZING FULL SENTENCES

Publisher: RIGHT ON PROGRAMS

Date: July 82

Grade: 1

Format: cassette or diskette

Hardware: Apple II; 48K with Applesoft in ROM (DOS 3.2 or 3.3) • PET; 16K

Language: BASIC

Price: $13.00/cassette; $15.00/diskette

Object of program is to have child learn to recognize full sentence. Tutorial part of program, written in very simple language, explains what a sentence is and gives examples. Child has several chances to choose between two samples, and pick one that is complete sentence. Second part of program contains game which encourages child to give right answer. Correct answers are rewarded and incorrect answers are corrected with no penalty.

ID: H165

RECOGNIZING NOUNS

Publisher: RIGHT ON PROGRAMS

Date: July 82

Grade: 1

Format: cassette or diskette

Hardware: Apple II; 48K with Applesoft in ROM (DOS 3.2 or 3.3) • PET; 16K

Language: BASIC

Source Code: yes

Price: $13.00/cassette; $15.00/diskette

Object of program is to have child learn to recognize noun in sentence. It is explained that noun is "person, place or thing" word. Examples are given to help child understand. Second part of program has game that rewards child for correct answer. There is no penalty for an incorrect answer.

ID: H166

RECOGNIZING VERBS

Publisher: RIGHT ON PROGRAMS

Date: July 82

Grade: 1

Format: cassette or diskette

Hardware: Apple II; 48K with Applesoft in ROM (DOS 3.2 or 3.3) • PET; 16K

Language: BASIC

Source Code: yes

Price: $13.00/cassette; $15.00/diskette

Object of program is to have child learn to recognize verb in sentence. It is explained that verb is "doing" word. Examples are given to help child understand. Second part of program has game that rewards child for correct answer. There is no penalty for an incorrect answer.

ID: H167

RIDDLE ME THIS

Publisher: Data Command

Also available from: EISI (Educational Instructional Systems, Inc.) • Opportunities For Learning, Inc.

Grade: 5-6; Junior High remedial

Format: 9 cassettes or 3 diskettes

Hardware: Apple II; 48K with Applesoft in ROM • Apple II Plus; 48K • TRS-80 MOD I; 16K (cassette) or 32K (diskette) with Level II BASIC • TRS-80 MOD III; 32K with MOD III BASIC

Language: BASIC

Source Code: no

Price: $85.25/set; $29.95/program (1 diskette or 3 cassettes/program)

Computer gives student a riddle based on word relationships and meanings, and challenges student to figure out answer. Programs build word skills using animated graphics and self-paced, menu-driven, interactive learning techniques. Each program is available individually and consists of three rounds of 12 riddles each. Student may select round he or she wishes to play. Summary of student progress is retained for review by teacher. Average running time is 15-20 minutes.

HOMONYMS - Student gains valuable word recognition practice by working with 31 different homonym pairs.

CONTRACTIONS - Program gives student valuable practice in identifying correct two-word forms of 26 contractions.

POSSESSIVES - Program allows student to gain experience in correct usage of singular and plural possessives to show relationship between person or animal and object used in riddle, as "cat's pajamas."

ID: H168

ROOTS/AFFIXES

Publisher: Hartley Courseware, Inc.

Also available from: Academic Software

Grade: 3-8

Format: 1 diskette

Hardware: Apple II; 48K with Applesoft in ROM (DOS 3.2 or 3.3);

Language: Applesoft BASIC

Price: $39.95

Twenty-one lessons on roots, prefixes, and suffixes for multiple reading levels gradated in readability and vocabulary level. Emphasis is placed on use of affixes to help decipher word meaning and increase vocabulary.

ID: H169

RUN-ON SENTENCES

Publisher: Micro-Ed, Inc.

Also available from: Academic Software • EISI (Educational Instructional Systems, Inc.) • MARCK • Queue, Inc.

Grade: Elementary

Format: cassette or diskette

Hardware: Commodore 64 • PET • TI 99/4; extended BASIC module

Language: BASIC

Source Code: no

Price: $7.95; $9.95/TI ed.

Each problem consists of a group of words that should be divided into two sentences. Using the space bar, the learner moves an arrow across the screen and places it after the word that should end the first sentence. At the bottom of the problem screen, the learner and computer have a race. Each lesson consists of from eleven to sixteen problems, depending on the outcome of the race. At the end of the lesson, the learner's performance is summarized.

ID: H170

SAT ENGLISH I

Publisher: Aquarius Publishers Inc.

Date: Aug. 82

Grade: High School-College Prep

Format: diskette

Hardware: Apple II; 48K with Applesoft in ROM (DOS 3.3)

Language: Applesoft BASIC

Source Code: no

Price: $30.00

Program is designed as study aid for those preparing to take Scholastic Aptitude Test or College Entrance Examination Boards. Four sections of verbal SAT exam are included: Antonyms, Analogies, Sentence Completion, and Reading Comprehension. Instruction is provided through use of instruction and testing modes. Program teaches students meanings of words, why one answer is preferred over another, and how to choose correct answers.

ID: H171

SCRAMBLED LETTERS

Publisher: Educational Activities, Inc.

Also available from: Academic Software • MARCK • Opportunities For Learning, Inc. • Queue, Inc.

Grade: Adjustable

Format: cassette or diskette

Hardware: Apple II Plus; (DOS 3.2.1 or 3.3) • TRS-80 MOD I or III; with Level II BASIC • PET • Commodore 2001 • Commodore 4000; 40 or 80 column • Commodore 8000; 80 column

Source Code: no

Price: $14.95/cassette; $33.50/diskette (includes FLASH SPELLING)

The computer presents spelling words with the letters scrambled. Two students compete to unscramble the letters keying in the correctly spelled word. The computer "rewards" the student who spells the word correctly. At the end of the program, all words are displayed on the screen with the correct spelling. Instructions which describe how teachers may add their own words to the program are included.

ID: H172

SENIOR HIGH VOCABULARY

Publisher: Microphys Programs

Also available from: Academic Software • EISI (Educational Instructional Systems, Inc.) • K-12 Micromedia • MARCK

Grade: 10-12

Format: 15 cassettes or 1 diskette

Hardware: PET; 8K; cassette or 4040 dual disk drive • Apple II; 24K (DOS 3.2 or 3.3) • TRS-80 MOD I or III;16K • Bell & Howell

Language: BASIC

Source Code: yes

Price: $180.00/diskette; $20.00/cassette

Package consists of 15 interactive vocabulary programs which present approximately 30 words each in contextual usage. Individualized-instruction versions generate a unique set of problems for each student, including exams and homework assignments. Grades and overall evaluation are compiled by programs for each student. Complete instructions are included.

VOCABULARY I-V: 12TH GRADE (PC401-405)

VOCABULARY I-V: 11TH GRADE (PC406-410)

VOCABULARY I-V: 10TH GRADE (PC411-415)

ID: H173

SENTENCE DIAGRAMMING

Publisher: Avant-Garde Creations

Also available from: Academic Software • Opportunities For Learning, Inc. • Queue, Inc.

Format: diskette

Hardware: Apple; 48K with Applesoft in ROM

Price: $24.95

This package contains four separate exercises, each designed to enforce grammatical ideas and aid the student in diagramming. The first exercise, Parts of Speech, presents the user with a sentence and s/he must identify the part of speech each word pertains to. In the second exercise, the student is given a numbered list of word usages (appositives, gerunds, etc.) and asked to match each word in the sentence to a usage. Then the student is asked to identify the type of sentence being displayed (declarative, interrogative, etc.). Any of these three initial exercises may be bypassed if desired. Finally, the skeleton diagram is given and the student must type the appropriate word in each blank as a quesiton mark appears under it. The Sentence Diagramming exercise consists of three levels of difficulty, each containing 20 different sentences. Other features include optional record-keeping, teacher-formatted requirements for advancement, and teacher-formatted options to exclude actual sentence diagramming.

ID: H174
SENTENCE STRUCTURE ERRORS
Publisher: RIGHT ON PROGRAMS

Also available from: Queue, Inc. • SouthWest EdPsych Services

Grade: High School

Format: 5 programs on 5 cassettes or diskette

Hardware: Apple II; 48K with Applesoft in ROM (DOS 3.2 or 3.3) • PET; 16K

Language: BASIC

Source Code: yes

Price: $13.00/cassette; $15.00/diskette; $70.00/5 programs on 1 diskette

These 5 programs review and provide exercises to correct most common sentence structure errors.

SENTENCE FRAGMENTS - A sentence fragment is defined and the user is shown two ways to correct the error. The program emphasizes recognition and correction of fragments.

FRAGMENTS - The user is given additional practice in recognizing and correcting sentence fragments in both sentences and paragraphs.

MISPLACED MODIFIERS - The user is given practice in identifying dangling modifiers and correcting phrase and clause modifiers to improve clarity of sentences.

RUN-ON SENTENCES (A) - This program reviews the basics of use of commas and endmarks to avoid run-on sentences and comma errors.

RUN-ON SENTENCES (B) - The user is given additional practice in the basics of proper sentence phrasing with practice in coordinating conjunctions and conjunctive adverbs.

ID: H175
SENTENCES
Publisher: Micro Power & Light Company

Also available from: Academic Software • K-12 Micromedia

Grade: 5 and up

Format: diskette

Hardware: Apple II; 32K with Applesoft in ROM

Price: $24.95

The program covers the following topics: the subject of a sentence; the predicate, highlighting both action and being verbs; and the fragmented sentence. Each of these three topics consists of instruction, practice exercises, and a mastery quiz in game format. Each topic requires 10-15 minutes.

ID: H176
SILENT CONSONANT BASKETBALL
Publisher: Little Bee Educational Programs

Grade: 1-2

Format: cassette

Hardware: TRS-80 MOD I or III; 16K with Level II BASIC

Price: $10.95

Correctly identifying the silent consonant or consonants results in the silent letter or letters being shot through the hoop for a basket. The student is shown a word with a silent consonant and a sentence containing that word. The student selects the silent consonant from the choices given. Scoring is given at the end of the session.

ID: H177
SIMS
Publisher: TIES, Minnesota School Districts Data Processing Joint Board

Date: Sept. 80

Grade: 1-6

Format: 4 programs on 1 diskette with backup

Hardware: Apple II; 32K with Applesoft in ROM (DOS 3.3) • Apple II Plus

Price: $49.95; $5.50/documentation

The SIMS diskette contains lists of words which are useable with any of four included programs. This collection is based on the Systematic Instructional Management Strategies Reading curriculum which incorporates and integrates a number of educational principles. The curriculum was designed to provide remediation of reading skills for learning-disabled students. It utilizes a structured phonetic sequence encompassing the basic coding skills of reading and spelling. It follows a "Schmerler" approach which teaches the structure of one vowel before introducing other vowels. Each of the word lists contained on the SIMS diskette comprise fifteen of the thirty Accuracy Words from each of the 53 categories in the SIMS Reading curriculum.

HANGMAN - The student is allowed a certain number of chances to guess a word.

SCRAMBLE - A timed drill to unscramble a word.

SPELL - This is a spelling memory drill.

WORDER - This program generates a word puzzle (if a printer is attached).

ID: H178
SIT/SET
Publisher: Micro-Ed, Inc.

Also available from: EISI (Educational Instructional Systems, Inc.) • Queue, Inc.

Grade: Elementary and up

Format: cassette or diskette

Hardware: Commodore 64 • PET

Language: BASIC

Source Code: no

Price: $7.95

The proper uses of verbs sit and set are explained. Twenty problems are given, requiring the student to select the appropriate verb to use. As each problem is answered, a "word machine" processes what the learner has chosen, and responds accordingly. The lesson may be terminated at any point, at which time the learner's performance is summarized.

ID: H179

SOCIAL STUDIES WORD LIST: REGIONS

Publisher: Micro-Ed, Inc.

Also available from: EISI (Educational Instructional Systems, Inc.) • K-12 Micromedia

Grade: Elementary

Format: 2 programs on cassette or diskette

Hardware: Commodore 64 • PET

Language: BASIC

Source Code: no

Price: $49.95

Classroom teachers feel that although vocabulary exercises are a standard feature of instruction in the area of reading, more work in vocabulary development is needed in subjects such as science and social studies. This initial set of programs marks the beginning of a series designed to address this perceived need. REGIONS presents basic drill and practice social studies word list lessons for the following regions: FOREST, DESERT, FARMING, OCEAN, MANUFACTURING, TRADING, and POLITICAL. Each program works with a vocabulary commonly used when discussing a particular region. At the end of each lesson, the student's performance is summarized. If the student does all the problems in a lesson without having to review the word list, a special visual sequence will be presented on the screen.

ID: H180

SOLVING WORD PROBLEMS (I AND II)

Publisher: Aquarius Publishers Inc.

Also available from: Academic Software

Date: 1982

Grade: 3-5, 6-7

Format: cassette or diskette

Hardware: Apple II; 48K with Applesoft in ROM (DOS 3.2 or 3.3) • TRS-80; 16K

Source Code: no

Price: $24.95/cassette; $45.00/both $29.95/diskette; $55.00/both

Programs abandon traditional drill and practice method of solving word problems in favor of carefully planned instruction which teaches students to read and solve word problems using a logical progression of thought. Each program is menu driven and graded for reading level, allowing students to concentrate on problem solving rather than reading. Average running time is 20 minutes. Documentation is provided.

ID: H181

SPEAK & SPELL[T.M.] PROGRAM

Publisher: Texas Instruments

Also available from: Scott, Foresman and Co.

Format: diskette

Hardware: TI

Source Code: no

Price: $29.95

Offers the same features as the popular TI learning aid. Children can hear a word pronounced correctly as they learn to recognize and spell it. Five activities provide valuable tools to make learning fun. "Spell" pronounces a word and asks the child to type the correct spelling. "Mystery Word" selects a word and the child tries to guess it by spelling it correctly. "Say it" prompts a child to say a word and then spell it. "Secret Code" codes a word so that no one can read it until the coded word is entered and decoded by the computer.

ID: H182

SPECIAL NEEDS - VOLUME 1

Publisher: Minnesota Educational Computing Consortium

Also available from: Academic Software • Creative Computing • K-12 Micromedia • Opportunities For Learning, Inc.

Date: June 82

Grade: 1-6, Handicapped

Format: diskette

Hardware: Apple II; 32K with Applesoft in ROM (DOS 3.3)

Language: Applesoft BASIC

Source Code: no

Price: $35.40

Programs are designed to drill physically handicapped students on frequently misspelled primary and intermediate words. Students answer problems by using either game buttons, game turn knobs, or any key on keyboard. Support booklet (included) gives teacher instructions on changing words and sentences.

ID: H183

SPEED READER

Publisher: Apple Computer, Inc.

Date: Feb. 82

Grade: 6 and up

Format: master and backup diskettes, data diskette

Hardware: Apple II Plus; 48K (DOS 3.3) • Apple II; 48K with Applesoft in ROM (DOS 3.3)

Language: Applesoft BASIC

Source Code: no

Price: $70.00

SPEED READER is a complete reading development course, containing exercises to help build reading speed and increase comprehension. Lessons and exercises are designed to correct sluggish eye movements and sharpen peripheral vision. Offers 10 increasingly difficult practice sessions; measures reading speed; includes quizzes after each lesson; and provides numerous exercises. Instruction manual included.

ID: H184

SPEED READING AND COMPREHENSION

Publisher: Abbott Educational Software

Also available from: K-12 Micromedia • MARCK

Format: 6 cassettes or 2 diskettes

Hardware: PET; 16K; CBM model 16B recommended for standard keyboard

Language: BASIC

Source Code: yes

Price: $49.95/cassette; $59.95/diskette

Versatile and flexible system may be used by reading teachers and others to improve and monitor speed reading and comprehension. Heart of system is three programs that use different methods to place story lines on screen, or remove them from screen. Directions allow teacher to alter programs to meet needs of teaching situation. User may be allowed to choose own reading speed, and to change same during session. Disk version is menu-driven. Includes six programs, sample story cassette or disk file, manual, and album or binder. Average running time of lessons 5-15 minutes.

READA, READB, READC CREATE, EDIT, COPY - Programs present various user-controlled options of flashing and blanking story lines on screen to promote sound reading comprehension techniques. Reader may increase or decrease speed during read scan. Average reading rate is then calculated, and multiple choice questions for comprehension are asked and tallied. All statistics and results are then shown on screen.

ID: H185

SPELL-BOUND

Publisher: Robert R. Baker, Jr.

Also available from: Queue, Inc.

Date: June 82

Grade: 6-12

Format: cassette or diskette

Hardware: TRS-80 MOD I or III; 16K

Language: BASIC

Source Code: yes

Price: $19.85

Provides introduction to new words and practice in spelling words in any subject area. Student competes against computer in ten-word spelling contest. When student wins, computer challenges student to higher level of difficulty. Starting at beginner and working up through intermediate and advanced levels, student masters spelling words by beating computer at expert level. Average program running time is 2-3 minutes at each level of difficulty. Written documentation is provided, and program is self-documented as well.

ID: H186

SPELLING

Publisher: Orange Cherry Media

Also available from: Academic Software • K-12 Micromedia • Queue, Inc.

Grade: 2-6

Format: cassette or diskette

Hardware: PET 2000 or 4000; 16K • TRS-80 MOD I or III; 16K • Apple; 16K • Apple II; 16K

Price: $15.00/cassette; $28.00/cassette set of 2; $34.00/diskette

SEE AND SPELL - Uses the computer as a tachistoscope, flashing commonly misspelled words on the screen. Word then disappears and students are asked to spell it correctly. A correct answer brings an approving response from the computer and the next word. If a word is misspelled, the computer asks the student to try again. Teachers can select words for each grade.

SPELLING BEE - Presents three spellings of a word and gives the student the opportunity to select the correct spelling. Words are presented in the context of a sentence. The computer calculates the number and percentage of correct answers. Troublesome words are brought back later in the program. Word difficulty range 2.0 to 5.5.

ID: H187

SPELLING

Publisher: RIGHT ON PROGRAMS

Also available from: Academic Software • Queue, Inc.

Grade: 11

Format: 10 programs on 5 cassettes or diskette

Hardware: Apple II; 48K with Applesoft in ROM (DOS 3.2 or 3.3) • PET; 16K

Language: BASIC

Source Code: yes

Price: $13.00/cassette; $15.00/diskette; $70.00/10 programs on 2 diskettes

This series reviews specific spelling rules with their most common exceptions. Additional spelling practice is provided for commonly misspelled words.

IS IT "IE" OR "EI"? - Review of rules and practice exercises are provided.

PREFIXES AND SUFFIXES - Review is provided for specific rules on prefixes and suffixes.

THOSE NASTY DEMONS - Exercises are provided to recognize and correct frequently misspelled words.

MORE NASTY DEMONS - Exercises are provided to recognize and correct frequently misspelled words.

STILL MORE NASTY DEMONS - Exercises are provided to recognize and correct words most frequently misspelled.

SPELLING THOSE PLURALS - Exercises are provided giving the user practice in correct spelling of plurals.

HEARING THE HOMONYMS - The user receives practice in selecting the right word from 2 or 3 choices of words that sound alike but are spelled differently.

POSSESSING THE POSSESSIVES - These programs review the rules and exceptions governing possessives. The user is taught to recognize and correct the errors.

BATCH OF ENDINGS - Review is given of the rules for sentence endings.

END OF ENDINGS - Rules are given governing the addition of prefixes and suffixes. The emphasis is on words ending in silent "e" or "y", doubling of final consonant words ending in a "seed" sound and suffix endings most commonly confused.

ID: H188

SPELLING - VOLUME 1

Publisher: Minnesota Educational Computing Consortium

Date: June 82

Grade: 1-6, Adult Remedial

Format: diskette

Hardware: Apple II; 32K with Applesoft in ROM (DOS 3.3)

Language: Applesoft BASIC

Source Code: no

Price: $34.90

Package includes twenty spelling drills on frequently misspelled primary and intermediate words. Teachers can replace words and sentences included on programs with those of their own. Support booklet (included) shows teachers how to do so.

ID: H189

SPELLING - VOLUME 2

Publisher: Minnesota Educational Computing Consortium

Date: June 82

Grade: High School and up

Format: diskette

Hardware: Apple II; 32K with Applesoft in ROM (DOS 3.3)

Language: Applesoft BASIC

Source Code: no

Price: $36.50

Package includes 30 spelling drills on words most commonly misspelled by adults. Teacher can change sentences to include new lists of words. Support booklet (included) shows teacher how to enter unique words and sentences to create additional drills.

ID: H190

SPELLING BEE WITH READING PRIMER™

Publisher: Edu-Ware Services

Also available from: Academic Software • K-12 Micromedia • McKilligan Supply Corp. • Opportunities For Learning, Inc. • Queue, Inc.

Grade: K-1

Format: diskette

Hardware: Apple; 48K (DOS 3.3)

Language: Applesoft BASIC

Price: $39.95

These two programs introduce the learner to spelling and reading by linking familiar objects with words and identifying basic word groupings. Units cover simple 2-, 3-, and 4-letter words, double vowels and consonants, hard c's and silent e's, one-syllable words with diphthongs, multi-syllable words, directions, and numbers.

ID: H191

SPELLING MACHINE

Publisher: SouthWest EdPsych Services

Also available from: K-12 Micromedia • Queue, Inc.

Date: 1982

Grade: 1-6

Format: 1 diskette with backup

Hardware: Apple II; 48K with Applesoft in ROM (DOS 3.3); color monitor; printer optional

Language: Applesoft BASIC

Source Code: no

Price: $49.95; $9.95/manual

Program supplements classroom instruction to improve spelling skills of elementary students by offering step-by-step individualized lessons on 700 words and sentences encompassing approximately 85% of most frequently used vocabulary words. Immediate feedback and innovative reinforcement games utilize color graphics and sound to help make learning fun and improve hand-eye coordination. Management system allows students to progress at their own rate; record-keeping system permits convenient progress reviews and listings of each child's misspelled words. Powerful text editing system facilitates insertion of user-selected words. Manual included.

ID: H192

SPELLING RULES

Publisher: Micro Power & Light Company

Also available from: Academic Software • Queue, Inc.

Grade: 5 and up

Format: diskette

Hardware: Apple II; 32K with Applesoft in ROM

Price: $29.95

COVERAGE: The program addresses rules related to: (1) IE or EI; (2) Final E; (3) Adding K; (4) Final consonant; (5) -SEDE, -CEED, -CEDE; (6) Final Y. The principal intended users of this program include students 5th grade and up and an adult "refresher course". Each of six rules consists of: INSTRUCTION with illustrative examples; EXERCISES affording practice opportunities; MASTERY QUIZ in a game format; a concluding mastery exercise, made up of: you...and 'dab yug'! Each rule usually requires about 10-15 minutes. The entire program requires about .5-1.5 hours. Start with any rule. Take them in order. Do 1, 2,...any number.

ID: H193

SPELLING SORCERY

Publisher: SouthWest EdPsych Services

Also available from: K-12 Micromedia

Date: 1982

Format: diskette

Hardware: Apple II; 48K with Applesoft in ROM (DOS 3.3); color monitor

Language: Applesoft BASIC

Source Code: no

Price: $29.95

Three exciting color graphics programs harness power of arcade games to make spelling fun for children and adults. Powerful text-editing system permits easy insertion of user-selected words. Difficulty level of games and words is also controlled by user.

QUICK SPELL - User improves spelling and hand-eye coordination by capturing color graphic letters as they flash onto screen.

LETTER BLASTER - Employs spelling ability and visual-motor coordination by inviting user to shoot high-resolution letters with laser gun as they march across screen.

HIDE 'N SPELL - Exercises spelling and visual memory by requiring user to remember location of hidden high-resolution graphic letters.

ID: H194

SPELLING STRATEGY

Publisher: Apple Computer, Inc.

Date: Feb. 82

Grade: 1 and up

Format: master diskette, backup diskette

Hardware: Apple II Plus; 48K (DOS 3.3); color monitor • Apple II; 48K with Applesoft in ROM (DOS 3.3); color monitor

Language: Applesoft BASIC

Source Code: yes

Price: $45.00

Program provides challenging, interactive drills and exercises that utilize Apple's sound and color graphics capabilities to encourage effective habits of visualization and memorization of words. Exercises followed by multiple- choice quizzes encourage children to use mental images to arrive at correct answers. Author options allow parents and teachers to create an unlimited number of lessons, each containing up to 10 words. Instruction manual included.

ID: H195

SPELLTRONICS

Publisher: Educational Activities, Inc.

Also available from: Academic Software • K-12 Micromedia • Opportunities For Learning, Inc. • Queue, Inc.

Grade: 4

Format: cassette or diskette

Hardware: Apple II Plus; (DOS 3.2.1 or 3.3) • TRS-80 MOD I or III; with Level II BASIC • PET • Commodore 2001 • Commodore 4000; 40 or 80 column • Commodore 8000; 80 column

Source Code: no

Price: $59.00/cassette set of 3; $65.00/diskette

This program utilizes a systematic approach to spelling that uses the letter cloze technique to reinforce correct spelling and build visual memory. The microcomputer makes use of this technique in an interesting, personal, and non- fault-finding manner. SPELLTRONICS is useful for all students who have trouble spelling. The entire program teaches 240 new words and also allows the teacher to add additional words if desired. Each word is presented 3 separate times with different letters deleted. The student adds the missing letters. Finally, the student must type the entire word into a sentence so that the word is used in context. If the student is unable to provide the correct spelling after two opportunities, the correct answer is displayed and the student tries again. Correct answers are rewarded in all drills. Words are grouped based on linguistic,

phonic, or spelling concepts. The student advances from simple to more complex patterns. Each linguistic pattern has four units containing ten programmed words and a review unit.

    VOWEL PATTERNS
    LONG VOWEL
    CONSONANT PATTERNS
    WORD ENDINGS
    USEFUL WORDS
    UNEXPECTED SPELLINGS

ID: H196

STORY BUILDER/WORD MASTER

Publisher: Program Design, Inc.

Also available from: Academic Software • GRAFex Company • K-12 Micromedia • MARCK • Queue, Inc.

Date: Apr. 81

Grade: 4 and up

Format: cassette or diskette

Hardware: PET • TRS-80 MOD I; with Level II BASIC; cassette • Atari; 8K cassette; 16K diskette • Apple II Plus; 32K • Apple II; 32K with Applesoft in ROM

Price: $16.95/PET and TRS-80; $16.95/Atari cassette, $23.95/ diskette; $23.95/Apple

STORY BUILDER is series of partially constructed verses that child completes. Program teaches grammar skills in enjoyable way. WORD MASTER is logic game in which child tries to guess 3-letter word generated by computer. Program teaches reasoning and vocabulary.

ID: H197

STORYWRITER & STORYTELLER

Publisher: Comaldor

Format: cassette or diskette

Hardware: PET

Price: $25.00

STORYWRITER allows teachers and students to write stories or articles with questions for readers to answer. When the tape is played via STORYTELLER, others may read it at individual rates and answer the questions. Later the teacher can enter a code to have names, reading times, and answers displayed on the screen or printer.

ID: H198

STRANGE ENCOUNTERS: YOU DECIDE

Publisher: Orange Cherry Media

Also available from: Academic Software • K-12 Micromedia • Queue, Inc.

Grade: 4-8

Format: cassette or diskette

Hardware: PET 2000 or 4000; 16K • TRS-80 MOD I or III; 16K • Apple; 16K • Apple II; 16K

Price: $15.00/cassette; $56.00/cassette set of 4; $67.00/diskette set of 2

The four phenomena explored in these computer programs have been the subject of much debate and curiosity. Students read and analyze the evidence on both sides and make decisions as to what they think. This set will captivate all students, even reluctant readers.

BERMUDA TRIANGLE
BIGFOOT OF THE MOUNTAINS
LOCH NESS MONSTER
SNOWMAN OF THE HIMALAYAS

ID: H199
STUDENT WORD STUDY

Publisher: Hartley Courseware, Inc.

Grade: 2-6

Format: 1 diskette

Hardware: Apple II; 48K with Applesoft in ROM (DOS 3.2 or 3.3)

Language: Applesoft BASIC

Price: $29.95

Enables students to take a list of spelling or vocabulary words and build a "study list" of sentences around those words. Blank is left in each sentence where given word should be, enabling student to call up his own lists or those of other students and fill in missing words. Holds up to 15 sentences for each of 30 students.

ID: H200
SUBJECT AND PREDICATE

Publisher: Micro-Ed, Inc.

Also available from: Academic Software • EISI (Educational Instructional Systems, Inc.) • K-12 Micromedia • MARCK

Grade: Elementary and up

Format: cassette or diskette

Hardware: Commodore 64 • PET

Language: BASIC

Source Code: no

Price: $7.95

First, the subject matter is defined. Then the computer presents in random order twenty problems for the student to solve. Each problem is a sentence. For each sentence, the student is asked to identify the complete subject, the simple subject, the complete predicate, or the simple predicate. At the end of the lesson, the learner's performance is summarized.

ID: H201
SUFFIXES

Publisher: Micro-Ed, Inc.

Also available from: EISI (Educational Instructional Systems, Inc.) • K-12 Micromedia

Grade: Elementary

Format: cassette or diskette

Hardware: Commodore 64 • PET • TI 99/4; extended BASIC module

Language: BASIC

Source Code: no

Price: $7.95; $9.95/TI ed.

The problems in this program consist of incomplete words and suggested suffixes. The student must choose the right suffix. The problems are randomly selected by the computer, and there are ten problems in a lesson. At the end of the lesson, the student's performance is summarized. The suffixes treated in this program are NESS, MENT, TION, SION, ANCE, and ENCE.

ID: H202
SYLLABLE BREAKAWAY

Publisher: Little Bee Educational Programs

Also available from: K-12 Micromedia • Queue, Inc.

Grade: 2-4

Format: cassette

Hardware: TRS-80 MOD I or III; 16K with Level II BASIC

Price: $10.95

Breaking the word apart by moving the arrow enables the student to reinforce the syllabication process while providing an absorbing drill. The instructor has the option of using the word list supplied or making new word lists. Scoring is obtained at the end of the program.

ID: H203
SYNONYM SERIES

Publisher: Micro-Ed, Inc.

Also available from: MARCK • Opportunities For Learning, Inc. • Queue, Inc.

Grade: High School and up

Format: 3 programs on cassette or diskette

Hardware: Commodore 64 • PET

Language: BASIC

Source Code: no

Price: $21.00

This program series consists of fifteen lessons dealing with a total of 450 words. Each lesson works with thirty words divided into Columns A and B. Each word in Column A must be matched with the expression which is its synonym (i.e. having an equivalent meaning) in Column B. At the end of each lesson, the synonyms from Column A that gave the learner trouble are listed.

ID: H204
SYNONYMS

Publisher: RIGHT ON PROGRAMS

Also available from: Queue, Inc.

Grade: 11

Format: 5 programs on 5 cassettes or diskette

Hardware: Apple II; 48K with Applesoft in ROM (DOS 3.2 or 3.3) • PET; 16K

Language: BASIC

Source Code: yes

Price: $13.00/cassette; $15.00/diskette; $70.00/5 programs on 1 diskette

This program emphasizes the correct selection of words similar in meaning to the given word. Different words appear in each program and answers are explained. This program is part of a series designed to help students improve their performance on standardized examinations.

ID: H205

TACHISTOSCOPE

Publisher: Micro-Ed, Inc.

Also available from: Academic Software • EISI (Educational Instructional Systems, Inc.) • K-12 Micromedia • MARCK • Queue, Inc.

Grade: Elementary

Format: cassette or diskette

Hardware: Commodore 64 • PET • TI 99/4; extended BASIC module

Language: BASIC

Source Code: no

Price: $7.95

This program flashes small groups of words on the screen in random order. The student attempts to read each group at a glance, and then to reproduce it correctly at the computer keyboard. The speed at which the words are flashed on the screen can be set by the student. Five speeds are available. At the end of each run, the student's performance is summarized.

ID: H206

TANK TACTICS

Publisher: Data Command

Also available from: EISI (Educational Instructional Systems, Inc.) • K-12 Micromedia

Grade: 5-6; Junior High remedial

Format: 21 cassettes or 7 diskettes

Hardware: Apple II; 48K with Applesoft in ROM • Apple II Plus; 48K • TRS-80 MOD I; 16K (cassette) or 32K (diskette) with Level II BASIC • TRS-80 MOD III; 32K with MOD III BASIC

Language: BASIC

Source Code: no

Price: $197.50/set; $29.95/program (1 diskette or 3 cassettes/program)

Computer game pits student's word skills against those of computer adversary called "Super Tank." Programs build word skills using animated graphics and self-paced, menu-driven, interactive learning techniques. Each program is available individually and consists of 3 rounds of 6 games each. Student may select round he or she wishes to play. Summary of student's progress is retained for review by teacher. Average running time is 15-20 minutes.

CONTRACTIONS - Student improves word-recognition abilities by working with 50 contractions and their two-word forms. "Super Tank" fires contraction or two-word form, and student must select one correct match from four choices shown under his or her own tanks to block "Super Tank's" shots. Difficulty progresses sequentially through 3 rounds.

SUFFIXES, PART I - Student uses word-recognition skills to correctly match 24 different suffixes with as many as 205 different base words.

SUFFIXES, PART II - Program uses same instructional methods as PART I; however, there are an additional 321 different base words and 24 suffixes in this program.

PREFIXES - Student is challenged to match 12 different prefixes with assortment of around 325 base words.

BASE WORDS - Student learns to identify bases of up to 228 affixed words.

HOMONYMS - Program gives student valuable practice with "identical sound/different spelling" characteristics of up to 162 homonyms.

PLURALS - Student gains proficiency in correct formation of plural endings "s," "es," "y" to "ies," and "f" to "ves" with up to 276 different base words.

ID: H207

TENNIS, ANYONE?

Publisher: Data Command

Also available from: EISI (Educational Instructional Systems, Inc.) • Opportunities For Learning, Inc.

Grade: 5-6; Junior High remedial

Format: 18 cassettes or 6 diskettes

Hardware: Apple II; 48K with Applesoft in ROM • Apple II Plus; 48K • TRS-80 MOD I; 16K (cassette) or 32K (diskette) with Level II BASIC • TRS-80 MOD III; 32K with MOD III BASIC

Language: BASIC

Source Code: no

Price: $170.75/set; $29.95/program (1 diskette or 3 cassettes/program)

Student pits word recognition abilities against computer in game that is played and scored like tennis. Programs build word skills using animated graphics and self-paced, menu-driven, interactive learning techniques. Each program is available individually. Play consists of 3 rounds of 6 games each. Teacher can see summary of student's performance. Teacher's guide is provided. Average running time is 15-20 minutes.

PLURALS - Program gives student valuable practice in correctly spelling plural endings of up to 126 widely assorted singular words. Difficulty level increases through 3 rounds of play.

PREFIXES - Program builds student proficiency in understanding and correctly using 12 different prefixes with up to 126 widely assorted base words.

SUFFIXES - Program helps student grow in ability to recognize and correctly use suffixes meaning "one who." In course of games student uses six different suffixes with as many as 118 assorted base words. Difficulty increases sequentially through 3 rounds of play.

CONTRACTIONS - Student gains valuable practice in understanding structure and use of 50 different contractions.

HOMONYMS - Program gives student meaningful experience in seeing "identical sound/different spelling" characteristics of up to 126 pairs of homonyms. Difficulty increases through 3 rounds of play.

BASE WORDS - Program helps student see "building block" structure of many words in English language. To play, student must correctly identify and type bases of up to 126 affixed words given by computer.

ID: H208

THEIR WORLD

Publisher: Aquarius Publishers Inc.

Date: Aug. 82

Grade: Special ed., Preschool

Format: 5 diskettes

Hardware: Apple II; 48K with Applesoft in ROM (DOS 3.2 or 3.3)

Language: Applesoft BASIC

Source Code: no

Price: $160.00; $34.95/diskette

These five programs contain words taken from vocabulary of young children. Vocabulary covers range of everyday topics such as food, toys, and colors. Each program includes disk lesson, accompanying books (single copy of each title) and games. Programs feature large print on screen display; sound; multicolor rewards and reinforcement games; simple ''space bar only'' operation; automatic advancement after three tries; random word selection from pool of 31 words; and full-color, controlled vocabulary books.

THEIR WORLD I - Toys, clothes, food

THEIR WORLD II - Furniture, animals and insects, transportation

THEIR WORLD III - About us, what are they doing?

THEIR WORLD IV - Outside, inside, things we like to do

THEIR WORLD V - Colors and numbers

ID: H209

THERE/THEIR/THEY'RE

Publisher: Micro-Ed, Inc.

Also available from: EISI (Educational Instructional Systems, Inc.) • MARCK • Queue, Inc.

Grade: Elementary

Format: cassette or diskette

Hardware: Commodore 64 • PET

Language: BASIC

Source Code: no

Price: $7.95

These homonyms are often troublesome to students. This program provides drill and practice using these three words. Each lesson consists of ten problems. At the end of the lesson, the student's performance is summarized.

ID: H210

TIME BOMB

Publisher: Program Design, Inc.

Date: June 82

Grade: 3 and up

Format: cassette or diskette

Hardware: Atari 400/800; 16K, cassette or 24K, diskette

Language: BASIC

Source Code: no

Price: $16.95/cassette; $23.95/diskette

Program challenges player to uncover secret word before bomb goes off. Contains hundreds of words to guess plus high-resolution and player missile graphics. Diskette version allows user to add word lists.

ID: H211

TO/TOO/TWO

Publisher: Micro-Ed, Inc.

Also available from: EISI (Educational Instructional Systems, Inc.) • MARCK

Grade: Elementary

Format: cassette or diskette

Hardware: Commodore 64 • PET

Language: BASIC

Source Code: no

Price: $7.95

These homonyms are often troublesome for students. This program provides drill and practice problems using these words. Each lesson consists of ten problems. Because these problems are randomly sequenced and drawn from a larger bank of problems, it is highly unlikely that any two lessons in a row will display exactly the same sets of problems. At the end of each lesson, the student's performance is summarized.

ID: H212

TROUBLESOME PRONOUNS

Publisher: Micro-Ed, Inc.

Also available from: EISI (Educational Instructional Systems, Inc.)

Grade: Elementary and up

Format: cassette or diskette

Hardware: Commodore 64 • PET • TI 99/4; extended BASIC module

Language: BASIC

Source Code: no

Price: $7.95; $9.95/TI ed.

Most errors in using pronouns have to do with sentences that use a pronoun along with a noun, a proper noun, or another pronoun. This program presents an easy way for the learner to decide which usage is correct. Then, using a game format, twenty problems are given to the student to solve. At the end of the lesson, the learner's performance is summarized.

ID: H213

TYPE TO READ

Publisher: Micro-Ed, Inc.

Also available from: EISI (Educational Instructional Systems, Inc.) • K-12 Micromedia

Grade: 1-3

Format: 4 sets of programs on cassette or diskette (77 programs)

Hardware: VIC

Language: BASIC

Source Code: no

Price: $105.00/Set A; $119.00/Set B; $147.00/Set C; $168.00/Set D

TYPE TO READ is designed for students who have yet to master the basic word attack patterns essential to the business of learning to read. It is based on the principle that there is usually a dependable relationship between the sounds of the English language and the ways these sounds are represented in writing. Of the more than one thousand words taught in this series, only three do not have a regular correspondence between symbol and sound: of, to, and the. These three words first appear in Lessons 71 and 72 of Set B. In all other instances, once the students have linked certain letter arrangements with their corresponding patterns of sound, they can rely on this association as they proceed. Each lesson begins with a sentence printed on the screen by the computer. The learner types this sentence at the computer keyboard as indicated by an arrow that appears in turn under each letter or space of the problem sentence. As the student types, only correct responses are reproduced on the screen. In this way, the learner's performance is shaped in a positive manner so as to produce results that are always correct. As each word is typed, the learner should pronounce it. For this reason, it is recommended that the learner be accompanied by a partner whose job it is to monitor the learner's reading of each word that is typed.

SET A - Introduces short-vowel sounds between single consonants.

SET B - Focuses on consonant clusters at the beginning and endings of words.

SET C - Continues the work with consonant clusters at the beginnings and ends of words.

SET D - Deals with the regular sounds of some common vowel digraphs and dipthongs, some of them r-controlled; the last two groups of lessons teach silent e at the end of a word.

ID: H214
UPPER/LOWER CASE MATCHING
Publisher: Little Bee Educational Programs

Grade: K-1

Format: cassette

Hardware: TRS-80 MOD I; 16K with Level II BASIC • TRS-80 MOD III

Price: $10.95

This program reinforces the relationship between lowercase letters and their corresponding uppercase letter. The student is greeted by a "thinking face" who challenges him/her to select the correct uppercase letter for the large lowercase letter displayed on the screen. The student is given two chances to correctly identify the letter, then the correct uppercase letter is displayed as a continuous border around the screen. Scoring is given at the end of a session.

ID: H215
USAGE
Publisher: RIGHT ON PROGRAMS

Also available from: Academic Software • Queue, Inc.

Grade: High School

Format: 5 programs on 5 cassettes or diskette

Hardware: Apple II; 48K with Applesoft in ROM (DOS 3.2 or 3.3) • PET; 16K

Language: BASIC

Source Code: yes

This series reviews the correct use of various sentence parts, including noun, verb, adverb, etc.

SUBJECT/VERB AGREEMENT (A&B) AND AGREEMENT OF PRONOUN/ANTECEDENT - The rules are given for agreement of subject/verb and pronoun/antecedent. Users are given practice in identifying and correcting related errors.

IRREGULAR VERBS - The user is given review and practice in using irregular verbs by choosing the correct form for the sentence. Spelling is counted.

USING ADJECTIVES/ADVERBS CORRECTLY - This program reviews correct usage of adverbs with action verbs, adjectives with linking verbs, comparative and superlative form of modifiers and double negatives.

ID: H216
USAGE BONERS
Publisher: Micro-Ed, Inc.

Also available from: EISI (Educational Instructional Systems, Inc.) • K-12 Micromedia • MARCK • Queue, Inc.

Grade: Elementary and up

Format: 15 programs on cassette or diskette

Hardware: Commodore 64 • PET • Apple II Plus; 48K (DOS 3.3) • TRS-80 Color Computer; 32K • TI 99/4; extended BASIC module • VIC

Language: BASIC

Source Code: no

Price: $99.00

This drill and practice series focuses on common mistakes in usage, such as lack of agreement between subject and verb, double negatives, etc. For each problem, the computer not only states whether the student's response is right or wrong, but also shows how the mistake in English usage presented in the problem should be corrected. There are ten problems in each lesson. The problems are randomly sequenced. At the end of each lesson, the student's performance is summarized. The format employed is frequently used in standardized achievement tests. Additionally, in order to prevent the student from identifying a mistake because of the content of a given problem sentence, many of the problem sentences are identical in content except for a specific mistake in usage.

ID: H217
VERB
Publisher: Micro-Ed, Inc.

Also available from: Academic Software • EISI (Educational Instructional Systems, Inc.) • K-12 Micromedia • MARCK • Queue, Inc. • Texas Instruments

Grade: Elementary and up

Format: cassette or diskette

Hardware: Commodore 64 • PET • TI 99/4

Language: BASIC

Source Code: no

Price: $7.95; $9.95 TI ed.

This program covers action verbs, linking verbs, and verb phrases. First, the subject matter is defined and taught through examples. Then the learner is tested on what has been presented. At the end of the lesson, the learner's performance is summarized.

ID: H218

VERB USAGE 1 & 2

Publisher: Hartley Courseware, Inc.

Grade: 2-6

Format: 2 diskettes

Hardware: Apple II; 48K with Applesoft in ROM (DOS 3.2 or 3.3)

Language: Applesoft BASIC

Price: $49.95

Forty lessons and 8 tests provide simple, repetitive work on verb usage. Lessons require student to discriminate between present, past, and past participle forms of commonly used and misused verbs. Missed sentences are presented again to student at later time.

ID: H219

VERBAL SKILLS

Publisher: SEI (Sliwa Enterprises Inc.)

Also available from: Queue, Inc.

Date: May 82

Grade: 8-12

Format: 3 diskettes

Hardware: Apple II; 32K with Applesoft in ROM (DOS 3.2 or 3.3)

Language: Applesoft BASIC

Source Code: yes

Price: $25.00/program; $60.00/all three

Verbal skills programs were developed as aid for students preparing for college board exams. Multiple-choice format is used to drill and gain experience with sample problems from such tests. Files range in difficulty from eighth grade through college levels. Menu-driven programs require no documentation. Each program comes with resident editor for easy modification, updating, or expansion of data base by teacher or student.

VOCABULARY BUILDER - Over 1600 entries are stored, with synonyms and antonyms. User selects desired mode: synonyms for drill and antonyms for test practice. Program is useful tool for all age levels.

WORD ANALOGY - Over 1200 word relationships are saved in data base, with many questions coming directly from sample aptitude tests. After attempting to answer each problem, student has option of viewing a hint.

SENTENCE COMPLETION - Over 300 entries are arranged in completion, construction, and correction question formats. Program requires knowledge of vocabulary, usage, verb tenses, and even spelling.

ID: H220

VERBS

Publisher: Hartley Courseware, Inc.

Also available from: Academic Software • Opportunities For Learning, Inc.

Grade: 2-9

Format: 1 diskette

Hardware: Apple II; 48K with Applesoft in ROM (DOS 3.2 or 3.3)

Language: Applesoft BASIC

Price: $32.95

Comprehensive, multilevel program of lessons on verb recognition and usage, with controlled vocabulary to allow for each skill to be presented at different reading levels. Each lesson includes introductory frame followed by simple example, in gradually increasing level of difficulty. Includes verb recognition and identification, tense of regular and irregular verbs, subject-predicate correspondence, contractions, and correct usage.

ID: H221

VERBS I

Publisher: Convergent Systems Inc.

Grade: Upper Elementary and up

Format: diskette

Hardware: Apple II; 48K with Applesoft in ROM; shift key adapter • Apple II Plus; shift key adapter

Source Code: no

Price: $60.00

This package consists of 5 lessons covering identification of verbs, classification of tenses, auxiliary verbs, "being verbs", and action and linking verbs. Part of the Basic English Skills Series, these programs take 120 minutes to run. A specific learning objective is selected for each lesson. To accomplish the objective the lessons are programmed in several stages: the first is the tutorial section, which provides the learner with definitions, examples and clues for use and identification of parts of speech. Student performance is then evaluated through a practice session. Review options are available during the practice session if the learner has difficulty with a particular area. To proceed, the student must respond correctly. After 3 or 4 attempts, the student is given the correct answer. Upon completion of the basic skills lesson, scores are given and problem areas are identified with recommendations for review. To enhance learning reinforcement, feedback is given for both correct and incorect answers.

ID: H222

VERBS II

Publisher: Convergent Systems Inc.

Grade: Upper Elementary and up

Format: diskette

Hardware: Apple II; 48K with Applesoft in ROM; shift key adapter • Apple II Plus; shift key adapter

Source Code: no

Price: $45.00

The three lessons in this package cover irregular verbs. Taking approximately 90 minutes to run, this software is part of the Basic English Skills Series. A specific learning objective is selected for each lesson. To accomplish the objective the lessons are programmed in several stages: the first is the tutorial section, which provides the learner with definitions, examples and clues for use and identification of parts of speech. Student performance is evaluated through a practice session during which review options are available if the learner has difficulty with a particular area. To proceed, the student must respond correctly. After three or four attempts, the student is given the correct answer. Upon completion of the basic skills lesson, scores are given and problem areas are identified with recommendations for review. To enhance learning reinforcement, feedback is given for both correct and incorrect responses.

ID: H223

VERBS III

Publisher: Convergent Systems Inc.

Grade: Upper Elementary and up

Format: diskette

Hardware: Apple II; 48K with Applesoft in ROM; shift key adapter • Apple II Plus; shift key adapter

Source Code: no

Price: $20.00

This program takes about 40 minutes to run. It covers regular and irregular verbs in the past, present and future tenses. A specific learning objective is selected for each lesson. To accomplish the objective the lessons are programmed in several stages: the first is the tutorial section, which provides the learner with definitions, examples and clues for use and identification of parts of speech. Student performance is then evaluated through a practice session during which review options are available if the learner has difficulty with a particular area. To proceed, the student must respond correctly with the aid of clues. After three or four attempts, the student is given the correct answer. Upon completion of the basic skills lesson, scores are given and problem areas are identified with recommendations for review. To enhance learning reinforcement, feedback is given for both correct and incorrect responses.

ID: H224

VIDEO SPEED-READING TRAINER

Publisher: Instant Software^T.M.

Also available from: Academic Software • MARCK • Opportunities For Learning, Inc. • Queue, Inc.

Grade: 1-Adult

Format: cassette

Hardware: TRS-80 MOD I; 16K with Level II BASIC

Language: BASIC

Source Code: no

Price: $9.95

This three-part package uses scientific principle behind tachistoscope (a mechanical device used to flash characters or words on a screen) to train user's eyes and mind to quickly recognize numbers, letters, words, and phrases. Written documentation is provided.

ID: H225

VOCAB

Publisher: TYCOM Associates

Also available from: K-12 Micromedia • MARCK

Grade: Junior High-College

Format: 2 programs on cassette

Hardware: PET; 8K; 40 column screen; C2N cassette recorder

Price: $15.95

This program is an English vocabulary builder. Through the use of synonyms, the student learns to associate the meanings of new words. The programs can be operated in two modes. The first mode presents a list of synonyms a page at a time for student study. The second mode quizzes the student by asking questions such as "I am thinking of a 5 letter word meaning severe, what is the word?" The student has several chances to answer, and may be given clues such as "My word starts with 'AC'". The program may also suggest that the student has the correct word, but has spelled it improperly. On exiting this mode, the student is graded.

ID: H226

VOCABULARY SERIES

Publisher: Micro-Ed, Inc.

Also available from: EISI (Educational Instructional Systems, Inc.) • K-12 Micromedia • MARCK • Opportunities For Learning, Inc. • Queue, Inc. • Texas Instruments

Grade: Upper Elementary-High School

Format: 24 programs on cassette or diskette

Hardware: Commodore 64 • PET • TI 99/4 • Apple II Plus; 48K (DOS 3.3) • TRS-80 Color Computer; 48K • VIC; 3K memory enhancement

Language: BASIC

Source Code: no

Price: $168.00

This program consists of seventy-two lessons dealing with words commonly found in daily newspapers and weekly news magazines. Each problem presents a definition and sample sentence. The learner then chooses the vocabulary word that best fits. At the end of each lesson, the learner's results are summarized, including a listing of the specific words that gave trouble during the lesson.

ID: H227

VOCABULARY - DOLCH

Publisher: Hartley Courseware, Inc.

Also available from: Academic Software • Queue, Inc.

Grade: K-3

Format: 1 diskette

Hardware: Apple II; 48K with Applesoft in ROM (DOS 3.2 or 3.3); CCD required

Language: Applesoft BASIC

Price: $39.95

Lesson drills for common words, including all Dolch words from prereading through third grade. Student sees and says word, then hears word and indicates if he or she knows word. Computer stores responses for review by teacher. Teacher records words or words in context on any cassette recorder, using cassette control device (CCD).

ID: H228
VOCABULARY BUILDER
Publisher: Micro Learningware

Format: diskette

Hardware: TRS-80 MOD I or III; 32K

Language: BASIC

Source Code: yes

Price: $24.95

Package consists of series of five programs that offer three different formats of vocabulary drills: (1) definition is given and user selects word from list of alternatives; (2) word is given and user selects definition from list of alternatives; and (3) user matches words and definitions. Package contains over 1000 words. Written instructions provided.

ID: H229
VOCABULARY BUILDER
Publisher: Instant Software[T.M.]

Also available from: Academic Software • Queue, Inc.

Format: cassette

Hardware: TRS-80

Source Code: no

Price: $9.95

An educational vocabulary-building package for all ages uses crossword puzzle format to hold attention of even the most reluctant student. Written documentation is provided.

POLONIUS - Program offers 140 crossword puzzles.

VEEBEEGEE - Program provides letters and allows student to construct puzzle on game board.

ID: H230
VOCABULARY BUILDERS
Publisher: Orange Cherry Media

Also available from: Academic Software • K-12 Micromedia • Queue, Inc.

Grade: 3-8

Format: cassette or diskette

Hardware: PET 2000 or 4000; 16K • TRS-80 MOD I or III; 16K • Apple; 16K • Apple II; 16K

Price: $15.00/cassette; $56.00/cassette set of 4; $67.00/diskette set of 2

The computer guides students through various activities which expand their skill of analyzing word meanings. Continuous student involvement insures a high level of reinforcement. Vocabulary-building skills are introduced, explored and reinforced through review questions and games.

RECOGNIZING HOMONYMS

SYNONYMS AND ANTONYMS

IDENTIFYING MEANINGS THROUGH CONTEXT CLUES

VOCABULARY BUILDING SKILLS

ID: H231
VOCABULARY EDU-DISKS[T.M.]
Publisher: Readers Digest

Date: Oct. 82

Grade: Upper Elementary-High School

Format: 3 programs on diskette

Hardware: Apple II • Apple II Plus • TRS-80 MOD I or III

Source Code: no

Price: $48.96/disk

These 3 programs provide practice and self-instruction in vocabulary and related language arts skills. To play the games, students must connect words and meanings. They learn to pronounce the words they encounter and also develop related skills such as decoding, context clues, word parts, and recognizing synonyms and antonyms. Each game is presented at three vocabulary levels: upper elementary, junior high, and senior high. Includes 8-page User's Guide.

KEY LINGO

TRICKSTER COYOTE

THE CHAMBERS OF VOCAB

ID: H232
VOCABULARY GAME FOR THE APPLE II
Publisher: J & S Software, Inc.

Also available from: Academic Software • K-12 Micromedia • MARCK • McKilligan Supply Corp. • Queue, Inc.

Grade: 8-12

Format: diskette

Hardware: Apple II; 48K with Applesoft in ROM (DOS 3.2 or 3.3)

Language: BASIC

Source Code: no

Price: $29.50

An exciting, motivating game designed to help students in grades 8-12 improve their vocabulary in a fun, competitive way. A student has a choice of playing three baseball games: a one-inning game (3 outs), a two-inning game (6 outs), or a three-inning game (9 outs). Students compete against the previous high scorer whose name and score is shown. A student has a choice of trying for a single (an easy word), a double, or a triple (a hard word). If the student identifies the correct meaning of the word, he observes his player advance to that base. A student always sees the number of outs, runs, and the inning. Always displayed is the name of the high scorer for each game. Whenever he or she chooses, the teacher can use a password to eliminate these scores and start from the beginning. Words are chosen from a bank of almost 1000 SAT-type words. No words are repeated in the same game.

ID: H233
VOCABULARY PROGRAMS
Publisher: Microphys Programs

Also available from: MARCK • Queue, Inc.

Grade: 7-12

Format: 60 cassettes

Hardware: VIC-20; 3K expansion cartridge

Language: BASIC

Source Code: yes

Price: $15.00/cassette

Series of 60 vocabulary programs consists of ten programs at each of six grade levels. Each program randomly generates graded words which are to be defined. A sentence in which a word is used properly is displayed when an incorrect response is made. Using this contextual clue, a second opportunity to define the word is given. Reading and spelling skills are also reinforced as a more powerful vocabulary is developed. Complete instructions are included.

GRADE 12 (PV401-405 and PV431-435)

GRADE 11 (PV406-410 and PV436-440)

GRADE 10 (PV411-415 and PV441-445)

GRADE 9 (PV416-420 and PV446-450)

GRADE 8 (PV421-425 and PV451-455)

GRADE 7 (PV426-430 and PV456-460)

ID: H234

VOCABULARY PROMPTER

Publisher: Jagdstaffel Software

Date: 1981

Format: diskette

Hardware: Apple II Plus • Apple II; 32K with Applesoft in ROM (DOS 3.3)

Language: Applesoft BASIC

Source Code: no

Price: $29.95; $12.95/supplemental data diskette

Programmed learning software utility package may be used by language arts student and/or instructor to create simple data files and lists, and then use them for study and/or testing purposes. Under study and test options, program presents prompt and response in random sequences. Given data files can have from one to fifty pairs of prompts and responses at one time. All study and test options are scored with percentage of correct to incorrect responses. Supplemental data diskettes available are listed below. Written documentation is provided.

ENGLISH - RUSSIAN

ENGLISH - FRENCH

ENGLISH - GERMAN

ENGLISH - SPANISH

ID: H235

VOCABULARY SKILLS: CONTEXT CLUES

Publisher: Milton Bradley

Also available from: McKilligan Supply Corp. • Opportunities For Learning, Inc.

Grade: 6-8

Format: 1 diskette

Hardware: Apple II; 48K with Applesoft in ROM (DOS 3.3)

Language: Applesoft BASIC

Price: $44.95

This program covers the development of vocabulary through context, definition, contrast, educated guesses, and example. The three modes of instruction - rule explanation, practice, and review and reward - allow the student to progress at his own pace. Includes a Teacher's Guide and reproducible activity sheets.

ID: H236

VOCABULARY SKILLS: PREFIXES, SUFFIXES, ROOT WORDS

Publisher: Milton Bradley

Also available from: McKilligan Supply Corp. • Opportunities For Learning, Inc.

Grade: 6-8

Format: 1 diskette

Hardware: Apple II; 48K with Applesoft in ROM (DOS 3.3)

Language: Applesoft BASIC

Price: $44.95

This program includes introductory concepts, a prefix tutor, an easy suffix tutor, a hard suffix tutor, a root word tutor, and word building. Three instructional modes allow for rule definition, practice and review and a reward game. Includes Teacher's Guide and reproducible activity sheets.

ID: H237

VOWEL SOUND SPACE SHIPS

Publisher: Little Bee Educational Programs

Also available from: Queue, Inc.

Grade: 2-4

Format: cassette

Hardware: TRS-80 MOD I or III; 16K with Level II BASIC

Price: $10.95

The student is "Commander" of the space station and must defend against the "alien vowel sounds." In the lower left hand corner a word with the "alien vowel sound" is shown. From among three spaceships moving across the top of the screen, the student must zap the spaceship carrying a word with the same vowel sound as that shown at the bottom of the screen. Scoring is given at the end of the session.

ID: H238

VOWELS

Publisher: Hartley Courseware, Inc.

Also available from: Academic Software • Opportunities For Learning, Inc. • Queue, Inc.

Grade: 1-3

Format: 1 diskette with backup

Hardware: Apple II; 48K with Applesoft in ROM (DOS 3.2 or 3.3); CCD required

Language: Applesoft BASIC

Price: $93.05

Fifty-three lessons of twenty presentations each, covering long and short vowels, double vowels, diphthongs, r-controlled vowels, schwa sound, and related language skills. Cassette control device (CCD) enables teacher to record examples or instructions to play with program.

ID: H239

VOWELS TUTORIAL

Publisher: Hartley Courseware, Inc.

Grade: 1-3

Format: 3 diskettes

Hardware: Apple II; 48K with Applesoft in ROM (DOS 3.2 or 3.3); CCD required

Language: Applesoft BASIC

Price: $120.00

Extensive series of lessons for vowel instruction, presenting student with visual and auditory stimuli. Pictures are shown of words with same vowel sounds. Program branches to tutorial if error is made; student planning feature saves errors for review by teacher. Cassette control device (CCD) enables teacher to record examples or instructions to play with program. Developed under grant from Apple Education Foundation. Includes 1 disk for short vowels and 2 for long vowels.

ID: H240

WHEEL-OF-FORTUNE WORD GAMES

Publisher: Microphys Programs

Also available from: EISI (Educational Instructional Systems, Inc.) • MARCK • Queue, Inc.

Format: 6 cassettes or 1 diskette

Hardware: VIC-20; 3K expansion cartridge • PET; 8K • Commodore 64; 8K • Apple II; 24K • TRS-80 MOD I or III; 16K • Bell & Howell

Source Code: yes

Price: $15.00/cassette; $80.00/diskette

Series of six programs challenges players to try to fill in missing letters in a randomly generated title or phrase and earn or lose points according to graphic display on ''Wheel-of-Fortune''. Scores of as many as four players are displayed, 1000 points being required to win a given game. Complete instructions are included. Also available on diskette for price noted above, along with ten ANAGRAM programs. User must specify machine for which diskette is intended.

    SONG TITLES (PV375)

    FAMOUS PLACES (PV376)

    ENTERTAINERS (PV377)

    STATESMEN (PV378)

    SCIENTISTS (PV379)

    SPORTS FIGURES (PV380)

ID: H241

WHICH LETTER COMES NEXT

Publisher: Micro-Ed, Inc.

Also available from: Academic Software • Queue, Inc.

Grade: Primary

Format: cassette or diskette

Hardware: Commodore 64 • PET; light pen optional (specify program RE-6)

Language: BASIC

Source Code: no

Price: $7.95

A large capital letter appears on the screen, followed by a box with a question mark on it. What letter is hidden by the box? It is the letter that should come next in alphabetical order. At the bottom of the screen, two little rectangles of light have a

race. One belongs to the computer. The other belongs to the student. Which one will win? It all depends on how well the student supplies the missing letters asked for during the lesson. (If the student does not know the answer, and types the question mark, the computer will give the answer.)

ID: H242

WHICH LETTER IS MISSING

Publisher: Micro-Ed, Inc.

Grade: 1-3

Format: cassette or diskette

Hardware: VIC

Language: BASIC

Source Code: no

Price: $7.95

The computer presents a row of capital letters on the screen. But one of them is covered up. Which one is it? The student tries to find and press the key with the missing letter. If the student does not know the answer and presses the up-arrow key (the one just to the right of the asterisk), the computer will give the answer. At the end of the lesson, the student's performance is summarized.

ID: H243

WHICH NUMBER COMES NEXT?

Publisher: Micro-Ed, Inc.

Also available from: Academic Software • EISI (Educational Instructional Systems, Inc.) • MARCK • Queue, Inc.

Grade: Elementary

Format: cassette

Hardware: PET; 3G Light pen

Language: BASIC

Source Code: no

Price: $7.95

For each problem, three numbers in sequence between 1 and 20 are presented, followed by a blank. What number belongs in the blank? It is the next number in sequence. Two possible answer choices are presented. The student places the point of the light pen on a small square associated with the answer of his/her choice. Each completed lesson consists of sixteen problems randomly presented. However, the program may be terminated at any time simply by pressing the space bar. Then the student's performance is summarized.

ID: H244

WHO, WHAT, WHERE, WHEN, WHY

Publisher: Hartley Courseware, Inc.

Also available from: Academic Software • Queue, Inc.

Grade: 1-5

Format: 1 diskette

Hardware: Apple II; 48K with Applesoft in ROM (DOS 3.2 or 3.3)

Language: Applesoft BASIC

Price: $35.95

Fourteen lessons are carefully written and sequenced from easy to difficult. Each lesson contains 20 presentations on combinations of these easy-to-confuse words and concepts.

ID: H245

WHOLE BRAIN SPELLING

Publisher: SubLOGIC Communications Corporation

Grade: K-adult

Format: diskette

Hardware: Apple II Plus; 48K; color monitor • Apple II; 48K with Applesoft in ROM

Language: Applesoft BASIC

Source Code: no

Price: $34.95; same price each word list

Program is designed to help user develop internal visualization skills for improving spelling, through combination of self-paced, menu-driven instruction and color graphics capabilities of Apple. Contains 2000 study words in 200 lists. Includes sections on lesson operation, goals, study and practice words. Is also available with supplementary words in following categories: scientific, secretarial, fairy tale and child's garden of words. User's manual included.

ID: H246

WORD CATEGORIES

Publisher: RIGHT ON PROGRAMS

Also available from: Queue, Inc.

Grade: 11

Format: 5 programs on 5 cassettes or diskette

Hardware: Apple II; 48K with Applesoft in ROM (DOS 3.2 or 3.3) • PET; 16K

Language: BASIC

Source Code: yes

Price: $13.00/cassette; $15.00/diskette; $70.00/5 programs on 1 diskette

The user is given practice in grouping words by specific categories. This practice is designed to help the student retain definitions through associations with a particular subject area. The series is designed to help students improve their performance on standardized tests.

HISTORY

HUMANITIES

SCIENCE/MATH

LITERATURE

WORDS OF SIMILAR APPEARANCE

ID: H247

WORD ELEMENTS - SERIES FOUR

Publisher: BrainBank, Inc.

Also available from: Academic Software • Queue, Inc.

Grade: 5 and up

Format: 6 programs on cassette or diskette

Hardware: Apple; 16K • PET; 16K • TRS-80; 16K

Price: $60.00

Spelling, reading, grammar and vocabulary skill levels increase. Comprehension of language improves by recognizing component parts of speech. This series covers suffixes. Includes Courseware Kit with Teacher's Guide.

SUFFIX - ESS

SUFFIX - FY

SUFFIX - IZE

SUFFIX - IC

SUFFIXES - ICAL/ICALLY REVIEW TEST

ID: H248

WORD ELEMENTS - SERIES ONE

Publisher: BrainBank, Inc.

Also available from: Academic Software • K-12 Micromedia • Queue, Inc.

Grade: 5 and up

Format: 5 programs on cassette or diskette

Hardware: Apple; 16K • PET; 16K • TRS-80; 16K

Price: $50.00

Increases spelling, reading, grammar, and vocabulary skills. Includes Courseware Kit with Teacher's Guide.

PREFIX SUB-

PREFIXES UNI-, BI-, TRI-

PREFIXES SEMI-, HEMI-, DEMI-, INTER-, TRANS-, INTRA-

REVIEW TEST

ID: H249

WORD ELEMENTS - SERIES SIX

Publisher: BrainBank, Inc.

Also available from: Academic Software • Queue, Inc.

Grade: 5 and up

Format: 6 programs on cassette or diskette

Hardware: Apple; 16K • PET; 16K • TRS-80; 16K

Price: $60.00

Spelling, reading, grammar and vocabulary skill levels increase. Comprehension of language improves by recognizing component parts of words. This series covers prefixes. Includes Courseware Kit with Teacher's Guide.

PREFIX AUDI

PREFIX TELE

PREFIX PHONO

PREFIX PHOTO

PREFIXES STEREO/VIDEO

ID: H250

WORD ELEMENTS - SERIES THREE

Publisher: BrainBank, Inc.

Also available from: Academic Software • K-12 Micromedia • Queue, Inc.

Grade: 5 and up

Format: 5 programs on cassette or diskette

Hardware: Apple; 16K • PET; 16K • TRS-80; 16K

Price: $50.00

Increases spelling, reading, grammar and vocabulary skills. Includes Courseware Kit with Teacher's Guide.

SUFFIX - METER

SUFFIX - METER IN THE METRIC SYSTEM

SUFFIX - GRAM

SUFFIX - GRAM IN THE METRIC SYSTEM

REVIEW TEST

ID: H251

WORD ELEMENTS - SERIES TWO

Publisher: BrainBank, Inc.

Also available from: Academic Software • K-12 Micromedia • Queue, Inc.

Grade: 5 and up

Format: 5 programs on cassette or diskette

Hardware: Apple; 16K • PET; 16K • TRS-80; 16K

Price: $50.00

Increases spelling, reading, grammar, and vocabulary skills. Includes Courseware Kit with Teacher's Guide.

PREFIX MAL

PREFIX MIS

PREFIX DIS

PREFIX DYS

REVIEW TEST

ID: H252

WORD FACTORY

Publisher: Orange Cherry Media

Also available from: Academic Software • K-12 Micromedia • Queue, Inc.

Grade: 3-6

Format: cassette or diskette

Hardware: PET 2000 or 4000; 16K • TRS-80 MOD I or III; 16K • Apple; 16K • Apple II; 16K

Price: $15.00/cassette; $56.00/cassette set of 4; $67.00/diskette set of 2

A delightful set of programs which gives students the opportunity to change words and create new ones.

ADDING PREFIXES

FUN WITH SUFFIXES

LET'S USE CONTRACTIONS

RHYMING MACHINE

ID: H253

WORD FAMILIES

Publisher: Hartley Courseware, Inc.

Also available from: Academic Software • K-12 Micromedia • Opportunities For Learning, Inc.

Grade: 1-4

Format: 1 diskette

Hardware: Apple II; 48K with Applesoft in ROM (DOS 3.2 or 3.3)

Language: Applesoft BASIC

Price: $29.95

Includes 300 separate presentations in 3 different skill categories: beginning consonant substitution; final consonant substitution; and medial vowel substitution. For each presentation, a word is shown to student along with four additional letters from which student chooses to make another word. Incorrect responses are recorded on student's file; graphic reinforcer is provided when student successfully completes 10 presentations.

ID: H254

WORD FAMILY HOUSE

Publisher: Little Bee Educational Programs

Grade: 1-2

Format: cassette

Hardware: TRS-80 MOD I or III; 16K with Level II BASIC

Price: $10.95

This is a program that develops auditory discrimination and provides an exercise for rhyming words by changing the first letter/letters of the word. The student is presented with the word family and is given 3 choices from which to make a selection. As the words are correctly constructed they move into the house. Four words are constructed for each word family. Two levels of difficulty are provided with 30 different word families. Scoring is given at the end of the session.

ID: H255

WORD FLASH

Publisher: Ideatech Company

Also available from: K-12 Micromedia • MARCK

Grade: 1-8

Format: diskette

Hardware: Apple II; 16K with Applesoft in ROM • Apple II Plus; 16K

Language: BASIC

Price: $12.95

The program enables the student to increase spelling and visual memory skills. The student may choose the level of difficulty of the words and may choose the speed of presentation of each set of words. A student may play the game by matching the flashed word to one of three words provided as clues or may type the flashed word from memory without using the clue words. After two incorrect answers, the correct answer is given to the student. The score is kept on a scoreboard throughout the game and feedback is given after each answer. Ten words which are randomly chosen from a bank of words at the specified difficulty level are presented during each game. The bank of words can be changed by anyone with beginning programming knowledge. Directions for adding and changing words are given in the program listing.

ID: H256

WORD PREP (BASIC)

Publisher: Micro Power & Light Company

Grade: Upper Elementary-Junior High

Format: diskette

Hardware: Apple II; 32K with Applesoft in ROM

Price: $24.95

The program disk for WORD PREP (BASIC) includes: (1) 500 vocabulary-expanding words and associated definitions, appropriate for use by students at the upper elementary, middle school, and junior high levels; (2) randomization routines which ensure a novel selection of words and purported definitions, each time the program is used; (3) facilities permitting modification of the word list, to better fit a set of preferred words or definitions; and (4) instructions and facilities enabling the user to create word lists.

ID: H257

WORD RELATIONSHIPS

Publisher: RIGHT ON PROGRAMS

Also available from: Queue, Inc.

Grade: 11

Format: 5 programs on 5 cassettes or diskette

Hardware: Apple II; 48K with Applesoft in ROM (DOS 3.2 or 3.3) • PET; 16K

Language: BASIC

Source Code: yes

Price: $13.00/cassette; $15.00/diskette; $70.00/5 programs on 1 diskette

This program reviews the types of relationships that exist between pairs of words in analogies. Each program provides practice in all types of word relationships. Answers and different vocabulary in each program are explained. Part of a series designed to help students improve their performance on standardized exams.

ID: H258

WORD SCRAMBLER AND SUPER SPELLER

Publisher: Avant-Garde Creations

Also available from: Academic Software • Opportunities For Learning, Inc. • Queue, Inc.

Grade: K-College

Format: diskette

Hardware: Apple; 48K with Applesoft in ROM

Price: $19.95

This program includes practice drills for missed words, optional word unscrambling, and comprehensive scoring. The disk contains 3 word files - one K-3, one 4-8, and one 9-16 and up. The program also allows input of word files selected by user.

ID: H259

WORD SEARCH

Publisher: Micro-Ed, Inc.

Also available from: Academic Software • MARCK

Grade: Elementary

Format: cassette or diskette

Hardware: Commodore 64 • PET

Language: BASIC

Source Code: no

Price: $7.95

Ten words are entered by the student, one at a time. The computer then hides these words within a grid of scrambled letters. Where is each word located? At the end of the exercise, the student's performance is summarized.

ID: H260

WORD STRUCTURE

Publisher: Borg-Warner Educational Systems

Grade: A-D Elem., E-H Jr. High and up

Format: up to 8 diskettes

Hardware: Apple II Plus; 48K; printer optional

Language: Applesoft BASIC

Source Code: no

Price: $600.00/series A-H; $300.00/series A-D; $300.00/series E-H. $120.00/annual subscription; $60.00/yearly renewal

The Word Structure series helps students communicate more effectively by providing individualized instruction in basic word analysis. Each lesson, providing individualized instruction in one or more specific language skills, is structured according to increasing levels of difficulty. As a result of this spiral approach, each program introduces new material which builds upon previously acquired information. The variety of materials covered will be motivational for elementary through adult students who require instruction in language skills. Student records are maintained for review in the management system and may be permanently recorded with the use of an optional printer. Includes Teacher's Guide.

DISK A - CAPITALIZATION/ABBREVIATION

DISK B - SPELLING/SYLLABLES; SINGULARS/PLURALS

DISK C - POSSESSIVES; POSITIVES/COMPARATIVES/SUPERLATIVES

DISK D - PREFIXES; SUFFIXES

DISK E - CAPITALIZATION/ABBREVIATION

DISK F - SPELLING/SYLLABLES; SINGULARS/PLURALS

DISK G - POSSESSIVES; POSITIVES/COMPARATIVES/SUPERLATIVES

DISK H - PREFIXES/SUFFIXES

ID: H261

WORD WISE BASAL 1

Publisher: TIES, Minnesota School Districts Data Processing Joint Board

Date: Sept. 81

Grade: 1-3

Format: 8 diskettes with backup

Hardware: Apple II; 48K with Applesoft in ROM (DOS 3.3) • Apple II Plus

Price: $199.95; $6.50/documentation

The word lists used in this package are designed to correlate with the word lists used in the GINN Rainbow Series. WORD WISE is designed as a sight vocabulary exercise for primary-level students. The students either fill in a blank in a sentence with a word (or phrase) or match a word (or phrase) with a picture. After the student completes a lesson, a bar graph is displayed which illustrates the number of questions the student answered right and wrong. Support material includes sample picture and sentence lessons to show what a student might *see* when using the package. There is also a listing of all the lessons and the words used in each lesson. A student recording sheet is provided in the manual.

ID: H262

WORD WISE BASAL 2

Publisher: TIES, Minnesota School Districts Data Processing Joint Board

Date: Sept. 81

Grade: 1-3

Format: 33 diskettes with backup

Hardware: Apple II; 48K with Applesoft in ROM (DOS 3.3) • Apple II Plus

Price: $374.95; $6.50/documentation

The word lists used in this package are designed to correlate with the word lists used in the Harcourt, Brace, Jovanovich 1980 Basal Series. WORD WISE is designed as a sight vocabulary exercise for primary-level students. The students either fill in a blank in a sentence with a word (or phrase) or match a word (or phrase) with a picture. After the student completes a lesson, a bar graph is displayed which illustrates the number of questions the student answered right and wrong. Support materials include sample picture and sentence lessons to show what a student might *see* when using the package. There is also a listing of all the lessons and the words used in each lesson. A student recording sheet is provided in the manual.

ID: H263

WORD WISE BASAL 3

Publisher: TIES, Minnesota School Districts Data Processing Joint Board

Date: Sept. 81

Grade: 1-3

Format: 12 diskettes with backup

Hardware: Apple II; 48K with Applesoft in ROM (DOS 3.3) • Apple II Plus

Price: $224.95; $6.50/documentation

The word lists used in this package are designed to correlate with the word lists used in the Houghton Mifflin 1979 Basal Series. WORD WISE is designed as a sight vocabulary exercise for primary-level students. The students either fill in a blank in a sentence with a word (or phrase) or match a word (or phrase) with a picture. After the student completes a lesson, a bar graph is displayed which illustrates the number of questions the student answered right and wrong. Support materials include sample picture and sentence lessons to show what a student might *see* when using the package. There is also a listing of all the lessons and the words used in each lesson. A student recording sheet is provided in the manual.

ID: H264

WORD-A-TACH

Publisher: Hartley Courseware, Inc.

Grade: K-4

Format: 1 diskette

Hardware: Apple II; 48K with Applesoft in ROM (DOS 3.2 or 3.3)

Language: Applesoft BASIC

Price: $26.95

Presents words tachistoscopically to student for recognition and repetition into tape recorder for later review by teacher. Teacher may assign common sight words already on lessons or may devise own word lists, and may select different time durations for visual stimulus.

ID: H265

WORDGUESS

Publisher: Comaldor

Format: cassette or diskette

Hardware: PET

Price: $20.00

A game-drill to help weak spellers while they have fun. The student races against the computer to put in correct letters. Results are shown by a tug-of-war event. Time allowed per guess depends on which of 9 levels is chosen. The teacher may put in 4 different word sets at once from tapes made previously. An unlimited library can be built up of units from the Speller, vocabulary from lessons, or words from trips and events. In this way there could even be different levels of difficulty in the words selected from the same story.

ID: H266

WORDRACE

Publisher: Comaldor

Format: cassette or diskette

Hardware: PET

Price: $20.00

With this spelling program, a number of players can have a race identifying words. Rather than the hangman system, the contestants race in "track and field" lanes. It comes with lists of words built in, but allows the teacher to add a special list for that day. A timing sequence prevents unfair delays.

ID: H267

WORDS FOR THE WISE

Publisher: TYC Software (Teach Yourself by Computer)

Also available from: K-12 Micromedia • MARCK • Queue, Inc.

Grade: 1-6

Format: 3 cassettes

Hardware: TRS-80 MOD I or III; 16K, with Level II BASIC; amplifier/speaker optional

Price: $24.95

Complete spelling tutorial system for elementary school student features updatable list of 1000 words that may be presented through five types of activities listed below. Correct answers are reinforced throughout; students are rewarded and corrected through animated graphics and optional sound. Teaching/instruction manual contains list of words keyed by grade level.

MISSING LETTERS - Activity picks word from word list and asks student to fill in missing word.

SCRAMBLED WORDS - Word is chosen from word list and letters are scrambled. Student must give correct word.

MATCH THE LETTERS - Computer chooses two words from word list and highlights particular letter in first word. Student is asked to identify letter in second word which is in same position.

ALPHABETIZING - Student is given list of five words from word list to be put in alphabetical order.

HANGMAN - Standard hangman game is played with graphics using words from word list. Student may guess entire word and/or each letter.

ID: H268

WORDS IN CONTEXT SPELLING SERIES - LEVEL A

Publisher: Micro-Ed, Inc.

Also available from: EISI (Educational Instructional Systems, Inc.) • K-12 Micromedia • MARCK • Scholastic Software • Texas Instruments

Grade: 2

Format: 7 programs on cassette or diskette

Hardware: Commodore 64 • PET • Apple II Plus; 48K (DOS 3.3) • TRS-80 Color Computer; 32K • TI 99/4 • VIC

Language: BASIC

Source Code: no

Price: $49.95

This drill and practice series is designed to supplement regular classroom instruction. Each program works as follows. First, the student selects the desired lesson from the 5 or 6 offered in the program. This is done by means of a selection menu describing the rules or patterns taught by each lesson. After a lesson has been chosen, the computer displays 10 words that will be used during the lesson. This list of words may be recalled to the screen by the student throughout the lesson. A total of 10 problems are then presented. Each problem consists of a sentence with a word missing. The correct word to be supplied in each instance will be one of the ten spelling words listed for the lesson. If the student does not know the answer, the spelling list may be recalled to the screen, or the computer may be asked to give the answer. At the end of each lesson, the student's performance is summarized, including a listing of the specific words that gave trouble.

PROGRAM 1 - The 10 words in this lesson cover short A, short E, short I, short O, short U, and short-vowel words with double consonants.

PROGRAM 2 - This lesson covers short-vowel words ending with K, and with SH, CH, TH, and NG.

PROGRAM 3 - The lessons in this program cover long-vowel words: A with AI or AY; with A-consonant letter-E; E with E, EE, or EA; I with Y or IE; I with I-consonant letter-E.

PROGRAM 4 - This lesson covers long I words with I or IGH, long O words with O, OA, OW, or O-consonant letter-E words, words with vowel sounds spelled by UE, UI or EW, OO, or U-consonant letter-E.

PROGRAM 5 - This lesson covers some irregularly spelled words, words using U or OO, words starting with WH, words using AU, AW or A before L to spell the vowel sound in "small" or "haul" or "hawk", and words using OU or OW to spell the vowel sound in "sound" or "cow".

PROGRAM 6 - This lesson covers OI or OY to spell the vowel sound in "voice" or "joy", EAR or EER for ending sounds in "year" or "dear", AIR or ARE for ending sounds in "pair" or "rare", OR or ORE for vowel-R sound in "sort" or "sore", using AR to spell vowel-R sound in "farm".

PROGRAM 7 - This lesson covers IR, UR and ER to spell words like "chirp", "curve", or "perch", using AR, ER or OR for endings that sound alike, using Y to spell the long E ending sound, words with silent consonant letters, words sounding the same, but with different spelling and meaning.

ID: H269

WORDS IN CONTEXT SPELLING SERIES - LEVEL B

Publisher: Micro-Ed, Inc.

Also available from: EISI (Educational Instructional Systems, Inc.) • K-12 Micromedia • MARCK • Scholastic Software • Texas Instruments

Grade: 3

Format: 7 programs on cassette or diskette

Hardware: Commodore 64 • PET • Apple II Plus; 48K (DOS 3.3) • TRS-80 Color Computer; 32K • TI 99/4 • VIC

Language: BASIC

Source Code: no

Price: $49.95

This drill and practice series is designed to supplement regular classroom instruction. Each program works as follows. First, the student selects the desired lesson from 5 or 6 offered in the program. This is done by means of a selection menu describing the rules or patterns taught by each lesson. After a lesson has been chosen, the computer displays 10 words that will be used during the lesson. This list of words may be recalled to the screen by the student throughout the lesson. A total of 10 problems are then presented. Each problem consists of a sentence with a word missing. The correct word to be supplied in each instance will be one of the ten spelling words listed for the lesson. If the student does not know the answer, the spelling list may be recalled to the screen, or the computer may be asked to give the answer. At the end of each lesson, the student's performance is summarized, including a listing of the specific words that gave trouble.

PROGRAM 1 - This lesson covers short-vowel words, using two consonant letters to spell one consonant sound, doubling the last letter before adding ED or ING, two-letter consonant sounds, using QU and the combinations CK, NK and TCH, spelling the long A sound with AI, AY or A-consonant letter-E.

PROGRAM 2 - Covers long E with E, EA or EE, long I with I, I-consonant- E, IGH, or Y, long O with O, O-consonant-E, OA, or OW, adding ING to words ending with E, using G, J, GE, or DGE for the soft G sound.

PROGRAM 3 - This lesson covers using S, C, CE or SS to spell the sound at the beginning of the word "sun", words ending with silent E, using OO, using AL, AU or AW to spell words such as "source" or "fall", words that have the vowel sound spelled by OU or OW.

PROGRAM 4 - Covers some irregularly spelled words with OU, spelling vowel-R sounds with ER, IR, UR, AR, OR, ORE, AIR, ARE, EAR, or EER, and spelling contractions.

PROGRAM 5 - This program covers homonyms, words with silent consonant letters, using Y at the end of a word, changing Y to I and adding ES.

PROGRAM 6 - This lesson covers vowel-R sounds in 2-syllable words with OR, AR and ER, compound words, and 2-syllable words with double consonant letters.

PROGRAM 7 - This lesson covers two-syllable words divided between consonant letters, a vowel and a consonant, a consonant between two vowels, after a consonant between two vowels, and with three connected consonant letters.

ID: H270

WORDS IN CONTEXT SPELLING SERIES - LEVEL C

Publisher: Micro-Ed, Inc.

Also available from: EISI (Educational Instructional Systems, Inc.) • K-12 Micromedia • MARCK • Scholastic Software • Texas Instruments

Grade: 4

Format: 7 programs on cassette or diskette

Hardware: Commodore 64 • PET • Apple II Plus; 48K (DOS 3.3) • TRS-80 Color Computer; 32K • TI 99/4 • VIC

Language: BASIC

Source Code: no

Price: $49.95

This drill and practice series is designed to supplement regular classroom instruction. Each program works as follows. First, the student selects the desired lesson from the 5 or 6 offered in the program. This is done by means of a selection menu describing the rules or patterns taught by each lesson. After a lesson has been chosen, the computer displays 10 words that will be used during the lesson. This list of words may be recalled to the screen by the student throughout the lesson. A total of 10 problems are then presented. Each problem consists of a sentence with a word missing. The correct word to be supplied in each instance will be one of the ten spelling words listed for the lesson. If the student does not know the answer, the spelling list may be recalled to the screen, or the computer may be asked to give the answer. At the end of each lesson, the student's performance is summarized, including a listing of the specific words that gave trouble.

PROGRAM 1 - This lesson covers long and short sounds of A, E, I, O, U and vowel sounds with AL, AU, OI, OY, OU, OW or OO.

PROGRAM 2 - This lesson includes words with various vowel-R sounds, three patterns for ING endings, and compound words.

PROGRAM 3 - Covers irregularly spelled words, contractions, two- syllable words ending with Y, and words ending in AL, EL, LE, AR, ER, or OR.

PROGRAM 4 - Covers using C to spell the sound of K or S, words with silent consonant letters, homonyms, and two-syllable words with a vowel on each side of two consecutive consonant letters.

PROGRAM 5 - This lesson covers two-syllable words with a vowel on each side of two consecutive consonant letters or with a syllable break before or after the two consonant letters,

and vowel- consonant patterns with breaks before or after the consonant.

PROGRAM 6 - Covers words with two consecutive vowels where the syllable break is between the vowels, vowel sounds in soft syllables, irregularly spelled words, and words with a soft-syllable suffix.

PROGRAM 7 - Covers words with soft-syllable suffixes or prefixes, 3 syllable words, and some names of days and months.

ID: H271

WORDS IN CONTEXT SPELLING SERIES - LEVEL D

Publisher: Micro-Ed, Inc.

Also available from: EISI (Educational Instructional Systems, Inc.) • K-12 Micromedia • MARCK • Scholastic Software • Texas Instruments

Grade: 5

Format: 7 programs on cassette or diskette

Hardware: Commodore 64 • PET • Apple II Plus; 48K (DOS 3.3) • TRS-80 Color Computer; 32K • TI 99/4 • VIC

Language: BASIC

Source Code: no

Price: $49.95

This drill and practice series is designed to supplement regular classroom instruction. Each program works as follows. First, the student selects the desired lesson from the 5 or 6 offered in the program. This is done by means of a selection menu describing the rules or patterns taught by each lesson. After a lesson has been chosen, the computer displays 10 words that will be used during the lesson. This list of words may be recalled to the screen by the student throughout the lesson. A total of 10 problems are then presented. Each problem consists of a sentence with a word missing. The correct word to be supplied in each instance will be one of the ten spelling words listed for the lesson. If the student does not know the answer, the spelling list may be recalled to the screen, or the computer may be asked to give the answer. At the end of each lesson, the student's performance is summarized, including a listing of the specific words that gave trouble.

PROGRAM 1 - This lesson covers long and short sounds of A, E, I, O, and U, and words with OO, OU, and OW.

PROGRAM 2 - Covers words with AL, AU, AW or OI, AR or ARE, OAR, OR or ORE, RE, IR or UR, words with silent consonant letters, and some homonyms.

PROGRAM 3 - Covers words ending in ED, ING, AL, EL or LE, AR, ER or OR, Y or EY, and some compound words.

PROGRAM 4 - Covers compound words, and words with a vowel on each side of two consonants.

PROGRAM 5 - Covers words with a vowel-consonant-vowel pattern, words with a vowel on each side of three consonants, words with two vowels together where the syllable break comes between the vowels, ending with AGE, TURE or IVE.

PROGRAM 6 - Covers words with prefixes of EX, RE, UN, COM, CON, PRE, and PRO, and with suffixes of ANCE, ENCE, MENT, NESS, ABLE, IBLE, ANT, ENT, FUL, and LESS.

PROGRAM 7 - Covers three- and four-syllable words, words with ION, SION, and TION suffixes, and words with both a prefix and a suffix.

ID: H272

WORDS IN CONTEXT SPELLING SERIES - LEVEL E

Publisher: Micro-Ed, Inc.

Also available from: EISI (Educational Instructional Systems, Inc.) • K-12 Micromedia • MARCK • Scholastic Software • Texas Instruments

Grade: 6

Format: 7 programs on cassette or diskette

Hardware: Commodore 64 • PET • Apple II Plus; 48K (DOS 3.3) • TRS-80 Color Computer; 32K • TI 99/4 • VIC

Language: BASIC

Source Code: no

Price: $49.95

This drill and practice series is designed to supplement regular classroom instruction. Each program works as follows. First, the student selects the desired lesson from the 5 or 6 offered in the program. This is done by means of a selection menu describing the rules or patterns taught by each lesson. After a lesson has been chosen, the computer displays 10 words that will be used during the lesson. This list of words may be recalled to the screen by the student throughout the lesson. A total of 10 problems are then presented. Each problem consists of a sentence with a word missing. The correct word to be supplied in each instance will be one of the ten spelling words listed for the lesson. If the student does not know the answer, the spelling list may be recalled to the screen, or the computer may be asked to give the answer. At the end of each lesson, the student's performance is summarized, including a listing of the specific words that gave trouble.

PROGRAM 1 - This lesson covers one-syllable words with long- or short- vowel sounds, some compound words, and words with AL, AW, AU, OI, OO, OU, OW, AR, AIR, ARE, EAR, EER, ER, IR, UR, OAR, and OR.

PROGRAM 2 - Covers compound words with a vowel-R sound, vowel sounds in soft-syllable endings, two-syllable words with vowel- multiple consonant-vowel patterns or vowel-single consonant- vowel patterns, and words in which a syllable ends between two vowels.

PROGRAM 3 - This lesson includes two-syllable words in which the first syllable has the sound of short A, short E, short I, short O, or short U.

PROGRAM 4 - Covers two-syllable words in which one syllable has the long sound of A, E, I, O, or U.

PROGRAM 5 - Covers two-syllable words in which one syllable has the sound of OO, or the vowel sound in COW, BOY, SAW, or CAR.

PROGRAM 6 - Covers two-syllable words in which one syllable has the vowel sound in FOR or HER, words with the vowel sounds in AIR, CARE, EAR or HERE, words with the prefixes COM, CON, EN, EX, IN and RE, and words with the suffixes ANCE, ENCE, MENT, NESS, SION, and TION.

PROGRAM 7 - Covers words with four syllables, words with both prefixes and suffixes, words with the prefixes DE, DIS, PRE, PRO, and UN, and with the suffixes ABLE, ANT, ENT, FUL, IBLE, LESS and OUS.

ID: H273

WORDS PER MINUTE

Publisher: Comaldor

Format: cassette or diskette

Hardware: PET

Price: $20.00

This program helps calculate the number of words in a reading selection. From the time START is pressed, the screen displays in large numerals the number of words per minute that the students have read as they are reading the selection. When finished, the student notes the number displayed on the screen.

ID: H274

WORDSEARCH

Publisher: Hartley Courseware, Inc.

Also available from: Academic Software • Opportunities For Learning, Inc.

Grade: 2-10

Format: 1 diskette

Hardware: Apple II; 48K with Applesoft in ROM (DOS 3.2 or 3.3); printer

Language: Applesoft BASIC

Price: $26.95

Allows teacher to enter series of words to create word search puzzle to specifications of user, with options of overlapping words, rendering words frontwards, backwards, or diagonally, or rendering them left to right and top to bottom only. Prints completed puzzle; also prints answer key on request.

ID: H275

WORDWATCH

Publisher: Instant Software[T.M.]

Also available from: Academic Software • MARCK • Queue, Inc.

Format: cassette

Hardware: TRS-80

Source Code: no

Price: $9.95

WORDWATCH consists of four different programs, each designed to enhance students' understanding of word relationships, resulting in improved vocabulary and decreased dictionary dependency. Written documentation is provided.

WORD-RACE - A program in which student must choose proper definition of given word.

HIDE 'N SPELL - Asks students to find misspellings.

SPELLING BEE - Student takes pre-recorded quiz in which words are played aloud.

SPELLING TUTOR - Words are jumbled, reversed, or otherwise altered, and student must straighten them out.

ID: H276

WORKING WITH THE ALPHABET

Publisher: Orange Cherry Media

Also available from: Academic Software • Queue, Inc.

Grade: K-3

Format: cassette or diskette

Hardware: PET 2000 or 4000; 16K • TRS-80 MOD I or III; 16K • Apple; 16K • Apple II; 16K

Price: $15.00/cassette; $28.00/cassette set of 2; $34.00/diskette

ALPHABET SOUP - This is a program which helps students who are just learning the alphabet. Children are given individual practice in identifying the letters and their sequence. The program has various exercises, including filling in letters missing in the alphabetical sequence and putting 26 letters in proper alphabetical order in a race against the clock.

ALPHABETICAL ORDER - This program offers a short review of the sequence of the alphabet and then goes on to illustrate how words are placed into alphabetical order. The instructor or the student may also select the level of difficulty in exercises.

ID: H277
WRITING SKILLS: SENTENCE COMBINING

Publisher: Milliken Publishing Company

Grade: 4-8

Format: 2 diskettes

Hardware: Apple II Plus; 48K

Price: $95.00

The package is based upon the strategy of sentence combining - a proven method of leading students toward writing more fluent, "adult" sentences. The program is designed to increase each student's repertory of sentence structures and to encourage, through example and practice, the transfer of these structures to the student's independent writing. The package includes two diskettes, duplicating masters for supplementary activity, and a comprehensive Teacher's Guide. Topics covered are - And in predicates, And in subjects, 'S and S', Regular Adjectives and Adverbs, Who, Which, and That, Good and Well, Using Because, But with predicates and sentences, Where, When and How, Subject and Verb Agreement, Pronouns with and, using Before and After, And with predicates and sentences, Multiple Combinations. Each lesson uses the following instructional sequence: 1. Concept Introduction - the computer provides a brief, objective-based introduction to the concept presented in the lesson. Graphics are often used to illustrate key points. 2. Interactive Examples - the computer then leads students through carefully selected and structured examples followed by concise skill-building exercises and immediate feedback to student responses. Use of a step-by-step approach ensures a fuller understanding of the concept. 3. Motivating Practice - Students are now ready to demonstrate understanding of the comcept by seeing, reading, and manipulating complete sentences. Each lesson uses a highly interactive and motivating format to evaluate student mastery and to provide immediate feedback and reinforcement. Students in need of help are branched to sections providing remedial instruction. Students demonstrate mastery or weakness according to performance criteria set by teacher. Each diskette in the package contains a Manager Program which allows teacher to maintain records for up to 100 students. The teacher can make individual or class assignments, review student progress, and identify student problem areas.

LIBRARY SKILLS

ID: I1
ADVANCED DEWEY DECIMAL SYSTEM
Publisher: RIGHT ON PROGRAMS

Date: July 82

Grade: 1-6

Format: cassette or diskette

Hardware: Apple II; 48K with Applesoft in ROM (DOS 3.2 or 3.3) • PET; 16K

Language: BASIC

Source Code: yes

Price: $13.00/cassette; $15.00/diskette

Program explains in detail principles behind Dewey Decimal System and exactly how numbering system works. It takes one section of system, SPORTS, and shows how each sport, depending upon how it is played and equipment used, has its own "place" and correct number in the system. Game follows. Correct answers are rewarded and incorrect answers are corrected with no penalty.

ID: I2
ALMANACS
Publisher: Computer Assisted Library Instruction Co., Inc. (CALICO)

Grade: 7-12

Format: 1 diskette

Hardware: Apple II; 48K (DOS 3.3)

Language: Applesoft BASIC

Price: $25.00

A self-paced tutorial for use in library instruction. Gives immediate reinforcement to correct answers.

ID: I3
BARTLETT'S FAMILIAR QUOTATIONS
Publisher: Computer Assisted Library Instruction Co., Inc. (CALICO)

Grade: 7-12

Format: 1 diskette

Hardware: Apple II; 48K (DOS 3.3)

Language: Applesoft BASIC

Price: $25.00

A self-paced tutorial for use in library instruction. Gives immediate reinforcement to correct answers.

ID: I4
BASIC FICTION SKILLS
Publisher: RIGHT ON PROGRAMS

Date: July 82

Grade: 1-6

Format: cassette or diskette

Hardware: Apple II; 48K with Applesoft in ROM (DOS 3.2 or 3.3) • PET; 16K

Language: BASIC

Source Code: yes

Price: $13.00/cassette; $15.00/diskette

Program designed for very young children will teach them basic principles of shelving fiction books in library. It will explain meaning of fiction and show children various letters which appear on spines of library books and their meanings. Game follows, rewarding correct answers, and correcting incorrect answers with no penalty.

ID: I5
BIOGRAPHIES
Publisher: RIGHT ON PROGRAMS

Date: July 82

Grade: 1-6

Format: cassette or diskette

Hardware: Apple II; 48K with Applesoft in ROM (DOS 3.2 or 3.3) • PET; 16K

Language: BASIC

Source Code: yes

Price: $13.00/cassette; $15.00/diskette

Program is devoted exclusively to locating biographies in library. It explains why biographies are shelved as they are, what spine markings mean, and how to find books wanted from biography section of library. Game follows.

ID: I6
CURRENT BIOGRAPHY
Publisher: Computer Assisted Library Instruction Co., Inc. (CALICO)

Grade: 7-12

Format: 1 diskette

Hardware: Apple II; 48K (DOS 3.3)

Language: Applesoft BASIC

Price: $25.00

A self-paced tutorial on a popular library reference series.

ID: I7
DICTIONARY SKILLS
Publisher: RIGHT ON PROGRAMS

Date: July 82

Grade: 1-6

Format: cassette or diskette

Hardware: Apple II; 48K with Applesoft in ROM (DOS 3.2 or 3.3) • PET; 16K

Language: BASIC

Source Code: yes

Price: $13.00/cassette; $15.00/diskette

Program shows a listing as it would appear in dictionary. Information given is highlighted and explained. Game gives student opportunity to test skills learned in part one. Correct answers are rewarded and incorrect answers are corrected with no penalty.

ID: I8
ESSAY AND GENERAL LITERATURE INDEX

Publisher: Computer Assisted Library Instruction Co., Inc. (CALICO)

Grade: 7-12

Format: 1 diskette

Hardware: Apple II; 48K (DOS 3.3)

Language: Applesoft BASIC

Price: $25.00

A self-paced tutorial on a popular library reference series.

ID: I9
LEARNING ABOUT CATALOG CARDS

Publisher: RIGHT ON PROGRAMS

Also available from: Academic Software • K-12 Micromedia • Queue, Inc.

Grade: 1-6

Format: cassette or diskette

Hardware: Apple II; 48K with Applesoft in ROM (DOS 3.2 or 3.3) • PET; 16K

Language: BASIC

Source Code: yes

Price: $13.00/cassette; $15.00/diskette

An actual catalog card is reproduced on the screen. The student is asked specific questions about the information on the card and types in his/her answers. A feature of this program is that if the student gives an incorrect answer, the computer not only tells the student the correct answer but, in reverse color, actually shows the student the exact location on the card where that information can be found.

ID: I10
LEARNING TO LOCATE BOOKS ON THE SHELF

Publisher: RIGHT ON PROGRAMS

Also available from: Academic Software • K-12 Micromedia • Queue, Inc.

Grade: 1-6

Format: cassette or diskette

Hardware: Apple II; 48K with Applesoft in ROM (DOS 3.2 or 3.3) • PET; 16K

Language: BASIC

Source Code: yes

Price: $13.00/cassette; $15.00/diskette

This program explains the different ways in which books are shelved in libraries. Fiction and non-fiction markings on the spines are explained, as well as how to find those books on the shelves.

ID: I11
LEARNING TO UNDERSTAND THE CARD CATALOG

Publisher: RIGHT ON PROGRAMS

Also available from: Academic Software • K-12 Micromedia • Queue, Inc.

Grade: 1-6

Format: cassette or diskette

Hardware: Apple II; 48K with Applesoft in ROM (DOS 3.2 or 3.3) • PET; 16K

Language: BASIC

Source Code: yes

Price: $13.00/cassette; $15.00/diskette

This program explains the 3 ways to look up a book in the card catalog. After providing all the basic information, the student is asked a series of questions about various books and is required to type the correct answers, indicating s/he knows which drawer to consult, depending on the information available.

ID: I12
LEARNING TO UNDERSTAND THE COPYRIGHT NOTICE

Publisher: RIGHT ON PROGRAMS

Date: July 82

Grade: 1-6

Format: cassette or diskette

Hardware: Apple II; 48K with Applesoft in ROM (DOS 3.2 or 3.3) • PET; 16K

Language: BASIC

Source Code: yes

Price: $13.00/cassette; $15.00/diskette

Program stresses meaning and importance of copyright notice. Program also discusses preface and acknowledgments page. Student answers questions about information given. In game, correct answers are rewarded and incorrect answers are corrected with no penalty.

ID: I13
LEARNING TO UNDERSTAND THE TITLE PAGE

Publisher: RIGHT ON PROGRAMS

Also available from: Academic Software • K-12 Micromedia • Queue, Inc.

Grade: 1-6

Format: cassette or diskette

Hardware: Apple II; 48K with Applesoft in ROM (DOS 3.2 or 3.3) • PET; 16K

Language: BASIC

Price: $13.00/cassette; $15.00/diskette

An actual Title Page is reproduced on the screen, and the student is asked questions pertaining to it. For each correct answer the student "earns" a portion of a picture. When the student answers all the questions correctly, the completed picture appears on the screen with appropriate comments on the student's success on completing the picture.

ID: I14
LEARNING TO USE AN INDEX

Publisher: RIGHT ON PROGRAMS

Also available from: Academic Software • K-12 Micromedia • Queue, Inc.

Grade: 1-6

Format: cassette or diskette

Hardware: Apple II; 48K with Applesoft in ROM (DOS 3.2 or 3.3) • PET; 16K

Language: BASIC

Source Code: yes

Price: $13.00/cassette; $15.00/diskette

A sample index is shown on the screen. The student is asked a series of questions and types in the correct answers. At the outset of the program the student is told s/he is "lost in the woods". Every correct answer brings a clue to help the student get home safely.

ID: I15

LEARNING TO USE THE TABLE OF CONTENTS

Publisher: RIGHT ON PROGRAMS

Also available from: Academic Software • K-12 Micromedia • Queue, Inc.

Grade: 1-6

Format: cassette or diskette

Hardware: Apple II; 48K with Applesoft in ROM (DOS 3.2 or 3.3) • PET; 16K

Language: BASIC

Source Code: yes

Price: $13.00/cassette; $15.00/diskette

An actual Table of Contents is reproduced on the screen, and the student is asked questions pertaining to it. For each correct answer, the student can take a turn in the "maze". If the student has all the right answers (and makes all the right turns), s/he completes the maze and gets "home" safely.

ID: I16

LIBRARY CATALOG

Publisher: Computer Assisted Library Instruction Co., Inc. (CALICO)

Grade: Elementary and up

Format: 1 diskette

Hardware: Apple II; 48K (DOS 3.3)

Language: Applesoft BASIC

Price: $25.00

A self-paced tutorial for use in library instruction.

ID: I17

LIBRARY SKILLS

Publisher: Micro Power & Light Company

Also available from: Academic Software • K-12 Micromedia • Queue, Inc.

Grade: 4 and up

Format: diskette

Hardware: Apple II; 32K with Applesoft in ROM

Price: $24.95

What's in the library and how to find it is the subject of this program. Subjects include fiction, nonfiction, biographies, the Dewey Decimal System, the card catalog and using reference materials. Following the tutorial presenting each new topic, the student has an opportunity to do a number of relevant exercises, intended to reinforce his or her understanding of the material just covered. Throughout, the student helps 'Allie Gator' select the right kind of reference material, and then further helps Allie find it! A concluding master quiz offers the student a chance to do away with Allie - provided the student can demonstrate his or her ability to now use the library without help!

ID: I18

LIBRARY TERMS

Publisher: Micro-Ed, Inc.

Also available from: Academic Software • Queue, Inc.

Grade: Elementary

Format: cassette or diskette

Hardware: Commodore 64 • PET

Language: BASIC

Source Code: no

Price: $7.95

The student is given sixteen library terms and a series of statements. The student is to match each statement with the term that best fits it. If the student does not know the answer to a problem, pressing the question mark key will cause the answer to be revealed. At the end of the lesson, the student's performance is summarized.

ID: I19

MEDIA SKILLS

Publisher: TIES, Minnesota School Districts Data Processing Joint Board

Date: Nov. 81

Grade: 5-8

Format: 4 programs on 3 diskettes with backup

Hardware: Apple II; 48K with Applesoft in ROM (DOS 3.3) • Apple II Plus

Price: $84.95; $7.50/documentation

This package is designed to provide instruction and practice in using the card catalog. It includes lessons on identifying the three major kinds of catalog cards, locating cards in the card catalog, using call numbers and the Dewey Decimal System, and finding specific information on a catalog card. To provide reinforcement, the student must answer questions which are interspersed throughout the lessons. The package also includes a simulation of using the card catalog. In this exercise, the student must apply all of the major concepts presented in the lessons consecutively, or individual lessons may be assigned to students who require additional instruction in a particular concept.

CONCENTRATION - This is a matching activity. The student matches Dewey Decimal numbers with the subject headings. One or two students may use this activity.

DEW IT WITH DEWEY - This is a matching activity. The student matches the Dewey Decimal numbers with the subject headings.

HANGMAN - This is a word game in which the computer randomly selects a media term from a file of 16 media terms.

The student guesses one letter at a time, attempting to correctly spell the word.

SCRAMBLE - This is a program in which the computer scrambles the letters of a media term. The student attempts to respond with the correct spelling within a specified length of time (90 seconds).

ID: 120

PERIODICAL INDEXES

Publisher: Computer Assisted Library Instruction Co., Inc. (CALICO)

Grade: 7-12

Format: 1 diskette

Hardware: Apple II; 48K (DOS 3.3)

Language: Applesoft BASIC

Price: $25.00

A self-paced tutorial for use in library instruction.

ID: 121

POETRY INDEXES

Publisher: Computer Assisted Library Instruction Co., Inc. (CALICO)

Grade: 7-12

Format: 1 diskette

Hardware: Apple II; 48K (DOS 3.3)

Language: Applesoft BASIC

Price: $25.00

A self-paced tutorial for use in library instruction.

ID: 122

PUTTING FICTION BOOKS IN ALPHABETICAL ORDER

Publisher: Micro-Ed, Inc.

Grade: Elementary

Format: cassette or diskette

Hardware: Commodore 64 • PET

Language: BASIC

Source Code: no

Price: $7.95

The rules for arranging fiction books alphabetically on library shelves are explained. Then two groups of fiction books are presented in sequence. The student is to list the books in each group in the order in which they would appear on library shelves. At the end of the lesson, the student's performance is summarized.

ID: 123

USING REFERENCE TABLES IN AN ALMANAC

Publisher: RIGHT ON PROGRAMS

Date: July 82

Grade: 1-6

Format: cassette or diskette

Hardware: Apple II; 48K with Applesoft in ROM (DOS 3.2 or 3.3) • PET; 16K

Language: BASIC

Source Code: yes

Price: $13.00/cassette; $15.00/diskette

Program shows several different lists and gives hypothetical information. Student is asked to answer questions about information given. In game, same type of questions are asked, using different basic information. Correct answers are rewarded and incorrect answers are corrected with no penalty.

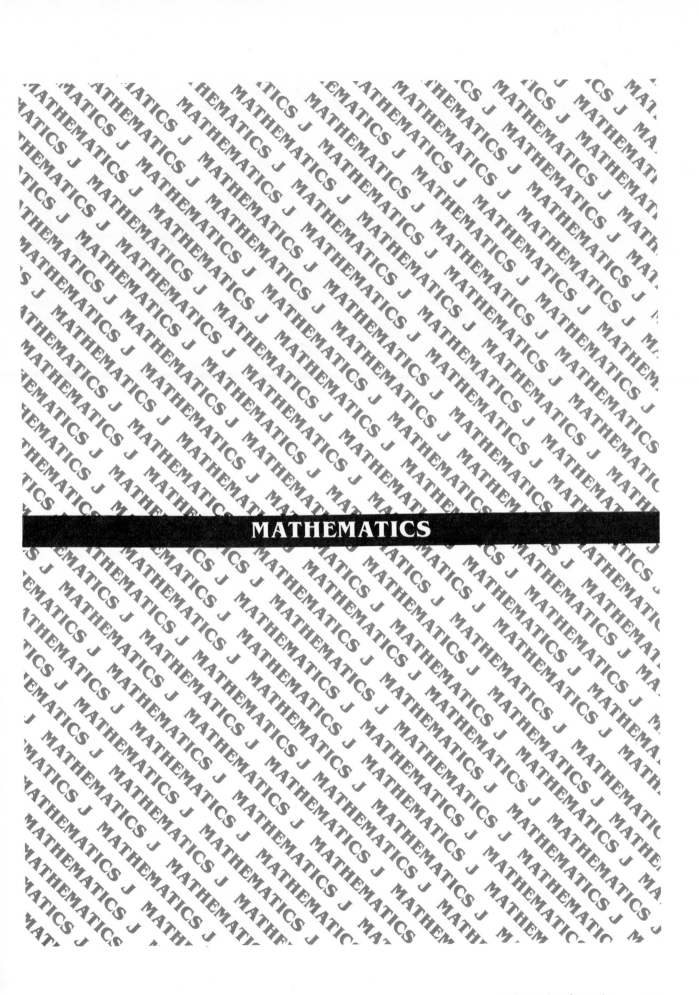

MATHEMATICS

ID: J1

1-2-3 DIGIT MULTIPLICATION

Publisher: Microcomputer Workshops

Also available from: Academic Software • EISI (Educational Instructional Systems, Inc.) • MARCK • Micro-Ed, Inc. • Queue, Inc.

Grade: Elementary

Format: cassette

Hardware: PET

Language: BASIC

Source Code: no

Price: $20.00

This program presents problems in multiplying a 3-digit number by a 1-, 2-, or 3-digit number at the option of the learner. All problems are generated randomly so that a different problem will be presented each time the program is run. The learner works with each problem just as if he/she were doing it on a piece of paper.

ID: J2

ABSOLUTE

Publisher: Cow Bay Computing

Format: 1 cassette

Hardware: PET; any model except VIC 20 or 8032

Price: $15.00

This program covers step-by-step solution of absolute value equations.

ID: J3

ADDING FRACTIONS

Publisher: Microcomputer Workshops

Date: July 82

Grade: 5-8

Format: cassette or diskette

Hardware: Apple II; 48K with Applesoft in ROM • PET; 16K; cassette • TRS-80 MOD I or III; 16K

Language: BASIC

Source Code: no

Price: $20.00/cassette; $24.95/diskette

Program generates problems randomly that give student practice in adding fractions with uncommon denominators. Program comes in both vertical and horizontal formats. All work is done on screen. If student is unable to find least common denominator, program branches to section that will explain how LCD is found. Student completes addition when denominators are equal. All errors are flagged immediately and explanations given. Written documentation is provided.

ID: J4

ADDING OR SUBTRACTING TWO AND THREE PLACE NUMBERS IN COLUMNS

Publisher: Micro-Ed, Inc.

Also available from: Academic Software • EISI (Educational Instructional Systems, Inc.) • MARCK • Queue, Inc.

Grade: Elementary

Format: cassette or diskette

Hardware: Commodore 64 • PET

Language: BASIC

Source Code: no

Price: $7.95

This program presents addition or subtraction problems using two and three place numbers in columns. The learner works with each problem beginning with the units column on the right, (as would be done with paper and pencil) and moving left as guided by an arrow displayed under the appropriate column. If the learner does not know the answer to a problem, the question mark key may be pressed and the computer will give the answer. The learner may terminate the lesson by pressing the letter "S." The computer will then summarize the student's performance.

ID: J5

ADDING WITH OBJECTS

Publisher: Micro-Ed, Inc.

Also available from: Academic Software • EISI (Educational Instructional Systems, Inc.) • MARCK • Queue, Inc.

Grade: 1-3

Format: cassette or diskette

Hardware: Commodore 64 • PET

Language: BASIC

Source Code: no

Price: $7.95

Each lesson presents ten randomly generated addition problems with sums up to twenty. Small diamond shapes representing the numbers to be added appear on the screen. If the learner's answer is wrong, the computer will give the right answer. If the learner presses the question mark, the computer will also give the right answer. At the end of each lesson, the learner's performance is summarized.

ID: J6

ADDITION AND SUBTRACTION OF WHOLE NUMBERS

Publisher: Orange Cherry Media

Also available from: Academic Software • Queue, Inc.

Grade: K-3

Format: cassette or diskette

Hardware: PET 2000 or 4000; 16K • TRS-80 MOD I or III; 16K • Apple; 16K • Apple II; 16K

Price: $15.00/cassette; $56.00/cassette set of 4; $67.00/diskette

This set is designed to help youngsters develop basic math skills in an effective and enjoyable way. In each program, concepts are introduced with simple, easily-grasped examples, followed by test questions of increasing difficulty. Computer calculates right and wrong answers. Immediate feedback and reinforcement are provided, together with provisions for differing levels and abilities of students.

ADDITION SUMS TO 10

SUBTRACTION DIFFERENCES TO 10

SUMS AND DIFFERENCES TO 30
WORD PROBLEMS WITH ADDITION AND SUBTRACTION

ID: J7

ADDITION DRILL/MULTIPLICATION DRILL

Publisher: Edu-Soft[T.M.]

Also available from: Academic Software

Grade: Elementary, Remedial

Format: 2 programs on cassette or diskette

Hardware: TRS-80 MOD I or III; 16K (cassette) or 32K (diskette), with with Level II BASIC

Price: $14.95/cassette; $19.95/diskette

The programs provide drilling in whole number addition and multiplication. Problems displayed in oversized numbers. Flashing digits emphasize focus of lesson or indicate correct answer. Student may choose from 5 levels of difficulty. In both programs, numbers carried from one column to next are displayed in small numbers above the columns. Student may choose from addition practice problem or quiz.

ID: J8

ADDITION WITH CARRY

Publisher: Microcomputer Workshops

Also available from: Academic Software • EISI (Educational Instructional Systems, Inc.) • MARCK • Micro-Ed, Inc. • Queue, Inc.

Grade: Elementary

Format: cassette

Hardware: PET

Language: BASIC

Source Code: no

Price: $20.00

This program gives the learner practice in addition with a carry and allows him to design any size of problem up to 9 rows and 9 columns. All problems are generated randomly so that a different problem will be presented each time the program is run. The learner works with each problem just as if he/she were doing it on a piece of paper.

ID: J9

ADDITION/SUBTRACTION 1

Publisher: Scott, Foresman and Co.

Also available from: McKilligan Supply Corp. • Texas Instruments

Date: Jan. 82

Grade: 1-2

Format: module

Hardware: TI 99/4A; speech synthesizer recommended

Source Code: no

Price: $44.95 ($39.95 from TI)

Teaches basic arithmetic skills and provides drills for reinforcement. Developed in conjunction with Texas Instruments. The program covers basic facts with sums through 9.

ID: J10

ADDITION/SUBTRACTION 2

Publisher: Scott, Foresman and Co.

Also available from: McKilligan Supply Corp. • Texas Instruments

Date: Jan. 82

Grade: 1-2

Format: module

Hardware: TI 99/4A; speech synthesizer recommended

Source Code: no

Price: $44.95 ($39.95 from TI)

Second in a series of addition and subtraction tutorial packages involving more difficult problems and techniques; developed in conjunction with Texas Instruments. Covers basic facts with sums through 18.

ID: J11

ADVANCED GRAPHICS

Publisher: Radio Shack®

Also available from: McKilligan Supply Corp.

Date: 1982

Grade: Secondary

Format: cassette or diskette

Hardware: TRS-80 MOD I; 16K with Level II BASIC • TRS-80 MOD III; 16K with Model III BASIC

Language: BASIC

Source Code: yes

Price: $29.95

Secondary math package contains two programs: PLOTTING FUNCTIONS, and PLOTTING POLAR AND PARAMETRIC EQUATIONS. Programs allow students to study and plot equations in a number of forms, and to change equations for a wide variety of applications. A selected investigations section allows extensive practice in problem solving. User's guide and programming guide are provided.

ID: J12

AESTHEOMETRY - VOLUME 1

Publisher: Minnesota Educational Computing Consortium

Also available from: Academic Software • Creative Computing • K-12 Micromedia

Date: June 82

Grade: Junior High and up

Format: diskette

Hardware: Apple II; 32K with Applesoft in ROM (DOS 3.3)

Language: Applesoft BASIC

Source Code: no

Price: $39.30

Geometry program deals with topic of curves by viewing them from two perspectives. First method demonstrates "space concepts" of elliptical, parabolic, and hyperbolic curves. Curve sketching designs are developed to provide aesthetic view of geometric shapes. Second method uses mathematical approach and defines curve as intersection of plane with cone. Support booklet included.

ID: J13
ALGEBRA

Publisher: TYCOM Associates

Also available from: K-12 Micromedia • MARCK • Queue, Inc.

Format: 7 programs on cassette

Hardware: PET; 8K; 40 column screen; C2N cassette recorder

Price: $19.95; $24.95/programs on 7 cassettes

This series of programs will assist the student with various topics of Algebra, including set operations, arithmetic operations with signed numbers, addition and multiplication of binomial expressions, solving linear equations, and factoring quadratic expressions. A lesson explaining each type of problem is given, followed by randomly generated problems to be solved by the student. After each problem, the correct answer is provided to check results. These programs may be used concurrently with a course or for review.

ID: J14
ALGEBRA 1

Publisher: Edu-Ware Services

Also available from: Academic Software • EISI (Educational Instructional Systems, Inc.) • K-12 Micromedia • McKilligan Supply Corp. • Queue, Inc.

Format: diskette

Hardware: Apple; 48K (DOS 3.3)

Language: Applesoft BASIC

Price: $39.95

This program is the first in a sequence of five independent systems. It teaches through positive reinforcement; learners are encouraged to experiment with "learning styles" (cognitive style differentiation) to discover which best suits their needs. Comprehensive documentation illustrates all procedures and explains the system's instructional model. The major content areas are definitions, number line operations, sets, evaluation expressions, and rules for equation reduction. Flow-charted "information maps" mark the learner's progress by designating concepts learned, those still to be learned, and those that need reinforcement.

ID: J15
ALGEBRA 2

Publisher: Edu-Ware Services

Also available from: Academic Software

Format: diskette

Hardware: Apple; 48K (DOS 3.3)

Language: Applesoft BASIC

Price: $39.95

The second in the series, this program elaborates on concepts developed in Algebra 1. New material covered includes rules for addition and multiplication, solving equations, and solving inequalities. The student is again given a choice of learning styles.

ID: J16
ALGEBRA BILLIARDS

Publisher: Curriculum Applications

Also available from: MARCK • Queue, Inc.

Grade: 8-12

Format: cassette

Hardware: TRS-80 MOD I or III; 16K with Level II BASIC

Language: BASIC

Price: $16.95

This program is a tutorial designed to instruct in the mechanics of algebra variable substitution. It is a drill for those familiar with the subject or a tutorial for those just beginning to understand algebra. The student will be presented with an equation to be solved, with one variable as the target of solution. Before beginning the game, the student is required to identify what he is trying to solve. Once underway, the student must solve for the unknown variable. Points are accumulated for correct answers. Should an incorrect answer be given, the program becomes tutorial by solving part of the equation, thus reducing its complexity, and the student can attempt another try at the answer. Major features include very extensive error-checking capabilities which do not allow bad keyboard entry, large printing for easy visual comprehension, a-priori parameter adjustments by teachers for number range, automatic difficulty level adjustment and signed numbers with sound for added student concentration and entertainment. Included is an extensive documentation package for teachers with complete details and recommendations for tailoring to specific student needs, with a suggested worksheet for students.

ID: J17
ALGEBRA DRILL & PRACTICE I

Publisher: CONDUIT

Also available from: MARCK • Queue, Inc.

Date: 1979

Grade: 9-College

Format: diskette

Hardware: Apple II; 48K with Applesoft in ROM (DOS 3.2.1)

Language: BASIC

Source Code: yes

Price: $125.00; $20.00/add'l software copy; $5.95/add'l instructor manual

This package will enable instructors to provide drill, practice, and help for students of algebra with little direct instructor involvement. Once the student knows how to manage the technical details of using the computer, the programs provide all the guidance necessary. The programs provide virtually unlimited example problems and their detailed, step-by-step solutions. Nine drills covering algebraic signs, operations with numeric and algebraic fractions, percents, equations of lines, simplification of algebraic expressions, and word problems are included with an Instructor's Manual (90 pages).

ID: J18
ALGEBRA WORD PROBLEMS

Publisher: TYCOM Associates

Also available from: K-12 Micromedia

Format: 2 programs on cassette

Hardware: PET; 16K; 40 or 80 column; C2N cassette recorder

Price: $19.95

This software is intended to help teach algebra students to set up and solve word problems. The student is led step by step through a logical problem-solving technique, and is asked several multiple-choice questions along the way. The student may then attempt randomly chosen problems in several formats, and with randomly generated values. The student is given the correct answer if a wrong answer is entered, and a score is given upon exiting this phase of the program. Finally, the student may choose to take a mastery test consisting of ten problems. Again, a score is given after all ten problems are attempted. Problem types include consecutive integers, sums and differences, multiples, and areas of rectangles. Students using this program should already know how to solve linear equations in one variable. The emphasis of this program is on interpreting word problems and setting up correct equations. A somewhat abbreviated version is also included which will run on all 8K machines.

ID: J19
APPLE DISSEMINATION DISK #8 - MATH I

Publisher: San Mateo County Office of Education and Computer-Using Educators

Format: 1 diskette

Hardware: Apple; 8 to 32K (DOS 3.2)

Language: INTEGER

Source Code: yes

Price: $10.00

This disk, written at the California School for the Deaf, includes 7 math programs. All may be copied.

BOXES - Student learns beginning algebra by supplying the missing number in an addition or subtraction problem (E 32K)INT

MAKING CHANGE - The student is given an amount of money and must make correct change. Use of high-resolution graphics for coins. (E 32K)INT

PIZZA - Delivering pizzas on a map helps student learn graphing on a coordinate system. (E 8K)INT

HURKLE - Student learns compass directions by looking for "hurkle" on graph. (E 32K)INT

SUPERMATH - Student practices elementary problems in addition, subtraction, multiplication and division. Program determines difficulty level of problems. (E 16K)INT

MASTERMIND - Teaches logical thinking in a "Bagels" format. The student must deduce a 4-color series, using hints from the computer. (S 8K)INT

OTHELLO - Thrilling board game of strategy where the player must leave more black chips on the board than the computer leaves white. (E/S 8K)INT

ID: J20
APPLE DISSEMINATION DISK #9 - MATH II

Publisher: San Mateo County Office of Education and Computer-Using Educators

Format: 1 diskette

Hardware: Apple; 8 to 32K (DOS 3.2)

Language: INTEGER

Source Code: yes

Price: $10.00

The 8 math programs on this were written by the California School for the Deaf; they are not copyrighted.

DRILL - Timed drill on multiplication, division, addition and subtraction. (E 16K)INT

ADRILL - Same as "Drill" but also drills with negative numbers. (E 16K)INT

APPLE BARREL - Estimation is taught by guessing number of apples in Farmer John's barrel. (E 32K)INT

APPLE ARRAY - Same as "Apple Barrel" but apples fall into rectangular shape, making estimations easier. (E 32K)INT

FRED FRACTION - Students are drilled in manipulating fractions, positive reinforcement with amusing animation. (E/S 32K)INT

X ZONE - Student tries to guess position of two lines on graph. The computer responds with a color that helps the student make a logical second guess.

COUNT TO 30 & COUNT TO ? - Student counts the number of marks on the screen. In "Count to?" the range for the number of symbols can be predetermined. (E 8K)INT

STALKER - Two students compete against each other to destroy star wars imperial stalkers. A stalker is destroyed by answering correctly an elementary math problem. (E/S 32K)INT

ID: J21
ARCHIMEDES' APPRENTICE

Publisher: Instant Software[T.M.]

Also available from: Academic Software • MARCK

Grade: 7 and up

Format: cassette

Hardware: TRS-80

Source Code: no

Price: $9.95

This geometry package teaches students formulas used to find volume of any solid object, including parallelopipeds (cubes and rectangular solids), prisms, pyramids, cylinders, cones, and spheres. It will even quiz student on how well a lesson was learned. Written documentation is provided.

ID: J22
ARITH-MAGIC

Publisher: Quality Educational Designs (QED)

Also available from: Activity Resources Company, Inc. • Queue, Inc.

Grade: 2-9

Format: 3 programs on cassette or diskette

Hardware: TRS-80; 16K (cassette) • TRS-80 MOD I or III; 32K • Apple; 32K (DOS 3.2) • Apple; 48K (DOS 3.3 Vers. 2.0) • PET; 16K (cassette or diskette)

Language: BASIC

Price: $35.00

This package includes three game programs and a teacher's manual. It is a versatile set of programs for independent use at various points in the math curriculum.

DIFFY - This game explores number differences. It is intended for grades 2 to 8.

TRIPUZ - This game covers multiplication for grades 3 to 8.

MAGIC SQUARES - For grades 5 to 9.

ID: J23

ARITHMETIC FUNDAMENTALS

Publisher: BLS Inc.

Date: Apr. 82

Grade: 2-5 (reading level 3-4)

Format: 29 diskettes

Hardware: Apple II; 48K with Applesoft in ROM (DOS 3.2 or 3.3)

Language: Applesoft BASIC

Source Code: no

Price: $1479.00/series; $60.00/diskette; $432.00/Addition lesson; $378.00/each other lesson

TUTORCOURSE BLS29 series has been designed by California Test Bureau. Series discusses addition, subtraction, multiplication, and division of whole numbers, as well as money and the addition and subtraction of like fractions. Four programs in series contain total of 29 lessons, each ending with summary and test. Programs utilize self-paced, branch-programmed instruction methods. Comprehensive user documentation provided. Series study time: 8-16 hours.

ADDITION - TUTORPROGRAM BLS29A includes eight lessons, covering two- place numbers; three- and four-place numbers; carrying to tens' and hundreds' place, and carrying more than once; column addition of three whole numbers; addition of money; addition of like fractions; and reducing fractions to lowest terms, and mixed numbers.

SUBTRACTION - TUTORPROGRAM BLS29B includes seven lessons, covering subtraction facts; two- and three-place numbers; borrowing; borrowing with a zero; zeroes in the minuend; borrowing in three and four places; subtraction of money; and subtraction of like fractions.

MULTIPLICATION - TUTORPROGRAM BLS29C includes seven lessons, covering multiplication by 0 and 1, multiplication facts, and two- place multiplicands with one-place multipliers; three-place multiplicands and place-holders; carrying to tens', hundreds', and both places; multiplication by 10 and by multiples of 10, and two-place multipliers; and multiplication of money.

DIVISION - TUTORPROGRAM BLS29D includes seven lessons, covering division facts and even division with two-place quotients; dividing with a zero and zero as a place-holder; finding a fractional part of a number; remainders with one- and two- place quotients and division of money; division by two- place numbers ending in zero; and division of money.

ID: J24

BACKFIRE

Publisher: Micro-Ed, Inc.

Grade: Elementary

Format: cassette or diskette

Hardware: Commodore 64 • PET • VIC; 3K memory enhancement

Language: BASIC

Source Code: no

Price: $14.95

BACKFIRE is an exercise in finding the divisors of a given number. Rockets fired from a battle station will attempt to destroy the divisors. If the wrong target is chosen, however, beware! Player gets "burned" from BACKFIRE.

ID: J25

BAKER MATH PACK

Publisher: Robert R. Baker, Jr.

Also available from: Queue, Inc.

Date: June 82

Grade: 5-12

Format: diskette

Hardware: TRS-80 MOD I or III; 16K

Language: BASIC

Source Code: yes

Price: $49.85

A complete math package including NUMBO-JUMBO, DECIMATION,, TENTRATION, FRACTION SERIES, and DECIMAL ADDITION AND SUBTRACTION WITH LINE NUMBER. Students can do same drill or return to menu. Average program running time is 2-3 minutes at each level of difficulty. Written documentation is provided, and program is self-documented as well.

ID: J26

BAR GRAPH

Publisher: Micro-Ed, Inc.

Also available from: Academic Software • EISI (Educational Instructional Systems, Inc.) • MARCK • Queue, Inc. • Texas Instruments

Grade: Elementary

Format: cassette or diskette

Hardware: Commodore 64 • PET • TI 99/4

Language: BASIC

Source Code: no

Price: $7.95; $9.95 TI ed.

This is a drill and practice exercise using a bar graph with different pieces of information on it. The information changes with every problem. There are ten problems in all. At the end of the lesson, the student's performance is summarized.

ID: J27

BASIC ARITHMETIC

Publisher: Minnesota Educational Computing Consortium

Date: June 82

Grade: 3-8

Format: diskette

Hardware: Atari 400/800; 16K with Atari BASIC in cartridge

Language: BASIC

Source Code: no

Price: $37.10

Module contains six drill and practice programs on arithmetic operations with whole numbers. Support booklet included.

BASE TEN - Program uses outerspace game format with three levels of multiplication problems, including decimals.

MATH GAME, SPEED DRILL - Level of difficulty of problems can be specified.

ROUND, ESTIMATE - Programs involve rounding numbers and estimating answers.

CHANGE - Gives practice in making change.

ID: J28

BASIC MATH COMPETENCY SKILL DRILLS COMPUTER

Publisher: Educational Activities, Inc.

Also available from: Academic Software • K-12 Micromedia • MARCK • Queue, Inc.

Grade: 7-12

Format: cassette or diskette

Hardware: Apple II Plus; (DOS 3.2.1 or 3.3) • TRS-80 MOD I or III; with Level II BASIC • PET • Commodore 2001 • Commodore 4000; 40 or 80 column • Commodore 8000; 80 column

Source Code: no

Price: $15.95/cassette; $173.00/complete cassette set of 12; $39.95/diskette; $203.00/complete diskette set of 6

These individualized programs will not only enhance students' basic math skills, but will also be a motivational tool to help teachers generate interest in math for poor as well as average students. Because these programs make full use of the computer graphics capability, students find the lessons fun to use. Even reluctant students become eager to begin class. In each program, the student or teacher can choose from a wide range of types of examples and levels of difficulty so that every program contains several lessons. All the examples given are randomly chosen by the computer, yet all examples are within specific ranges of difficulty. In programs that involve examples with more than one step (for example, Fractions), the student is guided through each example and can't continue until each step is done correctly. These programs take the boredom out of math drills! The students enjoy the "rewards," which are bold graphics, given for correct answers. The computer relates to each student by name, which personalizes the lessons.

PROGRAMS ON CASSETTES - Topics covered are: 1) addition and subtraction of whole numbers; 2) multiplication and division of whole numbers; 3) tables 1-12, addition, subtraction, multiplication, division; 4) rounding off numbers; 5) fractions - addition and subtraction; 6) fractions - multiplication and division; 7) decimals - addition, subtraction, multiplication, division; 8) graphs and mean, median, and mode; 9) converting fractions and percents; 10) percent word problems; 11) area, perimeter, circumference; and 12) linear measurement.

PROGRAMS ON DISKETTES - Topics covered are: 1) addition, subtraction, multiplication, and division of whole numbers; 2) tables 1-12 and rounding off numbers; 3) fractions - addition, subtraction, multiplication, and division; 4) decimals and graphs, and mean, median, and mode; 5) converting fractions and percents, and percent word problems; and 6) area, perimeter, circumference, and linear measurement.

ID: J29

BASIC MATH SYSTEM H

Publisher: Mathware/Math City

Also available from: MARCK • Queue, Inc.

Grade: 2-8

Format: 5 diskettes

Hardware: Apple II; 48K

Language: Applesoft BASIC

Price: $59.00/diskette

BASIC MATH SYSTEM H is a set of 5 disks which can be used individually. Each disk contains complete instructions, record storage, and more than 35 completely different teaching modules. A subset of up to 10 of the modules in a disk can be chosen for a lesson. Difficulty levels can be set, and are automatically adjusted as the student proceeds. Documentation included. (This is System S geared for home use.)

ADDITION AND SUBTRACTION

MULTIPLICATION AND DIVISION

FRACTIONS CONCEPTS AND OPERATIONS

DECIMAL CONCEPTS AND OPERATIONS

RATIOS, PERCENTS, AND NEGATIVE INTEGERS

ID: J30

BASIC MATH SYSTEM S

Publisher: Mathware/Math City

Also available from: Academic Software • K-12 Micromedia • MARCK

Grade: 2-8

Format: 8 diskettes

Hardware: Apple II; 48K; printer optional

Language: Applesoft BASIC

Price: $350.00

BASIC MATH SYSTEM S is a comprehensive and interactive system. It features: 1) five curriculum disks containing teaching modules which cover a 2nd through 8th grade math curriculum; 2) a class management disk which maintains records for a class of 50 students; 3) a diagnostic testing disk which administers tests at five different levels; 4) a data storage disk. An optional lesson selection feature will, on the basis of a diagnostic test, select a lesson plan for the student. Complete instructions for use of the computer are included on the diagnostic testing disk, so that a student can sit down at the computer and begin to use this software without any prior experience. A printout option is available for all class and individual records. SYSTEM S is sold with a licensing agreement; a backup disk for the class management disk is provided upon completion of the licensing agreement.

ID: J31

BASIC SECONDARY PACKAGE

Publisher: Math Software

Grade: 7-12

Format: diskette

Hardware: Apple II; 48K with Applesoft in ROM (DOS 3.3); game paddles needed for some programs • Apple II Plus; game paddles needed for some programs

Price: $175.00

This package is one of five offered by Math Software. The descriptions for the programs can be found in the SUPERMATH PACKAGE.

ARITHMETIC OF FUNCTIONS

ARITHMETIC RACING

BINOMIAL MULTIPLICATION

ECCENTRICITY FORM OF CONIC

FUNCTION GRAPHER

LIMACONS AND THEIR AREAS

LIMITS OF SEQUENCES

ORBITING AND ROTATING FIGURES

POLAR GRAPHING

SIMULTANEOUS LINEAR SYSTEMS

SINE AND COSINE GRAPHER

SOLVING LINEAR EQUATIONS

ID: J32

BEGINNING MATH CONCEPTS

Publisher: Orange Cherry Media

Also available from: Academic Software • Queue, Inc.

Grade: K-3

Format: cassette or diskette

Hardware: PET 2000 or 4000; 16K • TRS-80 MOD I or III; 16K • Apple; 16K • Apple II; 16K

Price: $15.00/cassette; $56.00/cassette set of 4; $67.00/diskette set of 2

A set of easy to use programs covering number concepts through intensive drill and structured activities. A choice of levels of difficulty accommodates below average, on-grade and above-grade students. Motivational activities, games and puzzles cleverly disguise structured drill.

COUNTING AND NUMBER VALUES: NUMBERS 1-10

COUNTING AND NUMBER VALUES: NUMBERS 10-30

BEGINNING ADDITION: CONCEPT OF PLUS ONE

COMPARING NUMBER VALUES

ID: J33

BELL RINGER

Publisher: Micro-Ed, Inc.

Grade: Elementary

Format: cassette or diskette

Hardware: Commodore 64 • PET • VIC; 3K memory enhancement

Language: BASIC

Source Code: no

Price: $14.95

BELL RINGER tests the student's ability to write fractions by their percent names. These fractions have either 5, 10 20, or 25 as denominators. If successful, a strong man appears on the screen and tries to ring a carnival bell with his mallet.

ID: J34

BRANDED

Publisher: Micro-Ed, Inc.

Grade: Elementary and up

Format: cassette or diskette

Hardware: Commodore 64 • PET • VIC; 3K memory enhancement

Language: BASIC

Source Code: no

Price: $14.95

The object is to recognize part of a whole and write it as a fraction. The student is shown a herd of cattle on the screen. After a certain number of cattle are branded, the student must express, as a fraction, the relationship of branded cattle to the total herd.

ID: J35

BUMBLE GAMES

Publisher: Learning Company

Date: 1982

Grade: K-5

Format: diskette

Hardware: Apple II; 48K with Applesoft in ROM (DOS 3.3); color monitor recommended • Apple II Plus

Language: Applesoft BASIC

Source Code: no

Price: $60.00

Set of six programs introduces use of number pairs to name positions in an array and points on a grid, while the student is guided by Bumble, an imaginary creature from the planet Furrin. Games are arranged from easy to hard, making ideas natural to learn. Games feature color graphics and music and sound effects that can be turned on and off. Plotting number pairs is a basic math skill for the computer age, needed to understand and build charts and graphs, locate places on a map, and design computer graphics.

ID: J36

BUMBLE PLOT

Publisher: Learning Company

Date: 1982

Grade: 3-8

Format: diskette

Hardware: Apple II; 48K with Applesoft in ROM (DOS 3.3); color monitor recommended • Apple II Plus; color monitor recommended

Language: Applesoft BASIC

Source Code: no

Price: $60.00

Set of five programs builds on graphic skills introduced in BUMBLE GAMES to enable child to use positive and negative numbers to name points in four quadrant grids. Games are arranged from easy to hard, making for natural progression of learning. They feature color graphics, as well as music and sound effects that can be turned on and off. Plotting number pairs is a basic math skill for the computer age, needed to understand and build charts and graphs, locate places on a map, and design computer graphics.

ID: J37
CALCULUS I

Publisher: Microphys Programs

Also available from: Academic Software • EISI (Educational Instructional Systems, Inc.) • MARCK • Queue, Inc.

Grade: High School and up

Format: 12 cassettes or 1 diskette

Hardware: PET; 8K; cassette or 4040 dual disk drive • Apple II; 24K (DOS 3.2 or 3.3) • TRS-80 MOD I or III; 16K • Bell & Howell

Language: BASIC

Source Code: yes

Price: $180.00/diskette; $20.00/cassette

Package consists of 12 interactive introductory calculus programs. Computer-assisted instruction versions guide student through series of quantitative questions; individualized-instruction versions generate a unique set of problems for each student. Grades and overall evaluations are compiled by programs for each student. Complete instructions are included. Also available through Queue, Inc. in diskette format only.

DIFFERENTIATION OF ALGEBRAIC FUNCTIONS (PC726)

MAXIMA/MINIMA PROBLEMS PART I (PC727)

MAXIMA/MINIMA PROBLEMS PART II (PC728)

RELATIVE RATES PROBLEMS PART I (PC729)

RELATIVE RATES PROBLEMS PART II (PC730)

INTEGRATION OF ALGEBRAIC FUNCTIONS (PC731)

DIFFERENTIATION OF TRIGONOMETRIC FUNCTIONS (PC732)

INTEGRATION OF TRIGONOMETRIC FUNCTIONS (PC733)

INTEGRATION: AREAS OF PLANE FIGURES (PC734)

INTEGRATION: VOLUMES OF SOLIDS (PC735)

INTEGRATION: ARC LENGTHS (PC736)

INTEGRATION: SURFACE AREAS OF SOLIDS (PC737)

ID: J38
CATERPILLAR 500

Publisher: Micro-Ed, Inc.

Also available from: EISI (Educational Instructional Systems, Inc.) • K-12 Micromedia

Grade: Elementary

Format: cassette or diskette

Hardware: Commodore 64 • PET • VIC

Language: BASIC

Source Code: no

Price: $14.95

It's not a car but a caterpillar that speeds around the oval in this Indy 500 type of race. To get the worm moving, just solve expressions such as (8 X —) + 3 = 59, and it's worth 7 laps

around the track. A clock records total time in this 100-lap race.

ID: J39
COLOR MATH

Publisher: Radio Shack®

Date: 1982

Grade: K-8

Format: 2 cassettes

Hardware: TRS-80 Color Computer; 4K; color monitor

Language: BASIC

Source Code: yes

Price: $39.95

Self-paced drill and practice program in addition, subtraction, multiplication, and division contains skill- building exercises, test mode, and placement mode for each of basic math concepts. Intended for home use, program features automatic promotion and demotion of student, reinforcement messages for correct answers, and a comprehensive reporting function.

ID: J40
COMPLEX OPERATIONS

Publisher: BLS Inc.

Date: Apr. 82

Grade: 7 and up (reading level 6-7)

Format: 9 diskettes

Hardware: Apple II; 48K with Applesoft in ROM (DOS 3.2 or 3.3)

Language: Applesoft BASIC

Source Code: no

Price: $459.00/series; $60.00/diskette; $216.00/AVERAGES...; $162.00 /LOWEST COMMON...;$108.00/ORDER OF OPERATIONS

TUTORCOURSE BLS25E series has been designed for instruction or review in vocational or trade schools, preparation for college entrance exams, college remedial and adult education classes, and for job training. Three programs on complex operations involving whole numbers contain total of nine lessons, each ending with summary and test. Programs utilize self-paced, branch-programmed instruction methods. Comprehensive user documentation is provided. Series study time: 6-12 hours.

AVERAGES, ESTIMATING, AND FACTORING - TUTORPROGRAM BLS25E-1 includes four lessons, covering following topics: finding the average of a set of numbers; rounding off to nearest ten and nearest hundred; estimating to check answers and estimating sums, differences, products, and quotients; and prime numbers, composite numbers, factors, prime factors, and greatest common factors.

LOWEST COMMON MULTIPLES, EXPONENTS, AND SQUARE ROOTS - TUTORPROGRAM BLS25E-2 includes three lessons, covering multiples and lowest common multiples (L.C.M.s); exponents and bases; and perfect squares and square roots.

ORDER OF OPERATIONS AND PRACTICAL OPERATIONS - TUTORPROGRAM BLS25E-3 includes two lessons, covering order of operations, multiplication before addition, use of parentheses, and practical applications.

ID: J41

COMPU-MATH: ARITHMETIC SKILLS

Publisher: Edu-Ware Services

Also available from: Academic Software • EISI (Educational Instructional Systems, Inc.) • K-12 Micromedia • MARCK • McKilligan Supply Corp. • Queue, Inc.

Format: diskette

Hardware: Apple; 48K (DOS 3.2 or 3.3)

Language: Applesoft BASIC

Price: $49.95

This program builds entry-level arithmetic skills by allowing young children to interact with the computer. It uses high-resolution graphics and a minimum of text, covering counting, addition, subtraction, multiplication, and division. ARITHMETIC SKILLS employs positive reinforcement; repeated errors route the learner back for review. The teacher or parent can easily define the presentation sequence, pass-fail ratios, "child" or "remedial" format, and other parameters which remain inaccessible to the learner.

ID: J42

COMPU-MATH: DECIMALS

Publisher: Edu-Ware Services

Also available from: Academic Software • EISI (Educational Instructional Systems, Inc.) • K-12 Micromedia • MARCK • McKilligan Supply Corp. • Queue, Inc.

Format: cassette or diskette

Hardware: Apple; 48K with Applesoft in ROM (DOS 3.3) • Atari; 48K with BASIC

Price: $49.00

This program covers definitions, addition, subtraction, rounding off, multiplication, division, and percentage. It includes a Learning Manager that controls sequence of units, learning parameters (such as minimum/maximum values in examples), and test scoring criteria. A pre-test and post-test are part of the program, as is a fully animated small figure who walks, runs and directs the movement of numbers.

ID: J43

COMPU-MATH: FRACTIONS

Publisher: Edu-Ware Services

Also available from: Academic Software • EISI (Educational Instructional Systems, Inc.) • K-12 Micromedia • MARCK • McKilligan Supply Corp. • Queue, Inc.

Format: cassette or diskette

Hardware: Apple; 48K with Applesoft in ROM (DOS 3.3) • Atari; 48K with BASIC

Price: $49.00

Part of the Compu-Math series, this program covers both common fractions and mixed numbers. Topics are definitions and parts of a fraction, denominators, addition, subtraction, multiplication and division. These programs define goals, give immediate feedback, and test progress. FRACTIONS is fully animated, featuring a small figure who walks, runs, and directs the movement of numbers on the screen. The Learning Manager functions identically to that with the Compu-Math ARITHMETIC SKILLS program.

ID: J44

COMPUTER GRAPHING EXPERIMENTS - VOLUME 2 (TRIGONOMETRIC FUNCTIONS)

Publisher: Addison-Wesley Publishing Company

Format: 1 diskette, with backup

Hardware: Apple II; 32K (DOS 3.3) • Apple II Plus

Source Code: no

Price: $45.00

Using this program, students can create and compare computer generated graphs using sine, cosine, tangent, cotangent, period, amplitude, phase shift and polar coordinates. Black line masters and teacher's notes included.

ID: J45

COMPUTER GRAPHING EXPERIMENTS - VOLUME 3 (CONIC SECTIONS)

Publisher: Addison-Wesley Publishing Company

Format: 1 diskette, with backup

Hardware: Apple II; 32K (DOS 3.3) • Apple II Plus

Source Code: no

Price: $45.00

Using this program, students create and compare computer-generated graphs using parabolas, ellipses, hyperboles, general quadratic functions and inequalities. Black line masters and teacher's notes are included.

ID: J46

COMPUTER GRAPHING EXPERIMENTS - VOLUME I (ALGEBRA I AND II)

Publisher: Addison-Wesley Publishing Company

Format: 1 diskette, with backup

Hardware: Apple II; 32K (DOS 3.3) • Apple II Plus

Source Code: no

Price: $45.00

Students create and compare graphs of linear and quadratic functions and inequalities, absolute value, polynomials, exponential and logarithmic functions. Black line masters, answers and teacher's notes included. No programming knowledge required.

ID: J47

COMPUTER MATH ACTIVITIES - VOLUME 1

Publisher: Addison-Wesley Publishing Company

Date: Aug. 82

Grade: 1-9

Format: 5 programs on diskette, with backup

Hardware: Apple II; 32K (DOS 3.3) • Apple II Plus

Source Code: no

Price: $54.00

This program includes math activities for 1-4 players or teams focusing on fact reinforcement, skill practice and problem-solving. Included is a teacher's guide with master record sheets.

SKI MATH - This program provides timed practice of adding, subtracting, multiplying, or dividing whole numbers, decimals, or integers. (2 players/team)

HEX GAME - The first activity in this program involves developing a strategy for winning. No math is involved. HEX MATH provides practice adding, subtracting, multiplying, or dividing whole numbers, decimals, or integers. (2 players/team)

LINE 'EM UP - This program provides timed practice arranging a set of numbers from smallest to largest. (2 players/team)

FIND IT - This program provides practice writing mathematical sentences using only numbers 1 through 13 and any combination of addition, subtraction, multiplication, or division. (1 player/team)

METRIC 21 - This program provides practice estimating (or measuring) centimeter lengths and adding them for sums through 21. (1-3 players/team)

ID: J48
COMPUTER MATH ACTIVITIES - VOLUME 2
Publisher: Addison-Wesley Publishing Company

Date: Aug. 82

Grade: 1-9

Format: 5 programs on diskette, with backup

Hardware: Apple II; 32K (DOS 3.3) • Apple II Plus

Price: $54.00

This program includes math activities for 1-4 players or teams focusing on fact reinforcement, skill practice and problem-solving. Included is a teacher's guide with master record sheets.

DINOSAUR MATH - This program provides timed practice adding, subtracting, multiplying, or dividing whole numbers, decimals, or integers. (1-4 players/team)

SURROUND 'EM - This program provides timed practice using 2 or 3 numbers to write math sentences in addition, subtraction, multiplication, and division. (2-5 players/team)

MATH GALLERY - This program provides timed practice adding, subtracting, multiplying, or dividing whole numbers, decimals, or integers. (1-5 players/team)

MATH MEMORY - This program provides basic facts practice in addition, subtraction, multiplication and division, and recognition of the mathematical signs involving these operations. (1-2 players/team)

MATH MEMORY 2 - This program provides practice identifying polygons, understanding fractions, and solving rebus problems (1-2 players/team)

ID: J49
COMPUTER MATH ACTIVITIES - VOLUME 3
Publisher: Addison-Wesley Publishing Company

Date: Aug. 82

Grade: 1-9

Format: 6 programs on diskette, with backup

Hardware: Apple II; 32K (DOS 3.3) • Apple II Plus

Price: $54.00

This program includes math activities for 1-4 players or teams focusing on fact reinforcement, skill practice and problem-solving. Included is a teacher's guide with master record sheets.

TREASURE HUNT - This program provides timed practice adding, subtracting, multiplying, or dividing whole numbers, decimals, or integers. (1-5 players/team)

BUZZ - This program provides recognition of number patterns including multiples of selected whole numbers within a pattern. (1-8 players/team)

ONCE AROUND - This program provides practice adding, subtracting, multiplying, or dividing whole numbers, decimals, or integers. (1-4 players/team)

SEGMENTS AND TRIANGLES - This program provides practice developing problem-solving strategies and using line segments to construct triangles. (2 players/team)

SPINO - This program provides practice adding and multiplying whole numbers to three digits and supplying missing addends and multiplicands. (1-5 players/team)

UNLOCK IT - This program provides practice developing place-value understanding and logic skills using 2-, 3-, and 4-digit numbers. (1 player/team)

ID: J50
COMPUTER MATH ACTIVITIES - VOLUME 4
Publisher: Addison-Wesley Publishing Company

Date: Aug. 82

Grade: 1-9

Format: 5 programs on diskette, with backup

Hardware: Apple II; 32K (DOS 3.3) • Apple II Plus

Price: $54.00

This program includes math activities for 1-4 players or teams focusing on fact reinforcement, skill practice and problem-solving. Included is a teacher's guide with master record sheets.

MONEY GUESSER - This program provides practice in developing strategies for finding a particular number within a range of numbers. (1 or more players/team)

TOP OF THE MOUNTAIN - This program provides timed practice in translating numbers from English words to Arabic numerals. (2 players/team)

MIX AND MATCH - This program provides timed practice with basic facts and manipulation of fractions and percents. (1-5 players/team)

PINBALL MATH - This program provides timed practice adding, subtracting, multiplying, or dividing whole numbers, decimals, or integers. (1-5 players/team)

TABLO - This program provides practice adding, subtracting, multiplying, or dividing whole numbers, decimals, or integers. (1-5 players/team)

ID: J51
COMPUTER MATH ACTIVITIES - VOLUME 5
Publisher: Addison-Wesley Publishing Company

Date: Aug. 82

Grade: 1-9

Format: 5 programs on diskette, with backup

Hardware: Apple II; 32K (DOS 3.3) • Apple II Plus; 32K (DOS 3.3)

Price: $54.00

These are math activities for 1-4 players or teams focusing on fact reinforcement, skill practice, and problem-solving. Included is a teacher's guide with master record sheets.

STRATO MATH - This program provides timed practice adding, subtracting, multiplying, or dividing whole numbers, decimals, or integers. (1-5 players/team)

MATH RING TOSS - This program provides timed practice adding numbers such as 100, 10, 1, 0.1, etc. (1-5 players/team)

EQUATIONS AND INEQUALITIES - This program provides practice generating mathematical sentences using equality and inequality symbols and addition, subtraction, multiplication, and division. (1-5 players/team)

MATH FACTS - This program provides practice selecting the correct operation symbol in computation and solving word problems. (1-5 players/team)

NAME THAT NUMBER - FRACTION SHAPE - This program provides practice in basic number facts using addition, subtraction, multiplication, or division; identifying polygons; or in determining the meaning of fractions. (1-5 players/team)

ID: J52

COMPUTER MATH GAMES - VOLUME 1

Publisher: Addison-Wesley Publishing Company

Grade: 1-9

Format: 5 programs on diskette, with backup

Hardware: Apple II; 32K (DOS 3.3) • Apple II Plus

Price: $45.00

These are math games for 1-4 players or teams, focusing on fact reinforcement, skill practice, and problem-solving. This package gives the student addition, subtraction, multiplication, or division practice using whole numbers, decimals, fractions, or integers; practice finding the percent of a number, finding what percent one number is of another, or finding a number if a percent of it is known; practice with equivalent fractions, improper fractions, or mixed numerals.

APPLE SQUARE-OFF - This program provides practice plotting ordered pairs of whole numbers or integers.

DOT-DOT-PLOT - This program provides practice plotting ordered pairs of whole numbers or integers.

MATH BOXES - This program provides addition, subtraction, multiplication, or division practice using whole numbers, decimals, or integers.

BEANS AND PITS - This program provides practice with place value and formulating a problem-solving strategy.

ID: J53

COMPUTER MATH GAMES - VOLUME 2

Publisher: Addison-Wesley Publishing Company

Grade: 1-9

Format: 5 programs on diskette, with backup

Hardware: Apple II; 32K (DOS 3.3) • Apple II Plus

Price: $45.00

These are math games for 1-4 players/teams focusing on fact reinforcement, skill practice, and problem-solving. This package gives the student practice in addition, subtraction, multiplication and division using whole numbers, fractions, decimals, or integers. Topics also include finding the percent of a number, and practice with equivalent fractions. improper fractions and mixed numbers.

YOUR NUMBER'S UP - This program provides practice with place value of whole numbers or decimals.

MATH BASKETBALL - This program provides timed practice with basic addition, subtraction, multiplication, or division facts.

MATCH UP - This program provides practice combining three whole numbers using addition, subtraction, multiplication, division, or exponents.

TIC-TAC-MATH - This program provides addition, subtraction, multiplication, or division practice using whole numbers, decimals, or integers.

HORSE RACE - This program provides timed practice with basic addition, subtraction, multiplication, or division facts.

ID: J54

COMPUTER MATH GAMES - VOLUME 3

Publisher: Addison-Wesley Publishing Company

Grade: 1-9

Format: 7 programs on 1 diskette, with backup

Hardware: Apple II; 32K (DOS 3.3) • Apple II Plus

Price: $45.00

These are math games for 1-4 players or teams focusing on fact reinforcement, skill practice, and problem-solving. This package gives the student addition, subtraction, and division practice using whole numbers, decimals, fractions, or integers; practice finding the percent of a number; and practice with equivalent fractions, improper fractions, or mixed numbers.

WAR - This program provides practice recognizing, counting, and comparing whole numbers less than or equal to 13.

FLASH - This program provides timed practice with addition, subtraction, multiplication, or division of basic facts.

SQUARE IT - This program provides timed practice finding the square of one- or two-digit sums or differences.

REDUCE - This program provides practice recognizing whether or not a fraction can be reduced and timed practice with reducing fractions.

IN BETWEEN - This program provides practice with counting and the notion of "betweenness."

TWENTY-ONE - This program provides practice with addition of whole numbers less than or equal to 11; practice with formulating a strategy; and missing addends.

ZERO - This program provides practice finding the sum of integers.

ID: J55

COMPUTER MATH GAMES - VOLUME 4

Publisher: Addison-Wesley Publishing Company

Grade: 1-9

Format: 5 programs on 1 diskette, with backup

Hardware: Apple II; 32K (DOS 3.3) • Apple II Plus

Price: $45.00

These are math games for 1-4 players or teams focusing on fact recognition, skill practice, and problem-solving.

NIM 25 - This program provides practice counting to 25 and formulating a strategy.

MATH DARTS - This program provides timed practice in addition, subtraction, multiplication, and division of whole numbers from 0 through 100.

FIVE HUNDRED - This program provides timed practice with compact notation, expanded numerals, or place-value identification.

WOODCHUCK - This program provides practice in addition, subtraction, multiplication, or division of whole numbers up to 255.

COVER UP - This program provides practice in addition or subtraction of whole numbers from 0 to 100.

ID: J56
COMPUTER MATH GAMES - VOLUME 5

Publisher: Addison-Wesley Publishing Company

Grade: 4-9

Format: diskette, with backup

Hardware: Apple II; 32K (DOS 3.3) • Apple II Plus

Price: $30.00

This program provides math or computer vocabulary practice.

MIX UP

ID: J57
COMPUTER MATH GAMES - VOLUME 6

Publisher: Addison-Wesley Publishing Company

Grade: 2-9

Format: 4 programs on diskette, with backup

Hardware: Apple II; 32K (DOS 3.3) Apple II Plus

Price: $45.00

These are math games for 1-4 players or teams focusing on fact recognition, skill practice, and problem-solving.

ASTEROID - This program provides practice using the symbols for greater than, less than and equals to make true sentences involving whole numbers, fractions, decimals, or integers.

AROUND THE SCHOOLYARD - This program provides practice in addition, subtraction, multiplication, or division of whole numbers up to 100.

MATH BASEBALL - This program provides practice with basic addition, subtraction, multiplication, or division facts.

MATH TRIANGLES - This program provides addition, subtraction, multiplication, or division practice using whole numbers, decimals, or integers.

ID: J58
COORDINATE

Publisher: Microcomputer Workshops

Also available from: Academic Software • Micro-Ed, Inc.

Grade: Upper Elementary and up

Format: cassette

Hardware: PET

Language: BASIC

Source Code: no

Price: $20.00

This program is designed to give the learner practice in plotting points on a Cartesian coordinate system. A graph is displayed and the student is asked to plot a point picked at random. The cursor is moved by using the 2, 4, 6, and 8 keys. When the learner decides that the cursor is in the correct position, he/she presses the letter A. The learner is then told whether the answer is correct. If the answer is incorrect, the correct position of the point is shown on the screen. The student may stop the drill at any time by pressing the letter S. The number of correct points plotted will then be shown.

ID: J59
COUNT 'EM

Publisher: Micro-Ed, Inc.

Also available from: Academic Software • EISI (Educational Instructional Systems, Inc.) • Queue, Inc. • Texas Instruments

Grade: K-1

Format: cassette or diskette

Hardware: Commodore 64 • PET • TI 99/4 • VIC

Language: BASIC

Source Code: no

Price: $7.95; $9.95 TI ed.

From one to ten steam locomotives appear on the screen. Each problem presents a different number of locomotives. How many are there? If the student is right, a right answer locomotive chugs across the screen. If the student is wrong, a wrong answer locomotive falls apart. At the end of the lesson, the student's performance is summarized. (If the student does not know the answer, and types the question mark, the computer will give the answer.)

ID: J60
COUNT AND ADD

Publisher: Edu-Soft[T.M.]

Also available from: Academic Software

Format: 2 programs on cassette or diskette

Hardware: Apple II; 16K (cassette) or 32K (diskette) with Applesoft in ROM (DOS 3.2 or 3.3)

Price: $14.95/cassette; $19.95/diskette

Two programs are designed to help users with related skills of counting and adding.

COUNT - The computer shows colored shapes on the screen for the user to count. If user miscounts, the computer counts the shapes, beeping each number. Shapes increase in number to 35 as user's skill increases.

ADD - A sequence of add programs increases in difficulty as user's skill increases. In ADD 1, the user counts each of 2 groups of shapes. The groups become a single group and the user is asked for the sum. If the wrong answer is given, the computer counts them. In ADD 2, the user is asked for the sum before the groups merge. If the wrong answer is given, the groups merge and the user is given a second chance to sum. If the wrong answer is given, the computer counts. In ADD 3, the user is asked to add 2 numbers. If the answer is wrong, the appropriate number of shapes appear on the screen. The sequence then follows as for ADD 2.

ID: J61
CROSSBOW

Publisher: Hayden Book Company, Inc.

Also available from: K-12 Micromedia • Queue, Inc.

Format: cassette

Hardware: PET

Price: $9.95/cassette

Learn fractions via a challenging target game. There are 3 levels of play. Level 1 teaches recognition of fractional quantities and allows the player to use a ruler to determine the target position on the screen. Level 2 increases judgment of fractional quantities in that the ruler is not displayed until after 4 misses. Level 3 generates both a target and a fraction. The player must then add or subtract a fraction. The resulting sum or difference is where the arrow will strike.

ID: J62
DECIMAL ADDITION AND SUBTRACTION

Publisher: Robert R. Baker, Jr.

Also available from: Queue, Inc.

Date: June 82

Grade: 6-9

Format: cassette or diskette

Hardware: TRS-80 MOD I or III; 16K

Language: BASIC

Source Code: yes

Price: $24.85/cassette; $19.85/diskette

Number line on computer helps student add and subtract decimals in range of .1 to 1.2. Two attempts may be made to answer problem before computer displays correct answer. Elapsed time is displayed. Average program running time is 2-3 minutes at each level of difficulty. Written documentation is provided, and program is self-documented as well.

ID: J63
DECIMAL EQUIVALENTS OF FRACTIONS

Publisher: Micro-Ed, Inc.

Also available from: EISI (Educational Instructional Systems, Inc.) • K-12 Micromedia

Grade: Elementary

Format: cassette or diskette

Hardware: Commodore 64 • PET

Language: BASIC

Source Code: no

Price: $7.95

The computer displays a number line marked with fractions. What is the decimal equivalent of the highlighted fraction on the number line? At the end of the lesson, the student's performance is summarized.

ID: J64
DECIMAL SKILLS

Publisher: Milton Bradley

Also available from: McKilligan Supply Corp. • Opportunities For Learning, Inc.

Grade: 6-8

Format: 1 diskette

Hardware: Apple II; 48K with Applesoft in ROM (DOS 3.3)

Language: Applesoft BASIC

Price: $44.95

DECIMAL SKILLS includes drill, practice, and extra help (for those who have not mastered the work) or readiness skills. Addition, subtraction, multiplication, and division of decimals are covered. Includes a teacher's guide and reproducible activity sheets.

ID: J65
DECIMALS

Publisher: Quality Educational Designs (QED)

Format: 16 programs on cassette or diskette

Hardware: TRS-80; 16K (cassette) • TRS-80 MOD I or III; 32K • Apple; 32K (DOS 3.2) • Apple; 48K (DOS 3.3 Vers. 2.0) • PET; 16K (cassette or diskette)

Language: BASIC

Decimals uses the computer as a tutor, reinforcer and vehicle for expansion of learning through games and explorations. The programs are built in an interrelated fashion and are designed for sequential use. The tutorial programs are DRIFTS LEFT AND RIGHT, READING DECIMALS, ADDING DECIMALS, OLD FRIENDS NEW FACES, APPROXIMATELY DECIMALS, MULTIPLYING DECIMALS, DIVIDING DECIMALS, and ESTIMATING ANSWERS. Game/Exploration programs are ALL ABOARD, DOUBLE DOUBLE, DECI-GUESS, DECIMAL PATTERNS, RATIONAL NUMBERS, TRIPLE TROUBLE, E NOTATION, and PROGRESS TEST.

ID: J66
DECIMALS: A REVIEW COURSE

Publisher: BLS Inc.

Date: Apr. 82

Grade: 7 and up (reading level 6-7)

Format: 13 diskettes

Hardware: Apple II; 48K with Applesoft in ROM (DOS 3.2 or 3.3)

Language: Applesoft BASIC

Source Code: no

Price: $663.00/series; $60.00/diskette; $216.00/DECIMALS: FRACTIONS...and DIVISION OF DECIMALS; $270.00/DECIMALS: ADDITION...

TUTORCOURSE BLS25G series is designed to meet growing need for effective basic and remedial instruction in area of decimals. Three programs contain total of 13 lessons, at end of which is final exam. Programs utilize self- paced, branch-programmed instruction methods. Comprehensive user documentation is provided. Series study time: 9-15 hours.

DECIMALS: FRACTIONS, AND EQUIVALENTS - TUTOR-PROGRAM BLS25G-1 includes four lessons, covering following topics: whole numbers, base 10, and place value; decimal fractions, and changing common fractions and mixed numbers to decimals; decimal equivalents of some common fractions, denominators (2,4,6,8,16), and denominators (5, 20, 25, and 50).

DECIMALS: ADDITION, SUBTRACTION, AND MULTIPLICATION - TUTORPROGRAM BLS25G-2 includes five lessons, covering following topics: addition of decimals, zero as a place holder, and subtraction of decimals; rounding off decimals; multiplication of decimals, and placement of decimal point in product; multiplying and dividing by 10, 100, and 1000; and general review.

DIVISION OF DECIMALS - TUTORPROGRAM BLS25G-3 includes four lessons, covering following topics: division of decimals by whole numbers, and placement of decimals in the quotient; division of decimals by decimals; and general review, non-terminating decimals, and final exam.

ID: J67
DECIMATION

Publisher: Robert R. Baker, Jr.

Also available from: Queue, Inc.

Date: June 82

Format: cassette or diskette

Hardware: TRS-80 MOD I or III; 16K

Language: BASIC

Source Code: yes

Price: $19.85

Self-study program provides timed math drill in decimal addition, subtraction, multiplication, and division. Each problem has time limit, and entire exercise is timed. Four ability levels make program challenging to all. Average program running time is 2-3 minutes at each level of difficulty. Written documentation is provided, and program is self-documented as well.

ID: J68
DESCRIPTIVE STATISTICS

Publisher: Sheridan College

Grade: 6-12

Format: 1 diskette

Hardware: PET 2001-8 or 4016; 8K (DOS 1.0 or 2.0); 2040, 4040 or 8050 • Apple II Plus; 8K (DOS 3.1)

Source Code: yes

Price: $100.00

This program covers the following topics: average - describes and defines the concept of the average; a graphical reinforcement of the concept is provided, as well as a sample problem; grouped data - provides a computational alternative for calculating the average of a large set of repetitive or grouped data; includes an example problem for the student; coding methods - a second computational problem is demonstrated, together with an example problem; frequency distribution and mode - describes the frequency distribution and mode of a data set, including the histogram; includes practice exercises for finding the mode of a distribution; median - calculates the me-

dian of a set of data and the procedure is simulated for randomly generated data; includes a machine language routine for ordering the data; a sample program is provided; and in a summary - the concepts of the 5 previous programs are brought together so that the student can see how these statistics effectively describe a set of data.

ID: J69
DIPT

Publisher: Micro Power & Light Company

Also available from: Queue, Inc.

Format: diskette

Hardware: Apple II; 32K with Applesoft in ROM

Price: $34.95

Delusions, Illusions, Puzzles and Tricks (DIPT) - it's fun, challenging, disturbing, and rewarding! A potpourri of mind-benders. Center stage is a big puzzle, daring the student to guess its secret. It explores the misconceptions and resulting illusions stemming from the use of directional terms appropriate to plane geometry, in solid geometry situations. In addition the program produces mazes, some of which are quite impossible. An occasional one-liner pops out. A variety of puzzles, and what would a puzzle be without a puzzle within a puzzle? Illuminating records are kept of each student's use of the program.

ID: J70
DISCOVERY LEARNING IN TRIGONOMETRY

Publisher: CONDUIT

Also available from: Queue, Inc.

Date: 1981

Grade: 9-College

Format: diskette

Hardware: Apple II; 48K with Applesoft in ROM (DOS 3.2.1)

Language: BASIC

Source Code: yes

Price: $75.00; $5.95/add'l student guide

This package uses discovery learning techniques to introduce students to trigonometric functions and their visual representations. Following the exercises in the User's Guide, students use the programs to discover how trigonometric functions are represented graphically and the cause-and-effect relationships between parts of equations and their graphs. Students are also led to analyze equations, taking into consideration such factors as amplitude, period, phase shift, and patterns; to prove that both sides of an identity are equal by transforming one side of the identity into a graph representing the other side; and to graph polar equations. Includes Student Guide.

ID: J71
DIVISION 1

Publisher: Scott, Foresman and Co.

Date: Jan. 82

Grade: 3-5

Format: module

Hardware: TI 99/4A; speech synthesizer recommended

Source Code: no

Price: $52.95

Math tutorial teaches basic facts of division, with divisors through 9; developed in conjunction with Texas Instruments. Includes both tutorial and practice activities; automatically selects appropriate tutorial activities when practice results indicate need. Teacher's guide included.

ID: J72
DIVISION OF NUMBERS

Publisher: Orange Cherry Media

Also available from: Academic Software

Grade: 3-6

Format: cassette or diskette

Hardware: PET 2000 or 4000; 16K • TRS-80 MOD I or III; 16K • Apple; 16K • Apple II; 16K

Price: $15.00/cassette; $56.00/cassette set of 4; $67.00/diskette set of 2

This program is available as part of a package through Queue, Inc.

DIVISION TABLES REVIEW AND ACTIVITIES

DIVISION CONCEPTS AND FACTS

SHORT AND LONG DIVISION

WORD PROBLEMS WITH DIVISION

ID: J73
DIVISION SKILLS

Publisher: Milton Bradley

Also available from: McKilligan Supply Corp. • Opportunities For Learning, Inc.

Grade: 6-8

Format: 1 diskette

Hardware: Apple II; 48K with Applesoft in ROM (DOS 3.3)

Language: Applesoft BASIC

Price: $44.95

Program allows student to move at his own pace; focuses on specific learning needs. DIVISION SKILLS includes 90 basic facts, one- and two-digit divisors, whole and fractional remainders, and decimal remainders. Includes Teacher's Guide and reproducible activity sheets. Three modes provide rapid drills, practice, and extra help.

ID: J74
DRILL/FLASHMATH

Publisher: Cow Bay Computing

Format: 1 cassette

Hardware: PET; any model except VIC 20 or 8032

Price: $15.00

In using DRILL, the student can select addition, subtraction, multiplication or division of whole numbers. The number of problems and size of the numbers can also be set. FLASHMATH works in the same way as DRILL, but the student is timed.

ID: J75
EDUCATIONAL PACKAGE III

Publisher: Micro Learningware

Also available from: Academic Software • MARCK

Format: diskette

Hardware: Apple II; 32K with Applesoft in ROM

Language: Applesoft BASIC

Source Code: yes

Price: $24.95

Package consists of four programs offering drill and practice on numerical and mathematical relationships. Written instructions provided.

TEMPERATURE - Drill and practice session on use of thermometer includes graphic illustrations and rewards.

NUMBER READING - Drill in conversion of numbers to written form. Number is displayed on screen, which user must key as it would be read. For example, 1267 would be read as One Thousand Two Hundred Sixty Seven.

NUMBER COMPARISONS - True or false drill on use of greater than, less than, and equal symbols. User is asked to determine if statement using one of these symbols is true or false.

MONEY COUNTING - Varying quantities of common monetary denominations are displayed on screen. User responds with total of amounts displayed.

CHANGE MAKER - Provides drill and practice on making change, based on randomly selected purchase and payment amounts. Available as an individual program from K-12 Micromedia.

ID: J76
ELEMENTARY - VOLUME 1

Publisher: Minnesota Educational Computing Consortium

Also available from: Academic Software • Creative Computing • K-12 Micromedia • Scholastic Software

Date: June 82

Grade: 1-6

Format: diskette

Hardware: Apple II; 32K with Applesoft in ROM (DOS 3.3)

Language: Applesoft BASIC

Source Code: no

Price: $38.80

Package contains a variety of programs for use in elementary mathematics classroom. Support booklet included.

BAGELS, TAXMAN, NUMBER - Games of logic.

SPEED, DRILL, ROUND, CHANGE - Drill and practice programs.

METRIC ESTIMATE, METRIC LENGTH, METRIC 21 - Programs about metric system.

ID: J77
ELEMENTARY - VOLUME 10

Publisher: Minnesota Educational Computing Consortium

Date: June 82

Grade: 4-6

Format: diskette

Hardware: Apple II; 32K with Applesoft in ROM (DOS 3.3)

Language: Applesoft BASIC

Source Code: no

Price: $34.50

Package consists of three geometry programs. Two quizzes are provided to test student's knowledge. Support booklet included.

QUADRILATERAL - Defines different types of quadrilaterals, including parallelograms, trapezoids, rectangles, squares, and rhombuses.

AREA, PERIMETER - Defines properties of geometric shapes, including area and perimeter.

ID: J78

ELEMENTARY - VOLUME 8

Publisher: Minnesota Educational Computing Consortium

Date: June 82

Grade: 3-5

Format: diskette

Hardware: Apple II; 32K with Applesoft in ROM (DOS 3.3)

Language: Applesoft BASIC

Source Code: no

Price: $33.90

Package consists of two geometry progams. Two quizzes are provided to test student's knowledge. Support booklet included.

POINTS, ANGLES - Teaches concepts of point, line, line segments, rays, and types of angles.

ID: J79

ELEMENTARY - VOLUME 9

Publisher: Minnesota Educational Computing Consortium

Date: June 82

Grade: 4-6

Format: diskette

Hardware: Apple II; 32K with Applesoft in ROM (DOS 3.3)

Language: Applesoft BASIC

Source Code: no

Price: $35.10

Package consists of two geometry programs. Two quizzes are provided to test student's knowledge. Support booklet included.

LINES - Defines parallel, perpendicular, and intersecting lines.

TRIANGLES - Defines different types of triangles, including scalene, isosceles, equilateral, acute, right, obtuse, and equiangular.

ID: J80

ELEMENTARY MATH

Publisher: TIES, Minnesota School Districts Data Processing Joint Board

Date: Oct. 81

Grade: 4-6; 1-6 Super Drill only

Format: 4 programs on diskette with backup

Hardware: Apple II; 32K with Applesoft in ROM (DOS 3.3) • Apple II Plus

Price: $49.95; $5.00/documentation

These programs are designed to develop skills in logic and reasoning, provide practice in estimating lengths in centimeters, develop speed and accuracy in computation in the four basic functions, develop problem-solving strategies, and determine the factor property of prime versus composite numbers. SUPER DRILL allows the teacher to set any or none of 3 parameters controlling this program. These options allow the teacher to define a specific set of problems and type of exercise to meet particular needs of an individual or group of students. A comprehensive manual accompanies these programs and includes instructions on how to use the program background information, etc.

BAGELS - BAGELS is designed to develop skills in reasoning and logic. The computer randomly selects a three-digit number and the student has up to 18 tries to guess the number.

ESTIMATE - ESTIMATE is a drill and practice exercise on estimating the lengths of random line segments in centimeters. The student is given two tries to correctly estimate the length. The program responds with various messages to indicate whether the estimation is "TOO HIGH", "TOO LOW", "CLOSE" or "RIGHT ON".

SUPER DRILL - SUPER DRILL is an arithmetic drill and practice program on the four basic operations of addition, subtraction, multiplication, and division. The objective is to improve computation skills and speed while maintaining accuracy.

TAXMAN - TAXMAN is a whole-number factor exercise. The student selects a number from a numeric list and the Taxman (computer) takes all the factors of that number remaining on the list. Points are scored by summing the numbers that the student gains with each move. The goal of the activity is to score more points than the Taxman.

ID: J81

ELEMENTARY MATH PACKAGE I

Publisher: Micro Learningware

Also available from: Academic Software • MARCK • Opportunities For Learning, Inc. • Queue, Inc.

Grade: Elementary

Format: cassette or diskette

Hardware: PET; 8K cassette • TRS-80 MOD I or III; 16K cassette or 32K diskette • TRS-80 Color Computer; 16K with extended BASIC cassette • Apple II; 32K with Applesoft in ROM (DOS 3.2 or 3.3)

Language: BASIC

Source Code: yes

Price: $24.95

Package contains programs designed to introduce basic math concepts and give students drill and practice in their use. Certain programs are for certain models of computers only, as noted in descriptions. TRS-80 Color Computer version is known as ELEMENTARY MATH PACKAGE III.

PLACE VALUE - Introduces basic concepts of decimal number system and place value with graphic illustrations. Concludes with drill and practice session on place value. Written instructions included.

NUMBER STRINGS - Drill and practice program provides drills on addition of strings of numbers, with user providing number of digits in each of numbers and how many numbers will be in each string.

MATH DRILL - Provides drills with graphics in addition, subtraction, and multiplication. User specifies type of problem, with total control over level of difficulty.

DIVISION DRILL - Drill and practice program with graphics provides division problems at level of difficulty specified by user. All problems are designed to result in dividends without fractions. Color Computer version has color graphics and sound.

SPEED DRILL - Similar to MATH DRILL program; provides drills on addition, subtraction, multiplication, and division with difficulty determined by user. Also times user and scores answer wrong if it is not given rapidly enough. Time limit is also determined by user. For TRS-80 MOD I or III, Color Computer, and Apple II only.

ID: J82

ELEMENTARY MATH PACKAGE I (TRS-80 COLOR COMPUTER VERSION)

Publisher: Micro Learningware

Grade: Elementary

Format: cassette

Hardware: TRS-80 Color Computer; 16K

Language: BASIC

Source Code: yes

Price: $24.95

Package contains drills in multiplication, division, subtraction, and addition. Written instructions provided.

MULTIPLICATION DRILL - Has 9 levels of speed and 4 levels of difficulty, with graphics used for timing.

DIVISION DRILL - Has 9 levels of speed and 4 levels of difficulty. Uses color graphics and sound. All problems are designed to result in dividends without fractions.

SUBTRACTION DRILL - Has 9 levels of sound and 4 levels of difficulty. Uses sound and color graphics.

ADDITION DRILL - Has 9 levels of speed and 4 levels of difficulty. Uses color graphics and sound.

ID: J83

ELEMENTARY MATH PACKAGE II

Publisher: Micro Learningware

Also available from: Academic Software • Opportunities For Learning, Inc. • Queue, Inc.

Grade: Elementary

Format: cassette or diskette

Hardware: PET; 8K cassette • TRS-80 MOD I or III; 16K (cassette) or 32K (diskette) • TRS-80 Color Computer; 16K with extended BASIC; cassette • Apple II; 32K with Applesoft in ROM (DOS 3.2 or 3.3)

Language: BASIC

Source Code: yes

Price: $24.95

Package provides a number of drill and practice and game format programs designed to introduce and reinforce math concepts. For all computers listed unless otherwise noted in descriptions. Written instructions provided.

FRACTIONS - Introduces concept of fractions, with numerous graphic illustrations followed by various drill and practice problems on fractions.

DECIMALS - Introduces user to decimal numbers with graphic illustrations, then proceeds to drill and practice using decimal numbers.

BAGELS - Math game in which user tries to guess three-digit number with clues provided by computer.

STONES - User plays against computer in trying to pick up last stone without picking up more than 10 stones each turn.

FACTOR - Game makes learning factoring fun and easy. Computer displays string of up to 50 consecutive numbers (actual number is determined by user) and player selects a number. That number is added to player's points, and computer gets all factors of number. Number selected and all factors thereof are deleted from list and play continues. For TRS-80 MOD I or II only.

METRIC BLACKJACK - Makes learning metrics fun. User plays blackjack with computer; but instead of using cards, lines are drawn on screen. In order to determine value of hand, player must estimate length in centimeters of each of lines, then decide whether or not to take another "hit". For TRS-80 MOD I or III only.

ID: J84

ELEMENTS OF MATHEMATICS

Publisher: Electronic Courseware Systems, Inc. (ECS)

Format: diskette

Hardware: Apple II; (DOS 3.2 or 3.3)

Price: $90.00

This lesson series is a drill and practice approach presented in a progressively structured manner. The program includes instruction in adding fractions (common denominators), reducing fractions and adding fractions (unlike denominators). All lessons have been developed with a student router and data-keeping options for collecting student progress.

ID: J85

EQUATIONS

Publisher: Educational Activities, Inc.

Also available from: Academic Software • Queue, Inc.

Grade: 7-12

Format: cassette or diskette

Hardware: Apple II Plus; (DOS 3.2.1 or 3.3) • TRS-80 MOD I or III; with Level II BASIC • PET • Commodore 2001 • Commodore 4000; 40 or 80 column • Commodore 8000; 80 column

Source Code: no

Price: $15.95/cassette; $45.00/cassette set of 3; $45.00/diskette

Each of the programs in this set provides the student with an unlimited supply of random equations which s/he must solve for the variable. Correct solutions are heralded with animated rewards, and a step-by-step display and explanation of how to find the solution are supplied if indicated by poor student performance.

SOLVING EQUATIONS LEVEL I - Provides random equations of one variable and one operation.

SOLVING EQUATIONS LEVEL II - Provides random equations of one variable and two operations, and frequent use of parentheses.

SOLVING EQUATIONS LEVEL III - Provides random equations which include the variable on both sides.

ID: J86
EQUATIONS

Publisher: Microcomputer Workshops

Also available from: Micro-Ed, Inc.

Grade: 7-10

Format: cassette

Hardware: PET

Language: BASIC

Source Code: no

Price: $20.00

This program generates random equations in the form AX - B = C, where A, B, and C are integers. All solutions are integer values. Students solve the equations step by step on the screen. All errors, including incorrect use of algebraic axioms, are immediately flagged and appropriate messages are given explaining the student's error. The student continues solving the equations until the correct solution is reached. The student is then told the number of errors made and is given the option of working with a new problem.

ID: J87
ESSENTIAL MATH PROGRAM, VOLUME ONE

Publisher: Radio Shack®

Also available from: McKilligan Supply Corp.

Date: 1982

Grade: 7-12

Format: 4 cassettes or 2 diskettes

Hardware: TRS-80 MOD I; 16K with Level II BASIC • TRS-80 MOD III; 16K with Model III BASIC

Language: BASIC

Source Code: yes

Price: $199.00

Self-paced drill and practice package consists of series of programs designed to reinforce math concepts introduced by classroom teacher. Contains skill-building exercises in addition, subtraction, multiplication, division, and number concepts. Includes placement mode of operation with optional promotion/demotion feature. Reinforcement messages keyed to correct and incorrect responses provide constant feedback to student. Comprehensive reporting function provides student progress reports on record sheet forms. Teacher's manual included.

ID: J88
ESSENTIAL MATH PROGRAM, VOLUME TWO

Publisher: Radio Shack®

Date: 1982

Grade: 7-12

Format: cassette or diskette

Hardware: TRS-80 MOD I; 16K with Level II BASIC • TRS-80 MOD III; 32K with Model III or Disk BASIC

Language: BASIC

Source Code: yes

Price: $199.00

Program is designed to reinforce math concepts introduced by classroom teacher. Covers fractions, decimals, and percentages, as well as pre-algebraic concepts. Features automatic promotion and demotion through lessons, and reinforcement messages which provide constant feedback to student.

ID: J89
EUCLID GEOMETRY TUTOR

Publisher: Radio Shack®

Also available from: McKilligan Supply Corp.

Date: 1982

Grade: Secondary

Format: cassette or diskette

Hardware: TRS-80 MOD I; 16K with Level II BASIC • TRS-80 MOD III; 16K with Model III BASIC

Language: BASIC

Source Code: yes

Price: $29.95

Program is designed to reinforce geometrical concepts introduced by teacher. Students practice constructing proofs using nine basic postulates of Euclidean geometry. Self-paced program allows students to progress according to individual ability through automatic, practice, quiz, and test modes of operation. Option is available to re-prove theorem in different mode. Selected exercises section gives students opportunity for drill and practice in wide variety of problems.

ID: J90
EXPANDED NOTATION

Publisher: Hartley Courseware, Inc.

Also available from: Academic Software • K-12 Micromedia • Opportunities For Learning, Inc. • Queue, Inc.

Grade: 2-5

Format: 1 diskette

Hardware: Apple II; 48K with Applesoft in ROM (DOS 3.2 or 3.3)

Language: Applesoft BASIC

Price: $29.95

Numerals are presented in expanded form and student must type numerical equivalent; simple arithmetic operations are performed using expanded numerals. Ten lessons of twenty presentations each build in difficulty from ones and tens to hundreds and thousands. Place values are also introduced.

ID: J91

FABULOUS L-C-M MACHINE AND THE GENEROUS JACKPOT MINE

Publisher: Micro-Ed, Inc.

Also available from: EISI (Educational Instructional Systems, Inc.) • K-12 Micromedia

Grade: Elementary and up

Format: cassette or diskette

Hardware: Commodore 64 • PET • VIC; 3K memory enhancement

Language: BASIC

Source Code: no

Price: $14.95

The purpose of this program is to win at the L-C-M Machine. This is done by finding the Least Common Multiple of three numbers randomly generated by the computer. If the student wins enough during nine tries, the Big Dollar Board will fill up, and the computer will take the student to see a Big Event at the Jackpot Mine.

ID: J92

FACTORING WHOLE NUMBERS

Publisher: Quality Educational Designs (QED)

Also available from: Activity Resources Company, Inc. • Queue, Inc.

Format: 12 programs on 18 cassettes or 9 diskettes

Hardware: TRS-80; 16 K (cassette) • TRS-80 MOD I or III; 32K • Apple; 32K (DOS 3.2) • Apple; 48K (DOS 3.3 Vers. 2.0) • PET; 16K (cassette or diskette)

Language: BASIC

Price: $90.00

This program uses the computer as a tutor, reinforcer and vehicle for expansion of learning through games and explorations. The programs are built in an interrelated fashion and are designed for sequential use. The tutorial programs are THE RECTANGLE GAME, GUESS AND TEST, THE SIEVE OF ERATOSTHENES, HOW MANY FACTORS, THE EUCLID GAME, and FACTORING FINALE. The game programs are FACTOR PAIRS, PAIRS AND SQUARES, EXPONENTS, HIGHEST COMMON FACTOR, and LEAST COMMON MULTIPLE.

ID: J93

FACTORING; TEACH ME AND SHOW ME

Publisher: Micro Power & Light Company

Also available from: Academic Software • Queue, Inc.

Format: diskette

Hardware: Apple II; 32K with Applesoft in ROM

Price: $34.95

This program teaches the student how to factor polynomial expressions, containing a single variable, with the highest degree two. From a readily-accessible main menu, the student is able to go directly to any of four sections of the program: (1) The Distributive Property. This section demonstrates how to remove and insert parentheses in the factoring process. FOIL is illustrated. Practice problems are generated and presented by

the program, and the correct answer is given when requested by the student having difficulty. (2) The Factoring Game. This section of the program affords the student unlimited practice opportunities. Students working 10 or more exercises become participants in the ongoing "contest" monitored by the program. The student who gets all correct answers in the briefest period of time, holds the winner's title- until someone else does better! (3) The Scheduled Quiz. The "teacher mode", accessible by password only, enables teachers to specify the type and number of factoring exercises to be presented each student in the class. In student mode, the program generates and presents the exercises, keeps score, and subsequently (back in teacher mode) shows the results to the teacher. (4) The Factoring Machine. In this section, the student can enter an expression to be factored - and the program does it, step by step, at the student's pace!

ID: J94

FAT CHANCE

Publisher: Micro-Ed, Inc.

Also available from: EISI (Educational Instructional Systems, Inc.)

Grade: Elementary and up

Format: cassette or diskette

Hardware: Commodore 64 • PET • VIC; 3K memory enhancement

Language: BASIC

Source Code: no

Price: $14.95

An understanding of multiples is needed to make the student's "FAT CHANCE" pay off. The player must predict the chances of a certain number being the multiple of another number.

ID: J95

FRACTION - ADDITION

Publisher: Robert R. Baker, Jr.

Date: June 82

Format: cassette or diskette

Hardware: TRS-80 MOD I or III; 16K

Language: BASIC

Source Code: yes

Price: $23.85

Self-study program builds student's confidence in adding fractions. Different skill levels and timed problems make fractions interesting to students of differing abilities. Summary scores and times are displayed at end of program. Average program running time is 2-3 minutes at each level of difficulty. Written documentation is provided, and program is self-documented as well.

ID: J96

FRACTION AND MIXED NUMBER ARITHMETIC

Publisher: Educational Micro Systems Inc.

Also available from: MARCK • Queue, Inc.

Grade: 4-9

Format: cassette or diskette

Hardware: Apple II Plus; 48K (DOS 3.3) • TRS-80 MOD I; 32K (DOS 2.3)/MOD III; 32K (DOS 1.2) • TRS-80 MOD I or III; 16K (cassette)

Price: $23.95/diskette; $18.95/cassette

This program was developed to provide a powerful tool for teaching mixed number arithmetic. It is not meant to replace the generally accepted methods of introducing students to fractions and mixed number concepts, but rather to shorten the period of time from initial awareness of the concepts to mastery of related computational skills. This is accomplished through interactive practice sessions which provide the student with immediate evaluation of the problem solving ability, and the detailed step-by-step solution for review and reinforcement. The program works in Instruction Mode or Calculator Mode. In instruction mode a student enters a problem; the program edits and formats it; the student(s) calculates the answer with pencil and paper; a student enters the answer; the program then evaluates the answer and displays the step-by-step result for review; and the cycle is then repeated. In calculator mode a problem is entered and the final solution is immediately displayed. Note: In either mode, this program generates exact answers. It does not convert the problem operands to decimal fractions, perform decimal arithmetic, or try to convert an approximate decimal answer back to a mixed number. For this reason, in calculator mode, the program has many uses outside the classroom: home construction (estimating material requirements and costs), stock market (trading stocks and options, exact portfolio evaluation), and cooking/catering (menu and recipe calculation).

ID: J97

FRACTION RECOGNITION/MIXED NUMBER RECOGNITION

Publisher: Edu-Soft[T.M.]

Also available from: Academic Software • K-12 Micromedia

Format: 2 programs on cassette or diskette

Hardware: Apple II; 16K (cassette) or 32K (diskette) with Applesoft in ROM (DOS 3.2 or 3.3) • Atari 400 or 800; 16K (cassette) or 24K (diskette)

Price: $14.95/cassette; $19.95/diskette

Two programs focus on fraction recognition, comprehension and facility of use.

FRACTION RECOGNITION - The user is introduced to the concept of fractions through the use of rectangles, parts of which are shaded. The user is taught to add up shaded and unshaded parts to make the fraction. The terms ''numerator'' and ''denominator'' are introduced. As the user gets right answers he moves on to more complicated problems. User errors are corrected by the computer counting the parts and beeping as it counts.

MIXED NUMBER RECOGNITION - Each problem involving mixed numbers is displayed as a series of rectangles, some of which are completely shaded and one of which is only partly shaded. The user is aided in calculating the mixed number represented by each rectangle series. If the user gives the wrong answer, the computer counts the appropriate part of the diagram with beeping numbers. The terms ''whole number'', ''numerator'' and ''denominator'' are introduced. Whole numbers are represented by large numerals and fractions by small numerals.

ID: J98

FRACTION SERIES

Publisher: Robert R. Baker, Jr.

Also available from: Queue, Inc.

Date: June 82

Format: 4 cassettes or 1 diskette

Hardware: TRS-80 MOD I or III; 16K

Language: BASIC

Source Code: yes

Price: $34.85/cassette; $19.85/diskette

Program provides fraction drill in addition, subtraction, multiplication, and decimal conversion. Time for entire exercise is given as well as score. Average program running time is 2-3 minutes at each level of difficulty. Written documentation is provided, and program is self-documented as well.

ID: J99

FRACTIONS

Publisher: Quality Educational Designs (QED)

Also available from: Activity Resources Company, Inc. • Queue, Inc.

Format: 24 programs on 12 cassettes or 6 diskettes

Hardware: TRS-80; 16K (cassette) • TRS-80 MOD I or III; 32K • Apple; 32K (DOS 3.2) • Apple; 48K (DOS 3.3 Vers. 2.0) • PET; 16K (cassette or diskette)

Language: BASIC

Price: $175.00

FRACTIONS uses the computer as a tutor, reinforcer and vehicle for expansion of learning through games and explorations. The programs are built in an interrelated fashion and are designed for sequential use. The tutorial programs are CONCEPTS, EQUIVALENT FRACTIONS, DIVISION MEANING, FRACTIONS AND MEASUREMENT, MULTIPLYING FRACTIONS, MULTIPLICATION SHORTCUTS, ADDING FRACTIONS, COMPARING FRACTIONS, MIXED NUMBERS, DIVISION THE SAFE WAY, DIVISION AND MINUSES, and COMPOUND FRACTIONS. The game and exploration programs are A PLACEMENT TEST, FRAC TAC TOE, DECIMAL PATTERNS, CURIOUS MEASUREMENTS, TARGET, FACTOR FRACTURE, THE ANOW PROBLEM, FAREY SEQUENCES, FRACJACK, DIVIDE AND CONQUER, TAKE A WALK, and CONTINUED FRACTIONS. A teacher's manual is included.

ID: J100

FRACTIONS - DECIMAL CONVERSIONS

Publisher: Robert R. Baker, Jr.

Date: June 82

Format: cassette or diskette

Hardware: TRS-80 MOD I or III; 16K

Language: BASIC

Source Code: yes

Price: $23.85

Self-study program gives students practice converting fractions to decimal equivalents. Different skill levels and time limits build student confidence in solving fraction decimal conversions. Total time and score are displayed at completion of program. Average program running time is 2-3 minutes at each level of difficulty. Written documentation is provided, and program is self-documented as well.

ID: J101

FRACTIONS - IMPROPER TO MIXED

Publisher: Robert R. Baker, Jr.

Date: June 82

Format: cassette or diskette

Hardware: TRS-80 MOD I or III; 16K

Language: BASIC

Source Code: yes

Price: $23.85

Self-study program gives students practice in converting improper fractions to mixed numbers. Different ability levels and timed problems make exercises interesting to all. Score and total time are displayed at end of drill. Average program running time is 2-3 minutes at each level of difficulty. Written documentation is provided, and program is self-documented as well.

ID: J102

FRACTIONS - LCD SELECTION

Publisher: Robert R. Baker, Jr.

Date: June 82

Format: cassette or diskette

Hardware: TRS-80 MOD I or III; 16K

Language: BASIC

Source Code: yes

Price: $23.85

Self-study program provides practice finding lowest common denominator. Timed program drills students at different skill levels. Total time and score are displayed at completion of program. Average program running time is 2-3 minutes at each level of difficulty. Written documentation is provided, and program is self-documented as well.

ID: J103

FRACTIONS - MIXED ADDITION

Publisher: Robert R. Baker, Jr.

Date: June 82

Format: cassette or diskette

Hardware: TRS-80 MOD I or III; 16K

Language: BASIC

Source Code: yes

Price: $23.85

Program gives students practice in adding mixed fractions. Different ability levels provide transition from easy to difficult problems. Timed problems and exercises encourage students to try harder to increase their scores. Average program running time is 2-3 minutes at each level of difficulty. Written documentation is provided, and program is self-documented as well.

ID: J104

FRACTIONS - MIXED MULTIPLICATION

Publisher: Robert R. Baker, Jr.

Date: June 82

Format: cassette or diskette

Hardware: TRS-80 MOD I or III; 16K

Language: BASIC

Source Code: yes

Price: $23.85

Self-study program gives students practice in multiplying mixed fractions. Different ability levels provide transition from easy to difficult problems. Timed problems and exercises encourage students to try harder to increase their scores. Average program running time is 2-3 minutes at each level of difficulty. Written documentation is provided, and program is self-documented as well.

ID: J105

FRACTIONS - MIXED SUBTRACTION

Publisher: Robert R. Baker, Jr.

Date: June 82

Format: cassette or diskette

Hardware: TRS-80 MOD I or III; 16K

Language: BASIC

Source Code: yes

Price: $23.85

Self-study program gives students practice in subtracting mixed fractions. Different ability levels provide transition from easy to difficult problems. Timed problems and exercises encourage students to try harder to increase their scores. Average program running time is 2-3 minutes at each level of difficulty. Written documentation is provided, and program is self-documented as well.

ID: J106

FRACTIONS - MIXED TO IMPROPER

Publisher: Robert R. Baker, Jr.

Date: June 82

Format: cassette or diskette

Hardware: TRS-80 MOD I or III; 16K

Language: BASIC

Source Code: yes

Price: $23.85

Self-study program gives students practice in converting mixed numbers to improper fractions. Different ability levels and timed problems make exercises interesting to all. Score and total time are displayed at end of drill. Average program running time is 2-3 minutes at each level of difficulty. Written documentation is provided, and program is self-documented as well.

ID: J107
FRACTIONS - MULTIPLICATION
Publisher: Robert R. Baker, Jr.

Date: June 82

Format: cassette or diskette

Hardware: TRS-80 MOD I or III; 16K

Language: BASIC

Source Code: yes

Price: $23.85

Self-study program builds student's confidence in multiplying fractions. Different skill levels and timed problems make fractions interesting to students of differing abilities. Score and time are displayed at end of exercise. Average program running time is 2-3 minutes at each level of difficulty. Written documentation is provided, and program is self-documented as well.

ID: J108
FRACTIONS - REDUCING
Publisher: Robert R. Baker, Jr.

Date: June 82

Format: cassette or diskette

Hardware: TRS-80 MOD I or III; 16K

Language: BASIC

Source Code: yes

Price: $23.85

Self-study program provides practice in reducing fractions to lowest terms. Computer times each problem as well as exercise as a whole. Different skill levels provide motivation for each student to persist. Average program running time is 2-3 minutes at each level of difficulty. Written documentation is provided, and program is self- documented as well.

ID: J109
FRACTIONS/DECIMALS
Publisher: Cow Bay Computing

Format: 1 cassette

Hardware: PET; any model except VIC 20 or 8032

Price: $15.00

This program teaches which number in a fraction is the divisor, how to add a decimal point and zeros, and how to divide and round off.

ID: J110
FRACTIONS/RATIONAL NUMBERS
Publisher: Comaldor

Format: 4 programs on cassette or diskette

Hardware: PET

Price: $60.00/set

Each program takes students step by step through solutions to addition, subtraction, multiplication, and division of rational numbers. Each step is explained. Students put in their own questions making it suitable for fractions in the junior level and rationals in the intermediate. Ideally suited for checking solutions or reviewing method.

ID: J111
FRACTIONS: A REVIEW COURSE
Publisher: BLS Inc.

Date: Apr. 82

Grade: 7 and up (reading level 6-7)

Format: 15 diskettes

Hardware: Apple II; 48K with Applesoft in ROM (DOS 3.2 or 3.3)

Language: Applesoft BASIC

Source Code: no

Price: $765.00/series; $60.00/diskette; $216.00/INTRO. TO FRACTIONS and ADDITION OF FRACTIONS...; $378.00/FRACTIONS: SUBTRACTIONS...

TUTORCOURSE BLS25F series is designed to meet growing need for effective basic and remedial instruction in area of fractions. Three programs contain total of 15 lessons, each ending with summary and test. Programs utilize self-paced, branch-programmed instruction methods. Comprehensive user documentation is provided. Series study time: 9-15 hours.

INTRODUCTION TO FRACTIONS - TUTORPROGRAM BLS25F-1 includes four lessons, covering following topics: fraction idea, numerator and denominator, parts of a unit, parts of a group, and diagrams of fractions; fractions equal to 1, equal fractions, fractions greater than 1, and proper and improper fractions; prime and composite numbers, and factors; and multiples, and lowest common multiples (L.C.M.'s).

ADDITION OF FRACTIONS AND MIXED NUMBERS - TUTORPROGRAM BLS25F-2 includes four lessons, covering following topics: addition of like fractions, addition of unlike fractions, fraction method, and column method.

FRACTIONS: SUBTRACTION, MULTIPLICATION, AND DIVISION - TUTORPROGRAM BLS25F-3 includes seven lessons, covering following topics: subtraction of like and unlike fractions, and subtraction of mixed numbers; multiplication of fractions by whole numbers and by fractions, cancellation, and multiplication of mixed numbers; division of like and unlike fractions, and division by inverting the divisor and multiplying; and general review, practice exercises, and finding fractional parts.

ID: J112
FUNDAMENTALS OF ALGEBRA
Publisher: Aquarius Publishers Inc.

Date: Aug. 82

Format: 3 diskettes

Hardware: Apple II; 48K with Applesoft in ROM (DOS 3.3)

Language: Applesoft BASIC

Source Code: no

Price: $115.00; $39.95/diskette

Powerful computer mediated instructional system is suitable for both adjunct and stand-alone learning. Programs in series offer choice of "learning styles" - definitions, rules, examples, and sample problems to solve. Choice gives student opportunity to discover most effective methods for gaining information and to achieve certain level of self- management in learning. Programs feature high resolution graphics, custom designed upper/lower case font, and flow- charted information maps. Written documentation is provided.

ALGEBRA I - Program presents definitions, number line operations, sets, evaluation expressions, and rules for equation reduction.

ALGEBRA II - Program presents rules for addition, multiplication, solving equations, and solving inequalities.

ALGEBRA III - Program provides instruction in monomials, polynomials, simple factoring, factoring and binomials, and quadratic trinomials.

ID: J113
GENERAL MATHEMATICS - 1
Publisher: Hayden Book Company, Inc.

Format: cassette

Hardware: PET • TRS-80; with Level II BASIC • Apple II • Sorcerer

Language: BASIC

Price: $14.95/cassette

Contains 15 programs useful to anyone who wants to improve their math skills and accelerate their computations.

LOG TO ANY BASE
NEW COORDINATES
RECTANGULAR/POLAR COORDINATES
PERMUTATIONS
COMBINATIONS
VECTOR CROSS-PRODUCTS
VECTOR SCALAR PRODUCTS
MAX/MIN LOCATOR
NUMBER ROUNDER
DIMENSION SCALAR
HISTOGRAM
CIRCLE FINDER
Nth ROOT OF A NUMBER
NORMALLY DISTRIBUTED RANDOM NUMBERS
RATIONAL FRACTIONS

ID: J114
GEOMETRY MEASUREMENT DRILL & PRACTICE
Publisher: Apple Computer, Inc.

Date: Feb. 82

Grade: Junior High and up

Format: 2 program diskettes, backup diskettes

Hardware: Apple II Plus; 32K (DOS 3.3) • Apple II; 32K with Applesoft in ROM (DOS 3.3)

Language: Applesoft BASIC

Source Code: yes

Price: $50.00

Programs use high-resolution graphics to provide study information, drill options, and correct answers on areas, perimeters, lengths, angles, polygons, volumes, circles, and clock time intervals. Material is presented on separate elementary and advanced diskettes. Menu-driven programs permit user selection of number of problems to be worked on. Program summarizes number of correct answers on first and second tries, as a gauge of progress. User instructions included.

ID: J115
GRAPHICAL ANALYSIS OF DATA
Publisher: Merlan Scientific Ltd.

Grade: High School and up

Format: cassette or diskette

Hardware: PET; 8K

Language: BASIC

Source Code: no

Price: $60.00

Program teaches student how to take table of data relating two variables and, by graphical techniques, to determine mathematical equation linking them. In conjunction with student study guide, program addresses itself to three kinds of mathematical functions--direct proportion, simple power law, and simple inverse relationships. Program will plot graph of pre-programmed data (or student data) on computer screen, then replot data using modified x-axis chosen from listing by student. Once student has chosen appropriate axes to obtain straight-line plot, he or she can find equation of line from slope and y-intercept. Program is fully documented, including detailed teacher's guide, as well as student guide which includes set of student worksheets (which may be duplicated for each student using program). Apart from teaching graphical analysis techniques, program can be used as aid in analyzing experimental data.

ID: J116
GRAPHICAL ANALYSIS OF EXPERIMENTAL DATA
Publisher: Radio Shack®

Date: 1982

Grade: Secondary

Format: cassette or diskette

Hardware: TRS-80 MOD I; 16K with Level II BASIC • TRS-80 MOD III; 16K with Model III BASIC

Language: BASIC

Source Code: yes

Price: $29.95

Secondary math and physics program allows students to solve problems by analyzing experimental data graphically. Program computes equation of line of best fit to data points on graph, and predicts value of dependent variable or function thereof based on values of independent variable or function thereof. Program allows individual data points to be removed from data set, and features a "stopwatch" timer for timing experiments. User's guide and programming guide are included.

ID: J117
GRAPHING
Publisher: Educational Activities, Inc.

Also available from: Academic Software • K-12 Micromedia • Queue, Inc.

Grade: 7-12

Format: cassette or diskette

Hardware: Apple II Plus; (DOS 3.2.1 or 3.3) • TRS-80 MOD I or III; with Level II BASIC • PET • Commodore 2001 • Commodore 4000; 40 or 80 column • Commodore 8000; 80 column

Source Code: no

Price: $17.95/cassette; $34.95/cassette set of 2; $39.95/diskette

INTRODUCTION TO GRAPHING ON THE COORDINATE PLANE - After reviewing basic terms, such as coordinate plane, X and Y axes, origin, and ordered pair, this program provides instruction on writing an ordered pair for a point displayed on a graph. Random points are displayed on a coordinate plane, allowing the student to input the correct X and Y coordinates for each. If the student completes the example correctly, a random textual reward is given. If the student is unable to answer the example as required, the computer provides the answer.

PLOTTING POINTS ON THE COORDINATE PLANE - This program gives the student the opportunity to plot random ordered pairs, designated by the computer, on a coordinate plane. By using specified keys on the keyboard, the student is able to move the cursor on the screen to the proper location. An unlimited number of ordered pairs, motivating rewards for correct answers, and (after two unsuccessful attempts by the student) an explanation of how to locate the point and a display of the correct location, make this program a valuable teaching tool.

ID: J118
GRAPHING CAN BE FUN!

Publisher: Aquarius Publishers Inc.

Also available from: Academic Software

Date: 1982

Format: cassette or diskette

Hardware: Apple II; 48K with Applesoft in ROM (DOS 3.2 or 3.3) • TRS-80; 16K

Source Code: no

Price: $24.95/cassette; $45.00/both $29.95/diskette; $55.00/both

Separate programs on pie and line graphs and on bar and picture graphs provide students with simplified instruction on purpose of graphs and on how to interpret and draw them. Self-directed skill sheets assist students in designing their own graphs based on data given and then interpreting data properly. Teacher's guide is included. Average running time is 20 minutes.

ID: J119
GREAT TIMES HOTEL

Publisher: Micro-Ed, Inc.

Also available from: EISI (Educational Instructional Systems, Inc.) • K-12 Micromedia

Grade: Elementary

Format: cassette or diskette

Hardware: Commodore 64 • PET

Language: BASIC

Source Code: no

Price: $14.95

This hotel is filled with mystery and intrigue. Certain clues will lead the player to the floors where strange things are happening. The greatest challenge of all is to discover the secret of the multiple elevators. In so doing, the learner will master the concept of common multiple.

ID: J120
GREATER THAN / LESS THAN

Publisher: Micro-Ed, Inc.

Also available from: Academic Software • EISI (Educational Instructional Systems, Inc.) • K-12 Micromedia • MARCK • Queue, Inc.

Grade: Elementary

Format: cassette or diskette

Hardware: Commodore 64 • PET; light pen optional (specify program MA-16)

Language: BASIC

Source Code: no

Price: $7.95

This program is designed to give practice in using the math symbol meaning greater than and the math symbol meaning less than. Ten problems of the following type are presented for each lesson: (8 + 6) ? (19 - 4). The student's job is to make a true statement by substituting the proper symbol for the question mark. At the end of the lesson, the student's performance is summarized.

ID: J121
GUESS THE NUMBER/REVERSE

Publisher: Edu-Soft[T.M.]

Also available from: Academic Software

Format: 2 programs on cassette or diskette

Hardware: Atari 400 or 800; 16K (cassette) or 24K (diskette)

Price: $14.95/cassette; $19.95/diskette

These are two programs designed to help users learn relative sizes of numbers and to play an educational strategy game.

GUESS THE NUMBER - Program aids users in recognizing relative size of different numbers. Computer asks user to guess a number between 1 and 500. The guess will "sink" or "float" on the screen depending on whether it is too large or too small. The speed of the sinking or floating varies according to how close the guess is to the computer's secret number.

REVERSE - This is an educational strategy game using a list of digits. The digits are scrambled and the object is to get them in the correct order through a series of moves called "reverses."

ID: J122
GUESSTIMATOR A

Publisher: Micro-Ed, Inc.

Also available from: EISI (Educational Instructional Systems, Inc.)

Grade: Elementary and up

Format: cassette

Hardware: PET

Language: BASIC

Source Code: no

Price: $14.95

This program gives the student an opportunity to learn to estimate proportion by having the computer respond appropriately to estimates. For each problem, a rectangle appears which is partly filled at random by the computer. What proportion of the box is filled? Make a guesstimate! The student may choose the level of difficulty: easy or hard.

ID: J123
GUESSTIMATOR B
Publisher: Micro-Ed, Inc.

Also available from: EISI (Educational Instructional Systems, Inc.)

Grade: Elementary and up

Format: cassette

Hardware: PET

Language: BASIC

Source Code: no

Price: $14.95

The purpose of this program is to encourage the student to ESTIMATE answers before working them out by calculator or with paper and pencil. The student makes an estimate by moving a pointer to an appropriate position on a number line, using the + key and the - key. The SCALE of the number line may be changed by pressing the = key. Five levels of difficulty are available, and problems are presented in sets of five.

ID: J124
GUZINTA HOTEL
Publisher: Micro-Ed, Inc.

Also available from: EISI (Educational Instructional Systems, Inc.)

Grade: Elementary

Format: cassette or diskette

Hardware: Commodore 64 • PET

Language: BASIC

Source Code: no

Price: $14.95

This hotel has a special set of "multiple" elevators that stop only on certain floors. The player must decide what elevator to use to reach several floors in one ride. Making the right decisions leads to an understanding of the concept of greatest common factor.

ID: J125
HIGH SCHOOL COMPETENCY MATH SERIES
Publisher: Microcomputer Workshops

Date: July 82

Grade: 9-12

Format: diskette

Hardware: TRS-80 MOD I or III; 32K

Language: BASIC

Source Code: no

Price: $99.00

Computer-based drill and remediation program in basic math skills is based on New York state curriculum guidelines for competency in mathematics. Diskette contains fourteen subprograms. Written documentation is provided.

WHOLE NUMBERS
FRACTIONS
DECIMALS
BASIC PERCENT
PRIMES AND FACTORS
INTEGERS
ALGEBRA
GEOMETRY
RATIO AND PROPORTION
PROBABILITY
STATISTICS
PERCENT WORD PROBLEMS
MONEY PROBLEMS
MISCELLANEOUS PROBLEMS

ID: J126
INTEGERS
Publisher: Comaldor

Format: 4 programs on cassette or diskette

Hardware: PET

Price: $60.00/set

Using a number line approach, students are guided through solutions of addition, subtraction, multiplication, and division questions. Sample questions are followed by the opportunity for students to question input.

ID: J127
INTEGERS/EQUATIONS
Publisher: Hartley Courseware, Inc.

Also available from: Academic Software • Queue, Inc.

Grade: 5-8

Format: 1 diskette

Hardware: Apple II; 48K with Applesoft in ROM (DOS 3.2 OR 3.3)

Language: Applesoft BASIC

Price: $35.95

Provides practice lessons for intermediate students in three concept areas: variables, integers, and elementary equations. Separate pre/post-tests are provided for placement into particular areas or for additional review. Total of 23 lessons, each with 20 different presentations.

ID: J128
INTEGERS/ESTIMATION DRILL
Publisher: Edu-Soft[T.M.]

Also available from: Academic Software • K-12 Micromedia

Format: 2 programs on cassette or diskette

Hardware: TRS-80 MOD I or III; 16K (cassette) or 32K (diskette) with with Level II BASIC

Price: $14.95/cassette; $19.95/diskette

Two programs of math drill are included. ESTIMATION DRILL focuses on multiplication, while INTEGERS works with four basic arithmetic operations.

INTEGERS - User is taught the four basic arithmetic functions on both positive and negative integers. User chooses 1 of 6 problem types. Feedback is provided in multiplication/division when correct rule is shown on screen before correct answer is given. For addition/subtraction, the solution is demonstrated on the number line.

ESTIMATION DRILL - The program presents the user with a multiplication problem to which he is to estimate the answer. The user starts with 1000 points and loses points depending on accuracy and speed of answer. Problems are presented in a series of ten, and the user may choose one of three skill levels.

ID: J129

INTERMEDIATE MATH SKILLS

Publisher: Orange Cherry Media

Also available from: Academic Software

Grade: 3-8

Format: cassette or diskette

Hardware: PET 2000 or 4000; 16K • TRS-80 MOD I or III; 16K • Apple; 16K • Apple II; 16K

Price: $15.00/cassette; $56.00/cassette set of 4; $67.00/diskette set of 2

This set provides an effective review of intermediate math skills and a quick appraisal of student's level of understanding. Enjoyable activities and computer graphics help reinforce concepts and pinpoint problem areas.

FRACTIONS: ADDITION AND SUBTRACTION

FRACTIONS: MULTIPLICATION AND DIVISION

USING DECIMALS

WORKING WITH PERCENT

ID: J130

INTERPRETING GRAPHS IN PHYSICS: POSITION VERSUS TIME AND VELOCITY VERSUS TIME

Publisher: Radio Shack®

Date: 1982

Grade: Secondary

Format: cassette or diskette

Hardware: TRS-80 MOD I; 16K with Level II BASIC • TRS-80 MOD III; 16K with Model III BASIC

Language: BASIC

Source Code: yes

Price: $29.95

Secondary math and physics program allows students to solve problems in kinematics using position vs. time and velocity vs. time simulations. Randomly generated problems provide endless variety of questions for drill and practice. Helpful hints aid student in solving problems. Student progress reports evaluate student performance by number and type of problems worked, and percentage of problems correctly answered on one or two tries. User's guide and programming guide are included.

ID: J131

INTRODUCTION TO DECIMALS ON THE COMPUTER

Publisher: Educational Activities, Inc.

Also available from: Academic Software • K-12 Micromedia • MARCK • Opportunities For Learning, Inc. • Queue, Inc.

Grade: Level 2-5; Remedial

Format: cassette or diskette

Hardware: Apple II Plus; (DOS 3.2.1 or 3.3) • TRS-80 MOD I or III; with Level II BASIC • PET • Commodore 2001 • Commodore 4000; 40 or 80 column • Commodore 8000; 80 column

Source Code: no

Price: $34.95/cassette; $39.95/diskette

This program is modeled on INTRODUCTION TO MATHEMATICS ON THE COMPUTER, except that it deals with decimals. It covers addition, subtraction, multiplication and division of decimals. Each area has six levels of difficulty. This program was designed to help slow learners and learning disabled students increase their mathematical abilities by decreasing the distractibility factor and increasing the students' interest. The student makes her/his own choice. Each area has twenty randomly selected problems. If the student gets the problem wrong twice, the computer is programmed to show the same problem as a word problem. This is a self-scoring program. When the student gets 85% correct the computer will allow the student to go on to the next area. If the area is complete, it will go up to the next level of difficulty. The only prerequisite for the student is that s/he must be taught to type in "RUN" and to press the ENTER key. The program runs itself.

ID: J132

INTRODUCTION TO MATHEMATICS ON THE COMPUTER

Publisher: Educational Activities, Inc.

Also available from: Academic Software • K-12 Micromedia • MARCK • Opportunities For Learning, Inc. • Queue, Inc.

Grade: 1-4, Remedial

Format: cassette or diskette

Hardware: Apple II Plus; (DOS 3.2.1 or 3.3) • TRS-80 MOD I or III; with Level II BASIC • PET • Commodore 2001 • Commodore 4000; 40 or 80 column • Commodore 8000; 80 column

Source Code: no

Price: $34.95/cassette; $39.95/diskette

This program was designed to help slow learners and learning disabled students increase their mathematical abilities by decreasing the distractibility factor and increasing the students' interest. This program covers addition, subtraction, multiplication, and division. Each area has six levels of difficulty. The student makes her/his own choice. Each area has twenty randomly selected problems. If the student gets the problem wrong twice, the computer is programmed to show the same problem as a word problem. This is a self-scoring program. When the student gets 85% correct the computer will allow the student to go on to the next area. If the area is complete, it will go up to the next level of difficulty. The only prerequisite for the student is that s/he must be taught to type in "RUN" and to press the ENTER key. The program runs itself.

ID: J133

JUNIOR HIGH MATH

Publisher: Microphys Programs

Also available from: Academic Software • EISI (Educational Instructional Systems, Inc.) • MARCK • Queue, Inc.

Grade: Junior High

Format: 15 cassettes or 1 diskette

Hardware: PET; 8K; cassette or 4040 dual disk drive • Apple II; 24K (DOS 3.2 or 3.3) • TRS-80 MOD I or III; 16K • Bell & Howell

Language: BASIC

Source Code: yes

Price: $180.00/diskette; $20.00/cassette

Package consists of 15 interactive math programs. Computer-assisted instruction versions guide student through series of quantitative questions; individualized-instruction versions generate a unique set of problems for each student. Grades and overall evaluation are compiled by programs for each student. Complete instructions are included. Also available through Queue, Inc. in diskette format only.

MAGIC SQUARES (PJ801) - Computer randomly generates 3X3 magic squares. Value of six of nine elements will be displayed, and student is required to compute values of remaining three elements.

MULTIPLICATION (PJ802) - Enables student to develop facility in dealing with simple multiplication problems.

DIVISION (PJ803) - Enables student to develop facility in dealing with simple division problems, some involving two- to seven-digit integers.

MODULAR ARITHMETIC (PJ804) - Enables student to develop facility in dealing with addition, subtraction, and multiplication problems in randomly generated modular systems.

PROPORTION PROBLEMS (PJ805) - Enables student to develop facility in dealing with solution of problems involving proportional relationships of type x/a = b/c.

PERCENT PROBLEMS (PJ806) - Enables student to develop facility in dealing with solution to verbal problems involving percent relationships.

ADDITION OF FRACTIONS (PJ807) - Enables student to develop facility in dealing with addition of randomly generated fractions.

SUBTRACTION OF FRACTIONS (PJ808) - Enables student to develop facility in dealing with subtraction of randomly generated fractions.

MULTIPLICATION OF FRACTIONS (PJ809) - Enables student to develop facility in dealing with multiplication of randomly generated fractions.

DIVISION OF FRACTIONS (PJ810) - Enables student to develop facility in dealing with division of randomly generated fractions.

MODE, MEDIAN, AND MEAN (PJ811) - Enables student to develop facility in statistically analyzing table of randomly generated data. Greatest, smallest, and range of values, and mode, median, and mean are six quantities student must determine.

BAR GRAPH ANALYSIS (PJ812) - Enables student to develop facility in statistically analyzing a bar graph of randomly generated data values.

DECIMALS I (PJ813) - Enables student to develop facility in dealing with addition and subtraction of decimals. Each numerical value may have one, two, or three places to right of decimal point.

DECIMALS II (PJ814) - Enables student to develop facility in dealing with multiplication and division of decimals. Each numerical value may have one, two, or three places to right of decimal point.

NUMERICAL RELATIONSHIPS - VERBAL PROBLEMS I (PJ815) - Enables student to develop facility in dealing with solution to verbal problems involving simple numerical relationships.

ID: J134

JUNIOR HIGH MATH PACKAGE I

Publisher: Micro Learningware

Also available from: Academic Software • MARCK • Queue, Inc.

Grade: Junior High

Format: cassette or diskette

Hardware: TRS-80 MOD I or III; 16K cassette or 32K diskette

Language: BASIC

Source Code: yes

Price: $24.95

Package contains four math programs in "magic square" format. Written instructions provided.

MAGIC SUMS - WHOLE NUMBERS - Student must identify whether whole numbers placed in 3x3 matrix are series that form "magic square" (sums of all rows, columns, and diagonals add up to same number).

MAGIC SQUARES - WHOLE NUMBERS - Four of the nine numbers forming a "magic square" are given. The student must determine and enter the other five numbers needed to form the magic square.

MAGIC SUMS - DECIMAL NUMBERS - Just like the first program, but with decimal rather than whole numbers.

MAGIC SQUARES - DECIMAL NUMBERS - Just like the second program, but with decimal rather than whole numbers.

ID: J135

JUNIOR HIGH PACKAGE

Publisher: Math Software

Grade: 7-9

Format: diskette

Hardware: Apple II; 48K with Applesoft in ROM (DOS 3.3) • Apple II Plus

Price: $100.00

This package is one of five offered by Math Software. The descriptions for the programs can be found in the SUPERMATH PACKAGE.

ARITHMETIC RACING

BINOMIAL MULTIPLICATION

FUNCTION GRAPHER

ORBITING AND ROTATING FIGURES
SIMULTANEOUS LINEAR SYSTEMS
SOLVING LINEAR EQUATIONS

ID: J136
K-8 MATH PROGRAM
Publisher: Radio Shack®

Also available from: McKilligan Supply Corp.

Date: 1982

Grade: K-8

Format: 5 cassettes or 3 diskettes

Hardware: TRS-80 MOD I; 16K with Level II BASIC • TRS-80
MOD III; 16K with Model III BASIC

Language: BASIC

Source Code: yes

Price: $199.00

Program is designed for use in classroom environment as
supplement to regular instruction. Part One contains skill-
building exercises in numeration, addition, and subtraction for
grades K-3. Part Two contains skill-building exercises, test
mode, and placement mode for addition, subtraction,
multiplication, and division for grades 1-8. Self-paced instruction features reinforcement messages keyed to correct and incorrect answers. Comprehensive reporting function displays
results at end of student session. Teacher's manual included.

ID: J137
K-8 MATH PROGRAM WITH STUDENT MANAGE-MENT, VOLUME ONE
Publisher: Radio Shack®

Date: 1982

Grade: K-8

Format: 10 diskettes

Hardware: TRS-80 MOD I; 32K with Level II BASIC • TRS-80
MOD III; 32K with Model III BASIC

Language: BASIC

Source Code: yes

Price: $199.00

Program consists of original K-8 MATH PROGRAM enhanced by student management capability. This capability
automatically tracks lesson promotions and demotions and
sends student to correct lesson when student logs on; maintains complete ongoing record on disk of student performance;
and allows teacher to review and print out student reports. Program features placement, skill building, and test modes, and
stores all results on disk for later viewing by teacher. Teacher's
manual included.

ID: J138
LAST OF THE NINTH
Publisher: Micro-Ed, Inc.

Also available from: EISI (Educational Instructional Systems,
Inc.) • K-12 Micromedia • Opportunities For Learning, Inc.

Grade: Elementary

Format: cassette or diskette

Hardware: Commodore 64 • PET • VIC

Language: BASIC

Source Code: no

Price: $14.95

It's the last of the 9th and one's team is trailing by 10 runs.
Does one play it safe and just try to get on base, or does one
gamble for the home run? The greater the risk, the more difficult will the problem be in this test of the learner's ability to
solve a variety of multiplication problems.

ID: J139
LAWN OF THE LOST RINGS
Publisher: Micro-Ed, Inc.

Grade: Elementary and up

Format: cassette or diskette

Hardware: Commodore 64 • PET • VIC; 3K memory enhancement

Language: BASIC

Source Code: no

Price: $14.95

The student is given a series of decimal fractions -
denominators are either 10, 100, or 1,000 - and must write
their decimal and percent names. A lawn mower appears on
the screen and the math solutions help to locate valuable rings
lost in the grass.

ID: J140
LEARNING CAN BE FUN #2
Publisher: Jensen Software

Grade: K-3

Format: cassette or diskette

Hardware: TRS-80 MOD I or III; with Level I or II BASIC

Price: $19.95/cassette; $24.95/diskette

This package includes five programs that teach counting, addition, and subtraction skills.

HOW MANY - Prints random blocks on the screen. The child
must count the blocks and enter the correct number.

ADD ON - Simple problems in addition are aided by graphic
display of blocks. The beginner can count the blocks to get the
answer.

TAKE AWAY - Graphic block display aids in learning subtraction.

MATH RACE - A game for 1 or 2 players using simple problems in addition geared to the age of the players. Choice of
animals and vehicles to race to the finish.

MATH RACE II - More advanced racing game using addition
and subtraction.

ID: J141
LEARNING CAN BE FUN #4
Publisher: Jensen Software

Grade: 2-7

Format: cassette or diskette

Hardware: TRS-80 MOD I or III; with Level I or II BASIC

Price: $19.95/cassette; $24.95/diskette

This package contains five programs that teach multiplication, division, fractions, decimals, and test memory.

MULTIPLY - An aid to learning the basic multiplication tables. Problems are displayed similar to flash cards. Percentage of correct answers will adjust difficulty of problems.

DIVIDE - Problems in short division. Reinforces multiplication tables.

FRACTIONS - Fractional values are graphically shown with their numeric counterparts, followed by practice in identification of fractional sizes and quantities.

DECIMALS - Decimal values are explained with special emphasis on place values. Fractions are also changed to decimal value.

ZOO BREAK - A game of concentration and memory.

ID: J142
LIGHTS OUT
Publisher: Micro-Ed, Inc.
Grade: Upper Elementary and up
Format: cassette or diskette
Hardware: Commodore 64 • PET • VIC; 3K memory enhancement
Language: BASIC
Source Code: no
Price: $14.95

This is a timed exercise in which the student practices arranging a computer-generated group of decimals, in order, from largest to smallest. As the student proceeds, the lights in a building on the screen go out, one by one.

ID: J143
LOCOMOTIVE
Publisher: Micro-Ed, Inc.
Also available from: Academic Software • EISI (Educational Instructional Systems, Inc.) • MARCK • Queue, Inc.
Grade: Elementary
Format: cassette
Hardware: PET; 3G Light pen
Language: BASIC
Source Code: no
Price: $7.95

From one to ten steam locomotives appear on the screen. How many are there? Two possible answer choices are presented. The student places the point of the light pen on a small square associated with the answer of his/her choice. If the choice is correct, a little steam locomotive chugs across the screen. If the choice is not correct, a bad face appears and the problem is repeated. The lesson consists of ten problems, randomly presented. However, the program may be terminated at any time simply by pressing the space bar. Then the student's performance is summarized.

ID: J144
LONG DIVISION
Publisher: Educational Activities, Inc.

Grade: Junior High
Format: cassette or diskette
Hardware: Apple II Plus; (DOS 3.2.1 or 3.3) • TRS-80 MOD I or III; with Level II BASIC • PET • Commodore 2001 • Commodore 4000; 40 or 80 column • Commodore 8000; 80 column
Source Code: no
Price: $16.95/cassette; $19.95/diskette

A tutorial and drill approach to teach, review, practice, and reinforce the process of long division. Correct answers are reinforced; an incorrect answer lets the computer show the student how to solve the problem by explaining and illustrating each step of the solution. Similar problems are then generated until the subject is mastered. A patient, interested and nonjudgmental way of conveying this often difficult subject.

ID: J145
LONG DIVISION
Publisher: Microcomputer Workshops
Also available from: Academic Software • EISI (Educational Instructional Systems, Inc.) • MARCK • Micro-Ed, Inc. • Queue, Inc.
Grade: Elementary
Format: cassette
Hardware: PET
Language: BASIC
Source Code: no
Price: $20.00

This program presents problems in long division allowing the learner to choose a 1-, 2-, or 3-digit divisor. All problems are generated randomly so that a different problem will be presented each time the program is run. The learner works with each problem just as if he/she were doing it on a piece of paper.

ID: J146
MARATHON
Publisher: Santa Cruz Educational Software
Date: May 82
Grade: 3-10
Format: cassette or diskette
Hardware: Atari 400; 16K; cassette; joysticks • Atari 400; 24K; diskette; joysticks • Atari 800; 16K; cassette; joysticks • Atari 800; 24K; diskette; joysticks
Source Code: yes
Price: $19.95

A unique math quiz for one or two players. One is in a race to move runner across the screen first! There are four levels of play with five modes of operation for each. The game uses joysticks for all input, so play is easy for young children.

ID: J147
MATH - ADDITION AND SUBTRACTION
Publisher: RIGHT ON PROGRAMS
Also available from: Academic Software • Queue, Inc.

Grade: 2

Format: cassette or diskette

Hardware: Apple II; 48K with Applesoft in ROM (DOS 3.2 or 3.3) • PET; 16K

Language: BASIC

Source Code: yes

Price: $13.00/cassette; $15.00/diskette

Children are introduced to the basic concepts of adding things together. Then, simple examples are introduced, with student typing in correct answers, and computer correcting errors, as well as offering motivation for correct answers.

ID: J148

MATH - MATCHING AND USING NUMBERS

Publisher: RIGHT ON PROGRAMS

Also available from: Academic Software • Queue, Inc.

Grade: 1

Format: cassette or diskette

Hardware: Apple II; 48K with Applesoft in ROM (DOS 3.2 or 3.3) • PET; 16K

Language: BASIC

Source Code: yes

Price: $13.00/cassette; $15.00/diskette

This program is divided into three sections so the student can progress from one to another as each skill is mastered. In separate sections, the concept of matching graphic symbols with numerals is introduced.

ID: J149

MATH - MATCHING GEOMETRIC FIGURES

Publisher: RIGHT ON PROGRAMS

Also available from: Academic Software • Queue, Inc.

Grade: 4

Format: cassette or diskette

Hardware: Apple II; 48K with Applesoft in ROM (DOS 3.2 or 3.3) • PET; 16K

Language: BASIC

Source Code: yes

Price: $13.00/cassette; $15.00/diskette

Geometric figures are reproduced on the screen, facing in different directions. Student is shown how the figures are the same, regardless of the direction in which they face. Game, requiring accurate matching, helps motivate the student to pay attention and "find the match".

ID: J150

MATH - MEASUREMENTS

Publisher: RIGHT ON PROGRAMS

Also available from: Academic Software • Queue, Inc.

Grade: 6

Format: cassette or diskette

Hardware: Apple II; 48K with Applesoft in ROM (DOS 3.2 or 3.3) • PET; 16K

Language: BASIC

Source Code: yes

Price: $13.00/cassette; $15.00/diskette

There is a brief review of estimating common measures, as well as formulas for finding perimeters and areas. Graphics will help the student understand volume and measurement of squares, triangles, circles, etc.

ID: J151

MATH - MULTIPLICATION AND DIVISION

Publisher: RIGHT ON PROGRAMS

Also available from: Academic Software • Queue, Inc.

Grade: 4

Format: cassette or diskette

Hardware: Apple II; 48K with Applesoft in ROM (DOS 3.2 or 3.3)

Language: BASIC

Source Code: yes

Price: $13.00/cassette; $15.00/diskette

The student is introduced to basic multiplication facts; then is brought up to the fourth-grade level. A random series of examples requires answers to be typed in by student. Incorrect answers are corrected.

ID: J152

MATH - PROBLEM SOLVING

Publisher: RIGHT ON PROGRAMS

Also available from: Academic Software • Queue, Inc.

Grade: 5

Format: cassette or diskette

Hardware: Apple II; 48K with Applesoft in ROM (DOS 3.2 or 3.3) • PET; 16K

Language: BASIC

Source Code: yes

Price: $13.00/cassette; $15.00/diskette

Introduces the student to the very simple basics of problem solving. Shows students the various ways in which a math problem can be written. Then shows how same problem would appear "in words". Shows student how, though it might seem confusing at first, it is really quite simple and shows how to change word problem into number problem. Random problems appear at end so student can have fun solving problems.

ID: J153

MATH - SETS

Publisher: RIGHT ON PROGRAMS

Also available from: Academic Software • Queue, Inc.

Grade: 5

Format: cassette or diskette

Hardware: Apple II; 48K with Applesoft in ROM (DOS 3.2 or 3.3) • PET; 16K

Language: BASIC

Source Code: yes

Price: $13.00/cassette; $15.00/diskette

This program introduces basic concepts of sets to the students and then provides examples of not only what they are but how they are used, how they relate to math and how they relate to "real life".

ID: J154
MATH - SIMPLE MULTIPLICATION AND DIVISION
Publisher: RIGHT ON PROGRAMS

Also available from: Academic Software • Queue, Inc.

Grade: 3

Format: cassette or diskette

Hardware: Apple II; 48K with Applesoft in ROM (DOS 3.2 or 3.3) • PET; 16K

Language: BASIC

Source Code: yes

Price: $13.00/cassette; $15.00/diskette

Student is introduced to the concepts of multiplication, division, and numbers. Simple examples are given.

ID: J155
MATH BASEBALL
Publisher: Educational Activities, Inc.

Grade: Upper Elementary-Junior High

Format: cassette or diskette

Hardware: Apple II Plus; (DOS 3.2.1 or 3.3) • TRS-80 MOD I or III; with Level II BASIC • Commodore 2001 • Commodore 4000; 40 or 80 column • PET • Commodore 8000; 80 column

Source Code: no

Price: $19.95/cassette; $24.95/diskette

A baseball game format used to motivate the student to do the repetitive drill and practice problems necessary to build addition, subtraction, multiplication, and division skills. To play, the student must correctly answer arithmetic problems. Each correct answer is a hit, and each incorrect answer is an out. The more difficult the question, the better the hit (double, triple, home run). The program is designed so that two students can play each other, or a single student can play against the computer.

ID: J156
MATH BID
Publisher: Micro-Ed, Inc.

Also available from: Academic Software • EISI (Educational Instructional Systems, Inc.) • K-12 Micromedia • MARCK • Queue, Inc.

Grade: Elementary

Format: cassette or diskette

Hardware: Commodore 64 • PET • VIC

Language: BASIC

Source Code: no

Price: $7.95

Drill and practice problems in addition, subtraction, multiplication, or division are presented. A different choice can be made for each game. The difficulty level for each game can

also be set. The unique feature of this program lies in the fact that it is an achievement motivation game. That is, before the computer gives a student a problem to solve, the student must make a bid on his/her ability to solve the problem. A player starts with fifty points, and wins the game when 1,000 points have been accumulated. The student then watches the Bad Math Mac Monster get wiped out. (If the student does not know the answer, and types the question mark, the computer will give the answer.)

ID: J157
MATH COMPUTATION
Publisher: TSC® , A Houghton Mifflin Company

Grade: 1-8

Format: sealed disk

Hardware: Dolphin

Language: PASCAL

Source Code: no

Price: $1300.00/year license

This program promotes mastery of 125 computational skills. Made of four clusters, subdivided into 14 strands, containing a total of 534 separate drills, this software constitutes a competency-based system of skills instruction with a built-in management system. First a survey test checks competency for each skill. The number of drills provided depends on the difficulty of the skill. Problems are randomly selected to make sure each session is individualized. The instructor predetermines the length of time that the student will be given to complete each drill. To move from skill to skill, students must demonstrate mastery by scoring 80 to 100%. A score of 60-70% initiates more practice. Below 59%, a special drill sheet is printed, or the instructor can direct the computer to refer the student to other specific manuals. The four clusters are: basic skills - addition, subtraction; whole numbers - addition, subtraction, multiplication, division; fractions - basic skills, addition, subtraction, multiplication, division; and decimals, rates, ratios, proportions, percents. Documentation includes a "skill booklet" which details exactly each skill in the program.

ID: J158
MATH CONCEPTS
Publisher: Hartley Courseware, Inc.

Also available from: Academic Software • K-12 Micromedia • Queue, Inc.

Grade: 2-6

Format: 1 diskette

Hardware: Apple II; 48K with Applesoft in ROM (DOS 3.2 or 3.3)

Language: Applesoft BASIC

Price: $39.95

Presents elementary mathematical concepts. Includes lessons on before-after, prime numbers, less than-greater than, place value, odd-even, decimal words, rounding, and counting by 2s, 5s, and 10s. Simple introductory presentations are made for each concept; lessons gradually increase in difficulty. Three pre/post-tests may be used to determine lessons on which student needs additional work.

ID: J159
MATH FACTS

Publisher: Little Bee Educational Programs

Also available from: Queue, Inc.

Grade: K-6

Format: cassette

Hardware: TRS-80 MOD I or III; 16K with Level II BASIC

Price: $10.95

This program provides drill for students in addition, subtraction, division or multiplication. Any or all of the math operations may be set at the start of the program, as well as the number limits for each operator. The student fills in the blanks in an equation presented on the screen. This program employs large-sized graphically formed numbers. One to four students can be drilled at the same time. Scoring for each student is given at the end of the session.

ID: J160
MATH GOLF

Publisher: Micro-Ed, Inc.

Also available from: EISI (Educational Instructional Systems, Inc.) • K-12 Micromedia

Grade: Elementary

Format: cassette or diskette

Hardware: Commodore 64 • PET • VIC

Language: BASIC

Source Code: no

Price: $14.95

The purpose of this program is to give the student practice in forming equations with different math operations. The challenge is to place numbers in an order-of-operations arrangement that will better par. Club selection is very important. If a student is really good, he or she might make a hole-in-one every time on this 9-hole course.

ID: J161
MATH LAB I

Publisher: EduTech

Also available from: Academic Software • Queue, Inc.

Grade: 6-7

Format: diskette

Hardware: Apple II Plus; 48K (DOS 3.2 or 3.3) • Apple II; 48K with Applesoft in ROM (DOS 3.2 or 3.3)

Source Code: yes

Price: $65.00/program with manual

Each math unit drills the student on basic skills and illustrates the concept through simulation. Records are kept on diskette of each student's performance.

TIME - RATE - DISTANCE - Student is drilled separately on distance, time, and rate problems and then takes a final drill on mixed problems. After each response, the true motion is displayed.

GRAPHS - Student is drilled on reading points from a graph and plotting points on a graph. The plotting of linear and quadratic equations is also drilled. Student response is compared graphically to the correct response.

ID: J162
MATH MACHINE

Publisher: SouthWest EdPsych Services

Also available from: K-12 Micromedia • Queue, Inc.

Date: 1982

Grade: K-6

Format: 1 diskette with backup

Hardware: Apple II; 48K with Applesoft in ROM (DOS 3.3); color monitor; printer optional

Language: Applesoft BASIC

Source Code: no

Price: $79.95; $9.95/manual

Program fosters math skills on multiple-skill levels in pre-math, subtraction, division, addition, and multiplication. Step-by-step approach to drill and practice sessions supplements classroom instruction and presents individualized lessons with immediate feedback and an innovative reinforcement system to help maximize learning. Reinforcement games utilize color graphics and sound to help make learning fun and improve hand-eye coordination. Record- keeping system allows convenient progress reivews. Manual and student record forms included.

ID: J163
MATH PROBLEM SOLVING

Publisher: TSC® , A Houghton Mifflin Company

Grade: 5-8

Format: sealed disk

Hardware: Dolphin

Language: PASCAL

Source Code: no

Price: $1500.00/year license

This program teaches problem-solving skills. Techniques used to accomplish this are: the use of "reverse video" or highlighting to point out crucial information within a word problem and the use of concealed multiple choice questions. The computer presents only one possible answer at a time, forcing the student to accept or reject each answer on its own merits. This eliminates comparison judgments, focusing the child's attention and speeding up the learning process. A four-step approach teaches problem solving: 1. Get to know a problem; 2. Complete a plan to solve the problem; 3. Solve the problem; and 4. Look back at the solution. Problem solving is taught in relation to basic computational skills. These skills are arranged in five sections - whole numbers, fractions, decimals, geometry and miscellaneous (rates & proportions, percents). Correlations to five nationally recognized achievement tests are available. Documentation includes a "drill booklet" which details each skill in the program.

ID: J164
MATH SAFARI

Publisher: Micro-Ed, Inc.

Also available from: Academic Software • EISI (Educational Instructional Systems, Inc.) • K-12 Micromedia • MARCK

Grade: Elementary

Format: cassette

Hardware: PET

Language: BASIC

Source Code: no

Price: $20.00

Hunt awful ADDCHNIDS, slashing SUBSLIMPS, malicious MULGRILAS, and daring DIVAGLONS in this Mathematical Safari! The evil beasts move across the screen, challenging the student who must get them before they get away. Large bold numbers make it easy for the hunter to aim his/her math gun. However, as the safari progresses, the animals move faster. Fortunately, there is a quick plane back to civilization in case the safari needs to be shortened. At the end of each hunt, the results are summarized. Different levels of difficulty make this program appropriate for students of varying abilities.

ID: J165

MATH SEQUENCES

Publisher: Milliken Publishing Company

Also available from: EISI (Educational Instructional Systems, Inc.) • McKilligan Supply Corp.

Grade: 1-8

Format: 12 cassettes or diskettes

Hardware: Atari 800 • Apple II Plus; 48K • TRS-80; 16K with Level II BASIC (grades 1-6) • PET; 8K (grades 1-6) • TI 99/4

Price: $450.00/set; $675.00/set with backup; $200.00/set of cassettes (grades 1-6)

This package provides a wide variety of highly motivating exercises based on a comprehensive, objective-based curriculum. Students move through precisely defined sequence levels by achieving individualized mastery criteria. Both skill and performance objectives may be individualized by the teacher. Student interaction requires a minimum of direct supervision, so the sequences may be implemented in various learning environments. A teacher management program and comprehensive documentation are included with the package. The package contains a Manager Program which enables teachers to maintain individual records for up to 100 students on each diskette. The teacher can make personalized assignments for individuals or general assignments for an entire class. Student performance records are automatically updated and hard-copy printouts may be generated. Progress graphs make it very easy to identify student problem areas. The sequences provide a highly motivating, success-oriented approach to mastering pre-algebra mathematics skills. Work is self- paced and may be individualized through skill and performance objectives. The rate at which the students move through the sequence levels may also be personalized by the teacher. Feedback is immediate and positive reinforcements may be varied for primary or older students. Topics include number readiness, addition, subtraction, multiplication, division, laws of arithmetic, integers, fractions, decimals, percents, equations, and measurement formulas. The cassette packages have an abbreviated curriculum and contain no management. Also, student interaction is not as sophisticated.

ID: J166

MATH SHOOTOUT

Publisher: Micro-Ed, Inc.

Also available from: Academic Software • EISI (Educational Instructional Systems, Inc.) • MARCK • Queue, Inc.

Grade: Elementary

Format: cassette or diskette

Hardware: Commodore 64 • PET • VIC; 3K memory enhancement

Language: BASIC

Source Code: no

Price: $7.95

The idea of this program is to have the learner practice doing math exercises as fast as possible. If the learner is swift enough, he/she can beat Bad Math Mac who is waiting to draw first. Difficulty levels and time requirements can be set for any of the four areas: addition, subtraction, multiplication, and division. Each lesson consists of ten problems, at the conclusion of which the learner's performance is summarized.

ID: J167

MATH SKILLS

Publisher: SEI (Sliwa Enterprises Inc.)

Also available from: Queue, Inc.

Date: May 82

Grade: 9-12 and up

Format: 2 diskettes

Hardware: Apple II; 32K with Applesoft in ROM (DOS 3.2 or 3.3)

Language: Applesoft BASIC

Source Code: yes

Price: $25.00/MATH I; $35.00/MATH II; $50.00/both

Math skills programs are ideal as study aids for college board-type exams. Subject areas include algebra, geometry, and trigonometry at high school and college levels. Students may select to view a hint after attempting to answer each question, which shows the most efficient approach to a solution. Menu-driven programs require no documentation. Each program comes with resident editor for easy modification, updating, or expansion of data base by teacher or student.

MATH I - Program groups over 300 problems into categories such as fractions, exponents, equations, geometry, and word problems. Several files are available with a mixed assortment of types of problems.

MATH II - Program offers over 150 problems with graphic displays of problems. Questions require students to interpret line plots, flow charts, bar graphs, pie charts, and geometric constructions. MATH II requires use of a MATH I diskette as well.

ID: J168

MATH SPEED TUTOR

Publisher: Aquarius Publishers Inc.

Date: Aug. 82

Format: cassette or diskette

Hardware: TRS-80 MOD I or III

Language: BASIC

Source Code: no

Price: $14.95

Computer randomly selects simple math and algebra problems for student to solve, including addition, subtraction, multiplication, and division. Unknown variables provide added challenge. One in series of programs authored by The Programming Force and distributed exclusively by vendor.

ID: J169
MATH SPIN

Publisher: Micro-Ed, Inc.

Also available from: EISI (Educational Instructional Systems, Inc.)

Grade: Elementary

Format: cassette or diskette

Hardware: Commodore 64 • PET

Language: BASIC

Source Code: no

Price: $7.95

This is an exercise in multiplication. The object is to win 21 points before the computer does. Using a random choice technique, the student will create problems both for himself and for the computer. Game points can then be won in various ways.

ID: J170
MATH STRATEGY

Publisher: Apple Computer, Inc.

Date: Feb. 82

Grade: 1 and up

Format: master and backup diskettes

Hardware: Apple II Plus; 48K (DOS 3.3); color monitor • Apple II; 48K with Applesoft in ROM (DOS 3.3); color monitor

Language: Applesoft BASIC

Source Code: yes

Price: $45.00

Program provides challenging, interactive drills and exercises that utilize Apple's sound and color graphics capabilities to encourage effective habits of visualization and memorization of equations in addition, subtraction, multiplication, and division. Exercises followed by multiple-choice quizzes encourage children to use mental images to arrive at correct answers. Author options allow parents and teachers to create an unlimited number of lessons, each containing up to 10 equations. Instruction manual included.

ID: J171
MATH WARS

Publisher: SouthWest EdPsych Services

Also available from: K-12 Micromedia

Date: 1982

Format: diskette

Hardware: Apple II; 48K with Applesoft in ROM (DOS 3.3); color monitor

Language: Applesoft BASIC

Source Code: no

Price: $39.95

Program combines fast, high-resolution color animation with sound educational content to produce truly educational game.

Computations ranging from simple whole number addition to more complicated fractions and decimals are practiced in format guaranteed to maintain motivation and interest while concurrently improving math skills.

ID: J172
MATHEMATIC-TAC-TOE

Publisher: APX (Atari Program Exchange)

Also available from: Academic Software

Date: June 82

Grade: 3-11

Hardware: Atari 400 or 800; 16K (cassette) or 24K (diskette); Atari BASIC language cartridge

Language: BASIC

Source Code: no

Price: $15.95

Program provides addition, subtraction, multiplication, and division drills on 15 difficulty levels and 15 time-limit levels, from 2 to 23 seconds, within framework of tic-tac-toe game. Correct answer marks designated square with player's symbol (X or O). Most difficult levels go beyond point at which children normally memorize answers. User manual is included.

ID: J173
MATHEMATICS - VOLUME 1

Publisher: Minnesota Educational Computing Consortium

Also available from: Academic Software • Creative Computing • K-12 Micromedia • Opportunities For Learning, Inc. • Scholastic Software • Sunburst Communications

Date: June 82

Grade: 7-12

Format: diskette

Hardware: Apple II; 32K with Applesoft in ROM (DOS 3.3)

Language: Applesoft BASIC

Source Code: no

Price: $40.80

Package contains eight programs that provide exercises in various aspects of mathematics. Support booklet (included) provides laboratory-type activities for POLYGRAPH, POLAR, and SLOPE programs.

BAGELS, SNARK, ICBM, RADAR - Programs teach student logical methods while reinforcing concepts of plotting points or angle measurements.

ALGEBRA - Provides drill and practice in solving equations.

SLOPE - Designed to plot equations on grid using simple linear functions.

POLYGRAPH - Will plot any equation on a rectangular coordinate system.

POLAR - Graphs functions on polar coordinates.

ID: J174
MATHEMATICS - VOLUME 2

Publisher: Minnesota Educational Computing Consortium

Date: June 82

Grade: Junior High

Format: diskette

Hardware: Apple II; 32K with Applesoft in ROM (DOS 3.3)

Language: Applesoft BASIC

Source Code: no

Price: $36.90

Programs provide lessons and drills on English measurement system. Tutorials include conversion with English system and addition/subtraction of measurements. Support booklet included.

LIQUIDS, LENGTHS, TIME, WEIGHTS, ADDITION DRILL, SUBTRACTION DRILL

ID: J175
MATHEMATICS - VOLUME 3

Publisher: Minnesota Educational Computing Consortium

Also available from: Sunburst Communications

Date: June 82

Grade: 6-8, Adult Remedial

Format: diskette

Hardware: Apple II; 32K with Applesoft in ROM (DOS 3.3)

Language: Applesoft BASIC

Source Code: no

Price: $37.30

Package covers geometric concepts of area and perimeter. Support booklet (included) contains handouts referenced in programs.

GEOMETRIC SHAPES

PERIMETER

RECTANGLE AND SQUARE AREAS

PARALLELOGRAM AREAS

TRAPEZOID AND TRIANGLE AREAS

ID: J176
MATHEMATICS - VOLUME 4

Publisher: Minnesota Educational Computing Consortium

Date: June 82

Grade: High School and up

Format: diskette

Hardware: Apple II; 32K with Applesoft in ROM (DOS 3.3)

Language: Applesoft BASIC

Source Code: no

Price: $51.20

Module is designed for use in higher education mathematics, linear algebra, and calculus. Concepts covered include numerical integration, limits of functions, least squares techniques of approximating functions, graphing system of equations, solving linear programs, matrix operations, and solving polynomial equations. Support booklet (included) contains sample problems, worksheets, and background information.

ID: J177
MATHEMATICS ACTION GAMES

Publisher: Scott, Foresman and Co.

Grade: 1-8

Format: 3 modules

Hardware: TI 99/4A

Price: $222.95/set of 3 modules; $75.95/module

Set of 3 graded computer modules augment instruction and give practice in fundamental mathematics skills. Variety of game formats motivates learning and encourages students to develop mental computation ability. Four different games and four different mathematics topics make up each module. Mathematics content is progressively more complex from module to module. Special features, such as outstanding color, graphics, animation, music, and sound effects, motivate and assist students. Each package includes teacher's guide.

PACKAGE A - For grades 1-3, module covers place value, ordering numbers, basic facts, and money.

PACKAGE B - For grades 4-6, module covers numeration, multiplication, division, and decimals.

PACKAGE C - For grades 7-8, module covers order of operations, decimals and fractions, percents, and integers.

ID: J178
MATHEMATICS ASSESSMENT/PRESCRIPTIVE EDU-DISKS[T.M.]

Publisher: Readers Digest

Date: 1982

Grade: 1-7

Format: 7 programs and 1 correlation on 15 diskettes

Hardware: Apple II • Apple II Plus • TRS-80 MOD I and III

Source Code: no

Price: $876.00/set of 15 disks; $129.00/grade level set (2 disks); $36.00/correlation disk

This set can be used at levels 1-7 or for remedial testing and practice on the secondary level. Format includes pretest, practice and post-test. Records of student's activities are automatically entered into the student data base. Each level includes 1 student and 1 administrative disk. 32-page teacher's guide is included. The optional correlation disk correlates the entire program to nine leading basals.

ID: J179
MATHEMATICS DRILL - ELEMENTARY

Publisher: Educational Courseware

Also available from: Academic Software

Grade: Elementary

Format: diskette

Hardware: Apple; 48K (DOS 3.3 or 3.2)

Price: $24.00

A series of programs provide remedial drill and practice with addition, subtraction, multiplication and division of integers and/or fractions. Displays problems at increasing levels of difficulty. Students' progress is evaluated. Each question is produced from a random number generator within the range of difficulty specified. Mathematics skills are improved with practice. Word problems are introduced at the end. Simple to use and user- friendly.

ID: J180

MATHEMATICS FOR SCIENCE, SERIES 2: BASIC MATH TECHNIQUES

Publisher: Merlan Scientific Ltd.

Grade: High School and up

Format: 4 cassettes or 1 diskette

Hardware: PET; 16K; cassette or diskette • Apple II Plus; 48K (DOS 3.3)

Language: BASIC

Source Code: no

Price: $20.00/cassette; $72.00/diskette; $180.00/4 diskettes in series

Series of four programs on basic math techniques is part of larger series designed primarily for science students who need specific mathematics skills. Series features alternating lesson exercises and drills in each subject area. Many parts of lessons and all drill questions are randomly generated so that student repeating exercise will be presented with different questions each time through. Written documentation is provided.

SIGNIFICANT FIGURES - Program teaches student how to judge number of significant digits in a given number. This basic concept is essential in dealing with measured quantities.

ROUNDING OFF - Program teaches proper rounding off techniques by asking student to round off variety of numbers to specific numbers of significant digits, analyzing mistakes, and prompting student to give correct answer.

CALCULATIONS AND ROUNDING OFF (ADDITION AND SUBTRACTION) - Students are asked to perform addition and subtraction calculations, with calculator simulated on computer screen, and they write their answers rounded off to appropriate number of digits. Answers are analyzed and feedback is provided.

CALCULATIONS AND ROUNDING OFF (MULTIPLICATION AND DIVISION) - Students are asked to perform multiplication and division calculations, with calculator simulated on computer screen, and they write their answers rounded off to appropriate number of digits. Answers are analyzed and feedback is provided.

ID: J181

MATHEMATICS FOR SCIENCE, SERIES 3: EXPONENTIAL NOTATION

Publisher: Merlan Scientific Ltd.

Grade: High School and up

Format: 3 cassettes or 1 diskette

Hardware: PET; 16K; cassette or diskette • Apple II Plus; 48K (DOS 3.3)

Language: BASIC

Source Code: no

Price: $20.00/cassette; $54.00/diskette; $180.00/4 diskettes in series

Series of three programs on scientific notation is part of larger series designed primarily for science students who need specific mathematics skills. Series features alternating lesson exercises and drills in each subject area. Many parts of lessons and all drill questions are randomly generated so that student repeating exercise will be presented with different questions each time through. Written documentation is provided.

SCIENTIFIC NOTATION - Program teaches student to convert numbers from ''ordinary'' form to scientific notation and vice versa.

EXPONENTIAL CALCULATIONS (ADDITION AND SUBTRACTION) - Program teaches addition and subtraction of numbers expressed in scientific notation. Student is encouraged to express answers with correct number of significant digits.

EXPONENTIAL CALCULATIONS (MULTIPLICATION AND DIVISION) - Program reviews multiplication and division of powers of ten, then moves on to examples involving numbers expressed in scientific notation. Student is encouraged to express answers with correct number of significant digits.

ID: J182

MATHEMATICS FOR SCIENCE, SERIES 4: MISCELLANEOUS

Publisher: Merlan Scientific Ltd.

Grade: High School and up

Format: 2 cassettes or 1 diskette

Hardware: PET; 16K; cassette or diskette • Apple II Plus; 48K (DOS 3.3)

Language: BASIC

Source Code: no

Price: $20.00/cassette; $36.00/diskette; $180.00/4 diskettes in series

Two programs on metrics and graphing are part of larger series designed primarily for science students who need specific mathematics skills. Series features alternating lesson exercises and drills in each subject area. Many parts of lessons and all drill questions are randomly generated so that student repeating exercise will be presented with different questions each time through. Written documentation is provided.

METRIC CONVERSIONS - Program teaches method of converting numbers expressed with one metric prefix to another. Largest prefix used is mega; smallest is micro.

SLOPES OF GRAPHS - Program teaches student how to find slope of straight-line graphs and provides many examples. Problems involve both negative and positive slope in first quadrant.

ID: J183

MATHEMATICS SERIES

Publisher: Spectrum Software

Also available from: MARCK

Grade: High School and up; Gifted

Format: diskette

Hardware: Apple II Plus or Apple II with Applesoft in ROM; 32K (DOS 3.2 - Muffinable to 3.3)

Language: BASIC

Source Code: yes

Price: $49.95

Package of four mathematical analysis routines makes maximal use of Apple's high-resolution plotting capabilities to augment math routines and display results. Programs are menu-driven and employ extensive prompting for ease of use. Entire series is shipped on single disk with demo routines and instruction manual. Running times vary according to complexity of calculations, but are generally in 5-10 minute maximum range.

STATISTICAL ANALYSIS I - General-purpose menu-driven statistics package allows user to analyze numerical data bases. Program computes and displays mean, standard deviation, frequency distribution plot, simple linear regression, SLR equation coefficient and data points. Includes routines for disk data file I/O, editing, and printer output.

NUMERICAL ANALYSIS - Program plots any two variable equations user can write, using standard BASIC arithmetic functions. Program will plot equation, its integral, and its derivative. It will determine and list roots, maxima or minima encountered, and integral value over plot range.

MATRIX - Program allows user to solve for inverse, determinant, and solution matrix for linear systems of up to 54 equations in 54 unknowns. It uses standard Gauss elimination with pivoting for maximum efficiency. Includes standard data base management routines for editing, disk I/O, and printer reports of both data and results.

3D SURFACE PLOTTER - Program does general-purpose three-dimensional plotting of any three-variable equations that user can write using standard BASIC arithmetic functions. Performs either hidden line or transparent plotting. Includes disk I/O routines for saving plot pictures on diskette.

ID: J184
MATHFLASH
Publisher: Comaldor

Format: cassette or diskette

Hardware: PET

Price: $20.00

This arithmetic drill can be set on 5 levels of difficulty. Addition, subtraction, multiplication or division, or a mix, can be selected. A summary is printed at the end of the sequence, recommending a change in level if needed.

ID: J185
MATHGRID
Publisher: Ideatech Company

Also available from: K-12 Micromedia • MARCK

Grade: 3-5; Remedial

Format: diskette

Hardware: Apple II Plus; 16 K • Apple II; 16 K with Applesoft in ROM

Language: BASIC

Price: $14.95

The program is designed to improve the student's accuracy with the 0 to 9 multiplication tables, in addition to reinforcing the concept of identifying unique points on an x-y coordinate system. Mathgrid provides drill and practice with the 0 to 9 multiplication tables for one or two players. A 10-by-10 grid is drawn on the screen, with the horizontal and vertical axes labeled 0 to 9. The student selects one to forty problems to be worked and the computer randomly chooses and marks that number of locations on the grid. The student selects a problem by identifying the correct x and y coordinates for the desired problem location. The computer then presents the problem and accepts the student's answer. The computer provides the correct answer if the problem is missed twice. A running score is kept on the screen and the total score is provided at the end of the game. Auditory feedback is used throughout the program.

ID: J186
MATHMADNESS
Publisher: Comaldor

Format: cassette or diskette

Hardware: PET

Price: $20.00

This is a super multiplication or addition drill. Pairs of randomly selected numerals are displayed in large format. The range of the tables from 1 to 9 is selected by the teacher. Teacher may enter code for display or printout of results in ranked order. Develops speed and accuracy.

ID: J187
MATHMASTER
Publisher: Instant Software[T.M.]

Also available from: Academic Software • Queue, Inc.

Format: cassette

Hardware: TRS-80 MOD I; 16K with Level II BASIC

Language: BASIC

Source Code: no

Price: $49.95

This program is designed to aid in process of understanding concepts of math by repetitive problem solving. First of program's two parts is MathCard, an addition, subtraction, multiplication, and division drill based on flash card principle. A second part, MathFrac, permits student to practice arithmetic functions using fractions only, and makes use of large, on-screen graphics which are easily read. Written documentation is provided.

ID: J188
MATHPACK - I
Publisher: Ideatech Company

Also available from: Queue, Inc.

Format: 3 programs on diskette

Hardware: Apple II; 16K with Applesoft in ROM • Apple II Plus; 16K

Price: $29.95

This package contains three programs also available separately. See individual program entries for descriptions.

SPEED FACTS

MATH GRID

MULTIPLICATION & DIVISION FUN

ID: J189
MATHRACE

Publisher: Comaldor

Format: cassette or diskette

Hardware: PET

Price: $20.00

This drill allows a number of players to have a race with questions in addition, subtraction, multiplication, division, or a mix of these. Four levels of difficulty may be selected. Should the students experience difficulty, the program automatically changes to a lower level. In "track and field" fashion, players race toward the end. Speed determines distance travelled.

ID: J190
MATHWAR

Publisher: Comaldor

Format: cassette or diskette

Hardware: PET

Price: $20.00

With the screen divided into "battleship" zones, players attempt to decimate their opponent's fleet. Opportunity to fire a salvo is earned via math questions. Different levels are available, controlling time allowed to answer.

ID: J191
MEDAL WINNER

Publisher: Micro-Ed, Inc.

Also available from: EISI (Educational Instructional Systems, Inc.) • K-12 Micromedia

Grade: Elementary

Format: cassette or diskette

Hardware: Commodore 64 • PET • VIC

Language: BASIC

Source Code: no

Price: $14.95

Here is a math exercise that can be used on either a group or individual basis! The object is to create a multiplication problem with three digits to produce the largest product. The computer will display three random digits (such as 5, 3, 9) and a product (39 X 5 = 195) that can always be bettered (for example, 53 X 9 = 477). Each learner will meet the challenge with his/her own arrangement. The computer will then print all the winning arrangements and award a gold, silver, or bronze medal for a player's performance. Each learner has an opportunity to win medals in ten events.

ID: J192
METRIC ADVENTURE

Publisher: Sunburst Communications

Grade: 3 and up

Format: diskette

Hardware: Apple II; 32K

Price: $29.00

This program creates a space colony for students to explore. Their success depends on their judgment of metric lengths, weights and volumes. Speedy decisions are important since time is counted. Support booklet is included.

ID: J193
METRIC AND PROBLEM SOLVING

Publisher: Minnesota Educational Computing Consortium

Also available from: APX (Atari Program Exchange)

Date: June 82

Grade: 1-6

Format: diskette

Hardware: Atari 400/800; 16K with Atari BASIC in cartridge

Language: BASIC

Source Code: no

Price: $36.80

Package combines practice in working with metric units, estimation, and conversion, as well as educational games in logic, coordinate systems, factors of a number, and prime numbers. Support booklet included.

METRIC ESTIMATE - Timed drill for estimating lengths and line segments in centimeters and millimeters.

METRIC LENGTH - Drill for converting from one metric unit to another using millimeters, centimeters, meters, and kilometers.

METRIC 21 - Lets students play game of metric blackjack with computer. Skill is improved in approximating metric lengths by determining when their line segments add up to 21 centimeters.

BAGELS - Game of logic in which student uses clues to guess two- to four-digit number selected randomly by computer.

HURKLE - Game for learning to locate points on number line, or for teaching coordinate system.

NUMBER - Game of logic in which computer chooses number and gives clues. Game can use various ranges of numbers to accommodate different grade levels.

TAXMAN - Game for teaching factors and prime numbers. Students choose number from list, and "taxman" collects all factors of that number remaining on list. Play continues until no factors are left. Students compete with "taxman" for highest score.

ID: J194
METRIC DRILL

Publisher: Hartley Courseware, Inc.

Also available from: Academic Software

Grade: 4-8

Format: 1 diskette

Hardware: Apple II; 48K with Applesoft in ROM (DOS 3.2 or 3.3)

Language: Applesoft BASIC

Price: $49.95

Drill/practice program is designed to reinforce the skills students must learn to use the metric system. Contains over 600 different presentations in areas of length, mass, and capacity of common objects or quantities, grouped into beginning, termediate, and advanced levels of lessons. Pre/post-tests are included for student placement or for exam and review purposes.

ID: J195
METRIC/ENGLISH CONVERSION
Publisher: Educational Micro Systems Inc.

Also available from: MARCK

Grade: 6-10

Format: cassette or diskette

Hardware: TRS-80 MOD I; 32K (DOS 2.3) or 16K cassette TRS-80 MOD III; 32K (DOS 1.2) or 16K cassette

Price: $19.95/diskette; $14.95/cassette

This program converts commonly used Metric measurements to English equivalents, and vice versa. The program is menu- driven, straightforward, and easy to use.

ID: J196
MICROMATH
Publisher: Sheridan College

Grade: Remedial, 6-12

Format: 5 diskettes (PET); 10 (Apple); 8 (TRS-80)

Hardware: PET; 16K, 40 or 80 column; 4040 or 8050 disk drive • Apple II Plus; 16K (DOS 3.3) • TRS-80 MOD II; 16K

Source Code: yes

Price: $500.00; $100.00/additional copy

A comprehensive one-semester remedial mathematics course for students in grades 6 through 12. Topics covered are: operations with signed numbers; order of operations; factoring of integers; multiplication, division, addition, and subtraction of fractions; complex fractions; manipulations of percents; working with positive, negative, and zero exponents; basic algebraic operations; algebraic substitution; simple linear equations in one unknown; percentages; algebraic simplification and linear equation solving; algebraic solution of systems of linear equations in two variables; linear relations and their graphs; solving quadratic equations by formula; and ratio and proportion. The full package includes 93 lessons and a 152-page workbook which reviews the material. A demonstration diskette is available for $25.00, which will be deducted from the cost of MICROMATH.

ID: J197
MISSILE MATH
Publisher: Microphys Programs

Grade: K-9

Format: cassette

Hardware: VIC-20; 3K expansion cartridge

Language: BASIC

Source Code: yes

Price: $15.00

Program presents in game format an opportunity to develop and practice basic skills of addition, subtraction, multiplication, and division. Four levels of difficulty may be selected in each skill area. Problems in given skill are randomly generated, and missiles launched at correct answers. Computer displays results

on each program run, and may be directed to generate same sequence of problems, so that review and match play against opponent are possible. Complete instructions are included.

ID: J198
MISSING MATH FACTS
Publisher: Educational Activities, Inc.

Also available from: Academic Software • K-12 Micromedia • MARCK • Opportunities For Learning, Inc. • Queue, Inc.

Grade: 3-6, Remedial Secondary

Format: cassette or diskette

Hardware: Apple II Plus; (DOS 3.2.1 OR 3.3) • TRS-80 MOD I or III; with Level II BASIC • PET • Commodore 2001 • Commodore 4000; 40 or 80 column • Commodore 8000; 80 column

Source Code: no

Price: $34.95/cassette; $39.95/diskette

MISSING MATH FACTS contains addition, subtraction, multiplication, and division examples on four levels of ascending difficulty. The student chooses the level s/he wishes to work on (Level 1,2,3 or 4). Each example is presented with the answer, but missing another component. The student must determine the missing number. Correct answers are "rewarded." If the student is unable to give the correct answer by the third try, the complete problem with the answer is displayed. Students may need paper and pencil to work out the problems, especially at the higher levels.

ID: J199
MISSING NUMBER
Publisher: Little Bee Educational Programs

Grade: K-1

Format: cassette

Hardware: TRS-80 MOD I or III; 16K with Level II BASIC

Price: $10.99

A program to provide drill in the sequence of numbers. The student is presented with a sequence of numbers with one of the numbers missing. He/she must respond with the missing number in the sequence. The student has two opportunities to correctly identify the missing number, then the number is identified for the student. The instructor can set the range of numbers at the start of the program. Scoring is given at the end of the program.

ID: J200
MIXED NUMBERS
Publisher: Milton Bradley

Also available from: McKilligan Supply Corp. • Opportunities For Learning, Inc.

Grade: 6-8

Format: 1 diskette

Hardware: Apple II; 48K with Applesoft in ROM (DOS 3.3)

Language: Applesoft BASIC

Price: $44.95

Program includes readiness skills, addition, subtraction, multiplication, and divison of mixed numbers. Allowing student to move at his own pace, it focuses on specific deficiencies. Includes Teacher's Guide and reproducible activity sheets. MIXED NUMBERS has three modes: Readiness, or drill; Practice, during which the student caluculates on paper; and Instruction, which gives extra help to students who have not mastered the skills.

ID: J201
MORE ALGEBRA
Publisher: TYCOM Associates

Also available from: MARCK • Queue, Inc.

Format: 5 programs on cassette

Hardware: PET; 8K; C2N cassette recorder

Price: $19.95; $26.95/programs on 5 cassettes

This series of programs is a continuation of the TYCOM ALGEBRA series described elsewhere. Topics presented include slope of a line, distance between points, solving pairs of simultaneous linear equations, solving quadratic equations by factoring, the use of the discriminant, and solving for complex roots using the quadratic formula. A lesson explaining each type of problem is given, followed by randomly generated problems to be solved by the student. After each problem incorrectly answered, the correct answer is provided. Upon exiting a program, the student is informed of how many problems were attempted and given a grade. These programs may be used concurrently with a course or for review.

ID: J202
MULTIPLICATION & DIVISION FUN
Publisher: Ideatech Company

Also available from: MARCK

Grade: 3-5, Remedial

Format: diskette

Hardware: Apple II Plus; 16K • Apple II; 16K with Applesoft in ROM

Language: BASIC

Price: $12.95

This program provides practice in multiplication and division facts, and improves the student's performance by drilling on missed problems at the end of the lesson. The student may choose which operation to practice or to practice a specific table within the operation or problems randomly chosen from all the tables of the specified operation. Twenty problems are presented to the student. After the second error on a problem, the answer is given to the student. Feedback is given after each answer, and the score is shown throughout the game in the form of the number correct and as a percentage. After all 20 problems have been attempted, the problems which were answered incorrectly are presented again as a review.

ID: J203
MULTIPLICATION 1
Publisher: Scott, Foresman and Co.

Also available from: McKilligan Supply Corp. • Texas Instruments

Date: Jan. 82

Grade: 3-5

Format: module

Hardware: TI 99/4A; speech synthesizer recommended

Source Code: no

Price: $44.95 ($39.95 from TI)

Math tutorial teaching the basics of multiplication; developed in conjunction with Texas Instruments. Includes both tutorial and practice activities for basic facts with factors through 9. Teacher's guide included.

ID: J204
MULTIPLICATION OF WHOLE NUMBERS
Publisher: Orange Cherry Media

Also available from: Academic Software

Grade: 3-6

Format: cassette or diskette

Hardware: PET 2000 or 4000; 16K • TRS-80 MOD I or III; 16K • Apple; 16K • Apple II; 16K

Price: $15.00/cassette; $56.00/cassette set of 4; $67.00/diskette set of 2

This set of programs is available as part of a package from Queue, Inc.

MULTIPLYING FROM 0 TO 5

MULTIPLYING FROM 6 TO 12

MULTIPLES OF 10, 100, AND 1000

WORD PROBLEMS WITH MULTIPLICATION

ID: J205
MULTIPLYING FRACTIONS
Publisher: Microcomputer Workshops

Date: July 82

Grade: 5-8

Format: cassette or diskette

Hardware: Apple II; 48K with Applesoft in ROM • PET; 16K; cassette • TRS-80 MOD I or III; 16K; cassette

Language: BASIC

Source Code: no

Price: $20.00/cassette; $24.95/diskette

This program generates problems randomly that give students practice in multiplying fractions and in canceling or reducing. All work is done on screen. Errors are flagged immediately and appropriate explanations given. When all cancellations are finished, student then completes multiplication. Errors are categorized and totals are given at the end of each problem and at the end of the lesson. Written documentation is provided.

ID: J206
NUMBER JUMPER
Publisher: Micro-Ed, Inc.

Also available from: EISI (Educational Instructional Systems, Inc.) • K-12 Micromedia

Grade: Elementary

Format: cassette or diskette

Hardware: Commodore 64 • PET • VIC

Language: BASIC

Source Code: no

Price: $14.95

The learner practices the skill of adding numbers quickly. The goal is to start small but, eventually, to be able to add nine numbers in a row. Watch the jumper hurdle the numbers after each success! One miss, though, and it's back to the beginning!

ID: J207

NUMBER MAGIC

Publisher: Texas Instruments

Also available from: McKilligan Supply Corp. • Scholastic Software • Scott, Foresman and Co.

Grade: 1 and up

Format: module

Hardware: TI

Source Code: no

Price: $19.95

A basic drill and practice in arithmetic; quite similar to Little Professor[T.M.] and Dataman[T.M.].

ID: J208

NUMBER TREE

Publisher: Little Bee Educational Programs

Grade: K-1

Format: cassette

Hardware: TRS-80 MOD I or III; 16K with Level II BASIC

Price: $10.95

This program reinforces the relationship between a numeral and the word for that numeral. If the student enters the proper numeral for the word displayed beneath tree, then the tree fills with that number of numerals. The student is given two opportunities to answer correctly before the correct numeral is displayed. Scoring is given at the end of the session.

ID: J209

NUMBER WORDS - LEVEL 1

Publisher: Hartley Courseware, Inc.

Also available from: Academic Software • Queue, Inc.

Grade: K-2

Format: 1 diskette

Hardware: Apple II; 48K with Applesoft in ROM (DOS 3.2 or 3.3)

Language: Applesoft BASIC

Price: $26.95

Lessons randomly present thirty words representing numbers from 0 to 99 in five levels of difficulty, and require students to type numerical equivalents. One- or two-digit numbers may be selected. Easy for beginning students to use.

ID: J210

NUMBER WORDS - LEVEL 2

Publisher: Hartley Courseware, Inc.

Also available from: Academic Software • Queue, Inc.

Grade: 2-5

Format: 1 diskette

Hardware: Apple II; 48K with Applesoft in ROM (DOS 3.2 or 3.3)

Language: Applesoft BASIC

Price: $29.95

Ten lessons of 20 presentations each present students with written numbers from 100 to 1,000,000 and require that student type correct numerical equivalent. Lessons are graduated in difficulty.

ID: J211

NUMBER/NUMERAL

Publisher: Little Bee Educational Programs

Also available from: Queue, Inc.

Grade: K-1

Format: cassette

Hardware: TRS-80 MOD I or III; 16K

Price: $10.95

The acrobat performs a somersault when the student correctly counts the dots and enters the proper numeral. If the entry is incorrect, the acrobat falls down. Teaches number/ numeral relationships and number sequencing for the numbers 1 to 10. The score is given at the end of the session.

ID: J212

NUMBO-JUMBO

Publisher: Robert R. Baker, Jr.

Also available from: Queue, Inc.

Date: June 82

Format: cassette or diskette

Hardware: TRS-80 MOD I or III; 16K

Language: BASIC

Source Code: yes

Price: $19.85

Self-study program provides timed math drill in integer addition, subtraction, multiplication, and division. Each problem has time limit, and entire exercise is timed. Four ability levels make program challenging to all. Average program running time is 2-3 minutes at each level of difficulty. Written documentation is provided, and program is self-documented as well.

ID: J213

NUMBOWL

Publisher: Micro-Ed, Inc.

Also available from: EISI (Educational Instructional Systems, Inc.) • K-12 Micromedia

Grade: Elementary

Format: cassette or diskette

Hardware: Commodore 64 • PET • VIC

Language: BASIC

Source Code: no

Price: $14.95

The computer presents three random numbers. The student must put these into an equation so that the total is as near to 30 as possible. The total must not be more than 30, however. For example, if the computer generated the numbers 3, 5, and 9, the student might create the equation (3 X 5) + 9 = 24. There are ten turns (bowling frames) to a game, and a perfect score (attainable only through a combination of skill and luck) would be 300 points.

ID: J214
NUMERATION 1

Publisher: Scott, Foresman and Co.

Date: Jan. 82

Grade: 1-2

Format: module

Hardware: TI 99/4A

Source Code: no

Price: $52.95

This program covers numeration and place value with one-, two- and three-digit numbers. Teacher's guide is included.

ID: J215
NUMERATION 2

Publisher: Scott, Foresman and Co.

Date: Jan. 82

Grade: 3-5

Format: module

Hardware: TI 99/4A; speech synthesizer recommended

Source Code: no

Price: $52.95

Math tutorial presents basics of numeration and place value with 2-6 digit numbers; developed in conjunction with Texas Instruments. Includes both tutorial and practice activities; automatically selects appropriate tutorial activities when practice results indicate need. Teacher's guide included.

ID: J216
OIL WELL

Publisher: Micro-Ed, Inc.

Also available from: EISI (Educational Instructional Systems, Inc.)

Grade: Elementary and up

Format: cassette or diskette

Hardware: Commodore 64 • PET • VIC; 3K memory enhancement

Language: BASIC

Source Code: no

Price: $14.95

This is an exercise in drilling for oil by finding the prime factors of a number. Refine a number into its prime factors (24 = 2

X 2 X 2 X 3) and watch the oil flow! From oil well to pipeline to tank truck, the learner will have many opportunities to become an oil millionaire.

ID: J217
OMNI-CALCULATOR

Publisher: Instant Software[T.M.]

Also available from: Academic Software

Format: diskette

Hardware: TRS-80 MOD I or III

Source Code: no

Price: $19.95

This package provides solutions to complex problems on different units of measurement. It provides rapid means of conversion from one unit of measure to another in any of ten categories: length, volume, mass, velocity, area, density, power, energy, pressure/stress, and temperature. Gives students learning advantage in understanding complex relationships between different units of measurement. Written documentation is provided.

ID: J218
ON THE AVERAGE

Publisher: Micro Power & Light Company

Also available from: Academic Software • K-12 Micromedia

Grade: High School and up

Format: diskette

Hardware: Apple II; 32K with Applesoft in ROM

Price: $29.95

This program covers scores and variables, frequency tables, frequency graphs and curves, the measures - recognition and calculation by mean, mode, or median. It teaches how to recognize the center of a set of numerical scores, how to find the center, by calculating the mean, mode or median, what the center (or average) shows about the group of scores and what the average shows about individual scores within the group.

ID: J219
ON THE LINE

Publisher: Micro-Ed, Inc.

Grade: Elementary and up

Format: cassette or diskette

Hardware: Commodore 64 • PET • VIC; 3K memory enhancement

Language: BASIC

Source Code: no

Price: $14.95

ON THE LINE spotlights mixed numbers and improper fractions that appear on football jerseys. The object is to pick 22 uniforms for the Stars pro team by identifying a number's other name. Mistakes are reported.

ID: J220
PAIL GREEN

Publisher: Micro-Ed, Inc.

Grade: Elementary and up

Format: cassette or diskette

Hardware: Commodore 64 • PET • VIC; 3K memory enhancement

Language: BASIC

Source Code: no

Price: $14.95

The player "goes to the well" to earn buckets of money. Lower the pail and, if one is math-perfect on matching equal fractions, one will scoop all the dollars out of the well. Any mistakes, though, and some of the money drops back in.

ID: J221

PARTING SHOTS

Publisher: Micro-Ed, Inc.

Also available from: EISI (Educational Instructional Systems, Inc.)

Grade: Elementary

Format: cassette or diskette

Hardware: Commodore 64 • PET • VIC; 3K memory enhancement

Language: BASIC

Source Code: no

Price: $14.95

A box with 36 squares appears on the screen. The computer randomly places four kinds of characters in these squares. Shooting at the box by pressing the RETURN key will cause all but one kind of character to be erased. Problem for the student: What fraction tells how many characters remain in relation to the total number of squares? The student tries to express this fraction in its lowest terms. Game points are scored depending on how many characters are in the squares and whether the student can express the fraction in its lowest terms.

ID: J222

PERCENTAGE: A REVIEW COURSE

Publisher: BLS Inc.

Date: Apr. 82

Grade: 7 and up (reading level 6-7)

Format: 13 diskettes

Hardware: Apple II; 48K with Applesoft in ROM (DOS 3.2 or 3.3)

Language: Applesoft BASIC

Source Code: no

Price: $663.00/series; $60.00/diskette; $162.00/FRACTIONS, DECIMALS, AND PERCENTAGE; $270.00/EXERCISES...and DISCOUNT,TAXES,...

TUTORCOURSE BLS25H series is designed to meet growing need for effective basic and remedial instruction in area of percentage. Three programs contain total of 13 lessons, at end of which is final exam. Programs utilize self-paced, branch-programmed instruction methods. Comprehensive user documentation is provided. Series study time: 9-15 hours.

FRACTIONS, DECIMALS, AND PERCENTAGE - TUTOR-PROGRAM BLS25H-1 includes three lessons, covering following topics: fractions and percent; percent as hundredths; changing fractions to percentages and vice versa; decimals and percent; changing decimals to percent and vice versa; and bank interest.

EXERCISES ON PERCENTAGE - TUTORPROGRAM BLS25H-2 includes five lessons, covering following topics: finding a percent of a number; percents less than 1% and greater than 100%; the three types of percentage problems; base percent and percentage; and finding one term when the other two are given.

DISCOUNT, TAXES, SALARIES, AND PROFITS - TUTOR-PROGRAM BLS25H-3 includes five lessons, covering following topics: discount; selling price; sales, income, and admissions taxes; commissions: interest and net proceeds; increase and decrease; and final test.

ID: J223

PERCENTAGES

Publisher: Educational Activities, Inc.

Also available from: Academic Software • K-12 Micromedia • Queue, Inc.

Grade: 7-12

Format: cassette or diskette

Hardware: Apple II Plus; (DOS 3.2.1 or 3.3) • TRS-80 MOD I or III; with Level II BASIC • PET • Commodore 2001 • Commodore 4000; 40 or 80 column • Commodore 8000; 80 column

Source Code: no

Price: $15.95/cassette; $45.00/cassette set of 3; $45.00/diskette

This series of programs provides both instruction and reinforcement in solving percent problems. The programs utilize both tutorial and drill formats to develop skill in percent conversion and computation. All problems given are randomly selected by the computer.

INTRODUCTION TO PERCENT - Involves rewriting a decimal as a percent and a percent as a decimal.

FRACTIONS AS A PERCENT - Explains and provides practice in rewriting fractions as a percent.

FINDING A PERCENT OF A NUMBER - Instruction and practice from the previous programs are used to find a percent of a given number.

ID: J224

PET DISSEMINATION DISK #2

Publisher: San Mateo County Office of Education and Computer-Using Educators

Format: 1 diskette

Hardware: PET; 8K; disk drive 2031, 2040, 4040, 8050

Source Code: yes

Price: $10.00

This disk includes 28 math programs that are in the public domain.

ADD FAST - Student must add 2 place problems, sometimes regrouping mentally. (E 8K)

BIG MATH - Student has choice of operations (+, -, X, ÷) and works 5 randomly selected problems. (E 8K)

CASH REGISTER - User counts out correct change after a purchase. (E 8K)

COMBINATION WARS - Student tries to "beat" the alien enemy by accurately answering multiplication facts. (E/S 16K)

DECIMAL DIVISION - Checks student's answers for problems in division with decimals. (E/S 8K)

DIVISION DRILL - Drill on simple division facts. (E 8K)

DRILL - Choice of +, -, X, ÷ problems with simple one and two-digit numbers. (E/S 8K)

FRACTION LINE - Practice in estimating fractions between 0 and 1. (E/S 8K)

GROSS PAY - Generates 6 problems, with random amounts, to provide practice in computing gross pay with overtime. (S 8K)

GUESS-A-NUMBER - Guessing game for numbers between 1 and 10. (E 8K)

HANG MATH - Guess the digits in a multiplication problem. (E 8K)

HI-LO - Computer guesses number between 1 and 1,000,000. (E 8K)

HOW MANY? - Student counts 1 to 10 squares that are displayed on screen. (E 8K)

HOW MANY BOXES? - Count the boxes (from 1 to 12). (E 8K)

LINEAR EQUATIONS - Plots linear equations $AX + BY = C$. (S 8K)

MARBLESTAT - Drops marbles into slots -- player selects number of slots and displays results as a bar graph. (E/S 8K)

MATCH THE NUMBER - Match the numeral to the number of objects displayed. (E 8K

MATH DICE - Student counts the dots on dice and adds them to give correct response. (E 8K)

MATH FACTS DRILL - Drill on math facts -- user selects operation (+, -, X, ÷.) (E/S 8K)

MATH TEST - Timed drill with sets of 10 problems (X, ÷, +, -, or any combination of these. (E/S 8K)

MISSING NUMBER - Using numerals from 0 to 10, user types in missing number. (E 8K)

MIXED NUMBERS - Student adds from one to five mixed numbers and reduces the fractions. (E/S 8K)

MORTGAGE - Computes mortgage payments and prints table of payments, interest, etc.

MULT DRILL - Timed drill on multiplication facts -- gives score and average time. (E/S 8K)

REVERSE - Arranges digits 1-9 in correct sequence by reversing. (E/S 8K)

SIGNIFICANT DIGITS - Drill on recognizing number of significant digits in a randomly selected decimal number. (E/S 8K)

TAX COLLECTOR - Drill in factoring whole numbers. (E/S 8K)

+-*/ FRACTIONS - Sets of 10 problems in +, -, X and ÷ of fractions at choice of difficulty level. (E/S 8K)

ID: J225

PET DISSEMINATION DISK #4

Publisher: San Mateo County Office of Education and Computer-Using Educators

Format: 1 diskette

Hardware: PET; 8K; disk drive 2031, 2040, 4040, 8050

Source Code: yes

Price: $10.00

The disk contains 23 math programs in the public domain.

EQUATIONS - Math drill and practice. (8K)

P.DICE (DICE) - Simulates distribution of dice throws. (8K)

BROWNIAN - Simulation of molecular movement. (8K)

BUGGY - Practice in debugging errors in computer-generated math problems. (8K)

ABLOCKS - Computerized exercise with Attribute Blocks. (8K)

FRACTION PRACTICE - Math drill and practice. (8K)

PRIMES - Searches for primes, beginning with any number; factors any number. (8K)

COMPARE - Draws zig-zag line representing the first and then the second of two numbers, allowing user to compare relative sizes. (8K)

GUESS MY FRACTION - Strategy game. (8K)

OPERATIONS - Math drill and practice. (8K)

HELP! - Uses In-Out machine to evaluate algebraic expressions. (8K)

POSTAL - Choosing a route through a maze. (8K)

SPIDER - Programming language for creating graphic designs. (8K)

PICTURES - Small pictures, already programmed into the computer, can be positioned on the screen to create a larger picture. (8K)

CHICK - Simulates diet control experiment in raising chickens. (8K)

TOMATO - Simulation of a tomato farm; user seeks to discover best variety of tomato and optimum conditions of heat and light. (8K)

CHICK RESULTS - Tests results obtained in #15. (8K)

TOMATO RESULTS - Tests results obtained in #16. (8K)

GUESS MY MEAN - Math strategy game. (8K)

FOREST - Use sampling techniques to discover percentage of diseased trees in different forests. (8K)

FISH - Simulates catching and marking trout as a means of estimating total number of fish in each of several lakes. (8K)

SELECT - Agricultural simulation in which user selects a variety of plants that together will yield the largest crop. (8K)

PLUG - Determine whether a coin is a plug or is a good coin by flipping coins and noting percentages. (8K)

ID: J226

PET PROFESSOR

Publisher: Cow Bay Computing

Also available from: K-12 Micromedia

Format: 40 cassettes

Hardware: PET; any model except VIC 20 or 8032

Price: $499.00; $235.00/whole numbers only; $175.00/fractions only

A complete arithmetic software package of 77 programs. Each lesson includes: an objective or concept stated clearly; a step-by-step example; explanation of vocabulary; a sample problem; a five-question test: repetition of random sample problems or tests throughout the program; and an advancement option to go directly to the test without instruction. Topics covered are addition, subtraction, multiplication, decimals and fractions.

ID: J227
PINBALL I.Q.
Publisher: Micro-Ed, Inc.

Also available from: EISI (Educational Instructional Systems, Inc.) • K-12 Micromedia

Grade: Elementary

Format: cassette or diskette

Hardware: Commodore 64 • PET • VIC

Language: BASIC

Source Code: no

Price: $14.95

This program gives the learner practice in finding the whole number part of a quotient in division. Correct answers will light up bumpers on a pinball machine and build up the player's score. The game is over when all the bumpers are lighted.

ID: J228
PLOT/GUESS THE RULE
Publisher: Edu-Soft[T.M.]

Also available from: Academic Software • K-12 Micromedia • Queue, Inc. • Scholastic Software

Format: 2 programs on cassette or diskette

Hardware: Apple II; 16K (cassette) or 32K (diskette) with Applesoft in ROM (DOS 3.2 or 3.3) • TRS-80 MOD I or III; 16K (cassette) or 32K (diskette) with with Level II BASIC • Atari 400 or 800; 16K (cassette) or 48K (diskette)

Price: $14.95/cassette; $19.95/diskette

Two programs focus on algebra and graphing and attempt to familiarize player with concept of functions.

GUESS THE RULE - Computer shows student ordered pairs of numbers that satisfy an equation. Player can score points by guessing equation or additional ordered pairs. Player may choose from eleven levels of difficulty, from elementary through high school.

PLOT - Player can display graph of any chosen function. Graphs may be programmed one after another in the same axes and special provisions are given for graphing simultaneous equations and conic sections. Player can choose limits of axes.

ID: J229
PRESCRIPTIVE MATH DRILL
Publisher: Hartley Courseware, Inc.

Also available from: Opportunities For Learning, Inc. • Scholastic Software

Grade: 1-4

Format: 1 diskette with backup

Hardware: Apple II; 48K with Applesoft in ROM (DOS 3.2 or 3.3)

Language: Applesoft BASIC

Price: $79.95

Menu-driven math drill and practice program enables teacher to set level of achievement necessary for advancement to higher level of difficulty and to analyze student performance based on last three lessons student has completed in each of four categories: addition, subtraction, multiplication, and division. Computer will store records for up to 100 students, with password protection for each student.

ID: J230
PRIME FACTORS
Publisher: Comaldor

Format: cassette or diskette

Hardware: PET

Price: $20.00

This teaching/drill program gives the choice of a lesson on factors and prime factors or a series of questions which the student may attempt to solve. During the lesson, "factor" and "prime factor" are explained with examples. Good use of graphics adds interest and fun. During the question portion of the program, the student's knowledge of the process is tested by means of a game much like a shooting gallery. At the end of a series of questions the program reports to the student his degree of success.

ID: J231
PRIME FISHIN'
Publisher: Micro-Ed, Inc.

Also available from: EISI (Educational Instructional Systems, Inc.)

Grade: Elementary

Format: cassette or diskette

Hardware: Commodore 64 • PET • VIC; 3K memory enhancement

Language: BASIC

Source Code: no

Price: $14.95

This is an exercise in identifying prime and composite numbers. The student goes fishing in Lake Eratosthenes to catch prime fish. Composite fish are illegal. The computer keeps a fishing scorecard for the student.

ID: J232
PRIME NUMBER
Publisher: Micro-Ed, Inc.

Also available from: EISI (Educational Instructional Systems, Inc.)

Grade: Elementary

Format: cassette or diskette

Hardware: Commodore 64 • PET

Language: BASIC

Source Code: no

Price: $7.95

For each problem, the computer will display a grid of numbers from 1 to 100. One of these numbers, selected at random by the computer, will flash on and off on the screen. The student's job is to identify the number as being prime or composite. At the end of the lesson, the student's performance is summarized.

ID: J233
PROBLEM SOLVING

Publisher: Comaldor

Format: 6 programs on cassette or diskette

Hardware: PET

Price: $90.00/set

A "How to" series in which the student enters problems of his choice. These may be from any source. The program checks the student's work, step by step. Especially helpful for review or drill. Perimeter, Area, Volume, Coins, Age, Consecutive Numbers.

ID: J234
PROBLEM SOLVING IN EVERYDAY MATH

Publisher: Interpretive Education, Inc.

Grade: 1-12

Format: 4 diskettes

Hardware: Apple II Plus; 48K • Apple II; 48K with Applesoft in ROM

Language: Applesoft BASIC

Source Code: no

Price: $225.00 with backup; $165.00 without

This process-oriented program takes a step-by-step approach to analyzing practical everyday mathematical problems. It provides interactive experiences in determining the processes to be used in solving the problems. The disk covers: how to solve problems; solving addition and multiplication problems; solving subtraction and division problems; and other problem-solving processes, such as reasoning without numbers, estimating solutions and analyzing multiple-step problems. Program has optional music or sound. Branching automatically places student in one of 4 reading levels - 2nd, 3rd, 5th, and 7th. There is also an enrichment level with simulation and problem- solving. The teacher may control the entry reading level. Content of this program makes it especially useful for special education.

ID: J235
PROOFS AND PROPERTIES

Publisher: Micro Power & Light Company

Also available from: K-12 Micromedia

Format: diskette

Hardware: Apple II; 32K with Applesoft in ROM

This program should be of real benefit to the beginning student in plane geometry. It addresses a number of basic concepts and principles normally covered early in a first year course. Topics include: (1) Properties, descriptions and examples of the transitive property, as well as the properties of substitution, addition and subtraction; (2) Pictures, a number of geometric shapes and drawings which are meant to provoke a sense of recognition in the student - suggesting a particular property or definition; (3) Proofs, from a large number of exercises, the student is shown a simple geometric configuration, with the "givens" and the "conclusion" to be derived, together with all necessary intermediate steps. The student is then invited to arrange those steps into an orderly valid proof; and (4) Amsterdam avuncularism, an imaginative conceptual aid to help the student get the idea of what is involved in deriving a proof - getting from here to there, trying first one path and then another.

ID: J236
PUMPING IRON

Publisher: Micro-Ed, Inc.

Grade: Elementary and up

Format: cassette or diskette

Hardware: Commodore 64 • PET • VIC; 3K memory enhancement

Language: BASIC

Source Code: no

Price: $14.95

Subtracting mixed numbers properly - borrowing or reducing when necessary - brings on PUMPING IRON. As each problem is solved, a weight-lifter appears on the screen and lifts a heavier weight each time. A summary identifies the student's trouble spots.

ID: J237
PYTHAGOREAN PROOFS

Publisher: Micro Power & Light Company

Also available from: Academic Software

Format: diskette

Hardware: Apple II; 32K with Applesoft in ROM

Price: $29.95

This program covers proofs of the Pythagorean theorem, by (1) Lengendre, (2) Bezout, (3) Garfield, (4) Euclid, (5) Pythagoras, and (6) the Chinese. Each proof consists of the proof's history, graphically displayed constructions, and the proof itself. The program provides the rationale for each step of each proof. To see this information, the user runs the program from the beginning, entering the word "solution" in place of his name (when asked for it by the program).

ID: J238
QUADRATIC AND THE PARABOLA

Publisher: Avant-Garde Creations

Also available from: Academic Software • Queue, Inc.

Grade: 11-12

Format: diskette

Hardware: Apple; 48K with Applesoft in ROM

Price: $29.95

Topics covered are quadratic polynomials, roots of quadratic equations, definitions, graphs, and equations of parabolas, tangent and normals.

ID: J239
QUANTITATIVE COMPARISONS

Publisher: Program Design, Inc.

Also available from: Academic Software • GRAFex Company •
MARCK

Date: June 82

Grade: High School-College Prep

Format: cassette or diskette

Hardware: Atari 400/800; 16K

Language: BASIC

Source Code: no

Price: $19.95/cassette; $26.50/diskette

Course reviews priciples that form basis of mathematics,
from beginning arithmetic through elementary algebra and
plane geometry. Prepares students for types of math problems
commonly found on SAT and other aptitude or intelligence
tests, using multiple-choice questions. Includes lessons in areas
of numbers and arithmetic, roots and exponents, fractions,
decimals and percent, angles and plane geometry, algebra, and
graphs and units of measurement. Also includes exam at end of
course. Course booklet contains explanations of the various
types of problems, keyed by number on screen to the problems
themselves, for the benefit of students who do not understand
particular problems.

ID: J240
READ AND SOLVE MATH PROBLEMS

Publisher: Educational Activities, Inc.

Also available from: Academic Software • K-12 Micromedia •
MARCK • Opportunities For Learning, Inc. • Queue, Inc.

Grade: 4-6, Remedial Secondary

Format: cassette or diskette

Hardware: Apple II Plus; (DOS 3.2.1 or 3.3) • TRS-80 MOD I or
III; with Level II BASIC • PET • Commodore 2001 • Commodore 4000; 40 or 80 column • Commodore 8000; 80 column

Source Code: no

Price: $78.00/cassette set $85.00/diskette set

A progressive tutorial and drill program that teaches students
the important elements of word problems and the conversion
of written problems to number problems. The program allows
interaction between the student and the computer and provides reinforcement of all concepts and reteaching where
necessary. Interesting animated graphics reward the student
when he/she is correct. The program is self-scoring and will not
allow the student to progress to higher level concepts until the
previous lesson has been mastered. Included with the program
are 10 reproducible activity masters to reinforce concepts and
four reproducible activity masters for a pre- and post-test.

KEY WORDS IN ADDITION PROBLEMS

KEY WORDS IN SUBTRACTION OR ADDITION PROBLEMS

WRITING EQUATIONS

USING EQUATIONS TO SOLVE ADDITION OR SUBTRAC-
TION PROBLEMS

MORE ADDITION AND SUBTRACTION PROBLEMS

USING EQUATIONS TO SOLVE MULTIPLICATION, ADDI-
TION, AND SUBTRACTION PROBLEMS

MORE MULTIPLICATION, ADDITION, AND SUBTRAC-
TION PROBLEMS

USING EQUATIONS TO SOLVE DIVISION, MULTIPLICA-
TION, ADDITION, AND SUBTRACTION PROBLEMS

MORE DIVISION, MULTIPLICATION, ADDITION, AND
SUBTRACTION PROBLEMS

PROBLEMS WITHOUT NUMBERS

ID: J241
REAL NUMBER SYSTEM

Publisher: Avant-Garde Creations

Also available from: Academic Software • Queue, Inc.

Grade: 11-12

Format: diskette

Hardware: Apple; 48K with Applesoft in ROM

Price: $29.95

Topics covered include rational and irrational numbers, inequalities, absolute values, and number line graphs.

ID: J242
RIEMANN INTEGRAL

Publisher: Micro Power & Light Company

Also available from: Academic Software • Queue, Inc.

Format: diskette

Hardware: Apple II; 32K with Applesoft in ROM

Price: $29.95

The topics available from a master menu are a history of the
integral, the theory of the integral, development of the integral,
numerical techniques of approximation and summary review
quiz. The principal intended users include calculus students
about to study this topic, any students needing integral approximations and those interested in math, seeking enrichment!

ID: J243
ROUNDING OFF

Publisher: Cow Bay Computing

Format: 1 cassette

Hardware: PET; any model except VIC 20 or 8032

Price: $15.00

With ROUNDING OFF the student learns to round off
decimals to the nearest millionth.

ID: J244
ROUNDOFF ROUNDUP

Publisher: Comaldor

Format: cassette or diskette

Hardware: PET

Price: $20.00

Drill and review in game form give a lesson in rounding off numbers, reviewing rules, then taking student through a number of questions which drill each rule. One, two, or three players may participate, with a choice of Canadian or American spellings offered at beginning of game. Graphics maintain interest, and sound is optional for 12'' PETs. If errors occur, student is taken back for review of rules. Challenge is to make it through program to mastery of rounding off.

ID: J245

SAMPLER

Publisher: Math Software

Format: diskette

Hardware: Apple II; 48K with Applesoft in ROM (DOS 3.3) • Apple II Plus

Price: $50.00

This is one of five packages offered by Math Software. SAMPLER includes the two programs listed here and one other of the purchaser's choice. Descriptions of the programs can be found in the SUPERMATH PACKAGE.

FUNCTION GRAPHER

SIMULTANEOUS LINEAR SYSTEMS

ID: J246

SECTOR FIVE

Publisher: Micro-Ed, Inc.

Also available from: EISI (Educational Instructional Systems, Inc.)

Grade: Elementary and up

Format: cassette or diskette

Hardware: Commodore 64 • PET • VIC; 3K memory enhancement

Language: BASIC

Source Code: no

Price: $14.95

This is an exercise in estimation. The student's job is to locate and turn back hordes of Kuminons that roam the galaxy. The key to success is estimating correctly the number of space invaders appearing on the player's scanner.

ID: J247

SENIOR HIGH MATH I

Publisher: Microphys Programs

Also available from: Academic Software • EISI (Educational Instructional Systems, Inc.) • MARCK • Queue, Inc.

Grade: High School

Format: 13 cassettes or 1 diskette

Hardware: PET; 8K; cassette or 4040 dual disk drive • Apple II; 24K (DOS 3.2 or 3.3) • TRS-80 MOD I or III; 16K • Bell & Howell

Language: BASIC

Source Code: yes

Price: $180.00/diskette; $20.00/cassette

Package consists of 13 interactive math programs. Computer-assisted instruction versions guide student through series of quantitative questions; individualized-instruction versions generate a unique set of problems for each student. Utility programs are designed to provide solutions to time-consuming problems often given on exams and homework assignments. Grades and overall evaluation are compiled by programs for each student. Complete instructions are included. Also available from Queue, Inc. in diskette form only.

QUADRATIC EQUATIONS (PC701) - Program enables student to develop facility in solving quadratic equations.

TRIGONOMETRY I (PC702) - Enables student to develop facility in dealing with definitions of basic trig functions and employing laws of sines and cosines.

SIMULTANEOUS EQUATIONS (2X2) (PC703) - Enables student to develop facility in obtaining solutions to sets of two simultaneous linear equations.

SIMULTANEOUS EQUATIONS (3X3) (PC704) - Enables student to develop facility in obtaining solutions to sets of three simultaneous linear equations.

GEOMETRICAL AREAS (PC705) - Enables student to develop facility in determining areas of various plane figures.

TRIGONOMETRY II (PC706) - Enables student to develop facility in dealing with properties of right triangle and six basic trig functions: sine, cosine, tangent, secant, cosecant, and cotangent.

NUMBERS - VERBAL PROBLEMS I (PC707) - Enables student to develop facility in arriving at solutions to verbal problems involving numerical relationships. Student must construct, from statement of problem, an algebraic equation which he or she then proceeds to solve for the unknown.

COINS - VERBAL PROBLEMS II (PC708) - Enables student to develop facility in arriving at solutions to verbal problems involving numerical relationships among various U.S. coins.

AGES - VERBAL PROBLEMS III (PC709) - Enables student to develop facility in arriving at solutions to verbal problems involving numerical relationships related to age.

INTEREST - VERBAL PROBLEMS IV (PC710) - Enables student to develop facility in arriving at solutions to verbal problems involving numerical relationships relating to simple interest.

MIXTURES - VERBAL PROBLEMS V (PC711) - Enables student to develop facility in arriving at solutions to verbal problems involving numerical relationships related to mixtures.

GEOMETRY - VERBAL PROBLEMS VI (PC712) - Enables student to develop facility in arriving at solutions to verbal problems involving simple geometric relationships.

RATES - VERBAL PROBLEMS VII (PC713) - Enables student to develop facility in arriving at solutions to verbal problems involving rate relationships.

ID: J248

SENIOR HIGH MATH II

Publisher: Microphys Programs

Also available from: Academic Software • EISI (Educational Instructional Systems, Inc.) • MARCK • Queue, Inc.

Grade: High School

Format: 12 cassettes or 1 diskette

Hardware: PET; 8K; cassette or 4040 dual disk drive • Apple II; 24K (DOS 3.2 or 3.3) • TRS-80 MOD I or III; 16K • Bell & Howell

Language: BASIC

Source Code: yes

Price: $180.00/diskette; $20.00/cassette

Package consists of 12 interactive math programs. Computer-assisted instruction versions guide student through series of quantitative questions; individualized-instruction versions generate a unique set of problems for each student. Grades and overall evaluation are compiled by programs for each student. Complete instructions are included. Available from Queue, Inc. in diskette format only.

DIGITS - VERBAL PROBLEMS VIII (PC714) - Program enables student to develop facility in arriving at solutions to problems involving relationships among various digits of randomly generated numbers.

WORK - VERBAL PROBLEMS IX (PC715) - Enables student to develop facility in arriving at solutions to problems involving rates at which work may be accomplished.

ARITHMETIC PROGRESSIONS I (PC716) - Enables student to develop facility in dealing with various arithmetic progressions. Among concepts dealt with are common difference, nth term, and number of terms.

ARITHMETIC PROGRESSIONS II (PC717) - Enables student to develop facility in dealing with various arithmetic progressions. Concepts dealt with include common difference, nth term, and sum of an arithmetic progression.

GEOMETRIC PROGRESSIONS I (PC718) - Enables student to develop facility in dealing with various geometric progressions. Concepts dealt with include common ratio, nth term, and geometric mean.

GEOMETRIC PROGRESSIONS II (PC719) - Enables student to develop facility in dealing with various geometric progressions. Concepts dealt with include common ratio, nth term, and sum of progressions.

TYPES OF VARIATION (PC720) - Enables student to develop facility in dealing with direct, indirect, and joint relationships.

LINEAR EQUATIONS (PC721) - Enables student to develop facility in dealing with solution of simple linear equations for a single unknown.

FORMULA EVALUATION (PC722) - Enables student to develop facility in algebraically solving a randomly generated implicit relationship for some unknown variable.

COORDINATE GEOMETRY (PC723) - Enables student to develop facility in dealing with elementary concepts of coordinate geometry. Among concepts dealt with are distance between two points and slope and intercept of line passing through these points.

EXPONENTS AND LOGARITHMS (PC724) - Enables student to develop facility in dealing with definition of logarithmic equations and use of exponents.

VERBAL PROBLEMS X - GENERAL (PC725) - Enables student to develop facility in arriving at solutions to verbal problems involving various types of numerical relationships.

ID: J249

SIGNED1/SIGNED2

Publisher: Cow Bay Computing

Format: 1 cassette

Hardware: PET; any model except VIC 20 or 8032

Price: $15.00

This program gives rules and quizzes for addition, subtraction, multiplication, and division of signed whole numbers. A rule review is given after each error.

ID: J250

SLAM DUNK

Publisher: Micro-Ed, Inc.

Also available from: EISI (Educational Instructional Systems, Inc.) • K-12 Micromedia • Opportunities For Learning, Inc.

Grade: Elementary

Format: cassette or diskette

Hardware: Commodore 64 • PET • VIC

Language: BASIC

Source Code: no

Price: $14.95

Challenge shooting eye and swish the net in this basketball competition. Make five shots in a row and watch player rise to the occasion with a slam dunk. Upon a miss, opponent scores. There's a time clock in this drill and practice game on subtraction facts.

ID: J251

SOCCER MATH

Publisher: COMPU-TATIONS, Inc.

Also available from: Academic Software • Opportunities For Learning, Inc.

Grade: Elementary-Intermediate

Format: diskette

Hardware: Apple II; (DOS 3.2 or 3.3)

Price: $24.95; $29.95 for disk compatible with the VOTRAX speech synthesizer

This is a math teaching program which utilizes graphically displayed soccer players to test for the correct answer. A choice of addition/subtraction/multiplication problems is available in ten skill levels. A correct answer makes the soccer player score a goal. A wrong answer means a missed shot and the correct answer is displayed on the screen.

ID: J252

SOLVING QUADRATIC EQUATIONS

Publisher: Microcomputer Workshops

Date: July 82

Grade: 8-11

Format: cassette

Hardware: PET; 16K

Language: BASIC

Source Code: no

Price: $20.00

Program generates random quadratic equations in form $AX^2 + BX + C = 0$ that are solvable by factoring. Student solves equation by factoring quadratic expression, setting both factors equal to zero and solving resultant equations for all values of X. If student is unable to factor expression, detailed explanation is given. Errors are also flagged immediately and appropriate response is made. All work is done on screen, using screen as interactive worksheet step by step. Written documentation is provided.

ID: J253

SPEAK & MATH[T.M.] PROGRAM

Publisher: Texas Instruments

Also available from: Scott, Foresman and Co.

Format: diskette or cassette

Source Code: no

Price: $29.95/diskette; $24.95/cassette

Offers the same practice in addition, subtraction, multiplication, division, number relationships and problem-solving that is available with the popular hand-held learning aid. Activities include "Solve It and Mix It", "Greater/Less", "Write It", and "Number Stumper".

ID: J254

SPEED DRILL/ GUESS THE NUMBER/ ARITHMETIC DRILL

Publisher: Edu-Soft[T.M.]

Also available from: K-12 Micromedia

Grade: Elementary-High School

Format: 3 programs on cassette or diskette

Hardware: TRS-80 MOD I or III; 16K (cassette) or 32K (diskette) with with Level II BASIC

Price: $14.95/cassette; $19.95/diskette

Three programs are provided that focus on improving numerical facility through drills of arithmetic functions.

SPEED DRILL - Program drills students in individual or mixed arithmetic operations. Provides same drills for algebra students using positive and negative integers. Score is based on speed and accuracy of answer. This program is also available individually from Queue, Inc., and Academic Software.

GUESS THE NUMBER - Aids students in recognizing relative size of different numbers. Computer asks youngster to guess number between 1 and 500. The guess will "sink" or "float" on the screen depending on whether it's too large or too small. The speed of the sinking or floating varies according to how close the guess is to computer's secret number.

ARITHMETIC DRILL - Program provides untimed drill for whole number arithmetic operations. Student may choose specific operation of assorted problems. Student may also choose size of numbers. Each choice of round includes 10 problems of chosen type.

ID: J255

SPEED DRILL/ NUMBER LINE

Publisher: Edu-Soft[T.M.]

Also available from: Academic Software • K-12 Micromedia • Scholastic Software

Format: 2 programs on cassette or diskette

Hardware: Apple II; 16K (cassette) or 32K (diskette) with Applesoft in ROM (DOS 3.2 or 3.3)

Price: $14.95/cassette; $19.95/diskette

Two programs focus on improving arithmetic skills of user.

SPEED DRILL - Program drills users in individual or mixed arithmetic operations. Provides same drill for algebra students using positive and negative integers. Score is based on speed and accuracy of answer. This program is available individually from Queue, Inc.

NUMBER LINE - This program teaches the addition/subtraction of positive and negative numbers. The user chooses the type of problem. If the user gives a wrong answer to an addition problem, the correct answer is shown on the number line, using a beeping arrow and flashing numbers. The user is helped to change a subtraction problem, incorrectly solved, into an addition problem, which is then answered. If the answer is still wrong, correct answer is shown on number line.

ID: J256

SPEED FACTS

Publisher: Ideatech Company

Also available from: MARCK

Grade: 1-5, Remedial

Format: diskette

Hardware: Apple II Plus; 16K • Apple II; 16K with Applesoft in ROM

Language: BASIC

Price: $14.95

SPEED FACTS is designed to improve the student's accuracy and rate of response for addition, subtraction, multiplication and division facts. The program provides practice for one to three students at a time. The students may choose the operation, the level of difficulty of the problems and the speed of problem presentation for a set of ten problems. If a student does not answer a problem within the selected time limit, he/she is told, "you took too long!" After the second error on a problem, the student is given the answer. The score for all players is shown throughout the game on a scoreboard.

ID: J257

STATISTICS

Publisher: Avant-Garde Creations

Also available from: Academic Software • Queue, Inc.

Grade: Up to 10

Format: diskette

Hardware: Apple; 48K with Applesoft in ROM

Price: $29.95

This program covers mode, mean, median, histograms, and cumulative frequency.

ID: J258

STORY PROBLEMS IN ADDITION AND SUBTRACTION

Publisher: Micro-Ed, Inc.

Also available from: Academic Software • EISI (Educational Instructional Systems, Inc.) • K-12 Micromedia • MARCK • Queue, Inc.

Grade: Elementary

Format: cassette or diskette

Hardware: Commodore 64 • PET • TI 99/4; extended BASIC module

Language: BASIC

Source Code: no

Price: $7.95; $9.95/TI ed.

The computer presents an assortment of story problems in addition and subtraction. Many of these are about a Great Castle with lords and knights in some of its 103 rooms. Because the settings of these story problems are often repeated, the student cannot know simply on this basis what operations to perform. The student must read and understand what is being asked before the problem can be correctly solved. At the end of each lesson, the student's performance is summarized. (If the student does not know the answer, and types the question mark, the computer will give the answer.)

ID: J259

SUBTRACTING WITH OBJECTS

Publisher: Micro-Ed, Inc.

Also available from: Academic Software • EISI (Educational Instructional Systems, Inc.) • MARCK • Queue, Inc.

Grade: 1-3

Format: cassette or diskette

Hardware: Commodore 64 • PET

Language: BASIC

Source Code: no

Price: $7.95

Each lesson presents ten randomly generated subtraction problems with numbers from one to ten being subtracted from each other. Small arrows and diamond shapes represent this operation. If the learner's answer is wrong, the computer will give the right answer. If the learner presses the question mark, the computer will also give the right answer. At the end of each lesson, the learner's performance is summarized.

ID: J260

SUBTRACTION

Publisher: Microcomputer Workshops

Also available from: Academic Software • EISI (Educational Instructional Systems, Inc.) • Micro-Ed, Inc.

Grade: Elementary

Format: cassette

Hardware: PET; 16K

Language: BASIC

Source Code: no

Price: $20.00

This program presents problems in subtraction allowing the learner to pick the amount of digits in each number. The learner is also given the option of problems involving borrowing or no borrowing. All problems are generated at random. The learner works with each problem just as if he/she were doing it on a piece of paper.

ID: J261

SUM-IT MOUNTAIN

Publisher: Micro-Ed, Inc.

Also available from: EISI (Educational Instructional Systems, Inc.) • K-12 Micromedia

Grade: Elementary

Format: cassette or diskette

Hardware: Commodore 64 • PET • VIC

Language: BASIC

Source Code: no

Price: $14.95

Carry the flag to the top of SUM-IT-MOUNTAIN in the fastest time possible. Success depends on the learner's ability to add numbers rapidly. Any mistake means starting all over from the bottom. A clock records the climb time.

ID: J262

SUPER MATH PACKAGE

Publisher: Math Software

Grade: Junior High-College

Format: diskette

Hardware: Apple II; 48K with Applesoft in ROM (DOS 3.3), game paddles needed for some programs • Apple II Plus; game paddles needed for some programs

Price: $250.00

This large package is one of five offered by Math Software. As many programs are repeated in the packages, their descriptions will only be listed here. SUPERMATH includes all the programs available.

AREA UNDER A CURVE - This program demonstrates the method of lower sum, upper sum, and Riemann sum approximations. The user may choose the type of summation process desired as well as the number of rectangles to be used for the approximation. The curve is graphically represented; the rectangles are shown in color and areas are quantitatively expressed. After completing the approximations the accuracy of that particular process is shown relative to the actual area under the curve. This program is ideal for introducing the definite integral to a beginning calculus class.

ARITHMETIC OF FUNCTIONS - This program provides a display of the computer potential in function graphing. It graphs the function f, the function g, and then the function h = function f operation function g. This process also generates some exciting relationships which can be seen from the graphic displays. The menu selections also generate graphic verification of certain trig relationships including a double angle formula, some half-angle formulas, and some quotient relationships. The eight menu selections for each function followed by the four choices for the operation provide 256 choices. The additional option for user-supplied functions enables a very wide spectrum of both classroom instruction and also individual learning.

ARITHMETIC RACING - Here is a game that students can play as often as they wish because they will be developing basic arithmetic skills. ARITHMETIC RACING is game of timed arithmetic practice with the versatility to be appropriate for students from the early grades through the early high school years. The player first selects either addition, subtraction, multiplication, or division and then specifies the largest number that he wants the computer to give him. He also selects a speed level from 1 to 5. The computer then assigns a point value to each problem based on these selections. A twenty-five point bonus is added to the score for answering each of the ten questions correctly. ARITHMETIC RACING provides subtle incentive for the development of arithmetic skills.

BINOMIAL MULTIPLICATION - This program uses the Apple's high-resolution screen and color graphics to demonstrate that (1) $(X + A) (X + B) = X^2 + AX + BX + AB$ is really a true equation. This equality is shown through the use of a very convincing area argument. The user may input any value of "A" or "B" from -5 to 5 inclusive. Then through the use of Apple's high-resolution graphics, the equivalence of the right- and left-hand sides of the equation (1) is shown through the use of the areas. Once students have seen this demonstration, their appreciation and understanding of BINOMIAL MULTIPLICATION will be greatly enhanced.

DERIVATIVE OF SINE - This program is for use as a teacher demonstration, giving a very convincing argument that the derivative of the sine function is indeed the cosine function. Initially the sine function is graphed and then moving tangents to the sine function are drawn and the values of the slopes recorded. The graph of the slope values is plotted as the tangents again move along the curve. Finally, the cosine function is plotted and shown to coincide with the slope values which were plotted earlier. This program will enhance the students' understanding of the relationships between a function, its derivatives and the tangent lines to a function. It will also provide a convincing geometric argument that the derivative of the sine function is indeed the cosine function.

ECCENTRICITY FORM OF CONIC - An outstanding program for introducing and reinforcing the definition of a conic section from an eccentricity point of view. The first section defines a conic in terms of the focus, the directrix, and the eccentricity and then shows these relationships on the high-resolution screen. The second section enables the user to pick a value for the eccentricity and see the points of the conic generated using this value of the eccentricity. The high-resolution screen is used to show the focus, the directrix, and the points generated using the definition and the given eccentricity. The third section enables the user to choose not only the eccentricity but also the initial distance between the focus and the directrix. The graph is then generated as in the second section.

FUNCTION GRAPHER - The opening menu offers the user the choice of circular (trig) functions, absolute value functions, greatest integer functions, polynomial functions, or user-supplied functions. Once inside the circular function category, the user may select either sine, cosine, tangent, cotangent, secant, cosecant or choose to supply his own circular function. If the user selects the polynomial function category, he is offered the choice of linear, quadratic, cubic, or quartic function or the opportunity to supply a special function.

GRAPHIC INTEGRATION THEORY - This program places the graphic theory at the user's fingertips, and frees him to develop the important notions of inner (lower) rectangular sum, outer (upper) rectangular sum, and integration as the limit of rectangular sums. It features a graphic inner rectangular display and a graphic outer rectangular display. These displays are followed by a very valuable numerical listing of the inner rectangular sum, the outer rectangular sum, and the numerical evaluation of the corresponding integral. The six menu selections provide for choice of graph and number of intervals and also allow the user to supply both the lower limit and the upper limit of integration. The dual program, MIDPOINT RULE AND TRAPEZOIDAL RULES, is an excellent extension which provides graphic interpretation of these two approximation techniques.

LIMACONS AND THEIR AREAS - This program consists of three parts. The first section describes limacons whose equations are r = a + b sin(t) or r = a + b cos(t). The effects of changing the values of a and b are described in written form and also shown graphically. Also the effects of using the sine function or the cosine function are shown. The second section allows the user to choose the values of a and b and cosine or sine. The program then graphs the limacon on the high-resolution screen. The third section allows the user to calculate various areas enclosed by the limacon. The program will give an approximate value of this area.

LIMITS OF SEQUENCES - The program graphically displays approximately fifty-five terms of a sequence selected by the user. The epsilon neighborhood of the limit is drawn with the value of epsilon which is supplied by the user. The threshold value, M, is then computed and printed. This provides a graphic interpretation of the definition of the limit of sequences which shows that the nth sequence terms are indeed within the epsilon neighborhood of the limit when n ⁶ M. The five menu selections enable the user to choose a suggested sequence or to specify his own sequence choice.

MIDPOINT RULE AND TRAPEZOIDAL RULE - This dual program is an excellent extension of GRAPHIC INTEGRATION THEORY and provides both graphic interpretation and numerical evaluation of the Midpoint Rule and also the Trapezoidal Rule. The six menu selections provide for choice of graph and number intervals. It also allows the user to supply the lower limit and the upper limit of integration. After graphically displaying the midpoint rectangles or the trapezoids, the numerical listing of the appropriate approximation is listed along with the numerical evaluation of the corresponding integral.

ORBITING AND ROTATING FIGURES - An excellent demonstration program for introducing solid figures in geometry, discussing orbital mechanics in physics, and for visualizing the solids generated when a planar or 3-D object is rotated in space. The demonstrations include cones (both one and two nappes), cubes, cylinders, pyramids, and octahedrons as well as several others. Through the use of the game paddles and keyboard one can rotate the objects about their attitudes or a central axis as well as rotate them about an elliptical orbit. One can also change the object's colors and the speed of the rotation. Moreover, it is possible to leave a trail of the object as it is rotated so that one can see where the object was as well as where the object is at the present time.

POLAR GRAPHING - The intent of POLAR GRAPHING is to help the student learn about polar graphing and to provide an instructional tool for the introduction of polar areas. It is also a very interesting method for checking answers after an assignment has been completed. The menu selections include both the traditional polar graphs which provide opportunity for the study of symmetry and polar graphs of the ellipse, hyperbola, and the parabola. The menu selection also provides the framework for the user to supply a polar equation which is then graphed.

RATIONAL FUNCTION GRAPHER - This program allows the user to enter any rational function of the formula: $y = [(ax^2 + bx + c)^d] \div [(ex^2 + fx + g)^h]$. After entering the values of a,b,c,d,e, f,g, and h, the roots, horizontal asymptotes, and vertical asymptotes are shown. The function is then graphed with the asymptotes drawn. The x and y coordinates are shown as they are graphed. This program can be used to graph linear and quadratic functions as well as more complicated rational functions. Experimentation with various functions will demonstrate the versatility of this program.

SOLVING SIMULTANEOUS LINEAR SYSTEMS - An excellent demonstration program for the teacher to use. It also may be used as a drill and practice program for individual students to reinforce the Multiplication-Addition method of solving two linear equations in two unknowns. The program allows students to interact with the computer to solve the given randomly generated linear system of equations. If the student correctly solves the system, a high-resolution graph of the two equations is given to demonstrate that his algebraic solution is identical to the intersection of the original two equations. This program reinforces the geometric and algebraic equivalence of finding the ordered pair where the linear equations intersect. If the student is having difficulty solving the system, appropriate error messages are produced. As the student or teacher solves the system by the Multiplication- Addition method, the resulting intermediate equations of his partial solution are produced.

SINE AND COSINE GRAPHER - Ideal for demonstrating the effect that the constants A, B, and C have on the graphs of the functions $y = A \sin(Bx + C)$ and $y = A \cos(Bx + C)$. The user can choose either the "sin" or "cos" function as well as the values of A, B, and C. The program graphs this chosen function on the high-resolution screen. Several such graphs can be superimposed on the coordinate system in different colors so that the effects of changing A, B, and C can be readily distinguished by the students. Hence the student can see the effects of amplitude, period, and phase shift changes quickly, dramatically, and in color on the screen.

SOLIDS OF REVOLUTION - This program allows the user to choose from various objects, such as triangles, squares, rectangles, etc., and use the areas enclosed within these objects as areas to be revolved about an axis. The user can also choose whether he wants the object revolved around an axis touching the area or an axis removed a distance from this area. By using the paddle controls the object is revolved about the chosen axis and the solid of revolution is formed. The paddles adjust the speed of the rotation of the area, the color of the solid generated, and several other functions.

SOLVING LINEAR EQUATIONS - This program provides a graphic model of linear equations and provides for a computer solution as well as a user solution to isolate the variable. This graphic model of a linear equation provides a very vivid picture and is excellent for classroom presentation as well as individual "tutorial" use. The second part of the program provides individual practice to solve equations of the form $Ax + B = C + Dx$. The user can select either rational or integral coefficients depending upon his skill level. Of course, appropriate error messages are included throughout the program to guide the user. This program is intended for individual use as well as classroom introduction and will be especially helpful to the student who requires assistance.

TAYLOR'S SERIES APPROXIMATIONS - This program demonstrates how Taylor series expansions approximate the following functions: 1) $F(x) = \sin(x)$; 2) $F(x) = \cos(x)$; 3) $F(x) = \ln(1 + x)$; 4) $F(x) = e^x$. The function is plotted and then several TAYLOR SERIES APPROXIMATIONS are plotted on the same graph using different colors. Each successive plot uses more terms of the Taylor series expansion. Moreover, the accuracy of the approximation and the rapidity of the convergence of the Taylor series is clearly demonstrated.

ID: J263

SURFACE

Publisher: CONDUIT

Date: 1981

Grade: 9-College

Format: diskette

Hardware: Apple II; 48K with Applesoft in ROM (DOS 3.2.1)

Language: BASIC

Source Code: yes

Price: $40.00; $2.50/add'l student manual

This package is intended for students to use as a supplementary study aid for topics which require graphic representations of plane projections from three-space. The unit relies heavily on the numerous exercises in the Student Guide for its instructional value. The exercises lead students to illustrate interesting portions of functions of two variables. In the process of using the program, students sharpen their ability to visualize three-dimensional surfaces and become familiar with the parameters affecting how such a surface is represented in two dimensions -- the position of the viewer relative to the object and the position of the plane upon which the object is projected. Includes Student Manual (37 pages).

ID: J264

SURFACES FOR MULTIVARIABLE CALCULUS

Publisher: CONDUIT

Date: 1981

Grade: 9-College

Format: diskette

Hardware: Apple II; 48K with Applesoft in ROM (DOS 3.2.1)

Language: BASIC

Source Code: yes

Price: $40.00; $2.50/add'l instructor manual

This package is a multiprogram utility for producing three-dimensional graphics on the Apple. It is intended primarily for use by the instructor for classroom demonstrations, but it could also be useful for students in a lab setting. Includes Instructor's Guide.

DISPLAY SURFACES - Displays eight pictures, either one at a time or in cyclic order, including quadric surfaces, a dog saddle, a bivariate normal, and others. Can also be used in animation mode to display crude line drawings of nine different surfaces. The user can select the desired curve, rotate the surface in two directions, and expand and contract the surface.

DIRECTIONAL DERIVATIVES - Displays a complicated surface, an intersecting vertical plane, and the curve of intersection. The purpose of this program is to assist the instructor in showing that any directional (or partial) derivative is only an ordinary derivative for some curve in some plane. Can also be used in animation mode to display crude line drawings of nine different surfaces. The user can select the desired curve, rotate the surface in two directions, and expand and contract the surface.

SURFACE SKETCHING - Illustrates the construction of a surface by curves parallel to any of the coordinate planes.

SURFACE CONSTRUCTION - Permits the user to quickly sketch a user-defined function of two variables from various viewpoints without removing hidden lines once an appropriate perspective is determined.

SKETCH SURFACE - Permits a high-resolution drawing with hidden lines removed.

ID: J265

SURVIVAL MATHEMATICS

Publisher: Aquarius Publishers Inc.

Date: Aug. 82

Format: 3 cassettes or diskettes

Hardware: TRS-80 MOD I or III; 16K • Apple II; 48K with Applesoft in ROM (DOS 3.2 or 3.3)

Source Code: no

Price: $24.95/cassette, $70.00/set; $29.95/diskette, $85.00/set

Series introduces and gives opportunities for practice of real-life mathematical skills. Written documentation included.

REAL COST - Program teaches about sale prices, special offers, and comparative shopping.

UNDERSTANDING CHECKBOOKS/STATEMENTS - Program teaches how to manage checking account and keep up with bank statements.

FRACTIONS, PERCENTS, AND DECIMALS - Program compares common fractions, percents, and decimals using real-life examples.

ID: J266

TARGET MATH

Publisher: Micro-Ed, Inc.

Also available from: Academic Software • EISI (Educational Instructional Systems, Inc.) • MARCK • Queue, Inc.

Grade: Elementary

Format: cassette or diskette

Hardware: Commodore 64 • PET • TI 99/4; extended BASIC module • VIC; 3K memory enhancement

Language: BASIC

Source Code: no

Price: $7.95; $9.95/TI ed.

The learner selects problems in addition, subtraction, multiplication, or division at a difficulty level of his/her choice. A target area appears at the bottom of the screen, along with a math problem. When the learner types an answer, a plane flies over and a parachute jumper floats down over the landing strip. If the jumper hits the target area, the next problem is presented. If the learner's answer is too large, the jumper lands to the right of the target. The learner may terminate the lesson

at any point. The learner's performance is then summarized according to the following categories: number of jumps, hit the target, missed the target, target area, difficulty level, and time used.

ID: J267

TENTRATION

Publisher: Robert R. Baker, Jr.

Also available from: Queue, Inc.

Date: June 82

Format: cassette or diskette

Hardware: TRS-80 MOD I or III; 16K

Language: BASIC

Source Code: yes

Price: $19.85

Self-study program enables students to learn not to do long multiplication and division when working with powers of ten. Each problem has time limit, and overall exercise is also timed. Average program running time is 2-3 minutes at each level of difficulty. Written documentation is provided, and program is self-documented as well.

ID: J268

TUTTI FRUTTI

Publisher: Micro-Ed, Inc.

Grade: Elementary and up

Format: cassette or diskette

Hardware: Commodore 64 • PET • VIC; 3K memory enhancement

Language: BASIC

Source Code: no

Price: $14.95

This program is an exercise in adding mixed numbers. The goal is to find five sums and win a giant ice cream cone.

ID: J269

TWO-MINUTE WARNING

Publisher: Micro-Ed, Inc.

Also available from: EISI (Educational Instructional Systems, Inc.) • K-12 Micromedia • Opportunities For Learning, Inc.

Grade: Elementary

Format: cassette or diskette

Hardware: Commodore 64 • PET • VIC

Language: BASIC

Source Code: no

Price: $14.95

This program features a football race-against-the-clock as the player subtracts yardage on the way to the goal line. The runner moves across the screen each time he carries the ball. Any mistake, however, leads to a fumble and an automatic touchdown for the other team. In this learning game, the student practices the skill of successive subtraction.

ID: J270

UPS 'N DOWNS

Publisher: Micro-Ed, Inc.

Grade: Elementary and up

Format: cassette or diskette

Hardware: Commodore 64 • PET • VIC; 3K memory enhancement

Language: BASIC

Source Code: no

Price: $14.95

UPS 'N DOWNS puts the player on a ten-step staircase - adding fractions on the way up, subtracting fractions on the way down. Every answer, of course, must be reduced to lowest terms before taking another step. Errors are recorded.

ID: J271

VIDEO MATH FLASHCARDS

Publisher: APX (Atari Program Exchange)

Date: June 82

Grade: 1-5

Format: cassette or diskette

Hardware: Atari 400 or 800; 8K (cassette) or 16K (diskette); Atari BASIC language cartridge

Language: BASIC

Source Code: no

Price: $15.95

Program presents two-minute math drills in addition, subtraction, multiplication, division, or a combination of these, enlivened by simple sound, color, and graphics features. Goal for individual or team is to answer as many questions correctly as possible within two minutes. Program keeps running total of right and wrong answers, and displays player's rank at end according to number of questions attempted and number answered correctly. Review cycle prompts students on questions missed. User manual is included.

ID: J272

WHAT NUMBER IS MISSING

Publisher: Micro-Ed, Inc.

Also available from: Academic Software • EISI (Educational Instructional Systems, Inc.) • Queue, Inc.

Grade: K-1

Format: cassette or diskette

Hardware: Commodore 64 • PET

Language: BASIC

Source Code: no

Price: $7.95

Digits from 1 to 9 appear in sequence on the screen. But one of the digits is missing. Which one? Each lesson consists of ten problems randomly presented. At the end of each lesson, the student's performance is summarized. If the student does not know the answer to a problem, typing the question mark will cause the right answer to be revealed.

ID: J273

WHOLE NUMBER ARITHMETIC SERIES BY TEACHING OBJECTIVE

Publisher: Educational Micro Systems Inc.

Also available from: K-12 Micromedia • MARCK • Queue, Inc.

Grade: 2-8

Format: 4 programs on cassette or diskette

Hardware: Apple II Plus; 48K (DOS 3.3) • TRS-80 MOD I; 32K (DOS 2.3) • TRS-80 MOD III; (DOS 1.2) • TRS-80 MOD I or III; 16K (cassette)

Price: $29.95/diskette; $24.95/cassette; $109.95/package on diskette; $99.95/package on cassette

Each program has a 10- to 12-page teacher's guide. The use of the program requires frequent teacher intervention. This series was developed to teach whole number arithmetic. It is not meant to replace the generally accepted methods of introducing students to arithmetic concepts, but rather to shorten the period of time from initial awareness of specific concepts to mastery of related computational skill objectives. There is one program for each arithmetic operation and each one works on the same set of principles. (1) The teacher initializes a micro-assisted student session to reinforce a specific objective. (2) The student "takes" the session. (3) The teacher records the results, reviews the End of Session Analysis and decides what the next step should be - another session, or reinforcement of concepts with conventional teaching methods.

WHOLE NUMBER ADDITION

WHOLE NUMBER SUBTRACTION

WHOLE NUMBER MULTIPLICATION

WHOLE NUMBER DIVISION

ID: J274

WHOLE NUMBER ARITHMETIC WORKSHEET/TEST GENERATOR SERIES

Publisher: Educational Micro Systems Inc.

Also available from: MARCK

Grade: 2-8

Format: 4 programs on cassette or diskette

Hardware: TRS-80 MOD I; 32K (DOS 2.3) • TRS-80 MOD III; 32K (DOS 1.2) • TRS-80 MOD I or III; 16K (cassette)

Price: $23.95/diskette; $18.95/cassette; $79.95/package on diskette $69.95/package on cassette

This series was developed to extend the Whole Number Arithmetic Series by Teaching Objective. It generates standard 8 1/2-by-11 "hard copy" worksheets which may be used to practice or evaluate mastery of computational skills in the conventional class atmosphere or in conjunction with the computer. There is one program for each arithmetic operation and each one works in the same manner. The teacher answers a few questions displayed on the screen and the program prints out worksheets custom-tailored to his specifications. Up to 20 copies of the same worksheet may be requested and a teacher answer sheet is automatically produced. Teachers with classes where students tend to check their neighbor's answers can let the computer generate separate tests for each row - even for each student. Each test will have its own teacher answer sheet.

ID: J275

WORKING WITH BASIC ADDITION FACTS

Publisher: Micro-Ed, Inc.

Also available from: Academic Software • EISI (Educational Instructional Systems, Inc.) • MARCK • Queue, Inc.

Grade: 1-3

Format: cassette or diskette

Hardware: Commodore 64 • PET

Language: BASIC

Source Code: no

Price: $7.95

Each lesson consists of fifteen problems. If the learner wishes, he/she may practice adding only a certain number. Problems are posed at random and are not repeated unless they are missed. They may be repeated more than once. At the end of each lesson the learner's performance is summarized according to the following categories: number of problems, number of errors, answers given by the computer, average correct response time, total lesson time, specific problems that gave trouble.

ID: J276

WORKING WITH BASIC MULTIPLICATION FACTS

Publisher: Micro-Ed, Inc.

Also available from: Academic Software • EISI (Educational Instructional Systems, Inc.) • MARCK • Queue, Inc.

Grade: Elementary

Format: cassette or diskette

Hardware: Commodore 64 • PET

Language: BASIC

Source Code: no

Price: $7.95

Each lesson consists of fifteen problems. If the learner wishes, he/she may practice multiplying by a certain number. Problems are posed at random and are not repeated unless they are missed. They may then be repeated more than once. At the end of each lesson, the learner's performance is summarized according to the following categories: number of problems, number of errors, answers given by the computer, average correct response time, total lesson time, specific problems that gave trouble.

SCIENCE

ID: K1

ACID-BASED CHEMISTRY

Publisher: Programs For Learning, Inc.

Also available from: MARCK • McKilligan Supply Corp. • Queue, Inc.

Format: cassette or diskette

Hardware: Wang • HP-3000 • PDP-8 • Prime • PDP-11 • Apple • PET • TRS-80

Price: $150.00/package (Queue, Inc - $100.00)

Package of eleven programs offers drill and practice and simulation exercises in problems involving acid-base chemistry. Instructor's guide gives individual descriptions, sample runs, and specific suggestions for classroom implementation.

ABEQ - Demonstrates acid-base equilibria; students vary initial concentrations and dissociation constants to observe effects on equilibrium concentrations, pH and percent dissociation.

BUFFER - Demonstrates pH changes in buffer solutions; students establish initial conditions and observe pH values as a strong acid or base is added to both the buffer and a comparison sample of pure water.

BRNSTD - Drill on recognition of Bronsted acids and bases in a randomly selected sequence of reactions.

DRILL1 - Drill on a variety of fundamental concepts in multiple-choice format such as identifying conjugate acids/bases and interpreting relative strengths of acids from a table of equilibrium constants.

DRILL2 - Practice problems concerning pH, pOH for solutions of acids, bases and buffers of varying strengths.

ENDPT - Titration simulation in which student tries to analyze an unknown acid sample in the most efficient manner.

KHP - Practice with problems concerning standardization with potassium acid phthalate and determination of equivalent weight of unknown acid.

MOLAR - Practice problems concerning moles, grams and molarity of solutions.

PH - PH problem exercise presented in stages arranged in order of increasing complexity.

TCPLOT - Plots a titration curve demonstrating pH changes as strong base or acid is added to any weak acid or base with up to eight dissociation constants.

TCPROB - Practice problems of the type encountered in plotting a titration curve.

ID: K2

ASTRONOMY - PLANETS

Publisher: Educational Courseware

Format: diskette

Hardware: Apple; 48K (DOS 3.3 or 3.2)

Price: $32.00

The orbits of the planets are displayed in high-resolution graphics in this simulation of earth's solar system. Students can alter the speed of the inner and then outer planets as they orbit the sun. Displays are in the correct scale, and the orbiting periods are in their correct relationship to the earth's period of one year. Studies in orbiting distances, speeds, and Kepler's laws are presented for students to "see" the planets as they might be seen by an observer in deep space. Conjunction, opposition, and the geometry of sighting the planets from earth are easy concepts to discover with the aid of the programs.

ID: K3

ASTRONOMY I - INTRODUCTIONS

Publisher: Educational Courseware

Also available from: Queue, Inc.

Format: diskette

Hardware: Apple II; 48K (DOS 3.3 or 3.2)

Price: $32.00

This disk introduces features of the stars and constellations for study. High-resolution graphics are used. The Big Dipper and Orion start the study of stars and some constellations. Properties of stars, meteors, satellites and constellations and the celestial coordinates of right ascension and declination are presented. The 12 zodiac constellations set the background of stars for a display of the sun's motion in the heavens.

ID: K4

ASTRONOMY II - CONSTELLATIONS

Publisher: Educational Courseware

Also available from: Academic Software • MARCK

Format: diskette

Hardware: Apple II; 48K (DOS 3.3 or 3.2)

Price: $32.00

More than 24 constellations are displayed in graphics to aid in identifiying stars and locating objects in the sky. Includes Cepheus, Andromeda, Gemini, Aquarius, Scorpius, Virgo, Aquila, Cassiopeia, Cygnus, Pisces, Leo, Taurus, Aries, Capricornus, Cetus, Cancer, Ophiuchus, Canis Major, Libra, Bootes, Perseus, Sagittarius, Orion, and others. A quiz is included. Excellent displays help the user learn how to locate regions of the night sky without getting cold outside. A quiz is included.

ID: K5

ATOM

Publisher: Micro-Ed, Inc.

Also available from: EISI (Educational Instructional Systems, Inc.) • K-12 Micromedia

Grade: Upper Elementary and up

Format: cassette or diskette

Hardware: Commodore 64 • PET; 8K or 16K (8K is slightly abridged)

Language: BASIC

Source Code: no

Price: $14.95

Text, tables, and graphics are used to present the basic principles of atomic structure. Protons, electrons, neutrons, and the atomic number and weight of atoms are introduced, and the student is asked to apply the principles being learned. Following the lesson, the student is quizzed, the questions being randomly selected from a bank of thirty. The program ends with a summary of student performance. This is the first in a

K

projected science series that will include programs on the molecule, the cell, simple machines, and others.

ID: K6
ATOMIC PHYSICS
Publisher: Micro Learningware

Also available from: Academic Software

Grade: 9 and up

Format: diskette

Hardware: Apple II; 48K with Applesoft in ROM (DOS 3.3)

Language: Applesoft BASIC

Source Code: yes

Price: $30.00

Package includes six programs that discuss and illustrate major aspects of atomic theory. Documentation booklet included.

ATOMIC MODELS - Historical review of atomic theory discusses Democritus, Dalton, Brownian motion, Thompson, Rutherford, Bohr, quantum mechanics, and neutrons. No math is used; program can be understood by students from ninth grade through college, in either physics or chemistry classes.

PARTICLES AND WAVES - Program gives student the following choices: (1) watch everything; (2) Newton vs. Huygens; (3) dual nature of light; (4) matter waves.

ELECTRON CLOUDS IN HYDROGEN - Program plots electron density diagrams for six lowest energy states of hydrogen.

RUTHERFORD SCATTERING - Program presents the following options: (1) introduction; (2) distance of closest approach; (3) scattering angle; (4) game instructions; (5) play the scattering game.

RADIOACTIVE DECAY - Illustrates and discusses decay by alpha emission, beta emission, positron emission, and K shell electron capture.

NUCLEAR REACTIONS - Program presents binding energy curve. It discusses fusion and shows reaction of hydrogen with helium-3. Finally, it discusses fission, showing an example of a neutron exciting fission of Uranium-235.

ID: K7
ATOMIC STRUCTURE
Publisher: Programs For Learning, Inc.

Also available from: MARCK • McKilligan Supply Corp. • Queue, Inc.

Format: cassette or diskette

Hardware: Apple • TRS-80 • PET • Prime • Wang • HP-3000 • PDP-8 • PDP-11

Price: $150.00/package (Queue, Inc - $100.00)

Package of nine programs provides drill and practice and simulation exercises on problems of atomic structure. Instructor's guide gives individual descriptions, sample runs, and specific suggestions for classroom implementation.

ATOMIC - Drill on the number of protons, neutrons and electrons in atoms with atomic numbers through 22.

IP - Drill on predicting relative ionization energies for different atoms and ions, based on their positions in the Periodic Table.

LEWIS - Drill to develop mastery of the octet rule.

MILKAN - Simulation of the oil drop experiment; by varying voltage across plates, student finds conditions which keep drops stationary.

NUCLER - Practice interpreting equations for nuclear reactions in which one of the sub-atomic particles has been omitted.

SPDF - Drill on determining the number of electrons with given principles and azimuthal quantum numbers in a particular atom selected at random from a range determined by the student.

RYDBRG - Questions concerning the relationship between the energy levels and spectral lines in a hydrogen atom.

TRENDS - Questions concerning various trends and relationships between atoms based on their relative positions in the Periodic Table.

VSEPR - Practice using the VSEPR method to predict hybridization and geometry of simple molecules and ions.

ID: K8
BALANCING CHEMICAL EQUATIONS
Publisher: Microcomputer Workshops

Date: July 82

Grade: 9-12

Format: cassette

Hardware: PET; 16K

Language: BASIC

Source Code: no

Price: $20.00

Program introduces correct procedure for balancing elementary chemical equations, then offers equations of increasing difficulty. Student chooses number of problems attempted, then proceeds to balance equation using screen as worksheet and interacting step by step with computer. All errors are flagged immediately and appropriate explanations provided. After student has corrected error, problem continues until equation is correctly balanced. Number of errors made is given at end of each problem. Written documentation is provided.

ID: K9
BASIC ELECTRICITY
Publisher: Ideatech Company

Also available from: K-12 Micromedia • MARCK • Queue, Inc.

Grade: 2-8

Format: diskette

Hardware: Apple II Plus; 48K • Apple II; 48K with Applesoft in ROM

Language: BASIC

Price: $19.95

The program is designed to introduce the student to the fundamental aspects of electricity. The student interacts with the computer as diagrammatic representations are used to introduce the concept of current flow and open, closed, and short circuits. The program also stimulates logical thinking as the student must extrapolate from the presentation information in order to solve a switch puzzle presented within the lesson. BASIC ELECTRICITY presents a lesson on fundamental concepts through the use of mixed screen text and high-resolution graphics. The program is constructed of four parts - the lesson, a puzzle, a quiz and a demonstration. The lesson is presented through a drawing of a battery, lightbulb, switch and interconnecting wires. The student interacts with the program to gain an understanding of current flow and open, closed and parallel switches between the battery and the lightbulb.

ID: K10

BASIC ELECTRICITY

Publisher: Programs For Learning, Inc.

Also available from: MARCK • McKilligan Supply Corp. • Queue, Inc.

Format: cassette or diskette

Hardware: Apple II Plus; 48K (DOS 3.2 or 3.3)

Price: $50.00/package

This package contains a set of three programs, SERIES, PARALLEL, NETWORK, which provide practice in calculating current, voltage and resistance in D.C. circuits. Instructor's guide included.

        SERIES

        PARALLEL

        NETWORK

ID: K11

BEGINNING GEOGRAPHY

Publisher: RIGHT ON PROGRAMS

Date: July 82

Grade: 1

Format: cassette or diskette

Hardware: Apple II; 48K with Applesoft in ROM (DOS 3.2 or 3.3) • PET; 16K

Language: BASIC

Price: $13.00/cassette; $15.00/diskette

Students are introduced to basic map skills and directions. North, east, south, west are introduced. Mountains, rivers and cities are shown, and students learn to understand their symbols. Game follows.

ID: K12

BIOLOGY PROGRAMS FOR THE APPLE II

Publisher: J & S Software, Inc.

Also available from: Academic Software • K-12 Micromedia • MARCK • McKilligan Supply Corp. • Queue, Inc.

Grade: High School

Format: 8 diskettes

Hardware: Apple II Plus; 48K • Apple II; 48K with Applesoft in ROM

Language: BASIC

Source Code: yes

Price: $28.00/program; $105.00/5 programs; $250.00/15 programs

This program teaches 15 major biology concepts, requiring 20 minutes to 1 hour per unit. Lesson format uses question, information, more information, then branches to questions in subprogram on any concept with which student has difficulty.

Student names and grades are stored. Average running time of programs 30 min.-1 hr.

        TRANSPORT

        ASEXUAL REPRODUCTION

        CELLS

        NERVOUS SYSTEM

        EXCRETION

        ENDOCRINE SYSTEM

        DIGESTION

        BIOCHEMISTRY

        LOCOMOTION

        PHOTOSYNTHESIS AND TRANSPORT

        RESPIRATION

        GENETICS

        CLASSIFICATION

        REPRODUCTION - PLANTS

        ANIMAL REPRODUCTION

ID: K13

BIRDBREED

Publisher: EduTech

Also available from: Academic Software

Grade: High School-College

Format: diskette

Hardware: Apple II Plus; 48K (DOS 3.2 or 3.3) • Apple II; 48K with Applesoft in ROM (DOS 3.2 or 3.3)

Source Code: no

Price: $95.00/program with manual

Designed for exploration of genetic principles. Provides 16 breeding groups of birds of defined phenotypes. Student breeds up to 100 birds for analysis of genotypes and inheritance patterns. Illustrates phenomena of dominance, codominance, sex linkage, independent assortment, multiple alleles, gene interaction, and gene linkage. Complements laboratory experiments in genetics.

ID: K14

BIRDS

Publisher: RIGHT ON PROGRAMS

Date: Aug. 82

Grade: 4

Format: cassette or diskette

Hardware: Apple II; 48K with Applesoft in ROM (DOS 3.2 or 3.3) • PET; 16K

Language: BASIC

Source Code: yes

This general overview tells why birds are important; how they are born, what makes a bird a bird, about their beaks and feet and more. A game follows which tests the student's retention of the material given. Right answers are rewarded and incorrect answers are corrected with no penalty.

ID: K15
CATLAB

Publisher: CONDUIT

Date: Sept. 82

Grade: 9-College

Format: diskette

Hardware: Apple II; 48K with Applesoft in ROM

Language: BASIC

CATLAB is a computer simulation that allows students to mate domestic cats, selected on the basis of coat color and pattern. The program then produces genetically valid litters of kittens. From observing the coat color and patterns of these kittens, students may run any number of subsequent matings and again observe the litters, then develop and test hypotheses related to these observations. CATLAB is appropriate for students who have been introduced to the basic principles of Mendelian genetics, principally students at the university level. The program is open-ended and simply acts as a vehicle for investigation within the genetics field. Although a number of sample investigations are suggested in the Student Guide, in general the problem to be investigated, the starting point, the sequence of investigations, and the finishing point can all be defined and controlled by the student. In using this simulation, students also are freed from some of the problems of real laboratory investigations: successive generations can be produced with virtually no delay and cultures of breeding stocks do not have to be housed and maintained. This package is designed to complement laboratories, lecture materials, and textbook problems in genetics. Investigations using the program can run concurrently with hands-on laboratory activities using Drosophilia. It includes one copy of Student Guide and one Instructor Guide.

ID: K16
CELLS

Publisher: Educational Activities, Inc.

Also available from: Academic Software

Grade: 3-9

Format: cassette or diskette

Hardware: Apple II Plus; (DOS 3.2.1 or 3.3) • TRS-80 MOD I or III; with Level II BASIC • PET • Commodore 2001 • Commodore 4000; 40 or 80 column • Commodore 8000; 80 column

Source Code: no

Price: $39.00/cassette set of 2; $39.00/diskette

In these two programs, a presentation which is informative, motivational, and fun has been created to illustrate and explain the fundamental parts and functions of a cell. Animated graphics are used in both programs to aid in teaching about the cell. The programs contain both tutorial and drill formats.

BASIC CELL STRUCTURE - In this almost totally graphic presentation of the cell, the viewer is introduced to the basic parts of a cell (cell membrane, cytoplasm, and nucleus), shown how small particles of dissolved nutrients may pass through a cell membrane while larger particles are kept out, and is shown an amoeba extending a pseudopod. A drill section completes the lesson. The program responds to incorrect answers by branching to clear and complete explanations.

CELL DIVISION (BINARY FISSION) - The subject of cell reproduction by binary fission is explored in a step-by-step animated view of mitosis, cell membrane expansion and pinching together, and the resulting two daughter cells. The tutorial is followed by a drill section which utilizes branching to provide easily understandable explanations to incorrect student responses.

ID: K17
CHEM LAB SIMULATION #1

Publisher: CONDUIT

Also available from: McKilligan Supply Corp. • Queue, Inc.

Date: 1979

Grade: 9-College

Format: diskette

Hardware: Apple II; 48K with Applesoft in ROM (DOS 3.2.1) • Atari 800; 48K (DOS 2.0); Model 810 drive

Language: BASIC

Source Code: no

Price: $75.00

This set of programs simulates several common lab applications and can be used to demonstrate actual lab procedure and to assist students in gaining a better understanding of the typical calculations needed to process the lab data obtained. The package begins by simulating an acid-base titration. Base from a buret is delivered into an acid solution until the endpoint is reached and the titration is stopped. The student determines when the indicator color change shows the endpoint has been reached and then must determine the volume delivered (enters initial and final buret readings). The concentration of the weak acid is calculated next. The titration procedure may be repeated to obtain consistent readings. Next follows a simulation of several partial neutralizations, as monitored by a pH meter, in order to determine the equilibrium constant for a weak acid. From a list of unknown acids, the student finally selects which acid was used. Another option is to determine by titration the molecular weight of a fatty acid as it spreads across an oil slick to form a monolayer. The concentration of the acid solution, the number of drops of solution dispensed, and the area of the fatty acid surface are used to determine a value for Avogadro's number. Includes User's Manual (19 pages).

ID: K18
CHEM LAB SIMULATION #2

Publisher: CONDUIT

Also available from: McKilligan Supply Corp. • Queue, Inc.

Date: 1979

Grade: 9-College

Format: diskette

Hardware: Apple II; 48K with Applesoft in ROM (DOS 3.2.1)

Language: BASIC

Source Code: no

Price: $75.00

This package contains two simulations dealing with the behavior of ideal gases. The accompanying manual includes discussions of the theories behind the experiments, formulas and example calculations, and the procedures used to conduct each experiment. Methods notes explain the experimental process in general terms and further clarify the screen instructions. A set of study guides for the experiments is also included in the manual--exercises and discussions which direct the student from simple principles toward an understanding of the theories and laws demonstrated in the simulations. Includes User's Manual (35 pages).

IDEAL GAS LAW SIMULATION - Portrays the behavior of an ideal gas according to the kinetic molecular theory of gases. The simulation consists of visible particles of a gas within a container. The student may vary the pressure, volume, temperature, or number of moles of gas, and the simulation graphically demonstrates the gas' behavior.

ENTROPY SIMULATION - Program shows that entropy of a system in a given state is a measure of the amount of disorder of that state. The simulation displays a compartment divided by a barrier. In one option of the simulation two gases are allowed to mix, while in the second option a gas is allowed to expand from one side of the compartment into the other.

ID: K19
CHEMICAL EQUILIBRIUM

Publisher: Programs For Learning, Inc.

Also available from: MARCK • McKilligan Supply Corp. • Queue, Inc.

Format: cassette or diskette

Hardware: Apple • PET • TRS-80 • Wang • HP-3000 • PDP-8 • PDP-11 • Prime

Price: $150.00/package

Package of ten programs offers drill and practice and simulation exercises in various chemical equilibrium problems. Instructor's guide gives individual descriptions, sample runs, and specific suggestions for classroom implementation.

ACIDEQ - Practice problems on pH, phOH with strong and weak acid/base/buffer solutions.

EQCALC - Practice estimating equilibrium concentrations for any reaction with known equilibrium constant.

EQUIL - Investigation of two systems, one with a large Keq, the other with a small constant (PCL_5, phosgene) to develop understanding of relation between constant and concentrations.

EQPROB - Drill and practice computing concentrations from initial data and equilibrium constant, or constant from concentrations.

HABER - Simulation of ammonia synthesis allowing variations in temperature, pressure and catalyst to show effects on speed of reaction and equilibrium concentrations.

HIEQ - Simulation of hydrogen-iodine-HI equilibrium system to introduce concept of equilibrium constant.

H2S - Practice problems with concentrations of various species present in hydrogen sulfide solutions at varying pH values.

KSP - Practice problems with solubility product calculations.

KSP2 - Practice problems using solubility product to predict precipitation when mixing dilute solutions containing ions of slightly soluble compounds.

LECHAT - Drill on applications of Le Chatelier's principle.

ID: K20
CHEMICAL NOMENCLATURE SERIES

Publisher: Merlan Scientific Ltd.

Grade: High School and up

Format: 4 cassettes or 1 diskette

Hardware: PET; 8K cassette or 16K diskette • Apple II Plus; 48K (DOS 3.3)

Language: BASIC

Source Code: no

Price: $22.00/cassette; $66.00/diskette of 4 programs

Series consists of four programs presenting nomenclature of organic and inorganic substances. Written documentation is provided.

ORGANIC COMPOUND NOMENCLATURE - Program displays choice of nine different types of organic compounds on screen. Compound type (e.g. alkene, aromatic, ester, amine, etc.) is selected by user. Length of chain, position of functional group, and position of branch are changed randomly by computer, creating hundreds of possible combinations. User is then asked for IUPAC name and is corrected if answer is wrong.

HYDROCARBON NOMENCLATURE - Computer randomly creates alkenes from thousands of possible combinations. Variables include chain length, number of branches, position of branches, and length of branches. Program includes three levels of difficulty, with recent best scores for each printed on screen. User is asked to enter correct IUPAC name for hydrocarbon displayed. If incorrect the second time, correct answer is given.

INORGANIC NOMENCLATURE (NAME TO FORMULA) - Student is given name of binary compound or acid salt, and must type in its formula. Program uses sophisticated input routine, including capital and small letters, and computer automatically places numerals below line in correct subscript position. Student can be drilled only on IUPAC names, or icous method names can be included. Computer keeps score, and gives hints to help student learn correct nomenclature.

INORGANIC NOMENCLATURE (FORMULA TO NAME) - Student is given formula and must type in name of compound. Advanced input technique is used to minimize typing skill required. Computer scores and gives hints to help.

ID: K21
CHEMISTRY I

Publisher: Microphys Programs

Also available from: Academic Software • EISI (Educational Instructional Systems, Inc.) • MARCK • Queue, Inc.

Grade: High School and up

Format: 13 cassettes or 1 diskette

Hardware: PET; 8K; cassette or 4040 dual disk drive • Apple II; 24K (DOS 3.2 or 3.3) • TRS-80 MOD I or III; 16K • Bell & Howell

Language: BASIC

Source Code: yes

Price: $180.00/diskette; $20.00/cassette

Package consists of 13 interactive chemistry programs. Computer-assisted instruction versions guide student through series of quantitative questions; individualized-instruction versions generate a unique set of problems for each student. Utility programs are designed to provide solutions to time-consuming problems often given on exams and homework assignments. Grades and overall evaluation are compiled by programs for each student. Complete instructions are included. Also available through Queue, Inc. in diskette format only.

CALORIMETRY (PC8) - Program generates series of four questions dealing with principle of calorimetry, thereby reviewing definition of specific heat capacity and principle of conservation of energy.

SPECIFIC HEAT CAPACITY (PC9) - Generates series of four questions dealing with definition of specific heat capacity.

HEATS OF FUSION/VAPORIZATION (PC10) - Generates series of three questions dealing with concepts of fusion and vaporization.

SPECIFIC GAS LAWS (PC11) - Generates series of three questions dealing with gases undergoing isothermal, isobaric, and isovolumic processes, thereby reviewing Boyle's, Charles', and Gay-Lussac's laws.

GENERAL GAS LAW (PC12) - Generates series of questions dealing with behavior of gas undergoing general process in which all three thermodynamic variables may change.

FARADAY'S LAW (PC22) - Generates series of questions dealing with analysis of an electrolytic solution.

GRAM-MOLECULAR MASS (PC23) - Randomly synthesizes inorganic compounds whose gram-molecular masses are to be determined, thereby reviewing the writing of chemical formulas.

MOLE CONCEPT (PC24) - Generates series of questions dealing with mole concept and writing of chemical formulas.

SYMBOLS AND VALENCES DRILL (PC37) - Students are given practice in learning symbols and valences of common ions and radicals encountered in elementary courses.

NAMING COMPOUNDS DRILL (PC38) - Students are given practice in learning to name randomly synthesized compounds whose formulas are given.

FORMULAS OF COMPOUNDS DRILL (PC39) - Students are given practice in learning to write formulas of randomly synthesized compounds.

GAS LAW ANALYSIS (PC303) - Utility program is designed to solve large variety of problems in which gases undergo isothermal, isobaric, isovolumic, and general processes.

CALORIMETRY ANALYSIS (PC306) - Utility program is designed to solve various time-consuming problems involved in study of calorimetry. Substances undergoing changes in phase, as well as changes in temperature, may be dealt with by this problem.

ID: K22
CHEMISTRY II

Publisher: Microphys Programs

Also available from: Academic Software • EISI (Educational Instructional Systems, Inc.) • MARCK • Queue, Inc.

Grade: High School and up

Format: 13 cassettes or 1 diskette

Hardware: PET; 8K; cassette or 4040 dual disk drive • Apple II; 24K (DOS 3.2 or 3.3) • TRS-80 MOD I or III; 16K • Bell & Howell

Language: BASIC

Source Code: yes

Price: $180.00/diskette; $20.00/cassette

Package consists of 13 interactive chemistry programs. Computer-assisted instruction versions guide student through series of quantitative questions; individualized-instruction versions generate a unique set of problems for each student. Utility programs are designed to provide solutions to time-consuming problems often given on exams and homework assignments. Grades and overall evaluation are compiled by programs for each student. Complete instructions are included. Also available through Queue, Inc. in diskette format only.

MOLARITY CONCEPT (PC25) - Program generates series of three questions dealing with concept of molarity; mole concept is also reviewed.

NORMALITY CONCEPT (PC26) - Generates series of questions dealing with concepts of gram-molecular mass, gram-equivalent mass, and normality.

MOLALITY CONCEPT (PC27) - Generates series of questions dealing with concepts of gram-molecular mass and molality.

STOICHIOMETRY: MASS/MASS (PC28) - Generates series of questions permitting development of facility in solving problems involving mass/mass relationships in various chemical reactions.

STOICHIOMETRY: MASS/VOLUME (PC29) - Generates series of questions permitting development of facility in problems involving mass/volume relationships in various chemical reactions.

STOICHIOMETRY: VOLUME/VOLUME (PC30) - Generates series of questions permitting development of facility in problems involving volume/volume relationships in various chemical reactions.

STOICHIOMETRY: GENERAL (PC31) - Generates series of questions dealing with stoichiometric relationships in chemical reactions. Randomly generates mass/mass, mass/volume, and volume/volume problem types.

PERCENT CONCENTRATION (PC32) - Generates series of questions relating to computation of percent or fraction concentration of randomly generated solutions.

PH CONCEPT (PC33) - Generates series of questions dealing with concept of pH and pOH. Student gains facility in working with logarithmic scales.

EMF OF ELECTROCHEMICAL CELLS (PC34) - Generates series of questions in which student determines EMF of randomly synthesized electrochemical cell.

CHEMISTRY ANALYSIS I (PC307) - Utility program is designed to provide solutions to problems involving mole concept and molarity.

CHEMISTRY ANALYSIS II (PC308) - Utility program is designed to provide solutions to problems involving normality, molality, and changes in freezing and boiling points of solutions.

STOICHIOMETRIC ANALYSIS (PC309) - Utility program is designed to provide solutions to problems involving mass/mass, mass/volume, and volume/volume relationships in chemical reactions.

ID: K23

CHEMISTRY PROGRAMS

Publisher: Dr. Daley's Software

Also available from: Queue, Inc.

Grade: High School and up

Format: cassette or diskette

Hardware: PET; 8K • Apple II Plus; 32K (DOS 3.2 or 3.3) • Apple II; 32K (DOS 3.2 or 3.3)

Language: BASIC

Price: $119.95/set

Seven programs for drill in organic chemistry are designed to assist student in mastering specific concepts. All compounds are named using IUPAC rules.

NAMING - General review of naming of organic compounds, in which computer randomly selects compounds containing from one to ten carbons and attaches one of ten functional groups. Student is asked to identify functional group and then name compound.

ALKANES - Program gives student practice naming branched alkanes, with up to ten carbons on main chain and zero to ten side chains. Program can generate over 200,000 apparently different alkanes. When student enters incorrect answer, computer offers help and redraws compound so that student can see numbering of substituents. This feature is found on following two programs as well.

ALKENES - Much like ALKANES, but deals with alkenes, using EZ system of naming. Program can generate over 50,000 apparently different alkenes.

AROMATIC - Similar in format to ALKANES and ALKENES for aromatic compounds. Program randomly generates around 100,000 apparently different aromatic compounds and asks student to name them.

STEREOCHEMISTRY - Program drills student in concepts of stereochemistry, using concepts of chirality and Fischer projections as well as R, S, and meso designations.

NMR - Gives student practice using basics of interpreting NMR spectra. Can be used with 12 practice spectra coded in program or with one of student's spectra.

IR - Gives practice with interpreting infrared spectra. Can be used with 12 practice spectra coded in program or with one of student's spectra.

ID: K24

CHEMISTRY SIMULATIONS I & II

Publisher: Aquarius Publishers Inc.

Also available from: Academic Software

Date: 1982

Grade: 9-12

Format: cassette or diskette

Hardware: Apple II; 48K with Applesoft in ROM (DOS 3.2 or 3.3)

Source Code: no

Price: $29.95 each; $55.00/both

Two sets of chemistry programs for high school classes feature student-tested high-resolution animated graphics lab simulations that provide randomly generated initial values to insure that the experiments can be used repeatedly without arriving at same results each time. Set I includes acid-base titration and determination of molecular weight of a gas. Set II includes replacement of hydrogen by a more active metal and 50 common ions quiz (drill and practice). Average running time is 20 minutes; documentation is provided.

ID: K25

CHEMISTRY SIMULATIONS, VOLUME 1

Publisher: Radio Shack®

Date: 1982

Grade: Secondary

Format: cassette

Hardware: TRS-80 Color Computer; 16K with extended BASIC • CTR-80A cassette recorder

Language: BASIC

Source Code: yes

Price: $199.00

Set of chemistry laboratory experiment simulations allows student to control and *see* results of basic and classic experiments again and again. Titles in VOLUME 1 are Kinetic Theory, Charles' Law, Boyle's Law, Titration, Conductivity, and Solubility. Package includes instruction manual and student experiment books.

ID: K26

CHEMISTRY WITH A COMPUTER

Publisher: Programs For Learning, Inc.

Also available from: MARCK • McKilligan Supply Corp. • Queue, Inc.

Format: cassette or diskette

Hardware: Apple • TRS-80 • PET • Wang • Prime • HP-3000 • PDP-8 • PDP-11

Price: $150.00/package (Queue, Inc - $100.00)

Package of eleven programs provides drill and practice and simulation exercises. Includes a copy of *Chemistry with a Computer*, by Paul Cauchon.

EQPROB - Program has practice problems concerning equilibrium constants; given reaction type and concentrations, determine constant, or, given constant, determine concentrations.

GASES - Program has conventional assortment of pressure - volume - temperature problems for practice with Boyle's, Charles' and the combined gas laws.

KSP - Program has problems concerning solubility product calculations.

MOLES - Program is drill on problems concerning percent composition and gram-mole relationships in common compounds.

EXP19 - Program is simulation of ChemStudy experiment concerning the development of a scheme of analysis based on three solutions and four test reagents.

EXP20 - Program is simulation of ChemStudy experiment concerning an introduction to qualitative analysis with metals of the second group.

REDOX - Program has practice on various topics concerning oxidation- reduction systems such as identifying electrodes losing or gaining electrons, direction of electron flow, and potential difference in a given cell.

SOLUBLE - Program has practice problems requiring interpretations of typical solubility curves.

SOLUTIONS - Program is drill on moles, molarity, molecules and dilution.

STATE - Program is simulation of system in which a substance is to be identified by observing changes of state when it is heated or cooled.

SYSTEM - Program is drill on metric units of length, mass and volume.

ID: K27

CIRCULAR MOTION

Publisher: Micro Learningware

Also available from: Academic Software

Format: diskette

Hardware: Apple II; 48K with Applesoft in ROM

Language: Applesoft BASIC

Source Code: yes

Price: $15.00

Package consists of five programs which explain and illustrate aspects of circular motion. Documentation booklet included.

CIRCLE 1 (CONSTANT SPEED) - Program explains differences between angular velocity, tangential velocity, angular acceleration, tangential acceleration, and radial acceleration or circular motion with constant speed. It draws a picture with object moving around circle. Text appears on screen to explain different vectors.

CIRCLE 2 (ROTATION WITH INCREASING SPEED) - Program begins by showing picture of accelerating circular motion. Program also explains velocity and acceleration.

SIMPLE HARMONIC MOTION - Program illustrates simple harmonic motions and reference circle. It often shows picture of object moving in circle beside projection of same object moving vertically in simple harmonic motion. Includes detailed solution to problem as well as student problem.

ORBIT THEORY - Program provides two explanations of orbit theory with graphic illustrations. Program teaches concepts of gravity, centrifugal force, apogee, and perigee. Quiz at end includes graphics.

CIRCULAR ORBIT GAME - Program makes astronautical mid-flight changes in shape of orbit into computer game. Player is given initial elliptical orbit, and must change it into a circular orbit using limited amount of fuel.

ID: K28

CIRCULATION ORGANS

Publisher: Micro Power & Light Company

Also available from: Academic Software • Queue, Inc.

Grade: 5 and up

Format: diskette

Hardware: Apple II; 32K with Applesoft in ROM

Price: $29.95

The program addresses the blood, heart, arteries, capillaries, veins, and lungs. Each of six topics consists of a tutorial with color motion and sound; a quiz with entertaining and challenging questions; and a review opportunity with summary statements. Each topic usually requires about 5-15 minutes.

ID: K29

CIRCULATION SYSTEM

Publisher: Micro Power & Light Company

Also available from: Academic Software • Queue, Inc.

Grade: 8 and up

Format: diskette

Hardware: Apple II; 32K with Applesoft in ROM

Price: $29.95

This program covers preliminary descriptions of key organs: blood, heart, arteries, capillaries, veins, and lungs, and the circulatory system - the heart, blood, pulmonary circulation, and systemic circulation. A short (and entertaining) quiz follows the instruction, covering each new topic. There are numerous review opportunities. Much use is made of the computer's graphic capabilities.

ID: K30

COEXIST - POPULATION DYNAMICS

Publisher: CONDUIT

Also available from: K-12 Micromedia • MARCK • Queue, Inc.

Date: 1975

Grade: 9-College

Format: diskette

Hardware: Apple II; 48K with Applesoft in ROM (DOS 3.2.1) • TRS-80 MOD I; 32K with Level II BASIC • TRS-80 MOD III; 32K with Disk BASIC • PET 2000 or 4000 series; 8K (cassette) or 16K (disk) with 2040 or 4040 drive

Language: BASIC

Source Code: yes

Price: $35.00; $10.00/add'l copy of software; $1.50/add'l student manual; $1.50/add'l teacher manual

This unit simulates two biological situations. In the first, up to three populations are modeled to grow independently on identical, limited food resources. The student can then investigate organisms competing only with members of their own species. The second simulates two populations in competition with each other for the same limited resources. In each situation the student controls a number of parameters such as initial population, number of offspring, generation times, initial and saturation points, and inhibiting factors which influence the outcome of species competition. Includes six copies of Students' Notes (15 pages), one copy of Teachers' Guide (15 pages).

ID: K31

COMPETE - PLANT COMPETITION

Publisher: CONDUIT

Also available from: K-12 Micromedia • MARCK • Opportunities For Learning, Inc. • Queue, Inc.

Date: 1975

Grade: 9-College

Format: diskette

Hardware: Apple II; 48K with Applesoft in ROM (DOS 3.2.1) •
TRS-80 MOD I; 32K with Level II BASIC • TRS-80 MOD III;
32K with Disk BASIC • PET 2000 or 4000 series; 8K (cassette)
or 16K (disk) with 2040 or 4040 drive

Language: BASIC

Source Code: yes

Price: $35.00; $10.00/add'l software copy; $1.50/add'l student
manual; $1.50/add'l teacher manual

This simulation enables students to plan and carry out investigations of interactions between flowering plants without
the long delay usually associated with growth experiments.
The unit includes investigations with both real and simulated
plants and other relevant data in the form of graphs, tables and
descriptions. The seven investigations deal with effects of
crowding on plant growth, measurement growth, simulated
growth in a monoculture, interaction between clover varieties,
simulated growth in a mixture, interaction below the ground,
and direct plant interaction. Includes six copies of Students'
Notes (15 pages), one copy of Teachers' Guide (11 pages).

ID: K32
COMPUTER CHEMISTRY

Publisher: J & S Software, Inc.

Also available from: Academic Software • K-12 Micromedia •
MARCK • McKilligan Supply Corp. • Opportunities For
Learning, Inc. • Queue, Inc.

Grade: 10-12

Format: cassette or diskette

Hardware: Apple II; 48K with Applesoft in ROM • Apple II; 32K
• TRS-80 MOD I or III; 16K with Level II BASIC

Source Code: yes

Price: Apple II, 48K $28/program; $105/5 prog.; $250/15 prog.
Apple II, 32K or TRS-80 $23/prog; $90/6 prog; $185/15 prog.

This program includes 15 chemistry programs that review
and teach the main concepts in each topic. No two students
receive the same questions. Each program requires 20 to 30
minutes to complete. Names and grades can be stored on an
optional disk file.

GAS RELATIONSHIPS

MOLES AND FORMULAS

CHEMICAL EQUATIONS

SOLUTIONS

PERIODIC TABLE

ELECTRON STRUCTURE

BONDING IN MOLECULES

BONDING BETWEEN MOLECULES

KINETICS

EQUILIBRIUM

ELECTROCHEMICAL CELLS

OXIDATION - REDUCTION

ACID-BASE THEORIES

ACID-BASE PROBLEMS

ORGANIC CHEMISTRY

ID: K33
COMPUTERS IN THE BIOLOGY CURRICULUM

Publisher: CONDUIT

Also available from: K-12 Micromedia • MARCK • Opportunities For Learning, Inc.

Date: 1978

Grade: 9-College

Format: diskette (Apple) or 8 in. flexible disk for Standard
BASIC version (CONDUIT Level 0 BASIC), 12 programs

Hardware: Apple II; 48K with Applesoft in ROM (DOS 3.2.1)

Language: BASIC

Source Code: yes

Price: $95.00; $10.00/additional software copy; $41.00/addi-
tional documentation

The computer programs included in this package provide the
facility for simulation gaming and model building, and computation and data retrieval. The intent of the materials is to
create activities for students which are primarily seen as problem solving. The documentation for this package is divided into
eight chapters. The first chapter provides instructors with a
good overview of instructional computing in biology with
numerous examples. Later chapters deal with specific curriculum topics.

INHERITANCE - Two distinct parts comprise this unit. In the
first part, inheritance of characters is simulated for three species
of animals (fruit flies, mice and humans) and one species of
plant (tomatoes). In the second part, multifactorial inheritance
is simulated. Students can then use the simulations in both
parts to carry out breeding investigations to supplement those
which they can undertake in the laboratory.

PREDATOR - PREY RELATIONSHIPS - A simple model of
predator-prey relationships is provided to support the students'
study of inter-species relationships in ecosystems.

POND ECOLOGY - This unit is based on a computer simulation of a freshwater community consisting of three trophic
levels - phytoplankton, herbivores, and fish. Fishing can be per-
mitted, which introduces man as a fourth trophic level. Included in the extensive questions for student discussion in this
unit are questions dealing with whaling statistics for four
species of whales from 1929 through 1975.

TRANSPIRATION - This unit covers the simulation of water
loss by leaves. Included are a thorough description of a suggested preliminary laboratory experiment and a lucid explanation of the mathematical models employed in the computer
program.

COUNTERCURRENT SYSTEMS - Two types of countercurrent systems found in the bodies of animals are simulated: ex-
changers and multipliers. Both the simplified mathematical
models and their biological counterparts, kidneys, and the gas
glands and swim bladders of Teleost fish are discussed.

HUMAN ENERGY EXPENDITURE - This unit allows students
to explore human energy requirements in relation to activity,
sex and body mass. It contains data for men and women under-
taking 72 different activities.

STATISTICS FOR BIOLOGISTS - The program described in
this unit computes simple statistics (means, standard deviations
and values of chi-squared) which covers the needs of most introductory courses.

ID: K34
CONSERVATION LAWS

Publisher: Micro Learningware

Also available from: Academic Software

Format: diskette

Hardware: Apple II; 48K with Applesoft in ROM (DOS 3.3)

Language: Applesoft BASIC

Source Code: yes

Price: $12.00

Package consists of eight programs illustrating principles relating to conservation of energy. Documentation booklet included.

LINEAR MOMENTUM - Program first divides momentum problems into RECOIL and COLLISIONS, then illustrates each type with graphics. Momentum conservation law is presented and discussed. Finally, program solves some typical recoil problems.

ANGULAR MOMENTUM - Program shows point mass rotating around axis. Motion is shown for short and long radius. This gives viewer a feeling for how angular velocity decreases when radius increases. Program next calculates what happens to angular and tangential velocity when a radius changes.

ONE DIMENSIONAL COLLISIONS - Program begins by defining ''inelastic'' and ''elastic.'' It shows examples of both, using graphics. It then solves typical problems for both types.

INELASTIC COLLISIONS - Program solves problem of two point masses colliding. All components of velocity and momentum are calculated.

CONSERVATION OF ENERGY - Conservation law is presented and example problem solved.

CONSERVATION OF FORCES - Problems on conservation forces are illustrated and solved.

NON-CONSERVATIVE FORCES - Problems involving non-conservative forces are illustrated and solved.

ENERGY OF A BOUNCING BALL - Ball bounces around on high-resolution screen with gravity. There is small energy loss on each bounce. Beneath picture is running readout of kinetic, potential, and total energy.

ID: K35
CONSTELLATIONS

Publisher: Comaldor

Format: 4 programs on cassette or diskette

Hardware: PET

Price: $20.00/program; $60.00/set of 4

The constellations are introduced with a written description which is accompanied by a graphic presentation highlighting the major star of each constellation. Each unit has teaching and testing modes.

8 WINTER CONSTELLATIONS

8 MORE WINTER CONSTELLATIONS

10 SUMMER CONSTELLATIONS

12 ZODIAC CONSTELLATIONS

ID: K36
DIFFUSION

Publisher: Microcomputer Workshops

Date: July 82

Grade: 6 and up

Format: cassette

Hardware: PET; 16K

Language: BASIC

Source Code: no

Price: $20.00

Chemistry program displays definitions of diffusion, concentration, gradient, and final concentration, followed by examples utilizing these concepts. Graphics are used for observation of resulting changes that take place after selected responses are made. Written documentation is provided.

ID: K37
DIGESTIVE SYSTEM

Publisher: Avant-Garde Creations

Also available from: Academic Software • Queue, Inc.

Grade: 11-12

Format: diskette

Hardware: Apple; 48K with Applesoft in ROM

Price: $29.95

Covering the anatomy and process of the digestive system, this lesson's topics include structure, processing, absorption and byproducts.

ID: K38
EAR

Publisher: Micro Power & Light Company

Grade: Upper Elementary and up

Format: diskette

Hardware: Apple II; 32K with Applesoft in ROM

Price: $24.95

The various parts of the outer, middle and inner ear are presented in logical working order. The shape and location of each part can be seen, as well as vibration and movement! And for those who have black and white monitors rather than color, the disk includes a separate set of program modules to present the ear in successive outline drawings. As in color, each drawing includes a tutorial on a particular part of the ear. A further sophistication of the program allows the student to learn about the ear using either common or Latin terms. THE EAR describes basic anatomy and physiology. It covers the following topics: 1. The Outer Ear - including the pinna, ear canal and eardrum; 2. The Middle Ear - including the ossicles, (hammer, anvil and stirrup), and eustacian tube; and 3. The Inner Ear - includes the cochlea, vestibule, semicircular canals, round and oval windows, and auditory nerve. Because of its primary reliance on pictures and allowing for the use of either common or advanced terminology, THE EAR can be used effectively by interested upper elementary students as well as college students! The program is menu-driven. It is also interactive, requiring frequent user responses. Correct responses are reinforced! Incorrect responses are not acknowledged by the program. There three types of questions asked the student: true/false, numeric and fill-in-the-blank. In the case of true/false, if the correct answer is not "true", it must be "false". In the case of numeric, the correct answer can eventually be discovered by trying each of the ten digits, 0-9. And in the case of fill-in, if the student cannot supply the missing term, he is given the option to review.

ID: K39

EARTH SCIENCE

Publisher: Minnesota Educational Computing Consortium

Date: June 82

Grade: Junior High-High School

Format: diskette

Hardware: Atari 400/800; 16K with Atari BASIC in cartridge

Language: BASIC

Source Code: no

Price: $37.40

Earth science lessons include three programs covering astronomy topics of distance in space and rotation of constellations. Remaining programs are listed below. Support booklet included.

EARTHQUAKES - Provides instruction on locating epicenter of earthquakes.

MINERALS - Provides instruction on identifying 29 common minerals.

ID: K40

EARTH SCIENCE SERIES

Publisher: TYC Software (Teach Yourself by Computer)

Also available from: MARCK

Grade: 7-12

Format: 4 cassettes

Hardware: TRS-80 MOD I or III; 16K, with Level II BASIC

Language: BASIC

Price: $68.50

Series contains 11 independent teaching modules plus a lab aid program. Each was designed by educators as a supplement to teacher's regular curriculum or for use in general resource room. Tutorial information is presented and illustrated with graphics, and learning is reinforced with problems or simulations. Drills and quizzes provide further reinforcement. Series comes complete with teacher/student manual objectives, student worksheets, formulas covered, questions and answers, and instructions.

GRADIENT - Student is presented with simulated temperature field. Student measures distance between two points using graphic scale and determines gradient.

HEAT ENERGY LOST OR GAINED - Student is presented with simulation of beaker of water and thermometer. Student takes readings and calculates heat energy lost or gained.

LATITUDE AND LONGITUDE - Student is presented with map of imaginary island. Latitude and longitude grid is superimposed on map. Points are flashed on map and student must give correct latitude and longitude to nearest minute.

BASIC CHEMISTRY - Using worksheet included in manual,

student reviews eight elements using periodic table, and emphasizing terms element, compound, atom, snd molecule, and their definitions.

STREAM EROSION - Map is given of stream valley with various regions and features lettered. Student matches areas with terms which are presented based on previously given definitions.

WATER BUDGET - Student uses precipitation and potential evapotranspiration values to complete yearly water budget for given area. Water budget information is also determined from graph of precipitation, potential evapotranspiration, and actual evapotranspiration values.

SEISMIC WAVES - Computer simulates earthquake data. Student uses information to determine time of quake, distance to epicenter, and exact location of epicenter.

EARTH HISTORY - Using worksheet included in manual, student uses geologic timetable to relate geologic time periods and events which occurred in them. Student will also determine relative ages of geologic events using geologic cross-section, and determine absolute age of a rock using radioactive delay process.

SEASONS - Earth is shown at four different positions in its orbit. Various information is presented for each position and tests given.

METEOROLOGY - Student associates weather instruments and units with factors they measure and interprets information on a station model. Student then analyzes weather changes which occur as different fronts move through an area.

PERCENT ERROR - Using formula given, student determines which value is experimental value and which is accepted value; then uses formula to calculate percent error.

LAB AID PROGRAM - Program transforms computer into intelligent calculator, preprogrammed with 21 of most common formulas used in lab experiments. After student chooses calculations needed, computer then presents correct formula, prompts for missing values, and gives correct answer. This technique helps student with calculations and at same time teaches and reinforces formulas used. In addition, student may choose GRAPHIC routine with which to create graphs of lab results.

ID: K41

EARTHQUAKES/LATITUDE-LONGITUDE

Publisher: Aquarius Publishers Inc.

Date: Aug. 82

Format: diskette

Hardware: Apple II; 48K with Applesoft in ROM (DOS 3.2 or 3.3)

Source Code: no

Price: $34.95

Earth science package provides hands-on experience in plotting earthquakes and latitude-longitude lines. Use of high-resolution graphics, sound, and color "flash" enables program to depict location and intensity of hundreds of earthquakes on world map, as well as showing related geographical features. Section on latitude-longitude allows student to plot locations on map of world. Versatile, adaptable, expandable package includes detailed Teacher's Guide with instructions for program use, suggested activities, and instructions for modifying program to include new seismic data.

ID: K42

ECOLOGICAL MODELING

Publisher: CONDUIT

Also available from: K-12 Micromedia • MARCK • Queue, Inc.

Date: 1973

Grade: 9-College

Format: diskette

Hardware: Apple II; 48K with Applesoft in ROM (DOS 3.2.1) •
TRS-80 MOD I; 32K with Level II BASIC • TRS-80 MOD III;
32K with Disk BASIC • PET 2000 or 4000 series; 8K (cassette)
or 16K (disk) with 2040 or 4040 drive

Language: BASIC

Source Code: yes

Price: $65.00; $10.00/add'l software copy; $4.00/add'l user
manual

This package introduces students to techniques for modeling
ecological systems and processes on the computer. By controlling certain parameters, such as initial population size, growth
rate, time length of the simulation, and others, students test
hypotheses and predict results about ecosystems. Population
growth is first considered as unlimited growth of a single
species, using an analytical solution for the differential equations; and then is considered using difference equations for in-
crementing growth. Additional factors introduced are environmental carrying capacity, random environmental factors,
and competitive interaction between species. Each of these
concepts builds toward the last program, a simulation of the
growth and interactions of trophic levels within an arctic tundra
ecosystem. Includes three copies of User's Manual (76 pages).

ID: K43

ECOLOGY SIMULATIONS - I

Publisher: Creative Computing

Also available from: Academic Software • K-12 Micromedia •
Opportunities For Learning, Inc. • Queue, Inc.

Format: diskette

Hardware: Apple II; 48K with Applesoft in ROM • Apple II Plus
• PET; 16K • TRS-80; 16K (cassette) or 32K (diskette)

Price: $24.95

This package includes background material, sample exercises, study guides, and specially developed graphic displays.

STERL - STERL allows the student to investigate the effectiveness of two different methods of pest control: the use of
pesticides and the release of sterile males into a screw-worm fly
population. The concept of a more environmentally sound approach versus traditional chemical methods is introduced. In
addition, STERL demonstrates the effectiveness of an integrated
approach over either alternative by itself.

POP - The POP series of models examines three different
methods of population projection, including exponential, S-
shaped or logistical, and logistical with low density effects. At
the same time the programs introduce the concept of successive refinement of a model, since each POP model adds
more details than the previous one.

TAG - TAG simulates the tagging and recovery method that is
used by scientists to estimate animal populations. One attempts to estimate the bass population in a warm-water, bass-
bluegill farm pond. Tagged fish are released in the pond and

samples are recovered at timed intervals. By presenting a
detailed simulation of real sampling by "tagging and
recovery," TAG helps one to understand this process.

BUFFALO - BUFFALO simulates the yearly cycle of buffalo
population growth and decline, and allows one to investigate
the effects of different herd management policies. Simulations
such as BUFFALO allow one to explore "what if" questions
and experiment with approaches that might be disastrous in
real life.

ID: K44

ECOLOGY SIMULATIONS - II

Publisher: Creative Computing

Also available from: Academic Software • K-12 Micromedia •
Opportunities For Learning, Inc. • Queue, Inc.

Format: diskette

Hardware: Apple II Plus • Apple II; 48K with Applesoft in ROM
• PET; 16K • TRS-80; 16K (cassette) or 32K (diskette)

Price: $24.95

This package includes background material, sample exercises, study guide, and specially developed graphic displays.

POLLUTE - POLLUTE focuses on one part of the water pollution problem: the accumulation of certain waste materials in
waterways and their effect on dissolved oxygen levels in the
water. One can use the computer to investigate the effects of
different variables, such as the body of water, temperature, and
the rate of dumping waste material. Various types of primary
and secondary waste treatment, as well as the impact of scientific and economic decisions, can be examined.

RATS - In RATS, the student plays the role of a Health
Department official devising an effective, practical plan to control rats. The plan may combine the use of sanitation and slow
kill and quick kill poisons to eliminate a rat population. It is
also possible to change the initial population size, growth rate,
and whether the simulation will take place in an apartment
building or an entire city.

MALARIA - With MALARIA, the student plays the role of a
health official trying to control a malaria epidemic while taking
into account financial considerations in setting up a program.
The budgeted use of field hospitals, drugs for the ill, three types
of pesticides, and preventative medication must be properly
combined for an effective control program.

DIET - DIET is designed to explore the effect of four basic
substances--protein, lipids, calories and carbohydrates--on diet.
One enters a list of the type and amounts of food eaten in a
typical day, as well as age, weight, sex, health and a physical
activity factor. DIET is particularly valuable in indicating how a
diet can be changed to raise or lower body weights and provide proper nutrition.

ID: K45

EDUTECH SAMPLER

Publisher: EduTech

Format: 1 diskette

Hardware: Apple II Plus; 48K (DOS 3.2 or 3.3) • Apple II; 48K
with Applesoft in ROM

Price: $50.00/package with 4 manuals

Consists of programs and manuals from 4 different EduTech series. The programs are: FOURIER SYNTHESIS (PHYSICS DEMOS); TWO POINT CHARGES (COMPULAB); ARTILLERY COMMANDER (INTERACT); and PLOTTING A LINE (MATH LAB I). SAMPLER is ideal for workshops and teacher groups studying the uses of computer simulation in science education.

ID: K46
ELECTRICITY
Publisher: Micro Learningware

Also available from: Academic Software

Format: diskette

Hardware: Apple II; 48K with Applesoft in ROM (DOS 3.3)

Language: Applesoft BASIC

Source Code: yes

Price: $12.00

Package comprises seven programs applying electrical laws and principles. Documentation booklet included.

GAUSS'S LAW - Program applies Gauss' Law to sphere. Electric field is calculated both inside and outside sphere. All integrals are discussed in detail.

AMPERE'S LAW - Ampere's Law is applied to find magnetic field inside coaxial cable. Cable has uniform current flowing one way in inside core, and opposite current flowing in outer covering.

RESISTOR COMBINATIONS - Applies rules for combining series and parallel resistors.

CAPACITOR COMBINATIONS - Program gives practice in combining series and parallel capacitors and in applying Q = CV.

RESISTOR-CAPACITOR CIRCUITS - Program lets viewer pick R and C, then draws graphs of charge and current from time equals zero to one second. R and C can be changed as often as desired until viewer has acquired feeling for how capacitor will charge up under any combination of parameters.

RESISTOR-CAPACITOR-INDUCTOR RCL CIRCUITS - Program shows how to calculate reactances and total impedance, root-mean-square current, phase angle, and power factor. Secondly, program works on concept of resonant frequency.

LORENTZ FORCE - Program teaches vector nature of Lorentz force law. It draws coordinate system, then puts in charge and electric or magnetic field, then asks for direction of force.

ID: K47
ELECTRICITY
Publisher: RIGHT ON PROGRAMS

Date: Aug. 82

Grade: 3

Format: cassette or diskette

Hardware: Apple II; 48K with Applesoft in ROM (DOS 3.2 or 3.3) • PET; 16K

Language: BASIC

Source Code: yes

Price: $13.00/cassette; $15.00/diskette

Electricity gives light and heat. How that happens is explained along with explanations of electrons, filaments, static and current electricity. Safety rules for electricity are stressed. Game follows.

ID: K48
ELEMENTARY BIOLOGY
Publisher: Minnesota Educational Computing Consortium

Also available from: APX (Atari Program Exchange)

Date: June 82

Grade: 6-8

Format: diskette

Hardware: Atari 400/800; 16K with Atari BASIC in cartridge

Language: BASIC

Source Code: no

Price: $37.80

Module contains three elementary biology simulations. Support booklet included.

CIRCULATION - Program is tutorial-based simulation on blood circulation in animals having two-chambered hearts.

ODELL LAKE, ODELL WOODS - Tutorial-based simulations in which students discover food- chain relationships as they role-play animals in food chain.

ID: K49
ELEMENTS
Publisher: Instant Software[T.M.]

Also available from: Academic Software • Queue, Inc.

Grade: 7-8

Format: cassette

Hardware: TRS-80

Source Code: no

Price: $9.95

This program can be used to introduce students to periodic table of elements, or for review by students or adults who wish to refresh their memories in chemistry. Program includes elements' name, atomic number, weight, and symbol, as well as acid/base and normal physical state. Written documentation is provided.

ID: K50
ENZKIN - ENZYME KINETICS
Publisher: CONDUIT

Also available from: MARCK • Queue, Inc.

Date: 1976

Grade: 9-College

Format: diskette

Hardware: Apple II; 48K with Applesoft in ROM (DOS 3.2.1) • TRS-80 MOD I; 32K with Level II BASIC • TRS-80 MOD III; 32K with Disk BASIC • PET 2000 or 4000 series; 8K (cassette) or 16K (disk) with 2040 or 4040 drive

Language: BASIC

Source Code: yes

Price: $35.00; $10.00/add'l software copy; $1.50/add'l student manual; $1.50/add'l teacher manual

This unit permits students to obtain realistic results using a computer program to simulate enzyme-catalyzed reactions. The introduction to the Students' Notes describes some of the features of enzyme-catalyzed reactions. In later sections, students are asked to plot progress curves and calculate initial velocities of reactions. Six enzymes with different properties are simulated. Includes six copies of Students' Notes (15 pages), and one copy of Teachers' Guide (15 pages).

ID: K51
EVOLUT - EVOLUTION AND NATURAL SELECTION

Publisher: CONDUIT

Also available from: K-12 Micromedia • MARCK • Queue, Inc.

Date: 1975

Grade: 9-College

Format: diskette

Hardware: Apple II; 48K with Applesoft in ROM (DOS 3.2.1) • TRS-80 MOD I; 32K with Level II BASIC • TRS-80 MOD III; 32K with Disk BASIC • PET 2000 or 4000 series; 8K (cassette) or 16K (disk) with 2040 or 4040 drive

Language: BASIC

Source Code: yes

Price: $35.00; $10.00/add'l software copy; $1.50/add'l teacher manual; $1.50/add'l student manual

This introductory unit in evolution and population genetics is intended to teach (1) mechanisms generating variation and the selective process leading to adaptations, (2) adaptation to environmental conditions in relation to survival value, (3) manipulation of models of selection acting on populations, and (4) investigation of the power of selection in producing certain frequencies of alleles in a given environment and relation of adaptation to survival. Students select various parameters, such as zygote type, percent of green alleles, and number of generations, and observe the simulated process of natural selection and evolution. Includes six copies of Students' Notes (19 pages), and one copy of Teachers' Guide (11 pages).

ID: K52
FUNDAMENTAL SKILLS FOR GENERAL CHEMISTRY

Publisher: Programs For Learning, Inc.

Also available from: MARCK • McKilligan Supply Corp. • Queue, Inc.

Format: cassette or diskette

Hardware: PET • Apple • TRS-80 • Wang • Prime • HP-3000 • PDP-11 • PDP-8

Price: $150.00/package (Queue, Inc - $100.00)

Package of twelve programs provides tutorials, and drill and practice exercises. Instructor's guide gives individual descriptions, sample runs, and specific suggestions for classroom implementation.

BALEQ - Drill on balancing equations.

CONVERT - Drill on Metric/English conversion.

DENSITY - Practice with problems concerning density, mass, and volume.

ELEMENT - Drill on symbols, atomic number, electron configuration of first 20 elements.

EXPO - Tutorial exercise explaining exponential notation.

IONS - Drill concerning symbols and charges for common ions.

METRIC - Drill on SI units of mass, length, and volume.

MOLWT - Practice in computing formula weights.

NOMEN

SIGHELP - Drill on significant figures.

SYMBOL - Drill on names and symbols of elements.

TEMP - Practice with temperature conversions.

ID: K53
GAS LAWS

Publisher: Avant-Garde Creations

Also available from: Academic Software • Queue, Inc.

Format: diskette

Hardware: Apple; 48K with Applesoft in ROM

Price: $29.95

Specific gas laws covered in this program are Boyle's Law, Charles' Law, the Ideal Gas Law, and piston experiments.

ID: K54
GAS LAWS AND KINETIC MOLECULAR THEORY

Publisher: Merlan Scientific Ltd.

Grade: High School and up

Format: 7 cassettes or 1 diskette

Hardware: PET; 16K cassette or diskette • Apple II Plus; 48K (DOS 3.3)

Language: BASIC

Source Code: no

Price: $60.00/cassette for GAS LAW SERIES; $20.00/cassette for other programs; $99.00/diskette for all 6 programs in series

Series of programs provides instruction in basic chemistry of gas laws and kinetic molecular theory. Written documentation is provided.

BOYLE'S LAW - Simulated experiment for classroom demonstration or individual student use leads user through experiment in which various numbers of blocks are placed onto a piston. Using high-resolution graphics, piston moves, compressing gas beneath it. User must measure resulting volume and enter its value into computer. After results and conclusions are reached, sample problems are worked out.

CHARLES' LAW - Simulated experiment for classroom demonstration or individual student use uses animated graphics to lead user through experiment in which bead of mercury traps a gas in a capillary tube. Various temperatures are chosen which cause bead to move. Resulting volumes of trapped gas must be measured on screen and entered into computer. Conclusions are drawn from graph displaying results and user is then led through sample programs.

GAS LAW DRILL - Program provides drill in mathematical and non-mathematical gas law problems. Variables include volume, pressure, temperature, density, and mass. Explanations and correct solutions are provided when errors are encountered; calculator mode is included for convenience.

GAS LAW SERIES - Combines above three programs onto single cassette for convenience of user. Not included in series package as whole.

EQUILIBRIUM I - High-resolution bar graphs are used to display relative amounts of nitrogen, hydrogen, and ammonia in Haber process as equilibrium shifts. Objective is to learn how temperature and pressure affect equilibrium in opposite ways, and to try and obtain "ideal" compromise without having display "explode". Along with bar graphs, temperature, pressure, rate, and economical situation are constantly displayed.

KINETIC MOLECULAR THEORY - INTRODUCTION - Program displays molecules in constant motion, illustrating various concepts of kinetic molecular theory. Relationship between temperature and molecular speeds of molecules in a gas is established, and effect of temperature on gas volume is introduced. By viewing and answering questions, student works through pictorial lesson and gains intuitive grasp of what goes on at molecular level.

KINETIC MOLECULAR THEORY - CHANGES OF STATE - Student follows molecules in crystal of ice as melting occurs, evaporation occurs, and finally as water boils. Equilibrium situations at melting and boiling points are displayed.

ID: K55
GEIGER COUNTER
Publisher: Comaldor

Format: cassette or diskette

Hardware: PET

Price: $20.00

This program constitutes a safe method of conducting experiments with radioactive materials. Students select the type of material, lead shield, vacuum, and distance. All are represented graphically as the animated experiment accompanied by sound is completed. Questions are presented for the student to answer as a result of the exercise.

ID: K56
GENETICS
Publisher: TIES, Minnesota School Districts Data Processing Joint Board

Date: Sept. 81

Grade: 6-9

Format: 2 programs on diskette with backup

Hardware: Apple II; 32K with Applesoft in ROM (DOS 3.3) • Apple II Plus

Price: $49.95; $10.50/documentation

These two programs are designed to teach the student to identify and correctly use the rules for determining parental gene traits that will be transmitted to offspring and to correctly determine the blood type of an offspring using the rules for identifying blood types, blood typing test results and the parents genotypes. The accompanying comprehensive manual includes background information, instructions on how to use the programs, a sample run of the programs and directions on how to retrieve student files. Special activity sheets are included.

CHROMY BUG - Chromy Bugs are little insects with 15 gene traits on their chromosomes. The students first determine the 15 gene traits for the parent Chromy Bugs by choosing the (D) dominant, (S) semi-dominant, or (R) recessive traits. Each time the students select a gene trait, the body part will be drawn. After the parent bugs have been drawn, the students use the rules of dominance to decide which of the parents' gene traits will be dominant and will be transmitted to the offspring. After the students have determined the traits of the offspring, they have the option of changing the gene traits of the parent bugs and determining how the changes affect the offspring. At the end of the program, students name their bugs. Students' bugs and summary scores are saved in a file for teacher access and evaluation.

BLOOD TYPING - BLOOD TYPING is a program designed to have students identify blood types in a simulated hospital laboratory. Students are given the rules for inheriting blood types and simulated procedures for typing bood with Anti-A and Anti-B serums. This information is used as the basis for identifying the blood type of a baby Chromy Bug. Students assume the role of the doctor in charge of A-B-O Lab. They are given the blood type genes of the mother and father Chromy Bugs. In order to identify the blood type of the baby Chromy Bug, the students must first determine the possible gene combination(s) for the baby. Then, they identify the blood type for each of the possible gene combination(s). Finally, the students *see* the baby's blood test. They use the test results and the list of possible blood types to determine the baby's blood type.

ID: K57
GENETICS
Publisher: Microcomputer Workshops

Also available from: Academic Software • EISI (Educational Instructional Systems, Inc.) • Micro-Ed, Inc.

Grade: High School

Format: cassette

Hardware: PET; optional sound

Language: BASIC

Source Code: no

Price: $20.00

This program is a classroom tool for health, biology, and advanced placement biology classes. It is designed for use with either a full class or by individual students. Once a student is taught the basic laws of inheritance, he/she can run GENETICS to test his/her knowledge. The program will draw a family tree on the screen (up to three generations). Persons on the screen with a specific genetic trait are marked. The learner is then asked whether the trait is caused by a dominant, recessive, or sex-linked gene. If an incorrect answer is entered, the learner has the option of getting an explanation supplied by the computer. Detailed documentation is supplied with each program.

ID: K58
GEOLOGY PACKAGE I
Publisher: Micro Learningware

Also available from: Academic Software • MARCK • Opportunities For Learning, Inc.

Format: cassette or diskette

Hardware: TRS-80 MOD I or III; 16K cassette or 32K diskette

Language: BASIC

Source Code: yes

Price: $24.95

Package of four programs pertaining to geological questions. Written instructions provided

TIME DURATION OF EPOCHS & PERIODS - Question is asked and four possible answers are presented. Correct response yields congratulations, whereas incorrect response causes computer to present reason(s) why response is incorrect. Same question is presented until correct answer is given.

TYPES OF ANIMAL LIFE PRESENT - Similar to the first program except that the questions pertain to animal life present within the geologic timetable.

TYPES OF PLANT LIFE PRESENT - Questions pertain to plant life present within the geologic timetable.

GEOLOGICAL CONDITIONS PRESENT - This program contains questions that pertain to geological conditions.

ID: K59

GROUP VELOCITY

Publisher: CONDUIT

Also available from: MARCK • Queue, Inc.

Date: 1980

Grade: 9-College

Format: diskette

Hardware: Apple II; 48K with Applesoft in ROM (DOS 3.2.1); game paddles

Language: BASIC

Source Code: yes

Price: $45.00; $10.00/add'l software copy; $2.50/add'l student manual

In this program students use game paddles to control wave velocity and wave length to demonstrate a traveling sine wave and two types of wave groups by controlling wave velocity and group velocity. Students select values for frequency, time and wave number to display velocity, oscillation, cosine waves, moving waves, and group waves. Includes Student Guide (19 pages).

ID: K60

HABER - AMMONIA SYNTHESIS

Publisher: CONDUIT

Also available from: MARCK • Queue, Inc.

Date: 1978

Grade: 9-College

Format: diskette

Hardware: Apple II; 48K with Applesoft in ROM (DOS 3.2.1) • TRS-80 MOD I; 32K with Level II BASIC • TRS-80 MOD III; 32K with Disk BASIC • PET 2000 or 4000 series; 8K (cassette) or 16K (disk) with 2040 or 4040 drive

Language: BASIC

Source Code: yes

Price: $35.00; $10.00/add'l software copy; $1.50/add'l student manual; $1.50/add'l teacher manual

This simulation allows students to study the Haber process and how the various conditions (temperature, pressure, catalyst and reactant concentration ratios) influence the course of the reaction (the time required to reach equilibrium and the equilibrium yield of ammonia). Includes six copies of Students' Notes (11 pages), and one copy of Teachers' Guide (15 pages).

ID: K61

HEART

Publisher: Avant-Garde Creations

Also available from: Academic Software • Opportunities For Learning, Inc. • Queue, Inc.

Grade: 11-12

Format: diskette

Hardware: Apple; 48K with Applesoft in ROM

Price: $29.95

This program covers the anatomy of the heart; specific topics include blood flow structure, circulation, identification of heart chambers, and causes of heart attack.

ID: K62

HEART LAB - SIMULATION MODEL OF A FUNCTIONING HUMAN HEART

Publisher: Educational Activities, Inc.

Also available from: Academic Software • Opportunities For Learning, Inc. • Queue, Inc.

Grade: Secondary

Format: cassette or diskette

Hardware: Apple II Plus; (DOS 3.2.1 or 3.3) • TRS-80 MOD I or III; with Level II BASIC • PET • Commodore 2001 • Commodore 4000; 40 or 80 column • Commodore 8000; 80 column

Source Code: no

Price: $24.95/cassette; $29.95/diskette

This innovative program uses animated graphics to produce a simulation model of a functioning human heart. It provides the student with an opportunity to observe, through simulation, the heart in action. The program illustrates the various parts and functions of the heart by showing the pumping action and tracing the blood flow through the arteries, veins, and chambers. The program is divided into three sections: 1) TUTORIAL - Reviews the various vessels and chambers of the heart while identifying their locations on a graphic model; 2) DRILL - The computer indicates specific parts of the heart on the graphic model, and the student must type in the correct name of the vessel or chamber; 3) PULSE SIMULATION EXERCISE - Demonstrates how the heart responds to work. The students enter their own pulse rates, before and after exercising, into the computer. The animated, graphic heart demonstrates how their hearts would function using a visual simulation.

ID: K63

HEAT SOLVER

Publisher: Comaldor

Format: cassette or diskette

Hardware: PET

Price: $20.00

This program is for the physics class. In graph form, the program handles MASS, TEMPERATURE, and SPECIFIC HEAT of 5 items and FINAL TEMPERATURE. Using cursor movement, students fill in all known data with an ''X'' in one box. The program then calculates the missing information.

ID: K64

HUMAN BODY: AN OVERVIEW

Publisher: BrainBank, Inc.

Also available from: Academic Software • K-12 Micromedia • Queue, Inc.

Grade: 6 and up

Format: 8 programs on cassette or diskette

Hardware: Apple; 16K • PET; 16K • TRS-80; 16K

Price: $80.00

This package consists of 8 programs - an introduction, units on the muscular, digestive, respiratory, skeletal, circulatory and nervous systems, and a 67 question review test. Each lesson takes about 10 - 20 minutes to run. At intervals, multiple-choise, true-false, and short-answer questions must be answered correctly before the student can proceed. Graphics help to explain concepts that might otherwise be difficult to understand. The accompanying Courseware Kit includes a teacher's manual.

ID: K65

INTERP - WAVE SUPERPOSITION

Publisher: CONDUIT

Also available from: MARCK • Queue, Inc.

Date: 1976

Grade: 9-College

Format: diskette

Hardware: Apple II; 48K with Applesoft in ROM (DOS 3.2.1) • TRS-80 MOD I; 32K with Level II BASIC • TRS-80 MOD III; 32K with Disk BASIC • PET 2000 or 4000 series; 8K (cassette) or 16K (disk) with 2040 or 4040 drive

Language: BASIC

Source Code: yes

Price: $35.00; $10.00/add'l software copy; $1.50/add'l teacher manual; $1.50/add'l student manual

This unit on wave superposition is designed to improve students' understanding of the use of models in physics using the wave theory of light. The Students' Notes provide information to guide students through three investigations of interference and diffraction phenomena, using the program. The simple model of the program calculates the intensity due to the superposition of radiation from two sources, or two slits, each having two secondary sources. The complex model allows students to investigate the effects of the number of secondary sources in each slit. Includes six copies of Students' Notes (11 pages), and one copy of Teachers' Guide (15 pages).

ID: K66

INTRODUCTION TO ORGANIC CHEMISTRY

Publisher: COMPress

Also available from: Academic Software

Grade: High School-College

Format: 7 diskettes

Hardware: Apple II Plus; 48K with Applesoft in ROM (DOS 3.2, 3.2.1 or 3.3) • Bell & Howell; 48K

Language: BASIC

Source Code: no

Price: $350.00; $60.00/diskette

These programs are designed as a supplement to a first course in organic chemistry. They provide an introduction, with practice on nomenclature and simple reactions of alkenes, alkyl halides, alcohols, aldehydes and ketones, carboxylic acids and arenes. In addition, the programs allow students to practice single functional group multistep aliphatic synthesis and the preparation of arenes with one or two substituents. Infrared and proton nuclear magnetic resonance spectroscopy is introduced and practice provided in the identification of simple unknowns from their IR and NMR spectra. Spectroscopy is used throughout the programs in the development of functional group chemistry. The relative reactivity of alkyl halides and the stereochemistry of bimolecular displacement reactions is demonstrated through simulated experiments and animations. Other simulated experiments include the determination of the mechanism of aromatic nitration, lithium aluminum hydride reductions, aldol condensations, the relative acidity of carboxylic acids, the hydrolysis of esters, and the product of the oxidation of a primary alcohol.

ALKANES AND ALKENES - This diskette includes nomenclature rules and practice, formula drawing, reactions, and problems.

SUBSTITUTION REACTIONS - Covers bimolecular reactions, reactivity of alkyl halides, a racemization and exchange experiment, and the stereochemistry of substitution.

IR AND NMR SPECTROSCOPY - Includes infrared problems, nuclear magnetic resonance, NMR spin-spin splitting, and problems.

ARENES - Covers aromatic compounds, nomenclature, reactions, a nitration experiment, and multistep aromatic synthesis.

ALCOHOLS - Topics covered are nomenclature, reactions and oxidation of alcohols, Grignard reagents and problems, and multistep aliphatic synthesis.

ALDEHYDES AND KETONES - Includes introduction, nomenclature, acetals and ketals, mechanism of oxime formations, reduction of carbonyl groups, hydrogen-deuterium exchange, aldol condensations, and carbonyl chemistry problems.

CARBOXYLIC ACIDS - Topics include nomenclature, acidity and reactions of carboxylic acids, esterification experiment, ester hydrolysis, and RCOOH chemistry problems.

ID: K67

INTRODUCTION TO WEATHER CHARTS

Publisher: Avant-Garde Creations

Also available from: Academic Software • Opportunities For Learning, Inc. • Queue, Inc.

Grade: Up to 10

Format: diskette

Hardware: Apple; 48K with Applesoft in ROM

Price: $29.95

Topics covered on this program include air masses, pressure zones, synoptic charts and detailed graphics.

ID: K68

INTRODUCTORY MECHANICS DRILL PACKAGE

Publisher: Merlan Scientific Ltd.

Grade: High School and up

Format: cassette or diskette

Hardware: PET; 8K

Language: BASIC

Source Code: no

Price: $20.00/cassette; $110.00/diskette for this and six other programs on MERLAN PHYSICS I package

Series of four programs is presented on one tape. Each program is designed to drill student on use of one specific formula or concept. Drill is presented in game-like atmosphere in which student is challenged to work quickly. Student receives feedback on accuracy and time taken.

ID: K69

INTRODUCTORY MECHANICS FOR THE APPLE II

Publisher: CONDUIT

Also available from: MARCK

Date: 1981

Grade: 9-College

Format: diskette

Hardware: Apple II; 48K with Applesoft in ROM (DOS 3.2.1)

Language: BASIC

Source Code: yes

Price: $45.00; $10.00/add'l software copy; $3.00/add'l instructor manual; $8.00/add'l student manual

This package epitomizes the simplicity and power of applying the computer to solving problems in physics. The materials focus on the application of Newton's Second Law to the simple harmonic oscillator and to the motion of particles in two dimensions, under the influence of uniform fields or one or more force centers. The materials emphasize problem solving: students start with some example programs and make modifications to meet their specific needs. The exercises and examples use graphics throughout. Includes Student Guide (30 pages) and Instructor Guide (35 pages).

ID: K70

LABORATORY SIMULATIONS SERIES

Publisher: Merlan Scientific Ltd.

Grade: High School and up

Format: 6 cassettes or 1 diskette

Hardware: PET; 8K (except where noted)

Language: BASIC

Source Code: no

Price: $99.00/diskette; cassettes of individual programs - $20.00/ ACCELERATION DUE TO..., MILLIKAN'S EX. (Version 1), and RADIOACTIVITY-HALFLIFE; $22.00/GRAVITATIONAL...; $24.00/ LINEAR AIR TRACK; $26.00/MILLIKAN'S EX. (Version 2).

Series provides animated simulations of laboratory experiments in which students make measurements and prepare laboratory reports. Each exercise is organized under following headings--purpose, apparatus, method, observations, and conclusions. Students are guided to end of observation stage, then left with series of questions upon which to base conclusions. Written documentation provided.

ACCELERATION DUE TO GRAVITY - Program shows animated real-time simulation of dense object falling from rest. By showing fall one frame at a time, student may make measurements of displacement-time data from which to show that g is constant and to calculate its value. Computer checks accuracy of student's measurements and requires student to redo poor ones.

GRAVITATIONAL POTENTIAL ENERGY - Real-time simulation of projectile moving in two-dimensional path is used to guide student through series of measurements from which to calculate kinetic energy of projectile as function of its height above ground. Student is led to draw conclusions about nature of energy stored as height of projectile increases and to deduce equation delta Ep = mg delta h.

MILLIKAN'S EXPERIMENT (VERSION 1) - Core of program is animated simulation of latex sphere falling between pair of charged plates. Fall rate of sphere depends upon charge on sphere. Program randomly generates series of fall rates corresponding to various possible charges on sphere. By using stopwatch to measure fall rates, student may draw conclusions about quantum nature of electric charge.

MILLIKAN'S EXPERIMENT (VERSION 2) - Program simulates original oil drop experiment. Particle is injected into chamber and then ionized. By increasing or decreasing voltage on plates, particle is brought to equilibrium and voltage is recorded. After five successful attempts, the computer assists student in analyzing experiment data to determine charge on particle. 16K minimum required.

RADIOACTIVITY - HALF LIFE - Program simulates radioactive decay of short-lived radioisotope. Data is collected for seven-minute period, then student is guided through analysis to determine half life of isotope. Program includes sound to enhance presentation.

LINEAR AIR TRACK - MOMENTUM IN ELASTIC COLLISIONS - Program displays real-time simulation of motion of objects of different mass along frictionless air track. Objects collide elastically, allowing student to make measurements and do calculations leading to confirmation of law of conservation of momentum.

ID: K71

LATENT HEAT

Publisher: Comaldor

Format: cassette or diskette

Hardware: PET

Price: $20.00

This program for the physics class covers latent heat of steam and ice in graph form. Using cursor movement, students fill in all known data with an "X" in one box. The program then calculates the missing information.

ID: K72

LESSON-TUTORGRAPHS

Publisher: TYC Software (Teach Yourself by Computer)

Also available from: K-12 Micromedia • MARCK • Queue, Inc.

Grade: 9-College

Format: 2 diskettes

Hardware: Apple II Plus • Apple II; 48K with Applesoft in ROM or language card (DOS 3.3)

Language: Applesoft BASIC

Price: $24.95/diskette

Series consists of single-topic tutorials offering programmed presentation of lesson material, with branching and review based on student response to questions. Student or teacher can also access any page of text or illustration for further review independently of standard presentation. Animation and full-color high-resolution illustrations complement each lesson presentation. Computer-graded testing feature is included. Multipurpose manual includes lesson objectives, program operations, answer key, and suggestions for classroom use.

WEATHER FRONTS - Program provides introduction to concepts of weather fronts, their structure and nature. Concepts presented include front characteristics, frontal movement, and weather associated with different kinds of fronts. Color cross-sectional diagrams illustrate cold, warm, and occluded frontal structures.

SHORE FEATURES - Acquaints student with geographic features of shore/beach area of coast, enabling student to identify and define following features: beach/shore, berm, dunes, backshore, foreshore, low/high tide marks, low tide terrace, offshore area, trough, and bar. Illustrations highlight location of each type of feature. Excellent for classes in geography, geology, or oceanography.

ID: K73
LIFE

Publisher: Instant Software[T.M.]

Also available from: Academic Software

Format: cassette

Hardware: TRS-80

Source Code: no

Price: $9.95

This program presents computerized simulation of life cycle of a colony of bacteria. Although based on only a few simple concepts, program provides captivating and enlightening introduction to world of biology and genetics through use of animated graphics. Written documentation is provided.

ID: K74
LIFE IN THE OCEANS

Publisher: RIGHT ON PROGRAMS

Date: Aug. 82

Grade: 3

Format: cassette or diskette

Hardware: Apple II; 48K with Applesoft in ROM (DOS 3.2 or 3.3) • PET; 16K

Language: BASIC

Source Code: yes

Price: $13.00/cassette; $15.00/diskette

Program explains why oceans and life in oceans are so important to human survival. Animals, fish, birds, mammals, and weather are discussed. Dependence on the ocean is stressed. Game follows in which right answers are rewarded and incorrect answers are corrected with no penalties.

ID: K75
LINKOVER - GENETIC MAPPING

Publisher: CONDUIT

Also available from: MARCK • Queue, Inc.

Date: 1975

Grade: 9-College

Format: diskette

Hardware: Apple II; 48K with Applesoft in ROM (DOS 3.2.1) • TRS-80 MOD I; 32K with Level II BASIC • TRS-80 MOD III; 32K with Disk BASIC • PET 2000 or 4000 series; 8K (cassette) or 16K (disk) with 2040 or 4040 drive

Language: BASIC

Source Code: yes

Price: $35.00; $10.00/add'l software copy; $1.50/add'l teacher manual; $1.50/add'l student manual

Students plan and execute genetic mapping experiments to reinforce the concepts of linkage and crossing-over. Students specify a series of genetic crosses and, from the resulting data, build a linkage map for 10 genes of a hypothetical diploid species using the three-point testcross technique. Includes six copies of Students' Notes (11 pages), and one copy of Teachers' Guide (15 pages).

ID: K76
LIVING THINGS

Publisher: RIGHT ON PROGRAMS

Also available from: Academic Software • K-12 Micromedia • Queue, Inc.

Grade: 2

Format: cassette or diskette

Hardware: Apple II; 48K with Applesoft in ROM (DOS 3.2 or 3.3) • PET; 16K

Language: BASIC

Source Code: yes

Price: $13.00/cassette; $15.00/diskette

This program takes a brief look at the living things that exist here on earth -- plants, people, animals -- and how they live together, helping each other. Simple questions and a matching game complete this program.

ID: K77
MAMMALS

Publisher: RIGHT ON PROGRAMS

Date: Aug. 82

Grade: 4

Format: cassette or diskette

Hardware: Apple II; 48K with Applesoft in ROM (DOS 3.2 or 3.3) • PET; 16K

Language: BASIC

Source Code: yes

Price: $13.00/cassette; $15.00/diskette

This program discusses animals in general, and then, more specifically, mammals. It gives four things that make a mammal a mammal, and discusses and gives examples of each. A game follows which tests student's retention of material. Correct answers are rewarded and incorrect answers are corrected with no penalty.

ID: K78
MAPS AND GLOBES
Publisher: Micro-Ed, Inc.

Grade: Elementary and up

Format: 19 programs on cassette or diskette

Hardware: Commodore 64 • PET • Apple II Plus; 48K (DOS 3.3) • TRS-80 Color Computer; 32K • TI 99/4; extended BASIC module • VIC

Language: BASIC

Source Code: no

Price: $136.00; $2.95/additional student booklets

This maps and globes series is designed to be used directly with the booklet, *Skills for Understanding Maps and Globes*, by Kenneth Job and Lois Wolf (Follett Publishing Company). Each program in this series works as follows: The student brings the student booklet to the computer, loads the program, and begins the lesson. The computer now poses questions to the student concerning the subject matter in the booklet. The student is free to use the booklet in order to respond to questions from the computer. For example, the computer may refer the learner to a map on a particular page, and ask questions about the specific symbols being used. The computer thus becomes a sophisticated response device, providing immediate feedback to the student, keeping track of student progress, and so on. Each program covers one chapter in the booklet.

- MAP IS MADE
- FINDING OUR WAY
- FINDING OTHER DIRECTIONS
- METRIC SYSTEM
- HOW FAR IS IT?
- FINDING CITIES AND COUNTRIES
- WATER, WATER, EVERYWHERE
- EARTH'S LAND MASSES
- NEW WORLD
- OLD WORLD
- GUIDELINES ON THE EARTH
- USING THE EARTH'S GUIDELINES
- FLAT MAPS OF A ROUND EARTH
- HIGH LANDS AND LOW
- WHAT'S THE WEATHER?
- WORLD'S CLIMATES
- WHAT GROWS ON THE LAND
- PEOPLE AND PRODUCTS
- TRADE AND TRAVEL

ID: K79
MATHEMATICS FOR SCIENCE, SERIES 1: MEASURE-MENT
Publisher: Merlan Scientific Ltd.

Grade: High School and up

Format: 3 cassettes or 1 diskette

Hardware: PET; 16K; cassette or diskette • Apple II Plus; 48K (DOS 3.3)

Language: BASIC

Source Code: no

Price: $20.00/cassette; $54.00/diskette; $180.00/4 diskettes in series

Series of three programs on measurement techniques is part of larger series designed primarily for science students who need specific mathematics skills. Series features alternating lesson exercises and drills in each subject area. Many parts of lessons and all drill questions are randomly generated so that student repeating exercise will be presented with different questions each time through. Written documentation is provided.

SCALE READING - Program teaches student how to read linear scale, emphasizing need to show correct number of digits in measurements and how to estimate between scale divisions.

LINEAR SCALES - Program is extension of SCALE READING. It teaches student how to read variety of scales in which markings increase incrementally (i.e. go up by 1's, 2's, 10's, 50's, etc.), with different numbers of markings between gradations.

VERNIER SCALES - Program teaches student how to interpret readings on vernier scale. Scale shown on screen is straight, although concepts learned can easily be adapted to curved scales found on some laboratory equipment.

ID: K80
MATTER AND ENERGY
Publisher: RIGHT ON PROGRAMS

Date: July 82

Grade: 1

Format: cassette or diskette

Hardware: Apple II; 48K with Applesoft in ROM (DOS 3.2 or 3.3) • PET; 16K

Language: BASIC

Source Code: yes

Price: $13.00/cassette; $15.00/diskette

Beginning look at concepts of matter and energy. For curious, intellectually advanced first-grader, this is stimulating, thought-provoking program. Game follows.

ID: K81
MECHANICS AND MOTION
Publisher: Avant-Garde Creations

Also available from: Academic Software • Queue, Inc.

Grade: 11-12

Format: diskette

Hardware: Apple; 48K with Applesoft in ROM

Price: $29.95

This program covers vectors, distance/time graphs, acceleration units, and ticker tape experiments. Revision questions reinforce principles.

ID: K82
MOTION

Publisher: Micro Learningware

Also available from: Academic Software

Format: diskette

Hardware: Apple II; 48K with Applesoft in ROM

Language: Applesoft BASIC

Source Code: yes

Price: $12.00

Package consists of eight programs illustrating problems and solutions relating to physics of motion. Documentation booklet included.

GRAPHING MOTION PART 1 - Program demonstrates that velocity versus time graph is slope of position graph, and acceleration graph is slope of velocity graph.

GRAPHING MOTION PARTS 2 AND 3 - Programs are opposite of PART 1. They start with graph of acceleration vs. time and take its integral to obtain graphs of velocity and position. These concepts are applied to additional graphs. Viewer is asked questions in the process.

ONE DIMENSIONAL KINEMATICS - Long program gives practice in using equations of motion. Provides examples of accelerated motion with graphics. Numerous problems are solved in detail.

GRAVITY PROBLEMS (KINEMATICS AND GRAVITATIONAL ACCELERATION) - Program gives practice in applying equations of motion to problems of free-fall.

PROJECTILE - Program shows motion with moving picture, then repeats it with markers and slow motion. Next it solves some typical problems.

DYNAMICS - GENERAL METHOD - Program applies step-by-step process (graphically illustrated) of coming up with equations.

ROTATIONAL ACCELERATION - Computer sets up equations of motion for three free-body diagrams. It then substitutes given data and solves equations to arrive at correct acceleration.

MOTION ON AN INCLINED PLANE - Picture and free-body diagrams are shown. Program leads student through all details of driving equations and solving them.

ID: K83
NEWTON - SATELLITE ORBITS

Publisher: CONDUIT

Also available from: MARCK • Opportunities For Learning, Inc. • Queue, Inc.

Date: 1975

Grade: 9-College

Format: diskette

Hardware: Apple II; 48K with Applesoft in ROM (DOS 3.2.1) • TRS-80 MOD I; 32K with Level II BASIC • TRS-80 MOD III; 32K with Disk BASIC • PET 2000 or 4000 series; 8K (cassette) or 16K (disk) with 2040 or 4040 drive

Language: BASIC

Source Code: yes

Price: $35.00; $10.00/add'l software copy; $1.50/add'l teacher manual; $1.50/add'l student manual

This unit is designed to help students achieve an appreciation of how the application of Newton's Second Law and Law of Gravitation lead to the prediction of satellite orbits. The computer program on which the unit is based uses an iterative method to calculate the path of a projectile launched horizontally. The student is instructed to find the initial velocity needed for the minimum (circular) orbit. Includes six copies of Students' Notes (10 pages), and one copy of Teachers' Guide (11 pages).

ID: K84
OPTICS

Publisher: Micro Learningware

Also available from: Academic Software

Format: diskette

Hardware: Apple II; 48K with Applesoft in ROM

Language: Applesoft BASIC

Source Code: yes

Price: $30.00

Package consists of six programs illustrating principles of optics. Includes documentation booklet.

MIRROR RAY DIAGRAMS - Program discusses three types of rays reflecting from concave and convex mirrors. Program draws all three rays from a concave mirror.

LENS RAY DIAGRAMS - Program builds on previous one. Illustrates converging (convex) lens, convex lens with object arrow between lens and left focal point, and diverging lens illustrated with three types of rays.

TYPES OF IMAGES - Experiment which helps student discover kinds of images that occur when objects are placed at different positions in front of lenses and mirrors. Illustrates (1) convex lens, (2) concave lens, (3) convex mirror, and (4) concave mirror.

HELIUM-NEON LASER - Program discusses phenomenon of "light amplification by stimulated emission of radiation". Student learning options include: (1) Stimulated Emissions (discussing difference between spontaneous and stimulated emission); (2) Helium and Neon Energy Levels; (3) Laser Construction; (4) Watch It Operate (pulse of light bounces back and forth inside gas discharge tube containing red, helium, and neon gas).

WAVES - Program was written by optics teacher to show fundamental wave phenomena needed to study physical optics, including: (1) Explanation of simple waves; (2) Definitions; (3) Superposition of waves; (4) Standing waves; and (5) Complex waves.

INTERFERENCES AND DIFFRACTION - Program covers two-slit interference; multiple-slit interference (phasor review, two slits, three slits, four slits, five slits, and many slits); single-slit diffractions; putting it together; and phasor calculator.

ID: K85
ORGANIC NOMENCLATURE

Publisher: Programs For Learning, Inc.

Also available from: MARCK • McKilligan Supply Corp. • Queue, Inc.

Format: cassette or diskette

Hardware: PET • Apple • TRS-80 • Wang • HP-3000 • Prime • PDP-11 • PDP-8

Price: $100.00/package

Package of five programs offers drill and practice exercises in organic chemistry nomenclature. Instructor's guide gives individual descriptions, sample runs, and specific suggestions for classroom implementation.

ALKANE - Drill and practice with IUPAC nomenclature for alkanes. Structures are derived by random substitutions of hydrogen by methyl, ethyl or propyl groups on butane. An incorrect response results in redrawing the structure with the longest chain straightened and numbered.

ALKYL - Drill and practice classifying and naming alkyl derivatives selected at random from among twelve different types of compounds, ranging from alcohols to thiols.

AMINO - Drill and practice with names and properties of twenty amino acids.

AROMATIC - Drill and practice with IUPAC nomenclature for arenes. Compounds involve the substitution of one or more randomly selected substituents such as halides, nitro, methyl, etc.

OPTISO - Drill and practice with stereoisomerism.

ID: K86

PARTS OF THE MICROSCOPE

Publisher: Educational Activities, Inc.

Also available from: Academic Software

Grade: Intermediate-Junior High

Format: cassette or diskette

Hardware: Apple II Plus; (DOS 3.2.1 or 3.3) • TRS-80 MOD I or III; with Level II BASIC • PET • Commodore 2001 • Commodore 4000; 40 or 80 column • Commodore 8000; 80 column

Source Code: no

Price: $14.95/cassette; $19.95/diskette

Using an excellent graphic representation of a microscope, this program teaches the student to identify the various parts by location and function. The lesson begins with each part of the microscope being highlighted as its purpose is explained. This is followed by a drill section where the student must recall each part and its function. If the student answers incorrectly, the program branches to an explanation which encourages learning. Animated graphic rewards are used to reinforce correct responses. Graphics, personal responses, branching, and animated rewards are all ingredients that make this lesson one that will generate enthusiasm and interest in the subject in the classroom.

ID: K87

PH METER

Publisher: Programs For Learning, Inc.

Also available from: McKilligan Supply Corp. • Queue, Inc.

Format: cassette or diskette

Hardware: Apple II Plus; 48K (DOS 3.2 or 3.3); game paddle

Price: $30.00

Simulation is designed to introduce measurement techniques. Because there is a prescribed sequence of steps which must must be followed carefully, the program focuses on executing the steps properly. Game control knobs and paddles are used to turn switches on and off, and to adjust settings, enabling the student to acquire a "feel" for each instrument. Program is therefore particularly useful for pre-lab orientation, as well as class demonstrations.

ID: K88

PHYSICS - FREE FALL

Publisher: Educational Courseware

Also available from: Academic Software • MARCK

Format: diskette

Hardware: Apple II; 48K (DOS 3.3 or 3.2)

Price: $32.00

This disk introduces concepts associated with free-fall and provides simulation studies for various physical situations in graphics. Examples include: dropping water bombs on a forest fire; trajectories of falls on other planets; shooting arrows at a target; restitution of a bouncing ball; and vertical flight path near the earth. A real-time stopwatch is also included for laboratory work. This can be used to time events and can be calibrated. A program that turns the Apple into a powerful calculator is also provided. Students can learn how gravity affects the fall of objects near the earth.

ID: K89

PHYSICS - LAB PLOTS

Publisher: Educational Courseware

Also available from: Academic Software

Format: diskette

Hardware: Apple; 48K (DOS 3.3 or 3.2)

Price: $32.00

This disk is designed to teach students how to analyze experimental data with graphs. A method of graphic analysis is presented as a tutorial study, and then students can use the computer to help in their analysis of any experimental data gathered in the class or laboratory. Covers empirical method for power laws, tutorial for this method of analysis, text-in-graphics plots, and real-world experimental data. Some sets of experimental data are also included so that students can discover some "laws of nature". Real-world data for their analysis are: storm duration vs. storm size; antenna height vs. range of transmission; star illumination vs. distance; violin string length vs. the pitch of the note played; radius of a planet's orbit vs. the period of its solar orbit; molecular speeds vs. gas temperature; period of a pendulum vs. cord length; relativistic mass vs. speed; and rocket fuel left vs. rocket speed.

ID: K90

PHYSICS - LINEAR MOMENTUM

Publisher: Educational Courseware

Format: diskette

Hardware: Apple; 48K (DOS 3.3 or 3.2)

Price: $32.00

This series of programs is designed to illustrate the collision of hard spheres in graphics. These simulations provide students with a wide variety of two-dimensional collisions for study. Elastic and inelastic collisions are used to illustrate the conservation of linear momentum and the special cases of kinetic energy conservation. The coefficient of restitution is also included as a special case. Allows for student interaction with the computer. Superior graphics are used in this wide range of two-body interactions.

ID: K91

PHYSICS - WAVE AND OPTICS

Publisher: Educational Courseware

Also available from: Academic Software

Format: diskette

Hardware: Apple; 48K (DOS 3.3 or 3.2)

Price: $32.00

This disk contains simulation programs in graphics that are used by students during their study of the introduction to optic and wave properties. Topics covered are: light beam reflections off mirrors; refraction of light in water; properties of waves; superposition of waves; radar and sonar beams; and the electromagnetic spectrum. These programs will teach students about the relationships between waves and light.

ID: K92

PHYSICS COMPULAB PACKAGE

Publisher: EduTech

Also available from: Academic Software • Queue, Inc.

Grade: High School-College

Format: 6 programs on 6 diskettes

Hardware: Apple II Plus; 48K (DOS 3.2 or 3.3) • Apple II; 48K with Applesoft in ROM (DOS 3.2 or 3.3) • Some programs require use of game paddles

Source Code: yes

Price: $495.00/package with 6 student manuals and 1 guide; $95.00/ program with manual; $5.50/manual; $10.00/ Instructor's Guide

This provides students an opportunity to experimentally investigate concepts and phenomena that are difficult or impossible to investigate in a conventional lab. Students make measurements of simulated events in the same way they would measure real events. Consequently, COMPULAB experiments can be used in conjunction with conventional experiments to enhance the students' overall laboratory experience.

STATISTICS - The computer augments the student's own data with sufficient simulated data to permit the student to make a 100-trial histogram. The computer plots the same histogram for comparison, and then adds 500 more trials. The student measures the average and standard deviation of the 600-trial histogram. Full explanation of the necessary concepts is included in the laboratory manual.

PARABOLIC MOTION - Game control paddles are used to vary the initial speed and initial height (or angle) of a projectile. Students calculate the acceleration of gravity from time and distance measurements. This experiment also includes a simulation of the hunter-monkey demonstration, which illustrates that the acceleration of a projectile is independent of the projectile's velocity.

NONCONSTANT ACCELERATION - Laboratory manual explains how to write simple programs in BASIC to solve for the motion of a mass moving with arbitrary acceleration. Iterating the equations for constant acceleration, the student first solves the problem of a falling body subjected to air resistance. The results of this calculation are compared to measurements made of simulated motion. The student then solves problems of harmonic and anharmonic motion, and compares these results to the measurements of simulated motion of the same kind. For the oscillatory motions, students use a simple variation of the Euler approximation. This experiment includes enough work for several laboratory sessions. Knowledge of calculus is not required.

PLANETARY MOTION - Measurements are made of the orbits and periods of different planets orbiting the same star. Tests are made of Kepler's second and third laws. (A simple discussion of Kepler's laws is provided in the laboratory manual.) The stable and unstable orbits of a planet orbiting two stars are also studied.

WAVE MOTION - Students measure the speed, wavelength, and frequency of various traveling sine waves. A study is then made of the superposition of several waves, with emphasis on superpositions that produce beats, standing waves, and the first few terms of a Fourier series. Standing waves are studied further by observing the superposition of two sine waves traveling in opposite directions.

ELECTRIC FIELD - Using the game controls, students can move a dot anywhere on the screen. By pressing a button, a short line segment is drawn in the direction of the electric field (or equipotential) at the position of the dot. In this way, students can map the lines of force and equipotentials for several distributions of point charges. As a final exercise the point charges are not displayed. The student is asked to determine their position, magnitudes, and signs by plotting the lines of force they produce.

ID: K93

PHYSICS DEMOS PACKAGE

Publisher: EduTech

Also available from: Academic Software

Grade: High School-College

Format: 4 programs on 4 diskettes

Hardware: Apple II Plus; 48K (DOS 3.2 or 3.3) • Apple II; 48K with Applesoft in ROM (DOS 3.2 or DOS 3.3) • Some programs require use of game paddles

Source Code: yes

Price: $225.00/package with manual; $65.00/program; $10.00/Addl. teachers manual; $165.00/any 3 programs

Demonstrates several different physical phenomena including mechanics, optics, wave motion, electricity, and advanced physics. Allows parameters to be varied to show how they affect the process under investigation. For instructor's use while lecturing. Teacher's manual included.

MECHANICS - Demonstrates the hunter-monkey paradox, vertical fall with and without air resistance, and planetary motion. Rifle angle is adjusted using a game paddle.

OPTICS, WAVE MOTION AND ELECTRICITY - Demonstrates the lens formula, superposition of waves, and the electric field. In the electric field demonstration, game paddles are used to move test charge around two point charges.

When game paddle button is pressed, short line is drawn in direction of electric field at position of test charge.

GEOMETRICAL OPTICS - Demonstrates many basic concepts of geometrical optics such as reflection, refraction, reversibility, and convex lenses. Includes a game in which a laser beam must be correctly refracted through a semi-circular lens in order to hit an enemy alien.

ADVANCED PHYSICS - Demonstrates Fourier series, the Millikan oil drop experiment, and three-body motion. The Fourier series demo allows synthesis of various waveforms using a variable number of Fourier components. Complete spectra of the waveforms can be displayed.

ID: K94
PHYSICS I

Publisher: Microphys Programs

Also available from: Academic Software • EISI (Educational Instructional Systems, Inc.) • MARCK • Queue, Inc.

Grade: High School and up

Format: 14 cassettes or 1 diskette

Hardware: PET; 8K; cassette or 4040 dual disk drive • Apple II; 24K (DOS 3.2 or 3.3) • TRS-80 MOD I; 16K • TRS-80 MOD III; 16K; cassette or disk drive • Bell & Howell

Language: BASIC

Source Code: yes

Price: $180.00/diskette; $20.00/cassette

Package of computer-assisted instruction, individualized- instruction, and utility physics programs consists of 14 interactive programs. C-A-I versions guide student through series of quantitative questions. Individualized- instruction versions generate a unique set of problems for each student. Utility programs are designed to provide solutions to time-consuming problems often given on exams and homework assignments. Complete documentation is included.

LINEAR KINEMATICS (PC1) - Program generates series of 5 questions dealing with linear motion and the analysis of a graph of instantaneous speed vs. time.

PROJECTILE MOTION (PC2) - Generates series of 11 questions dealing with analysis of a projectile in flight, thereby reviewing basic definitions of kinematics.

MOMENTUM AND ENERGY (PC3) - Generates series of 11 questions dealing with concepts of linear momentum, impulse, and kinetic energy.

ENERGY AND THE INCLINED PLANE (PC4) - Generates series of 10 questions dealing with analysis of motion of a particle on an inclined plane, thereby reviewing concepts of work, kinetic energy, and potential energy.

INELASTIC COLLISIONS (PC5) - Generates series of seven questions dealing with analysis of an inelastic collision, thereby reviewing concepts of linear momentum and kinetic energy.

CENTRIPETAL FORCE (PC6) - Generates series of six questions dealing with analysis of motion of a particle undergoing uniform circular motion.

PULLEY SYSTEM - MACHINES (PC7) - Generates series of seven questions dealing with analysis of pulley system consisting of single, double, or triple fixed and movable blocks, thus reviewing concepts of work and efficiency.

CALORIMETRY (PC8) - Generates series of four questions dealing with principle of calorimetry, thereby reviewing definition of specific heat capacity and principle of conservation of energy.

SPECIFIC HEAT CAPACITY (PC9) - Generates series of four questions dealing with definition of specific heat capacity.

HEATS OF FUSION/VAPORIZATION (PC10) - Generates series of three questions dealing with concepts of fusion and vaporization.

VECTOR ANALYSIS I (PC301) - Utility program generates problems in which student is asked to determine magnitude and direction of resultant of concurrent system of three to five vectors.

VECTOR ANALYSIS II (PC302) - Utility program is designed to determine magnitude and direction of system of concurrent vectors.

PROJECTILE ANALYSIS (PC305) - Utility program is designed to solve general projectile motion problem. Time of flight, horizontal range, final velocity, and angle of impact are among values determined.

CALORIMETRY ANALYSIS (PC306) - Utility program is designed to solve various time-consuming problems involved in study of calorimetry. Substances undergoing changes in phase, as well as changes in temperature, may be dealt with by this problem.

ID: K95
PHYSICS II

Publisher: Microphys Programs

Also available from: Academic Software • EISI (Educational Instructional Systems, Inc.) • MARCK • Queue, Inc.

Grade: High School and up

Format: 17 cassettes or 1 diskette

Hardware: PET; 8K; cassette or 4040 dual disk drive • Apple II; 24K (DOS 3.2 or 3.3) • TRS-80 MOD I; 16K • TRS-80 MOD III; 16K; cassette or disk drive • Bell & Howell

Language: BASIC

Source Code: yes

Price: $180.00/diskette; $20.00/cassette

Package consists of 17 interactive physics programs. Computer-assisted instruction versions guide student through series of quantitative questions; individualized-instruction versions generate a unique set of problems for each student; utility programs are designed to provide solutions to time- consuming problems often given on exams and homework assignments. Complete instructions are included, and grades and overall evaluation are compiled by program for each student.

SPECIFIC GAS LAWS (PC11) - Program generates series of three questions dealing with gases undergoing isothermal, isobaric, and isovolumic processes, thereby reviewing Boyle's, Charles', and Gay- Lussac's laws.

GENERAL GAS LAW (PC12) - Generates series of questions dealing with behavior of a gas undergoing a general process in which all three thermodynamic variables may change.

THERMODYNAMICS I (PC13) - Generates series of five questions dealing with a confined gas which undergoes an isobaric process, thereby reviewing concepts of molar heat capacity, Charles' Law, and the first law of thermodynamics.

THERMODYNAMICS II (PC14) - Generates series of five questions dealing with a confined gas which undergoes an isobaric compression during which a quantity of heat is removed.

TRANSVERSE STANDING WAVES (PC15) - Generates series of four questions dealing with study of standing wave pattern established in wire which is fastened at both ends.

LONGITUDINAL STANDING WAVES (PC16) - Generates series of four questions dealing with longitudinal wave pattern established in open and closed organ pipes.

MIRRORS AND LENSES (PC17) - Generates series of five questions dealing with image- forming properties of convex and concave mirrors and lenses.

REFRACTION OF LIGHT (PC18) - Generates series of three questions dealing with behavior of light rays striking a planar interface between two optical media.

SERIES CIRCUIT ANALYSIS (PC19) - Generates series of ten questions dealing with analysis of series circuit consisting of three resistors and a battery, thereby reviewing concepts of resistance, potential difference, and power.

PARALLEL CIRCUIT ANALYSIS I (PC20) - Generates series of ten questions dealing with analysis of parallel circuit consisting of three resistors and a battery, thereby reviewing concepts of resistance, potential difference, and power.

PARALLEL CIRCUIT ANALYSIS II (PC20A) - Generates series of six questions dealing with analysis of circuit in which single resistor is in series with parallel combination of two resistors.

SERIES/PARALLEL CIRCUIT ANALYSIS (PC21) - Generates series of six questions dealing with analysis of circuit in which single resistor is in series with parallel combination of two resistors.

ELECTRIC FIELD ANALYSIS (PC35) - Generates series of six questions dealing with work done in transferring charged particle between two points in uniform electric field.

PHOTOELECTRIC EFFECT (PC36) - Generates series of four questions dealing with analysis of photoelectric emission from surfaces of various randomly selected metallic cathodes.

TOTAL INTERNAL REFLECTION (PC40) - Generates series of questions dealing with reflection of light at appropriate interfaces.

GAS LAW ANALYSIS (PC303) - Utility program is designed to solve large variety of problems in which gases undergo isothermal, isobaric, isovolumic, and general processes.

OPTICS ANALYSIS (PC304) - Utility program is designed to solve variety of problems involving image-forming properties of thin lenses and convex and concave mirrors.

ID: K96

PHYSICS INSTRUCTION SERIES

Publisher: Merlan Scientific Ltd.

Grade: High School and up

Format: cassette or diskette

Hardware: PET; 8K

Language: BASIC

Source Code: no

Price: $24.00/cassette for AVERAGE SPEED and AVERAGE

VELOCITY; $20.00/SUPERPOSITION; $15.00/PHOTON INTERFERENCE; $110.00/diskette for these and three other programs on MERLAN PHYSICS I PACKAGE.

Series of four packages presents basic concepts in physics. Written documentation provided.

AVERAGE SPEED - Program leads student from definition of average speed through series of problems designed to reinforce concept. Many of problems are illustrated by animated diagrams. Throughout program, student is provided with feedback appropriate to answers given. Program concludes with self test which scores student on progress.

AVERAGE VELOCITY - Similar to program on AVERAGE SPEED, these exercises explore concept of average velocity, providing many examples and feedback.

SUPERPOSITION PACKAGE - Series of two programs on one tape helps illustrate how two or more waves add together to produce superposed waveforms. SUPERPOSITION I is static presentation in which two or more waves may be added. For each wave, wavelength, attenuation, and phase display may be specified. SUPERPOSITION II is dynamic presentation in which two waves and their resultant waveform are shown rolling up screen continuously. For each wave, wavelength, attenuation, and phase delay must be specified.

PHOTON INTERFERENCE - Program simulates random behavior of photons passing through double slit and gradually produces statistical pattern of familiar bright and dark bars.

ID: K97

PHYSICS INTERACT PACKAGE

Publisher: EduTech

Also available from: Academic Software • Queue, Inc.

Grade: High School

Format: 3 programs on 3 diskettes

Hardware: Apple II Plus; 48K (DOS 3.2 or 3.3) • Apple II; 48K with Applesoft in ROM (DOS 3.2 or 3.3) • Some programs require use of game paddles

Source Code: yes

Price: $250.00/package with manuals; $95.00/program with manual

Provides individualized computer instruction to a class with only one computer. Provides entire class with interactive problem-solving activities. Keeps track of each student by name. Each diskette comes with teacher notes and student manual which can be reproduced. Topics are vectors, projectile motion, and the Millikan Oil Drop Experiment.

VECTORS - Students calculate the direction in which an airplane must fly to reach a specified point, given the magnitude and direction of the cross wind. Calculations are done away from the computer, allowing many students to participate simultaneously. When a student has an answer, the computer will simulate it. With limited fuel and treacherous mountains, calculational errors have disastrous results.

TARGET - Students take turns firing at an enemy, using initial conditions obtained by solving an individualized projectile-motion problem. Since the enemy is prepared to fire back, the student must be ready with the answer when he/she gets to the computer. A direct hit leads to a promotion, but a miss allows the enemy to fire back. A student may be "killed in action" or retired as a general. Full records are kept of each student's performance for teacher review. The three programs of TARGET give students practice with projectile-motion problems of increasing complexity. In addition, within Parts 1 and 2, a wind factor is added once the student reaches a certain rank. Thus, TARGET can be effectively used with students with very different levels of mastery. Furthermore, it can be used over any period of time, since the position of each student, after each shot, is stored on the diskette.

OIL DROP - Simulation of the Millikan Oil Drop Experiment. The game paddles are used to vary the voltage between two plates in order to stop a drop. When this is done, the student leaves the computer to compute the charge on the drop. (The mass or radius of the drop is given.) The student can stop another drop only after correctly entering the charge on the previous drop. Individual data files are maintained of each student's drops and a master file is kept of the entire class. A histogram can be shown of the pooled data.

ID: K98
PHYSICS LABORATORY EXPERIMENTS AND CORRELATED COMPUTER AIDS

Publisher: Metrologic Publications

Grade: High School and up

Format: cassette or diskette

Hardware: Apple II; 24K (DOS 3.2 or 3.3) • PET; 8K; cassette or 4040 dual disk drive • TRS-80 MOD I; 16K; cassette • Bell & Howell; 24K • TRS-80 MOD III; 16K; cassette or disk drive

Language: BASIC

Source Code: yes

Price: $10.50/copy for lab book; less than $30.00/program on cassette or diskette

Lab manual contains 49 dynamic experiment descriptions. Using conventional laboratory apparatus, student makes measurements and enters data into computer, which provides student with immediate feedback as to whether measurement precision is adequate and calculations correct for that particular experiment. Student then completes experiment by reentering data and calculations specified. Computer prints out complete evaluation of student's work and gives suggested grade for experiment.

ID: K99
PHYSICS PROGRAMS FOR THE APPLE II

Publisher: J & S Software, Inc.

Also available from: Academic Software • K-12 Micromedia • MARCK • McKilligan Supply Corp. • Queue, Inc.

Grade: High School

Format: 8 diskettes

Hardware: Apple II; 48K with Applesoft in ROM

Language: BASIC

Source Code: yes

Price: $25/program; $125/complete set

Programs review and teach main problem areas in physics, emphasizing experiments and problems. Includes high-resolution graphs and experimental setups. Each program has changing variables in questions and experiments. Student names and grades are stored. Each program requires 30-45 minutes.

CIRCULAR MOTION

NEWTON'S LAWS
ACCELERATION
UNIFORM MOTION
FREE FALL
PROJECTILE PROBLEMS
MOMENTUM
WORK AND ENERGY

ID: K100
PHYSICS VECTORS & GRAPHING

Publisher: Micro Learningware

Also available from: Academic Software

Format: diskette

Hardware: Apple II; 48K with Applesoft in ROM (DOS 3.3)

Language: Applesoft BASIC

Source Code: yes

Price: $10.00

Package consists of seven programs presenting material on vectors and graphing. Written instructions provided.

VECTOR RESOLUTION - Program begins with magnitude and direction of vector and shows how to convert it into X and Y components. Color vectors are drawn with low-resolution graphics.

VECTOR ADDITION - Given magnitude and direction of vectors, computer finds X and Y components and adds them together.

DOT PRODUCTS - Program starts with magnitude and direction of two vectors, and illustrates their dot product.

CROSS PRODUCTS - Program illustrates directions of original two vectors and their cross-product.

VECTOR PRODUCTS - UNIT VECTORS - Starts with vectors in form of x, y, and z components. Dot and cross-products are calculated by multiplying components of two given vectors.

VECTORS AND SCALARS QUIZ - Multiple-choice test with thirty questions, in which student presses V or S to tell whether given quantity is vector or scalar.

GRAPHING DATA - Program teaches how to scale axes of graph to fix lab data on it, then goes into details about fitting straight line to data. Both slope and intercept are calculated in standard form.

ID: K101
PLANTS AND HOW THEY GROW

Publisher: RIGHT ON PROGRAMS

Date: July 82

Grade: 2

Format: cassette or diskette

Hardware: Apple II; 48K with Applesoft in ROM (DOS 3.2 or 3.3) • PET; 16K

Language: BASIC

Source Code: yes

Price: $13.00/cassette; $15.00/diskette

Basic introduction to plants shows students parts of plants and trees, what each part does and how seeds are carried to reproduce. Game follows.

ID: K102
RAIN

Publisher: COMPress

Also available from: Academic Software

Grade: High School-College

Format: diskette

Hardware: Apple II Plus; 48K • Bell & Howell; 48K

Language: BASIC

Source Code: no

Price: $25.00

RAIN is a game format program. The object of the game is to keep inorganic compounds at the top of the screen from reaching the bottom by choosing organic compounds with which they will react. Points are deducted for each wrong choice and are given for each reaction caused. The rain falls more quickly as the game progresses.

ID: K103
REPRODUCTION ORGANS

Publisher: Micro Power & Light Company

Also available from: Queue, Inc.

Grade: Upper Elementary

Format: diskette

Hardware: Apple II; 32K with Applesoft in ROM

Price: $29.95

This program does a fine job of guiding the student through the material yet allowing the student a real measure of control over the actual sequencing of topics, reviews, and exercises. This is possible through the use of a readily-accessible master menu, together with control options presented to the student with nearly every display. When the student elects to take control of lesson sequencing, a master menu offers the following choices: (1) end the program; (2) test your knowledge; (3) choose what to review next; (4) choose what to study next; and (5) look up the definition of terms.

ID: K104
REPRODUCTION PROCESS

Publisher: Micro Power & Light Company

Grade: Upper Elementary and up

Format: diskette

Hardware: Apple II; 32K with Applesoft in ROM

Price: $29.95

The program is sensitive to the learning process. It guides the user, suggesting an appropriate next topic, and recommending review when too few questions are answered correctly. Yet, at nearly any point, the user is able to take control of lesson sequencing by calling forth a menu that offers the following choices: (1) look up the definition of a term; (2) end the program altogether; (3) return to the last idea covered, (4) take a quick quiz; (5) get a capsule review of organs; (6) go on to the next idea; and (7) choose the idea to be covered next. When the user chooses to determine the idea to be covered next by the program, the following topic-selection menu is presented for that purpose: (1) general introduction, (2) sperm, (3) ovum, (4) copulation, (5) fertilization, (6) embryo, (7) umbilical cord,

and (8) months 1-3, 4-6, 7-birth. Upper elementary, middle school and junior high students find this program great! The related program entitled REPRODUCTION ORGANS affords the student-user an insight into the essential function of each organ playing a major role in the reproduction process.

ID: K105
RKINET - REACTION KINETICS

Publisher: CONDUIT

Also available from: MARCK • Queue, Inc.

Date: 1975

Grade: 9-College

Format: diskette

Hardware: Apple II; 48K with Applesoft in ROM (DOS 3.2.1) • TRS-80 MOD I; 32K with Level II BASIC • TRS-80 MOD III; 32K with Disk BASIC • PET 2000 or 4000 series; 8K (cassette) or 16K (disk) with 2040 or 4040 drive

Language: BASIC

Source Code: yes

Price: $35.00; $10.00/add'l software copy; $1.50/add'l teacher manual; $1.50/add'l student manual

This simulation is intended to extend students' laboratory experience and understanding of reaction kinetics by enabling them to carry out a wider range of investigations. It will also help students understand the relationship between a mathematical model and reality. The model, based on data from real experiments, will broaden students' knowledge of first- and second-order reactions, rate constants, concentrations, and the effect of variation of temperature on reaction rate. Includes six copies of Students' Notes (10 pages), and one copy of Teachers' Guide (10 pages).

ID: K106
SCATTER - NUCLEAR SCATTERING

Publisher: CONDUIT

Also available from: MARCK • Queue, Inc.

Date: 1975

Grade: 9-College

Format: diskette

Hardware: Apple II; 48K with Applesoft in ROM (DOS 3.2.1) • TRS-80 MOD I; 32K with Level II BASIC • TRS-80 MOD III; 32K with Disk BASIC • PET 2000 or 4000 series; 8K (cassette) or 16K (disk) with 2040 or 4040 drive

Language: BASIC

Source Code: yes

Price: $35.00; $10.00/add'l software copy; $1.50/add'l teacher manual; $1.50/add'l student manual

Because of the experimental difficulties in performing certain nuclear scattering investigations, models of three experimental situations have been programmed for computer simulation. The programs give students experience in deducing the size, shape and force law of a single scattering center, and the scattering of alpha particles by a metal foil. Includes six copies of Student's Notes (15 pages), and one copy of Teachers' Guide (17 pages).

ID: K107
SCIENCE
Publisher: RIGHT ON PROGRAMS

Also available from: Academic Software • K-12 Micromedia • Queue, Inc.

Grade: 5

Format: cassette or diskette

Hardware: Apple II; 48K with Applesoft in ROM (DOS 3.2 or 3.3) • PET; 16K

Language: BASIC

Source Code: yes

Price: $13.00/cassette; $15.00/diskette

This program provides a greater in-depth study of the systems of the body, their functions, and the importance of proper care of each. The body's reactions to daily living are explained. The student learns to understand "what makes him tick".

ID: K108
SCIENCE - COMMUNICATIONS
Publisher: RIGHT ON PROGRAMS

Also available from: Academic Software • K-12 Micromedia • Queue, Inc.

Grade: 6

Format: cassette or diskette

Hardware: Apple II; 48K with Applesoft in ROM (DOS 3.2 or 3.3) • PET; 16K

Language: BASIC

Source Code: yes

Price: $13.00/cassette; $15.00/diskette

Basic facts about communication, how it is used, its importance and how its speed has changed our lives are covered. The student is taken on a trip through time from the simplest beat of the tom-tom to the most sophisticated laser beam communications system.

ID: K109
SCIENCE - INSECTS
Publisher: RIGHT ON PROGRAMS

Also available from: Academic Software • K-12 Micromedia • Queue, Inc.

Grade: 4

Format: cassette or diskette

Hardware: Apple II; 48K with Applesoft in ROM (DOS 3.2 or 3.3) • PET; 16K

Language: BASIC

Source Code: yes

Price: $13.00/cassette; $15.00/diskette

This program provides the student with some interesting background information on insects. A series of questions will help the student check to see if s/he has remembered the information. Provides a good beginning with enough information to start the student searching further for an in-depth research report.

ID: K110
SCIENCE - OUR BODIES
Publisher: RIGHT ON PROGRAMS

Also available from: Academic Software • K-12 Micromedia • Queue, Inc.

Grade: 2

Format: cassette or diskette

Hardware: Apple II; 48K with Applesoft in ROM (DOS 3.2 or 3.3)

Language: BASIC

Source Code: yes

Price: $13.00/cassette; $15.00/diskette

This is a very simple and basic approach to the different systems in human bodies and what each one does. Also included is information on maintaining the health of these bodies. A game at the end checks the student's knowledge of the material given and rewards the correct answers.

ID: K111
SCIENCE - SOUND
Publisher: RIGHT ON PROGRAMS

Also available from: Academic Software • K-12 Micromedia • Queue, Inc.

Grade: 6

Format: cassette or diskette

Hardware: Apple II; 48K with Applesoft in ROM (DOS 3.2 or 3.3) • PET; 16K

Language: BASIC

Source Code: yes

Price: $13.00/cassette; $15.00/diskette

The student is introduced to basic concepts in the science of sound. Examples are given of everyday sound experiences to help the child relate the scientific concept to his/her everyday life. A simple game will encourage the child to learn and recall the information given.

ID: K112
SCIENCE - THE EARTH AND ITS COMPOSITION
Publisher: RIGHT ON PROGRAMS

Also available from: Academic Software • K-12 Micromedia • Queue, Inc.

Grade: 3

Format: cassette or diskette

Hardware: Apple II; 48K with Applesoft in ROM (DOS 3.2 or 3.3) • PET; 16K

Language: BASIC

Source Code: yes

Price: $13.00/cassette; $15.00/diskette

The student is introduced to the basic components that make up the earth on which we live. Water, mountains, air, volcanoes, etc. are explained, as are the ways in which they are formed, eroded, changed and "reborn" in other places as "other things". Relationships of one to the other are explained where appropriate.

ID: K113
SCIENCE - THE SOLAR SYSTEM
Publisher: RIGHT ON PROGRAMS

Also available from: Academic Software • K-12 Micromedia • Queue, Inc.

Grade: 1

Format: cassette or diskette

Hardware: Apple II; 48K with Applesoft in ROM (DOS 3.2 or 3.3) • PET; 16K

Language: BASIC

Source Code: yes

Price: $13.00/cassette; $15.00/diskette

The child is introduced to the basic concepts of the planets, the sun, moon and stars. Simple questions and a matching game are designed to reward the student when the material is mastered.

ID: K114
SCIENCE - VOLUME 1
Publisher: Minnesota Educational Computing Consortium

Date: June 82

Grade: 7-12

Format: diskette

Hardware: Apple II; 32K with Applesoft in ROM (DOS 3.3); printer optional for some programs

Language: Applesoft BASIC

Source Code: no

Price: $35.90

Package contains some of physics and ecology programs developed by Huntington II project. Support booklet (included) provides instructions and lesson plans. Huntington II documentation is also useful for successful running of programs.

BUFFALO - Ecology program concerning control of buffalo population.

SLITS - Studies Young's double-slit experiment.

TAG - Program simulates fish tagging procedure.

CHARGE - Simulation of Millikan's oil drop experiment.

WHALES - Simulation on whale migration, developed by San Diego schools.

DECAY1 - Casino game enables student to understand exponential decay.

NEWTON2 - Game reinforces concept of vectors.

ID: K115
SCIENCE - VOLUME 2
Publisher: Minnesota Educational Computing Consortium

Also available from: Academic Software • Creative Computing • K-12 Micromedia • Opportunities For Learning, Inc. • Scholastic Software

Date: June 82

Grade: 9-12

Format: diskette

Hardware: Apple II; 32K with Applesoft in ROM (DOS 3.3)

Language: Applesoft BASIC

Source Code: no

Price: $40.90

Package consists of programs on science, many of them developed by Minnesota teachers for use in biology and physics classrooms. Support booklet included.

PEST - Program deals with use of pesticides.

CELL MEMBRANE - Program in which user assumes the part of a cell.

SNELL - Demonstrates Snell's Law by plotting light refraction.

COLLIDE - Simulates collision between two bodies.

DIFFUSION - Deals with diffusion rates of various gases.

NUCLEAR SIMULATION - Shows radioactive decay of nine different radioisotopes.

ICBM, RADAR - Teach angles and projections on coordinate system.

ID: K116
SCIENCE - VOLUME 3
Publisher: Minnesota Educational Computing Consortium

Also available from: Academic Software • Creative Computing • K-12 Micromedia • Opportunities For Learning, Inc. • Scholastic Software

Date: June 82

Grade: Junior High-High School

Format: diskette

Hardware: Apple II; 32K with Applesoft in ROM (DOS 3.3)

Language: Applesoft BASIC

Source Code: no

Price: $35.90

Package consists of five science programs. Support booklet included.

FISH - Program uses graphics to show circulatory system of a fish.

ODELL LAKE - Simulation is used to explore food chains.

URSA - Program teaches about constellations.

QUAKES - Simulates earthquakes.

MINERALS - Can be used in area of earth science to identify 29 minerals by simple tests.

ID: K117
SCIENCE - VOLUME 4
Publisher: Minnesota Educational Computing Consortium

Date: June 82

Grade: High School and up

Format: diskette

Hardware: Apple II; 32K with Applesoft in ROM (DOS 3.3)

Language: Applesoft BASIC

Source Code: no

Price: $40.20

Programs in module are designed to serve primarily as support for teacher lecture/demonstrations on topics of solubility, gas laws, and determining basic unit of electrical charge. Support booklet included.

DEFINITION, SOLUBILITY PRODUCTS, PRECIPITATES - Solubility programs.

CHARLES' LAW, BOYLE'S LAW - Gas law programs.

ELECTRON CHARGE - Program is based on Millikan's oil drop experiment for determining basic unit of electrical charge.

ID: K118
SCIENCE PACKAGE I

Publisher: Micro Learningware

Also available from: Academic Software • MARCK • Queue, Inc.

Format: cassette or diskette

Hardware: TRS-80 MOD I or III; 16K cassette or 32K diskette

Language: BASIC

Source Code: yes

Price: $24.95

Package consists of four programs designed to stimulate student's interest in physics and other scientific disciplines. Written instructions provided.

ELECTRONICS - Ohm's Law practice program graphically displays both series and parallel circuits for student to solve. All voltages and resistances are picked at random.

METRIC QUIZ - Thirty-question quiz tests metric prefixes, conversion, significant figures, and scientific notation. Program is structured in such a way that it is easy to modify questions and answers.

LOST ON THE MOON - Student must select items most useful for survival on moon.

CUP THE BALL - Simulation of physics lab project in which student must calculate the necessary speed a ball placed randomly on a table must have to roll off the table and fall into a cup below. Computer graphically displays ball, table, and cup. Available as an individual program from K-12 Micromedia.

ID: K119
SCIENCE PACKAGE II

Publisher: Micro Learningware

Also available from: Academic Software • MARCK • Opportunities For Learning, Inc.

Format: cassette or diskette

Hardware: TRS-80 MOD I or III: 16k cassette or 32K diskette • TRS-80 Color Computer; 16K with extended BASIC; cassette

Language: BASIC

Source Code: yes

Price: $24.95

Package consists of five chemistry drill and practice programs. Written instructions provided.

VALENCE - Program quizzes student on most stable valence of up to 97 comment elements. If student answers incorrectly, computer displays correct valence. When student has completed quiz, computer displays number correct.

ELEMENTS - Student is given name of element and asked to identify it as metal, nonmetal, or inert gas. If student answers incorrectly, computer displays correct answer. Computer keeps track of number correct and displays that number when student is finished.

SYMBOL - Program drills students on chemical names and symbols. Student has choice of being given name of chemical and responding with symbol and responding with name.

ATOMIC WEIGHT - Program drills student on atomic weights of elements. Student has choice of being given name of element and responding with atomic weight or vice versa (weights are given as integers to make memorization easier).

ATOMIC NUMBER - Program drills students on atomic numbers of elements. Student has choice of being given name of element and responding with atomic number or vice versa.

ID: K120
SCIENCE PACKAGE III

Publisher: Micro Learningware

Also available from: Academic Software • MARCK • Queue, Inc.

Format: cassette or diskette

Hardware: TRS-80 MOD I or III; 16K cassette or 32K diskette • PET; 8K cassette

Language: BASIC

Source Code: yes

Price: $24.95

Series of five programs provides drill and practice with various formulas dealing with physics of motion. In each program, problem is presented and answer is solicited. If response is correct, student is congratulated and asked to try another problem involving different variation of formula. Should response be incorrect, student is taken through step-by-step solution with appropriate corrections along way. In each program, student may use own calculator or one offered by computer. Written instructions provided.

ID: K121
SCIENTIFIC MEASUREMENTS

Publisher: Micro Power & Light Company

Also available from: Queue, Inc.

Grade: Advanced Elementary and up

Format: diskette

Hardware: Apple II; 48K with Applesoft in ROM

Price: $24.95

This program offers examples and exercises in reading three instruments found in most science laboratories, the graduated cylinder, the metric ruler, and the triple beam balance. The program shows the correct method for reading the amount of liquid in a graduated cylinder, indicating that liquid level should be read at the meniscus bottom. The student is given an example of taking such a reading, and then is invited to do ten exercises. The program computes each successive liquid height randomly. If the student answers incorrectly, he receives a second chance. Should the second try also be incorrect, the correct answer is then provided by the program. The program follows a similar instructional strategy relative to reading lengths by a metric ruler. Answers are to be given in both centimeters and millimeters. Several examples are provided to show the student how to correctly balance and read a triple beam balance. The student has the opportunity to complete five exercises in balancing the scale and entering the associated weight. The student has to balance each of the three sections of the balance individually - hundredths, tenths and units.

ID: K122
SCIENTIFIC METHOD
Publisher: Micro Power & Light Company

Also available from: Academic Software • K-12 Micromedia • Queue, Inc.

Grade: Upper Elementary-High School

Format: diskette

Hardware: Apple II; 48K with Applesoft in ROM

Price: $19.95

This program covers observation - use of the senses, generalization - stating a hypothesis, measurement - seeking precision, and verification - involving experimentation. The student is led through an entire process, simulating an experiment, to arrive at an empirical law. The program requires 15-30 minutes.

ID: K123
SIMPLE MACHINES
Publisher: Micro Power & Light Company

Also available from: Academic Software • Queue, Inc.

Grade: 5 grade reading level

Format: diskette

Hardware: Apple II; 32K with Applesoft in ROM

Price: $29.95

The six simple machines covered are; lever, pulley, wheel and axle, inclined plane, wedge, and screw. Upon successful completion of the program, the student should be able to select the appropriate simple machine to use to solve any number of real-life situations. Instruction and an illustrative example of an application are presented for each machine. The student then has an opportunity to work several exercises intended to further reinforce his or her understanding of how each machine can be used. There are review opportunities throughout the program. A concluding mastery quiz affords the student a chance to evaluate his or her own basic understanding of the principles and uses that are presented.

ID: K124
SIMPLE MACHINES I
Publisher: Micro-Ed, Inc.

Grade: Upper Elementary and up

Format: cassette or diskette

Hardware: Commodore 64 • PET; 16K

Language: BASIC

Source Code: no

Price: $14.95

Combining text with animated graphics, this program introduces the principles and some of the applications of three simple machines: the inclined plane, the screw, and the wedge. The program concludes with a quiz (from ten to thirty problems as requested) and a summary of student performance.

ID: K125
SKIES ABOVE/WATERS BELOW
Publisher: Aquarius Publishers Inc.

Date: Aug. 82

Format: 4 cassettes or diskettes

Hardware: Apple II; 48K with Applesoft in ROM (DOS 3.2 or 3.3) • TRS-80 MOD I or III

Language: BASIC

Source Code: no

Price: $95.00, or $24.95/cassette; $115.00, or $29.95/diskette

Series introduces students to exciting world of physical science. Colorful graphic simulations depict series of fascinating voyages ranging from planets and stars of outer space to waterways of earth. Students learn basic facts about areas they explore through dynamic drill techniques. Each program includes testing section and student management system. Detailed Teacher's Guide accompanies each program.

  PLANETS

  STARS

  STREAMS AND RIVERS

  OCEANS

ID: K126
SOLAR SYSTEM ASTRONOMY
Publisher: Micro Learningware

Also available from: Academic Software

Format: diskette

Hardware: Apple II; 48K with Applesoft in ROM (DOS 3.3)

Language: Applesoft BASIC

Source Code: yes

Price: $30.00

Package consists of five programs on aspects of Earth's solar system. Documentation booklet included.

INNER PLANETS - Menu offers choice of viewing orbits of Mercury, Venus, Earth, Mars, or all of these. It draws all four inner planets against arc of sun for comparison.

OUTER PLANETS - Menu-driven program presents pictures of outer planets and offers the following choices: (1) orbits; (2) Jupiter; (3) Saturn; (4) Uranus and Neptune; and (5) Pluto.

GREENHOUSE EFFECT - After discussing (with illustrations) the greenhouse effect in parked car and on Venus, program outlines how Earth could enter ice age or tropical age.

LIFE IN THE SOLAR SYSTEM - Program discusses conditions necessary for life and their presence or absence on various planets. It concludes with discussion of space colonies.

COMETS - Program shows three scenarios: (1) view from Earth, as distant comet approaches and grows tail; (2) close-up of nucleus, gas cloud, and tail, describing dirty snowball theory; and (3) orbit of typical comet.

ID: K127
SPECTRO

Publisher: Programs For Learning, Inc.

Also available from: McKilligan Supply Corp. • Queue, Inc.

Format: cassette or diskette

Hardware: Apple II Plus; 48K (DOS 3.2 or 3.3); game paddle

Price: $30.00

Simulation designed to introduce measurement techniques. There is a prescribed sequence of stops which must be followed carefully, hence the program focuses on executing the steps properly. Game control knobs and paddles are used to turn switches on and off, and adjust settings, thus a student can acquire a "feel" for each instrument. The program is therefore particularly useful for pre-lab orientation, as well as class demonstrations.

ID: K128
STARWARE

Publisher: APX (Atari Program Exchange)

Date: June 82

Grade: 7 and up

Format: diskette

Hardware: Atari 400 or 800; 40K with Atari BASIC language cartridge

Language: BASIC

Source Code: no

Price: $22.95

Program uses high-resolution graphics to create maps of constellations in both hemispheres visible from any location at any date and time this century. Handy features for telescope owners include calculation of local sidereal time, and user specification of right ascension and declination of center of map, as well as size of field of view. Beginner and advanced quizzes test student's progress in learning to identify program's 66 constellations. User manual is included.

ID: K129
STATICS

Publisher: Micro Learningware

Also available from: Academic Software

Format: diskette

Hardware: Apple II; 48K with Applesoft in ROM

Language: Applesoft BASIC

Source Code: yes

Price: $12.00

Package of five programs on principles of statics, making extensive use of graphics. Documentation booklet included.

STATICS METHOD

BEAM PROBLEMS

EASY BEAM PROBLEM

LADDERS

INCLINED PLANES

ID: K130
STELLAR ASTRONOMY

Publisher: Micro Learningware

Also available from: Academic Software

Format: diskette

Hardware: Apple II; 48K with Applesoft in ROM (DOS 3.3)

Language: Applesoft BASIC

Source Code: yes

Price: $30.00

Package consists of eight programs that describe many aspects of stellar astronomy. Documentation booklet included.

TYPES OF STARS - High-resolution diagram fills top of screen, at bottom of which is menu. Each menu choice explains stars found in one region of diagram with emphasis on stellar evaluation and lifetimes of stars.

GALAXIES - Provides discussion and graphic illustrations of: (1) origins of galaxies; (2) elliptical galaxies; (3) spiral and barrel galaxies; (4) other galaxies (irregular galaxies, radio galaxies, seyferts and quasars).

CONSTELLATIONS - Program teaches names and shapes of 30 constellations.

SIRIUS AND THE WHITE DWARF - Program discusses and illustrates these two stars and compares both with the sun; includes picture of Canis Major and Orion to show how to find Sirius in sky.

DEATH OF A STAR - Program describes and graphically illustrates what happens at time star uses up its nuclear fuel.

DOPPLER EFFECT - Program presents sound waves in terms of their spread from stationary and moving sources, toward and away from human ear. Viwer is asked whether frequency will increase or decrease when source moves toward ear. Program then derives formula for observed frequency. Sound effects used.

COSMOLOGY AND ORIGIN OF THE ELEMENTS - First part of program discusses scientific theories for origin of the universe, including dark night sky, Hubble's law, and three degree microwave background. It then presents both Steady State and Big Bang models. Second part deals with creation of elements.

COSMOLOGY II - Program explores (with many graphic illustrations) the following philosophical theories for origin of universe: (1)Genesis; (2)Deism; (3)Theistic existentialism; (4) Naturalism; (5)Nihilism; (6)Polytheism; (7)Astrology; (8) Chinese mysticism; (9)Pantheism; and (10)New Consciousness.

ID: K131
TARGET PRACTICE

Publisher: Merlan Scientific Ltd.

Grade: High School and up

Format: cassette or diskette

Hardware: PET; 8K

Language: BASIC

Source Code: no

Price: $20.00/cassette; $110.00/diskette for this and six other programs on MERLAN PHYSICS I package

Program takes form of game designed to test student's knowledge of projectile motion equations. Student is given three or four flight parameters (range, muzzle velocity, firing angle, and height above ground level) and asked to calculate fourth. Graphics simulate flight of projectile. Points are awarded for accuracy, and student's final score is displayed as percent. Written documentation provided.

ID: K132

THERMODYNAMICS

Publisher: Micro Learningware

Also available from: Academic Software

Format: diskette

Hardware: Apple II; 48K with Applesoft in ROM

Language: Applesoft BASIC

Source Code: yes

Price: $20.00

Package consists of seven programs designed to enable student to gain familiarity with thermodynamic processes. Documentation booklet included.

THERMODYNAMIC PROCESSES - Program draws isobaric, adiabatric, isometric, and isothermal processes and asks questions about them. Next it draws families of curves for an ideal gas with different numbers of molecules going through each process.

THERMODYNAMIC CYCLES - Program builds on previous one to combine basic processes into cycles.

HEAT ENGINES - THEORY - Program shows animated heat flow diagram for an engine, with hot reservoir on top, cold on bottom, and work being extracted at side. It then explains that a heat pump is the opposite, and draws pump with heat moving from cold to hot area.

HEAT ENGINES - APPLICATIONS - Program applies theory of heat engines to particular problems involving ideal engines and refrigerators.

CALORIMETRY - Starting with hot sample and placing it into cup of cool liquid, both will come to same temperature. Program illustrates this process, then solves six problems.

IDEAL GAS CYCLES - Program simulates ideal gas enclosed in cylinder with moveable piston. Several processes may be performed on monatomic, diatomic, or polyatomic ideal gas.

MOLECULAR MOTION AND GAS PRESSURE - Program simulates motion of ideal gas modules. They bounce around at random in cylinder, sometimes hitting pressure gauge on right side.

ID: K133

TRIBBLES

Publisher: CONDUIT

Also available from: K-12 Micromedia • MARCK

Grade: 9-College

Format: diskette

Hardware: Apple II; 48K with Applesoft in ROM (DOS 3.2.1)

Language: BASIC

Source Code: yes

Price: $35.00; $10.00/add'l software copy; $1.50/add'l student manual

This introductory unit on the scientific method consists of a written tutorial and a computer simulation. The tutorial presents students with a problem and guides them to its solution. The computer simulation provides the data for making observations and for forming tentative explanations and testing predictions. To eliminate the variable of background knowledge, the problem takes place on an alien planet inhabited by tribbles. Includes five copies of Student Tutorial (30 pages).

ID: K134

VECTOR ADDITION

Publisher: Radio Shack®

Date: 1982

Grade: Secondary

Format: cassette or diskette

Hardware: TRS-80 MOD I; 16K with Level II BASIC • TRS-80 MOD III; 16K with Model III BASIC

Language: BASIC

Price: $29.95

Secondary math and physics program allows students to solve problems on vector addition. An edit feature allows students to add to list of vectors, or to change vector components. Vectors may be drawn by either tip-to-tail or common origin method. A problems section covers fundamentals of vectors, displacement, velocity and acceleration, force, gravitation, conservation of momentum, and electric forces and fields. User's guide and programming guide are included.

ID: K135

WAVES AND VIBRATION SERIES

Publisher: Merlan Scientific Ltd.

Grade: High School and up

Format: 7 cassettes or 1 diskette

Hardware: PET; 8K • Apple II Plus; 32K (DOS 3.3)

Language: BASIC

Source Code: no

Price: $138.00/series cassette or diskette; indiv. programs - $24.00/cassette and $32.00/diskette for WAVES IN A LINEAR MEDIUM: SUPERPOSITION, PERIODIC WAVES: INTERFERENCE..., LONGITUDINAL WAVE..., and WAVE DEMONSTRATIONS; $28.00/ cassette and $36.00/diskette for WAVES IN A LINEAR MEDIUM: INTRO. and PERIODIC WAVES: BASIC CONCEPTS; $32.00/cassette and $40.00/diskette for PERIODIC MOTION.

Sequence of seven programs teaches fundamentals of periodic motion and waves, making extensive use of graphics and animation. Students are required to perform experiments and draw conclusions from animated displays on screen. Many problems are presented. Teacher notes are included for each program in package.

PERIODIC MOTION - Five programs teach concepts of periodic motion, cycle, longitudinal and transverse vibration, amplitude, phase, period, and frequency.

WAVES IN A LINEAR MEDIUM: INTRODUCTION - Series of three lessons in which nature of wave pulses in medium are examined. Student is led to draw conclusions based on animated displays of pulses reflected from fixed and free ends and pulses hitting boundary between two mediums.

WAVES IN A LINEAR MEDIUM: SUPERPOSITION - Concepts of constructive and destructive interference of pulses are explored in series of two programs. Student will be taught details of how to use superposition principle to construct wave patterns resulting from interference of two pulses.

PERIODIC WAVES: BASIC CONCEPTS - Sequence of three programs concentrates on periodic waves, introducing ideas of wavelength, amplitude, period, and frequency. Although lessons stress transverse waves, segment at end demonstrates longitudinal waves and related vocabulary.

PERIODIC WAVES: INTERFERENCE AND STANDING WAVES - Final sequence of two programs analyzes production of standing waves on stretched spring by applying ideas of interference to case of periodic wave motion.

LONGITUDINAL WAVE DEMONSTRATOR - Program demonstrates both single pulses and periodic longitudinal waves moving along spring. Program allows viewer to stop and restart motion, show motion at different speeds, and highlight movement of single coil. With computer interfaced to large TV monitor, program is excellent aid in teaching entire class.

WAVE DEMONSTRATIONS - Program is designed for teacher use in demonstrating wave phenomena. Routines include periodic transverse wave, ''reflection from a fixed end,'' constructive and destructive interference of pulses, and standing waves on a string. Program allows teacher to freeze waves in order to illustrate specific points of discussion such as wavelength and direction of particle motion.

ID: K136
WEATHER SCIENCE SET
Publisher: Orange Cherry Media

Also available from: Academic Software • K-12 Micromedia • Queue, Inc.

Grade: 3-8

Format: cassette or diskette

Hardware: PET 2000 or 4000; 16K • TRS-80 MOD I or III; 16K • Apple; 16K • Apple II; 16K

Price: $15.00/cassette; $28.00/cassette set of 2; $34.00/diskette

This set examines the major factors that affect climate, the basic vocabulary of weather observation and the instruments that are used to trace weather patterns.

FORECASTING THE WEATHER
WEATHER STATION

ID: K137
WHEATSTONE
Publisher: Programs For Learning, Inc.

Also available from: McKilligan Supply Corp. • Queue, Inc.

Format: cassette or diskette

Hardware: Apple II Plus; 48K (DOS 3.2 or 3.3); game paddle

Price: $30.00

A simulation designed to introduce measurement techniques. There is a prescribed sequence of steps which must be followed carefully, hence the program focuses on executing the steps properly. Game control knobs and paddles are used to turn switches on and off, and adjust settings, thus a student can acquire a ''feel'' for each instrument. The program is therefore particularly useful for pre-lab orientation, as well as class demonstrations.

ID: K138
WORLD CLOCK
Publisher: COMPress

Also available from: Academic Software

Format: diskette

Hardware: Apple II Plus; 48K • Bell & Howell; 48K

Language: BASIC

Source Code: no

Price: $40.00

Daylight and darkness can be seen on the globe at any time of the day and year chosen by the user. The globe display will continue to run as a real-time clock. Introduction shows and explains planets' relationship to the sun and each other. A demonstration displays the sun's effect on the world through one year, focusing on summer and winter solstice periods and spring equinox.

SOCIAL SCIENCES

ID: L1
ACROSS THE PLAINS

Publisher: Micro-Ed, Inc.

Grade: Upper Elementary-Adult

Format: 4 programs on cassette or diskette

Hardware: Commodore 64 • PET; 16K

Language: BASIC

Source Code: no

Price: $39.95

These programs are designed to provide students with information about that colorful period in American history, the westward movement, and to do so using a game-playing format that utilizes real places and events. Each program focuses on one stage of the journey. The first one has to do with the trail from St. Joseph, Missouri, to Fort Kearny, Nebraska. Stage Two encompasses the trip from Fort Kearny to Fort Laramie. The third stage takes the student from Fort Laramie to Fort Hall (by way of Fort Bridger). The fourth stage deals with the final leg of the journey - from Fort Hall to what is now Sacramento. Interspersed with events that occur on the trail are bonus questions about the westward movement. Correctly answering such questions enables a student player to acquire funds which may be used to purchase needed items at trading posts enroute. ACROSS THE PLAINS is intended to be played by two participants, each trying to complete the overland trip to California. The results from each part of the journey are carried over into the next phase. The exercise is thus an ongoing one that can be conducted over more than one session, if this seems desirable.

ID: L2
AMERICA'S HERITAGE

Publisher: Aquarius Publishers Inc.

Date: Aug. 82

Format: 6 cassettes or diskettes

Hardware: Apple II; 48K with Applesoft in ROM (DOS 3.2 or 3.3) • TRS-80 MOD I or III

Language: BASIC

Source Code: no

Price: $24.95/cassette, $139.00/6 in package; $29.95/diskette, $169.00/6 in package

Series is designed to promote student's appreciation of people and events that shaped development of United States. Instructional emphasis is on development of historical concepts, understanding of geography involved, and vocabulary enrichment. Student's knowledge of historical concepts presented is evaluated periodically throughout lesson and in separate testing sections. Test results are recorded in student management system. Series is accompanied by Teacher's Guide with suggested follow-up activities.

NEW CONTINENT IS DISCOVERED - Early Viking sagas tell of land beyond Greenland. Columbus seeks an ocean route to Asia.

JAMESTOWN, AN EARLY SETTLEMENT - Some made journey in search of wealth, while others sought new beginnings.

THIRTEEN COLONIES - Could thirteen separate colonies unite in common cause?

STRUGGLE FOR INDEPENDENCE - Colonies take first steps toward independence.

AMERICAN EXPLORERS - Rugged individualists help a young nation grow.

WESTERN EXPANSION - Bursting at its seams, a nation looks west.

ID: L3
AMERICAN HISTORY: THE DECADES GAME

Publisher: BrainBank, Inc.

Also available from: Academic Software • K-12 Micromedia • Queue, Inc.

Grade: 9 and up

Format: 3 series of 5 programs each on cassette or diskette

Hardware: Apple; 16K • PET; 16K • TRS-80; 16K

Price: $50.00/series

Players learn historical data as they determine the dates in America's politics, economics, technology, science and art. There are 5 different games in each series. Games are for 1 to 4 players.

ID: L4
ANNAM - THE STUDY OF A DEVELOPING COUNTRY

Publisher: Educational Activities, Inc.

Grade: 7 and up

Format: diskette

Hardware: Apple II Plus; (DOS 3.2.1 or 3.3) • TRS-80 MOD I or III; with Level II BASIC • Commodore 2001 • Commodore 4000; 40 or 80 column • PET • Commodore 8000; 80 column

Source Code: no

Price: $49.00

The player is the leader of a developing country, aided by a superpower and in rivalry with an aggressive Communist neighbor. The player has a small standing army, various different interest groups in his country, rivals at high levels and he must remain popular to govern. Many decisions must be made which invariably lead to a change in conditions and more decisions. An exciting way to promote understanding of leadership, problems a nation must face, the impact of a decision upon many facets of the country, and an understanding of contemporary world affairs. Conditions are presented at random so that there are many different possible endings. Students will use the game over and over to find the most appropriate responses to given situations.

ID: L5
COMMUNITY HELPERS

Publisher: RIGHT ON PROGRAMS

Date: July 82

Grade: 2

Format: cassette or diskette

Hardware: Apple II; 48K with Applesoft in ROM (DOS 3.2 or 3.3) • PET; 16K

Language: BASIC

Source Code: yes

Price: $13.00/cassette; $15.00/diskette

Students learn about community helpers and their jobs. Commonplace and unusual jobs are included, and both men and women are well represented in all jobs. Game follows.

ID: L6
DEMO-GRAPHICS

Publisher: CONDUIT

Also available from: MARCK

Date: 1978

Grade: 9-College

Format: diskette

Hardware: Apple II; 48K with Applesoft in ROM (DOS 3.2.1)

Language: BASIC

Source Code: yes

Price: $85.00; $10.00/add'l software copy; $3.50/add'l users manual

These programs can be used to present current and historical demographic data for many nations; project multinational populations given current trends; and facilitate understanding of demographic dynamics and the impact of both real and simulated factors affecting the growth of world populations. The programs include 1980 data on population, fertility, and mortality for 40 countries. The materials are suitable for students just beginning to learn the outlines of the population/resource relationship as well as for graduate students who are ready to attempt computer simulations to test hypotheses about the effects of various demographic variables. Includes User's Manual (120 pages), Instructor's Notes (13 pages).

ID: L7
ELEMENTARY - VOLUME 3

Publisher: Minnesota Educational Computing Consortium

Also available from: Academic Software • Creative Computing • K-12 Micromedia • Scholastic Software

Date: June 82

Grade: 3-8

Format: diskette

Hardware: Apple II; 32K with Applesoft in ROM (DOS 3.3)

Language: Applesoft BASIC

Source Code: no

Price: $40.60

Package consists of social studies programs for elementary classroom. Support booklet included.

SELL - Elementary economics programs include SELL APPLES, SELL PLANTS, SELL LEMONADE, and SELL BICYCLES.

CIVIL - Recreates Civil War battles.

STATES, STATES 2 - Provides drill and practice on locations of states in U.S. and their capitals.

ID: L8
ELEMENTARY - VOLUME 6

Publisher: Minnesota Educational Computing Consortium

Also available from: Academic Software • Creative Computing

• K-12 Micromedia • Scholastic Software • Sunburst Communications

Date: June 82

Grade: 5-7

Format: diskette

Hardware: Apple II; 32K with Applesoft in ROM (DOS 3.3)

Language: Applesoft BASIC

Source Code: no

Price: $41.60

Package contains social studies programs for elementary classroom. Support booklet included.

OREGON, VOYAGEUR, FURS - Historical simulations.

NOMAD - Teaches map reading.

SUMER - Simulation role-playing game features economics of running ancient kingdom.

ID: L9
GEOGRAPHY EXPLORER: USA

Publisher: Instant Software[T.M.]

Also available from: Academic Software • Opportunities For Learning, Inc. • Queue, Inc.

Grade: 1-Adult

Format: diskette

Hardware: TRS-80 MOD I; 16K with Level II BASIC, expansion interface; light pen optional

Language: BASIC

Source Code: no

Price: $49.95

This program teaches vital facts about each state of the Union, through computer-generated maps of the U.S., its seven regions, and the individual states. Questions may be in multiple-choice, recognition, or fill-in format. A unique TEACHER mode allows teacher or parent to choose multiple options of how material is to be presented, permitting directed learning for student. A variety of graphic displays flash on screen to reward correct responses. Compatible light pen may be used for input as alternative to keyboard. Written documentation is provided.

ID: L10
GROWTH OF THE UNITED STATES

Publisher: RIGHT ON PROGRAMS

Date: Aug. 82

Grade: 4

Format: cassette or diskette

Hardware: Apple II; 48K with Applesoft in ROM (DOS 3.2 or 3.3) • PET; 16K

Language: BASIC

Source Code: yes

Price: $13.00/cassette; $15.00/diskette

Because of its remarkable system of government, free enterprise, free schools, natural resources, industry, inventions, and the drive and determination of its citizens, the U.S. in its short history has become the greatest industrial nation in the world. Reasons, causes and famous people are discussed. Game follows.

ID: L11

HAIL TO THE CHIEF

Publisher: Creative Computing

Also available from: Opportunities For Learning, Inc. • Queue, Inc.

Format: cassette or diskette

Hardware: Atari 800 or 400 • TRS-80; 48K

Price: $24.95

The object in this simulation is to be elected president. Player sets campaign strategy and carries it out week by week, running TV or magazine ads, traveling to different states, holding news conferences, and participating in a debate. Candidate must take a position on ten campaign issues such as energy policy, unemployment, taxes, Mid-East policy and strategic arms limitations. Candidate must manage fund-raising efforts to business and labor and handle direct-mail solicitations. The package includes four models of varying complexity; each can be used at ten levels of difficulty. The more complex models introduce the influences of incumbency, campaign finance and spending limits. HAIL TO THE CHIEF has been used as a teaching aid in political science, voting behavior, and computer science at the university level since 1976. It is a well proven package which includes a comprehensive manual.

ID: L12

HAT IN THE RING: A PRESIDENTIAL ELECTION GAME

Publisher: Micro-Ed, Inc.

Also available from: K-12 Micromedia • Opportunities For Learning, Inc. • Queue, Inc. • Texas Instruments

Grade: Elementary and up

Format: cassette or diskette

Hardware: Commodore 64 • PET • TI 99/4

Language: BASIC

Source Code: no

Price: $9.95

HAT IN THE RING is a two-player exercise designed to acquaint students with some of the political considerations involved in running a presidential candidate - one for the Republicans, the other for the Democrats. Throughout the exercise, each candidate makes decisions intended to result in a successful campaign. At the outset, each candidate has 9 units of priority resources that can be assigned as needed in order to bolster the campaign in any of the states. The overall campaign ends after each candidate has made, in alternating turns, 10 decisions. Within each state, the outcome of the campaign hinges upon four factors: 1) media exposure; 2) personal campaigning; 3) domestic issues; and 4) international issues. Although the weight of these four factors is randomly determined by the computer, the probabilities are that media exposure and domestic issues will prove to be substantially more powerful in their impact than will the factors of personal campaigning and international issues. The political situation in each state keeps changing as the game progresses. As the campaign begins, the computer randomly chooses the candidate who will have the first turn. The computer may be commanded to do one of six things: 1) raise funds (increase resources); 2) list the states in which the Republican candidate leads; 3) list the states in which the Democratic candidate leads; 4) list the current probable electoral count for each candidate; 5) list each candidate's remaining resources; and 6) get ready to display the political situation in a state.

ID: L13

HISTORY & GEOGRAPHY PACKAGE

Publisher: Micro Learningware

Also available from: Academic Software • MARCK • Opportunities For Learning, Inc. • Queue, Inc.

Format: cassette or diskette

Hardware: PET; 8K cassette • TRS-80 MOD I or III; 16K cassette or 32K diskette • TRS-80 Color Computer; 16K with expanded BASIC; cassette • Apple II; 32K with Applesoft in ROM (DOS 3.2 or 3.3)

Language: BASIC

Source Code: yes

Price: $24.95

Package consists primarily of drill and practice programs on U.S. and world history and geography. Programs are for all computers listed, unless otherwise noted in descriptions. Written instructions provided.

REVOLUTIONARY WAR QUIZ - In this game, two players compete in answering questions on Revolutionary War. Program is written in such a fashion that it would be relatively easy for user to substitute any questions, thus creating computer quiz on any subject.

REGIONS OF THE U.S. - Drill and practice exercise in which user is asked to identify region of U.S. where randomly selected states are located.

STATES AND CAPITALS - Program drills user on randomly selected states and their capitals. If user does not know capital, computer offers clues to help determine it.

PRESIDENTS - Drill and practice session on presidents of U.S.

COUNTRY - Drill and practice session on countries and continents where they are located. Not available for Commodore.

ID: L14

INVENTIONS THAT CHANGED OUR LIVES

Publisher: Radio Shack®

Date: 1982

Grade: Upper Middle-Secondary

Format: cassette

Hardware: TRS-80 Color Computer; 16K; CTR-80A cassette recorder

Language: BASIC

Source Code: yes

Price: $94.95

Package describes technological achievements through combination of graphics, text, and recorded speech. Topics covered include Edison's Electric Inventions, Bell and the Telephone, The Story of Railroads, and The Age of Television. Part of History of Technology series.

ID: L15
LEARNING CAN BE FUN #7

Publisher: Jensen Software

Grade: 4 and up

Format: cassette or diskette

Hardware: TRS-80 MOD I or III; with Level I or II BASIC

Price: $19.95/cassette; $24.95/diskette

These five programs test world population facts and world geography.

POPULATION OF WORLD CITIES - Object is to list urban areas according to population.

WORLD POPULATION BY COUNTRY - Tests knowledge of the most populated countries of the world.

WORLD AREA BY COUNTRY - Tests knowledge of countries with largest area. Is a take-off point for a more detailed study of the world.

WORLD RECORDS - Tests knowledge of the location of natural and man-made phenomena from Guinness book of records.

AIR DISTANCE BETWEEN CITIES - A chart of the principal cities of the U.S. which will give the distance between any two cities chosen.

ID: L16
OCEANS AND CONTINENTS

Publisher: Micro-Ed, Inc.

Grade: Elementary and up

Format: cassette

Hardware: PET

Language: BASIC

Source Code: no

Price: $14.95

Continents and oceans appear on the screen. The student works with problems that require the identification of each name according to location. Questions missed are placed back into the pool of problems until all are answered correctly.

ID: L17
PIONEERS IN TECHNOLOGY

Publisher: Radio Shack®

Date: 1982

Grade: Upper Middle-Secondary

Format: cassette

Hardware: TRS-80 Color Computer; 16K; CTR-80A cassette recorder

Language: BASIC

Source Code: yes

Price: $94.95

Package describes technological achievements through combination of graphics, text, and recorded speech. Topics covered include The Age of Flight, Space Exploration, The Electric Car, and History of Computers. Part of History of Technology series.

ID: L18
POPULATION

Publisher: Educational Courseware

Also available from: Academic Software • MARCK

Format: diskette

Hardware: Apple II; 48K (DOS 3.3 or 3.2)

Price: $24.00

This disk includes a series of brief studies for any student wishing to learn how various population growth rates affect the population of the world and the USA. Graphic displays of annual populations provide a quick projection into the future. Students can investigate the effects of various population growth rates on the future. The simulated educational "game of life" is also included. Population stability, as well as birth and death trends, can be altered by the student. LIFE, as first developed by *Scientific American*, is an example of a simulation game used in logic. BIRTHDAY, another program on this disk, predicts the probability of two persons in a group having the same birthday.

ID: L19
PRESIDENTS OF THE UNITED STATES

Publisher: APX (Atari Program Exchange)

Also available from: Academic Software

Date: June 82

Grade: 5 and up

Format: cassette or diskette

Hardware: Atari 400 or 800; 24K (cassette) or 32K (diskette)

Language: BASIC

Source Code: no

Price: $15.95

One-player quiz invites player to guess president's name from clues provided. Game operates at novice and advanced levels. Both levels give four clues: term of office, order of presidency, political party, and event or fact about president's term of office or personal life. Choices of clues vary from game to game. User's manual is included.

ID: L20
SOCIAL AND ECONOMIC SIMULATIONS

Publisher: Creative Computing

Also available from: Academic Software • Opportunities For Learning, Inc. • Queue, Inc.

Format: cassette or diskette

Hardware: Apple II Plus • Apple II; 48K with Applesoft in ROM • PET; 16K • TRS-80; 16K (cassette) or 32K (diskette)

Price: $24.95

This package includes background material, sample exercises, study guide, and specially developed graphic displays.

LIMITS - This program, based on the limits to growth study of the Club of Rome, is a world model with five major variables: population, pollution, food supply, industrial output, and resource usage. These are all linked by the birth rate, death rate, pollution generation rate, resource usage rate, industrial growth rate, and food production rate. Varying these can result in extraordinary insights into the possible future of the world.

MARKET - In this program, two people compete with each other in the bicycle manufacturing business. Each has to deal with the production, the advertising, and the pricing of their products and try to make more money than his opponent.

USPOP - This program allows the user to study many aspects of United States demography (population change). This means that the user can investigate the effect of many social changes on population.

ID: L21
SOCIAL STUDIES
Publisher: RIGHT ON PROGRAMS

Also available from: Academic Software • K-12 Micromedia • Queue, Inc.

Grade: 1

Format: cassette or diskette

Hardware: Apple II; 48K with Applesoft in ROM (DOS 3.2 or 3.3) • PET; 16K

Language: BASIC

Source Code: yes

Price: $13.00/cassette; $15.00/diskette

The child is introduced to the basic concepts of farms, farm animals and products raised on farms. The child is then asked a series of matching questions designed to show that s/he has understood the information given.

ID: L22
SOCIAL STUDIES - AMERICAN HISTORY THROUGH BIOGRAPHIES
Publisher: RIGHT ON PROGRAMS

Also available from: Academic Software • K-12 Micromedia • Queue, Inc.

Grade: 4

Format: cassette or diskette

Hardware: Apple II; 48K with Applesoft in ROM (DOS 3.2 or 3.3) • PET; 16K

Language: BASIC

Source Code: yes

Price: $13.00/cassette; $15.00/diskette

In this program, names of famous Americans are introduced with a brief fact or two about each. The period of the Pilgrims, Colonial America and the Westward Movement are covered. Vocabulary and matching games complete program.

ID: L23
SOCIAL STUDIES - AMERICAN INDIANS
Publisher: RIGHT ON PROGRAMS

Also available from: Academic Software • K-12 Micromedia • Queue, Inc.

Grade: 5

Format: cassette or diskette

Hardware: Apple II; 48K with Applesoft in ROM (DOS 3.2 or 3.3) • PET; 16K

Language: BASIC

Source Code: yes

Price: $13.00/cassette; $15.00/diskette

Students will be introduced to the various Indian tribes and the sections of the United States in which they lived. The students will learn new vocabulary and the ways of life of the American Indians. They will also learn about all the things the Indians taught the new Americans and how they helped the new Americans survive in this country.

ID: L24
SOCIAL STUDIES - EARLY CIVILIZATION
Publisher: RIGHT ON PROGRAMS

Also available from: Academic Software • K-12 Micromedia • Queue, Inc.

Grade: 6

Format: cassette or diskette

Hardware: Apple II; 48K with Applesoft in ROM (DOS 3.2 or 3.3) • PET; 16K

Language: BASIC

Source Code: yes

Price: $13.00/cassette; $15.00/diskette

The student is introduced to early Greek and Roman civilization. Famous names and places are given, with information about them.

ID: L25
SOCIAL STUDIES - HOLIDAYS AND FESTIVALS
Publisher: RIGHT ON PROGRAMS

Also available from: Academic Software • K-12 Micromedia • Queue, Inc.

Grade: 2

Format: cassette or diskette

Hardware: Apple II; 48K with Applesoft in ROM (DOS 3.2 or 3.3) • PET; 16K

Language: BASIC

Source Code: yes

Price: $13.00/cassette; $15.00/diskette

This program talks about the national holidays celebrated in this country (with a little basic information about similar holidays in other countries). Vocabulary, games, customs and gifts are included. A matching game tests student's recall of information given.

ID: L26
SOCIAL STUDIES - STATES OF THE UNITED STATES
Publisher: RIGHT ON PROGRAMS

Also available from: Academic Software • K-12 Micromedia • Queue, Inc.

Grade: 5

Format: cassette or diskette

Hardware: Apple II; 48K with Applesoft in ROM (DOS 3.2 or 3.3) • PET; 16K

Language: BASIC

Source Code: yes

This program provides background information on the United States: how many there are, how many there were in the beginning, largest, smallest, why states are famous, and more. Series of matching questions creates a game student enjoys playing and is challenging enough to make the student want to "keep trying" until s/he gets all the answers right.

ID: L27

SOCIAL STUDIES - THE MIDDLE AGES

Publisher: RIGHT ON PROGRAMS

Also available from: Academic Software • K-12 Micromedia • Queue, Inc.

Grade: 6

Format: cassette or diskette

Hardware: Apple II; 48K with Applesoft in ROM (DOS 3.2 or 3.3) • PET; 16K

Language: BASIC

Source Code: yes

Price: $13.00/cassette; $15.00/diskette

The student is introduced to the basic historical facts dealing with the Middle Ages. Political and economic "facts of life" are covered. A game and series of questions encourage the student to learn.

ID: L28

SOCIAL STUDIES - TRANSPORTATION

Publisher: RIGHT ON PROGRAMS

Also available from: Academic Software • K-12 Micromedia • Queue, Inc.

Grade: 2

Format: cassette or diskette

Hardware: Apple II; 48K with Applesoft in ROM (DOS 3.2 or 3.3) • PET; 16K

Language: BASIC

Source Code: yes

Price: $13.00/cassette; $15.00/diskette

A brief history of transportation will be given with emphasis on "how they got where they were going and how long did it take to get there". The program then brings the student to the present time, showing various types of transportation, how important each one is and what each is responsible for.

ID: L29

SOCIAL STUDIES - VOLUME 1

Publisher: Minnesota Educational Computing Consortium

Date: June 82

Grade: 8-12

Format: diskette

Hardware: Apple II; 32K with Applesoft in ROM (DOS 3.3); printer optional for some programs

Language: Applesoft BASIC

Source Code: no

Price: $36.80

Package contains some of programs developed by Huntington II project. Support booklet included.

LIMITS - Program simulates resource use of world of future.

ELECT1, ELECT2, ELECT3 - Election series simulates presidential elections.

POLICY - Simulates impact of special interest groups on policy formation.

USPOP - Program projects U.S. population into future.

ENERGY, FUTURE - Programs developed at N.W. Regional Lab deal with issues of energy supplies in future.

ID: L30

SOCIAL STUDIES - VOLUME 2

Publisher: Minnesota Educational Computing Consortium

Also available from: Scholastic Software

Date: June 82

Grade: 7-12

Format: diskette

Hardware: Apple II; 32K with Applesoft in ROM (DOS 3.3); printer optional for some programs

Language: Applesoft BASIC

Source Code: no

Price: $43.40

Package includes both simulation and drill and practice programs. Support booklet included.

STATES, STATES2 - Drill and practice programs which deal with U.S. states and capitals.

COUNTRY - Drill and practice program which identifies capitals of various countries.

CONTINENT - Drill and practice program which identifies continents and countries.

MINNAG - Allows users to explore factors in Minnesota agriculture.

BARGAIN - Simulates collective bargaining process in labor relations.

FAIL SAFE - Simulates nuclear war situation, based on novel of same name.

CRISIS - Simulates military confrontation in Berlin.

ID: L31

SOCIAL STUDIES - WORLD DESERT REGIONS

Publisher: RIGHT ON PROGRAMS

Also available from: Academic Software • K-12 Micromedia • Queue, Inc.

Grade: 3

Format: cassette or diskette

Hardware: Apple II; 48K with Applesoft in ROM (DOS 3.2 or 3.3) • PET; 16K

Language: BASIC

Source Code: yes

Price: $13.00/cassette; $15.00/diskette

Student is introduced to background information on this particular climate region of the world. Animals that live in that climate are discussed, as are birds, trees, and flowers, if appropriate. A series of matching questions provides a game which checks the student's retention of the material.

ID: L32

SOCIAL STUDIES - WORLD POLAR REGIONS

Publisher: RIGHT ON PROGRAMS

Also available from: Academic Software • K-12 Micromedia • Queue, Inc.

Grade: 3

Format: cassette or diskette

Hardware: Apple II; 48K with Applesoft in ROM (DOS 3.2 or 3.3) • PET; 16K

Language: BASIC

Source Code: yes

Price: $13.00/cassette; $15.00/diskette

Student is introduced to background information on this particular climate region of the world. Animals that live in that climate are discussed, as are birds, trees and flowers, if appropriate. A series of matching questions provides a game which checks the student's retention of material.

ID: L33

STATES AND CAPITALS

Publisher: Micro-Ed, Inc.

Also available from: Queue, Inc.

Grade: Elementary and up

Format: cassette or diskette

Hardware: Commodore 64 • PET

Language: BASIC

Source Code: no

Price: $7.95

This program randomly selects either the name of a state (in which case the learner is to supply the name of its capital), or the name of its capital (in which case the learner is to supply the name of the state). A game-like format is used. Six wizards appear with numbers on their foreheads. The student must try to erase all these numbers by answering questions correctly. At the end of the lesson, the student's performance is summarized.

ID: L34

STATES GAME

Publisher: BrainBank, Inc.

Also available from: Academic Software • K-12 Micromedia • Queue, Inc.

Grade: 4 and up

Format: cassette or diskette

Hardware: Apple; 16K • PET; 16K • TRS-80; 16K

Price: $50.00

THE STATES GAME includes five games for 1 to 4 players. Students can learn facts about history and geography as they guess the states from descriptive clues.

ID: L35

TRUCKER, STREETS OF THE CITY

Publisher: Creative Computing

Also available from: Academic Software • Opportunities For Learning, Inc. • Queue, Inc.

Format: diskette

Hardware: Apple II Plus • Apple II; 48K with Applesoft in ROM • PET; 32K • Atari 800 or 400; 40K

Price: $24.95

These simulations include background material, sample exercises and specially developed graphics.

TRUCKER - This program simulates coast-to-coast trips by an independent trucker hauling various cargos. The user may haul oranges, freight or U.S. mail. All have different risks and rewards. Maximum profit comes from prudent risk-taking. If all goes well, the driver can obey the speed limits, stop for eight hours of sleep each night and still meet the schedule. Bad weather, road construction or flat tires may put the rig behind schedule. The driver may try to increase profit by skimping on sleep, driving fast or carrying an over-weight load. Other factors are choice of routes, truck payments, fuel, food, tolls and fines. The simulation is engrossing and informative.

STREETS OF THE CITY - This simulation is modeled on Grand Rapids, Michigan, a metropolitan area with a population of 550,000. The budgeting, cost and work standard bases are derived from actual experiences of the city over the past five years. The objective of the simulation is to complete a ten-year plan of street and transit improvements while retaining the support of a majority of the City Commission. During one's tenure, the player must construct streets and interstate highways, repair existing streets, and improve traffic safety. For the Transit Authority one must upgrade and replace a dilapidated bus fleet, increase ridership, reduce maintenance downtime and improve on-schedule performance. Other factors to be considered are operating tax levies, construction bonding and labor negotiations. The simulation provides a substantial challenge and it is both educational and entertaining.

ID: L36

WHO BUILT AMERICA

Publisher: RIGHT ON PROGRAMS

Date: Aug. 82

Grade: 4

Format: cassette or diskette

Hardware: Apple II; 48K with Applesoft in ROM (DOS 3.2 or 3.3) • PET; 16K

Language: BASIC

Source Code: yes

Price: $13.00/cassette; $15.00/diskette

For over 300 years, men and women have come to America to begin new lives. Some came to escape persecution, others to seek fame and fortune. Why they came, what they brought and what they gave is discussed with emphasis on how they made America great and why they were all welcome. Game follows.

ID: L37

WORLD MOUNTAIN REGIONS

Publisher: RIGHT ON PROGRAMS

Date: Aug. 82

Grade: 3

Format: cassette or diskette

Hardware: Apple II; 48K with Applesoft in ROM (DOS 3.2 or 3.3) • PET; 16K

Language: BASIC

Source Code: yes

Price: $13.00/cassette; $15.00/diskette

Student is introduced to basic, background information on this particular climate region of the world. Animals that live in climate are discussed as are birds, trees, and flowers if appropriate. Series of matching questions provides game which is fun and checks student's retention of material.

ID: L38

YOUR COMMUNITY

Publisher: RIGHT ON PROGRAMS

Date: July 82

Grade: 1

Format: cassette or diskette

Hardware: Apple II; 48K with Applesoft in ROM (DOS 3.2 or 3.3) • PET; 16K

Language: BASIC

Source Code: yes

Price: $13.00/cassette; $15.00/diskette

Different types of neighborhoods are included in this program: urban, residential, suburban, rural. Different uses of land are shown: recreation, farms, industry, streets, homes, offices. The program shows how the type of land and its use influence the inds of neighborhoods that grow in vicinity. Game follows.

PUBLISHERS AND DISTRIBUTORS

APX (Atari Program Exchange)

Atari Inc.
P.O. Box 427
Sunnyvale, CA 94086

(800)538-1862

(800)672-1850 (CA)

APX - Atari Program Exchange - was created to distribute user written software for Atari computers. In many cases, the author provides support for the software. The quarterly catalog is sent free to all those who have sent in a warranty card for an Atari home computer. Others may purchase a catalog for $2.00.

Software may be ordered by mail, or by calling the toll free number. There is a $10.00 minimum order, and a $2.50 charge for shipping/handling. Acceptable means of payment are check, money order, VISA or MasterCard. Shipping is by UPS. APX programs are not guaranteed in any way. No returns are accepted, except for goods damaged in shipment. Some programs may be temporarily unavailable.

Abbott Educational Software

Richard A. Brown, PhD
334 Westwood Avenue
East Longmeadow, MA 01028

(413)525-3462

Schools desiring preview of Abbott software should contact Abbott; requests will be considered on a case-by-case basis.

Abbott software is available by mail from the publisher, J.L. Hammett, or K-12 Micromedia. Users are urged to make a backup copy of software when received.

Academic Computing Association

P.O. Box 27561
Phoenix, AZ 85061

Software produced by ACA is written with the COurseware DElivery System, or CODES, a processor for computer presented drill and instruction. CODES will run on most computers. ACA offers workshops, manuals, and starter kits on the use of CODES.

Minimum computer size is 16K with Floating Point arithmetic. For computers other than Apple, PET, or TRS-80, contact ACA for information.

All ACA software is copyrighted; one copy may be made by the purchaser for backup. For those needing multiple copies, a substantial discount is available. All materials are sold "as is", with no warranty.

Academic Software

Div. of Software City
22 E. Quackenbush Avenue
Dumont, NJ 07628

(201)385-2395

Academic Software is a distributor carrying programs from many different publishers and software houses. Catalogs are available by model; the prices of the catalogs vary.

While software is not available on approval, full refund or credit is available if the program is returned within 30 days. A brief note explaining why the program was not suitable should accompany the returned item.

Minimum order is $50.00. Discounts are as follows: 5% on orders over $500.00, 10% on orders over $1000.00, 15% on orders over $1500.00, and 20% on orders over $2000.00. Prepaid orders have an additional 2% discount on net cost.

Prices are identical to the manufacturers'. Orders will be shipped on open account upon receipt of authorized purchase order and bank reference. Invoice will accompany shipment and is payable within 10 days.

For Apple disks, specify DOS 3.2 or 3.3. For TRS-80 disks, specify Model I or III. For PET, specify Old ROM or New ROM.

Acorn Software Products, Inc.

634 North Carolina Ave, SE
Washington, DC 20003

(202)544-4259

Acorn does not have a preview policy. Programs will be replaced within 90 days of purchase free of charge if found to be defective. After 90 days, the replacement charge is $6.00.

Orders should be accompanied by check, money order or charge card information.

Activity Resources Company, Inc.

P.O. Box 4875
Hayward, CA 94540

Activity Resources is an educational supply house with a limited amount of software available (all from QED). Their prices are the same as those from the publisher.

Claims for returns should be made in writing within two weeks of receipt of order. Material should not be returned until buyer is instructed to do so.

Add $1.50 handling fee. For orders less than $15.00, add $1.00 shipping; for those over $15.00, add 8%.

Addison-Wesley Publishing Company

Reading, MA 01867

(617)944-3700

Addison-Wesley has six regional offices to serve their users; sales representatives in these offices will make arrangements for previews. Sales are subject to 30-day approval. All packages include a backup diskette. Defective diskettes will be replaced free of charge. Orders from individuals must be accompanied by payment. No shipping is charged for prepaid orders.

All 7 volumes of the COMPUTER MATH GAMES may be purchased as a set for $270.00. Volumes 1-3 of COMPUTER GRAPHING EXPERIMENTS may be purchased as a set for $120.00.

Advanced Learning Technology see Learning Company

Apple Computer, Inc.

Special Delivery Software
20525 Mariani Avenue
Cupertino, CA 95014

(408)996-1010

Apple programs may be previewed at Apple dealers. Software must be purchased from dealers. Most packages include a backup diskette.

Aquarius Publishers Inc.

P.O. Box 128
Indian Rocks Beach, FL 33535

(813)595-7890

All materials are copyrighted, and may not be reproduced without prior written permission. Requests for permission to reproduce, modify, or translate materials should be addressed to the Service Manager. Institutions will be granted a 30-day preview privilege upon request. Payment is net 30 days. Shipping and handling are 6% of invoice. For rush orders, call collect.

Atari Program Exchange *see* APX

Avant-Garde Creations

P.O. Box 30160
Eugene, OR 97403

(503)345-3043

All orders must be prepaid, COD or bankcard. Add a $2.00 postage and handling fee for the first disk; $.50 for each additional disk. Defective or nonloading disks will be replaced free of charge if returned within 30 days of invoice.

Avant-Garde is a software publisher, but also distributes software produced by other firms.

BLS Inc.

Random House School Division
2503 Fairlee Road
Wilmington, DE 19810

(302)478-2451

(800)638-6460

BLS programs may be previewed on a 30-day basis. They must be returned with invoice in salable condition for credit. Customers may also purchase sample lessons with price to be applied later to full purchase. Also, demonstration disks are available through dealers.

Prices for complete Tutorcourses reflect a 10% savings over single lesson prices. A 25% discount applies to orders of six or more copies of the same courseware. School prices reflect 25% discount off publisher's list prices. Purchase orders are honored. Defective courseware will be replaced free of charge within 60 days.

The current catalog includes 164 lessons of a 727-lesson series. An additional 187 lessons in Apple format will be available in September, 1982 (as well as some in TRS-80 format).

Basics and Beyond, Inc.

P.O. Box 10
Pinesbridge Rd.
Amawalk, NY 10501

(914)962-2355

Orders must be accompanied by a purchase order, check or credit card information. A 30-day money-back guarantee backs all software.

Bell & Howell Microcomputer Systems

Audio-Visual Products Division
7100 N. McCormick Road
Chicago, IL 60645

(312)262-1600

Bell & Howell offers a series of programs for computer-assisted instruction. Generalized Instructional Systems, or GENIS, is composed of two interrelated software systems that can be used independently or together. Bell & Howell's microcomputer is an Apple II Plus (48K). All Bell & Howell programs may be run on an Apple II Plus, and all programs compatible with the Apple will run on the Bell & Howell machine.

Borg-Warner Educational Systems

600 W. University Drive
Arlington Heights, IL 60004

(312)394-1010

(800)323-7577

Borg-Warner software is available through purchase or on a subscription basis to qualified institutions. After the first year, materials may be renewed for an annual fee of one-half the initial charge. Damaged disks will be replaced at no charge.

For those desiring a demonstration, a sales call may be arranged by calling the toll free number. Customer service at this number is excellent.

The teacher's guide included with all software explains specific procedures, while providing behavioral objectives. Management systems built into the programs keep student records.

All Borg-Warner software is for use with the Apple II Plus. New programs planned are SENTENCE STRUCTURE, COMPUTATION, and MATH PROBLEM SOLVING.

Brain Box *see* BrainBank, Inc.

BrainBank, Inc.

Suite 408
220 Fifth Ave
New York, NY 10001

(212)686-6565

A $30.00 demo disk with representative programs is available; purchase price will be deducted when two or more titles are ordered. BrainBank offers a discount plan. For each package ordered, up to five additional packages may be purchased for 60% off.

Each title is packaged in a Courseware Kit with a teacher guide. Graphics on the Apple are programmed in color, but will also be effective in black-and-white. All programs are written for 16K.

The BrainBank catalog offers very little descriptive information; published reviews, however, have been quite favorable.

COMPU-TATIONS, Inc.

P.O. Box 502
Troy, MI 48099

(313)524-3217

COMPU-TATIONS, Inc., software is not available for preview. Programs are sold through dealers and distributors, as well as by direct mail. Michigan residents must add sales tax; add $2.00 for shipping and handling. On purchases of 5-9 items, 10% may be deducted from total price; on purchase of 10 or more, 40% may be deducted.

All software is guaranteed to load and run. Defective software will be replaced. Specify DOS required when ordering.

COMPress
P.O. Box 102
Wentworth, NH 03282

(603)764-5831

COMPress, a division of Science Books International, produces software for high school, college and adult use. Materials are available for 30-day preview for a charge of $10.00, which will be applied to the purchase price.

Software is copyrighted, and may not be duplicated. Additional copies may be purchased for $10.00/diskette. All disks are warranted to be free of defects under normal use for 90 days.

CONDUIT
100 Lindquist Center
Univ. of Iowa P.O. Box 388
Iowa City, IA 52244

(319)353-5789

CONDUIT does not allow preview of specific software packages, but a demonstration kit for use with the Apple II may be borrowed or purchased. All material may be returned for refund within 30 days. After 30 days (up to 6 months), the purchaser will be charged $10.00. Also, if incorrect software is ordered, a $10.00 fee will be charged.

Software was originally intended for college level instruction, but more and more schools are finding the materials useful for senior high. All software included in this directory was recommended for senior high by the publisher. CONDUIT also publishes *Pipeline*, a biannual magazine on computer use in education.

Comaldor
P.O. Box 356
Postal Station O
Toronto, Ontario M4a2N9

(416)751-7481

Software is available on approval. Defective tape or disks will be replaced. Comaldor will revise programs for specific uses upon request. Most authors are teachers from Ontario who have classroom tested the software.

Compumax, Inc.
P.O. Box 7239
Menlo Park, CA 94025

(415)854-6700

Compumax offers a demonstration diskette for $30.00. No other previews are available. Defective software will be exchanged, but no other returns will be accepted.

Computer Assisted Library Instruction Co., Inc. (CALICO)
P.O. Box 15916
St. Louis, MO 63114

CALICO does not offer previews, but a $5.00 SAMPLER includes examples from all programs. The SAMPLER is available on loan for workshops; purchase price may be deducted from first software order.

All sales are final; add $1.50 for shipping and handling, and 4 5/8% sales tax in Missouri.

Convergent Systems Inc.
245 E. 6th Street
St. Paul, MN 55101

(612)221-0587

All software from Convergent Systems may be borrowed for a fee of $20.00, which will be taken off the purchase price. A 100-page instructor's manual, available for $10.00, includes prints of screens and commentary.

Defective disks will be replaced within 30 days. A preview policy has not been set.

The shift key adaptor required to use Convergent Systems software is included in the package price.

Cow Bay Computing
P.O. Box 515
Manhasset, NY 11030

Cow Bay Computing offers three workbooks for the PET users -- *Feed Me, I'm Your PET COMPUTER*, *Looking Good With Your PET*, and the *Teacher's PET*.

No preview or other policies are available.

Creative Computing
Dept. TS2
One Park Avenue, Room 458
New York, NY 10016

(800)345-8112

(800)662-2442 (PA)

Creative Computing publishes a popular microcomputer magazine in addition to distributing software. The software available from them is published by software houses which are not identified in the catalog.

Orders must be accompanied by payment or bankcard information. Credit card holders may order by phone. (Minimum is $10.00)

Curriculum Applications
P.O. Box 264
Arlington, MA 02174

Software from Curriculum Applications has been tested and modified in schools. Teachers or users can modify program complexity before use. Programs are written in upper and lower case; on systems without lower case, all display will be in upper case.

Any program that fails to load will be replaced (with a refund of mailing costs). There is no other warranty expressed or implied other than a guarantee that the courseware will load and work.

Copies of published reviews are included with the catalog material.

Data Command

P.O. Box 548
Kankakee, IL 60901

(815)933-7735

Data Command software is available on an "on approval" purchase option by special arrangement through dealers or distributors. Institutional purchase orders will be honored.

Dr. Daley's Software

Water Street
Darby, MT 59829

(406)821-3924

(800)548-3289

Dr. Daley's software has a demo disk, or "automated brochure" for $5.00; a software library demo disk with manual is available for $25.00. Institutional purchase orders, check, bankcard or COD orders are accepted. Shipping charges are 2% for the U.S.; 5% for Mexico and Canada.

Duxbury Systems, Inc.

77 Great Road
Acton, MA 07120

(617)263-7761

Duxbury Systems has become a leader in computerized braille systems. Contact Customer Relations for information on customized systems.

EISI (Educational Instructional Systems, Inc.)

2225 Grant Road
Suite 3
Los Altos, CA 94022

(415)969-5212

EISI distributes educational software from Eduware, Data Command, MicroEd, Microphys, Software Technology, Milliken, and Edu-Ware. Prices are the same as the publishers'.

All publishers represented guarantee the quality of their software. Faulty software will be replaced at no charge by EISI within 30 days if the defective software is returned. Contact EISI for individual backup policies. Specify model when ordering.

Edu-Soft^{T.M.}

Steketee Educational Software
4639 Spruce Street
Philadelphia, PA 19139

(215)747-1284

Edu-Soft software is guaranteed to load and run properly. Disks may be copied for backup only. Schools may prepay or order with valid purchase order. Add $2.00 shipping and handling for orders shipped within North America. Specify model when ordering.

Edu-Soft programs are classroom tested. Cassette versions may not include all features of the diskette version on the Atari programs.

Edu-Ware Services

28035 Dorothy Drive
Agoura, CA 91301

(213)706-0661

Edu-Ware® software is available through local computer stores or directly from Edu-Ware Services, Customer Sales Department. When ordering directly, include $2.00 for shipping and handling. Credit card orders are not accepted.

Software is supported after sale by a 30-day limited warranty, rapid service, and low-cost updates and replacements.

EduTech

634 Commonwealth Ave
Newton Centre, MA 02159

(617)965-4813

Selected software is available for a 30-day free trial. All material may be returned within 15 days for full credit. Diskettes damaged within 2 years of purchase can be returned for replacement at no charge.

Diskettes are copy protected

All orders must be prepaid or on an institutional purchase order form.

Educational Activities, Inc.

P.O. Box 392
Freeport, NY 11520

(516)223-4666 (NY)

(800)645-3739

All software is available for review to educational institutions. Consultants and programmers are available to help with software problems; consultants are also available for workshops.

All personal orders must be accompanied by check, money order or bankcard information. Any item found defective or damaged will be replaced at no charge. Direct inquiries to Customer Service. Specify model when ordering. Currently software is available for Apple, PET and TRS-80, and will be available soon for Atari.

Educational Courseware

3 Nappa Lane
Westport, CT 06880

All orders, except those from schools on a purchase order, must be prepaid. Add $2.00 ($3.50 foreign) for mailing costs to total order. Connecticut residents add 7.5% tax. Shipments will be made within 24 hours. All disks are DOS 3.3 unless 3.2 is specified in the order.

A sample of educational programs is available for $12.00. Examples include simulation, tutorial, CAI, and drill and practice.

Grade levels for software are not indicated in the catalog.

Educational Micro Systems Inc.

P.O. Box 471
Chester, NJ 07930

(201)879-5982

Educational Micro Systems does not allow preview for direct mail customers. All materials are copyrighted; one backup copy may be made.

The catalog descriptions for this publisher are very complete. Copies of published reviews are included with the catalog.

Educulture

1 Dubuque Plaza
Suite 803
Dubuque, IA 52001

(319)557-9610 (IA)

(800)553-4858

Educulture produces one software package, due to be released in 1982. They offer a free 30-day examination package which may be returned or purchased for $25.00 plus $3.00 postage and handling. Institutional purchase orders are accepted. Defective items may be returned for exchange within a reasonable period of time.

Eiconics, Inc.

P.O. Box 1207
211 Cruz Alta Road
Taos, NM 87571

(505)758-1696

A demonstration package for the Eureka learning system consists of a teacher's guide and four lessons.

Purchase of the system includes a perpetual license for use by one educational entity. Licenses are available free of charge to established educational software evaluation centers. One year of software maintenance is included; contracts for further maintenance are available.

Royalty contracts are available for duplication and distribution of courses developed using the system. Training is available for users at all levels of sophistication.

Eiconics is considering the establishment of a money-back guarantee or a 30- to 60-day preview period. Customers are encouraged to make copies of the program disk for backup.

Electronic Courseware Systems, Inc. (ECS)

P.O. Box 2374
Station A
Champaign, IL 61820

(217)359-7099

ECS will send software on preview for up to a month. Materials may not be copied for backup, nor are backup copies available. Any damaged disks will be replaced at nominal cost. Prepaid orders will be shipped postage free. Illinois residents add 5% sales tax.

Fireside Computing see MicroGnome

GRAFex Company

P.O. Box 1558
Cupertino, CA 95015

(408)996-2689

GRAFex is a distributor handling Atari software. They currently do not have a preview policy. Purchase orders are accepted.

Gregg/ McGraw-Hill

1221 Avenue of the Americas
New York, NY 10020

(800)223-4180

(212)997-2646 (NY)

Gregg software is available through license agreement rather than through purchase. Copyright restrictions permit one backup copy to be made; Gregg will supply one backup copy for those programs which are write-protected. All other copies or derivative works must be authorized by the publisher.

A hotline is provided for customer questions.

Programs are not available for preview; however, a demonstration disk is available for $6.00.

Hartley Courseware, Inc.

P.O. Box 431
Dimondale, MI 48821

(616)942-8987

Hartley provides a free backup copy of any disk priced over $50.00. There is no charge for replacement of damaged disks within 60 days, or for replacement of disks with program bugs. Within two years of purchase, replacement copies are available for $6.00/disk. Payment is due 30 days from shipment date.

Student records are automatically kept for each student using a disk. This Student Planning file will hold up to 100 students. It may be erased at any time to allow for new records.

Modification of lesson content is made easy by a special program on each disk. Most programs have a CREATE capability to allow the teacher to add lessons.

A cassette control device (CCD) is available for $79.95 for use with indicated courseware. It allows the teacher to present additional directions.

Hayden Book Company, Inc.

50 Essex Street
Rochelle Park, NJ 07662

(800)631-0856

Software is not available for preview. Check or money order must be enclosed with order. Hayden pays postage and handling. Residents of New Jersey and California add sales tax. Programs are warranted to load and run.

Houghton Mifflin see TSC[T.M.]

Ideatech Company

P.O. Box 62451
Sunnyvale, CA 94088

(408)985-7591

Software is not available for preview, however, any software may be returned within 10 days of receipt for refund, less shipping charges. Shipment must include a signed statement indicating that the software was not copied.

If software does not function properly, return with a note stating the nature of the difficulty. Ideatech will replace or repair the disk. Damaged disks will be replaced for $5.00. Replacement will be mailed within 10 days of receipt of the damaged disk.

Instant Software[T.M.]

Peterborough, NH 03458

(800)343-0728

Programs from Instant Software are not available for preview. Materials may be purchased from dealers or from the publisher by phone or mail. Purchase orders are accepted. Freight will be paid on prepaid orders. The Instant Software catalog, which costs $1.00, contains coupons redeemable from dealers. Defective products may be returned for exchange or credit.

Interpretive Education, Inc.

157 S. Kalamazoo Mall
P.O. Box 3176
Kalamazoo, MI 49003

(616)345-8681

Previews of Interpretive Education programs are not available, but a demonstration kit is available on loan for 10 days by special request. All materials are copyrighted and copy-locked.

J & S Software, Inc.

140 Reid Avenue
Port Washington, NY 11050

(516)944-9304

J & S Software provides a demonstration disk for purchasers who need preview. Science programs are not copy-protected. J & S approves copying and modification of programs by individuals within a school building, but not copying by school districts for distribution to schools within that district.

J.L. Hammett

Microcomputer Division
Box 545
Braintree, MA 02184

(800)225-5467

(800)972-5056 (MA)

Jagdstaffel Software

608 Blossom Hill Road
San Jose, CA 95123

(408)578-1643

Jagdstaffel has no formal preview policy. Institutional purchase orders are accepted. Individuals must enclose a check or money order for full amount, plus $2.50 for shipping and handling. California residents add state and local sales tax. Defective software will be replaced free of charge.

Jensen Software

Box 535
Happy, TX 79042

Jensen Software has no preview policy. Orders are shipped within 48 hours, and the company pays shipping in the continental U.S.

K-12 Micromedia

P.O. Box 17
Valley Cottage, NY 10989

(201)391-7555

K-12 Micromedia is a distributor carrying software from many educational publishers and software houses. Their catalog sells for $2.95. They also offer books, kits, filmstrips and blank cassettes and diskettes. Prices are generally identical to original publisher retail.

All K-12 Micromedia software orders that are prepaid or on a valid purchase order are available for 30-day approval. Individuals should include payment in full. Indicate type, model, memory, cassette or diskette, and DOS.

Krell Software Corporation

1320 StonyBrook Road
Stony Brook, NY 11790

(516)751-5139

Krell does not send software for preview. A demonstration can be arranged by calling the New York office. Shipping costs will be paid on prepaid orders. All defective software will be replaced within one year of purchase.

L & S Computerware

1589 Fraser Drive
Sunnyvale, CA 94087

(408)738-3416

(800)227-1617 EXT481

(800)772-3545 (CA)

L & S software carries a lifetime warranty. Defective software will be replaced free within 90 days; after 90 days, the replacement charge is $5.00.

Learning Company

4370 Alpine Road,
Portola Valley, CA 94025

(415)851-3160

Learning Company software is not available for preview. A demo disk with a sample of all programs is available for $50.00.

Learning Company software is based on a game format. Programs are very colorful; much would be lost on a noncolor monitor. All of the games are available from Apple dealers or directly from the publisher. Qualified schools are entitled to a 10% discount on the unit price.

California residents add 6.5% sales tax. Shipping and handling charge is $2.00. Defective programs will be replaced within 90 days of purchase.

Little Bee Educational Programs

P.O. Box 262
Massilon, OH 44648

Little Bee programs are guaranteed. If they do not meet specifications or do not work, they may be returned for replacement or refund. A note describing the reason for return must be included.

MARCK

280 Linden Avenue
Branford, CT 06405

(203)481-3271

MARCK is a distributor carrying software for Apple, Atari, PET and TRS-80. Their prices are identical to those of the original publishers. The MARCK catalog is $4.95, deductible from the first order. Minimum order is $50.00. 10% billing/handling charge should be added unless order is prepaid. Add 20% surcharge on orders outside of the U.S. or Canada. Connecticut residents add 7 1/2% sales tax.

MARCK also offers consulting services to provide assistance to educators and business people.

Math Software

1233 Blackthorn Place
Deerfield, IL 60015

Math Software sells their software only to schools. Terms are net 30 days with 1.5% service charge per month after 30 days. Discounts are available to school systems purchasing software for use in multiple locations.

Defective software returned within 7 days will be replaced provided software has not been altered. Software orders cannot be returned for credit or refund. If you purchase the SAMPLER, $40.00 will be credited to the purchase of any package made within 30 days.

Mathware/Math City

4040 Palos Verdes Drive N.
Rolling Hills Estates, CA 90274

(213)541-3377

(213)541-1570

Mathware is a private institution which specializes in teaching mathematics. They have been developing software for several years. Programs will be sent to educational institutions on a 2-week trial basis. If software is found to be inappropriate, it may be returned within 30 days of purchase, and full refund will be issued.

All diskettes are guaranteed unconditionally for 3 months. After 3 months, they will be replaced at $10.00/disk. Discounts are available for quantity purchases.

McGraw-Hill *see* Gregg/McGraw-Hill

McKilligan Supply Corp.

435 Main Street
Johnson City, NY 13790

(607)729-6511

McKilligan offers hardware, software, and books. Their catalog is free to schools, and $2.00 to individuals. Prices are generally about the same as the original publisher's. Publishers are not identified in the catalog.

Software is supplied "as is", without warranty. McKilligan assumes no liability or responsibility for loss or damage. Manufacturers' warranties are included with the software. Purchase orders and bankcard orders accepted. Minimum order is $15.00. Specify model, memory, and disk or cassette.

Merlan Scientific Ltd.

247 Armstrong Avenue
Georgetown, Ontario L7G 4X6,

(416)877-0171

(416)846-0646

Merlan Scientific software may be ordered on a 30-day approval basis with written confirmation that programs will not be copied. A demonstration disk is available for $100.00. Institutional purchase orders are honored.

Metrologic Publications

143 Harding Avenue
Bellmawr, NJ 08031

Metrologic Publications offers one program - PHYSICS LABS EXPERIMENTS - which was developed in conjunction with Microphys. Further information and free examination copies are available from Metrologic.

Micro Learningware

P.O. Box 2134
North Mankato, MN 56001

(507)625-2205

All software may be returned within 30 days. Orders must be prepaid or accompanied by a signed school district purchase order. VISA and MasterCard are accepted. Minnesota residents add 5% sales tax. Specify model when ordering.

Micro Music Software Library
Musitronic

P.O. Box 441
555 Park Drive
Owatonna, MN 55060

(507)451-7871

Micro Music software is available on 10-day preview upon request.

Micro Power & Light Company

12820 Hillcrest Road
Suite 224
Dallas, TX 75230

(214)239-6620

Micro Power & Light offers three purchase options: 1.) for one protected copy of disk, pay retail price; 2.) for two copies of each program (1 backup), pay retail price plus $15.00; 3.) for customer needing multiple copies, pay retail price plus $180.00; customer will receive one unprotected disk.

Educational institutions, government agencies, and nonprofit organizations receive a 10% discount. Payment options are prepaid, net 30 days (include $5.00 shipping and handling charge), and COD. (also a $5.00 charge). Defective disks will be replaced free within 60 days

Micro-Ed, Inc.

P.O. Box 24156
Minneapolis, MN 55424

(612)926-2292

Micro-Ed catalogs are available for Apple, TI, PET, VIC, TRS-80 and Commodore 64. The software covers a large range of subjects; most is on the elementary level.

Orders are payable within 30 days; software may be returned within that time. Defective software may be returned for replacement at any time.

Programs for the TI are currently available only on diskette, but cassettes will soon be available.

MicroGnome

Division of Fireside Computing, Inc.
5843 Montgomery Rd.
Elkridge, MD 21227

(301)796-4165

MicroGnome software may be previewed at state, city and county educational software centers. Programs may be purchased from computer dealers or through Fireside Computing.

Microcomputer Workshops

103 Puritan Drive
Port Chester, NY 10573

Software ordered by schools on a purchase order may be returned for full refund within 30 days of delivery. Microcomputer Workshops' software is written by classroom teachers and tested in the classroom environment.

Microphys Programs

2048 Ford Street
Brooklyn, NY 11229

(212)646-0140

Microphys Programs are available for preview to any teacher who requests one or two programs on school letterhead. A demonstration disk is available to school resource or computer centers. Purchase orders are honored. Returns allowed for defective disks only.

Milliken Publishing Company

1100 Research Blvd.
St. Louis, MO 63132

(314)991-4220

Milliken will arrange for a demonstration of their software upon request. All diskettes have a 30-day warranty. Defective diskettes will be replaced if mailed to Milliken. After warranty period, worn disks will be replaced for $10.00 (for up to 12 months). After that time, current retail price will be charged for replacements.

Milton Bradley

443 Shaker Road
East Longmeadow, MA 01028

(413)525-6411

Milton Bradley software is available through Apple dealers and major school suppliers. A demodisk containing portions of all seven programs is available from the publisher for $5.00 (teacher's guide $6.00).

Defective disks will be replaced free within 30 days of purchase. Disks damaged in use will be replaced for $20.00 if the old disk is sent to Milton Bradley.

Each software unit contains a built-in management system which holds up to 120 student records.

Minnesota Educational Computing Consortium

2520 Broadway Drive
St. Paul, MN 55113

(612)638-0627

A demonstration diskette and support booklet for the Apple computer are available to non-Minnesota customers for $34.60. The prices to MECC member agencies are $15.00 for the diskette, and $2.30 for the booklet. Atari versions are available to non-members for $35.00 (includes diskette and booklet), and to members for $15.00 for the diskette and $2.50 for the booklet.

MECC offers a Non-Minnesota Educational Institutional Agreement Policy for volume purchasing and distribution of software to non-profit educational agencies outside of Minnesota.

Minimum order is $5.00. Payment by check or money order must accompany orders of $20.00 or less. Orders over $20.00 may be accompanied by institutional purchase order. No telephone orders are accepted.

Incomplete orders or defective disks will be replaced only if MECC is notified within 30 days.

Prices listed are for users outside of Minnesota (i.e., non-consortium members); they are almost invariably twice that charged to members, since member agencies pay MECC development costs.

Opportunities For Learning, Inc.

8950 Lurline Ave.
Dept. 26C
Chatsworth, CA 91311

(213)341-2535

Opportunities for Learning is an educational supply house offering software for the Apple, TRS-80, Atari and PET machines. They do not have materials available for preview; however, items ordered on school purchase order forms or prepaid may be accepted for return within the first 30 days if they are found to be unsuitable. Before returning any items, contact the office; no items will be accepted for return without prior notification. Shortages and damaged or defective items must be reported within 15 days of receipt.

Minimum order is $25.00. A shipping and handling charge of 10% of the total will be added to invoices under $99.00. This charge will be 8% on invoices over $100.00. Orders from individuals must be accompanied by a check, money order, or credit card information.

Orange Cherry Media

7 Delano Drive
Bedford Hills, NY 10507

(914)666-8434

Orange Cherry Media does not send software for preview. Schools and institutions may order on purchase order; orders from individuals or businesses should be accompanied by payment. Payment must accompany all orders of $20.00 or less. Terms are net 30 days.

All materials are protected by copyright. Permission for a license for unlimited duplication is available to educational institutions on the following schedule: $36.00 - unlimited duplication of individual cassette program; $144.00 - unlimited duplication for set of four; $50.00 - unlimited duplication of individual cassette.

Orange Cherry Media has a Lifetime Replacement Policy. All software will be replaced free if damaged or accidentally erased at any time. A small handling and postage fee is charged.

A Complete Math Skills Series (25 programs) is available for $325.00.

Program Design, Inc.

11 Idar Court
Greenwich, CT 06830

(203)661-8799

PDI does not have a preview policy. Software is guaranteed; defective programs will be replaced free of charge. PDI products are available through dealers or by direct mail. Shipping and handling charges will be added. Volume discounts are available.

Programs For Learning, Inc.

P.O. Box 954
New Milford, CT 06776

(203)355-3452

Programs are sold with full return privileges; if programs do not meet expected needs, the invoice will be cancelled or payment refunded. Software that fails to load properly will be replaced. A special preview/demonstration disk is available if requested on school letterhead and signed by an authorized administrator. This disk contains 15 programs and may be kept for 15 days.

All software is copyrighted; only one backup copy may be made.

Terms are net 30 days; there is a service charge for past due accounts. The shipping/handling fees are 5% with a $5.00 minimum. Shipping/handling charges will be waived on all prepaid accounts.

Most programs and instructor's guides are also available in French.

Quality Educational Designs (QED)

P.O. Box 12486
Portland, OR 97212

(503)287-8137

QED programs are available for preview only in extenuating circumstances; make application in writing. The publisher will also provide the source code if the user's application requires drastic modification; however, modification attempts are not recommended.

All software is licensed with copying rights. Defective programs will be replaced within 14 days.

Queue, Inc.

5 Chapel Hill Drive
Fairfield, CT 06432

(203)372-6761

Queue, Inc., is a distributor handling software from many different sources. Each of their catalogs is unique to a model and is priced from $3.95 to $14.95. Generally, Queue prices are the same as those for the publisher. School purchase orders are accepted. Connecticut residents add 7 1/2% sales tax.

Queue also offers a newsletter, *Microcomputers in Education,* seminars, and books on microcomputers in education.

RIGHT ON PROGRAMS

Division of COMPUTEAM, Inc.
P.O. Box 977
Huntington, NY 11743

(516)271-3177

Right On software is not available on a preview basis. Defective disks will be replaced free of charge within 30 days of purchase, and for a nominal charge thereafter. Add $1.50 per order for shipping via UPS.

A complete SAT package is available for $370.00, containing 28 programs on 6 diskettes. A comprehensive English package with 41 programs on 8 diskettes is available for $550.00.

Radio Shack®

Education Division
1600 Tandy Center
Fort Worth, TX 76102

(817)390-3302

Prices of Radio Shack® software may vary at individual stores and dealers. Equipment and courseware may be placed in classrooms on a flexible leasing basis.

The source code for Radio Shack® programs is available in printed form.

Courseware developed by Radio Shack® has been field tested as a part of an effort to produce instructionally sound and properly validated software.

Random House *see* BLS, Inc.

Readers Digest

Educational Division
Pleasantville, NY 10570

(914)769-7000

Reader's Digest software may be previewed by arrangement with salesmen. All software is covered by a full 90-day warranty. Multiple copies of programs ordered are available at "preferred customer prices."

Robert R. Baker, Jr.

Educational CAI Programs
5845 Topp Court
Carmichael, CA 95608

(916)482-7771

Software is not available for preview. Specify model and format when ordering. Purchase orders from institutions are accepted. Payment must accompany orders from individuals.

The source code is available for Baker software at cost equivalent to that of the program ordered.

SEI (Sliwa Enterprises Inc.)

P.O. Box 7266
2013 Cunningham Dr., Suite 238
Hampton, VA 23666

(804)826-3777

SEI has no formal preview policy; individual accomodations will be made. A demonstration disk is available for $10.00. Software registration is available to purchasers in order to obtain product update information. Purchase orders are accepted.

A School Pak including all 10 diskettes is available to institutions for $215.00. This represents an additional 10% discount over package prices.

San Mateo County Office of Education and Computer-Using Educators

SOFTSWAP
333 Main St.
Redwood City, CA 94063

(415)363-5470

SMERC is a consortium that maintains SOFTSWAP, public domain software available for copying. Members of CUE

(Computer-Using Educators, $6.00 per year) receive a newsletter. Contributors of original programs can order one disk free of charge. All other orders must be prepaid.

Codes included in program listings refer to size of memory (K), grade level (secondary-S or elementary-E), and BASIC used (FP-floating point, or INT-integer.)

Santa Cruz Educational Software

5425 Jigger Drive
Soquel, CA 95073

(408)476-4901

Purchase price will be refunded if the customer is not satisfied. Santa Cruz accepts Bankcard or COD orders, and will bill by prior arrangement. Add $3.00 postage. California residents add 6.5% tax. Outside North America add $2.00 per program for air shipment.

Defective programs will be promptly replaced, and credit given for postage.

Specify cassette or diskette when ordering.

Scholastic Software

P.O. Box 2002
904 Sylvan Avenue
Englewood Cliffs, NJ 07632

Scholastic is a distributor that does not identify the producers of its software. All selections in their catalog have been reviewed before inclusion.

Software is available on a 30-day approval basis. Orders of $10.00 or less or orders from individuals must be accompanied by payment. For invoiced orders, shipping and handling are an estimated 6%.

Scott, Foresman and Co.

Electronic Publishing
1900 East Lake Avenue
Glenview, IL 60025

(312)729-3000

Scott, Foresman software is designed for use with classroom reading and math programs. No preview policy is available. Scott, Foresman sells through a dealer network rather than directly.

Sheridan College

Centre for Instructional Development
1430 Trafalgar Road
Oakville, Ontario L6H 2L1

(416)845-9430

Software from Sheridan College is not available for preview. There is a demo disk available for the Micromath program for $25.00, which will be deducted from the $500.00 total price. All defective software will be replaced. Payment is by check or purchase order. Specify hardware configuration when ordering.

Software City see Academic Software

SouthWest EdPsych Services

P.O. Box 1870
Phoenix, AZ 85001

(602)253-6528

SWEPS has discontinued free previews; however, copies will be provided at a substantial discount to schools which specify that they are considering adoption of the software. With most packages, two copies are furnished with purchase. Defective disks will be replaced free of charge within 30 days, and with a nominal charge within one year. Purchase orders, VISA and MasterCard accepted. Arizona residents add 5% sales tax.

All materials are copyrighted. Each product is field tested after development to ensure state-of-the-art performance. SWEPS welcomes feedback.

Special Delivery Software see Apple Computer, Inc.

Spectrum Software

P.O. Box 2084
142 Carlow
Sunnyvale, CA 94087

(408)738-4387

Spectrum software is not available for preview. Diskettes are warranted to be free from defects under normal use for a period of 90 days after purchase. Send a copy of receipt and defective diskette, and the diskette will be replaced without charge.

Materials ordered are provided under a license agreement. All items are copyrighted; copies may be made for backup only.

Institutional purchase orders are accepted; discounts are available for multiple orders by educational institutions. Mail and telephone orders are accepted with payment by check/money order, bankcard or COD ($1.50 extra per order). A flat rate of $1.50 per software package should be added for shipping. ($5.00 foreign orders.)

Steketee see Edu-Soft[T.M.]

SubLOGIC Communications Corporation

713 Edgebrook Drive
Champaign, IL 61820

(217)359-8482

SubLOGIC software is not available for preview. Purchase orders and bankcards are accepted. Programs are available from dealers or by mail (add $1.50 for shipping). Specify UPS or First Class. Illinois residents add 5% sales tax.

Sunburst Communications

P.O. Box 40
39 Washington Avenue
Pleasantville, NY 10570

(800)769-5030

(914)431-1934

Sunburst offers software produced by their company and by MECC (Minnesota Educational Computing Consortium.) All materials are sold on 30-day approval. For rush service, call collect.

TIES, Minnesota School Districts Data Processing Joint Board

1925 W. County Rd. B 2
St. Paul, MN 55113

TIES software is not available for preview. It is suggested that program documentation be purchased separately; sample screens and objectives will inform the user of content.

All diskettes are copy-protected unless otherwise noted. An archive copy is included with each order. Materials may not be transmitted by television or other processes or copies made without specific written authorization from TIES.

All materials are purchased "as is". Since courseware is documented, no changes will be made free of charge. Any product found defective in manufacture within 10 days of receipt will be replaced. After 10 days, $10.00/disk will be charged. Terms are net 60 days on school purchase orders.

Prices include one copy of the documentation.

TSC®, A Houghton Mifflin Company

Dept 65
Box 683
Hanover, NH 03755

(603)448-3838

TSC® software is contained on a sealed hard disk which runs only on the Dolphin^T.M. computer. The system includes up to 12 video terminals and a printer. Software is available on a license basis only. It is updated continuously and fully supported by TSC.

Contact TSC for arrangements to see the Dolphin educational system.

TYC Software (Teach Yourself by Computer)

40 Stuyvesant Manor
Genesco, NY 14454

(716)243-3005

TYC does not send software for preview. All defective software will be replaced. Purchase orders are accepted. New York residents add 7% sales tax.

TYCOM Associates

68 Valma Avenue
Pittsfield, MA 01201

(413)442-9771

TYCOM software is available from computer stores or directly from TYCOM. Programs are copyrighted and may not be copied to any other media.

When ordering by mail, include $1.50 for shipping and handling. Massachusetts residents should add 5% sales tax. TYCOM will replace defective programs within 30 days free of charge; after 30 days, $3.00 will be charged to rerecord, with an additional $1.50 if a new cassette is required. Original must be returned with claim.

Teach Yourself By Computer see TYC Software

Terrapin, Inc.

678 Massachusetts Avenue
Cambridge, MA 02139

(617)492-8816

Orders are accepted by Terrapin with check or bankcard. Massachusetts residents add 5% tax. Shipping in the U.S. is $5.00/program copy. Shipment is by UPS.

Terrapin also offers seminars designed to prepare teachers to use LOGO in the classroom.

Texas Instruments

P.O. Box 53
Lubbock, TX 79408

(800)858-4565

(800)692-4279

TI does not send software for preview; potential purchasers may visit dealer stores to use programs before purchase. The software is available through dealers or by phone or mail from Texas Instruments.

All software has a 90-day warranty; defective programs may be taken to TI service centers or returned to TI.

TI dealers offer many different brands of software available for use on their machines. Many programs are in the form of Solid State Software^T.M. Command Modules which plug right into the TI computer.

Universal Systems for Education, Inc. (USE)

2120 Academy Circle
Suite E
Colorado Springs, CO 80909

(303)575-4575

USE publishes the PAL reading program, which is available on five reading levels. A demodisk is available for $9.95 (applied to next order). Software may be returned within 10 days for full refund. Order through purchase order, check, money order, or bankcard. Colorado residents add 3% sales tax.

University Software

Division of Compumax
P.O. Box 4544
Stanford, CA 94305

(415)854-6700

University Software does not provide software for preview. Defective software will be exchanged; no other returns will be accepted.

Orders may be phoned into University Software. Mail orders should include name, address and phone number. Bankcard customers include card number and expiration date.

Add $1.00 per volume for shipping and handling. California residents add 6% tax.

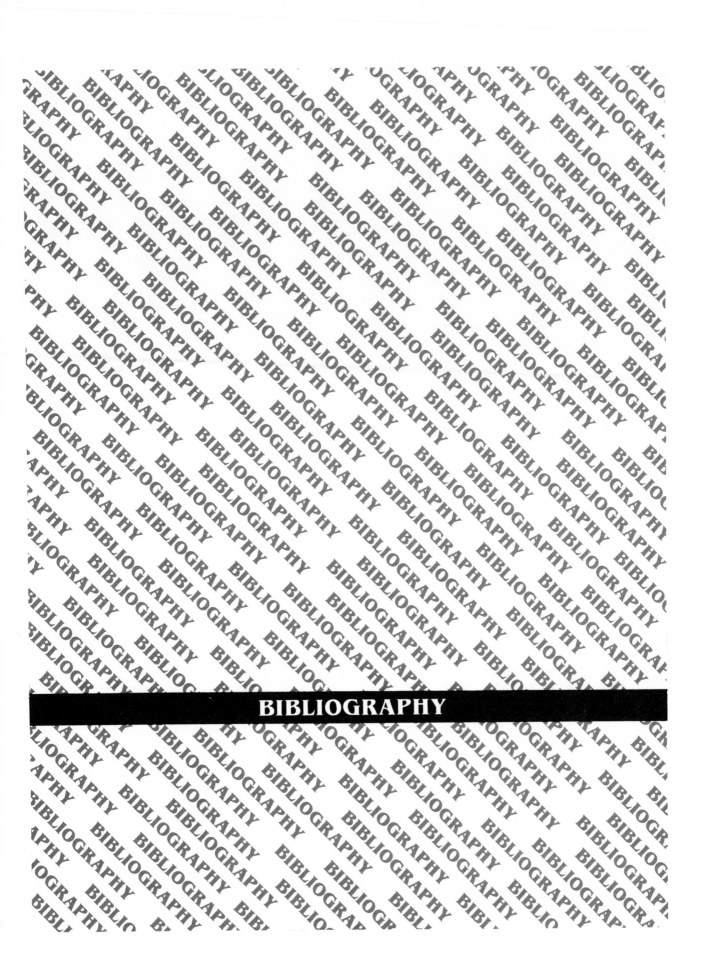

BIBLIOGRAPHY

Getting Started

Aiken, R.M. "The Golden Rule and Ten Commandments of Computer Based Education (CBE)." *Technological Horizons in Education*, vol. 8, no. 3, Mar. 1981, p39-42.

Ten factors to be considered in selecting and using computers in the classroom if the system is to be most effectively utilized as a teaching tool are examined. Topics include personnel, materials, services, and equipment.

"All Those Add-Ons." *Classroom Computer News*, vol. 1, no. 6, July-Aug. 1981, p14-18.

This article discusses peripherals available for microcomputers: keyboards, video monitors, mass storage (disks and cassettes), printers, clock/calendars, voice recognition and synthesis devices, graphics pads, and video projectors. Includes a list of peripherals suppliers.

Anderson, Cheryl A. *Microcomputers in Education. Paper presented at the State Convention of the Texas Association of Educational Technology (Dallas, TX, October 27, 1980).* Oct. 1980, 22p. ERIC Document Reproduction Service No. ED 198 812; MF-$.91/PC-$2.00.

Designed to answer basic questions about microcomputer hardware and software and their applications in teaching, this paper provides information on the major computer components, the cost and timesaving advantages of a microcomputer, the instructional advantages, and the various types of teaching strategies used with a computer.

Braun, Ludwig. "Help!!! What Computer Should I Buy???." *Mathematics Teacher*, vol. 74, no. 8, Nov. 1981, p593-598.

Criteria for selection of a microcomputer are given. A three-step decision-making procedure which enables educators to consider the uniqueness of their own environments is outlined. A table listing the hardware characteristics of several microcomputers is included.

Carter, Jim A., Jr. "How to Buy Microcomputers...and How & Where to Use Them." *School Shop*, vol. 40, no. 8, Apr. 1981, p28-33.

Microcomputer components, applications, input and output requirements, processing and storage requirements, determination of user needs, and purchase are discussed. Also included is a description of the development of a computer area for a multiple activity lab. The physical design of the equipment layout in the room is detailed.

Copple, Christine. *Computers in the Secondary Mathematics Curriculum.* June 1981, 34p. ERIC Document Reproduction Service No. ED 204 144; MF-$.91/PC-$3.65.

This annotated bibliography contains a glossary of commonly used computer terms; a section regarding attitudes toward computer use in the computer curriculum; and a section on computer uses in the mathematics classroom.

Douglas, S.; Neights, G. *Microcomputer Reference: A Guide to Microcomputers. Microcomputers in Education Series.* Harrisburg, PA: Pennsylvania State Dept. of Education, 1980, 37p. ERIC Document Reproduction Service No. ED 205 203; MF-$.91/PC-$3.65.

This guide for educational practitioners considers the purchase of a microcomputer. It discusses basic information about computers and criteria to use in conducting a needs assessment and in evaluating various microcomputers in relation to those needs.

Eisele, James E. "Computers in the Schools: Now That We Have Them...?." *Educational Technology*, vol. 21, no. 10, Oct. 1981, p24-27.

This article deals with recommended directions to be taken with microcomputers in education. These include the development of comprehensive instructional systems, the development of advanced instructional strategies; the promotion of universal computer literacy; and the use of microcomputers to teach problem-solving skills.

Eldredge, Bruce; Delp, Kenneth. "But What's a Software?." *Media & Methods*, Feb. 1981, p4.

The author provides basic definitions of software, hardware, documentation, computer-assisted instruction (CAI), computer management instruction (CMI), games, and simulation. CAI is examined in detail.

Feurzeig, W. et al. *Microcomputers in Education. Report No. 4798.* Cambridge, MA: Bolt, Beranek and Newman, Oct. 1981, 115p. ERIC Document Reproduction Service No. ED 208 901; MF-$.91/PC-$8.60.

This document contains a review of computer-assisted instruction and discussion of the current and potential roles of microcomputers in education. It also discusses the capabilities of state-of-the-art microcomputers and software currently available for them. Speculations about future trends and developments are given.

Fors, George (ed.). *Microcomputer Guide.* Bismarck, ND: North Dakota State Dept. of Public Instruction, Sept. 1979, 51p. ERIC Document Reproduction Service No. ED 205 169; MF-$.91/PC-$5.30.

Designed for use by school districts introducing computer mathematics into the curriculum, this manual provides guidelines for selecting a microcomputer system, as well as objectives and an outline for an introductory course in computer programming.

Frederick, F.J. *Guide to Microcomputers.* Washington, D.C.: Association for Educational Communications and Technology, 1980, 159p. ERIC Document Reproduction Service No. ED 192 818; MF-$.91/PC-$11.90.

This guide to microcomputers discusses their general nature, computer languages, operating and compatible systems, special applications and accessories, service and maintenance, computer-assisted and -managed instruction, graphics, time and resource sharing, potential instruction, and media center applications. An extensive resource list is included.

Gleason, G.T. "Microcomputers in Education: The State of the Art." *Educational Technology*, vol. 21, no. 3, Mar. 1981, p7-18.

This overview of instructional applications of CAI and microcomputer applications discusses current developments in hardware and software, the need for independent review and evaluation of programs, the growing importance of computer literacy, and projections for the future.

Harris, Diana (ed.) ; Nelson-Heern, Laurie (ed.). *Proceedings of the NECC 1981. National Educational Computing Conference (3rd, North Texas State University, Denton, Texas, June 17-19, 1981).* Iowa City, IA: University of Iowa, Weeg Computing Center, Jun 1981, 361p. ERIC Document Reproduction Service no. ED 207 526; MF-$.91/PC-$10.00 from Computer Science Dept., University of Iowa, Iowa City, IA 52242.

This volume includes texts of more than 50 papers presented at a conference organized to present in one forum all major work regarding computers in education in the United States. Topics covered include simulations, videodisc projects, administration, computer literacy, business, higher humanities, science, social science, computer science, preschool/elementary applications, graphics, mathematics, engineering, and health education.

Jay, Timothy B. "Computerphobia: What to Do about It." *Educational Technology*, vol. 21, no. 1, Jan. 1981, p47-48.

This article covers an often hidden problem - the symptoms, causes, and remedies for "computerphobia," a negative attitude toward computers.

Joiner, Lee Marvin; Silverstein, Burton J.; Ross, Jay Dee. "Insights from a Microcomputer Center in a Rural School District." *Educational Technology*, vol. 20, no. 5, May 1980, p36-40.

This article describes hardware problems discovered in the testing of TRS-80 Level I and III, PET, Tektronix 4051, Micro-33, NCR 7100, Digital 11V03, and the Apple II. Instructional applications in the Ortonville Public Schools, Ortonville, MN, are discussed.

Kosel, Marge. "Computer Bibliography." *Mathematics Teacher*, vol. 74, no. 8, Nov. 1981, p658-659.

This bibliography includes secondary school computer textbooks, background computer books, periodicals, and educational computing organizations.

Lathrop, A.; Goodson, B. "How to Start a Software Exchange." *Recreational Computing*, vol. 10, no. 2, Sept.-Oct. 1981, p24-26.

The authors describe the microcomputer display center and SOFTSWAP program developed by the San Mateo County (CA) Office of Education and the Computer Using Educators' group. SOFTSWAP disseminates teacher-produced, public domain courseware and is beginning evaluations of commercial products.

Lopez, Antonio M., Jr. "Teach Them Computing with a Pocket Computer." *Creative Computing*, vol. 8, no. 4, Apr. 1982, p141-145.

The use of "pocket computers" is presented as a low-priced solution to limited funds for microcomputer hardware in schools. Limitations as well as advantages are discussed.

Matthews, John I. "Considerations in Selecting Microcomputers for Instructional Design." *Journal of Industrial Teacher Education*, vol. 19, no. 1, 1981, p26-35.

Hardware, operating systems, programming languages, and applications software are discussed as important aspects of the selection of a microcomputer for educational use.

Michelsen, James (comp.). *A Survey of Selected Computer-Related Periodicals.* Lansing, MI: Michigan State Dept. of Education Bureau of Library Services, [1981], 9p. ERIC Document Reproduction Service No. ED 208 946; MF-$.91/PC-$2.00.

This report consists of an annotated bibliography of over 60 computer-related periodicals.

Prentice, W.P.; Beckelman, L. "Classroom Computer News." *Instructor*, vol. 91, no. 3, Oct. 1981, p85-90+.

The editors of *Classroom Computer News* prepared this compendium of news and tips for using computers in the classroom. Topics include computer literacy, the benefits of classroom computer use, programming of individualized education programs, selection of courseware, the basics of microprocessors, and new products.

Smith, Lorraine. "Choosing a Computer for Education." *Popular Computing*, vol. 1, no. 2, Dec. 1981, p108.

Maintenance, cost, file transfer capability, definition of needs, and amortization are presented as issues to be considered when selecting a computer for educational purposes.

Stewart, George. "How Should Schools Use Computers?." *Popular Computing*, vol. 1, no. 2, Dec. 1981, p104-108.

Issues on how computers should be used in the schools are presented. Discussions of "learning *from* computers," "learning *with* computers," and "learning *about* computers," are presented. Other questions, such as "what should a computer literacy curriculum consist of?", "where does computer literacy fit into the existing curriculum?", and "who should teach the subject?", are touched upon. Other issues discussed relate directly to the equipment itself.

Sturdivant, Patricia ; Finkel, LeRoy. "Selecting a Microcomputer: It's More than the Hardware." *Classroom Computer News*, vol. 1, no. 6, July-Aug. 1981, p10+.

Cost, maintenance, software, inservice training support, and minimum configurations are among the considerations discussed in selecting a microcomputer.

Watson, Nancy A. (ed.). *Microcomputers in Education: Getting Started. Conference Proceedings.* Tempe, AZ: Arizona State University, College of Education, Jan. 1981, 349p. ERIC Document Reproduction Service No. ED 205 216; MF-$.91. PC from Gary Bitter, Arizona State University, Payne 203, Tempe, AZ 85281.

This volume contains brief write-ups of 55 presentations given at a conference on microcomputer technology in elementary education, secondary education, special education, and school administration. Appended is a bibliography of BASIC computer books and lists of computer journals, microcomputer manufacturers, and software vendors.

Wright, A. *Microcomputers in the Schools: New Directions for British Columbia. Discussion Paper Number 05/80.* Victoria, British Columbia: Dept. of Education, Information Service; JEM Research, 1980, 42p. ERIC Document Reproduction Service No. ED 208 846; MF-$.91/PC-$3.65.

Plans for educational use of microcomputers in British Columbia are outlined. Hardware is discussed in terms of usage, context, location and educational level. The approach to software includes development of a standards manual for courseware evaluation, modification of courseware by JEM Research, new program development, and the development of programs by teachers.

Selecting and Designing Software

Barry, Tim. "Considering Software Reviews." *InfoWorld*, vol. 3, no. 24, Nov. 2, 1981, p20-21.

In the first of a two-part series, an *InfoWorld* columnist examines the considerations that should go into reviewing software. Qualifications for becoming a software reviewer are suggested, and documentation is discussed. Although it is not directed specifically toward the educational software market, the information presented could be helpful in evaluating educational software.

Barry, Tim. "Considering Software Reviews II." *InfoWorld*, vol. 3, no. 25, Nov. 9, 1981, p20-21.

Part II of a two-part series on reviewing software discusses how to try out a program and how to write a review. Although it is not directed specifically toward the educational market, the information presented could be helpful in evaluating educational software.

Douglas, Shirley; Neights, Gary. *Instructional Software Selection: A Guide to Instructional Microcomputer Software. Microcomputers in Education Series.* Harrisburg, PA: Pennsylvania State Dept. of Education, n.d., 33p. ERIC Document Reproduction Service No. ED 205 201; MF-$.91/PC-$3.65.

A guide for evaluating microcomputer instructional software, this report includes a hardware/software interface analysis sheet and an instructional software evaluation form for use in judging specific objectives, grade level, validation data, correlation data, instructional strategies employed in the software, and instructional design features.

Evaluator's Guide for Microcomputer-Based Instructional Packages. Portland, OR: Northwest Regional Educational Lab, 1981, 61p. ERIC Document Reproduction Service No. ED 206 330; MF-$.91• PC-$5.30.

Developed by MicroSIFT, a clearinghouse for microcomputer-based educational software and courseware, this guide provides background information to aid teachers and other educators in evaluating available microcomputer courseware. The evaluation process is described, which includes sifting/screening, package description, and courseware evaluation. Forms are provided for the second and third phases, together with explanations of information needed and discussions of factors to be considered in completing the forms.

Forman, Denyse et al. *Reference Manual for the Instructional Use of Microcomputers. Volume I (Release II).* Victoria, British Columbia: JEM Research, 1981, 873p. ERIC Document Reproduction Service No. ED 208 849; MF-$1.86/PC-$58.10; also available in PC from JEM Research, Discovery Park, PO Box 1700, Victoria, B.C. V8W 2Y2 for $75.00.

This manual is intended to provide educators with information and guidelines for locating, selecting, and purchasing com-

mercially available courseware for the Apple II microcomputer. An annotated bibliography of microcomputer periodicals and a list of selected compatible accessories and expansion options for the Apple II are also provided.

Glotfelty, Ruth. "Stalking Microcomputer Software." *School Library Journal*, vol. 28, no. 7, Mar. 1982, p91-94.

This review of Pontiac Township (IL) High School's assessment of various software packages includes comments on packages they previewed, plus a list of the packages that software publishers refused to release for preview.

Hannaford, A.; Sloane, E. "Microcomputers: Powerful Learning Tools for Proper Programming." *Teaching Exceptional Children*, vol. 14, no. 2, Nov. 1981, p54-57.

The potential uses of microcomputers in special education are considered. Cautions are noted regarding selection of software which will meet learner/teacher needs, possess instructional integrity, and be technically adequate and usable.

Holznagel, Donald C. "Which Courseware Is Right for You?." *Microcomputing*, vol. 5, no. 10, Oct. 1981, p138-140.

The Computer Technology Program of the Northwest Regional Educational Laboratory, Portland, OR, has developed a system for evaluating educational software packages. This MicroSIFT technique is described.

Kansky, Bob; Heck, William ; Johnson, Jerry. "Getting Hard-Nosed about Software: Guidelines for Evaluating Computerized Instructional Materials." *Mathematics Teacher*, vol. 74, no. 8, Nov. 1981, p600-604.

Overview of methods for evaluating educational software includes definitions of basic terms such as "software," "hardware," "documentation"; steps to follow in examining a program; and a list of periodicals, books, and organizations dealing with computers in education.

Kingman, James C. "Designing Good Educational Software." *Creative Computing*, vol. 7, no. 10, Oct. 1981, p72+.

The authors recommend the following characteristics of good educational software: educational soundness; ease of use; "bullet" proofing; clear instructions; appropriate language; appropriate frame size; motivation; and evaluation. Each point is discussed.

Kleiman, Glenn ; Humphrey, Mary M.; Van Buskirk, Trudy. "Evaluating Educational Software." *Creative Computing*, vol. 7, no. 10, Oct. 1981, p84+.

The following questions should be asked when evaluating educational software: 1) Does the software follow good educational practices? 2) Is it suitable for its intended purpose and audience? 3) Does it take advantage of the capabilities of the computer? Details are presented.

"A Level-Headed Guide to Software Evaluation." *Classroom Computer News*, vol. 1, no. 6, July-Aug. 1981, p22-23.

A suggested simple 5x7 card format for evaluating educational software is given.

Olds, Henry F., Jr. "The Making of Software." *Classroom Computer News*, vol. 1, no. 6, July-Aug. 1981, p20-21.

In order to avoid the weaknesses of traditional educational

materials, educational software must integrate knowledge of educational theory, educational practice, curriculum design, and computer capability.

Roblyer, M.D. "When Is It 'Good Courseware'? -- Problems in Developing Standards for Microcomputer Courseware." *Educational Technology*, vol. 21, no. 10, Oct. 1981, p47-54.

Two major courseware philosophies, the "PLATO model" and the "Stanford/CCC model," are compared. Several courseware criteria are categorized and discussed, including "essential characteristics" (statement of objectives, content integrity, etc.); "aesthetic characteristics" (spacing, format, use of color); and "differential characteristics" (amount of learner control, response format, etc.).

Case Studies

Barta, Ben Zion. "Microcomputers in the Israeli Educational System." *Educational Media International*, no. 3, 1981, p4-7.

The use of microcomputers in Israeli schools is outlined. Applications, software, hardware, and the role of the Centre for Educational Applications of Microcomputers are discussed.

Brown, R.W. "Microcomputing in an Educational Cooperative." *Microcomputing*, vol. 5, no. 10, Oct. 1981, p214-217.

Ohio Scientific microcomputers have replaced the mainframe system of the San Juan Board of Cooperative Services (BOCS), Durango, CO. BOCS has developed the most comprehensive test item data base in existence for secondary schools, as well as other successful applications on their microcomputer system.

Chambers, Jack A.; Bork, Alfred. *Computer Assisted Learning in U.S. Secondary/Elementary Schools*. New York, NY: Association for Computing Machinery, July 1980, 50p. ERIC Document Reproduction Service No. ED 202 461; MF-$.91/PC-$3.65.

A sample of 974 school districts was surveyed by mail to determine the current and projected use of computers in U.S. public secondary/elementary schools, with special reference to computer-assisted learning. Returned questionnaires provided a 62.3 percent response rate, and were balanced both geographically and by urban/rural distribution.

Gesshel-Green, Herb. "Getting Started in a High School: A Case Study." *Mathematics Teacher*, vol. 74, no. 8, Nov. 1981, p610-612.

This is a case study of a teacher's experience with the use of the computer for teaching in the Parkway Program, Philadelphia, PA. His experience began with the use of a terminal on a large Hewlett-Packard time-sharing system and has continued with the use of an Apple II.

Gras, Daniel. "The French Experiment." *Educational Media International*, no. 3, 1981, p8-12.

An overview of the "10,000 microcomputer experiment" is given. The goal of the project is to develop the use of computers as an educational tool in all subject areas and to familiarize all students with computer technology. The French

plan is that computers will be used as a teaching tool in all 1160 "lycees" in France by 1986-87.

Grossnickle, Donald R.; Laird, Bruce A. "Profile of Change in Education: A High School Uses Microcomputers." *Educational Technology*, vol. 21, no. 12, Dec. 1981, p7-11.

This article summarizes the development of microcomputer implementation at Palatine High School, Chicago, IL. Includes hardware selection (Apple II), the pilot site, goals of teacher training, and results of the project.

Gull, Randall L. "A Successful Transition from Mini- to Microcomputer-Assisted Instruction: The Norfolk Experience." *Educational Technology*, vol. 20, no. 12, Dec. 1981, p41-42.

This article describes Norfolk Public Schools' (Norfolk, VA) transition from the use of a Hewlett-Packard 2000 Access timesharing system with 32 terminals to the use of 29 Apple II Plus computers.

Humphrey, Mary M.; Kleiman, Glenn M. "Benefits of Using Computers in Special Education." *The Best of the Computer Faires, Volume VII. Conference Proceedings of the 7th West Coast Computer Faire*. Woodside, CA: Computer Faire, Mar. 1982, p89-92. Available from: Teaching Tools, Microcomputer Services, PO Box 50065, Palo Alto, CA 94303.

The implementation of the use of personal computers in two special education classrooms is discussed. The authors report the clearly positive effects achieved. They present the traditional arguments against the use of microcomputers in special education, countered by a set of strongly supporting arguments.

"Learning with LOGO at the Lamplighter School." *Microcomputing*, vol. 5, no. 9, Sept. 1981, p42-44+.

All teachers at the Lamplighter School (for pre-schoolers and grades 1-4), Dallas, TX, teach LOGO using TI 99/4 personal computers in their own schoolrooms. Computer use is only one of a wide range of learning activities. Individualization and improvement in students' self-concepts, peer relationships, and ability to communicate are just a few of the positive factors attributed to the use of the computer as a learning tool.

Loop, Liza; Christensen, Paul. *Exploring the Microcomputer Learning Environment. Independent Research and Development Project Reports. Report #5*. San Francisco, CA: Far West Laboratory for Educational Research and Development, Nov. 1980, 90p. ERIC Document Reproduction Service No. ED 201 307; MF-$.91/PC-$6.95.

The current state-of-the-art on the educational use of microcomputers was explored through a review of the literature, observations, and interviews with teachers and practitioners in the San Francisco Bay area.

Malsam, Margaret. "The Computer Replaces the Card Catalog in One Colorado Elementary School." *Phi Delta Kapan*, vol. 63, no. 5, Jan. 1982, p321.

Mountain View Elementary School, Broomfield, CO, may be the first elementary school in the U.S. to have its holdings entered on a microcomputer rather than filed in a traditional card catalog. In addition to enabling the children to find books faster and with less frustration, the new system provides students with hands-on computer experience, while increasing their library reference skills.

Miller, Benjamin S. "Bringing the Microcomputer into the Junior High: A Success Story from Florida." *Phi Delta Kappan*, vol. 63, no. 5, Jun 1982, p320.

Description of the introduction of microcomputers into Miami Lakes Junior High School, FL. Lists criteria used for selection of the Apple II.

Nelson, Harold. "Learning with LOGO." *onComputing*, vol. 3, no. 1, Sum. 1981, p14-16.

This article describes the use of LOGO on fifty TI 99/4s at Lamplighter School, Dallas, TX. One computer is placed in each preschool and kindergarten room; two, in each elementary classroom and in each shared space. All students from three and up use the computers. Use of LOGO in the "Computers in the Schools Project," New York City, is also described.

Noonan, Larry. "Computer Simulations in the Classroom." *Creative Computing*, vol. 7, no. 10, Oct. 1981, p132+.

The use of computer simulation in the classroom allows students to make judgments and, ultimately, decisions based on logic, observation, and their knowledge of the real world. This article describes the use of a game used in the classroom which gives a series of simulated real-life situations. The student must recognize and identify the cause-and-effect relationship involved by trying different solutions to the problems presented by the computer.

Petruk, Milton W. *Microcomputers in Alberta Schools. Final Report.* Alberta, Canada: Alberta Dept. of Education, Edmonton. Planning and Research Branch, Feb. 1981, 43p. ERIC Document Reproduction Service No. ED 205 214; MF-$.91/PC $3.65.

This study reports the nature and extent to which microcomputers have been introduced into Alberta.

Robbins, Bill; Taylor, Ross. "Getting Started in Junior High School: A Case Study." *Mathematics Teacher*, vol. 74, no. 8, Nov. 1981, p605-608.

This is an account of the use of computers in the classroom and for administration at Ramsey Junior High School, Minneapolis, MN. Tips for getting started and for expanding the use of computers in schools are given.

Sakamoto, Takashi. "The Educational Use of Microcomputers in Japan." *Educational Media International*, no. 3, 1981, p18-20.

Microcomputers are used in education in Japan for the following purposes: for teaching about hardware, software, and programming; for controlling educational devices such as slide projectors; for simulation; for computer-aided instruction; and for handling of administrative data.

Saltinski, Ronald. "Microcomputers in Social Studies: An Innovative Technology for Instruction." *Educational Technology*, vol. 21, no. 1, Jan. 1981, p29-32.

The use of the microcomputer for statistics and simulation in the social studies curriculum is discussed. Specific experiences at the Miller Creek Middle School, San Rafael, CA, are related.

Saracho, Olivia N. "Planning Computer Assisted Instruction for Spanish-Speaking Migrant Students." *International Journal of Instructional Media*, vol. 10, no. 3, 1981-82, p257-260.

Many Spanish-speaking migrant children have encountered difficulty with basic academic skills because they do not speak English. The Computer Curriculum Corp. has developed computer-based instruction for language arts, math, and reading. It has been used in several U.S. school districts for Spanish-speaking migrant students. The positive results achieved are reported.

Sheingold, Karen. *Issues Related to the Implementation of Computer Technology in Schools: A Cross-Sectional Study. Children's Electronic Laboratory Memo No. 1.* New York, NY: Bank Street College of Education, Feb. 19, 1981, 19p. ERIC Document Reproduction Service No. ED 205 165; MF-$.91/PC-$2.00.

Three school systems were examined to assess issues pertinent to microcomputer innovations in the schools and to determine whether a revolution in education was taking place because of this new technology.

Sheingold, Karen et al. *Study of Issues Related to Implementation of Computer Technology in Schools. Final Report. Children's Electronic Laboratory Memo No. 2.* New York, NY: Bank Street College of Education, July 1981, 141p. ERIC Document Reproduction Service No. ED 210 034; MF-$.91/PC-$10.25.

The study reported here was conducted in order to discover and identify ways in which microcomputers are now being used in schools, and the complex issues which surround their implementation. Three geographically distinct school districts, with a diversity of microcomputer applications at both elementary and secondary schools, were studied.

Stutzman, Carl R. *Computer Supported Instruction in California Elementary and Secondary Schools. A Status Report.* Paper presented at the Annual Fresno Research Symposium (2nd, Fresno, CA, April 24, 1981). Mar 1981, 39p. ERIC Document Reproduction Service No. ED 206 304; MF-$.91/PC-$3.65.

A survey was sent to superintendents of each school district in California in June 1980 to gather information about the uses of computers in instruction in the state's public elementary and secondary schools. Findings of the study are reported.

Terzian, Peter J. *Microcomputers in Public Schools: Albany, Schenectady and Saratoga Counties of New York State.* San Diego, CA: California University, Center for Human Information Processing, Dec. 1981, 9p. ERIC Document Reproduction Service No. ED 212 291; MF-$.91/PC-$2.00.

Results of a questionnaire distributed to 31 public school districts in New York State on the extent of microcomputer utilization and attitudes toward their use are presented.

Tinker, Robert; Naiman, Adeline. *Microcomputers in Education: Applications of Microprocessors in the Schools. A Report to the Northeast Regional Educational Planning Project.* Cambridge, MA: Technical Educational Research Center, May 15 1980, 100p. ERIC Document Reproduction Service No. ED 196 455; MF-$.91/PC-$6.95.

A three-month study of the role of microcomputers in the six New England states and New York State. Gives examples of current school applications and identifies 10 locations where schools have successfully integrated the use of microcomputers in the K-12 curriculum.

Vickery, Carol A. *Personal Experiences: Using Microcomputers in a Junior High School High-Potential Program. Paper presented at the Annual Meeting of the International Reading Association (26th, New Orleans, LA, April 27-May 1, 1981).* Apr. 30, 1981, 29p. ERIC Document Reproduction Service No. ED 208 860; MF-$.91/PC-$3.65.

A school district's involvement in the use of microcomputers and one teacher's experiences at the junior high level are described. Strategies for initiating teacher involvement are included. An analysis of microcomputer applications in an English class, in writing a school newspaper, an in a program for the academically gifted are presented.

SUBJECT INDEX

A

Abbreviations
ACRONYMS, H3
WORD STRUCTURE, H260

Acceleration (physics)
LABORATORY SIMULATIONS SERIES, K70
MOTION, K82
PHYSICS COMPULAB PACKAGE, K92
PHYSICS I, K94
PHYSICS PROGRAMS FOR THE APPLE II, K99
VECTOR ADDITION, K134

Accident procedures
LIFE CHALLENGES, B25

Accounting
ACCOUNTING EXAM, C2
ACCOUNTS PAYABLE POSTING DRILL, C3
ACCOUNTS RECEIVABLE POSTING DRILL, C4
BUSINESS - VOLUME 2, C6
BUSINESS - VOLUME 3, C7
BUSINESS PACKAGE I, C8
BUSINESS PACKAGE II, C9
BUSINESS PACKAGE III, C10
DECISION-MAKING SIMULATIONS IN AC-
    COUNTING FOR THE MICROCOMPUTER,
    C11
MICROCOMPUTER ACCOUNTING APPLICA-
    TIONS, C20
MICROCOMPUTER TESTING PROGRAM FOR
    ACCOUNTING: SYSTEMS AND PRO-
    CEDURES, FOURTH EDITION, C21
PET DISSEMINATION DISK #2, J224
T-ACCOUNTS, C26
TRS-80 DISSEMINATION DISK #3, A46

Acid-base equilibrium
ACID-BASED CHEMISTRY, K1

Acoustics
PHYSICS - LAB PLOTS, K89

Acronyms
ACRONYMS, H3

Addition
ADDING OR SUBTRACTING TWO AND THREE
    PLACE NUMBERS IN COLUMNS, J4
ADDING WITH OBJECTS, J5
ADDITION AND SUBTRACTION OF WHOLE
    NUMBERS, J6
ADDITION DRILL/MULTIPLICATION DRILL, J7
ADDITION WITH CARRY, J8
ADDITION/SUBTRACTION 1, J9
ADDITION/SUBTRACTION 2, J10
APPLE DISSEMINATION DISK #2, A3
BEGINNING MATH CONCEPTS, J32
COUNT AND ADD, J60
ELEMENTARY - VOLUME 7, A17
JUNIOR HIGH MATH PACKAGE I, J134
LEARNING CAN BE FUN #2, J140
MATH - ADDITION AND SUBTRACTION, J147
MATHEMATICS FOR SCIENCE, SERIES 2: BASIC
    MATH TECHNIQUES, J180
MATHMADNESS, J186
NUMBER JUMPER, J206
SCHOOLHOUSE I, A40
SUM-IT MOUNTAIN, J261
WHOLE NUMBER ARITHMETIC SERIES BY
    TEACHING OBJECTIVE, J273
WORKING WITH BASIC ADDITION FACTS,
    J275

Adjectives
ADJECTIVE, H5
ADJECTIVES, H6
ADVERBS, H9
BASIC LANGUAGE SKILLS, H23
READING LESSONS - SET TWO, H155
USAGE, H215
WRITING SKILLS: SENTENCE COMBINING,
    H277

Adverbs
ADVERB, H8
ADVERBS, H9
BASIC LANGUAGE SKILLS, H23
USAGE, H215
WRITING SKILLS: SENTENCE COMBINING,
    H277

Aestheometry
AESTHEOMETRY - VOLUME 1, J12

Affixes
MULTIPLE SKILLS, H121
READING LESSONS - SET ONE, H154
ROOTS/AFFIXES, H168

Alcohols
INTRODUCTION TO ORGANIC CHEMISTRY,
    K66

Aldehydes
INTRODUCTION TO ORGANIC CHEMISTRY,
    K66

Algebra
ALGEBRA, J13
ALGEBRA 1, J14
ALGEBRA 2, J15
ALGEBRA BILLIARDS, J16
ALGEBRA DRILL & PRACTICE I, J17
ALGEBRA WORD PROBLEMS, J18
APPLE DISSEMINATION DISK #8 - MATH I, J19
BASIC SECONDARY PACKAGE, J31
CALCULUS I, J37
COLLEGE ENTRANCE EXAMINATION PREPARA-
    TION, H36
COMPUTER GRAPHING EXPERIMENTS -
    VOLUME I (ALGEBRA I AND II), J46
ESSENTIAL MATH PROGRAM, VOLUME TWO,
    J88
FUNDAMENTALS OF ALGEBRA, J112
INTEGERS/EQUATIONS, J127
JUNIOR HIGH PACKAGE, J135
MATH SKILLS, J167
MATH SPEED TUTOR, J168
MICROCOSM II, A29
MICROMATH, J196
MORE ALGEBRA, J201
QUADRATIC AND THE PARABOLA, J238
SAMPLER, J245
SENIOR HIGH MATH I, J247
SUPER MATH PACKAGE, J262

Alkanes
INTRODUCTION TO ORGANIC CHEMISTRY,
    K66

Alkene compounds
INTRODUCTION TO ORGANIC CHEMISTRY,
    K66

Alphabetizing skills
ALPHABETIZE, H11
ALPHABETIZING, H12
ARC SEQUENCE, H22
EDUCATIONAL PACKAGE II, A15
LANGUAGE ARTS: STUDY SKILLS, H98

MISSING LETTER, H116
PUTTING FICTION BOOKS IN ALPHABETICAL
    ORDER, I22
READING LESSONS - SET ONE, H154
WHICH LETTER COMES NEXT, H241
WORKING WITH THE ALPHABET, H276

Alphabets
ABC, H2
ALPHABET/ GUESS THE NUMBER/ REVERSE, A1
ALPHAKEY, H13
APPLE DISSEMINATION DISK #6, A7
COMPU-READ[T.M.] 3.0, H40
EARLY ELEMENTARY II, A14
ELEMENTARY - VOLUME 7, A17
PET DISSEMINATION DISK #6, A33
WHICH LETTER IS MISSING, H242
WORKING WITH THE ALPHABET, H276

American Indians
see Native Americans

American history
ACROSS THE PLAINS, L1
AMERICA'S HERITAGE, L2
AMERICAN HISTORY: THE DECADES GAME, L3
APPLE DISSEMINATION DISK #1, A2
ELEMENTARY - VOLUME 3, L7
ELEMENTARY - VOLUME 6, L8
GROWTH OF THE UNITED STATES, L10
HISTORY & GEOGRAPHY PACKAGE, L13
INVENTIONS THAT CHANGED OUR LIVES,
    L14
LEARNING CAN BE FUN #6, A24
PIONEERS IN TECHNOLOGY, L17
QUESTION & ANSWER GROUP, E32
SOCIAL STUDIES - AMERICAN HISTORY
    THROUGH BIOGRAPHIES, L22
STATES GAME, L34
TRAIL WEST, A44
WHO BUILT AMERICA, L36

Analogies
see Convergent thinking
see Word analogies

Anatomy
see also Body organs
see also Circulation
see also Physiology
see also specific organs and systems
BIOLOGY PROGRAMS FOR THE APPLE II, K12
CIRCULATION ORGANS, K28
DIGESTIVE SYSTEM, K37
ELEMENTARY BIOLOGY, K48
HEART, K61
HEART LAB - SIMULATION MODEL OF A
    FUNCTIONING HUMAN HEART, K62
HUMAN BODY: AN OVERVIEW, K64
QUESTION & ANSWER GROUP, E32
REPRODUCTION ORGANS, K103
SCIENCE, K107
SCIENCE - OUR BODIES, K110
TRS-80 DISSEMINATION DISK #2, A45

Ancient history
SOCIAL STUDIES - EARLY CIVILIZATION, L24

Animal classification
QUESTION & ANSWER GROUP, E32

Antonyms
ANTONYM MACHINE, H17
ANTONYM/SYNONYM TIC-TAC-TOE, H18

BUSINESS PACKAGE I, C8
BUSINESS PACKAGE III, C10
GENERAL LEDGER POSTING DRILL, C13
INVENTORY POSTING DRILL, C15
PAYROLL POSTING DRILL, C22

Books

LEARNING TO UNDERSTAND THE TITLE
PAGE, I13
LEARNING TO USE AN INDEX, I14
LEARNING TO USE THE TABLE OF CONTENTS,
I15

Botany

see also Plants
COMPUTERS IN THE BIOLOGY CURRICULUM,
K33

Braille

MICRO BRAILLE TRANSLATOR, E27

Budgeting

see Personal budgeting

C

Calculus

ADVANCED GRAPHICS, J11
CALCULUS I, J37
MATHEMATICS - VOLUME 4, J176
RIEMANN INTEGRAL, J242
SUPER MATH PACKAGE, J262
SURFACE, J263
SURFACES FOR MULTIVARIABLE CALCULUS,
J264

Calendar skills

CALENDAR SKILLS, B2
CALENDAR TIC-TAC-TOE, H28
MONEY MANAGEMENT ASSESSMENT, B31
READING COMPREHENSION (BLS79), H150
USING A CALENDAR, B41

Capitalization

CAPITALIZATION, H29
CAPITALIZATION, H30
CAPITALIZATION, H31
CAPITALIZATION AND PUNCTUATION, H32
CAPITALIZATION SERIES, H33
ENGLISH LESSONS - SET ONE, H63
LANGUAGE ARTS, H97
LANGUAGE SKILLS, H100
MECHANICS, H111
MECHANICS OF ENGLISH, H112
MECHANICS OF ENGLISH, H113
UPPER/LOWER CASE MATCHING, H214
WORD STRUCTURE, H260

Carboxylic acids

INTRODUCTION TO ORGANIC CHEMISTRY,
K66

Cells (biology)

BIOLOGY PROGRAMS FOR THE APPLE II, K12
CELLS, K16
SCIENCE - VOLUME 2, K115

Centripetal force

PHYSICS I, K94

Checking accounts

SURVIVAL MATHEMATICS, J265
YOU CAN BANK ON IT, B44

Chemical equilibrium

CHEMICAL EQUILIBRIUM, K19

Chemical reactions

CHEMISTRY I, K21

CHEMISTRY II, K22
RAIN, K102

Chemistry

ACID-BASED CHEMISTRY, K1
APPLE DISSEMINATION DISK #1, A2
APPLE DISSEMINATION DISK #4, A5
ATARI VOL. II - EDUCATION & SCIENTIFIC,
A10
BALANCING CHEMICAL EQUATIONS, K8
CHEM LAB SIMULATION #1, K17
CHEM LAB SIMULATION #2, K18
CHEMICAL EQUILIBRIUM, K19
CHEMICAL NOMENCLATURE SERIES, K20
CHEMISTRY I, K21
CHEMISTRY II, K22
CHEMISTRY PROGRAMS, K23
CHEMISTRY SIMULATIONS I & II, K24
CHEMISTRY SIMULATIONS, VOLUME 1, K25
CHEMISTRY WITH A COMPUTER, K26
COMPUTER CHEMISTRY, K32
DIFFUSION, K36
EARTH SCIENCE SERIES, K40
ELEMENTS, K49
FUNDAMENTAL SKILLS FOR GENERAL
CHEMISTRY, K52
GAS LAWS, K53
GAS LAWS AND KINETIC MOLECULAR
THEORY, K54
HABER - AMMONIA SYNTHESIS, K60
ORGANIC NOMENCLATURE, K85
PET DISSEMINATION DISK #3, A31
PET DISSEMINATION DISK #6, A33
QUESTION & ANSWER GROUP, E32
RAIN, K102
SCIENCE - VOLUME 4, K117
SCIENCE PACKAGE II, K119

Circulatory system

CIRCULATION ORGANS, K28
CIRCULATION SYSTEM, K29
QUESTION & ANSWER GROUP, E32

Clauses

see Complex sentences

Clerical skills

see also specific skills, e.g., Dictation
ALPHABETIZE, H11
DISK STENO, E16
FILING TEST, C12
STENO, C25

Climate

SOCIAL STUDIES - WORLD DESERT REGIONS,
L31
SOCIAL STUDIES - WORLD POLAR REGIONS,
L32
WORLD MOUNTAIN REGIONS, L37

Clocks

see Telling time
see Time

Cognitive skills

CRITICAL READING, H46

Coins

MONEY! MONEY!, B32

Collision integral

PHYSICS - LINEAR MOMENTUM, K90

Colonial period

QUESTION & ANSWER GROUP, E32

Colons

PUNCTUATION SERIES, H142

PUNCTUATION SKILLS: END MARKS,
SEMICOLON, COLON, H144

Color

EARLY ELEMENTARY I, A13

Color discrimination

COLOR GUESS, B6
GERTRUDE'S PUZZLES, B16
GERTRUDE'S SECRETS, B17

Commas

COMMAS; TWELVE COMMON USES, H37
PUNCTUATION SERIES, H142
PUNCTUATION SKILLS: COMMAS, H143

Communication systems

SCIENCE - COMMUNICATIONS, K108

Community awareness

COMMUNITY HELPERS, L5
YOUR COMMUNITY, L38

Community economic systems

SOCIAL STUDIES - VOLUME 2, L30

Comparative government

ANNAM - THE STUDY OF A DEVELOPING
COUNTRY, L4

Comparison shopping

COMPARATIVE BUYING, B7
MARKET SURVEY, B27

Compass directions

APPLE DISSEMINATION DISK #8 - MATH I, J19
DIRECTION AND DISTANCE, B9

Complex sentences

PHRASES AND CLAUSES, H132

Compound words

COMPOUND WORD MATCHUP, H38
COMPOUND WORDS, H39
MULTIPLE SKILLS, H121

Computers

see Data Processing

Conic section

BASIC SECONDARY PACKAGE, J31
SUPER MATH PACKAGE, J262

Conjunctions

CONJUNCTIONS, H42

Consonant blends

CONSONANTS, H43

Consonants

see also Hard and soft consonants
CONSONANTS, H43
SILENT CONSONANT BASKETBALL, H176
SPELLING BEE WITH READING PRIMER[T.M.],
H190

Constellations

ASTRONOMY I - INTRODUCTIONS, K3
ASTRONOMY II - CONSTELLATIONS, K4
CONSTELLATIONS, K35
STARWARE, K128

Consumer mathematics

APPLE DISSEMINATION DISK #2, A3
APPLE DISSEMINATION DISK #5, A6
COMPARATIVE BUYING, B7
INCOME MEETS EXPENSES, B22
MARKET PLACE, C17
MARKET SURVEY, B27
MONEY MANAGEMENT ASSESSMENT, B31
PERCENTAGE: A REVIEW COURSE, J222
PERSONAL FINANCE, B34

H

Haiku poetry
HAIKU, H77
PET DISSEMINATION DISK #6, A33

Hard and soft consonants
SPELLING BEE WITH READING PRIMER[T.M.], H190

Health education
GOOD HEALTH HABITS, B18

Hearts
HEART, K61
HEART LAB - SIMULATION MODEL OF A FUNCTIONING HUMAN HEART, K62

Heat measurement
CHEMISTRY I, K21
PHYSICS I, K94
THERMODYNAMICS, K132

Heredity
BIRDBREED, K13
COMPUTERS IN THE BIOLOGY CURRICULUM, K33

History
see specific periods, e.g., Middle Ages

History, American
see American history

Holidays
HALLOWEEN JUMBLE/THANKSGIVING CROSSWORD/CHRISTMAS WORD SEARCH, H78
SOCIAL STUDIES - HOLIDAYS AND FESTIVALS, L25

Homonyms
ELEMENTARY - VOLUMES 11 & 12, H56
ENGLISH BASICS, H61
GRAMMAR PROBLEMS FOR PRACTICE, H75
HOMONYM JUGGLER, H83
HOMONYM MACHINE, H84
HOMONYMS, H85
HOMONYMS, H86
HOMONYMS II, H87
ITS/IT'S - YOUR/YOU'RE, H94
LEARNING CAN BE FUN #3, H102
MULTIPLE SKILLS, H121
RIDDLE ME THIS, H167
SPELLING, H187
TANK TACTICS, H206
TENNIS, ANYONE?, H207
THERE/THEIR/THEY'RE, H209
TO/TOO/TWO, H211
VOCABULARY BUILDERS, H230

I

Incomplete sentences
VERBAL SKILLS, H219

Independent living
CONTEMPORARY LIVING, B8
FACTS AND FORMULAS, A19
PERSONAL FINANCE, B34

Indexes
ESSAY AND GENERAL LITERATURE INDEX, I8
PERIODICAL INDEXES, I20
POETRY INDEXES, I21

Indians
see Native Americans

Industrial arts
DRIVER'S EDUCATION/INDUSTRIAL ARTS - VOLUME 1, B14

Inelastic scattering
CONSERVATION LAWS, K34
PHYSICS I, K94

Inferential thinking
see Convergent thinking

Infrared spectroscopy
INTRODUCTION TO ORGANIC CHEMISTRY, K66

Inheritance
see Heredity

Inorganic chemistry
CHEMICAL NOMENCLATURE SERIES, K20
RAIN, K102

Insects
SCIENCE - INSECTS, K109

Integers
INTEGERS/EQUATIONS, J127
MICROMATH, J196

Inventions
INVENTIONS THAT CHANGED OUR LIVES, L14

Italian
LANGUAGE TEACHER SERIES, G11

J

Japanese
SUPER PROMPTER (JAPANESE KATAKANA), G17

Job interviews
see Employment interviews

Job training programs
WORK SERIES, B43

Judgment
READING COMPREHENSION, H149

K

Ketones
INTRODUCTION TO ORGANIC CHEMISTRY, K66

Keypunching
see Data Processing

Kinematics
ATARI VOL. II - EDUCATION & SCIENTIFIC, A10
INTERPRETING GRAPHS IN PHYSICS: POSITION VERSUS TIME AND VELOCITY VERSUS TIME, J130
MOTION, K82

Kinetic energy
PHYSICS - LINEAR MOMENTUM, K90
PHYSICS I, K94

Kinetic theory
GAS LAWS AND KINETIC MOLECULAR THEORY, K54

Kinetics
COMPUTER CHEMISTRY, K32
RKINET - REACTION KINETICS, K105

L

LOGO
ALICE IN LOGOLAND, D1
MIT-LOGO FOR APPLE, D8
TERRAPIN LOGO LANGUAGE, D17
TI LOGO, D18

Labels and signs
GRADUATED CYLINDER, B19

Land features
MAPS AND GLOBES, K78

Latin
ROMAN BANQUET, G13

Left-right concept
JUGGLES' RAINBOW, B24

Legal rights
LIFE CHALLENGES, B25

Lesson development
ADAPTABLE SKELETON, E1
BLOCKS AUTHOR LANGUAGE SYSTEM AND GRAPHICS LIBRARY, E3
CREATE - ELEMENTARY, E9
CREATE - FILL IN THE BLANK, E10
CREATE - INTERMEDIATE, E11
CREATE - SPELL IT, E12
CREATE VOCABULARY, E13
DIETING DINOSAUR, H50
EDUCATORS' LESSON MASTER, E17
FACTORING; TEACH ME AND SHOW ME, J93
FLASH SPELL HELICOPTER, H68
GENIS (GENERALIZED INSTRUCTIONAL SYSTEMS), E22
GUESS THAT WORD, H76
HISTORY & GEOGRAPHY PACKAGE, L13
INDIVIDUAL STUDY CENTER, E25
K-8 MATH WORKSHEET GENERATOR, E26
MEDALIST SERIES, A26
MICROTEACH, E28
PILOT ANIMATION TOOLS, E30
PROCTOR, E31
PROFIT AND LOSS: A MICROCOMPUTER SIMULATION, C23
PUNCTUATION CIRCUS, H141
QUESTION, ANSWER & VOCABULARY FACILITIES, E33
QUIZ MASTER, E34
READABILITY ANALYSIS, H147
READABILITY; FORMULA RESULTS, GRAPHS AND STATISTICS, E35
SPELL WRITER, D15
STUDY QUIZ FILES, E37
SUPER PROMPTER (JAPANESE KATAKANA), G17
SUPER PROMPTER (RUSSIAN CYRILLIC), G18
TEACHER'S AIDE, E41
TRS-80 DISSEMINATION DISK #3, A46
TRS-80 PILOT PLUS, E43
VOCABULARY - ELEMENTARY, E44
VOCABULARY PROMPTER, H234
WORD PREP (ADVANCED); VOCABULARY DRILL...MAKE YOUR OWN, E45
WORD PREP (BASIC), H256
WORD WISE AUTHORING, E46
WORDSEARCH, H274

Lesson writing
see Lesson development

Letter discrimination
ABC, H2

MONEY! MONEY!, B32
PET DISSEMINATION DISK #2, J224
PROBLEM SOLVING, J233
SENIOR HIGH MATH I, J247
SURVIVAL MATH, B37
USING MONEY AND MAKING CHANGE, B42

Money management
see Personal finance management

Months of year
CALENDAR SKILLS, B2

Morse code
PET DISSEMINATION DISK #3, A31

Mortgages
see Loans

Motion
CIRCULAR MOTION, K27
MECHANICS AND MOTION, K81
MOTION, K82
PHYSICS - LAB PLOTS, K89
PHYSICS COMPULAB PACKAGE, K92
PHYSICS I, K94
PHYSICS PROGRAMS FOR THE APPLE II, K99
TARGET PRACTICE, K131
WAVES AND VIBRATION SERIES, K135

Mountains
WORLD MOUNTAIN REGIONS, L37

Multiplication
1-2-3 DIGIT MULTIPLICATION, J1
ADDITION DRILL/MULTIPLICATION DRILL, J7
APPLE DISSEMINATION DISK #1, A2
APPLE DISSEMINATION DISK #3, A4
ARITH-MAGIC, J22
FABULOUS L-C-M MACHINE AND THE
GENEROUS JACKPOT MINE, J91
GREAT TIMES HOTEL, J119
GUZINTA HOTEL, J124
LAST OF THE NINTH, J138
LEARNING CAN BE FUN #4, J141
MATH - MULTIPLICATION AND DIVISION,
J151
MATH - SIMPLE MULTIPLICATION AND DIVI-
SION, J154
MATH SPIN, J169
MATHGRID, J185
MATHMADNESS, J186
MEDAL WINNER, J191
MULTIPLICATION & DIVISION FUN, J202
MULTIPLICATION 1, J203
MULTIPLICATION OF WHOLE NUMBERS, J204
TENTRATION, J267
WHOLE NUMBER ARITHMETIC SERIES BY
TEACHING OBJECTIVE, J273
WORKING WITH BASIC MULTIPLICATION
FACTS, J276

Music
APPLE DISSEMINATION DISK #3, A4
CHORD MANIA, F2
COMPOSE, F3
ELEMENTS OF MUSIC, F5
HARMONIOUS DICTATOR, F6
HIGHER, SAME, LOWER, F8
INSTRUMENT DRILL, F9
INTERVAL DRILLMASTER, F10
INTERVAL MANIA, F11
KEY SIGNATURE DRILLS, F12
KOLOSICK SERIES, F13
LINES AND SPACES OF THE TREBLE CLEF, F14
MATCHING EQUIVALENT NOTES, F15
MATCHING RHYTHMS, F16

MELODIOUS DICTATOR, F17
MICROCOSM I, A28
MODE DRILLS, F18
MUSIC I: TERMS AND NOTATIONS, F19
MUSIC III: SCALES AND CHORDS, F20
MUSIC LOVER'S GUIDES TO LEARNING
SERIES, F22
MUSIC MAKER, F23
MUSIC SKILLS TRAINER, F24
NAME THAT TUNE, F27
PET DISSEMINATION DISK #6, A33
PITCH DRILLS WITH ACCIDENTALS, F28
PITCH DRILLS WITHOUT ACCIDENTALS, F29
RHYTHM DRILLS, F30
RHYTHMIC DICTATOR, F31
SEBASTIAN, F32

Music appreciation
DOREMI, F4
HARMONY DRILLS: SET 1, F7
NAME THAT TUNE, F26

Music theory
MUSIC IN THEORY AND PRACTICE TUTOR
(VOLUME 1: 2ND EDITION): A COMPUTER-
ASSISTED SUPPLEMENT, F21
MUSIC THEORY SERIES, F25

Musical games
NAME THAT TUNE, F27

Musical instruments
INSTRUMENT DRILL, F9

N

Naming numbers
see Number words

Native Americans
SOCIAL STUDIES - AMERICAN INDIANS, L23

Negative numbers
see also Signed numbers
APPLE DISSEMINATION DISK #9 - MATH II, J20

BASIC MATH SYSTEM H, J29
BASIC MATH SYSTEM S, J30
BUMBLE PLOT, J36
INTEGERS/ESTIMATION DRILL, J128
MICROMATH, J196

Nouns
BASIC LANGUAGE SKILLS, H23
NOUN, H123
NOUNS, H124
NOUNS/PRONOUNS, H125
PLURAL NOUNS, H134
RECOGNIZING NOUNS, H165

Nuclear reactions
ATOMIC PHYSICS, K6

Number concepts
MATH CONCEPTS, J158

Number discrimination
ALPHABET/ GUESS THE NUMBER/ REVERSE, A1

LETTER RECOGNITION, H103
MATH - MATCHING AND USING NUMBERS,
J148

Number lines
ALGEBRA 1, J14

Number notation
MICROMATH, J196

Number patterns
COMPUTER MATH ACTIVITIES - VOLUME 3,
J49
MATH CONCEPTS, J158

Number values
BEGINNING MATH CONCEPTS, J32

Number words
BEGINNING MATH CONCEPTS, J32
EARLY ELEMENTARY I, A13
EDUCATIONAL PACKAGE III, J75
NUMBER TREE, J208
NUMBER WORDS - LEVEL 1, J209
NUMBER WORDS - LEVEL 2, J210

Numerical notation
EXPANDED NOTATION, J90
FACTORING WHOLE NUMBERS, J92

Nutrition
ELEMENTARY - VOLUME 13, B15
PERSONAL FINANCE, B34

O

Oceans
LIFE IN THE OCEANS, K74
OCEANS AND CONTINENTS, L16
SKIES ABOVE/WATERS BELOW, K125

Odd numbers
see Counting

Optics
OPTICS, K84
PHYSICS - WAVE AND OPTICS, K91
PHYSICS DEMOS PACKAGE, K93

Organic chemistry
CHEMICAL NOMENCLATURE SERIES, K20
COMPUTER CHEMISTRY, K32
INTRODUCTION TO ORGANIC CHEMISTRY,
K66
ORGANIC NOMENCLATURE, K85
RAIN, K102

Outlining
MAKING AN OUTLINE, H107

P

PASCAL
COMPUTER POWER: A FIRST COURSE IN US-
ING THE COMPUTER, D5

PILOT
APPLE PILOT, E2
CO-PILOT, E7
GENIS (GENERALIZED INSTRUCTIONAL
SYSTEMS), E22
SUPERPILOT, E39

Paleontology
GEOLOGY PACKAGE I, K58

Parametric equations
ADVANCED GRAPHICS, J11

Parts of speech
see also specific parts of speech, e.g., Nouns
ADJECTIVES, H6
ADVERBS, H9
BASIC LANGUAGE SKILLS, H23
BEGINNING GRAMMAR, H24
CONJUNCTIONS, H42
DRAGON GAME SERIES FOR LANGUAGE
ARTS, H52
ENGLISH - VOLUME 1, H59

Square roots

Squares

Stars

States

Statics

Statistics

Stock market

Stoichiometry

Story writing

Structural analysis

Study skills

Subject-verb agreement

Substitution reactions

Subtraction

Suffixes

Syllabication

Synonyms

Syntax

T

Taxes

Technology

Telling time

Temperature

Temperature gradients

Test construction

Test development

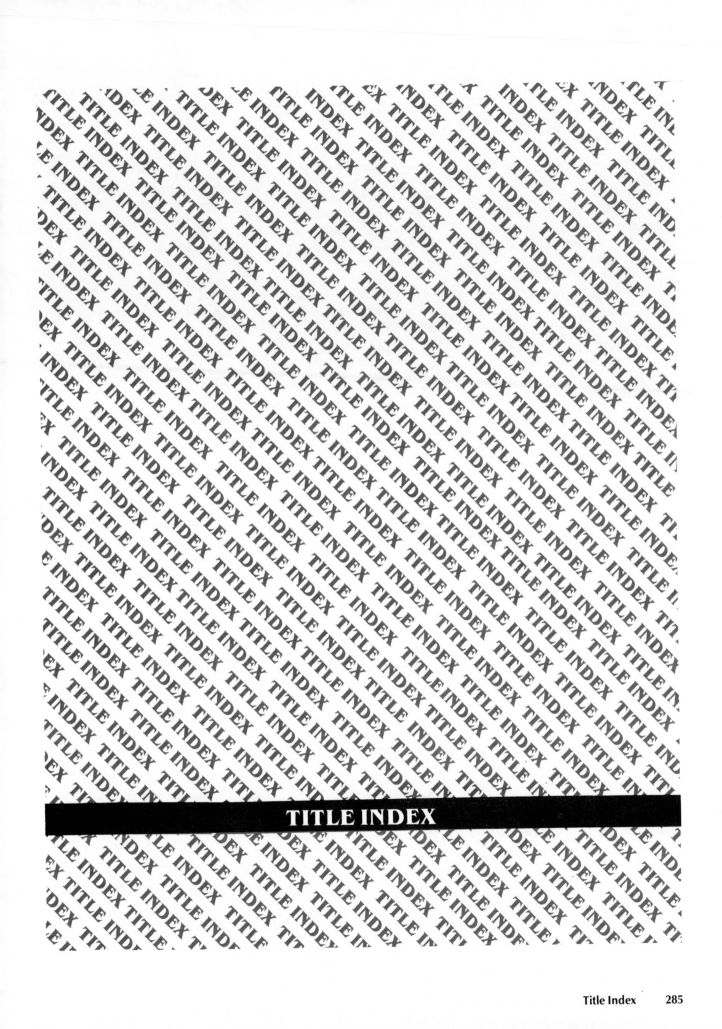

TITLE INDEX

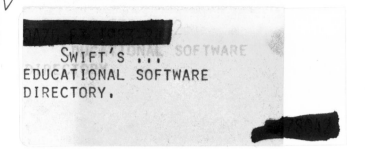